The global environment in the twenty-first century

The global environment in the twenty-first century: Prospects for international cooperation

Edited by Pamela S. Chasek

United Nations University Press

TOKYO · NEW YORK · PARIS

The views expressed in this publication are those of the authors and do not necessarily reflect the views of the United Nations University.

United Nations University Press
The United Nations University, 53-70, Jingumae 5-chome,
Shibuya-ku, Tokyo, 150-8925, Japan
Tel: +81-3-3499-2811   Fax: +81-3-3406-7345
E-mail: sales@hq.unu.edu
http://www.unu.edu

United Nations University Office in North America
2 United Nations Plaza, Room DC2-1462-70, New York, NY 10017, USA
Tel: +1-212-963-6387   Fax: +1-212-371-9454
E-mail: unuona@igc.apc.org

United Nations University Press is the publishing division of the United Nations University.

Cover design by Jean-Marie Antenen

Printed in the United States of America

UNUP-1029
ISBN 92-808-1029-4

Library of Congress Cataloging-in-Publication Data

The global environment in the twenty-first century : prospects for international cooperation / edited by Pamela S. Chasek.
     p.   cm.
   ISBN 92-808-1029-4
   1. Environmental policy-International cooperation. 2. Environmental protection—International cooperation. 3. Sustainable development—International cooperation. 4. Conservation of natural resources.
5. Pollution. I. Chasek, Pamela S., 1961– II. Title.
   HC79.E5   G5927   1999
   363.7'0526—dc21   99-050800

3/01

Contents

List of tables and figures ix

Note on measurements xi

Introduction: The global environment at the dawn of a new
millennium 1
    Pamela S. Chasek

States and sovereignty 13

  1 States and sovereignty: Introduction 15
     Jeannie Sowers, Atul Kohli, and Georg Sørensen

  2 States, markets, and energy use patterns in China and India .. 22
     Holly Sims

  3 Sustainability, degradation, and livelihood in third world
    cities: Possibilities for state-society synergy 42
     Peter Evans

  4 Global environment and the changing nature of states: The
    role of energy 64
     José Goldemberg

Civil society: Defining a new partnership 81

5 (I)NGOs and global environmental governance: Introduction 83
   Volker Rittberger

6 The transnational politics of environmental NGOs:
   Governmental, economic, and social activism 87
   Paul Wapner

7 Energy development and environmental NGOs: The Asian
   perspective 109
   Lin Gan

8 Environmental NGOs in an emerging global civil society 130
   Helmut Breitmeier and Volker Rittberger

Market forces and the environment 164

9 Market forces and environment: Introduction 167
   Chung-in Moon

10 Sustainable energy in a developing world: The role of
   knowledgeable markets 175
   Ken Wilkening, David Von Hippel, and Peter Hayes

11 Coping with the global fresh water dilemma: The state,
   market forces, and global governance 204
   Peter H. Gleick

12 Market forces and food security: The case of developing Asia 223
   Angelina Briones and Charmaine Ramos

Regional arrangements 253

13 Environmental governance – the potential of regional
   institutions: Introduction 255
   Muthiah Alagappa

14 Energy and the environment in Asia-Pacific: Regional
   cooperation and market governance 271
   Lyuba Zarsky

15 Regional environmental cooperation and preventive
   environmental policy in Central and Eastern Europe 301
   Egbert Tellegen

16 African regional organizations and environmental security ... 322
   Gregory W. Myers

International organizations and the environment................... 343

17 Intergovernmental organizations and the environment:
   Introduction 345
   Michael W. Doyle and Rachel Massey

18 The UN Environment Programme at a turning point: Options
   for change 355
   David L. Downie and Marc A. Levy

19 The UN Commission on Sustainable Development: The first
   five years... 378
   Pamela S. Chasek

20 The World Bank's environmental agenda 399
   Mikiyasu Nakayama

21 Intergovernmental organizations and the environment:
   Looking towards the future..................................... 411
   Michael W. Doyle and Rachel Massey

Conclusion: The global environment in the twenty-first century:
Prospects for international cooperation 427
   Pamela S. Chasek

Acronyms 442

List of contributors 447

Index 452

List of tables and figures

Table 4.1	Main environmental problems	65
Table 4.2	Total energy consumption	78
Table 7.1	Characteristics of social institutions	121
Table 8.1	Relationship between different types of environmental NGOs and economic actors	153
Table 10.1	World energy use trends, 1985–1995	178
Table 10.2	USDOE/EIA projections of world energy use, 1995–2015	182
Table 11.1	Availability of fresh water by continent	206
Table 11.2	Water requirements for basic human needs	214
Table 12.1	Average annual percentage change in production and population, 1971–1995	226
Table 12.2	Average annual percentage change in productivity, 1971–1995	227
Table 12.3	Grain self-sufficiency, various regions: Actual 1989–1991 and projected 2010	229
Table 12.4	Estimates of food-energy deficiency in developing regions	229
Table 12.5	Net trade balance in food, 1965–1995	231
Table 12.6	Key features of the GATT-UR	233
Table 12.7	Extent of major limitations for agriculture of soil resources in South East Asia	245

Figure 4.1   Per capita income: Selected countries in 1988
             compared with the United States, 1830–1988   67
Figure 4.2   Carbon emissions, 1950–2030   68
Figure 4.3   Long-term trends in the intensity of use of materials
             and energy   69
Figure 4.4   Energy intensity of industrialized countries   70
Figure 4.5   Frequency distribution of the progress ratio   75
Figure 4.6   Penetration curve for photovoltaics   76
Figure 10.1 1995 world energy use by fuel and region 177
Figure 10.2 Epistemic communities, energy markets, and public
             sector governance institutions........................ 195
Figure 10.3 Knowledge and market matrix for the energy sector   196
Figure 12.1 Food production and food production per capita
             indices, 1965–1995 227
Figure 12.2 Functional literacy in the Philippines................ 242
Figure 14.1 East Asia-Pacific region: Strategic energy resources   275
Figure 14.2 Primary commercial energy consumption by source,
             1995 277
Figure 14.3 APEC (non-binding) energy principles 289

Note on measurements

In this volume:

1 billion = 1,000 million
1 trillion = 1,000 billion
1 tonne = 1,000 kg
1 ton = 2,240 lbs

Introduction: The global environment at the dawn of a new millennium

Pamela S. Chasek[1]

After much anticipation and many clichés about the "dawn of a new millennium," the twenty-first century is here. But after the celebrations are over and the anticipation is but a mere memory, what kind of world will we be living in? The earth's physical and biological systems are facing an unprecedented strain. The human population reached 6 billion in 1999 and is still growing. The major components of the biosphere, including the atmosphere, the oceans, soil cover, the climate system, and the range of animal and plant species, have all been altered by the intensity of human exploitation of the earth's resources in the twentieth century. The by-products of economic growth – the burning of fossil fuels; the release of ozone-destroying chemicals; emissions of sulphur and nitrogen oxides; the production of toxic chemicals and other wastes and their introduction into the air, water, and soil; and the elimination of forest cover, among others – cause cumulative stresses on the physical environment that threaten human health and economic well-being.

At the same time, we are in a period of transition between two centuries. We are leaving a century shaped largely by world wars and ensuing cold wars and entering a new one shaped principally by ecological limits, redistributive politics, and the global reach of technology. While the future is certainly not going to be devoid of military threats, which may be compounded by the spread of biological, chemical, and nuclear weapons, it may be the conflict with the natural environment that will erupt on a world-war scale. And, as in the case of military conflict, it is

1

international cooperation that offers the best hope for bringing about a sustainable world peace (Hempel 1996).

International cooperation and the environment in the twentieth century

Environmental problems do not respect national boundaries. Transboundary air pollution, the degradation of shared rivers, and the pollution of oceans and seas are just a few examples of how one nation's or one factory's pollutants can have wide-ranging effects downstream or downwind. In fact, the international dimensions of certain environmental problems may even be worse than those at the site of the initial emissions. Population growth, in combination with resulting urbanization and industrialization, has served only to increase the amount and frequency of major international environmental problems. The cumulative impact that human beings have had on the earth, together with an increased understanding of ecological processes, means that the environment cannot be viewed as a relatively stable background factor. Rather, the interaction between economic development and the complex, often fragile ecosystems on which that development depends has become an international political and economic issue (Hurrell and Kingsbury 1992).

The nature of transboundary environmental problems has changed over the years. First, the number and scope of transboundary environmental problems has increased. Second, a new category of global environmental issues has emerged. These environmental problems, including climate change, depletion of the ozone layer, biodiversity loss, and overfishing of the high seas, are global in the sense that they affect everyone and can only be effectively managed on the basis of cooperation between most, if not all, countries in the world. Third, the increasing scale of many regional or local environmental problems, such as urban degradation, deforestation, desertification, salinization, denudation, or water or fuelwood scarcity, now have broader international repercussions. These problems can undermine the economic base and social fabric of weak and poor states, generate or exacerbate intra- or inter-state tensions and conflicts, and stimulate increased flows of refugees. As a result, environmental degradation in diverse parts of the developing or even the industrialized world can affect the political and security interests of countries thousands of miles away (Hurrell and Kingsbury 1992).

Over the last quarter of a century, the UN system has become the focal point for addressing global environmental issues at the international level. This is quite a development, particularly since the UN Charter makes no specific mention of environmental protection, preventing pollution, or conserving resources. Whereas in 1945 environmental awareness was low, the situation changed dramatically by 1972 when the concerns of private citizens and emerging environmental organizations led certain states to place environmental issues on their political agendas. Two events of particular importance occurred in the 1960s that sparked the industrialized world's awareness of the need for environmental concern. First, the publication of Rachel Carson's *Silent Spring* brought to light the devastating impact of DDT on bird populations and the deleterious effect of industrial chemicals on the earth's natural resources. Not long thereafter, in 1967, an oil tanker, the *Torrey Canyon*, spilled most of its cargo in the English Channel, killing hundreds of sea birds and polluting the British coast.

It was at this time that the industrialized countries identified the need for multilateral action. Even though the international community had already adopted a number of multilateral environmental treaties, there was no framework within the United Nations for comprehensive consideration of the problems of the human environment. Thus, in 1968, Sweden called for a UN environmental conference to encourage "intensified action at national and international levels to limit, and where possible eliminate, the impairment of the human environment" (UN Resolution 1346 (XLV), 30 July 1968). The General Assembly approved this proposal in 1969 and decided that the conference would take place in 1972 in Stockholm.

The UN Conference on the Human Environment began a process that resulted in the "piecemeal construction" of a number of international environmental institutions, the steady expansion of the environmental agenda, and increasing acceptance by states of international monitoring of environmental standards (Mingst and Karns 1995, 127). After more than two years of preparation, representatives from 113 states gathered in Stockholm from 5 to 16 June 1972. By the conclusion of the conference delegates had established a UN environment framework consisting of four major elements: an action plan; an environment fund to be established by voluntary contributions from states; a new UN mechanism (the UN Environment Programme – UNEP) for administering and directing the framework; and a declaration of 26 principles on the human environment. Not only did the Stockholm Conference legitimize environmental policy as an issue of international concern, but environmental issues received a place on many national agendas. Many governments created environment ministries and adopted environmental legislation for the first time.

Nevertheless, despite some progress, until the 1980s global environmental problems were still regarded by many states as minor issues that were marginal to their national interests and to international politics.

However, as a result of the rise of environmental movements in the industrialized countries and the appearance of well-publicized global environmental threats that could seriously affect the welfare of all humankind, global environmental issues began to assume a new status in world politics. Environmental issues were no longer viewed as merely scientific and technical problems, but as intertwined with central issues in world politics: the international system of resource production and use, the liberalization of world trade, North-South relations, and international conflict and internal social and political stability (Porter and Brown 1996).

The "new status" of global environmental issues was reflected in the fact that the first global summit meeting in world history was the 1992 UN Conference on Environment and Development (UNCED), held in Rio de Janeiro, Brazil. The conference – held 20 years after the Stockholm Conference – was convened to "elaborate strategies and measures to halt and reverse the effects of environmental degradation in the context of increased national and international efforts to promote sustainable and environmentally sound development in all countries" (General Assembly Resolution 44/228). At the top of the so-called Earth Summit's agenda was the adoption of five items: a "Rio Declaration" setting forth 27 principles for sustainable development; a 700-page non-binding action plan, known as "Agenda 21"; a global treaty on climate change; another global treaty on biodiversity; and a set of non-legally binding principles for sustainable forest management.

During the course of four preparatory committee (PrepCom) meetings between August 1990 and April 1992 and the conference itself, delegates from more than 150 countries negotiated the contents of Agenda 21, the Rio Declaration and the Forest Principles.[2] Agenda 21 was intended to stimulate cooperation on more than 120 separate initiatives for environmental and economic improvement, each commencing by the turn of the century. Having devoted 40 chapters to issues ranging from air pollution to waste management and the creation of a UN Commission on Sustainable Development, Agenda 21 represented "the most comprehensive framework ever devised by governments for global environmental policy making" (Hempel 1996, 31). Delegates also examined the underlying patterns of development that cause stress to the environment – poverty in developing countries, levels of economic growth, unsustainable patterns of consumption, demographic pressures, and the impact of the international economy, particularly trade and investment. This marked the first time that an intergovernmental conference addressed these crucial economic and social development issues in conjunction with the natural environment.

The Earth Summit, like the 1972 Stockholm Conference, provided an international framework for action that far exceeded in scope and ambition all prior initiatives in environmental governance. It also attempted to provide a mobilizing vision and motivational ethic that would persuade millions of individuals to take more responsibility for their environmental misdeeds and to welcome, or at least tolerate, added regulation in the interests of environmental protection. To the extent that any mobilizing vision and ethical framework was established, it was embodied in the principle of "sustainable development." Defined as development that "meets the needs of the present without compromising the ability of future generations to meet their own needs" (WCED 1987, 8), sustainable development was the major theme of the conference, representing a politically expedient compromise between the forces of economic growth and those of environmental protection (Hempel 1996, 39).

Despite the lofty goals and the supposed inauguration of a "new era of international ecological responsibility" (Hempel 1996, 42), the Earth Summit and the subsequent implementation of the Rio agreements have not lived up to expectations. The mobilization of financial resources for the implementation of Agenda 21 has not materialized, the UN Commission on Sustainable Development has not become a proactive forum for promotion and implementation of Agenda 21, deforestation and biodiversity loss continue at an alarming rate, and environmental health issues, including a lack of clean drinking water, still affect millions of people throughout the world.

Think globally, act locally

While cooperation among nation-states has proven to be necessary to address many transboundary environmental issues, virtually all policies must be implemented at the national or local level. There are no international governments, laws, or courts that can enforce binding decisions on sovereign nations (with the partial exception of the European Union). But equally important, actions taken by individual states or actors within states can have major international implications, such as activities that cause transboundary pollution. The growing interaction between national and international actors and levels of governance is an increasingly important aspect of international environmental policy (Vig 1999).

Lamont Hempel (1996, 5–11) argues that global environmental governance is needed to shape the environmental future of the planet and the quality of life that it makes possible. Global governance, according to Hempel (1996, 5), refers to the "people, political institutions, regimes and nongovernmental organizations at all levels of public and private policy making that are collectively responsible for managing world affairs." Environmental concerns, he continues, are "the latest in a series of threats to international security and development that have called attention to the political need for laws and institutions that operate beyond the zones of sovereignty." In order to achieve effective environmental governance, both the global and the local ends of the political spectrum must be strengthened. International institutions and organizations that have been established to address environmental concerns will need to be strengthened and will need to cooperate more with one another. National governments will need to recognize the importance of the natural environment and take the necessary measures to implement economically sound and environmentally sustainable development. Local communities must be educated to adopt sustainable lifestyles and empowered so that they can engage in dialogue with and, perhaps, influence national governments and international environmental initiatives. Furthermore, parliaments, popular assemblies, non-governmental organizations, business and industry, and professional associations also have a crucial role to play in global environmental governance.

At the international level, the United Nations is perhaps best placed to advise governments on policy-making and assess the state of the global environment, and to initiate the development of new treaties, policies, and institutions. As societies become ever more interdependent, individual nation-states find it increasingly difficult to deal with international or transnational problems. The United Nations, as the only truly global organization, stands a better chance.

The United Nations is also an arena where various national, subnational, and global actors manoeuvre – in other words, where the "local" can interact with the "global." While the United Nations is often seen as an arena for states to cooperate, in reality there are numerous non-state actors that also participate in UN politics, including non-governmental organizations, regional organizations, and other international organizations. In addition, the private sector has become increasingly engaged in UN activities, as global markets and multinational corporations exercise tremendous influence on the other actors. This is quite different from the early days of the organization. Peter Thacher (1992) noted that when the UN Charter was signed,

governments were the dominant actors on the international stage, and keeping the peace among member states was the primary task for the international community. As the 50th anniversary [of the United Nations] approaches, the end of the Cold War brings new issues to the fore in an organization whose membership – in terms of states – has more than trebled and is still growing. But the comparative influence of states on the international scene has diminished as significant roles are acquired in an interdependent and more transparent world by non-state actors of all sorts, including science, multinational corporations and financial institutions, media, as well as a host of international organizations.

This relationship between state and non-state actors at all levels is thus critical to the formulation of global environmental policies.

Overview of the book

This volume will examine the roles of state and non-state actors in safeguarding the environment and advancing sustainable development into the twenty-first century. The research for this volume was carried out by five groups. Each of the research groups focused on a different actor – states, civil society, market forces, regional arrangements, and international organizations. By examining the functions and capabilities of each of these actors, the research groups studied their effectiveness and their relationship with other actors both within and outside the UN system.

The first research group, coordinated by Atul Kohli, Georg Sørensen, and Jeannie Sowers, looks at the role of states and their policies, which are critical to the future of sustainable development. The three chapters in this section analyse the politics of environmental management in India, China, and Brazil, illuminating the conditions under which state-society interaction may produce environmental good or sustain environmental harm. While examining the political and institutional determinants of responses to environmental problems, these chapters help clarify why states so often fail to provide environmental protection as a public good and suggest ways in which the UN system might influence state behaviour towards more environmentally responsible policies.

Both legitimacy and capacity of states are important in understanding the likelihood of successful environmental policies. In the first chapter, Holly Sims tackles this issue by analysing the contrasting experiences of India and China as they attempted to alter energy policies in the 1970s with new standards of efficiency and environmental accountability in mind. In the second chapter, Peter Evans uses case studies of urban governance in Brazil to argue that for effective environmental governance, there must be a symbiotic relationship between civil society and public institutions. The final chapter, by José Goldemberg, examines the need for increased state capacity to guide markets and select appropriate and efficient energy systems.

The second research group, coordinated by Volker Rittberger, looks at the activities of environmental organizations; these have increased dramatically in the last three decades of the twentieth century. The three chapters in this section deal specifically with the roles of environmental non-governmental organizations (NGOs) in shaping international environmental policy-making at the regional and global levels. In the first chapter, Paul Wapner develops a definition of NGOs and separates them from international organizations. Wapner focuses on those actions of NGOs that are directed toward changing the behaviour of states, aim at engaging economic forces, or alter social mores. Lin Gan's chapter describes the role of environmental NGOs in energy sector development in Asia. This chapter further describes the activities of research-oriented NGOs providing scientific knowledge to decision-makers; lobbying NGOs, which have criticized and campaigned against projects like the Narmada Dam in India; and mediating NGOs establishing domestic and trans-national networks with the purpose of disseminating knowledge and coordinating joint activities. In the third chapter, Helmut Breitmeier and Volker Rittberger ask whether NGOs have already succeeded in chang-ing the relationship between states and civil society. This chapter also describes how the activities of environmental advocacy organizations put states and international organizations under political pressure to strengthen their efforts for the international management of environ-mental problems.

The third research group, coordinated by Chung-in Moon, examines the relationship between market forces and the environment. Free mar-kets are a powerful social invention for efficient allocation of scarce resources, but they cannot necessarily serve as a useful tool in ensuring sustainability. The chapters in this section all share the view that scarcity problems involving energy, fresh water, and food are real and present, and market forces and technology alone cannot resolve ecological dilemmas. In the first chapter, Ken Wilkening, David Von Hippel, and Peter Hayes postulate the idea that market forces cannot ensure long-term sustainability in energy use. The current operating logic of energy markets defies the issue of sustainability and is not ready to cope with future energy dilemmas. Peter Gleick analyses the global fresh water di-lemma in the second chapter. While there is a sufficient amount of water to meet the needs and wants of every human being, imbalances between overall availability and growth in need and demand have emerged as a serious problem. While market forces can serve as a valuable tool for conserving fresh water resources, the application of market approaches in situations where non-economic values are high or where certain types of water needs or uses cannot be quantified is bound to fail, and may even create new problems. Drawing on the experiences of the Philippines and selected Asian countries, the third chapter by Angelina Briones and Charmaine Ramos explores the dimensions of food insecurity in devel-oping countries. In their view market forces are the primary cause of food insecurity rather than a solution to it.

The fourth research group, coordinated by Muthiah Alagappa, analy-ses the role of regional organizations in environmental governance. In his introduction to this section, Alagappa defines a number of roles for regional institutions, including the provision of high-level forums to map the regional environmental agenda, facilitation of regional input into the formulation and implementation of global conventions, the development and management of regional initiatives and action plans to address regional transboundary environmental problems, mediation of disputes between member states, and harmonization of national efforts on issues that fall under the domestic jurisdiction of member states.

The three chapters in this section investigate the possibilities and limitations of regional cooperation in three regions: the Asia-Pacific, Central and Eastern Europe, and sub-Saharan Africa. Lyuba Zarsky's chapter advocates the case for the high-energy-consuming Asia-Pacific states to develop a long-term market-oriented regional energy plan that integrates environmental considerations. Egbert Tellegen's chapter investigates the role of regional cooperation in energy conservation and waste minimization in Central and Eastern Europe. Gregory Myers's chapter reviews the role of African regional organizations in addressing land and natural resource degradation.

The fifth and final research group, coordinated by Michael Doyle and Rachel Massey, looks at international organizations as actors in the international environmental arena. The chapters in this section examine the history, mandate, and activities of three intergovernmental organizations that have been active participants in the formation of the global environmental agenda. The first chapter, written by David Downie and Marc Levy, looks at the UN Environment Programme, the oldest and core UN agency with a specific environmental mandate. Pamela Chasek's chapter examines the UN Commission on Sustainable Development, a relatively new international environmental forum created in response to the sustainable development agenda set by UNCED. Mikiyasu Nakayama's chapter addresses the World Bank, an influential international organization whose core mandate is not concerned with environmental protection, but whose activities have a major effect on the prospects for the international coordination of environmental protection. These three chapters examine how the mandate, the configuration, and the resources of each organization have influenced its ability – as well as the collective ability of intergovernmental organizations in aggregate – to address global environmental problems. While each chapter evaluates one organization individually, the larger purpose of this section, as set forth in the final chapter by Michael Doyle and Rachel Massey, is to evaluate whether existing organizations together meet the need for a coordinated approach to protecting the global environment. This chapter describes the activities of other intergovernmental organizations that address environmental issues, and analyses the future of international environmental organizations and the arguments for establishing a "Global Environmental Organization."

Into the twenty-first century

Human demands on the environment continue to mount as poverty and affluence spread in parallel around the globe. Despite all of the efforts made at Stockholm and Rio and at national and local levels over the past quarter of a century, the environment continues to deteriorate in many parts of the world. Social, economic, and technological trends are exacerbating these problems. New and unexpected problems will certainly continue to arise. Much more vigorous and effective coordinated action will be required at all levels and by all actors. The ways of the past may not suffice. International action, including cooperation among states, civil society, market forces, regional arrangements, and international organizations, will continue to be essential in meeting these challenges. However, the nature of these future environmental challenges and the relationships among major actors *vis-à-vis* these challenges are not at all clear. What are the issues that we will have to address in the next century? Can the existing locus of actors find the proper solutions? What will be the role of the United Nations? Is there a better model for international cooperation to address environmental issues? These questions will be examined again in the Conclusion.

Notes

1. Special thanks to Michael Doyle and Rachel Massey for their helpful suggestions regarding both the Introduction and Conclusion to this volume.
2. The Framework Convention on Climate Change and the Convention on Biological Diversity were negotiated by separate negotiating committees that were convened in parallel to the UNCED PrepCom.

REFERENCES

Hempel, L. C. 1996. *Environmental Governance: The Global Challenge.* Washington, DC: Island Press.

Hurrell, A. and B. Kingsbury, eds. 1992. *The International Politics of the Environment.* New York: Oxford University Press.

Mingst, K. A. and M. P. Karns. 1995. *The United Nations in the Post-Cold War Era.* Boulder: Westview.

Porter, G. and J. W. Brown. 1996. *Global Environmental Politics*, 2nd edn. Boulder: Westview.

Thacher, P. S. 1992. "The Role of the United Nations." In *The International Politics of the Environment*, eds A. Hurrell and B. Kingsbury. Oxford: Oxford University Press.

Vig, N. J. 1999. "Introduction: Governing the International Environment." In *The Global Environment: Institutions, Law and Policy*, eds N. J. Vig and R. S. Axelrod. Washington, DC: Congressional Quarterly Press.

WCED (World Commission for Environment and Development). 1987. *Our Common Future*. Oxford: Oxford University Press.

States and sovereignty

1

States and sovereignty: Introduction

Atul Kohli, Georg Sørensen, and Jeannie Sowers

States and their policies remain critical to the future of sustainable development. The three chapters in this section analyse the politics of environmental management in such large countries as India, China, and Brazil, illuminating the conditions under which state-society interaction may produce environmental goods or sustain environmental harm. While examining the political and institutional determinants of responses to environmental problems, these chapters help clarify why states so often fail to provide environmental protection as a public good, and suggest ways in which the UN system might influence state behaviour towards more environmentally responsible policies.

States are certainly not the only actors crucial to environmental management. Global problems such as climate change require international cooperation and regimes, while localized degradation is often best addressed through subnational agents such as municipalities, regional air and water quality management authorities, and non-governmental organizations. Furthermore, transnational flows of capital, information, and trade (as well as competition between states to attract these flows, and the regional arrangements that have emerged to foster and monitor them) have eroded the traditional forms of environmental regulatory policy.

Precisely because of these globalizing and regionalizing trends, states must be encouraged to reinvent their roles in environmental management, rather than abandon them. Increasing public concern and growing scientific understandings of the complexity of environmental change have translated into expectations that states must find more effective ways of integrating environmental and developmental concerns. The chapters in this section suggest that environmental outcomes, no less than other public goods, depend on the ways in which political power is structured and used.

The following observations about the status of environmental priorities within most states can be taken as a starting point.

- The environment competes with other public goods for the state's attention. For many states, especially in the developing world, the link between environment and development is viewed as a competitive trade-off, where environmental considerations impose unnecessary costs and take much-needed resources, especially from economic growth. The low priority assigned to environmental issues is, in turn, often reflected in the low budgets, limited staff, and limited authority of many national environmental agencies.

- Powerful domestic and international interests, especially private sector interests, influence states. When faced with a trade-off between policies that may help the environment but may hurt profitability of firms, governments often further dilute their limited environmental commitments. Since states and businesses must work together, states should consider structuring markets in a way that rewards entrepreneurs who are willing to incorporate environmental concerns into corporate management strategies.

- The weakness of channels for popular participation is a crucial factor, particularly in developing countries. Less powerful groups, many of whom might benefit the most from the provision of environmental public goods, often face the greatest obstacles in organizing collectively. Poverty and environmental vulnerability are inextricably linked. Open politics and non-governmental organizations that may facilitate collective action are thus desirable from the standpoint of improving environmental outcomes.

- International actors, particularly transnational financial institutions and multilateral donors, can now play a critical role in the environmental field by channelling resources to environmentally friendly investments. While these institutions have unprecedented leverage to promote environmentally responsible projects, their practices often fall short. For example, whereas the IMF and World Bank increasingly advocate environmental considerations, their efficacy is limited by their suspicion of public regulatory authorities, and by lending priorities and portfolios still consisting of traditional investments in major infrastructure projects, with sometimes questionable environmental impacts. There are few incentives for private investment banks to use environmental criteria in financing or selecting investments, while trade treaties such as GATT have no formalized criteria for environmental accountability.

Developing countries face these challenges and more. Although the rise of environmental politics has been fairly well documented for industrialized countries, less attention has been paid to how this sequence and its actors often differ in developing countries. In industrialized countries, increasing public awareness and the formation of environmental interest groups led to the construction of national and international environmental regulatory regimes. In many developing countries the state itself, usually under pressure from donors and the dedicated efforts of local individuals, passes environmental laws, but these are rarely enforced as they often threaten the activities of influential private companies and state agencies.

Both the legitimacy and capacity of states, therefore, are important in understanding the likelihood of successful environmental policies. The legitimacy aspect is particularly overlooked, as many reports on environment stress capacity-building issues with little connection to how inclusionary political reforms might affect environmental accountability. Among the chapters that follow, Holly Sims tackles this question by analysing the contrasting experiences of India and China, especially as these two giants attempted to alter energy policies in the 1970s with new standards of efficiency and environmental accountability in mind. Although both countries maintained some overarching vision of equitable energy distribution, China's energy policies relied on cloistered decision-making, largely insulated from domestic politics and plagued by bureaucratic infighting. In India, by contrast, public opinion loudly and openly questioned the need for foreign investment, reduced subsidies, and massive dam construction projects. "States, markets, and energy use patterns in China and India" shows that China's centralized decision-making fostered "fast-track" investment approvals and reduced subsidies, while India succeeded in neither. Indian political debates, however, revealed a more substantive discussion of what environmental accountability actually meant, and who would benefit.[1] Sims points out that as the state's control over decision-making expands, establishing mechanisms of accountability, such as transparent and competitive bidding procedures, becomes ever more difficult.

Peter Evans stakes out even more explicitly the claim that inclusionary politics usually facilitate the equitable provision of environmental goods in his chapter, "Sustainability, degradation, and livelihood in third world cities: Possibilities for state-society synergy." Using case studies of urban governance in Brazil, Evans argues that for effective environmental governance there must be a symbiotic relationship between civil society and public institutions. Through both negative cases (the organizational demise of Rio de Janeiro's pollution control agency) and positive ones (the innovative public transport system of Curitiba and the extension of sewers to poor *favelas* in São Paulo), Evans argues that effective societal actions depend on public institutions, just as state actors depend on the ability to organize citizens. State attempts to either regulate pollution or provide public goods depend ultimately on "the character of the relations between public agencies and societal actors – whether societal actors play the role of co-producers of urban infrastructure, sources of political pressure to expand environmental action, or implementers of state-constructed strategies."

The final chapter by José Goldemberg shifts the attention away from specific country experiences to developing countries as a whole, and explores how states might structure market incentives so private interests will have incentives to use environmentally friendly technologies. Goldemberg argues that developing countries could "leapfrog" some of the energy-intensive production technologies that characterized earlier development pathways. However, as currently structured, international energy markets encourage fossil fuel use to the detriment of investments in other sources of energy. International financial institutions, including the World Bank, also contribute to this bias by being "colour-blind" in their lending, not explicitly considering whether proposed investments incorporate "green" innovations over polluting "brown" technologies. If states have the capacity to select appropriate technologies by structuring appropriate incentives in the design and regulation of markets, the rate of natural resource depletion can be reduced. This can be done through a variety of instruments: preferential financing for modern production processes; screening of donor and foreign investment projects for their ability to transfer appropriate technologies; and encouraging local research and innovation on alternative energy sources such as biomass, ethanol, and solar power.

A common thread linking the three chapters in this section is that environmental problems compete with other significant problems for public attention. This lack of consensus is apparent among individual states and international actors, including the UN system. Environmental problems thus struggle for political recognition with other issues internationally, within governments, and also within populations. People need a healthy environment, but they also need food, shelter, and a number of other things; in the short and medium run, these different objectives may conflict and lead to environmental damage.

Peter Evans very instructively points to one way of understanding how social and state consensus can emerge on the need for environmental reforms. The notion of "state-society synergy" suggests that solutions to environmental problems require both the collective goods provided by public institutions and the active participation of local communities.

It is important to emphasize the administrative and political preconditions for such state-society synergies to emerge. They include a trained, competent bureaucracy that is sufficiently well rewarded, political entrepreneurship by innovative leaders, and an engaged civil society permitted by the state to engage in public action. The implications of this are, regrettably, that there are many countries, especially in the developing world, where state-society synergy may not be easy to achieve. Those concerned with promoting constructive state-society synergy must then also consider the appropriate preconditions for such public and private cooperation.

In her analysis of energy use patterns in China and India, Holly Sims also stresses the importance of the political context in understanding how environmental concerns are incorporated into state policies. Authoritarianism in China facilitated certain measures improving energy efficiency, including reform of the energy price system and the promotion of private foreign investment. But this centralized system provided no checks on questionable energy investments such as the Three Gorges Dam. In India's more democratic system, in contrast, political leaders have had to face "the sometimes bracing test of Indian public opinion." The implication is by no means that authoritarianism is better equipped than democracy to address issues concerning the environment. Rather, the Indian case implies that state-society synergy will not necessarily be conducive to dramatic policy changes, but may work towards other goals, such as promoting a more open and susbstantive discussion of environmental issues.

José Goldemberg's analysis stresses the possibility for "technological leapfrogging" in the energy sector as a means of responding to urgent development problems in many countries. Examples include the adoption of cellular telephones instead of traditional telephone systems which require extensive wiring, electricity generation from biomass, and ethanol production from sugar cane. Yet further research is needed on the global market structures and domestic political objectives which reward using conventional rather than environmentally friendly technologies.

The contributors to this section thus point to a variety of ways in which the UN system can continue and enhance its contributions in the field of environmental accountability. The UN system has already played a proactive role in bringing environmental issues to international attention, particularly through member agencies such as the UN Development Programme (UNDP), UNEP, the United Nations University, and the UN Industrial Development Organization (UNIDO). Through publications, research, workshops, and training sessions, these agencies have sought to build and disseminate conceptual models and practical measures which integrate environmental and development concerns. These activities also provide an important networking function, bringing scientists and professionals from developing countries together to share ideas and difficulties, as well as providing additional training and funding.

How can the UN system influence governments of member countries to play more environmentally responsible roles? First, provision of information about environment-friendly technologies and modes of production must remain a key focus of UN endeavours, especially those which might deliver the simultaneous provision of competing public goods. As stressed by Peter Evans, "small injections of new knowledge can play an important role in arriving at positive resolutions." The United Nations has already assisted in the spread of alternative energy technologies, particularly wind and solar power community development projects, as Holly Sims notes. This role could be expanded from technical assistance *per se* to other forms of incentive-building. For instance, one of Goldemberg's most innovative suggestions is that developing countries aggregate their demand for environmentally friendly technologies such as photovoltaics; since most technologies exhibit exponentially declining cost curves when mass marketed, such demand might spur multinational and domestic energy companies to cheaper production and more research and development. Such a process could be facilitated by cooperation between UN agencies such as the UNDP or UNEP, on the one hand, and member states on the other.

The possibilities for "leapfrogging" that José Goldemberg describes for technological adaptation can also apply to governmental tasks. Institutional development concerning environmental supervision and the diffusion of knowledge about experiences with environment-friendly policies at all political levels is of paramount importance. Some initiatives have already emerged, such as UN sponsorship of guidelines to handle hazardous waste in developing countries; such tasks should be expanded.

Increasingly, the challenge for UN agencies is to address the potentially environmentally hazardous effects of globalization. This could be done by UN-sponsored proposals for reforms in international trade regimes, especially devising mechanisms to address issues of environmental accountability. Integral to such a project is the promotion of national systems of environmental accounting and auditing for investments, including the innovative use of tax incentives for environmental entrepreneurs.

The chapters by Sims and Evans address a lacuna in the discourse on environmental planning, by drawing explicit linkages between inclusionary politics, vital civil societies, and the resulting distribution of environmental goods. These authors draw attention to the ways in which relationships between public agencies and civil society can be synergistic or debilitating. The cooperative aspect was most prominent when there was a sizeable middle class, interested in the equitable provision of environmental goods, as in Curitiba, Brazil. More conflictual approaches amidst greater income inequalities, as in the case of the Rio *favelas*, still produced successful outcomes when linked to the constructive engagement of public authorities.

At least two conditions must be met for the emergence or survival of engaged and capable publics.[2] First, the public can be sustained only when the state or powerful private interests do not crowd out or dampen the articulation of other private interests, monopolizing public spheres. Second, and related to the first, the relevance of these expressed interests can only be tested when directed to audiences which can meaningfully participate. Neither of these enabling conditions is fully attained in most developing countries, but UN projects should extend their efforts to find new ways of involving civic organizations, public agencies, and the media in public decision-making.

Finally, it should be recognized that the environment remains a politically contested issue at global, national, and local levels. These three chapters highlight the need for the UN system, and researchers, to focus on the political and institutional factors which shape patterns of environmental degradation. These chapters suggest that environmental goods, like other public goods, are more likely to be provided when markets penalize environmental harm and states encourage participation by a variety of publics. To the extent that these conditions are not met, the UN system and other concerned parties should work to provide incentives for states and markets to become more environmentally accountable.

Notes

1. The case of large dams provides an interesting example of how the political systems of China and India have yielded different outcomes. While Nehru once categorized "big dams as the temples of India," the recent Narmada project was cancelled due to public protest, while in China the Three Gorges Dam is going ahead. The World Bank had originally provided financing for both projects, but pulled out in the Indian case when opposition mounted.
2. These conditions were suggested by Jurgen Habermas in a lecture at the American University in Cairo on 17 March 1997.

2

States, markets, and energy use patterns in China and India

Holly Sims[1]

During the second half of the twentieth century, states and private market-led forces emerged as key players in the production and distribution of the energy critical to the economic growth of pivotal developing countries, including China and India. In both countries, major responsibility for energy production and distribution was initially shouldered by states, with rapid industrialization as their overriding objective. The critical test of energy systems' performance was simple. They were to serve instrumental economic purposes, and to a much lesser extent political ones, since a share of scarce amenities was channelled to rural areas where most people lived.

A new criterion for assessing the systems'[2] performance – efficiency – became increasingly compelling in the 1970s and 1980s, due to global economic developments and domestic policy changes that widened scope for market-led forces. During roughly the same period, a third criterion for assessing energy systems – environmental responsiveness – arose from mounting international concern about the health of the planet. This chapter discusses the experience of China and India in developing energy systems since the 1950s, and compares their recent efforts to improve efficiency and environmental responsiveness. The argument may be summarized as follows. The political economy of Chinese and Indian energy policy evolved in broadly similar fashion from the 1950s until the 1970s. Thereafter, the two states responded to pressures for energy system efficiency and environmental responsiveness in different ways, reflecting their contrasting political systems. For example, China's authoritarian structure that combines economic liberalization with political control has facilitated official efforts to pursue market-led energy policies which have foundered in democratic India. Yet India's federal system highlights ambiguities in notions of environmental responsiveness, and conflicts between national and local perspectives in particular.

Despite constraints imposed by political economy and political structures, there is considerable scope in both countries to develop energy systems that could be widely seen as environmentally responsive, particularly in rural areas which often are poorly served by state-led instrumental or market-driven energy systems. Examples of such promising initiatives are briefly noted in the concluding section.

It is important to emphasize the parallel factors that shaped the initial design of Chinese and Indian energy policy systems. China and India are among the few major countries whose primary source of energy is coal. The "ignoble fuel" (Ramage 1997, 71) blamed for greenhouse gas production, acid rain, and serious air pollution and health hazards accounts for almost 70 per cent of industrial energy use in China, and over half of primary energy sources used in India. Coal use helps both countries retain claims to some of the world's most polluted cities.

The priority of economic development is underwritten by the striking gap between industrialized and even rapidly growing non-industrialized countries in terms of energy access, and by population pressure. Although the range of high and low temperatures is broadly similar in China and the United States, the average person in China uses only 3 per cent of the energy used by the average American (Lieberthal 1995). An estimated 100 million Chinese live without electricity. India's population is three times that of the United States, but the former's energy use is little more than 10 per cent of commercial energy consumption in the United States (Ramage 1997, 36). Population pressure upon shrinking resource bases makes development all the more urgent. By 2025, China and India may represent 37.5 per cent of the projected global population of 8 billion (Population Reference Bureau 1997).

Variations in the impact of dissimilar political systems upon energy policy are highlighted when their national policy-makers are viewed with reference to both domestic and international constituencies (Evans, Jacobson, and Putnam 1993). The need to view policy from both vantage points became particularly important in the 1970s, due to widening global economic integration and international environmental concerns. Both trends influenced the roles of states, market forces, and international agencies in economic development and energy production. The ensuing discussion explains why states took a leading role in energy policy in China and India, but first it is essential to clarify the criteria of energy policy systems' performance.

Criteria of performance

Contemporary Chinese and Indian energy systems evolved from broadly similar centralized, state-led production and distribution mechanisms that were primarily designed to be instrumental in economic growth via rapid industrialization. Since strategies to achieve that goal in low-income countries with vast and dispersed rural populations and limited infra- structure were not clear, policy-makers were concerned more with the goal of development than with specific means to achieve it (Thompson 1967, 83–98). Efficiency, denoting "ability to produce the desired effect with a minimum of effort, expense or waste" (Webster's 1983), was not a useful or even applicable test in the 1950s and 1960s. In the middle of the twentieth century, risks and costs of investment in the rural areas that predominated in most low-income countries were high and potential returns a distant mirage.

The efficiency of energy production and distribution can be judged only when standards of desirability and plausible relationships between causes and effects are clear and widely accepted. Specific problems and pres- sures that directed state leaders' attention to efficiency in energy pro- duction and distribution are noted in the ensuing section. Yet the pursuit of efficiency proved difficult in countries with elaborate state structures and real or potential political concerns.

The third criterion, environmental responsiveness, is potentially con- troversial, particularly when both standards of desirability, or goals, and strategies to pursue them are ambiguous or contested. Nuclear power offers a good example. People who broadly agree on the need for envi- ronmental responsiveness may disagree as to whether nuclear power's advantages relative to fossil fuels offset its intractable management risks and waste-disposal problems. Instead of proposing a narrow definition of "environmental responsiveness" based upon an exclusive list of such promising renewable energy sources as solar energy, wind power, bio- mass, and small hydropower projects, the definition of "environmental responsiveness" will be left broad, in order to focus more on policy change.

One of the most important obstacles to environmental responsiveness is persistent global reliance on coal, the earth's most abundant fuel. Coal generates about 35 per cent of the world's electricity, and the figure may rise to nearly 40 per cent by 2010. If coal remains the "fuel of choice for electricity generation in the foreseeable future" (CERI and TERI 1995, 67, 109), new "clean coal technologies" that limit environmental emissions deserve serious consideration as possible means to advance environmental responsiveness, even if longer-term strategies emphasize alternatives to coal.

In the short term, other practices or technologies are also available to make energy use more efficient and/or environmentally responsive. They include conservation, sometimes called "demand-side management," and cogeneration, which involves the simultaneous production of electrical or mechanical power and thermal energy from a single fuel source.

In sum, environmental responsiveness may accommodate a range of possible strategies whose absolute merit may be debated. In the meantime, clearer standards may crystallize as new technologies become available. Even when there is broad agreement on objectives and standards of environmental responsiveness, there may be trade-offs between efficiency and environmental responsiveness and also official instrumental goals.

For example, some might decry rising energy intensity in rural areas of India and China, as subsidized commercial fuels such as kerosene and coal encourage a shift from traditional biomass (Ishiguro and Akiyama 1995). Yet resulting losses in energy efficiency may be offset by gains in environmental responsiveness, since the use of commercial fuels obviates the need to collect biomass and thereby aggravate deforestation. Provision of subsidized fuels may also serve official instrumental goals related to the equitable distribution of critical resources (Shukla 1996). In short, prospects for improving efficiency may be limited by other important considerations. Yet the ensuing discussion of state-led instrumental energy systems suggests that there is broad scope for improving efficiency, in order to use energy with less pollution and waste.

State-led instrumental energy systems

The state-led energy production and distribution systems that emerged in China and India midway through the twentieth century bore the hallmarks of prevailing development theory. States and their public sectors took the leading role in economic growth, which was identified with rapid industrialization and import substitution through the centrally planned development of heavy industry. In India, the private sector was too limited in size and scope to orchestrate energy production and distribution on a large scale. The People's Republic of China established by Mao Zedong in 1949 envisaged no role for private participation in such a critical sector.

The priority task of industrialization-oriented power systems in low-income countries, including China, India, and Brazil, was large-scale energy production through massive dams, power plants, and oil refineries. Coal and oil, the fossil fuels that sparked eighteenth-century Britain's industrial revolution, were widely seen as "modern" energy sources, and critical ingredients for advanced large-scale production. China and India were well-endowed in terms of fossil fuel resources, and since they claimed some of the world's most majestic rivers, giant hydroelectric power plants offered another important energy option. In many rich and poor countries, major dam projects galvanized political and economic support as symbolic giant steps towards "modernization" (Reisner 1993). Indian Prime Minister Jawaharlal Nehru even called major dams "the temples of modern India."

The grandest hydroelectric project was conceived for China. For the Chinese political leadership, the Three Gorges Dam over the Yangtze River represented not only the source of 18,200 megawatts (million watts, or MW) of electricity, equivalent to energy produced by about 50 million tons of coal each year (*New York Times* 1997), but also a symbol of national pride and achievement.

If state leaders' ambitions for drastic change were sometimes heroic, their reach into the hinterlands was generally attenuated. Since benefits and opportunities of development were widely expected to trickle down gradually to widening constituencies, the countryside was often overlooked by urban-based policy-makers. Meanwhile, rural people overwhelmingly depended upon traditional biomass fuels, which were not traded in marketplaces but gathered from fields and forests (Shukla 1996; Yang and Yu 1996). Estimates of biomass use vary widely, reflecting difficulties of measuring trends beyond the market economy.

The importance of political factors – specifically, rural constituencies and official adherence to equity in China and India – served to extend both commercial energy and new industries to rural areas, particularly after the 1960s, when agricultural development drew increasing official attention. Economists might criticize "inefficient" uses of dispersed resources, but possible compensating advantages deserve note. In China and India, rural investment served to slow the pace of urban migration, thereby mitigating pressures of rapid urbanization. Brazil's rapid but regionally specific industrialization and relative concentration of energy resources in São Paulo and surrounding areas of south-east Brazil reflects state leaders' more narrowly focused priorities and constituencies. Also, while Brazil's concentrated efforts may have facilitated growth, its income equity contrasts unfavourably with that of India (Chaffee 1998; Ishiguro and Akiyama 1995).

On balance, Chinese and Indian state leaders' achievements merit recognition. Chinese leaders could take pride in mastering the design, manufacture, and operation of what became the world's third largest power system after those of the United States and Japan. In 1950, total annual electricity generation was only 4.6 terawatt hours (trillion watt, or TWh); by 1994, the figure had increased to 928 TWh (Yang and Yu 1996, 736). During the Ninth Five-Year Plan (1996–2000), officials hoped to increase annual electricity capacity by about 20 gigawatts (million kilowatts) per year, equivalent to adding a major power station every two to three weeks (USDOE 1997). India's power sector increased from production levels of 2,300 MW in 1950 to 69,618 MW by 1992. Officials said the country needed to add up to 8,000 MW of new capacity each year until 2013 (*India Abroad* 1997, 30).

Organization and management

Mid-century perspectives on the efficiency of centrally planned and orchestrated development significantly affected the organization of production and distribution of energy resources. In China, provincial and other subnational electricity providers in the country's 23 provinces and five autonomous regions operated within a nationally directed system. Until 1985, the Ministry of Water Resources and Electrical Power was the main official agency overseeing funding and management of power enterprises. Its annual investment and power-supply plans were prepared under guidelines of the State Planning Committee's Five-Year Plans (Yang and Yu 1996).

Central direction was diluted and diverted by India's democratic federal political system, which gave control of energy to constituent states. In general, India's 25 states and seven union territories are covered by a system of vertically integrated utilities that spans the administrative unit. Since states vary substantially in size and population, their leaders' energy goals and strategies reflected divergent interests and local socioeconomic power configurations.

State government officials have considerable influence over the activities and finances of state electricity boards (SEBs). Official reluctance to yield control over SEBs is reflected in the absence of provisions for effective regulation of the SEBs, by either central government or independent authorities (Salgo 1996; Ranganathan 1996).

Neither country has a power service that provides energy to all who might require it, and the distribution of existing supplies is unreliable. Both centralized and decentralized energy production and distribution systems have many shortcomings, including faulty distribution, inefficiency, and heavily polluting carbon intensity. Faulty distribution covers both sufficiency and reliability of supplies.

Faulty distribution

Even a casual visitor to Beijing or New Delhi may quickly experience a major shortcoming of state-led power systems. Power outages or black-outs, euphemistically called "load-shedding" in India, are a feature of daily life. Long-time residents of both capitals may attest to a deterioration in power supplies due to increased demand. In the 1960s and early 1970s, India produced more electrical power than it could use, but faced growing shortages in the 1990s. During peak hours in 1997, officials reported shortages of 20 per cent (CERI and TERI 1995; *India Abroad* 1997).

China also faced increasing and widening power shortages and gaps between supply and demand, even in such favoured areas as Shanxi Province, which has abundant energy resources. National average peak-hour power shortages ranged around 20 per cent. Losses in terms of economic output were high, and certain to increase, despite official efforts to expand supplies dramatically (Yang and Yu 1996).

The overall unreliability of energy supplies reflects such generic problems of underdevelopment as inadequate infrastructure, particularly transportation networks. China's coal production is centred in northern and north-western regions, whereas its booming industry is mainly in the south-east. The difficulties of transporting supplies from the world's richest coal region to south-eastern factories are ironically underscored by China's recent decision to import coal supplies from Australia (laGrange 1995). Production and transportation costs have also sobered potential private investors' enthusiasm regarding large oil reserves in China's land-locked Xinjiang region.

Ageing energy production facilities also impede reliability of distribution. About 40 per cent of India's power plants are more than 15 years old, and thus prone to repeated breakdowns. As in China, officials sometimes favoured investment in new plants instead of allocating adequate resources to plant renovation that could extend plant life and perhaps produce energy at far lower costs than those needed to build new plants (Purkayastha and Ghosh 1997).

Apart from technical problems related to transmission and distribution along power grid networks that are ill-equipped to adjust supplies and demand across regional jurisdictions, unreliable power distribution in India's constituent states also reflects extensive electricity theft. In many rural areas and surrounding towns, a power line is an inviting challenge for entrepreneurs who hijack power resources to the detriment of the financially strapped SEBs.

Inefficiency

The efficiency of energy use may be assessed by financial profits or losses to providers, and by energy intensity. Neither measure is entirely satisfactory, but they indicate patterns of production and use that might be improved. It bears repeating that Indian and Chinese energy systems were not designed to minimize costs and maximize outputs measurable by profits. Dismaying statistics on financial losses of state-led power systems, which are available for India, should be regarded in that light.

India's SEBs are widely seen as the inefficient Achilles heel of its state-led energy production and distribution system. The SEBs' spiralling annual losses rose to about US$1.7 million by 1995 (Purkayastha and Ghosh 1997). Such haemorrhages deterred further investment in the power sector and also effective maintenance of existing facilities.

Although poor management is reflected in the SEBs' deficient metering practices, bill collection, and widespread power theft (Salgo 1996), pricing policy for power is the major factor in massive SEB losses. Price policy is a key indicator of official economic and political goals. Subsidies to electricity used in agriculture reflect not only the 65 per cent of the population in various state politicians' constituencies but also an overriding national priority, since agriculture constitutes 34 per cent of India's GDP (Ranganathan 1996). The broadly similar political and economic weight of agriculture in China is reflected in its subsidized electricity prices that were suppressed for 30 years under the regime led by its former pre-eminent leader, Mao Zedong.

China performs poorly in relation to a second measure of the efficiency of energy use, energy intensity, denoting energy consumption per US dollar of gross domestic product (GDP). China's energy intensity is 18 times that of Japan, whose energy intensity is lowest among industrialized countries, while India's is four times that of Japan (Ishiguro and Akiyama 1995). Economists might offer several explanations, including obsolete facilities and processes, poor energy management, and lingering low energy prices that discourage efforts to improve energy efficiency (Ishiguro and Akiyama 1995). It is important to note that a developing country may use more energy per unit of output precisely because it is developing, rather than using larger proportions of energy to support such economically non-productive activities as watching television and driving automobiles (Ramage 1997).

Deficiencies of state-run energy systems became more obvious as economic growth and population pressure increased demand. Pressures for fundamental change arose from three major sources – energy price increases, and both domestic and global economic and political change.

Pressures for efficiency and market-led energy systems

Sharp increases in international oil prices during 1973 and 1979 represented the first major challenge to fossil-fuel-based industrial development strategies and heavily subsidized energy prices. National responses reflected their relative command of energy sources. China's fossil fuel reserves made it relatively invulnerable to international oil price increases in the 1970s; thus its energy policies did not change. At the other extreme, Brazil was profoundly shaken, and took decisive steps toward the development of indigenous renewable resources such as biomass-based fuels (Monaco 1991). Midway between those cases, India and the United States registered concern at enforced fuel economies. Both took small steps to support alternative energy sources but made no significant and lasting gains toward either energy efficiency or environmental responsiveness (Ramage 1997; Ishiguro and Akiyama 1995).

In different ways, domestic economic change constituted a second impetus for energy policy change in both China and India. China's major steps toward a market-led economy occurred almost a decade earlier than those of its Indian neighbour. They reflected deliberate policy initiatives to accelerate economic growth and thereby achieve state leaders' goals of technological modernization. The reforms initiated in 1978 by the late Vice Premier Deng Xiaoping decentralized economic administration, allowed scope for market forces, and opened China to the international economy (Lieberthal 1995). Because Chinese leaders were isolated from both major industrial powers in the international arena and domestic opinion, economic and political change was controlled to a degree unimaginable in democratic India.

In India, links between domestic and international politics and economics were as exposed and potentially hazardous as a wayward surging power line. Economic reforms were enacted in 1990–1991 in response to external crises, specifically in foreign exchange reserves, which followed a steep rise in world oil prices accompanying the war in Kuwait. Subsequent external pressure for economic policy change made state leaders vulnerable to criticism from attentive domestic constituencies who might contend that market-led growth and heightened foreign investment threatened important values of equity and self-reliance. The contrasting effects of authoritarian and democratic political systems are striking in the two cases of attempted market-based energy policy change discussed in the two ensuing sections.

Political systems and the domestic arena

In the 1980s and early 1990s, both Chinese and Indian leaders dramatically reversed state-controlled energy policies based upon administered prices and public ownership. Policy-makers endorsed efficiency as a criterion of energy system performance and solicited external foreign investment for energy needs made more urgent by global economic integration and increasing competitiveness. At first sight, state leaders' approaches to potential private foreign investors seemed parallel, and the unforeseen complications broadly similar (*The Economist* 1995). Yet market-based initiatives were shaped by very different political systems which yielded dissimilar results.

China's authoritarian system facilitated drastic price reform and foreign investment in its critical energy sector. Both issues were policy questions addressed in cloistered official deliberations; in a democratic political system, they became public and political issues.[3]

In India, as in the United States, energy prices are inherently political issues. Proposed price increases justified as a means to efficiency or environmental responsiveness invite criticism from opposition leaders. Indian officials' efforts to relinquish power over prices have been painfully slow due to the country's regular elections and anticipated violent protests by farmers (*The Economist* 1997).

Chinese officials' resolve to wield a key instrument of market-led economic reform was apparently not tempered by the political obstacles that daunted their Indian colleagues (Yang and Yu 1996; Ishiguro and Akiyama 1995). Price policy has been set largely by Communist Party and state leaders, without regard to electoral schedules. In 1984, for example, party leaders accepted a gradual introduction of market-based measures such as price liberalization; in 1988, senior government leaders pushed through more drastic reforms. Although subsequent unrest triggered a retrenchment, China's acceptance of market-based rather than administered energy prices nevertheless contrasts with the Indian experience (Starr 1997; Mann 1997; Ishiguro and Akiyama 1995).

Similarly, administrative reform seemed uncomplicated in China but fraught with political difficulties in India. China's once-mighty Ministry of Water Resources and Electrical Power was superseded by new, streamlined organizations including 30 provincial power companies and six power groups from 21 of the 30 provincial companies. As bodies only partly owned by government, they were encouraged to follow a popular trend to "jump into the sea," a colloquialism suggesting entry into the marketplace (Yang and Yu 1996, 737).

By contrast, India's SEBs seemed unready to either jump or be pushed into the sea. External pressure from Bretton Woods agencies to dismantle them angered members of India's sizeable attentive public (Purkayastha and Ghosh 1997). Many observers expressed scepticism about the World Bank's reform efforts undertaken in Orissa, one of India's poorest states, which involved increased electricity tariffs, dismantling the state's financially troubled SEB, and establishing an independent regulatory authority.

Few members of India's attentive public might challenge economists' arguments that investment in dispersed rural communities was inefficient, and subsidized energy distribution in the countryside egregiously so. But even fewer Indian political leaders would willingly shoulder the repercussions of rising energy prices and limitations on energy distribution, particularly if changes could be linked to external pressure that challenged Indian sovereignty and to the financial interests of external utility company shareholders. Domestic political fallout thus reflected back upon national leaders as they faced external economic and political actors.

Political systems and external economic interests

Differences in the two systems' patterns of interaction with international economic interests are illustrated by state leaders' efforts to attract foreign investment in energy production. Such "opening" exposed policymakers to generic problems involved in revamping non-commercial infrastructure (Salgo 1996), and to political and economic risks that may be dramatized in an open society. In India, neither the terms of contract negotiations nor the types of energy production invited could be kept from public view and discussion; thus officials faced a painful and public learning process.

Central leaders' attempts to attract foreign investment with "fast-track" approvals backfired as various projects, most notably a power station proposed by the US-based multinational Enron Development Corporation, were engulfed in domestic political maelstroms and scathing criticism by India's attentive public.[4] For example, an environmental journal charged that:

The incentives to attract foreign investment in India's power sector are iniquitous and make little commercial sense. Observers point out that if these projects go through, "India will soon have unaffordable, 'gold-plated' power, greatly increased dependence on imports and foreign-exchange outflow and a ruined power equipment-manufacturing sector, besides rendering many industries hopelessly uncompetitive" (Shrivastava 1994, 5).

Another commentator raised a common suspicion among India's attentive public that electricity privatization, like the economic liberalization initiated in 1991 in general, was "a decision imposed from outside" that was clumsily pursued by state officials (Ranganathan 1996, 825). Perhaps as a result of public criticism of national leaders' difficulties with both wary potential foreign investors and state-level politicians who traded subsidized power for political support, officials took steps to promote open competition for power contracts with foreign investors.

Senior Chinese officials' determination to monitor the location and nature of foreign energy investment was reflected in a statement by the Minister of Power and Industry: "Since power supply is of great importance to the national economy, foreign investment in it will proceed under the State's macro-control" (Shi 1994). Official ambivalence about external involvement was reflected in bureaucratic politics involving inter-agency and factional rivalries within government. Meanwhile, potential foreign investors consulted presumed experts on Chinese negotiating practices, and worried about the sanctity of contracts in a policy system with no tradition of formal law (Mann 1997).

With the exception of a major hydroelectric project discussed in the ensuing section, the type of energy project proposed did not emerge as a major public issue in China. In India, media and parliamentary discussions of alternative energy projects pursued a range of criticisms raised by external participation. Of gravest concern to environmentalists was the possibility that energy sources facing public opposition in Western democracies, such as nuclear power and coal, were being marketed instead in Asia, to policy-makers who discounted environmental and safety risks. Indian commentators also noted that many large power producers relied upon fossil fuels to maximize their convenience and profits (*Down to Earth* 1997a). Ironically, however, although India's abundant coal resources recalled those of fabled Newcastle, a multinational company's controversial Cogentrix plant proposed to bring imported coals to Karnataka because Indian coal is generally of inferior quality. The coal import proposal was duly denounced as a way to increase Indian dependency on fossil fuel imports despite an indigenously available resource.[5]

In sum, state leaders in China and India faced both domestic and external constituencies in different ways. In China, a small number of officials could arbitrarily raise energy prices or set a date for the phase-out of leaded gasoline. Domestic leaders' detachment from civil society also facilitated Chinese negotiations with external economic interests. In both cases, political conflict was played out within the state bureaucracy.

In India, national policy-makers faced open resistance in state political arenas and in rural society, where farmers' organizations sporadically but dramatically claim the public stage. Faced with an international marketplace, Indian representatives needed to anticipate close public scrutiny and potentially embarrassing questions that exposed pitfalls to negotiators and potential foreign investors. Indian debates raised questions about "efficiency" or "profitability" as absolute values, and as the ensuing discussion indicates, about perspectives on "environmental responsiveness."

Pressures for environmental responsiveness

Even as pressures for efficiency in terms of waste reduction and cost effectiveness drove efforts to deregulate and privatize instrumental energy systems in many parts of the world, environmental responsiveness emerged as an alternative criterion for their assessment. Concerns about environmental implications of energy use were fuelled by UN-sponsored global environmental meetings in Stockholm and Rio de Janeiro; the emergence of environmental problems as a public issue; and the development of institutional structures, including Chinese and Indian environmental agencies, to address unwelcome fallout from economic and social change.

As a criterion for energy system assessment, environmental responsiveness was limited by several factors. Like "sustainable development," the term is vague and subject to divergent interpretations. Cause-and-effect relationships are often unknown or disputed; thus costs and benefits are unclear. As a result, strong and sustained support for environmental responsiveness as a yardstick for energy systems has not emerged on a global scale in either public or private sectors. In sharp contrast, private business support for profitability as a measure for efficiency is strong and constant.

Although environmental responsiveness has not become a standard for energy system assessment in China and India, their political structures have shaped its manifestation in interesting ways. In a democratic political system, environmental responsiveness is not exclusively defined by state leaders in either domestic arenas or settings where domestic and international actors meet. The reverse may be true in an authoritarian system.

Costs, benefits, and domestic politics

In either setting, national policy-makers can make a strong case that major hydroelectric projects are considerably more environmentally responsive than coal-based power projects. Upon its completion, China's proposed US$25 billion Three Gorges project on the Yangtze River will be the world's biggest dam. Many smaller but still massive projects have been completed in India since the middle of the twentieth century, but their construction has stirred controversies almost unknown in China. In India's democratic political system, central pronouncements are challenged by state, regional, and local residents who ask, in essence, "environmentally responsive for whom and what?"

Engineers' and national leaders' calculations of proposed benefits of major hydroelectric projects have often discounted environmental and resettlement costs. In an authoritarian system such as China, criticism and public debate can be and has been banned, and opposition within both government and society has been suppressed.[6] As a result, Western scholars and the international media generally frame controversy surrounding the Three Gorges Dam, which may displace 1.2 million people, as a dispute between its major proponent, Prime Minister Li Peng, and Dai Qing, a journalist and environmental activist identified as "one of the few critics who dares to speak out" (*New York Times* 1997, 14).

In India, critics of major energy projects include not only famous veteran activists such as Chipko movement leader Sunderlal Bahuguna, who hugged trees to protest deforestation in the Himalayan mountains and fasted to register local concerns about the Tehri Dam project, but also many ordinary men and women whose names never appear in print. While mobilizing concern in local, national, and international arenas, Indian activists have drawn attention to the painful displacement of people who traditionally lack political power and financial resources. Such dramatic measures have deterred investment in potentially controversial projects by international agencies, including the World Bank.[7]

In sum, public debate in India underscores the subjective dimension of environmental responsiveness, and the competing values that restrain unilateral action by national and state officials. Prospects for active local initiatives in public arenas apart from the marketplace revitalize the world's largest democracy by stirring widening constituencies into an active rather than passive role in public life.

Political systems and external interests

The presence or absence of freedom of speech and association exerts important influences upon Chinese and Indian state leaders' positions in the international arena. Indian leaders must express and defend positions regarding energy alternatives and their costs and benefits to an attentive public. Indian commentators and non-governmental organizations (NGOs) put state representatives on notice by monitoring their positions at home and abroad. No official has been immune from criticism.[8]

Indian officials are vulnerable to potentially embarrassing domestic criticism that cannot be suppressed.[9] In international forums, this can strengthen Indian officials' claim to represent the world's second most populous nation. Thus, while Chinese and Indian negotiators may express similar misgivings about the equity of rich nations' proposals to apportion costs for remedying such transboundary problems as ozone depletion and global climate change among industrialized and rapidly growing low-income countries including China and India, for example, Indian concerns carry more moral authority. Commentary from within Indian society lends a democratic dimension to official policy positions, and because it is not controlled by government, it can influence constituencies beyond the horizons of the average state official.

Indian environmental activists play a critical educational role for a wide circle of NGOs and scholars throughout the world. Through mass media and more specialized forms of communication, Indian commentators have challenged easy assumptions about global environmental problems related to energy use held by both Northern NGOs and political leaders in the world's most profligate energy consumer, the United States.[10] In so doing, they raised important questions about strategies for reconciling possibly conflicting imperatives of economic growth and environmental protection. In particular, they have contested a widespread North American belief that "the market" discharges state responsibilities for agenda-setting and regulation by offering a range of painless and potentially profitable solutions to local and global environmental problems.

In sum, as a criterion for assessing energy systems, environmental responsiveness is weak in relation to the emerging efficiency criterion, which has strong economic and political support in both international and domestic policy circles. Environmental responsiveness is hindered by lack of consensus on goals and means. Like democracy or sustainable development, it is a process, not a fixed nostrum with supposedly universal validity (Fisher 1995). India's democratic political system facilitates debate about the nature of environmental responsiveness in ways foreclosed by an authoritarian system. In both systems, however, the spread of market-driven energy systems leaves vast scope for pursuit of environmental responsiveness in areas that yield neither wealth nor profits. As in the 1950s, such constituencies are overwhelmingly rural. Once again, they will need state support, but in ways that reflect intervening economic, technological, and political change.

Emerging arenas for clean and efficient energy development

Critical economic, technological, and political factors affecting areas where thousands of Chinese and Indian men and women live without modern energy resources may be summarized as follows. Economic con-

siderations include massive growth of demand for energy and the resources needed to meet it. Since neither state can mobilize such vast
sums, the private domestic and foreign investment that was uninterested
and perhaps unwanted in the 1950s is increasingly sought.

Private participation in energy systems has shifted attention from instrumental criteria of performance to efficiency and profitability considerations. Many rural areas would face continued delays in securing prized
energy connections, and meanwhile aggravate biomass depletion and coal-
based pollution, were it not for important technological developments.

Technological change since the 1950s entails a pronounced shift from
perspectives guided by the economies of scale of the industrial revolution, which placed large-scale coal, oil, and nuclear energy production
under centralized control. Contemporary planners have considered decentralized energy production and explored rather than assumed the
nature of emerging demand (CERI and TERI 1995). From such vantage
points, rural citizens' inexperience with the centralized power grids that
urban customers take for granted can be seen as advantageous, for it
facilitates innovation and an array of promising small-scale technological
possibilities.

For example, an Indian environmental journal reported the development in Britain of a simple solar-powered pump that is much cheaper to
run than conventional systems driven by fossil fuel engines. Due to the
absence of engineering – indeed, its inventor calls the device the "epit-
ome of minimalist engineering" – little maintenance is needed. The back-
breaking, time-consuming and wasteful practice that involves millions of
Asians, Africans, and Latin Americans in a daily grind of water extraction and delivery could be relegated to history if such promising developments are realized (*Down to Earth* 1996). Since Asia represents the
world's most dynamic markets for energy, the size of the potential market
may fortuitously be matched by the eagerness of their promoters.

An internationally funded project to increase energy efficiency and
affordability through the use of copper was scheduled for implementation
in both India and China beginning in 1998. The US$2.5 billion project,
which is supported in part by the UN Common Fund for Commodities,
will draw upon copper's power to conduct energy effectively to help meet
Chinese and Indian demand for energy at lower costs to society and individual users (*Down to Earth* 1998).

Political factors influencing Asia's new frontier of energy development
include a shift in perspectives on the role of the state, born of virtue
possibly learned from past experience and necessity imposed by contemporary resource scarcities. Since the 1970s, the centralized state structure
that specified and implemented presumed development through far-flung
line agencies has deflated in both theory and practice. Particularly in

democratic political systems, local communities seek to claim authority to decide such critical matters as energy supply and use, and to define environmental responsiveness themselves, instead of passively accepting national officials' judgements.

Political and administrative decentralization does not obviate the need for state support. An important assessment of rural energy planning in India concluded that:

intensive intervention, implemented at the cluster of villages level by block [administrative unit] institutions, supervised from the block, coordinated from the district, monitored at the state level and supported nationally appear to be the most promising combination for making effective interventions in the rural energy sector ..." (Sinha, Venkata, and Joshi 1994, 403–414).

Specific areas where official expertise is needed include planning and the reconciliation of local, regional, and national priorities and capabilities, and also in demonstrating, monitoring, maintenance, and evaluation of energy technologies.

Such tasks will draw upon the extensive experience of international agencies and, particularly, the United Nations, which has actively assisted the spread of energy technologies that are widely viewed as environmentally responsive, rather than the massive but environmentally controversial projects of the past. As a result, the United Nations offers vast experience with wind and solar energy technology and their use in rural areas of low-income countries. Its staff and advisers with general expertise in community development can assist both official and agency technical specialists and local community representatives. Perhaps one of the most critical emerging needs in the wake of energy deregulation and privatization is assistance in developing mechanisms for accountability that would make energy producers and distributors answerable to people beyond themselves.

Summary

In the middle of the twentieth century, states sought to develop energy for instrumental purposes. Initially, the political economy of energy production and distribution in China and India was broadly similar, because both states had abundant coal and shared perspectives on the need for a dominant, centralized state in promoting economic development. By the 1970s, however, key development objectives remained distant goals. As past strategies for achieving development were called into question by uncertain energy supplies, such as oil, and by technologies increasingly recognized as wasteful and environmentally unsound, two new criteria of energy system performance emerged: efficiency and environmental responsiveness.

The preceding discussion illustrates how political regimes affected Indian and Chinese approaches to alternative energy system criteria. China's authoritarian system facilitated measures taken in pursuit of efficiency, including energy price reform and private foreign investment. India's democratic system illustrated complications that may arise when political leaders derive power from citizens, who may criticize both domestic and external economic interests. A democracy also highlights the many-faceted nature of environmental responsiveness, and the importance of debate and reassessment. Both Indian state leaders and international constituencies have faced the sometimes bracing test of Indian public opinion.

If the pursuit of environmental responsiveness is inherently a collective enterprise, so too is the monitoring of emerging energy systems. Private interests have strong incentives to monitor profitability, which is one aspect of efficiency. States have incentives to measure the overall efficiency of energy use and the effectiveness of its distribution. Environmental responsiveness is a shared concern of states, market-led forces, and the citizens who use energy in their daily lives. Because of its extensive experience with environmental technology and informal education about its use and effects, the United Nations can and probably will be a catalyst in crystallizing both goals and standards for environmental responsiveness in the twenty-first century. In particular, it can help rural communities draw clean energy from renewable sources, including wind and the sun, and thereby consign the "ignoble fuel" and its fellow fossils to history.

Notes

1. The author would like to thank Brian Halber and Rochelle Perry for research assistance, and Joshua Foster and Jeannie Sowers for helpful suggestions.
2. Unless otherwise indicated, "systems" refers to energy production and distribution.
3. For a discussion of issues and policy processes, see Kingdon (1984).
4. Among the extensive material on Enron, see, for example, Shrivastava (1994); Bartels and Pavier (1997).
5. Purkayastha and Ghosh 1997, 99. The old expression, "bringing coals to Newcastle," refers to the introduction of unneeded resources to an area where they are abundant.
6. See Qing (1994); Starr (1997); *New York Times* (1997). Among the many books chronicling the history of major dam construction, see, for example, Reisner (1993).
7. See *Down to Earth* (1997b, 39). On the controversial Sardar Sarovar Dam across India's Narmada River, see Fisher (1995) and Caulfield (1996).
8. Successive prime ministers have drawn pot-shots in many publications. See, for example, "Narasimha Rao Visits Jurassic Park," *Economic and Political Weekly*, 28 May 1994.

9. The Indian state's inability to do so was evident in its unsuccessful efforts to contain protest within India over the controversial Narmada or Sardar Sarovar Dam. See Fisher (1995, 44).
10. See, for example, Agarwal and Narain (1991).

REFERENCES

Agarwal, A. and S. Narain. 1991. "Global Warming in an Unequal World: A Case of Environmental Colonialism." *Earth Island Journal* (Spring).

Bartels, F. and B. Pavier. 1997. "Enron in India: Developing Political Capability." *Economic and Political Weekly*, 22 February.

Caulfield, C. 1996. *Masters of Illusion.* New York: Henry Holt.

CERI and TERI (Canadian Energy Research Institute and Tata Energy Research Institute). 1995. *Planning for the Indian Power Sector: Environmental and Development Considerations.* New Delhi: TERI.

Chaffee, W. A. 1998. *Desenvolvimento: Politics and Economy in Brazil.* Boulder: Lynne Rienner.

Down to Earth. 1996. "Water: Through the Sun." *Down to Earth* 5(5): 49.

Down to Earth. 1997a. "Nuclear Power: The Privatisation Preamble." *Down to Earth* 5(20): 14–15.

Down to Earth. 1997b. "Campaign." *Down to Earth* 6(14): 39.

Down to Earth. 1998. "More Power." *Down to Earth* 6(24): 51.

Evans, P. B., H. K. Jacobson, and R. D. Putnam, eds. 1993. *Double-Edged Diplomacy: International Bargaining and Domestic Politics.* Berkeley: University of California Press.

Fisher, W. 1995. "Development and Resistance in the Narmada Valley." In *Toward Sustainable Development?* ed. W. Fisher. Armonk: M. E. Sharpe.

India Abroad. 1997. 10 October.

The Economist. 1995. "Asia Delivers an Electric Shock." 28 October.

The Economist. 1997. "Indian Farmers' Power Struggle." 1 November.

Ishiguro, M. and T. Akiyama. 1995. *Energy Demand in Five Major Asian Developing Countries.* Washington: World Bank Discussion Paper.

Kingdon, J. 1984. *Agendas, Alternatives and Public Policies.* New York: Little, Brown.

laGrange, M.-P. 1995. "Les Defis Energetiques de la Chine." *Revue de l'Energie* 470 (July–September): 474–484.

Lieberthal, K. 1995. *Governing China.* New York: W. W. Norton.

Mann, J. 1997. *Beijing Jeep,* 2nd edn. Boulder: Westview.

Monaco, L. C. 1991. "Ethanol as Alternative Transportation Fuel in Brazil." In *Energy Systems, Environment and Development: A Reader.* New York: United Nations.

New York Times. 1997. "China Diverts the Yangtze while Crowing About It." 1 November: 1, 14.

Population Reference Bureau. 1997. *1997 World Population Data Sheet.* Washington: Population Reference Bureau.

Purkayastha, P. and A. Ghosh. 1997. "Power Policies: Need for a National Debate." *Economic and Political Weekly* 32(3): 95–100.

Qing, D. 1994. *Yangtze! Yangtze!* London: Probe International.

Ramage, J. 1997. *Energy: A Guidebook*, 2nd edn. London: Oxford University Press.

Ranganathan, V. 1996. "Electricity Privatization Revisited." *Energy Policy* 24(9).

Reisner, M. 1993. *Cadillac Desert*, 2nd edn. New York: Penguin.

Salgo, H. 1996. "India Faces Restructuring: The Need is with the States." *The Electricity Journal* 9(3): 5–62.

Shi, D. Z. 1994. "Power Industry to Accelerate Reform." *China Daily*, 28 May, cited in M. Yang and Y. Xin 1996. "China's Power Management." *Energy Policy* 24(8): 747.

Shrivastava, R. 1994. "For a Few Units More." *Down to Earth*. 31 July.

Shukla, P. R. 1996. "Modelling of Policy Options: Greenhouse Gas Mitigations in India," *Ambio* 25(4): 240–248.

Sinha, C. S., R. Venkata, and V. Joshi. 1994. "Rural Energy Planning in India." *Energy Policy* 22(5): 403–414.

Starr, J. 1997. *Understanding China*. New York: Hill and Wang.

Thompson, J. 1967. *Organizations in Action: Social Science Bases of Administrative Theory*. New York: McGraw Hill.

USDOE (US Department of Energy). 1997. *International Activities with China*. Washington: Office of Industrial Technology (July).

Webster's New Universal Unabridged Dictionary. 1983. 2nd edn.

Yang, M. and X. Yu. 1996. "China's Power Management." *Energy Policy* 24(8): 735–757.

3

Sustainability, degradation, and livelihood in third world cities: Possibilities for state-society synergy

Peter Evans

The quality of life at the end of the twenty-first century will depend fundamentally on whether a way is found to solve the problems of third world cities. At least three-quarters of the new membership in the world's population during the twenty-first century will live in third world cities. Their hope of enjoying a liveable environment will depend on a fundamental transformation of the political economies of those cities. Without such transformation, degraded, debilitating living environments will confront most third world citizens. Economic growth and new technology may help, but will not resolve the problems of third world urban environments. Political and economic institutions must be reconstructed to confront the complex and contradictory challenges of making urban environments liveable.

Conventional approaches to the political economy of the state suggest little in the way of positive strategies. Realist analysis of the ways in which states use their power as sovereigns to maximize the "national interest" suggests pessimistic conclusions when it comes to environmental problems. It is not only global environmental issues, like the ozone layer, that will be neglected if the traditional logic of competing sovereign states prevails. States primarily concerned with enhancing their sovereign power are also unlikely to focus on domestic environmental issues. Economic and military prowess depend on sound environmental policy only in the long run.

If traditional state-centred politics have little to offer in the environmental arena, calls for curtailing the role of the state offer even less. The "natural" logic of markets leaves environmental improvements as under-supplied collective goods and degradation as a negative externality for which both producers and consumers will try to avoid responsibility. Shifting incentives in a way that forces private economic actors to pay real attention to environmental issues implies more state involvement, not less.

Efforts to analyse the role of the state in fostering livelihood and sus-tainability in third world cities may have to leave behind both pre-occupations with states as unitary geopolitical and military actors and outmoded "state versus market" debates. Such efforts are much more likely to profit from a focus on the myriad local manifestations of the state – the city governments and local public agencies that confront urban economic problems on a quotidian basis. Such organizations are certainly as important to third world cities as foreign ministries. Even the con-sequences of decisions made by finance ministries depend in part on the imagination and effectiveness of such local public institutions.

While no one understands clearly how to make third world cities work, some things are plain. First, solutions cannot be individual – they require the massive provision of collective goods and therefore depend on public institutions. Second, governments – local and national – while they must be a part of the solution, can only be a part. Excepting élites, most third world urban dwellers even supply their own housing, using their own labour, savings, and ingenuity. Public solutions will only be effectual if they are designed to complement the actions of communities.

Markets by themselves are not solutions either. While more effective markets certainly help solve the problems of affluent urban dwellers, they cannot solve the most pressing problems of the urban poor. By them-selves, more effective markets will neither give the urban poor secure tenure in the areas where they need to live in order to work, nor provide them with the infrastructure and urban services necessary to make cities liveable.

For solutions that speak to the needs of the urban population as a whole, popular initiatives and institutional responses must come together in a mutually supportive synthesis. Unfortunately, this proposition is easy to put forward as an abstract principle but extremely difficult to turn into systematic general practice. There are innumerable examples of commu-nity initiatives prospering with the support of official agencies, but an-tagonistic stalemates in which both state and society end up frustrated losers are just as prevalent.

The real question is whether the development of shared under-standings of the political dynamics of third world urban environments can outpace the changing reality of the problems themselves. Extracting commonalities from successful cases while delineating the contextual specificities that limit transferability is the first step toward successful strategizing. Most proposed generalizations will be shot down, but some will survive in reconstructed form. Generating and implementing useful ideas faster than urban environments degenerate is a daunting challenge, but that is no excuse for abandoning the effort.

This chapter will look at how variations in state capacity make a difference to urban degradation and sustainability, but it also starts from the assumption that the effectiveness of state action depends on how the state is connected to society. For empirical examples, this chapter will draw on some cases from Brazil. It will examine the provision of infrastructure, including transportation, sewers, and water, and problems of pollution control. Provision of infrastructure draws the state into a "productive" role, either organizing the delivery of the services in question or providing them directly. Trying to control pollution involves the state as a regulator. What is interesting is that in both cases success depends on the character of the relation between public agencies and societal actors, whether the societal actors play the role of "co-producers" of urban infrastructure,[1] sources of political pressure to expand environmental action, or implementers of state-constructed strategies. This chapter argues that, in all these cases, the exploitation of different kinds of possibilities for "state-society synergy" is crucial to fostering more sustainable outcomes.[2]

Brazil is a good laboratory in which to examine the relations between the state and urban sustainability or degradation, because it offers a range of political variation under the aegis of a single national state (Ames and Keck 1997, 2). In some regions, the structure of local politics has created space for imaginative local politicians to come up with innovations that are copied around the world. In other cases, the structure of local politics has had the opposite effect, crippling innovative efforts by state agencies and forcing imaginative public servants to abandon their efforts to improve the urban environment.

The discussion begins with a story of a failure, the breakdown of FEEMA (Fundação Estadual de Engenharia do Meio Ambiente), Rio de Janeiro's once promising regulatory agency. The case illustrates the ways in which lack of coherence in the overall organization of the state apparatus can destroy the capacity of even a technocratically solid individual agency, and undercut the efficacy of even massive infusions of external funding. It also illustrates the potential (ultimately unrealized in this case) for increasing efficacy by building ties with polluters themselves.

From FEEMA, the analysis moves to one of Brazil's most touted successes, its "ecological capital" of Curitiba. Here an innovative local state apparatus has achieved dramatic successes in the delivery of urban infrastructure, most clearly in the form of its system of collective transport. Curitiba's success immediately poses the question, "What were the sociopolitical prerequisites underlying effective state action?" At the same time, Curitiba's success as a city has been accompanied by an explosive growth in its urban periphery, much of which is still not served in terms of basic infrastructure like sewers and water. This in turn raises the question of how the structure of state-society relations, which has served the middle-class core of the city so well, can incorporate the marginalized poor whose problems are at the heart of urban dilemmas in any growing city.

To explore the possibility of state-society synergy even when the societal counterparts are marginalized communities, the analysis uses the prism of political struggles over the provision of sewers and water in the advanced industrial centre of São Paulo, a case that shows how mobilized communities (however economically marginal) can increase the efficacy of state agencies, even when the relations between these communities and the state is confrontational.

The overall result is more optimistic than the perspective provided by a conventional political economy of the state. Together these Brazilian stories suggest some potential propositions concerning the conditions under which state and society might come together in a productive, mutually supportive synthesis. These cases suggest, in short, that a "state-society synergy" perspective is a particularly appropriate way of looking at problems of sustainability and degradation in the urban contexts.

The concluding section of the chapter moves from the level of cases back to the level of general analysis. It highlights the variations in state-society synergy revealed in the individual cases, and returns to a more general discussion of the role of the state in relation to urban environmental issues. Finally, this concluding section comments on the possible implications of the analysis for the potential role of the United Nations in confronting problems of sustainability, degradation, and livelihood in third world cities.

Pollution control in Rio

The evolution of FEEMA during the late 1990s illustrates, sadly but well, the extent to which the capacity of state agencies depends on a stable and supportive political context.[3] Founded in 1975, FEEMA was the linchpin of the system of pollution abatement for the metropolitan region of Rio de Janeiro and the striking bay (Baía da Guanabara) around which the city sits. With an initial staff of 700 employees, it was in charge of monitoring air and water quality and regulating the roughly 6,000 industrial firms that discharged organic waste and heavy metals into the bay each day (GEDEG undated). Initially, FEEMA was well funded, able to pay good salaries, and therefore able to attract a high-quality body of professionals. It became a model environmental agency within the Brazilian context and was internationally recognized for its work on environmental management (Margulis and Gusmão 1997, 3).

In the 1980s, however, both the fiscal situation of the state government and the place of FEEMA in the government's priorities shifted, to the agency's disadvantage. Salaries declined and by 1992 were less than one-quarter the level they had been at when the agency was founded. Falling salaries made it impossible to maintain previous standards of excellence. The general level of commitment of the professional staff fell along with their salaries. Absenteeism reached the point at which only about half the staff was on duty at any particular time. Even worse, staff began to depend on private consulting jobs in the very sectors that FEEMA was supposed to be regulating. Gradually, FEEMA's reputation for professional excellence was corroded by allegations of corruption and its ability to perform even its routine monitoring tasks was compromised (Margulis and Gusmão 1996, 11).

Just how intractable FEEMA's problems had become was demonstrated by a failed attempt at reviving the agency in the mid-1990s. At the beginning of 1995, a newly inaugurated state government invited a young environmental economist, Sergio Margulis, to take over the presidency of FEEMA (and become simultaneously Sub-secretary for Environment in the state government). Margulis entered his office with the proclaimed aim of revitalizing FEEMA, recovering the full glory of its pioneering past, and making it again a centre of scientific excellence and an institutional model. While recovering the agency's past, he also wanted to transform and modernize its role. His goal was to leave behind the old "command and control" model of environmental management which focused the agency on policing tasks. Instead, he advocated building ties with entrepreneurial and community groups so as to "turn them into active participants in the execution of goals and strategies of environmental management" (Margulis 1995a, 3). He offered, in short, a vision that would go beyond the old "command and control" model of environmental management and move toward a "state-society synergy" model.

Sixteen months later Margulis' visions of a revitalized FEEMA were dust. He had resigned from the presidency, wiser but disillusioned by his experience. He had discovered that without being able to recuperate the basic capacity of the agency as a professional and bureaucratic organization, building state-society synergy was impossible, and without the support of a politically coherent, committed state government, recuperating the basic capacity of the agency was a goal beyond reach.

Lack of commitment was clear in the budgetary process. In order to recuperate staff morale and commitment, FEEMA would have had to make some progress in improving salaries, which in turn required that the state government commit new resources. Instead, the budgetary process proved disheartening. It began with the state legislature cutting FEEMA's proposed budget by 12 per cent. Worse still, only 40 per cent of the reduced budget allocation was actually transferred to FEEMA. (Margulis and Gusmão 1996, 7; 1997, 8). Lack of commitment to environmental issues was also illustrated by the fact that revenues specially earmarked in the Constitution for a fund for environmental control (FECAM – Fundo de Controle Ambiental) were at first not channelled into the fund at all and then channelled into the fund but not released to environmental agencies like FEEMA.

The state government's inability to project a coherent overall approach to environmental management was evident in the conflict-filled relationship between FEEMA and the state water company (CEDAE – Companhia Estadual de Águas e Esgotos). A contract with CEDAE for the regular analysis of water quality in CEDAE's system absorbed about 60 per cent of the resources that FEEMA could devote to water-quality monitoring. Instead of being a partnership between the service provider (CEDAE) and its technical auxiliary agency (FEEMA), this relationship was characterized by debilitating conflict. When FEEMA fulfilled its obligation for public disclosure by announcing water-quality problems in certain parts of the CEDAE system, CEDAE simply denounced FEEMA as unqualified to do the analysis. From the beginning of the 1990s, FEEMA was unable to collect payment for its monitoring services, a debt that amounted to over US$5 million by the middle of 1996 when FEEMA finally gave up monitoring the water quality in the state company's system (Margulis and Gusmão 1996, 7–8; 1997, 8–9).

The costly absence of a coherent shared project among state agencies whose work should have been inherently complementary was equally apparent in the operation of the massive (US$800 million) Programme for the Clean-up of Guanabara Bay. Funded by the InterAmerican Development Bank and Japan's Overseas Economic Cooperation Fund (OECF), this project consisted primarily of the construction (by private contractors) of sanitation and water supply infrastructure, mainly in the less privileged "suburbs" to the north of Rio city proper. Monitoring and assessing the changes in the bay's water quality, clearly a crucial function if the project was to succeed in accomplishing its goals, was FEEMA's obligation. The importance of FEEMA's role was underlined by the funders when they earmarked US$20 million of the project funds for strengthening FEEMA's institutional capacity. Yet the agencies implementing the project, in part because they were primarily concerned with its public works aspects, resisted the release of the environmental control part of the funding (FEEMA's part), aggravating rather than ameliorating FEEMA's institutional problems (Margulis and Gusmão 1996, 8; 1997, 10).

Ironically, FEEMA had greater success building productive alliances with the polluters it was in charge of regulating than it had with its sister agencies in the state government. Consistent with his view that FEEMA's chances of achieving results via a "command and control" strategy were unlikely, Margulis decided to work with the local industry association (FIRJAN – Federação das Indústrias do Estado do Rio de Janeiro) to see if a system could be devised that would make smaller demands on FEEMA's increasingly precarious organizational and professional capacity, but still promise a reduction in industrial pollution. In fact, the industry association was quite receptive and an interesting plan emerged. Potentially polluting industries were divided into five groups according to their location on different river basins which fed into the bay. Each group was constituted as a consortium with collective responsibilities for reducing pollution levels in their river basin. The plan meant that FEEMA could focus on enforcing lower pollution levels for each basin as a whole, leaving it up to individual firms to decide among themselves on the most economical means of meeting the goals, given each firm's capacity to respond to its specific emission problems (Margulis and Gusmão 1996, 13–14; 1997, 15–17).

While this effort at state-society synergy did reduce the demands on FEEMA (in comparison to what would have been required to produce the same results by means of monitoring specific emissions from each individual firm and then enforcing reductions), the system still depended critically on FEEMA's being able to sustain a certain minimal level of capacity and credibility. Collective responsibility for overall levels of pollution is attractive only as long as the alternative is enforcement of specific levels of emissions at each individual company. If FEEMA becomes too decrepit to enforce individual standards credibly in any case, then there is little incentive to participate in the collective consortia. In short, the same organizational and professional capacity that is the basis for successful execution of traditional pollution control tasks also underlies more innovative "state-society synergy" approaches.

Buses and parks in Curitiba

During the 1970s Curitiba, the capital of the southern Brazilian state of Paraná, was the fastest-growing city in Brazil. Between 1970 and 1990 a million people were added to the city's population, so that by 1990 what had been a quiet town of 140,000 at the eve of the Second World War had become a metropolis of 1.6 million people with another 650,000 living in the surrounding metropolitan region.[4]

Given such explosive growth, degradation in the quality of urban life would be a normal expectation. Curitiba's problems could certainly have been expected to follow this pattern since one of the major impetuses for the growth of its population was the shift from a more labour-intensive form of agricultural production (coffee) to a more capital-intensive one (soy) in the northern part of the state, which left massive numbers of untrained rural workers without a source of livelihood. Nor did Curitiba have any obvious natural advantages which might have allowed it to sustain such growth. It was not a port or a major industrial centre. Its relatively cold, damp climate did not lend itself in any obvious way to tourism. It was certainly not a major financial centre like Rio or São Paulo.

Despite its rather ordinary economic prospects and burden of rapid growth, Curitiba emerged from its growth period with a firm claim to the title of "Brazil's Ecological Capital." During the fanfare stimulated by the 1992 UN Conference on Environment and Development in Rio, Curitiba was touted by the full range of international media, including conservative business journals like *The Economist*, *The Financial Times*, and *The Wall Street Journal*, as being a model of ecological success.[5] While local critics who claimed that intensive marketing of the city's image played an important role in generating this international fanfare (e.g. Garcia 1997) are unquestionably correct, there is nonetheless substance underlying Curitiba's "ecological capital" claim.

An extraordinary system of public transportation is perhaps the single best example of the city's success. It is sufficiently efficient and inexpensive to attract 75 per cent of the city's commuters, 28 per cent of whom previously travelled to work by car. The result is not only less-congested city streets and lower transportation costs than in most Brazilian cities but also a 25 per cent saving in fuel consumption and consequently one of the "lowest rates of ambient air pollution in Brazil" (Rabinovitch and Leitmann 1993, 29).[6]

This surprisingly effective system was initiated in the early 1970s along with a new city plan that emphasized growth along particular "axes" spreading out from the city centre. Each axis is served by a "trinary" system of roads which includes two lanes restricted to buses only as well as lanes for local traffic (immediately adjacent to the bus lanes) and express roads for cars and trucks, one block away from the bus lanes on either side (Rabinovitch and Leitmann 1993, 21). Zoning rules helped ensure that high-density urban development (in the form of high-rise apartments, for example) would take place along the axes. The resulting pattern of land use made an efficient system of collective transportation possible.

To exploit the possibilities created by the urban design it had fostered, the city government created a remarkably efficient bus system. The choice of buses rather than a metro or light-rail system made it possible to build a comprehensive system without forcing the city into bankruptcy.[7] Because the buses were part of an urban plan which gave them exclusive traffic lanes rather than leaving them to fight their way through normal traffic, the time it took passengers to arrive at their destinations was cut in half. Other innovations cut commuting time even further. The local Volvo factory produced "articulated buses" which expanded the capacity of a single bus from 80 to 270 passengers. New "tube stations" allowed passengers to enter and pay their fares prior to the arrival of the bus and then board the bus at the level of seating, as though it were a metro train. The overall result was a bus system that rivalled a metro system in terms of efficiency, but could cover the entire city at a fraction of what a metro system would have cost.

Curitiba's bus system is a perfect example of how a capable, coherent public administration can make "state-society synergy" work. On the one hand, the creation of the system depended absolutely on the existence of a coherent, publicly enforced plan of roadways and land use designed to make collective transportation feasible. Yet the city government was acutely aware of the limits of its own capacity and the necessity of relying on private partners. A number of different private companies are licensed to operate different routes (ensuring that none of them has any monopoly power *vis-à-vis* the city). The payment they receive is based on the number of passenger/kilometres they deliver, giving them an interest in maximizing the utilization of the system. In addition, their return depends on the capital they have invested in the bus fleet, which helps account for the fact that the average bus in Curitiba is only three years old (as opposed to eight years old in other Brazilian cities) and therefore has substantially lower emissions levels (Rabinovitch and Leitmann 1993, 29).

Relying on private companies to undertake the operation of the system undoubtedly helps make Curitiba's buses run more efficiently than those of other cities. If the city had tried to operate the system by itself it would have risked the kind of bloated, clientelistic, 200-employees-per-vehicle public transport systems that plague some other Brazilian cities. Such a strategy would also have sapped scarce public managerial capacity which could be better used elsewhere. Nonetheless, the role of public authorities remains as central to the operational side of the system as it was in creating the initial preconditions for its success.

The city carefully regulates the private companies, to ensure that both the level of service is maintained and the companies get a sufficient level of return to make operating the system an attractive proposition from their point of view. With the assistance of the City Planning Institute (IPPUC – Instituto de Pequisa e Planejamento Urbano de Curitiba), a parastatal company (URBS – Urbanização de Curitiba; a parastatal organization is one which is separate from the normal bureaucratic machinery of government, but which is owned/controlled by public authorities) sets the parameters of the system, including "calculation of bus timetables and frequencies, development of new bus routes, determination of the necessary number of buses, monitoring the performance of the system, training drivers and conductors, and responding to suggestions and complaints from the bus users" (Rabinovitch and Leitmann 1993, 22). City Hall and URBS also set the level of fares for the system, managing to maintain some of the lowest fares in Brazil while still providing enough incentives so that the companies continue to invest. This is a market-oriented operation – Curitiba's bus system pays its own way on the basis of the fares collected – but it is a market carefully shaped by the visible hand of public planning and regulation.

In addition to public transportation, a variety of other successes validate Curitiba's claim to being an "ecological capital." The city's green space per inhabitant was expanded 100fold from 0.5 m²/inhabitant to 50 m²/inhabitant between 1970 and 1993 through an aggressive programme of recuperating underutilized and abandoned areas and turning them into parks (Rabinovitch and Leitmann 1993, 37). Over 70 per cent of the city's households participate in a recycling programme by sorting their solid waste (Rabinovitch and Leitmann 1993, 36). A carefully planned industrial zone on the edge of the city has generated 200,000 jobs with minimal negative impact on the environment by recruiting low-environmental-impact industries (Rabinovitch and Leitmann 1993, 43).

Looking at Curitiba's accomplishments, two questions remain. First, how can this extraordinary success be explained? What are its sociopolitical underpinnings? Second, can the admirable quality of life that has been provided to the middle-class population living within the city limits be extended to include the population of the metropolitan region surrounding the city, a population which is substantially poorer, still lacking in basic infrastructure like sewers, and expected to match Curitiba's projected population of a 1.5 million people with 1.5 million of its own over the course of the next 12 years (Samek 1996, 70, 158).

The sociopolitical roots of Curitiba's success probably begin with the fact that the city's politics were not dominated historically by a traditional oligarchy. As Ames and Keck (1997, 15) point out, "Paraná lacks the kind of traditional economic and social oligarchy that is common in much of Brazil." The *erva mate* (a bush whose leaves are used to make the *mate* tea commonly drunk in southern Brazil, Argentina, and Paraguay) growers who were the state's first agrarian élite never achieved the kind of semi-feudal level of domination enjoyed by sugar-growers in the northeast. The potential power of traditional agrarian élites was further diluted by the arrival in the latter half of the nineteenth century of a diverse set of immigrants, many of whom managed to make their way as independent farmers.

People who have some political and economic clout, but not enough to be able to rely solely on political connections and economic privilege to ensure that their needs are met, are more likely both to care about collective goods and to foster the public institutions that deliver them. So it is not surprising that a social structure like Curitiba's might generate the most robust public institutions.[8] Nonetheless, the particular pattern of institutional development that led Curitiba to its position as an "ecological capital" involves a combination of path-dependent institution building and political entrepreneurship that is worth underlining.

The "Plan Agache," created for the city by the French planner Alfred Agache, is usually cited as the beginning of Curitiba's transformation. While the centre of the contemporary city is still marked by some of the avenues created under this plan, its cultural legacy may have been more important than its physical one. It established the idea that growth could be directed rather than simply accepted. Thus, when the city later doubled in size over the course of the 10-year period between 1950 and 1960, the response was to turn again to the possibility of directing the pattern of growth. In 1963 URBS, the parastatal that would eventually manage the transportation system, was created. In 1964 two firms from São Paulo won the bid to provide a new city plan (IPPUC 1996, 45; Rabinovitch and Leitmann 1993, 8). The following year, IPPUC was created as a planning institute that would generate the local expertise required to implement the plan. IPPUC would eventually grow to an organization of over 200 people, including 100 professionals. It would also provide the incubator and training ground for Curitiba's most famous mayor, Jaime Lerner, as well as the current mayor, Cassio Taniguchi (Rabinovitch and Leitmann 1993, 10).

Curitiba's success, then, is built first of all on a socio-economic structure in which groups with a strong vested interest in the provision of urban collective goods have sufficient political weight. This socio-economic context made it easier to legitimize a culture in which collective responses to shared problems could be anticipatory rather than reactive. The legitimacy of planning allowed the institutionalization of a set of organizations devoted to the shaping of effective shared responses. A solid set of public institutions increases the likelihood that policies will be successful and successful policies reinforce, in turn, political support for public institutions.

If institutional advantages can be leveraged through imaginative political entrepreneurship, the possibility of positive outcomes is further enhanced, and Curitiba has certainly benefited from political entrepreneurship. Jaime Lerner, who moved from the presidency of IPPUC to become mayor of the city in 1971 and served as mayor for a total of 12 years over the course of the next two decades,[9] is without question a skilful and imaginative political entrepreneur whose creations (from the first pedestrian mall to the "tube stations") captured the imagination of the citizenry. While it is important to recognize the role of political entrepreneurship and creativity, however, it is also important to recognize that without the infrastructure provided by a robust set of public institutions, and the culture and personnel that go with them, the ability of even the most imaginative planner to "deliver the goods" is severely constrained.

If Curitiba were a small island, like Singapore, or located in a national context of high welfare and low population growth, like Sweden or Switzerland, then it might be appropriate to simply celebrate the city's victories and try to figure out how to copy them. But Curitiba is located in Brazil in an epoch where increasingly capital-intensive agriculture continues to push populations out of the countryside and an increasingly capital-intensive industrial sector lacks the capacity to generate a commensurate number of manufacturing jobs. In part precisely because its past success makes it an attractive destination, Curitiba must face the same problem as other third world cities: how to deal with a growing but impoverished peripheral population which can neither secure the private income to participate in the urban land market nor generate the tax revenues that are necessary to provide it with conventional urban services.

The city government clearly recognizes that its future as an "ecological capital" depends on its ability to extend its success to the poorer surrounding communities, yet it also recognizes that such an extension is a daunting challenge. Over the course of the two decades from 1991 to 2010, the population of Curitiba is expected to grow by only about 25 per cent. The population of some of the poorer communities in the surrounding metropolitan area, like Colombo and Almirante Tamandaré, will come close to tripling in size. Instead of representing almost 90 per cent of the population of the metropolitan region, as it did in 1970, Curitiba will represent less than half by 2015 (COMEC 1997, 8; Samek 1996, 158).

In 1991, over 90 per cent of heads of households with incomes greater than 10 minimum salaries lived in the city proper, whereas heads of household earning less than two minimum salaries a month were already close to becoming the majority in the surrounding communities. Once economic disparities are reflected in spatial segregation, the potential for overt political conflict between rich and poor, something which has been strikingly absent from public political debates in Curitiba,[10] is undeniable.[11]

Land occupations (or, as they are more pejoratively labelled in the press, "invasions") are a good example of how the governance of urban growth can be forced outside the boundaries of consensual planning into the arena of political struggle between the dispossessed and their more privileged fellow citizens. Obviously, Curitiba's city government could not sanction the take-over of land by those who don't own it without alienating its essentially middle-class constituency. Yet the popular movements that initiate occupations have little option but to "live outside the law." Participants in these occupations, like Sebastiana (Tiana) Oliveira Motta, an activist in the 1988 Xapinhal occupation, are convinced that urban real-estate markets hold only "the death of high rents." Successfully staking a non-market (and therefore illegal) claim to some land is viewed as the "passage from death to life" and pursued with corresponding fervour.[12] Dealing with the irreducible conflict of interest between those fortunate enough to own land and those, like Tiana, who know that they will not be able to afford decent housing requires a quite different definition of "state-society synergy" than the one that has worked so well for Curitiba in the past. Nor are the problems of city government likely to end with the regularization of an occupation. Tiana ends her diary of the Xapinhal occupation by saying, "This is only one successful step. Now it is the fight for water, electricity and the construction of a decent house. There is a lot of struggle ahead." (Motta 1991, 40). Political struggle is likely to become part of the process of infrastructure development as well as part of the process of land allocation.

Does this mean that Curitiba's efforts to become an ecological capital will inevitably be undermined by the larger contradictions of a society that current President Fernando Henrique Cardoso characterizes as "not underdeveloped but unjust"? Not necessarily. Dealing with land that is occupied by one set of people but owned by another set is a generic problem for third world "megacities" and has stimulated a variety of creative responses.[13] Curitiba's problems are less extreme than most and its public institutions are more robust and creative than most. There is no reason to believe that it will be incapable of dealing creatively with processes of urban growth that are more conflictual than those of the past. In fact, a quick look at struggles over infrastructure in Curitiba's much less ecologically successful neighbour, São Paulo, suggests that conflictual relations between poor communities and state agencies can be a source of productive state-society synergy.

Sewers in São Paulo[14]

The *favelas* (slums) of São Paulo are less famous than those of Rio de Janeiro, but their population is no less numerous and their living conditions no less difficult. In 1973, only 20 per cent of São Paulo's *favelas* had potable water. Fourteen years later, in 1987, 99 per cent did. During the same period there was also a 15 fold increase in the proportion of *favelas* served by sewers. For the Curitiba metropolitan region, where the proportion of the households served by sewers in 1993 was only 46 per cent[15] and some of the region's communities had no sewers at all,[16] the dynamics of São Paulo's phenomenal increase in the provision of basic collective goods are of obvious relevance.

The extension of sewer service to marginal communities is not necessarily conflictual. In other Brazilian contexts, the story of the extension of sewer systems began, like Curitiba's bus system, with the imagination of technocrats working inside the state and then proceeded through the construction of state-society synergy based on what Ostrom (1996) would call "co-production." "Condominial sewers," originated by Brazilian engineer José Carlos de Melo, have been very successful in giving poor communities an avenue for cooperating with state agencies in building their own sewer systems, and have enabled a considerable expansion of sewer systems to poor communities.[17]

In São Paulo in the 1970s and 1980s, however, the expansion of basic infrastructure to poor communities was based on a different sort of synergistic interaction of communities and state agencies. The starting point in São Paulo in the 1970s and 1980s was not an innovation promoted by progressive technocrats within the state. It was the poor communities themselves that took the initiative. Neighbourhood associations, originally mobilized to demand cost-of-living adjustments from an authoritarian military regime, began to fight for the provision of normal urban services. Neighbourhood women fought small battles for improvements in health care and schooling for their children (Watson 1992, 40–41).

These quotidian struggles were punctuated by larger confrontations with state agencies in which men were more likely to become involved. Over the course of such conflicts, communities learned to work together and to pressure government agencies in more sophisticated ways. Public demonstrations in which busloads of people from the *favelas* arrived at the headquarters of the state sanitation company (SABESP) with buckets full of undrinkable water were combined with small meetings in which association leaders proposed alternative technologies, discovered through contacts with university housing specialists, to SABESP technicians (Watson 1992, 34–35, 45).

What is most interesting about the contestation between these communities and the state agencies they were pressuring is that contestation was always combined with engagement. In their meetings with agency staff, neighbourhood activists learned about the technical and legal problems that stood in the way of state action. Having learned, they formulated new strategies that would circumvent these problems. Perhaps even more important, they learned about the organization of the public agencies with which they were dealing. They learned how to use more sympathetic state agencies to pressure less sympathetic ones, and which arguments were effective in which offices.

Eventually, as democratization replaced military appointees with elected mayors and governors, neighbourhoods found allies whose pressure from above would complement their own pressure from below. Pressure, channelled through sympathetic parts of the public sector, led to small organizational changes that made big differences.

SABESP, the state sanitation company, was a well-managed company with a high level of technical competence, but it was determined to stick to the provision of conventional water and sewer hook-ups and therefore very reluctant to serve *favelas* with dubious legal status and no real streets. Communities responded by focusing their efforts on other, more sympathetic organizations and gained their first successes. With the help of pressure from a new elected mayor, the Municipal Bureau of Social Welfare and the Municipal Development Agency were persuaded to set up a pilot organization (Profavela) that would work in poor neighbourhoods with neighbourhood associations and connect them up with SABESP's regular networks (Watson 1992, 57–67). Profavela not only succeeded in multiplying the number of *favela* water connections enormously (from 2,000 to 27,000) but also gave SABESP district offices some experience in dealing with *favelas* (Watson 1992, 63–64).

Later, with help from a newly elected state governor, SABESP was persuaded to set up its own internal "*favela* team," whose technocrats became insider allies for the outsider neighbourhood associations. These insiders figured out what techniques for the extension of water and sewer networks into *favelas* would be most acceptable to SABESP's engineers. They then used the threat of neighbourhood mobilization as a way of persuading the organization to adopt new techniques. Thanks to this insider/outsider combination SABESP began putting water connections into the *favelas* at an unprecedented rate, so that by 1987 99 per cent of all *favelas* had at least partial water connections and the majority had water service going to all households.

What the São Paulo example suggests is that state-society synergy need not always be consensual and conflict-free in order to be effective. As long as contestation between communities and the state is combined with engagement, conflict can play a vital role in creating synergy. Even more important, this case underlines the fact that the state is not a monolith.

There are likely to be some potential reformers in even the most hide-bound agencies. Aggressive community action empowers these internal reformers and helps transform the character of the agencies in which they work.

Conclusion: State, society, and the struggle for liveable cities

Examining the role of the state in relation to environmental issues in third world cities produces a discourse quite different from that which dominates most discussions of the state in the contemporary global political economy (Evans 1997c). The discussion here has been able to proceed without reference to the supposed evaporation of the power of the state. If the declining ability of nation-states to counterbalance the private power of transnational corporations played a role in the local urban dramas that were the focus of attention in this chapter, it was a diffuse and indirect one, not the centre of the story. Yet the authoritative legitimacy of public organizations and the fact that they can be held responsible for the realization of collective interests, both of which are at the essence of the concept of the state, were absolutely central to the unfolding of these local dramas. One of the implications of this analysis may well be that preoccupations with the changing relations of states to the global political economy should not distract analytical attention from the persistently essential role of public institutions in confronting collective dilemmas like the degradation of urban environment.

The organizational capacity of city governments to deliver public goods is crucial to making cities liveable, but public institutions also play a critical role because they articulate shared interests. Sometimes this means taking inchoate needs and aspirations and giving them a form that captures the imagination of the community, as in Curitiba. Even when public agencies are the targets of indignation because of their inability to meet obvious societal needs, as in the case of São Paulo, they are still lenses that help focus communities on the pursuit of their collective interests.

Because public institutions are so central to the dynamics of environmental politics, their capacity as institutions is a decisive determinant of whether environmental goals are likely to be realized. It is hard to overstate the importance of simple quotidian kinds of capacity in the form of trained, competent personnel, sufficiently well rewarded to be willing and able to devote themselves to carrying out organizational goals. The contrast between the devastation of organizational strength in the case of FEEMA and the gradual construction of institutional capacity in the case of Curitiba made the point nicely.

Public institutions are also sites for innovation, imagination, and political entrepreneurship. From José Carlos de Melo's invention of the condominial sewer to Jaime Lerner's genius for making ecological success a major source of civic identity, it is clear that changing urban environments depend on being able to transcend quotidian routines. Yet, as the experience of Sergio Margulis showed, attempting innovative public policy without basic organizational capacity is a formula for frustration. The FEEMA case also underlined the fact that the construction and sustenance of capacity is not simply a technical problem. The capacity of individual agencies, and ultimately the state apparatus as a whole, is rooted in political support.

However fundamental the capacity and entrepreneurial initiatives of the public sector are to the outcome of these cases, the cases also make it clear that government cannot confront urban environmental issues as an independent actor. Pursuing environmental agendas depends on engaging the interests and energies of communities and societal actors. Synergistic interaction of state and society does indeed seem to be what produces environmental results. The symbiotic relationship between the city government and private companies that produced collective transportation in Curitiba illustrates the point nicely. Less obvious types of state-society synergy are equally important. José Carlos de Melo and his shanty-town co-producers, SABESP and its community critics, and even Sergio Margulis and his industrial polluters are all examples of how the ability of the state to deliver basic collective goods depends on societal collaboration.

State-society synergy involves combining complementary public and private capacities to allow the production of collective goods that neither public nor private sector could produce by itself. It also involves uncovering shared interests in the creation of new collective goods. Private companies could never have created Curitiba's bus system, but it would have been foolish and wasteful for the city to try to operate the system on its own. URBS and IPPUC function as very "visible hands" channelling the private pursuit of profit into the satisfaction of public needs. They have structured the system so that private companies pursue their interests in profits via strategies which increase passenger numbers and decrease emissions.

The relationship between poor communities and SABESP illustrates a very different relationship between public and private interests. When poor communities realize their particular interests in gaining access to water and sewers, they are also furthering the general interests of the city in reducing the health and environmental hazards associated with open sewers and pit latrines. In this case, the realization of general interests depends on pushing the public organization, SABESP, to go beyond its particularistic organizational interest in preserving established routines and avoiding challenges that would stretch its capacity.

The FEEMA-FIRJAN relationship illustrates still another possibility.

FEEMA represents the collective interests in cleaning up Rio's air and water. Getting companies to commit their private resources to investments which will reduce emissions is a means to that end. Companies trying to minimize production costs have a private interest in avoiding such expenditure, whatever their general feelings about the environment. Public and private interests conflict. Yet as long as firms believe that pollution control will indeed be enforced, they have an interest in supporting an "efficient" form of regulation – one that will be least arbitrary, most predictable, and allow them to respond in ways that they feel minimize the private cost of a given reduction in pollution. At the same time, a regulator like FEEMA has a clear interest in finding forms of pollution reduction whose demands do not exceed its limited organizational capacity. As it turns out, there is a substantial overlap between these two particular interests. The intersection creates space for state-society synergy, despite the underlying conflict.

The point can be summarized simply. Societal actors play an important role in the struggle for more liveable urban environments in at least three ways. Private interests can be engaged in the implementation of environmental strategies, conserving scarce public capacity. The political energies of those most directly affected by degradation are important in pushing state agencies to make the most of their capacity to deliver collective goods. Even when particular societal interests are in conflict with the general interest in a cleaner environment, it is still possible to find space for state-society synergy. As long as societal actors are complemented by adequate state capacity, applied with some imagination and creativity, the problems of the urban environment are anything but intractable.

The analysis that has been presented here underlines the irreplaceable contribution of local public institutions to the struggle for more liveable third world urban environments. It demonstrates the importance of preserving the capacity and defending the legitimacy of the general system of public authority that is rooted in the idea of the state. But what, if anything, might this analysis have to say about supranational public institutions like the United Nations? It could be argued that it suggests a role which does not fit neatly into either the "global manager" or the "global counsel" archetypes.

A state-society synergy image suggests a fluid political arena in which solutions to environmental problems emerge out of creative conflicts between local communities and state agencies. Small injections of new knowledge can play an important role in arriving at positive resolutions. Indigenous innovation is the most likely source of such new knowledge, but if each locality has to "reinvent the wheel" then problems may evolve more rapidly than local innovations are replicated. Public institutions or community/NGO networks at the national level may help diffuse innovations across localities, but the degree to which cities in different countries and regions share similar problems is striking, and diffusing innovations across national boundaries is likely to depend on supranational organizations.

Since collective solutions to environmental problems involve, almost by definition, ideas from which the returns are not easily privately appropriated through markets, corporations won't do as vehicles. Ideas that could be put into practice by communities on their own may be most effectively spread by international NGOs. But if implementation depends on the joint action of communities and government agencies, UN agencies, which appear at the local level as a peculiar hybrid of global NGOs and supranational state agencies, may well have a special aptitude for complementing the local dynamics of state-society synergy.

Notes

1. See Ostrom (1996) for a discussion of the way in which citizens who are formally in the role of "clients" are often in fact "co-producers" of the services that they receive.
2. For an elaboration of the "state-society synergy" perspective see Evans (1996a; 1996b; 1997a; 1997b). For a very similar perspective which introduces some useful complementary concepts see Tendler (1997).
3. This section is based primarily on Margulis (1995a; 1995b) and Margulis and Gusmão (1996; 1997). The author would also like to thank Victor Coelho for sharing his extensive knowledge of the history of FEEMA as well as some of his archival material. Obviously, the way in which this material has been used to construct the interpretation of the FEEMA case presented here is solely the author's responsibility.
4. Figures cited in the text are from Rabinovitch and Leitmann (1993, 2). COMEC (1997, 8) gives slightly different figures.
5. See The Economist 1993; Kamm 1992; Lamb 1991; Maier 1991. All are cited in Rabinovitch and Leitmann 1993.
6. The interesting thing is that Curitiba has achieved its elevated use of collective transport and low emission levels despite having more cars per capita than any Brazilian city besides Brasilia. (Rabinovitch and Leitmann 1993, 18).
7. Per kilometre served, the capital costs of bus systems are about 1 per cent of light-rail systems and 0.2 per cent of the cost of metro systems (Rabinovitch and Leitmann 1993, 23). If total costs per passenger/kilometre are considered the difference is less overwhelming, but buses are still a fraction of the cost (World Resources Institute 1996, 93).
8. For example, in 1990 the income distribution in the city of São Paulo was bimodal because of the small proportion (18 per cent) of the population earning between US$290 and US$360 per month, whereas in Curitiba this middle group was half as large again, containing 28 per cent of the population, while the proportion with very high incomes in Curitiba (>US$1,500 per month) was only about 60 per cent of the proportion in São Paulo (4.3 per cent versus 7 per cent) (data are for 1990 from IBGE National Census and IPPUC, household survey cited in Rabinovitch and Leitmann 1993, 7). Yet at the same time it should be noted that Curitiba's social structure is hardly egalitarian. The city government reports the city's Gini index in 1991 to be 0.57 (Curitiba 1996, 7), only slightly less than Brazil's record level of 0.63 (World Bank 1997, 223).
9. 1971–1974, 1979–1983, 1988–1992 (Rabinovitch and Leitmann 1993, 13).

10. Ames and Keck (1997, 25), for example, contrast Paraná with Pernambuco, whose environmental politics reflects the "high level of left-right polarization in the state."
11. For a discussion of the way in which spatial segregation can stimulate class politics see Seidman (1993) on political mobilization in Brazil and South Africa in the 1970s and 1980s.
12. The quotes are from Tiana's diary (Motta 1991, 8). For her, the Xaphinal occupation was a perfect parallel to the flight of the children of Israel from bondage in Egypt to the promised land.
13. There is, of course, a very large literature on this issue. For example, Janice Perlman (1990, 6) goes so far as to argue that "it was recognized in the early 1960s that the self-built shanty towns of the Third World Cities were not the problem but the solution, and that giving land tenure to the squatters and providing urbanized lots in the peripheral areas yielded better results than the bulldozer." Douglass (1992, 19) notes some interesting Asian experiments and Pezzoli (1998) chronicles a particularly interesting case in Mexico City in which the occupying communities used a public commitment to developing more sustainable land use as one their political tools for maintaining their tenure.
14. The material that follows on São Paulo is drawn from Gabrielle Watson's (1992) MA thesis. For an earlier version of the author's interpretation of Watson's work see Evans 1997a.
15. COMEC 1997, 41, data from PNAD/93. Since the average for Brazil as a whole was 39 per cent (same source), this is an indicator on which Curitiba does not stand out as exceptionally advanced.
16. For example, Almirante Tamandaré and Colombo as of 1991; see Samek (1996, 70).
17. For an excellent description of the origination and expansion of condominial sewer systems in Brazil see Watson (1995). For a discussion of the export of the idea to Kenya, Paraguay, and Indonesia see Watson and Jagannathan (1995).

REFERENCES

Ames, B. and M. Keck. 1997. "The Politics of Sustainable Development: Environmental Policymaking in Four Brazilian States." *Journal of InterAmerican Studies and World Affairs* 39(4).
COMEC (Coordenação da Região Metropolitana de Curitiba). 1997. *A Base de Dados Sobre a Situação Ambiental da da Região Metropolitana de Curitiba.* Curitiba: COMEC.
Curitiba, Prefeitura da Cidade. 1996. *Curitiba: Economic and Social Indicators.* Curitiba: Department of Industry, Commerce, and Tourism.
Douglass, M. 1992. "The Political Economy of Urban Poverty and Environmental Management in Asia: Access, Empowerment and Community Based Alternatives." *Environment and Urbanization* 4(2): 9–32.
The Economist. 1993. "Home Remedies are the Best." 17 April.
Evans, P. 1996a. "Development Strategies Across the Public-Private Divide. *World Development* 24(6): 1033–1037.
Evans, P. 1996b. "Government Action, Social Capital and Development: Reviewing the Evidence on Synergy." *World Development* 24(6): 1119–1132.
Evans, P. 1997a. "Re-envisioning the Reform Process: A State-Society Synergy Perspective." Keynote address, ECLAC Conference on the Caribbean Quest: Directions for the Reform Process, 26 June, Port-of-Spain, Trinidad and Tobago.

Evans, P., ed. 1997b. *State-Society Synergy: Government and Social Capital in Development.* Berkeley: University of California.

Evans, P. 1997c. "The Eclipse of the State? Reflections on Stateness in an Era of Globalization." *World Politics* 50 (October): 62–87.

Garcia, F. E. S. 1997. *Cidade Espetáculo: Política, Planejamento e City Marketing.* Curitiba: Editora Palavra.

GEDEG (Grupo Executivo de Despoluição da Baía de Guanabara). Undated. *Baía de Guanabara, Espelho da Vida.* Rio de Janeiro: Governo do Estado do Rio de Janeiro.

IPPUC (Instituto de Pesquisa e Planejamento Urbano de Curitiba). 1996. *Curitiba em Dados.* Curitiba: IPPUC.

Kamm, T. 1992. "Urban Problems Yield to Innovative Spirit of a City in Brazil." *Wall Street Journal.* 10 January.

Lamb, C. 1991. "Brazil City in the Vanguard of Fight against Pollution." *Financial Times.* 10 August.

Maier, J. 1991. "From Brazil, the Cidade that Can." *Time.* 14 October.

Margulis, S. 1995a. "Resgatando o Pioneirismo." *Revista FEEMA* 4(17): 3.

Margulis, S. 1995b. "Resgatando o Pioneirismo." *Revista FEEMA* 4(17): 8–12.

Margulis, S. and P. P. de Gusmão. 1996. "Problems of Environmental Management in the Real World: The Rio de Janeiro Experience." Unpublished ms., translation of 1997 article below.

Margulis, S. and P. P. de Gusmão. 1997. "Problemas da Gestão Ambiental na Vida Real: A Experiência do Rio de Janeiro." Texto para discussão, No. 461. Rio de Janeiro: IPEA (Instituto de Econômica Aplicada).

Motta, S. O. 1991. *Diáro de Tiana: Uma experiência de fé na peripheria de Curitiba.* Paranavaí, Paraná: Gráfica Paranavaí.

Ostrom, E. 1996. "Crossing the Great Divide: Co-production, Synergy and Development." *World Development* 24(6): 1073–1088.

Perlman, J. 1990. "A Dual Strategy for Deliberate Social Change in Cities." *Cities* 7(1): 3–15.

Pezzoli, K. 1998. *Human Settlements and Planning for Ecological Sustainability: The Case of Mexico City.* Cambridge, MA: MIT Press.

Rabinovitch, J. and J. Leitmann. 1993. *Environmental Innovation and Management in Curitiba, Brazil.* UNDP/UNCHS(Habitat)/IBRD, Urban Management Program, Working Paper No. 1.

Samek, J. 1996. *A Curitiba do Terceiro Milênio.* Curitiba: Editora Palavra.

Seidman, G. 1993. *Manufacturing Militance: Workers Movements in Brazil and South Africa.* Berkeley: University of California Press.

Tendler, J. 1997. *Good Government in the Tropics.* Baltimore: Johns Hopkins University Press.

Watson, G. 1992. "Water and Sanitation in São Paulo, Brazil: Successful Strategies for Service Provision in Low-income Communities." Master's thesis, Department of Urban Studies and Planning, Massachusetts Institute of Technology.

Watson, G. 1995. *Good Sewers Cheap: Agency Customer Interactions in Low-cost Urban Sanitation in Brazil.* Washington: World Bank, Water and Sanitation Division.

Watson, G. and N. V. Jagannathan. 1995. "Participation in Water and Sanitation." Environment Department Papers Participation Series No. 002. Washington: World Bank.

World Bank. 1997. *World Development Report: The State in a Changing World.* New York: Oxford University Press.

WRI (World Resources Institute). 1996. *World Resources 1996–97, The Urban Environment,* New York: Oxford University Press.

FURTHER READING

Ard-Am, O. and K. Soonthorndhada. 1994. "Household Economy and Environmental Management in Bangkok: The Cases of Wat Chonglom and Yen-arkard." *Asian Journal of Environmental Management* 2(1): 37–48.

Bromely, D. 1989. "Property Relations and Economic Development: The Other Land Reform." *World Development* 17(6): 867–877.

Douglass, M. 1991. "Planning for Environmental Sustainability in the Extended Jakarta Metropolitan Region." In *The Extended Metropolis: Settlement Transition in Asia,* eds. N. Ginsburg et al. Honolulu: University of Hawaii Press.

Douglass, M. and M. Zoghlin. 1994. "Sustainable Cities from the Grassroots: Livelihood, Habitat and Social Networks in Suan Phlu, Bangkok." *Third World Planning Review,* 16(2): 171–200.

Drakakis-Smith, D. 1995. "Third World Cities: Sustainable Urban Development." *Urban Studies* 32(4–5): 659–677.

Eckstein, S. 1990. "Poor People vs the State and Capital: Anatomy of a Successful Community Mobilization for Housing in Mexico City." *International Journal of Urban and Regional Research* 14(2): 274–296.

Figueiredo, R. and B. Lamounier. 1996. *As Cidades que Dão Certo: Experiências Inovadores na Administração Pública Brasileira.* Brasília: MH Comunicação.

Furedy, C. 1992. "Garbage: Exploring Non-Conventional Options in Asian Cities." *Environment and Urbanization* 4(2): 42–60.

Hardoy, J. E., D. Mitlan, and D. Satterthwaite. 1992. *Environmental Problems in Third World Cities.* London: Earthscan.

McGranahan, G. and J. Songsore. 1994. "Wealth, Health, and the Urban Household: Weighing Environmental Burdens in Accra, Jakarta, and Sao Paulo." *Environment* 36(6): 4–17.

Morse, R. M. and J. E. Hardoy. 1992. *Rethinking the Latin American City.* Washington: Woodrow Wilson Center Press.

Rabinovitch, J. 1992. "Curitiba: Towards Sustainable Urban Development." *Environment and Urbanization* 4(2): 62–73.

Sinnatamby, G. 1990. "Low Cost Sanitation." In *The Poor Die Young: Housing and Health in Third World Cities,* eds J. E. Hardoy, S. Cairncross, and D. Satterthwaite. London: Earthscan.

Suryodipuro, L. 1995. *Towards an Environmentally Desirable Urban Form: The Case of Jabotabek.* Honolulu: Department of Urban and Regional Planning, University of Hawaii.

4

Global environment and the changing nature of states: The role of energy

José Goldemberg

Life on earth has shown a surprising resilience in withstanding changes in the environment, and humanity in particular has adapted well to changing climate after the last glaciation some 10,000 years ago when most of the northern hemisphere was covered by ice and snow. However, all the natural changes in our environment, except natural disasters, occurred slowly over long periods of time, typically centuries.

After the industrial revolution at the end of the eighteenth century, and particularly in the twentieth century, anthropogenic aggression to the environment has become more important due to population growth in developing countries and the enormous increase in personal consumption, mainly in the industrialized countries. What characterizes these environmental changes caused by man is that they took place in a short period of time, typically decades. As result, many new problems in the environmental area, mainly those indicated in Table 4.1, have become the object of study and great concern.

Broadly speaking all these problems have a multitude of causes, such as population increase, and the growth and changing patterns of industry, transportation, agriculture, and even tourism. The way energy is produced and used, however, is at the root of many of these causes.

For example, air pollution and acid rain are largely due to the burning of fossil fuels and urban transportation. Greenhouse warming and climate change are also due mainly to the burning of fossil fuels. Deforestation

Table 4.1 Main environmental problems

Environmental problem	Main source of problem	Main social group affected
Urban air pollution	Energy (industry and transportation)	Urban population
Indoor air pollution	Energy (cooking)	Rural poor
Acid rain	Energy (fossil fuel burning)	All
Ozone depletion	Industry	All
Greenhouse warming and climate change	Energy (fossil fuel burning)	All
Availability and quality of fresh water	Population increase, agriculture	All
Coastal and marine degradation	Transportation and energy	All
Deforestation and desertification	Population increase, agriculture, energy	Rural poor
Toxic chemicals and hazardous wastes	Industry and nuclear energy	All

and land degradation are due, in part, to the use of fuelwood for cooking. Such problems are also an important cause of the loss of biodiversity.

In some other environmental problems, energy does not play a dominant role but nevertheless is important in an indirect way, as in coastal and marine degradation which is due in part to oil spills. In the case of environmental hazards and disasters, the role of nuclear energy is paramount, as clearly demonstrated by the Chernobyl nuclear accident.

Why are these problems important today and not 100 years ago? The answer to that question in the words of the great Russian geochemist, V. I. Vernadsky, in 1929 is:

Man has become a large-scale geological force. The chemical face of our planet, the biosphere, is being sharply and consciously changed by man; even greater changes are happening unconsciously (Skinner 1994).

There are 6 billion people on the earth and their average consumption rate of mineral resources in 1994 was about 8 tonnes per capita, giving a total consumption of 44 billion tonnes a year. A century ago consumption was less than 2 tonnes/capita and population was four times smaller. So total consumption was 16 times smaller. These totals do not include all the material moved in order to facilitate mining, the soil disturbed during house building and parking-lot construction, nor any other disruptions to the crust. It is material dug out and used, directly or indirectly, to feed, clothe, transport, heat, cool, and entertain us. It is material humans dig up, move, process, use, and eventually put down somewhere else (Skinner 1994). Fossil fuels represent an appreciable part of that.

Annual mineral consumption can be contrasted with the mass of sediment transported to the sea by all rivers of the world. Suspended sediment is estimated to be about 14 billion tonnes per year and the dissolved load is about 2.5 billion tonnes, giving a total of 16.5 billion tonnes (Milliman and Meade 1983). This is only one-third of the total mass of mineral resources consumed.

Energy sources (coal, oil, gas, hydro, etc.) are distributed around the globe in a fashion that is frequently not matched to the location of the consumption centres. Access and distribution to most of them creates numerous problems such as global insecurity, of which the volatile political situation of the Middle East is an example. Other global problems are those originating in the use of nuclear energy for electricity generation, which creates the risk of nuclear weapons' proliferation.

Conventional wisdom says that economic growth is roughly proportional to the growth in consumption of raw materials and energy, and the resulting pollution. The empirical evidence for such correlation is in general based on studies over limited intervals of time. If such proportionality was to last for many decades the consequences would be disastrous, because the economies of a number of very populous developing countries are growing, as well as GDP per capita, and will soon approach the level of the developed countries. This would result in great strains in the access to raw materials and energy, as well as an increase in environmental degradation.

In the low-income economies of the developing world GDP per capita is at least 10 times smaller than in the OECD (Organization for Economic Cooperation and Development) countries, and consumption of raw materials and energy is also approximately 10 times smaller. Presently one-fifth of the world's population, in the OECD countries, has reached a standard of living that can be considered acceptable. Of the remaining four-fifths – spread out in more than 100 countries – only a small fraction of the population has reached a reasonable standard of living, with the remainder standing at a level little above absolute poverty.

Figure 4.1 shows the evolution of per capita income in the period 1830–1988 for the United States as well as a number of other countries in 1988 in US dollars corrected for parity purchase power. It is clear from this figure that some countries (such as Zaire) have a per capita income lower than the United States at the beginning of the nineteenth century. Brazil is at a stage corresponding to the United States in 1950.

Such disparities in income will not last forever.

The environmental consequences of industrial development and associated energy consumption in developing countries are beginning to

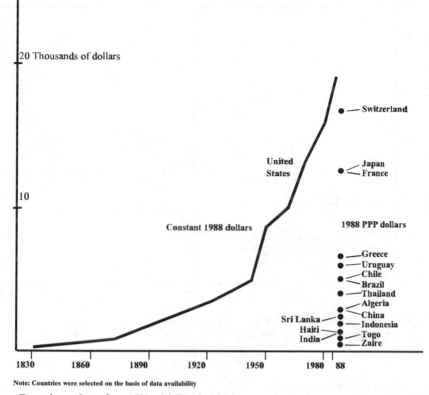

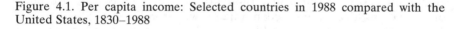

Note: Countries were selected on the basis of data availability

Based on data from World Bank 1991.

Figure 4.1. Per capita income: Selected countries in 1988 compared with the United States, 1830–1988

reach such proportions that they not only threaten the local population but represent a sizeable contribution to global climate change, mainly due to increased fossil fuel consumption.

As an example one can point out that, as far as carbon emissions are concerned, the emissions of industrialized countries levelled off at a rate of approximately 4 gigatonnes per year in 1980, growing at a rate of 1 per cent per year or less, while emissions in the developing countries have been growing at approximately 4 per cent per year or more (see Figure 4.2). If such trends are to continue, carbon emissions from this part of the world will surpass the emissions of industrialized countries around the year 2010.

To attenuate such problems one can introduce more rationality in the use of fossil fuels or search for carbon-free sources. This is indeed what

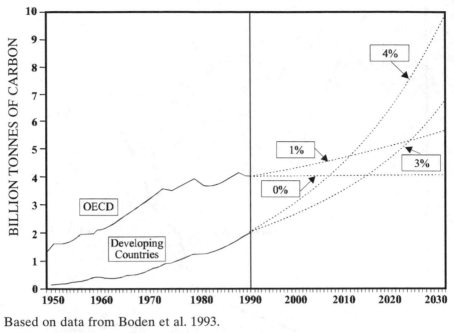

Based on data from Boden et al. 1993.

Figure 4.2. Carbon emissions, 1950–2030

happened after the "oil crisis" of the 1970s in the industrialized countries. In order to reduce their dependence on oil imports these countries made significant efforts to rationalize their productive systems and succeeded effectively in "decoupling" economic growth from energy consumption. Such efforts were duplicated in many other areas, with the result that there is a "dematerialization" trend in the world economy in the sense that more was achieved with a reduced consumption of raw materials.

Dematerialization is a general characteristic of industrialized countries as they reach higher income. The determinants of such dematerialization are:

• changes in the structure of final demand;
• technological innovations; and
• efficiency improvements in the use of materials and substitution by alternative materials.

Long-terms series studies of the intensity-of-use curves (in kilograms per unit of GDP) have demonstrated that in general they have a bell shape, as shown in Figure 4.3 for the United States and other countries (Malenbaum 1978).

What one learns from those curves is that the intensity of use of a given

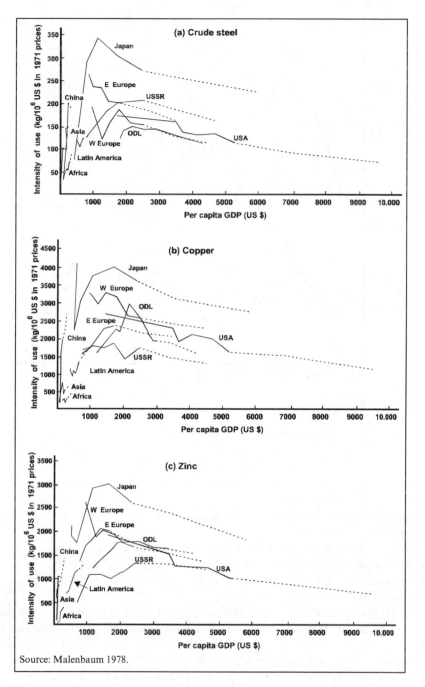

Source: Malenbaum 1978.

Figure 4.3. Long-term trends in the intensity of use of materials and energy

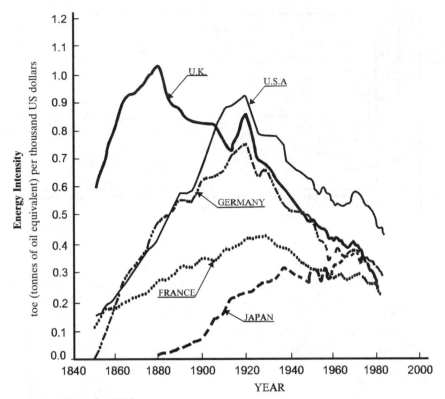

Source: Martin 1988.

Figure 4.4. Energy intensity of industrialized countries

material follows the same pattern for all economies, increasing with per capita GDP at first, reaching a maximum, and eventually declining; and that the maximum intensity of use declines the later in time it is attained by a given economy.

Such behaviour is particularly striking for the "energy intensity" (energy consumption per unit of GDP) of a number of industrialized countries, as shown in Figure 4.4 where only commercial energy was included in the analysis (Martin 1988).

What the data show is that the energy intensity increases during the initial phase of development when the heavy industrial infrastructure is put in place, reaches a peak, and then decreases. Latecomers in the development process follow the same pattern as their predecessors, but with less accentuated peaks: they do not have to reach high energy intensities in the initial stages of industrialization, because they benefit from modern methods of manufacturing and more efficient systems of transportation developed by others. This was true even before the oil crisis of 1973, and rising oil prices only accelerated the pace of structural changes in industrialized countries. This process is generally described as "technological leapfrogging," in which a number of stages of choices made by industrialized countries in the past are skipped by the early adoption of modern technologies in the process of development, avoiding the costly retrofits that are required when investment is made in obsolete technologies.

Enlightened governments can have an enormous success in accelerating this evolution, mobilizing local resources, investing in education, and establishing the indigenous capacity to develop or choose foreign technology selectively. This was to a large extent the case in Japan after the Meijii restoration during the last decades of the nineteenth century, which in 30 years converted Japan into a world power.

What is crucial in this approach is the capacity to choose among technologies and finance preferentially projects incorporating modern technologies, or conducting the necessary research for that. The best example of this approach is the one given by Japan after the Second World War with the creation of MITI (Ministry of International Trade and Industry), which is responsible for the support of research and development plus industrial development.

There are a number of examples of technological "leapfrogging" occurring in the developing countries today (Goldemberg 1998). The first is the adoption of cellular telephones to supplement, and sometimes replace completely, obsolete traditional telephone systems (which require extensive wiring) in cities such as Manila and some regions in China. Although cellular telephones were originally developed for mobile use or rural areas where wiring is very expensive, technical developments indicate that they can also be economically competitive for regular service.

A second example is the restructuring of the world steel industry, which is in a period of change, opening new possibilities for developing countries to enhance their comparative advantages. In the past five years large conventional, centralized, and integrated steels mills, which require the use of large blast furnaces, coke ovens, and sintering plants, have come under attack for their negative environmental impacts, including the production of toxic and carcinogenic by-products. In many parts of Europe, licences for new plant construction are impossible to obtain. Where plants are in operation, taxes are often applied. For example, an "ecotax" of US$25 per tonne of produced steel is levied on a sintering plant in Oxelosund, Sweden, because of its emissions of dioxin.

One result has been an increase in the number of electric arc furnaces, which were used in 35 per cent of total steel production worldwide in 1995 compared to 10 per cent in the 1960s and 22 per cent in 1980. This technology depends on the availability of low-cost electric energy, which is abundant in many of the developing countries to which the modern steel industry is migrating. Another trend has been toward descentralized medium-sized mills (production capacity less than 1 million tonnes per year). Still another result is the rebirth of charcoal-based pig-iron and steel production in Brazil: 19 per cent of all steel in the country (4.3 million tonnes) is produced in charcoal-based steel plants in addition to 4.5 million tonnes of pig-iron.

When one concentrates attention on energy there a number of opportunities to explore, the main ones being the modernization of the use of biomass and photovoltaics.

The modernization of the use of biomass

Biomass in the form of fuelwood, agricultural residues, dung, and bagasse provides 14 per cent of the world's primary energy (equivalent to 25 million barrels of oil per day). In developing countries – where it contributes approximately 35 per cent to all energy consumed – biomass is predominantly used as a non-commercial fuel. Modernization of the use of biomass is taking place through the conversion of biomass into liquid and gaseous high-quality fuels, such as ethanol from sugar-cane and low-BTU gas for combustion.

Ethyl alcohol (ethanol) is produced from fermented sugar-cane juice on a large scale in Brazil, and used as a substitute for gasoline in automobiles. Approximately 200,000 barrels per day of alcohol are in use, reducing by 50 per cent the amount of gasoline needed for Brazil's 10 million automobiles. Ethanol is an excellent motor fuel: it has a motor octane of 90, which exceeds that of gasoline, and its use in higher compression engines (12.1 to 1 instead of 8.1 to 1) compensates for its lower caloric content.

The expansion of the sugar-cane plantations from less than 1 million hectares to 4 million hectares between 1975 and 1990, and the nearly 400 processing plants needed to produce large amounts of alcohol, have resulted in the creation of approximately 700,000 jobs. The environmental problems encountered initially in the distilleries, such as disposing of liquid effluents and bagasse, have been solved by converting the stillage into fertilizers and bagasse into a fuel for electricity generation.

In addition, the substitution of the gasoline that would otherwise be consumed avoids emissions of 9.45×10^6 tonnes of carbon per year, which corresponds to 18 per cent of all carbon emissions in Brazil.

The amount of bagasse (and other agricultural residues) remaining after ethanol production is estimated to be 4×10^6 tonnes of dry matter, a significant portion of which is being used or could be used for electricity generation. Ethanol from sugar-cane is also used in Zimbabwe, and could play an important role in Cuba and other sugar-cane-producing countries.

Burning fuelwood, bagasse, and other agricultural residues to produce steam and generate electricity is a well-known technology in use in many countries. In the United States some 8,000 MW of electricity are generated per year. Present systems frequently use low-pressure boilers and their efficiency is usually below 10 per cent. The simplest improvement possible is to use condensing-extraction steam turbines (CESTs) and higher pressures. Efficiencies of up to 20 per cent can be reached this way.

Advanced technologies have been proposed to convert solid biomass into a low-BTU gas through gasification and use this gas to power gas turbines. Efficiencies higher than 45 per cent can be expected from a biomass integrated gasifier/gas turbine (BIG/GT) system. The merit of BIG/GT systems would be the ability to provide such high efficiencies in small units, in the range suitable for economical use of biomass (20–100 MW).

In a project in progress in Brazil for a 25 MW demonstration plant – with the financial support of the Global Environment Facility (GEF) – General Electric has adapted their aeroderivative turbines for the low-BTU gas to be used and TPS Termiska Processer AB, a Swedish company, has developed air pressure gasifiers. Once developed and fully tested the technology could be used worldwide. Producing fuelwood in large "energy farms" will be particularly significant to provide a basis for rural development and employment in developing countries.

This is a case in which multinational companies have developed the necessary technologies for use in a developing country, thus opening a market for their products. It is an example of a "leapfrogging" activity where international donors plus multinational companies join forces in stimulating development in a developing country. In the pilot plant being built in Brazil with a World Bank loan, Shell Brazil and local electricity companies are shareholders.

Photovoltaics

Photovoltaics (PV) technology could play an important role in tropical areas – where most of the developing countries are located – not only in decentralized but also in centralized units feeding directly into existing electricity distribution grids. While PV technology is perhaps the most inherently attractive of the renewable technologies it is also – due to its cost – the farthest from being commercial.

Estimates suggest that 2 billion people are without access to modern electricity, many of whom are willing to pay the full cost for the services it can provide. With suitable delivery systems, it is estimated that it may be possible to reach up to 50 per cent of the rural population with PV. In addition, wind for electricity production is also an attractive option.

All these new technologies have reached technological maturity – although new improvements are bound to take place – but suffer from the usual problem of initial high cost which is typical of new technologies.

Usually prices of any given manufactured products decline as sales increase according to "experience curves" (or "learning curves"), which reflect gains due to technological progress, economies of scale, and organizational learning. Experience shows that such decline is exponential as cumulative production grows. An indicator called progress ratio (PR) is often used to describe it. For example, a PR of 80 per cent means that the cost declines 20 per cent for each doubling of production. The lower the PR the faster the decline in cost.

Figure 4.5 shows the distribution of the PR observed for more than 100 industries, which indicates a cluster around a PR of 80 per cent (Dutton and Thomas 1984).

For photovoltaics costs are falling, as indicated in Figure 4.6, which corresponds to a learning curve with a PR of 81.6 per cent.

Aggregation of large international markets for PV sales in developing countries could be a mechanism for accelerating the rate of price reduction for PV systems produced in industrialized countries. Costs could be brought down quickly via mass purchases that could be facilitated by various national and international organizations, in conjunction with increased research and development.

What can governments do?

What can governments do to promote the adoption of better technologies and "technological leapfrogging"? To answer this question it must be realized that such problems fall into three distinct categories and the authorities responsible for solving them are different in each case: local, regional, or global.

Local pollution has to do with local governments since it deals with clean air, fresh supplies of clean water, the removal and disposal of solid wastes and liquid effluents, street cleaning, etc. This is what has characterized "good" small and medium-sized cities since Roman times. Yet in many developing countries a large fraction of the population lives among the rubble and residues it produces, due to the lack of resources to remove waste and build sewers and the engineering works needed for the

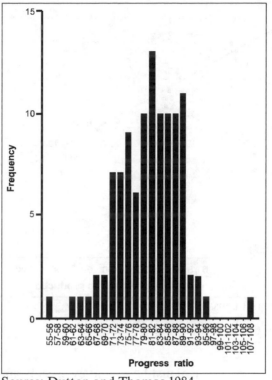

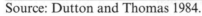

Source: Dutton and Thomas 1984.

Figure 4.5. Frequency distribution of the progress ratio

supply of water. This is quite evident in the slums of the big cities, which generally speaking surround "islands of prosperity" where the well-to-do succeed in reaching a quality of life that is comparable to that of Europe or the United States. Local pollution goes together with poverty.

Regional pollution is caused mainly by automobiles, energy production, and heavy industry, which are characteristic of more prosperous societies. Large cities and adjoining areas, such as Los Angeles, Mexico City, and São Paulo, have been "suffocating" under the pollution caused by the emissions and "smog" resulting from burning fossil fuels. Sometimes the amount of pollution produced is large enough to cause regional and even transborder problems, such as the acid rain that originates in the United States but is responsible for the destruction of life in Canadian lakes. The same happened to lakes in Scandinavia, due to industrial activities on the other side of the Baltic Sea. Regional pollution has to be

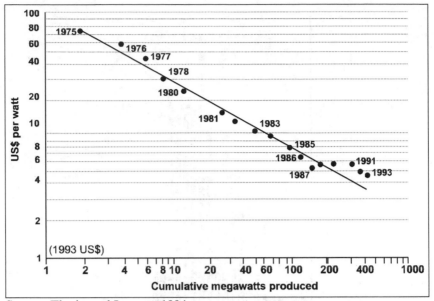

Source: Flavin and Lenssen 1994.

Figure 4.6. Penetration curve for photovoltaics

dealt with at the state or national level, and eventually among a number of countries.

The third category is global pollution, and its most obvious consequences to date are the destruction of the stratospheric ozone layer by CFCs and the "greenhouse effect." These problems result from changes in the composition of the atmosphere and have little to do with national borders. The causes of such global problems are gases originating anywhere in the world and are such that, for example, the well-being of people living in Switzerland might ultimately be affected by what takes place in India or China (and vice versa). Global pollution can only be tackled at the international level.

When dealing with local and regional pollution, governments can introduce incentives to stimulate better practices and guide markets; one of the most interesting methods for doing this is the one introduced in the United Kingdom, where it was decided that utilities should incorporate a minimum amount of renewable energy capacity into their portfolios even if they have less expensive alternative means of providing power.

The United Kingdom adopted the renewables' Non-Fossil Fuel Obligation (NFFO) in 1989 after privatization of the electric power sector. It evolved from the need to find a means of supporting nuclear power after it was realized that nuclear power could not survive privatization without subsidies. The British government was required to obtain a subsidy permission from the European Commission to levy a tax on electricity in order to do it. The government asked instead for permission for a levy on fossil-based electricity to support non-fossil-based electricity in an NFFO – a request that was granted by the Commission. The NFFO thus came to be understood to include both renewable and nuclear energy (Mitchell 1995).

There are other variations of such mechanisms (see Reddy, Williams, and Johansson 1997), one of which is the adoption of caps on emissions of pollutants such as was done for SO_2 in the United States; once they are established at a national level the agencies in charge, such as the US Environmental Protection Agency (EPA), can issue emission permits that are tradable and that encourage technological development of processes that avoid SO_2 emissions.

Dealing with global environmental problems is, however, the great challenge of our day: it requires international "hard" laws, such as setting mandatory targets and timetables for the reduction of emissions of the undesirable gases which will force technological change in the desired direction. In the case of CFCs, the Montreal Protocol was successful in doing that, but the same success was not achieved in the case of other "greenhouse gases" such as carbon dioxide (CO_2), methane (CH_4), and others. The UN Framework Convention on Climate Change (UNFCCC) adopted in Rio in 1992 can be clearly categorized as an international "soft law."

Industrialized countries announced in Rio their decision to reduce CO_2 emissions to 1990 levels by the year 2000, but that was not a binding commitment and nor will it be fulfilled. Actually emissions are growing in most of these countries. On the other hand, developing countries accepted no limitations on their future emissions since this could – in their perception – hurt their development goals.

In successive meetings of the Conference of the Parties (COP) of the UNFCCC, efforts were made to convert the Convention into a "hard law," the idea being that industrialized countries would stabilize emissions at the 1990 level and eventually reduce them by 5–15 per cent by the year 2010. Proposals to have developing countries accept binding or voluntary targets have also been made, mainly by the United States. Agreement was finally reached in December 1997 when COP-3 adopted the Kyoto Protocol, which contains the following key elements.
• A global Annex I target of 5.2 per cent emission reduction in the first five-year period, to run 2008–2012.

Table 4.2 Total energy consumption (GTOE)

Year	Scenario	Primary energy	Renewables
1990		8.8	0.32
2010	OECD/IEA*	11.59	<0.6 (<5%)
2020	WEC (ecologically driven)	11.3	3.4 (30%)
2025	RIGES	11.2	5.0 (45%)

Sources: OECD/IEA – IEA/OECD 1994; WEC – WEC 1993; RIGES – Johansson et al. 1992.
* Does not include non-commercial fuels such as wood or animal waste

- Coverage of six gases (CO_2, CH_4, N_2O, HFCs, PFCs, SF_6).
- Comprehensive coverage of sources and sinks.
- Annex I emission trading allowed.
- A clean development mechanism (CDM) that allows non-Annex I Parties to benefit from project activities resulting in certified emission reductions, while Annex I Parties can use these certificates to contribute to compliance.

As in the case of SO_2, the acceptance of caps on emissions will stimulate efforts to find alternative technologies to produce energy from carbon-free energy sources, such as renewable ones like wind, photovoltaics, biomass, hydrogen, etc. Estimates have been made of the possible role such sources could play early in the twenty-first century; one of the outstanding projections is that made by the World Energy Council in an "ecological-driven scenario" which predicts that by the year 2020 some 30 per cent of the total primary energy consumed could be renewable as compared to 3 per cent in 1990 (see Table 4.2).

There are significant technical opportunities to steer the present-day energy system, mainly based on the use of fossil fuel, to less carbon-dependent primary sources of energy (renewables) and more efficient energy use.

However, the obstacles to "technological leapfrogging" are considerable, since there are entrenched interests in industrialized countries which profit from supplying conventional technologies based on fossil fuel use to developing countries. Such interests have important allies in the international financial institutions, such as the World Bank, which are "colour-blind" regarding the technology involved in their loans and show no preference for innovations, which in general they consider very risky. Coupled with that is the passivity of governments which allow the import of machinery and even factories without any concern for their acceptability on environmental grounds. Enlightened governments and stricter criteria for funding in the World Bank and similar financing institutions could change that situation drastically.

REFERENCES

Boden, T. A., D. P. Kaiser, R. J. Sepanski, and F. W. Stoss. 1993. *Trends '93: A Compendium of Data on Global Change.* Oak Ridge: CDIAC.

Dutton, J. M. and A. Thomas. 1984. "Treating Progress Functions as a Managerial Opportunity." *Academy of Management Review* 1(9): 235–247.

Flavin, C. and N. Lenssen. 1994. *Power Surge: Guide to the Coming Energy Revolution.* New York: W. W. Norton.

Goldemberg, J. 1998. "Leapfrog Energy Technologies." *Energy Policy* 26(10): 729–741.

IEA/OECD. 1994. *World Energy Outlook.* Paris: OECD.

Johansson, T. B., H. Kelly, A. K. N. Reddy, and R. H. Williams, eds. 1992. *Renewable Energy – Sources for Fuels and Electricity.* Washington: Island Press.

Malenbaum, W. 1978. *World Demand for Raw Materials in 1985 and 2000.* New York: McGraw Hill.

Martin, J. M. 1988. "L'Intensité Energetique de l'Activité Economiques dans les Pays Industrialisées: Les Evolutions de Tres Longue Period Livrent Elles des Enseignements Utiles?" *Economie et Societés, Cahiers de L'ISMEA* 22(4): 9–27.

Milliman, J. D. and R. H. Meade. 1983. "World-wide Delivery of River Sediment to the Oceans." *Journal of Geology* 91: 1–21.

Mitchell, C. 1995. "The Renewables NFFO: A Review." *Energy Policy* 23(12): 1077–1091.

Reddy, A. K. N., R. H. Williams, and T. B. Johansson. 1997. *Energy After Rio – Prospects and Challenges.* UNDP.

Skinner, B. J. 1994. "Mineral Myopia." Paper presented at the Meyer Symposium on the Compatibility of Mining and Environment. Society of Economic Geologists, 25 October, Seattle, Washington.

WEC (World Energy Council). 1993. *Energy for Tomorrow's World – The Realities, the Real Options and the Agenda for Achievement.* New York: St. Martin's Press.

World Bank. 1991. *World Development Report.* Washington: World Bank.

Civil society: Defining a new partnership

5

(I)NGOs and global environmental governance: Introduction

Volker Rittberger

In the last three decades the world has experienced a marked increase in the activities of environmental non-governmental organizations (NGOs) at the local, national, regional, and global levels. The Western democracies, the former socialist countries in Eastern Europe, and the developing countries witnessed a change of state-society relationships. Early on the social sciences dealt with the causes of the rise of new social movements at the domestic level. They identified a change in Western societies toward post-materialist values and a growing demand in these societies for more political participation (Inglehart 1977; Abramson and Inglehart 1995). These new social movements reacted, *inter alia*, to environmental problems that were initially assumed to have mainly domestic causes and consequences. In the 1970s, "green" groups protested against the construction of nuclear power plants, the pollution of inland waters, or the smog in urban areas. The new social movements consisted not only of environmental groups but also civil rights groups and other actors protesting about acute social problems like housing shortages and gender discrimination. Their activities created a challenge for domestic governance in the Western democracies (Rucht 1994), which had to incorporate these new social movements in domestic political processes by establishing new, or improving existing, procedures of political participation. Furthermore, the transition to democracy in the former socialist countries and in many developing countries has also strengthened the political participation of these countries' civil societies in the 1990s.

When national governments and international organizations intensified the international management of environmental problems, domestic and international NGOs began to collaborate across the borders of nation-states. The societies of the industrially developed countries responded quickly to the internationalization of former domestic environmental policy-making in the 1980s. In addition, the UNCED process, following the work of the Brundlandt Commission (WCED 1987), alerted the societies of developing countries to the global character of many environmental problems. Thus the salience of these problems created a global awareness of the urgent need for environmental protection and global environmental cooperation. When (I)NGOs began to direct their attention more and more to international, particularly global, environmental problems they challenged governments' monopoly of responsibility for the making of foreign policy. At the end of the twentieth century, the UN system and regional organizations like the European Union face a strong debate about the role of civil society in global governance (Commission on Global Governance 1995). The three chapters in this section will deal specifically with the roles of environmental (I)NGOs in shaping international environmental policy-making at the regional and global levels.

In the first chapter, Paul Wapner develops a definition of (I)NGOs and separates them from international organizations. The activities of both (I)NGOs and international organizations reach beyond national borders. The points of view of both do not simply reflect the view of one or more nation-states but are non-territorial. However, international organizations are funded by governments and/or have their own sources of revenues; member states also influence their staffing and fill many of their positions, and they develop concrete guidelines for their activities. (I)NGOs, on the other hand, are much more independent of governments in all these respects. Wapner focuses on those actions of (I)NGOs which are directed towards changing the behaviour of states, or aim at engaging economic forces, or alter social mores. The activities of (I)NGOs are not only directed at states but also at international organizations, multinational corporations, various domestic groups, or individuals. Environmental (I)NGOs are aware that they can contribute to, and improve the effectiveness of, global governance when targeting their activities on states that dominate the processes of environmental policy-making and institution-building. (I)NGOs have also realized that the economy is a critical factor in the effectiveness of global environmental governance. Thus, transnational campaigns of (I)NGOs against industrial production damaging the environment or depleting natural resources ultimately seek to promote structural changes of the economic sector in favour of environmentally sound production. Further actions of (I)NGOs aim at changing the routine everyday behaviour of individuals impacting on the environment which they have acquired by their socialization. Therefore, altering social mores involves a process of educating individuals to become environmentally more conscious and responsible citizens.

Lin Gan's chapter describes the role of environmental NGOs in energy sector development in Asia. High economic growth rates have increased the demand for energy in many Asian countries in the last two decades, and Asian governments have thus developed plans for the construction of new power plants. Asian environmental NGOs became concerned about the environmental consequences of such large-scale energy development projects. They collaborated increasingly with Northern NGOs and put pressure on Asian governments and on international organizations like the World Bank as possible funding agencies to take environmental concerns into consideration when planning and executing these projects. In some cases, the politicization of these energy development projects by Asian and Northern NGOs prompted Asian governments and international organizations to reconsider construction plans and adjust them to the needs of sustainable development. This chapter further describes the activities of research-oriented NGOs providing scientific knowledge to decision-makers, lobbying NGOs which have criticized, and campaigned against, dam projects like the Narmada Dam in India, and mediating NGOs establishing domestic and transnational networks with the purpose of disseminating knowledge and coordinating joint activities.

Finally, Helmut Breitmeier and Volker Rittberger's chapter asks whether (I)NGOs have already succeeded in changing the relationship between state and civil society. The chapter argues that global civil society – despite the growing transnationalization of the activities of (I)NGOs – has not yet fully developed and remains a fragmented society at best. Furthermore, the authors conclude that the activities of (I)NGOs have not fundamentally changed state-society relationships. When discussing the possible contribution of NGOs to closing the democracy gap which occurs in the shifting of formerly domestic political processes to the international level, the authors deal with three models of global democracy, each offering different solutions to narrowing, if not closing, the democracy gap. The chapter then describes how the activities of environmental advocacy organizations put states and international organizations under political pressure to strengthen their efforts for the international management of environmental problems; and deals with environmental service organizations providing expertise that states and international organizations can make use of when managing environmental problems at the international and domestic levels. The authors then discuss the factors influencing the competence of (I)NGOs. They argue that the competence of (I)NGOs and their levels of participation depend, *inter alia*, on the availability of financial resources, on their readiness to follow specific environmental issues on a long-term basis, or on the expertise of their staff members. The authors finally address the relationship between environmental (I)NGOs and economic actors, which represents an underresearched topic and deserves more attention from the academic community. The chapter distinguishes different types of economic actors and environmental (I)NGOs. Coalition-building between economic actors and environmental (I)NGOs depends on the constellation of interests among the actors in both camps. The authors argue that the prospects for collaboration between economic actors and environmental (I)NGOs have improved due to converging interests of environmentally like-minded economic actors and (I)NGOs.

In sum, the chapters of Wapner and of Breitmeier and Rittberger seek to provide a theory-guided analysis of the role of (I)NGOs in global environmental governance, while Gan's description of NGOs' involvement in dealing with environmental problems in Asia provides a useful complement to both chapters.

REFERENCES

Abramson, P. R. and R. Inglehart. 1995. *Value Change in Global Perspective*. Ann Arbor: University of Michigan Press.

Commission on Global Governance. 1995. *Our Global Neighbourhood*. Oxford: Oxford University Press.

Inglehart, R. 1977. *The Silent Revolution: Changing Values and Political Styles Among Western Publics*. Princeton: Princeton University Press.

Rucht, D. 1994: *Modernisierung und neue soziale Bewegungen: Deutschland, Frankreich und USA im Vergleich*. Frankfurt: M. Campus.

WCED (World Commission for Environment and Development). 1987. *Our Common Future*. Oxford: Oxford University Press.

6

The transnational politics of environmental NGOs: Governmental, economic, and social activism

Paul Wapner

There is a widespread sense that NGOs greatly influence the way the international system addresses environmental issues.[1] This perception stems from the recognition that there are literally thousands of NGOs throughout the world working for environmental protection, and that they devote significant resources to their campaigns. While many sense that NGOs affect world environmental issues, there is, however, little understanding about the ways in which NGOs actually carry out their work. What strategies do NGOs utilize to advance their aims? Why do they choose these methods of political engagement? How do these efforts actually end up influencing the international system?

The most likely answers to these questions revolve around the viewpoint that NGOs are primarily interest groups that lobby governments to promote their causes. To put it differently, NGOs are pressure groups that work to influence the way states, and the international institutions states set up, address environmental issues. The guiding assumption of this orientation is that states constitute the seat of political power in the international system and that all sincere political effort must be directed at shaping the way they operate.

In many ways, this view is accurate. NGOs expend tremendous effort lobbying states and influencing international regime formation and implementation. But their efforts do not stop there, nor are such strategies undertaken separately from a host of other forms of political practice. In the most general sense, NGOs wish to advance the cause of environmental protection. They recognize that environmentally harmful human practices take place at the individual, group, corporate, and state levels, and aim to reorient human practices at all levels of collective life. To do so, they enlist the governing power not simply of states – which have a mixed record of shaping widespread behaviour with respect to environmental issues within their own territories (think, for example, of weak states like Somalia) – but also of economic and sociocultural forces that significantly influence human activity. These forces, like governmental power, can be understood as nodes of governance in that they shape widespread thought and behaviour.[2] They represent mechanisms that influence human activity in all areas of life, including human interaction with nature. Environmental NGOs recognize that environmentally harmful activities are carried out by a host of actors, all of whom are animated by and subject to various forms of governance. As a result, NGOs engage multiple levels of collective life and enlist numerous forms of political power to alter widespread practices.

This chapter outlines the range of strategies NGOs undertake to advance environmental protection. It does so by concentrating on three types of governance mechanisms and studying the way NGOs work to manipulate them. First, it looks at forms of state power. The state enjoys the ability to shape widespread behaviour based on its monopoly of legitimate coercive power within a given territory. It passes laws and backs them up through the threat of force. NGOs recognize the powerful capability of states to shape extensive practices and work to influence states' policies. Thus, while NGOs do more than lobby states, as mentioned, their lobbying efforts are essential to their activities and deserve attention. Hence, the chapter first catalogues and explains how NGOs engage states and the state system. Second, it looks at economic forms of power. People, as individuals and organized in groups, make decisions partially based on economic incentives. Many economic structures that establish incentives, however, fail to consider environmental issues and thus often support environmentally harmful practices. NGOs recognize this and strive to manipulate economic structures in the interest of environmental protection. These efforts make up an important strategy of NGO politics. Third and finally, the chapter focuses on social mores. People go through a socialization process wherein they learn to take cues from their peers and the institutions of social life. Like economic factors, these often support environmentally harmful activities or, put more positively, can be harnessed to advance environmental protection. As a result, NGOs target social proprieties in their campaigns for a healthier and more robust environment.

These three forms of governance represent conditioning factors that greatly shape widespread thought and action. Since NGOs aim, overall, to shift the way people think about and act toward the earth's ecosystem, they see themselves having to engage all forms. Appreciating the strategies they use to do so, and the overall frame of reference that informs such strategies, is crucial for understanding how and why NGOs influence world environmental affairs. The chapter, in short, aims to substantiate the assumption that NGOs influence the way the international system addresses environmental issues. It does so by providing a broad understanding of the meaning of the international system – through a discussion of forms of governance – and by delineating the role NGOs play in engaging it.

Environmental NGOs: Definitions

In the loosest sense of the term, NGOs are groups made up of people who come together to share interests, ideologies, cultural affinities, and so forth, outside the formal organs of the state. Substantively, NGOs may arise to promote economic interests, enjoy recreational or educational activities, undertake public service, or advance cultural and religious values. In each case, however, the term NGO is used in a negative sense: it means simply that people organize themselves on their own rather than under the rubric of state power. When the term is used in international politics, NGOs usually refer to groups that form on a voluntary basis with the aim of addressing a given problem in the world or advancing a particular cause (Weiss and Gordenker 1996, 19). Put differently, NGOs work to alleviate what they perceive to be hardships or misfortunes, or work to change the way people think and act with regard to public issues. As such, scholars tend to exclude for-profit economic actors in their understanding of NGOs. These entities aim foremost to produce financial wealth and are driven by the goal of maximizing profit. They are principally unconcerned with solving a certain problem or advancing a particular political agenda (Korten 1990, 96–98). Likewise, scholars tend to exclude intergovernmental agencies in their understanding. These entities – often called intergovernmental organizations (IGOs) – do, in fact, work to alleviate problems and promote certain agendas, but do so often only at the behest of, and remain fundamentally responsive to, states. Indeed, while the secretariats of IGOs are composed of civil servants who are free from state dictates, the decision-making organs of IGOs are composed of governmental delegates and this partially restricts IGO activities. NGOs, to put it concisely, are political organizations that arise and operate outside the formal offices of the state, and are devoted to addressing public issues.

While NGOs exist and operate at many levels of political life, those of interest to scholars of international politics are usually ones that are organized and take actions which have relevance across national boundaries. Some groups, such as Amnesty International or Medicins Sans Frontières, have actual offices in multiple countries and undertake campaigns outside the parameters of given states. Other groups, such as the Sierra Club in the United States or the Campaign for Nuclear Disarmament in the United Kingdom, staff offices within particular countries but address problems that have transnational and, at times, global significance. Grassroots movements of all sorts fall into this latter category. These groups are able to project extra-territorial relevance because the campaigns in which they are involved often relate to broader struggles in other countries or because communication technologies advertise their efforts and relate them to the sensibilities of citizens outside the domestic context.

For many scholars it is the transnational dimension, in addition to the political and non-governmental ones, that marks the notable character of NGOs. This allows NGOs to assume a certain perspective on issues and carry out untraditional activities. Organized across borders or projecting their efforts beyond their given territorial homes, NGOs assume a certain purchase point on issues that, at times, allows them the so-called "view from nowhere"; that is, a view from no given geographical place in particular. NGOs can focus upon issues and pursue aims free from the task of preserving and enhancing the welfare of a given, geographically situated population. This does not mean that they somehow assume a genuinely globalist perspective – in politics such a view is almost always a chimera – but simply notes the non-territoriality of their point of view. While not global in perspective, it certainly generates a non-national orientation. NGOs are, to use Rosenau's (1990) insightful phrase, "sovereignty-free actors."

A final definitional comment on NGOs in general is that they come in many political stripes and, although much of the literature focuses on so-called progressive NGOs, there are many right-wing organizations that have the same character and operate using the same strategies as their progressive counterparts. The organization Aryan Nations, for example, has offices in multiple countries and tries to generate solidarity across borders among white people of European descent and inspire hostility toward others (Ridgeway 1995). The National Rifle Association of the United States is also a bona fide NGO. Although headquartered in the United States, in 1997 it launched a transnational campaign to support unrestricted possession of firearms, in part to resist attempts to curb widespread trade in small arms. The term NGO, then, is a broad phrase that includes a wide variety of political organizations. The key is that these groups address given challenges in the world or advance certain causes that have transnational public relevance.[3]

Environmental NGOs are a subset of NGOs more generally. At the most generous level of attribution and using an ideal-typical formulation, one could say that these are groups dedicated to protecting the quality of air, land, and water throughout the world, and the continued existence and thriving of non-human species. This is generous because it suggests unconditional altruistic intentions when, in fact, we know that this is not the whole picture. Environmental NGOs are also bureaucratic organizations that often care as much about their own preservation – and therefore compete with each other – as other large organizations. The formulation is ideal-typical in that it suggests that environmental issues are easily distinguishable from other challenges when, in fact, this also is not always the case. In much of the world, protecting the environment is often a by-product of efforts to protect a community's economic base or resist severe social dislocations. Many so-called environmental NGOs do not conceptualize themselves as necessarily sensitive to non-human species or to the quality of water, land, and air but see themselves as campaigners for better living conditions (defined in an extremely broad manner).[4] Notwithstanding these qualifications, it is convenient and not all that inaccurate to say that groups falling under the rubric of environmental NGO have some connection to the protection of the non-human world and it is this character, however thin, that enables one to analyse them together as a distinct entity.[5]

Like other NGOs, environmental NGOs exist and operate at multiple levels. There are, for instance, local groups that address particular environmental threats within a given community or domestic region. In the village of Zom, Senegal, for example, grassroots groups work to protect the fertility of agricultural land. Many of these groups arose after a severe drought in 1984 and dedicated themselves to rebuilding topsoil and planting rice. As of the early 1990s, they were still working locally to protect land quality (Fisher 1993, 29). Likewise, the Anacostia Watershed Society in Maryland works to protect the well-being of the Anacostia River and its tributaries. Since its founding in 1989, it has worked continuously to remove debris from the riverbed, plant trees to restore habitat, and mobilize local volunteers in the District of Columbia and south-central Maryland.

In addition to local groups, there are national ones. These are organizations that focus their efforts on protecting environmental quality throughout a given state. The well-known Green Belt movement in Kenya, for instance, aims at combating desertification and alleviating famine throughout the country. It works mainly by establishing local tree nurseries and planting seedlings (Fisher 1993, 102–103). The Natural Resources Defense Council in the United States is similar in its focus on environmental quality in the United States.

Finally, there are transnational or global environmental NGOs. These are groups organized across state boundaries and committed explicitly to regional or global environmental protection. Greenpeace International, Friends of the Earth, and the Worldwide Fund for Nature (WWF) are probably the best known of these kinds of NGOs.

As mentioned, scholars of international politics are most interested in the last type of NGO. Transnational NGOs care about transboundary environmental phenomena and deliberately engage the international system. Nonetheless, it is important to point out that each of the other types of environmental NGOs can, at times, have transnational relevance. Depending on the issue area, domestic organizations can have a strong influence on international environmental affairs (Princen and Finger 1994). When Chico Mendes, the head of the National Council of Rubber Tappers (CNS, Brazilian acronym) in the western Amazon state of Acre, was killed while attempting to defend the rights of rubber tappers and protect the rain forest, his death produced an outcry from the international community that enhanced pressures on the Brazilian government to reverse its deforestation policies (Conca, Alberty and Dabelko 1995, 78). Thus, while CNS was a domestic NGO, Mendes's death had an impact on transnational issues such as biodiversity and, due to the relationship between deforestation and carbon sequestration, global climate change.

The power, presence, and character of environmental NGOs

Taken together, the host of environmental NGOs throughout the world represent a variegated presence through which voices and pressures in favour of environmental protection are being articulated and generated. While data are sketchy, it is estimated that there are tens of thousands of NGOs working in some capacity to protect the environment (Conca 1996, 106–107).[6] Moreover, in so far as some of these organizations have memberships in the millions and budgets of over US$200 million, at least on the surface, they represent a potentially powerful force in world environmental affairs. In fact, in 1994, the United Nations Environment Programme (UNEP) budget was roughly US$75 million while Greenpeace's was US$100 million and WWF's was US$200 million.[7] Finally, the number, membership figures, and financial power of NGOs fail to represent what is perhaps NGOs' most important strength – coalition-building between organizations. At least since the 1972 Stockholm Conference, and much more noticeably since the 1992 Earth Summit, NGOs have established networks among themselves to exchange information, share offices, and coordinate strategies. Although there is no way to measure the combined effects of NGO coordination, it is probably fair to say that the environmental NGO community as a whole is larger than the sum of its parts. In so far as it speaks and acts with a coordinated voice, its efforts can be directed toward multiple targets with similar effect. There are, for example, many formal networks established that organize activities. The Antarctic and Southern Oceans Coalition, for instance, coordinates activities among 200 NGOs in 40 countries with respect to Antarctica and its surrounding oceans. The Fifty Years is Enough Campaign (FYE) coordinates the efforts of dozens of NGOs to reform the World Bank. At an informal level, it is well known that many groups formulate policy and orientation together and project a common voice (Sale 1993, 33–34; Fisher 1993, 57–70).

While NGOs have much strength and represent an ostensibly important set of actors in world environmental affairs, they are not all alike nor above criticism. Notwithstanding the coordination just mentioned, some environmental NGOs have drastically opposing understandings of what would promote a healthy environment and work, at times, at cross-purposes. There are, for example, organizations linked to the "wise use" movement in the United States that claim to be environmentalists and insert themselves nationally and transnationally into environmental debates. Many of these are networked with industry-based groups who argue that they are committed to clean air, water, and so forth if these can be achieved purely through market mechanisms (Ehrlich and Ehrlich 1996; Kaufman 1994; Thiele 1999). Such groups are organized at the international level, playing an advocacy role for industries and businesses that oppose regulation on certain issues. The Global Climate Coalition and the Alliance for Responsible CFC Policy represent perhaps the best known of these organizations. Moreover, it is well known that Northern and Southern-based NGOs often have different visions of environmental protection and different understandings of the proper means for achieving such visions. This was demonstrated poignantly in the criticism launched by the Centre for Science and Environment (CSE) in Delhi against research undertaken by the World Resources Institute (WRI) concerning estimates of carbon production throughout the world. The CSE argued that the WRI's numbers failed to take into account per capita carbon production and thus portrayed many developing countries as heavy carbon producers when, if population is taken into account, they are actually much more environmentally benign. This criticism was important because the WRI's estimates were being accepted by many Northern NGOs and some states and sparked much debate about climate change. The CSE critique undermined the implicit notion of consensus among all environmental NGOs and underlined the sheer diversity of outlook (Agarwal and Narain 1991, 1992; Athanasiou 1996).

Environmental NGOs deserve careful scrutiny in so far as they are unelected and relatively unaccountable. The Worldwide Fund for Nature, Friends of the Earth, and other large NGOs speak with a tremendous amount of authority. A 1997 poll demonstrated this when it found that German youth placed more credibility in Greenpeace than in any other institutional authority. Among 14–18 year olds, Greenpeace ranked higher than political parties, unions, television personalities, and politicians in terms of public trust (Zitelmann 1997). Given the high profile of environmental NGOs, one might reasonably ask who they represent and on what grounds their authority rests. NGOs are ultimately accountable to their funders. And yet, those funders do not necessarily represent the public interest. Hence, while environmental NGOs work for the well-being of the environment, it is important to remember that their understanding of environmental protection is not above the fray of political life. It is, as mentioned, above statist orientations, and this is extremely important for locating their authority. This does not free them, however, from other types of loyalty that may skew their understanding of environmental issues.

Actions to change state behaviour

States are the most important actors in world politics and fundamentally constitute the international system. They have the ability to shape widespread behaviour significantly within their own territories and thus represent key mechanisms of global governance. The governing capacity of states is so impressive that the international system itself is often equated with the state system. Recognizing the significance of state power, NGOs focus much of their efforts on influencing states and the state system (Princen and Finger 1994; Wapner 1996). How do they do so?

Environmental NGOs influence state action primarily by pressuring government officials to support environmental protection efforts. At the international level, this entails NGOs inserting themselves into and manipulating the dynamics of public international regimes.[8] International regimes are rules, codes of conduct, principles, and so forth that inform inter-state behaviour; environmental regimes are those that guide inter-state behaviour with regard to environmental issues. States create environmental regimes to address transboundary environmental problems, since air, water, shifting soils, and migratory animals, for example, care little for passports or border patrol guards. As a result, environmental challenges call on states to coordinate their activities so as to fashion common responses to collective threats. While systematic understanding of the role of NGOs in regime life is still emerging, examples of NGO participation convey a sense of widespread involvement and impact. Preliminary findings suggest that NGOs play a significant role in all stages of regime formation, continuity, and modification.

Scholars explain regime formation in three ways: as arising as a result of power, interest, or knowledge (Hasenclever, Mayer and Rittberger 1996; Young 1994; Rowlands 1995). The first explanation emphasizes the distribution of power within the international system; the second focuses on forging common interests among states; the third points to the way in which new information reshapes state identities and interests. In each case, how a state understands and wishes to act with regard to environmental issues is crucial. For example, to the degree a hegemon is responsible for the emergence of a regime, it matters how the hegemon perceives and sees its interests being advanced or threatened by a given environmental issue. Likewise, to the degree that mutual interests drive regime formation, it matters how states perceive environmental issues and how they come to see them as common problems in which there is a shared stake that inspires cooperation. Finally, to the degree that new information is responsible for regimes, it matters how that information is understood and disseminated. NGOs draw attention to environmental issues – a task that includes interpreting scientific information and advertising given threats – and this helps create domestic and international pressure on states to establish environmental regimes. To be sure, NGOs are not single-handedly responsible for the creation of regimes, but their work as publicists on behalf of environmental challenges contributes to the formation of state understandings and interests, whether one is referring to those of a hegemon or a group of states.

The international toxic waste trade, for instance, involves the exportation of hazardous refuse from one country to another. In search of less expensive ways to dispose of hazardous wastes, countries have until recently allowed waste handlers to send materials outside the country of origin without monitoring or regulation. This practice took place largely because few people or states were aware of its magnitude or dangerous character. Starting in the mid-1980s, Greenpeace began a campaign that investigated and publicized instances of such exportation. Its offices around the world coordinated activities with shipping enterprises and governments to trace the dynamics of the international toxic waste trade. Among its most important efforts, Greenpeace alerted importing states about shipments, published a newsletter that, for years, was the only source of information on the waste trade, and raised the issue with national governments and multiple international organizations to draw attention to its hazardous effects on the planet. Due in large part to

Greenpeace's efforts, in the mid-1980s UNEP facilitated negotiations for controlling the toxic waste trade. The result was the Basel Convention on the Control of Transboundary Movements of Hazardous Wastes and Their Disposal. The Convention essentially outlaws the transportation of most toxic substances from member states of the OECD to non-OECD countries.[9]

In terms of monitoring and verification of environmental regimes, NGOs increasingly play both formal and informal roles in investigating and reporting violations. According to the US General Accounting Office and other sources, compliance with international environmental agreements is inadequate (General Accounting Office 1992; Ausubel and Victor 1992). States often fail to submit reports of relevant activity or live up to agreed-upon commitments. NGOs play an important role in trying to improve the record of compliance. In the case of the Convention on International Trade in Endangered Species (CITES), the International Union for the Conservation of Nature (IUCN) (with both government and non-government members) provides secretariat services on a UNEP contract (Ausubel and Victor 1992, 13; Young 1989, 26). Furthermore, in an unusual arrangement, the IUCN delegates research, monitoring, and technical assistance associated with its secretariat duties to an organization known as "TRAFFIC," which is staffed almost exclusively by WWF members and charged with CITES implementation. The WWF, with offices and long-standing working relationships with shipping docks around the world, is well positioned to discover CITES violations and report them to the secretariat. NGO monitoring activities in general often lead to tightening regime measures. For example, according to Peter Sand (1990), since the inception of the European Union more than half of the infringement proceedings relating to international environmental issues entered against member states were based on formal complaints from local and regional environmental NGOs. This mimics a similar dynamic with regard to transnational NGOs and international environmental agreements.

Finally, with regard to modifying existing regimes, NGOs play a key role in tracking new scientific evidence as to the nature and intensity of environmental degradation, publicizing it, and working to upgrade regimes to reflect new environmental realities. Due to the speed and complexity of environmental change, international accords are almost always in need of periodic revision. NGOs encourage such revision and have been responsible, in a few instances, for proposing the content of treaty upgrades. For example, after states established the Montreal Protocol on Substances that Deplete the Ozone Layer (brought about partially because of NGO efforts in the United States and United Kingdom (Wapner 1996, 127–128, 132)), there was a need to revise national commitments due to new scientific evidence of an expanding ozone hole over Antarctica and new discursive frames for understanding the severity of the threat (Litfin 1994). Friends of the Earth, the Environmental Defense Fund, and other NGOs worked vigorously to persuade state officials to enhance the Protocol. While not alone in their efforts – numerous scientists and policy-makers (part of a group of actors that Litfin (1994) calls "knowledge brokers") pressed for revisions – NGOs coordinated much of the effort and their activities won government support for establishing the 1990 London Amendments to the Protocol, which led eventually to the Copenhagen agreements that set the terms for a complete ban on ozone-depleting substances (Bramble and Porter 1992, 341). While not single-handedly responsible for the London and Copenhagen revisions, NGOs provided an essential component in the overall political effort.

NGOs thus play an important role in all phases of international environmental regimes. They recognize that such regimes, while imperfect mechanisms for environmental protection, greatly influence widespread behaviour. States have the ability to reach into and shape the activities of citizens throughout the world; NGOs see states and the international regimes they create, then, as efficient means of governance and appropriate targets of NGO political activity. However, states are not the only forms of global governance and thus not the only NGO targets in the international system.

Actions to engage economic forces

People are motivated not simply by government-sanctioned laws but also by economic forces. Likewise, structures of power throughout the world are not reducible simply to the actions of states but also arise as a result of economic activity. Economic forces, in other words, are forms of governance. They help set the character and define the dynamics of individual and collective life. Economic activity, by definition then, greatly determines how humans interact with the natural world and how they approach issues of environmental protection.

Economic systems are constituted by a process of production, distribution, exchange, and consumption. Each of these has to do with the way humans materially sustain themselves. However, the activities of production, distribution, and so forth are not simply about material survival and flourishing but, because they are so central to human existence, extend themselves into all aspects of human life. The way a society produces or exchanges goods, for instance, largely animates the way it understands itself and operates (Harvey 1996). It gives rise to, or sets the parameters of, certain identities that, in turn, create interests that translate into actual behaviour.

Economic forces, like ecological ones, inherently know no boundaries. Production, distribution, exchange, and consumption can, and increasingly do, take place across state boundaries. One result of this is the emergence of an integrated world economy based, according to many, on capitalist principles and dynamics (Harvey 1996; Wallerstein 1979). A related but different result is simply that economic activity shapes widespread behaviour beyond the territoriality of given states. It influences identity and interests throughout the world and leads to transnational dynamics that influence the day-to-day lives of individuals everywhere and the organization of transnational collective life. Given the powerful role of economic forces, it makes sense that NGOs try to intervene in and manipulate the character of economic affairs.

Engaging economic forms of governance is no easy matter. Given the constitutive role of economic forces, it is difficult for NGOs (or any other actor, for that matter) to develop a conceptually clear purchase point on economic issues and direct economic activities. NGOs undertake the challenge by conceptually "unpacking" the world economy and identifying certain nodes of power within it. They then target those nodes that most effectively engage environmental issues. A prime example of this is Greenpeace's work to eliminate waste dumping in the world's oceans and seas.

Throughout the 1970s, ocean dumping of waste was an accepted practice. For materials already at or close to bodies of water, it provided a relatively inexpensive form of disposal. For hazardous wastes, it provided a form of disposal that kept the terrestrial environment free from contamination. In both cases, it allowed waste to be kept out of sight and thus out of mind. Since the 1970s, Greenpeace, among other organizations, has worked to prevent and ultimately ban ocean dumping. One of its most dramatic campaigns along these lines has been to stop the dismantling of gas and oil rigs at sea, and force polluters to dismantle them on land. Key to its efforts has been the pressure it brought to bear on Shell Oil's Brent Spar installation in the North Sea.

There are over 400 gas/oil installations in the North Sea that will soon cease to be viable and will need dismantling. In the spring of 1995, Shell announced plans and received governmental approval to dispose of its Brent Spar by dumping it into the North Sea. Such a prospect became a significant concern for Greenpeace; the 4,000-tonne installation was believed to be loaded with toxic and radioactive sludge. According to Greenpeace, if Brent Spar were dismantled at sea, it would create a dangerous precedent for the disposal of other rigs and perhaps fuel an effort by many industries to turn to ocean dumping (Greenpeace 1998a). As a result, in May 1995 Greenpeace organized an intensive campaign against Shell. Over two dozen activists from six North Sea countries worked together to stage an on-site protest, with other Greenpeace members orchestrating the campaign from their home offices. Among its many activities, Greenpeace landed a helicopter on the oil platform and brought activists by sea to occupy the installation. This included unfurling a banner that read "Save the North Sea" to publicize the issue. Additionally, two Greenpeace ships circled the rig with photographers producing images of the occupation that were sent out electronically to media sources throughout the world, and occupiers wrote a diary of day-to-day activities that was also sent out electronically to world media sources. Finally, Greenpeace organized a boycott of Shell products that led, according to the London *Times*, to a 30 per cent reduction in sales throughout Europe (Millar 1995, 19). These efforts were well coordinated and took place across state boundaries. The Greenpeace campaign aimed to engage the public and Shell's subsidiaries throughout much of the world. Its efforts eventually paid off. In June 1995, after constant pressure, Shell reversed its decision and announced that it would bring the installation in and dismantle it on shore (Radford and White 1995, 1).

What is important to notice in this campaign is that Greenpeace did not target governments *per se* but rather Shell Oil. In fact, Shell apparently embarrassed former UK Prime Minister John Major by reversing its decision without first informing him. Hours before Shell's announcement, Major was in Parliament defending the decision to allow Shell to dismantle the rig in the North Sea (Nuttall and Leathley 1995, 1). Moreover, Shell had initially won approval from the Oslo and Paris Commission (OSPARCOM), an intergovernmental body that regulates pollution in the north-east Atlantic, and ignored this approval in its decision to bring the rig to shore (Nuttall and Leathley 1995, 1). Greenpeace targeted Shell as an economic actor and found ways to influence its behaviour. The campaign represents an attempt to target directly the economic sphere as opposed to the strictly governmental one.

The Brent Spar episode has proved to be important for setting the standard for dismantling oil and gas installations. Weeks after the Greenpeace campaign, all parties to OSPARCOM, with the exception of the United Kingdom and Norway, agreed to a moratorium on ocean dumping of oil and gas installations (which became a complete ban when OSPARCOM met again in July 1998). Moreover, since June 1995 12 decommissioned oil installations have come ashore for disposal even though at least three of these were in deep enough water conceivably to be left in situ, and a number of these were under the jurisdiction of the United Kingdom and Norway and thus not bound by the OSPARCOM agreement – for example, the Odin installation (Norway) (Greenpeace 1998b) and Shell's Leman BK (UK) (Greenpeace 1998a). In short, Greenpeace's campaign against Brent Spar reoriented ocean dumping practices. At a minimum, it set a standard of good conduct that has put in place a voluntary regime for corporate practice. Again, it represents an effort by an NGO to target the economic dimension of world collective life and understand the degree to which the economic realm represents a form of governance.

Another example of NGOs targeting the economic realm, in contrast to the strictly governmental one, is the NGO effort to hold corporations accountable to the general public. There is a long tradition of conceptualizing the economy as embedded in society (Polanyi 1957). That is, society itself – constituted by people understanding themselves as citizens as opposed to consumers or producers – has often been seen as primary in social ontology. Much critical thinking in the modern age has focused on the way in which economic forces have gained the upper hand in social relations, determining much of the character of collective life. Society is seen by many critical thinkers as now practically embedded in the economy. Environmental NGOs worry about the implications of such a reversal. For them, to the degree the economy dictates social affairs, environmental protection will tend to be neglected as it becomes marginalized under the commitment to profits, economic efficiency, and material productivity. NGOs have been working against this not only by pressuring specific corporations to change their practices but also by devising mechanisms for holding sets of corporations accountable to citizens.

One of the more prominent strategies for corporate accountability consists of establishing voluntary codes of conduct that corporations agree to abide by. In recent years, companies such as Levi Strauss, Reebok, J. C. Penny, and Wal-Mart have agreed to eliminate prison and child labour in their operations throughout the world. These agreements were initiated and are being monitored by labour and development NGOs (Broad and Cavanaugh 2000). A similar effort has taken place with regard to environmental issues. The best known was established in 1989 by the Coalition for Environmentally Responsible Economies (CERES). The CERES Principles provide concrete criteria against which corporations can strive to improve their environmental record and against which activist groups and citizens can evaluate corporate environmental performance. The code calls on companies, among other things, to minimize pollution, conserve non-renewable resources through efficient use and planning, and consider demonstrated environmental commitment as a factor in appointing members to the company's board of directors. The code has been embraced by at least one Fortune 500 company and a number of multinational corporations. Sun Company, General Motors, Polaroid, and a host of other multinational companies have pledged compliance or are at least seriously considering doing so. The effort to enlist companies in the CERES Principles (formerly known as the

"Valdez Principles," inspired by the *Exxon Valdez* oil spill) is an attempt by NGOs to work directly with corporations and find ways of holding them accountable for the impact they have on the environment (Ann-Zondorak 1991; Broad and Cavanaugh 2000). It represents another strategy of engaging directly the economic dimension of world collective life.

Environmental NGOs participate in the corporate accountability movement because it represents a way to guide corporate forces toward more environmentally sound types of practices. To be sure, the movement has not changed the essential character of corporate life, nor has it even, it is safe to say, resulted in significant changes that can be easily traced back to environmental protection. It has, however, played at the margins of global corporate understandings and practices, and holds promise as small successes might eventuate in large-scale transformations. NGOs are not holding their breath with regard to such promise, but they continue to engage corporate activities because they recognize the substantial governing power of economic forces and understand that *any* change in economic affairs will affect global environmental quality.

Actions to engage social mores

Governmental and economic forces clearly shape the way individuals and collectivities live their lives and reproduce themselves. Additionally, it is well known that social forces – constituted by cultural practices – shape the way people understand themselves and act in the world. A long tradition of social theory reminds us that humans are, seemingly by nature, social animals. On the whole, they seem to need others and, as communitarians well explain, find themselves being partially constituted by social interaction. People adopt ethical and practical orientations towards the world through the socialization process. The result is that they operate in the world informed by the sociohistorical context within which they find themselves. NGOs recognize the situated character of human life and, while influenced by it themselves, work to understand how social mores affect human attitudes and behaviour toward the environment. Their efforts along these lines lead to adopting a political strategy of social engagement wherein they try to manipulate the forces of socialization.

Environmentalism has been compared to religion and nationalism in so far as it calls for, according to some of its more radical advocates, adopting a certain world view based on philosophical and emotional foundations as well as scientific ones (Taylor 1995; Deudney 1995). At its most general level, environmentalism can be described as a sensibility that values nature and believes that the quality of life on earth depends upon the well-being of the planet's air, water, soil, and so forth. For many

environmentalists, environmental protection calls for others to adopt
such a sensibility. It involves winning over or literally converting people
to an environmental perspective. So many cultural practices reveal an
anti-ecological orientation; people throughout the world do things that
degrade the environment because they operate according to traditions or
within ideological structures that support anti-ecological practices. Environmental NGOs work to manipulate the factors that constitute such
traditions and structures with the aim of producing, as it were, environmentally conscious citizens.

In parts of Asia, there is a tradition of ingesting parts of certain wild
plants and animals to boost one's health. Because of increasing demand,
this tradition has been threatening the continued existence of certain
species. For example, in East Asia it is widely believed that the bile from
bear gall bladders acts as a health restorative, working as an antidote to
liver cancer, haemorrhoids, and conjunctivitis, as well as promoting general virility. In a grisly form of extraction, China has so-called bear farms
where bears live in captivity hooked up to intravenous systems that pull
just enough of the bile from their bladders to keep them alive while producing enough to sell. In general, the belief system threatens all bears
throughout the region and, due to international smuggling, the world.
This is also the case with tiger bones and rhinoceros horns, which are
thought to promote human health. One result of this belief is that the
number of bears, tigers, and rhinos throughout the world is decreasing.
All Asian species of bears, for instance, are presently on Appendix One
of CITES, and smuggling bears from other countries is endangering
North and South American bear populations (TRAFFIC 1997a.)

Environmental NGOs work to reduce the demand for bears, tigers, and
rhinos by engaging international regimes. One of their more important
efforts, already mentioned, is to increase compliance with CITES. Stopping the trafficking of endangered species at national borders represents
a key way to protect bears and other species. NGOs recognize, however,
that no matter how stringent international regimes are, if cultural practices still support exploitation of endangered species, bears, tigers, and
rhinos (as well as numerous other species) will be at risk. As a result,
NGOs try directly to change cultural practices. The Worldwide Fund for
Nature, for instance, has begun a dialogue with consumers and medical
practitioners throughout East Asia to alter the way they understand
endangered species and the necessity of using such species for medicinal
purposes. This has involved a contradictory strategy of, on the one hand,
trying simply to reacculturate people to different understandings of health
and the use of wild plants and animals, and, on the other, convincing
medical practitioners and consumers of the benefits of synthetic sub-
stitutes. The first involves changing the ideational context within which

traditional Eastern medicine operates; the second entails accommodating that tradition through technological intervention (TRAFFIC 1997a; 1997b). Both represent, however, the attempt to engage the social dimension of collective life.

One need not go to the East to discover the impact of social forces on environmental affairs. All cultures are animated by widespread understandings that support anti-ecological activities and, in an increasingly interdependent world where cultural forms are penetrating societies the world over, social forces are animating many anti-ecological practices across the globe. NGOs work to change social forces in general that they deem to be anti-ecological. One of the more obvious efforts along these lines is the ongoing campaign to endear certain animals to people so as to inspire people not to want to consume them – as clothing, food, and so forth – but to value their preservation in the wild. The best known of these campaigns are arguably the efforts to protect whales and harp seals.

For years, whales were seen as simply another resource to be used for human consumption. For the most part, they were hunted for food and oil. Greenpeace, Friends of the Earth, the Sea Shepherds Conservation Society, the WWF, and others have worked for years trying to change this image. Through photographs, films, and audio recordings, they have portrayed whales as a special species deserving not only protection but respect. NGOs have advertised whales' evident intelligence, gentleness, and unique vocalizations now known as whale "songs." Due in large measure to NGO efforts, whales have assumed a mystical character in many people's minds (Day 1989, 52). Such a view led to acts such as "Operation Rescue," wherein a US$5 million effort was waged to save three whales trapped in ice in Alaska (Rose 1989).

A similar campaign was waged to protect baby harp seals in northern Canada. For years there was an annual harp seal hunt in Canada that garnered hundreds of thousands of pure white pelts from newborn seals. Starting in the late 1960s, a host of NGOs including the International Fund for Animal Welfare, Greenpeace, the Sea Shepherds Conservation Society, and others focused attention on the hunt and tried to portray it as inhumane. Their main strategy was to personify the pups by photographing individual seals and representing them as cute, helpless victims. In the context of such personification, NGOs documented the brutal act of clubbing and skinning newborns (often in full view of mother seals). Seal pups are, like whales, "charismatic mega-fauna" – that is, large species that can be portrayed as having special qualities that enable people to extend to them care, concern, and simply relatedness (Wenzel 1991; Day 1989). NGOs played on this quality and worked to enhance it. NGO efforts worked, among other things, to dissuade customers from purchasing coats made out of the pelts, a move that reduced the Euro-

pean market considerably and made the seal trade essentially unprofit-
able (Wapner 1996, 66).

NGO attempts to portray animals in a particular manner or reacculturate the way people understand the health benefits of ingesting wild
animals are efforts to isolate and manipulate cultural formations. They
aim to change the way societies understand human relations with non-
human species and thus alter the sociohistorical context within which
people operate as they interact with the environment. The implicit understanding behind such a strategy is that sociocultural structures are
somewhat autonomous from economic and governmental forces – or at
least are able to be engaged directly – and thus represent worthy political
targets. NGOs recognize, in other words, the governing capability of
social structures and see their work as demanding political engagement
with them.

Dialectics by way of conclusion and qualification

This chapter has tried analytically to circumscribe three spheres of collective life that NGOs target to advance environmental protection. It has
presented these spheres as unproblematic in so far as they have been
portrayed in essentialist terms. It should be remembered, however, that
these spheres are not autonomous but overlap and, indeed, constitute
each other. Governmental life, for example, at the domestic and international levels is not separate or immune from economic and social
dynamics. Rather, in many ways it mirrors the qualities and patterns of
economic and social activity. This is also the case with economic and
social structures: they are infused with qualities that originate, or at least
find their greatest articulation, in the activities and imperatives of the
state and the state system. The idea here is that the three spheres outlined are in dialectical relation to each other. They are related to each
other as opposed to being self-subsisting entities with circumscribed
properties, and they have numerous contradictory tendencies within
them as opposed to being homogeneous realms of given character. It is in
this latter regard, by the way, that environmental NGOs can, in fact, engage them. If governmental, economic, and social forces completely supported anti-ecological practices, NGO efforts would be in vain. Openings
in the system arise from contradictions; NGOs work the contradictions.

Appreciating the dialectical character of governmental, economic, and
social relations allows for a clearer explication of environmental NGO
strategies. Environmental NGOs see themselves as committed to environmental protection. They seek to ensure the quality of the earth's air,
water, soil, and species. So committed, they care little in principle about

what routes to pursue when seeking environmental protection; they wish only to advance the cause.[10] The routes to environmental protection are many because the character of world political life is complex. The international system, as it were, is constituted not simply by the state system but by economic and social forces that animate widespread behaviour. The world, as it were, is governed by multiple sources of rule. Indeed, it is even somewhat unfair, from an analytical perspective, to circumscribe governmental, economic, and social forces as related realms and posit them as the most significant. As researchers well know, multiple forms of control, regulation, administration, and so forth exist that stabilize human life and condition understanding and action. Nonetheless, it often helps to delineate certain "permanences" (Harvey 1996) to identify categories of social analysis, even if one recognizes that these are simply convenient categories rather than concrete empirical realities. Environmental NGOs target each of these realms, then, as a realistic political strategy. They work for political change and thus find themselves targeting multiple realms that govern human interaction with the non-human world.

Notes

1. The author is grateful to American University for supporting this research through a University Research Award. An earlier version of this paper was presented at the American Political Science Association Annual Meeting, 29 August–3 September 1997. The author would like to thank Volker Rittberger, Judith Shapiro, and Sidney Tarrow for helpful comments on earlier drafts.
2. On the concept of governance, see Wapner 1996, 3ff.
3. It should be noted that the term NGO can be distinguished from what the United Nations and especially the Commission on Sustainable Development recognize as "major groups." "Major groups" include not only political organizations but also indigenous peoples, local authorities, business and industry, and other associations. The distinction is that some major groups may not have been established to induce political change, but either find themselves having a stake or role in the way certain public issues are understood or particular public problems are addressed. While recognizing the importance of "major groups" in world affairs and, in particular, in world environmental issues, this chapter restricts itself to a focus simply on what are conventionally understood as NGOs.
4. A good example of such environmental NGOs can be found in Dawson 1996.
5. For an insightful discussion of the interplay between, say, environment and development groups, see Durning 1989.
6. If one includes the host of organizations in the South that are not directly committed to environmental issues but which forge coalitions with environmental NGOs, this number jumps to hundreds of thousands. See Fisher, cited in Conca 1996.
7. For membership and budget figures, see Wapner 1996, 2, note 3.
8. On the distinction between private and public international regimes, see Haufler 1997, which is the first full-length exploration of private international regimes of which the author is aware.

9. See generally Wynne 1989; Agarwal and Narain 1992.
10. This is not to say that NGOs are unconcerned with how they undertake political action. Most environmental NGOs are committed, for example, to non-violent activities. See generally Taylor 1995.

REFERENCES

Agarwal, A. and S. Narain. 1991. "Global Warming in an Unequal World: A Case of Environmental Colonialism." *Earth Island Journal* (Spring).

Agarwal, A. and S. Narain. 1992. *Towards a Green World*. New Delhi: Centre for Science and Environment.

Ann-Zondorak, V. 1991. "A New Face in Corporate Environmental Responsibility: The Valdez Principles." *Boston College Environmental Affairs Law Review* 18.

Athanasiou, T. 1996. *Divided Planet: The Ecology of Rich and Poor*. Boston: Little, Brown.

Ausubel, J. H. and D. Victor. 1992. "Verification of International Environmental Agreements." *Annual Review of Energy and Environment* 17.

Bramble, B. J. and G. Porter. 1992. "Non-Governmental Organizations and the Making of US International Environmental Policy." In *The International Politics of the Environment*, eds A. Hurrell and B. Kingsbury. Oxford: Oxford University Press.

Broad, R. and J. Cavanaugh. 2000. "Global Backlash: Citizen Initiatives to Counter Corporate-Led Globalization." In *Principled World Politics: The Challenge of Normative International Relations at the Millennium*, eds P. Wapner and L. Ruiz. Lanham: Rowman and Littlefield.

Conca, K. 1996. "Greening the UN: Environmental Organizations and the UN System." In *NGOs, the UN and Global Governance*, eds T. G. Weiss and L. Gordenker. Boulder: Lynne Rienner.

Conca, K., M. Alberty, and G. D. Dabelko. 1995. "Ecology and the Structure of the International System." In *Green Planet Blues: Environmental Politics from Stockholm to Rio*, eds K. Conca, M. Alberty, and G. D. Dabelko. Boulder: Westview.

Dawson, J. I. 1996. *Eco-Nationalism: Anti-Nuclear Activism and National Identity in Russia, Lithuania and Ukraine*. Durham, NC: Duke University Press.

Day, D. 1989. *The Environmental Wars: Reports from the Frontline*. New York: Ballantine Books.

Deudney, D. 1995. "In Search of Gaian Politics: Earth Religion's Challenge to Modern Western Civilization." In *Ecological Resistance Movements: The Global Emergence of Radical and Popular Environmentalism*, ed. Bron Taylor. Albany: State University of New York Press.

Durning, A. 1989. *Action at the Grassroots: Fighting Poverty and Environmental Decline*. Worldwatch Paper 88. Washington: Worldwatch Institute.

Ehrlich, P. R. and A. H. Ehrlich. 1996. *Betrayal of Science and Reason: How Anti-Environmental Rhetoric Threatens Our Future*. Washington: Island Press.

Fisher, J. 1993. *The Road From Rio: Sustainable Development and the Non-Governmental Movement in the Third World*. Westport: Praeger.

General Accounting Office. 1992. *International Environment: International Agreements are Not Being Well Monitored* (CGAO/RCED-92-43). Washington: GAO. 27 January.

Greenpeace. 1998a. "Greenpeace Brent Spar Protest in the North Sea." Internet ⟨http://www.greenpeace.org/~comms/brent/brent.html⟩ (visited 25 January 1998).

Greenpeace. 1998b. "Greenpeace Applauds Norwegian Government Decision on Esso Rig." Internet ⟨http://www.greenpeace.org/~comms/brent/odinpr01.html⟩ (visited 25 January 1998).

Harvey, D. 1996. *Justice, Nature and the Geography of Difference*. Cambridge, MA: Blackwell.

Hasenclever, A., P. Mayer, and V. Rittberger. 1996. "Interests, Power, Knowledge: The Study of International Regimes." *Mershon International Studies Review* 40(2).

Haufler, V. 1997. *Dangerous Commerce: Insurance and the Management of International Risk*. Ithaca: Cornell University Press.

Kaufman, W. 1994. *No Turning Back: Dismantling the Fantasies of Environmental Thinking*. New York: Basic Books.

Korten, D. C. 1990. *Getting to the 21st Century: Voluntary Action and the Global Agenda*. Hartford: Kumarian Press.

Litfin, K. T. 1994. *Ozone Discourse: Science and Politics in Global Environmental Cooperation*. New York: Columbia University Press.

Millar, P. 1995. "Green Pressure, Plain Blackmail." *The Times*. 22 June.

Nuttall, N. and A. Leathley. 1995. "Shell Abandons: Ministers Furious over Capitulation to Greens." *The Times*. 21 June.

Polanyi, K. 1957. *The Great Transformation: Political and Economic Origins of our Time*. Boston: Beacon Press.

Princen, T. and M. Finger, eds. 1994. *Environmental NGOs in World Politics: Linking the Local and the Global*. New York: Routledge.

Radford, T. and M. White. 1995. "Shell Gives Up Battle for Oil Rig." *The Guardian*. 21 June.

Ridgeway, J. 1995. *Blood in the Face: The Ku Klux Klan, Aryan Nations, Nazi Skinheads, and the Rise of a New White Culture*, 2nd edn. New York: Thunder's Mouth Press.

Rose, T. 1989. *Freeing the Whales: How the Media Created the World's Greatest Non-Event*. New York: Birch Lane Press.

Rosenau, J. 1990. *Turbulence in World Politics: A Theory of Change and Continuity*. Princeton: Princeton University Press.

Rowlands, I. H. 1995. *The Politics of Global Atmospheric Change*. Manchester: Manchester University Press.

Sale, K. 1993. *The Green Revolution: The American Environmental Movement 1962–1992*. New York: Hill and Wang.

Sand, P. H. 1990. *Lessons Learned in Global Environmental Governance*. Washington: World Resources Institute.

Taylor, B. 1995. "Introduction: The Global Emergence of Popular Ecological

Resistance." In *Ecological Resistance Movements: The Global Emergence of Radical and Popular Environmentalism*, ed. B. Taylor. Albany: State University of New York Press.

Thiele, L. 1999. *Environmentalism for a New Millennium: The Challenge of Coevolution*. New York: Oxford University Press.

TRAFFIC. 1997a. *Traffic Dispatches*. February.

TRAFFIC. 1997b. *Traffic Bulletin* 16(3) (March).

Wallerstein, I. 1979. *The Capitalist World Economy*. Cambridge: Cambridge University Press.

Wapner, P. 1996. *Environmental Activism and World Civic Politics*. Albany: State University of New York Press.

Weiss, T. G. and L. Gordenker. 1996. "Pluralizing Global Governance: Analytical Approaches and Dimensions." In *NGOs, the UN and Global Governance*, eds T. G. Weiss and L. Gordenker. Boulder: Lynne Rienner.

Wenzel, G. 1991. *Animal Rights, Human Rights*. Toronto: University of Toronto Press.

Wynne, B. 1989. "The Toxic Waste Trade: International Regulatory Issues and Options." *Third World Quarterly* 11(3).

Young, O. R. 1989. *International Cooperation: Building Regimes for Natural Resources and the Environment*. Ithaca: Cornell University Press.

Young, O. R. 1994. *International Governance. Protecting the Environment in a Stateless Society*. Ithaca: Cornell University Press.

Zitelmann, R. 1997. "Greenpeace liegt weit vor den Politikern." *Die Welt*. 24 April. Internet ⟨http://www.welt.de/970424/0424de04.htm⟩.

FURTHER READING

Ross, M. 1996. "Conditionality and Logging Reform in the Tropics." In *Institutions for Environmental Aid*, eds R. O. Keohane and M. Levy. Cambridge, MA: MIT Press.

7

Energy development and environmental NGOs: The Asian perspective

Lin Gan[1]

Energy sector development is often identified as the focus of environmental action because of the severe environmental impacts of energy exploration and utilization, driven by the increasing demand for energy services (IPCC 1996). The conflict between energy production or use and environmental sustainability is seen as the main issue attracting the attention of nation-states worldwide. This chapter aims at analysing the role of NGOs in Asia in the energy sector. First, it will describe the characteristics and means of NGOs as they are involved in the conflict between energy production or use and environmental protection. Second, it will focus on NGOs' involvement in decision-making. Third, it will review the relationships of NGOs with governmental agencies, the private sector, the scientific community, and international aid agencies. Fourth, it will analyse the relationship of international NGOs with local and regional NGOs.

The development process in the energy sector is complex and includes many components. The issue area of energy production covers, for example, the construction of new power plants, including fossil-fuel-based power plants and hydroelectric dams. In this area of concern, NGOs often take radical approaches, such as lobbying and protesting against dominant development practices that are considered to be environmentally questionable. On the other hand, energy conservation, demand-side management, lifestyle changes, and the sustainable use of biomass resources have all become concerns of many stakeholders who are interested in changing energy consumption patterns and related development choices. In this area of NGO engagement, a participatory approach is often used to mobilize as many interested social groups as possible. The Green Movement in Korea is an example (Jeong and Lee 1996, 187–197).

Energy sector development and environmental protection in Asia have been integrated into development processes through the involvement of five different types of social institutions. They include governments, multilateral and bilateral aid agencies, the private sector, the scientific community, and NGOs. Their actions and interactions are the primary sources of societal response to critical development and environment issues (Gan 1995).

Governments traditionally play a leading role in shaping energy development and environmental protection. They often dominate development processes through a top-down approach, with command-and-control methods as a steering mechanism. This mechanism is often criticized as ineffective, and as operating as a barrier to greater energy efficiency and improved flexibility in operation, because it tends to diminish the potential for citizens' participation and discourages communities' self-involvement (Munasinghe 1991, 31). Multilateral and bilateral aid agencies cooperate with governments in large energy development projects. Many aid programmes are oriented toward large-scale projects that are often environmentally questionable, as often claimed by NGOs. The environment is a relatively new item on the agendas of development aid agencies. However, international organizations such as the World Bank (1997a) have increasingly considered environmental concerns when financing development aid projects. The private sector involved in energy development has traditionally been suspicious of environmental issues because of its business orientation, which often disregards environmental externalities. The private sector is increasingly being pushed by governmental regulations, and to a lesser extent by citizens' groups, towards an environmentally more benign approach. In general, environmental awareness has been increasing within the private sector, shaped both by internal environmental awareness and by external pressures such as governmental regulations. The scientific community includes scientists, engineers, and sectoral specialists. Scientists and policy advisers have moved many domestic and international organizations towards dealing with problems related to energy production or use and environmental protection, and towards changing their policy priorities. Scientists often play a critical role in fostering policy changes in environmentally benign directions.[2]

NGOs have established different working relationships with other actors in order to exchange information and collaborate on issues related to energy and environmental protection. Through formal and informal networks, NGOs shape the attitudes and operation of other social institutions.[3] NGOs often act from below and tend to engage in several issues at a time. Through advocating, opposing, negotiating, and consulting activities, NGOs contribute to setting up policy issue networks that link the general public from local communities upwards with governmental decision-making bodies at various levels.

Energy development and environmental NGOs in Asia

For the period 1980–1995, economic development in Asia was the most dynamic compared with other regions in the world. The East Asian and Pacific region had an average annual GDP growth rate of 7.6 per cent in the 1980s and of 10.3 per cent in 1990–1995. In the same periods, South Asia had relatively low rates of growth at 5.7 per cent and 4.6 per cent, respectively. Compared with world average growth rates of 3.1 and 2.0 per cent in the same periods, Asia performed relatively well as reflected in economic indicators (World Bank 1997b, 235). The high economic growth was sustained by increasing energy use. From 1981 to 1991, energy consumption in Asian developing countries doubled from 700 Mtoe (million tonnes of oil equivalent) to 1,350 Mtoe, and electricity consumption increased 2.5 times from 500 TWh (terawatt-hour) to 1,200 TWh (Sadiq 1996, 86).

Not surprisingly, rapid economic growth and increased dependency on energy use in Asia have been achieved at a great expense to the environment (Clad and Siy 1996, 52–58; ADB 1990, 40–50). The stark contrast between Asia's fast economic development and rapidly deteriorating environment, particularly in urban-industrial areas, makes this region the foremost test for sustainable development. Energy plays a central role in this process. The tension between energy sector development and associated environmental risks has led to increasing concerns for ecological sustainability in the region. In many countries of Asia, energy development is characterized by the expansion of fossil-fuel-based power generation and the development of large-scale hydroelectric power plants.[4] Industrialization and rapid urbanization are the main driving forces of this development.[5]

In rural areas, energy supply often does not meet demand. According to the World Bank, over 2 billion people in the world lack access to electricity and rely on biomass fuels as they have no better alternatives (World Bank 1996). The continuing conflict over the lack of fuelwood and commercial energy supply, i.e. electricity, has led to ecological imbalances in rural areas. With over 80 per cent of rural energy consumption based on non-commercial biomass in most Asian developing countries, such as China, India, Indonesia, and the Philippines (UNDP 1997, 196), the environment is bound to be severely affected. Burning biomass for cooking and heating in rural areas has intensified in some regions due to increasing population pressure (Brandon and Ramankutty 1993, 21–32). This creates further conflicts over natural resources and energy use.

Balancing energy development with environmental sustainability has become one of the greatest development challenges in Asia. There are uncertainties in achieving environmental objectives, such as improving urban air quality and providing clean water to urban and rural residents. This is mostly due to governmental subsidies to the energy sector and resources use (Daly 1994). There is little doubt that environmental risks in Asia, and elsewhere in the world, are not only associated with the complexities of the energy-environment interplay, but also related to the effects of economic growth, population pressure, poverty, and urbanization.

The costs of environmental externalities produced by the energy sector are often excluded from economic cost-benefit analyses when development projects are decided by governmental agencies. Monopoly is a common characteristic of energy development and service sector operation. The interest of the energy sector lies mostly in production expansion to maximize its influence and power. The recent trend of decentralization in the energy sector has legitimized private sector involvement in energy development (Munasinghe 1991, 31). With government support, and sometimes with the help of international development assistance agencies, public and, more recently, private utilities are bound to defend their common interests in energy sector expansion. For this to occur, great challenges in terms of environmental consequences of energy sector development are to be expected.

Asia's development has been characterized by the growing presence of the NGO community in political and social activities (Princen and Finger 1994, 1–3). NGOs have evolved into actors offering a social critique of political development processes. NGOs have also become a widely accessible provider of social services to millions of people in rural communities.[6] The development of environmental NGOs and their involvement in environmental activities must be interpreted from a historical perspective. NGOs can be considered as part of the massive social movements that challenge dominant structures and processes of authoritarian regimes through which political élites maximize their power and interests. The free associations of citizens in Asia have a long tradition, which can be traced back to the pre-colonial communal societies (Serrano 1994, 29).

Much of the growth of NGOs in Asia can be traced back to the post-Second World War period of the late 1940s and 1950s, when local residents and communities developed their networks of contacts. During the 1960s and 1970s, increased income in some Asian countries led to an expansion of the middle classes. These educated and better-informed social strata tend to exercise their influence through participatory social involvement. Environmental NGOs emerged in the 1970s as part of the global environmental movement. They developed further in the 1980s, and expanded rapidly in the early 1990s (Thomas 1992, 27–29). This phenomenon owes its origin and persistence, in part, to the deteriorating environmental situation in Asia following rapid economic development and the so-called modernization movements promoted by governments. Increasing industrialization has given rise to pollution problems that create environmental risks.[7] NGOs sometimes challenge dominant development activities when they see the risks to their interests, such as traditional rights of land use, being eroded and undermined by large-scale project development.

Three different types of NGOs

NGOs can influence energy development due to their expertise. Experts and expertise refer to those professionals with specific knowledge, training, and experience. In public policy-making, their knowledge is used to define policy priorities and set agendas for action. NGOs usually interact through networks that play a critical role in facilitating communication and cooperation between organizations and individuals. There are basically three types of Asian NGOs involved in the debates about energy production or use and environmental protection: research-oriented NGOs, lobbying NGOs, and mediating NGOs.

Research-oriented NGOs

Research-oriented NGOs are those with informational and advisory characteristics. They are motivated by the value of their service accomplished through scientific knowledge development, consultation, and policy advice. Many see their main function as knowledge providers to impart issue-relevant scientific knowledge to policy-makers and the general public. Their main interest is in research, to generate debate and knowledge within and between the scientific community, governments, the business community, and civil society. They intend to increase the scientific understanding of environmental risks of development. Many research-oriented NGOs are think-tanks with either public or private ownership. Their means of operation are through scientific publications, conferences or workshops, and media reporting. Traditionally, their roles are limited to being the agents that carry out projects designed by governments or international agencies. Increasingly, they have become independent players in decision-making processes with a more participatory perspective.

An important function of this type of NGO is to provide advisory services to governments with regard to the design and assessment of public policies aimed at increasing energy efficiency and reducing costs of energy consumption. For example, the Tata Energy Research Institute (TERI) in India is an influential research institute in the area of energy and the environment. It has played a critical role in informing the Indian government, and more broadly the international community, of the important environmental issues related to energy production and consumption. This type of NGO tends to act in a "soft" manner, often collaborating with their partners rather than opposing them. Another example is the Energy Research Institute of the State Development Planning Commission (SDPC) in China. However, this is a government-supported body providing advice to energy policy-makers rather than an independent think-tank.

Many NGOs of this type have grown out of governmental bodies. They prioritize research activities, instead of being action-oriented. The Beijing Energy Efficiency Centre grew out of the Energy Research Institute of the SDPC. Although it receives support from the Department of Energy (DOE) of the US government, it maintains close ties with governmental agencies and operates within the framework of official contacts. Its objective is to facilitate the transfer and dissemination of environmentally friendly energy technologies. In recent years, some technical assistance projects under the banner of capacity-building, funded by international aid agencies, have helped the growth of such institutions. In turn, this has given rise to what may be called the scientification, or professionalization, of decision-making processes (Jamison 1996).

Lobbying NGOs

Lobbying NGOs are those with critical, sometimes radical, attitudes toward development projects with major environmental impacts. They criticize important energy development activities that carry high environmental risks and have an impact on local communities and people. This type of NGO focuses on advocacy when they conduct lobbying activities against the policies of governments and international aid agencies.[8] They often attempt to attract media attention to inform the public and thereby exert pressure on governments. They also present themselves at international meetings to publicize their criticisms. The presence of the Greenpeace movement in Asia is a clear example. In large energy projects, such as hydroelectric dams, the role of lobbying NGOs cannot be underestimated, as their criticisms sometimes lead to reassessments of aid policies, as shown in an Indian case below.

Rapid industrialization and urbanization drastically increase demands for energy supply and services, especially for electricity. In response to the demand from the industrial and commercial sectors, governments in Asia have targeted the development of coal- and oil-based power plants, hydroelectric power stations, and, increasingly, nuclear power plants as main objectives for development. This is the clear case in China, where the use of coal dominates energy supply and demand (Gan 1998b). Increasing awareness of the potential environmental and social-ecological impacts of large hydroelectric dams has caused NGOs to respond strongly to this type of energy development. Resistance from affected local communities has made it difficult for governments to proceed with such projects. The best-known cases of hydroelectric dam projects are the Narmada Dam in India and the Three Gorges Dam in China. These projects have inspired strong public protest that led governments and international aid agencies to change their policies.

The Sardar Sarovar Dam and Power Project in western India, known as the Narmada Dam project, is one of the energy projects that have sparked the most public debate and protest. The project was proposed by the Indian government and strongly backed by governmental energy development institutions. The World Bank was originally involved, providing loans for the project. Largely concerned about the displacement of local tribal groups because of the construction of the dam, NGO lobbying activities across nation-states drew international attention. NGOs, such as the Narmada Bachao Andolan, criticized the anticipated environmental impact of the project, particularly the impact on the ecosystems upon which local people depended for their livelihood. Many Indian NGO groups, plus some concerned international NGOs, participated in this public protest, including research institutions, indigenous groups, and the mass media. Demonstrations and publicity campaigns were organized, putting pressure on the World Bank to stop its financing of the project. Eventually, the World Bank loan for this project was withdrawn at the request of the Indian government in 1993,[9] although the project is still supported by the government. NGO protest against this project helped shape the World Bank's policy on the environment and human settlements. The World Bank has now initiated a policy to encourage NGO participation in resettlement plans. It also requires consultation with potentially affected social groups and local NGOs in environmental assessments for large development projects (Malena 1995, 23).

After more than half a century of debate, the Chinese government decided in 1992 to build the world's largest hydroelectric dam at the Three Gorges of the Yangtze River. The project aims to generate 18,200 MW a year, which is enough to supply the power needs of 150 million people. The dam is expected to cost US$11 billion over an 18-year period (and, when interest charges are included, this figure goes up to US$25 billion). The main concern of opposition groups is that the dam will force the relocation of more than a million people. Opponents say it would be cheaper and less risky to build smaller dams upstream of the Three Gorges.[10] The project sparked protest among NGOs, mostly through lobbying activities. The International Rivers Network, Friends of the Earth, the Center for Marine Conservation, International Three Gorges Coalition, Probe International of Canada, the WWF in Hong Kong, and the Asian Pacific People's Network in Malaysia coordinated with several Chinese environmental groups to protest against the construction of the dam. Criticisms and protests against the dam have been made by prominent scientists in China and abroad. Dai Qing, a leading Chinese journalist, was jailed for a year after she published a book of essays criticizing the dam (Dai 1997). Despite the pressure from NGOs, the government decided to approve the project with full state support. The Chinese government muffled criticisms and unleashed pro-dam propaganda. In 1992, two-thirds of the 2,633-member Chinese People's Congress voted to build the dam, only 12 votes more than the minimum required. This is one of the lowest levels of support ever given to a government-backed project. The dam is now under construction, fully financed by the government. International agencies such as the World Bank and Asian Development Bank (ADB) have stayed away from financing the project, mostly for fear of criticism from NGOs (Magagnini 1992).

By contrast, the Xiaolangdi Dam on the Yellow River, China's second largest dam project, is well under construction. When completed in four years' time, the US$4 billion dam is expected to contain the type of "catastrophic" floods that have killed hundreds of thousands of locals over the past 2,500 years. The Xiaolangdi Dam project has "proceeded without [...] controversies" (*Greenwire* 1996). Many NGOs were preoccupied by the Three Gorges Dam and paid inadequate attention to the Xiaolangdi Dam project. The World Bank has offered a loan of US$430 million to the project, which is by far the largest loan ever provided to the Chinese government (*People's Daily* 1997).

Mediating NGOs

Mediating NGOs are those providing network services. They are usually competent in establishing networks of contacts, domestically and internationally. Their main interest lies in making connections and providing information on important issues to concerned interest groups and individuals. Networks play a critical role in facilitating communication and cooperation between organizations.

In the 1990s, it has become evident that the emerging information society provides opportunities to empower people at different levels of society (Baxter and Lisburn 1994; Willcocks and Currie 1998). The increasing accessibility of information through Internet services has provided a powerful means of communication for common people and social groups. This technological development has broken down the information monopoly traditionally maintained by governmental institutions. It also enables more widespread popular access to, and transfer of, information across national boundaries. The use of electronic mail has facilitated more networking and collaborating activities. As a result, many NGOs increasingly operate on a global scale rather than being restricted to a regional and local presence.

One example is the operation of the Professional Association for China's Environment (PACE), which was established in 1996. PACE has expanded rapidly since 1997, and it has now more than 300 members worldwide. Its operation consists of e-mail communications for sharing information and networking activities. PACE's work has, to some extent, facilitated contacts between the US and Chinese governments on issues related to energy and the environment.

The limitations of NGOs

There is an overlapping relationship among these three types of NGOs. Although TERI is basically a research NGO, it is also involved in networking activities. It acts as the secretariat for the Asian Energy Institute (AEI), a network organization with 13 member institutes across Asia. The AEI's work involves sustainable development and the use of energy resources. Its objectives are to promote information exchange, facilitate sharing and dissemination of knowledge, undertake research and training activities that are of common interest to its members, and analyse global energy developments and their implications.

Governments are often criticized for their lack of accountability in dealing with programmes for local energy development that sometimes benefit the rich instead of the poor.[11] Their means of governance are questioned by most NGOs as having a top-down approach with inadequate consultation with the local people concerned. Meanwhile, the strategy of NGOs offers an alternative approach with a bottom-up orientation. They provide services to local communities with flexible organizational structures and more democratic processes. Their objectives are to oppose dominant players and institutions with the intention of empowering the poor (*Civil Society* 1997).

NGOs have also limitations. Many Asian NGOs are small in both size and scope of operation. As most of them are rooted in local activities, lack of access to resources and information is common. NGOs can suffer from financial and technical constraints. Some of them depend on foreign donations and lack long-term financial security. Attracting funding is one reason for engaging in international activities.

Accountability and performance are interrelated issues. Many smaller NGOs are loosely structured and have limited accountability. Management and planning in these NGOs may be weak, or too flexible (Edwards and Hulme 1995). Many aid agencies are sceptical of the accountability of local NGOs because of the problem of measuring their performance. It has been increasingly realized that lobbying is not enough to generate proactive action for sustainable development. Therefore, more cooperation in project activities is needed at the local level.

Relationship between Asian NGOs and international NGOs

Asian NGOs are rapidly expanding their areas of activities across national boundaries and responding to issues with international orientations. They present themselves at international gatherings and conferences (Princen and Finger 1994, 4–5). They often act as advocates of international protest against dominant institutions. In this process, key persons play a central role and have gained international reputation. For example, the prominent environmental activist Vandana Shiva from India is recognized internationally as a leading spokesperson for Asian environmental NGOs. Her arguments often attack the policies of dominant international institutions, such as the IMF and the World Bank (Shiva 1991, 58–60). Khor Kok Peng from Malaysia, who also acts as an advocate for third world countries opposing unsustainable aid activities and policies, is another example.

NGOs in Asia are making their way into arenas traditionally occupied by NGOs from industrialized countries. Protest against international aid agencies is one area that attracts a lot of attention. There are differences in performance among Asian NGOs from industrialized countries, particularly Japan, and those from developing countries. Many South-East Asian NGOs are more actively involved in international environmental disputes than those from Japan. For example, many local residents in Japan have viewed global climate change as a relatively remote issue compared to others that immediately affect their health and livelihood, such as air and water pollution.

In the last few years, many NGOs in Asia have become involved in one way or another in climate-change-related activities. Interactions on global climate change have helped to improve the relationship between NGOs from different backgrounds and with different motivations. This has become a common phenomenon in transnational relations.

International NGOs have become more involved in Asia than ever before. This is mostly because of Asia's growing importance in the world economy, politics, and the environment. Many NGOs in the North are seeking partners from the South for collaborative activities, such as research, campaigning, and networking. This trend can be understood as an interdependent relationship, driven by demand for closer collaboration to link the local with the global, and vice versa. Large international NGOs, such as the WWF, Nature Conservancy, and Greenpeace International, have all established close contacts and collaborating relationships with local NGOs in Asia.

Since the early 1990s, a broadening and intensification of relationships between Asian NGOs and those from industrialized countries has been seen. In 1991, about 50 NGOs from Asia, North America, and Europe worked together in a campaign to protest against the establishment of the Global Environment Facility (GEF) and the operation of the multilateral aid agencies in their environmentally destructive activities in developing countries. In many respects, the operation of the GEF has provided an opportunity for many NGOs, including Asian NGOs, to be involved in activities that shape the global environmental agenda. This is evident from the NGO consultation meetings prior to the GEF meetings. These consultations have affected the formulation of GEF policy and strategies (Gan 1993a, 208).

One could argue that there is bound to be diminishing support from Northern NGOs for governments in developing countries. The main cause of this shift may be attributed to closer contacts between Southern and Northern NGOs. Although the WWF is committed to working with governments for its country programmes, increasing emphasis is being put on support for non-governmental conservation institutions. WWF Nepal assists a number of agencies in a variety of ways. Support includes funding staff training, purchasing field equipment, upgrading office facilities, and participating in national and international seminars and events. Following the democracy movement in 1990, hundreds of local NGOs are now registered in Nepal. Many of them function as pressure groups, catalysts, and educational forums, while others implement conservation and development projects. Many of these NGOs are committed to environmental conservation. The WWF is helping through its project "Support for Local NGOs." Supporting grassroots NGOs with practical and original ideas promotes conservation as part of the daily lives and actions of Nepal's people.

There is also increasing cooperation among NGOs across Asian countries. NGOs see the advantage of building up coalitions to strengthen their positions in international environmental movements. This is particularly seen in South-East Asia where networks of NGOs are blooming. NGOs come to define common interest areas for collective action. They have built up their collective alliance by holding large regional meetings and conferences.[12]

Interrelationships between NGOs and other social actors

In the following section, the interrelationships between NGOs and other societal institutions, such as governments, the private sector, the scientific community, and international development assistance agencies, will be reviewed. The purpose is to point to the interdependent relationships among these actors.

Governments

In the analysis of external forces that are shaping the environmental discourse, three social institutions have been distinguished: NGOs, governments, and the private sector. Table 7.1 shows the main characteristics of these three institutions interacting in energy production or use and environmental protection.

The relationship between governments and NGOs has gone through major changes in recent years. Concerns about sustainable development have brought governments and NGOs closer together than before as governments increasingly depend on NGOs for local consultation and professional assistance. Governments increasingly see NGOs' connections with local communities as an important factor for ensuring cost-effective implementation of projects.

On the other hand, NGOs realize the need to collaborate with governments for gaining financial support and legitimacy. The latter is important in countries with authoritarian regimes. Through establishing closer ties with the government, NGOs can minimize the risks that may arise from political uncertainties. NGOs' attitudes toward governments differ from country to country. In some countries in Asia, NGOs have been dependent on government subsidies for their activities. For example, NGOs in Viet Nam and China are usually semi-public in order to

Table 7.1 Characteristics of social institutions

	Environmental NGOs	Governments	Private sector
Characteristics	Social critique	Bureaucracy	Commercialization
Main interests	Defend local interests	Control of resources	Profit maximization
	Ideology/user interests	Retention of power	Market expansion
	Engage in politics		
Priorities	Poverty reduction	National economic development	Market share
	Natural resource conservation	National security	Risk minimization
	Environmental protection		
Instruments	Monitoring	Negotiation	Bidding
	Lobbying	Financial control	Accounting
	Public debate	Political pressure	Cost-benefit analysis
	Media reporting	Expropriation	
	Environmental impact assessment	Regulation	
		Incentives	

assure their legitimate rights and access to moral and financial support. The Chinese NGOs that attended UNCED were selected and sent by the government as part of the official delegation. This relationship is currently changing due to economic liberalization and decentralization of the political system and diminishing government support. New types of NGOs tend to distance themselves from government control and try to work on less sensitive issues, avoiding any challenge to governmental legitimacy.

Private sector

The private sector's relationship with NGOs has been little studied thus far. This is a complicated issue because it deals with diverse sectoral interests and, sometimes, conflicting organizational objectives. Many industrial enterprises find it difficult to agree with NGOs, especially on environmental aspects of development projects. The private sector has been criticized by NGOs for being responsible for severe environmental damage in development projects. Compared with international aid agencies, the industrial sector has made limited efforts to improve its relationship with NGOs.

Because of rapid industrialization in Asia, many NGOs have found it difficult to campaign effectively against major development projects funded by large international corporations which are perceived as having caused environmental damage. The ineffectiveness of NGOs in dealing with the private sector reflects the issue of legitimacy. NGOs feel incapable of pushing the business community toward responding to environmental externalities in their operations. However, there are cases of industrial pollution control, such as the Prokasih programme in Indonesia, which have proved successful, and at low cost. This programme for pollution control evaluation and rating identifies the level of industries' compliance with regulations on environmental management; improves environmental impact control efforts through active participation of the business community; motivates business operators to apply and implement cleaner technology; and creates self-confidence in the development of business through the presentation of awards to participating industries on their accomplishments.[13] It is claimed that part of the success in Prokasih is due to community participation as a watchdog of pollution control (Brandon and Ramankutty 1993, 80).

Scientific community

In many cases in Asia, NGOs and the scientific community are interrelated. Many scientific institutions regard themselves as NGOs, since they do not receive regular financial support from government and feel autonomous in their operations. Scientists play a critical role in fostering changes through their interactions with NGOs. In some cases, in Asia and elsewhere in the world, academics act as both scientists and environmental activists.[14]

Professionalization and specialization are two aspects in NGO development. NGOs become increasingly professionalized due to the increasing complexity of their objectives and the need for better scientific understanding of the issues. Consequently, this requires staff members with advanced educational backgrounds and professional training and experience. It can be argued that NGO staff members have become more specialized than ever before because of the demand for both disciplinary specialization and interdisciplinary collaboration in their work. NGOs have to deal with cross-sectoral issues, which requires interdisciplinary knowledge and training across traditional disciplinary boundaries. Compared to the relationship with other social institutions, the scientific community usually keeps relatively good relations with NGOs, since they have little conflict in their objectives.

International development assistance agencies

The relationship between NGOs and the international aid community has undergone drastic changes in recent years. Most aid agencies, such as the World Bank, have set policy guidelines with a view to providing NGOs with better access to information, consultation, and participation in project design and operation (Malena 1995).

Mostly because of the increasing pressure and criticism of NGOs with regard to aid policy and practice, improving relationships with NGOs has become a priority of aid agencies. NGOs have also realized the need to cooperate more with international aid agencies and the advantages resulting for them from such cooperation. The Small Grants Programme under the Global Environment Facility is an example. Many NGOs have found it useful to be involved in this framework of action, although grants for each project are rather limited (Gan 1993b).

Beginning in 1987, providing assistance to NGOs has become a policy priority in the ADB. This represents a marked departure, although still small, from its previous policies that put heavy emphasis on governments. Areas of cooperation include information-sharing, practical assistance in developing and implementing programmes and projects, and, where possible, co-financing projects with national governments (Kappagoda 1995, 159). The ADB asserts that participation in ADB activities helps NGOs expand their operations in areas such as project preparation and implementation, community organization, and social mobilization. Some specific advantages of working with NGOs are that NGOs, with direct knowledge of local communities, can share expertise with the ADB and governments in identifying, preparing, monitoring, and evaluating development policies, programmes, and projects; and that NGOs help the ADB and governments prepare and implement specific programmes and projects. For the ADB, NGO input is important for addressing specific concerns such as involuntary resettlement, protection of indigenous people, participation in development planning by beneficiaries and affected persons, and benefit monitoring and evaluation. Another advantage is that NGOs can provide co-financing in the ADB's loan and technical assistance activities, either by financing selected activities or by providing resources, such as consulting services, staff assistance, or facilities and equipment (ADB 1998).

Because of the social protest from NGOs, the ADB admitted that it has given little attention to alternative energy development, such as end-use energy conservation and efficiency improvement. The Meralco Distribution Project, approved in 1992, thus presents a major new development in the ADB's energy loans to the Philippines as it seeks to address electricity shortages in the country by looking at efficiency improvements, conservation measures, and demand-side management. The project was carried out between 1993 and 1996 with a US$230 million loan from the ADB. The remaining cost of US$92 million was met through a co-financing arrangement with local resources. With the Meralco Distribution Project as a major initiative, the ADB has begun to implement a comprehensive energy-lending strategy for the Philippines, with capital investments by both private and government agencies that focus on energy efficiency improvement and the development of renewable energy systems.

Conclusions

In summary, Asian NGOs play an important role in international and national energy and environmental activities. Their increasing presence in the world political arena has contributed to reshaping agendas of governments and international aid agencies. Their operations also affect their relationships with, and the behaviour of, the scientific community and the private sector. NGOs have facilitated the establishment of critical links between local communities on the one hand, and governments and international aid agencies on the other. Governments and aid agencies have benefited from interactions with the NGO community, but have also been puzzled about how to deal with them in proper and cost-effective ways.

NGOs' involvement in energy and environment issues cannot be considered in isolation. They constantly change their modes of involvement and participation, according to local and international circumstances. One example is their interest in global climate change debates and actions. Many have changed from sceptical to proactive attitudes. Their engagement in sustainable energy and environment activities has helped establish new and critical links among societal institutions. They base their strategy for survival on linking local with global perspectives.

NGOs' presence as a particular social phenomenon can be characterized as having been developed from below. NGOs have developed a public space that is not, and cannot be, filled by other societal institutions, such as governments, international aid agencies, the scientific community, and the private sector. In contrast to many institutions generated by governments from above, NGOs are deeply rooted in societal contexts. The development of NGOs as a social entity is crucial to the well-being of nation-states and international communities. The influence of NGOs across national boundaries can be seen as part of the globalization process and it will have far-reaching effects on public policy. Their influence on sustainable energy development in Asia is not unique; similar developments can also be seen in other regions of the world.

It is argued that this phenomenon of people's involvement is driven, on the one hand, by the growing democratization of the political systems in the region. More freedom of political choice because of relaxation of regulations has empowered NGOs to function as a source of social critique against dominant societal actors. On the other hand, increasing economic integration and liberalization between countries and within the region has provided incentives for the development of the NGO sector, with diversified sources of funding and opportunities for social intervention.

Several characteristics can be generalized from the involvement of Asian NGOs. First, NGOs will continue to create new social linkages, or webs of contacts. They will help establish and improve relationships between the general public and other social institutions: governments, international agencies, the private sector, and the scientific communities. Second, the diversification of NGOs will continue to increase in both scope and speed. Their influence will reach far more people in society, and their power will be further strengthened by wider participation of the general public. This will be seen especially in the fields of energy and the environment. One important question that needs further analysis is how to improve the accountability of NGOs with regard to their performance in projects. Workable methodologies and criteria for evaluating NGO performance need to be developed.

The increasing involvement of NGOs in environmental activities provides good opportunities for the United Nations and the international development assistance community. Through increasing participation of NGOs in the design, consultation, operation, and evaluation of projects, these institutions will be able to act as agents to empower people at the lower levels of society. With more incentives to support the NGO sector, greater social equilibrium could be achieved. It can be expected that NGOs will assume many of the conventional mandates that are usually undertaken by governments and specialized UN agencies. What represents the so-called global civil society is the inclusion of people's voices and needs.

Notes

1. The author is grateful to Professor Volker Rittberger and Dr Helmut Breitmeier at the University of Tuebingen, Dr Deborah Cornland at the Stockholm Environment Institute, and Dr Lasse Ringius and Dr Karen O'Brien at CICERO for their useful comments and editorial assistance.
2. In China, for instance, scientists have been instrumental in establishing policy priorities for the development of new and renewable energy technologies, and they were also important actors in emphasizing the need for energy conservation in the early 1980s and beyond (Gan 1998a).
3. Institutions are sets of rules or codes of conduct that serve to define social practices, assign roles to the participants in these practices, and guide the interactions among occupants of these roles. In this chapter, institutions refer to both international and domestic institutions. For further definition and description of institutional roles in international environmental politics, see Hasenclever, Mayer, and Rittberger (1997), Young (1994, 1–8; 1996), Haas, Keohane, and Levy (1993), and Keohane and Levy (1996).
4. One example is China's energy sector development, which has shown continuous growth in energy supply through the construction of large coal-burning power plants and hydroelectric power stations, despite progress in energy conservation. See Gan (1998b).
5. By 2025, the ADB estimates that Asia's urban population will more than double from 1.1 billion to 2.5 billion, as a result of population increase and rural migration, and will make up half the world's urban population. There will be some 20 megacities, each with more than 10 million inhabitants, and 10 of these will have populations of more than 20 million (Syman 1997).
6. In South Asia, for example, the Bangladesh Rural Advancement Committee (BRAC) has more than 17,000 full-time staff, and works with over 3 million people in rural communities. It reaches nearly 60 per cent of the country's 86,000 villages. India has more than 12,000 development NGOs. In Sri Lanka, the NGO Sarvodaya works in 7,000 villages. The Muslim Youth Movement of Malaysia (ABIM) has more than 50,000 members (Edwards and Hulme 1995, 3). The total number of NGOs in Indonesia has reached more than 10,000 (*Financial Times* 1997a). The Philippines has some 18,000 NGOs (Princen and Finger 1994, 2). In China, NGOs have mushroomed over the past 15 years, although environmental NGOs are small in proportion to the rest (Wang, Zhe, and Sun 1993).
7. Air pollution in Indian cities has reached a critical level, caused by increasing numbers of motor vehicles. It has contributed to severe human health problems (Jordan 1997).

8. One example is the citizens' campaign against the construction of the Naerinchon Dam project in South Korea, which has been supported by the government. This campaign is led by the Citizen's Coalition for Economic Justice. Local residents have shaved their heads as a means of public protest (Han 1997, 19–21).
9. According to a news release from the Environmental Defense Fund entitled "World Bank to Cancel Loan to Narmada Dam in India," 30 March 1993.
10. For a critic review of the Three Gorges Dam project, see Dai (1997).
11. For instance, demand for electricity in developing countries is doubling every eight years. So far, the majority of energy development programmes, supported by governments, private investors, and international aid agencies, have focused on large-scale coal, oil, and hydroelectric power. Meanwhile, more than 1.5 billion rural poor worldwide, who have no access to national and regional grids, have hardly benefited from such development (*Financial Times* 1997b).
12. Examples include the "Southeast Asia Regional Consultation on a People's Agenda for Environmentally Sustainable Development: Toward UNCED and Beyond," held in Los Banos, Laguna, the Philippines, in December 1991, and the "People's Participation in Environmentally Sustainable Development," held in Puncak Pass, Indonesia, in March 1990 (WWF International 1993, 49).
13. For further information, see: ⟨http://www.bapedal.go.id/profile/programs/proper.html⟩.
14. For example, Professor Madhav Gadgil, Indian Institute of Science, is a leading scientist, but also an environmentalist. See Gadgil 1997.

REFERENCES

ADB (Asian Development Bank). 1990. *Economic Policies for Sustainable Development*. Manila: Asian Development Bank.

ADB (Asian Development Bank). 1998. *The Asian Development Bank and Non-Governmental Organizations: Working Together*. Manila: Asian Development Bank.

Baxter, S. and D. Lisburn. 1994. *Reengineering Information Technology: Success through Empowerment*. New York: Prentice Hall.

Brandon, C. and R. Ramankutty. 1993. *Toward an Environmental Strategy for Asia*. World Bank Discussion Paper No. 224. Washington: World Bank.

Civil Society. 1997. January–February, 23.

Clad, J. and A. M. Siy. 1996. "The Emergency of Ecological Issues in Southeast Asia." In *Southeast Asia in the New World Order: The Political Economy of a Dynamic Region*, eds D. Wurfel and B. Burton. London: Macmillan.

Dai, Q. 1997. *The River Dragon Has Come: The Three Gorges Dam and the Fate of China's Yangtze River and its People*. Trykt, Armonk: M. E. Sharpe.

Daly, H., ed. 1994. *Farewell Lecture to the World Bank*. 14 January (mimeo).

Edwards, M. and D. Hulme, eds. 1995. *Non-Governmental Organizations: Performance and Accountability*. London: Earthscan.

Financial Times. 1997a. 30 December.

Financial Times. 1997b. 1 October.

Gadgil, M. 1997. "The Emerging Paradigm." *The Hindu Magazine*. 1 June, 1.

Gan, L. 1993a. "Global Environmental Policy and the World Bank: A System in Transition?" *Project Appraisal: Cost-benefit, Impact Assessment, Risk Analysis, Technology Assessment* 8(4): 198–212.

Gan, L. 1993b. "The Making of the Global Environment Facility: An Actor's Perspective." *Global Environmental Change: Human and Policy Dimensions* 3(3): 256–275.

Gan, L. 1995. "The Shaping of Institutions in Global Environmental Policy-making: International Development Assistance and China." PhD dissertation, Roskilde University Center.

Gan, L. 1998a. "Energy Conservation and GHG Emissions Reduction in China: The World Bank and UNDP Operation." In *China: Economic Growth, Population and the Environment*, ed. T. Cannon. London: Macmillan.

Gan, L. 1998b. "Energy Development and Environmental Constraints in China." *Energy Policy* 26(2): 119–128.

Greenwire. 1996. 9 July.

Haas, P. M., R. O. Keohane, and M. A. Levy, eds. 1993. *Institutions for the Earth: Sources of Effective International Environmental Protection*. Cambridge, MA: MIT Press.

Han, D.-H. 1997. "The Naerinchon Dam Problem." *Civil Society* 3 (June–August): 19–21.

Hasenclever, A., P. Mayer and V. Rittberger. 1996. "Interests, Power, Knowledge: The Study of International Regimes," *Mershon International Studies Review* 40(2).

IPCC (Intergovernmental Panel on Climate Change). 1996. *Climate Change 1995: Impacts, Adaptations, and Mitigation of Climate Change: Scientific-Technical Analyses, Contribution of Working Group II to the Second Assessment Report of the Intergovernmental Panel on Climate Change*. New York: Cambridge University Press.

Jamison, A. 1996. "The Shaping of the Global Environmental Agenda: The Role of Non-Governmental Organizations." In *Risk, Environment, Modernity: Towards a New Ecology*, eds S. Lash, B. Szerszynski, and B. Wynne. London: Sage Publications.

Jeong, H.-S. and S.-U. Lee. 1996. "The Green Movement in Korea and its Impact in the Policy Debate." In *Energy, Environment and the Economy: Asian Perspectives*, eds P. R. Kleindorfer et al. Cheltenham: Edward Elgar.

Jordan, M. 1997. "Environment: Capital Urgently in Need of Fresh Air." *Financial Times*. 1 August.

Kappagoda, N. 1995. *The Asian Development Bank*, Vol. 2. Ontario: The North-South Institute.

Keohane, R. O. and M. A. Levy. 1996. *Institutions for Environmental Aid*. Cambridge, MA: MIT Press.

Magagnini, S. 1992. "The Three Gorges Dam: Taming the Dragon or Destroying the Future." *China News Digest-Global*. 11 October.

Malena, C. 1995. *Working with NGOs: A Practical Guide to Operational Collaboration between the World Bank and Non-governmental Organizations*. Washington: World Bank.

Munasinghe, M. 1991. "Energy-Environmental Issues and Policy Options for Developing Countries." In *Global Warming: Mitigation Strategies and Perspectives from Asia and Brazil.* New Delhi: Asian Energy Institute.

People's Daily. 1997. 29 October, 1.

Princen, T. and M. Finger, eds. 1994. *Environmental NGOs in World Politics: Linking the Local and the Global.* New York: Routledge.

Sadiq, S. 1996. "Balancing Economic Growth, Energy Development and Environmental Impact." In *Energy, Environment and the Economy: Asian Perspectives,* eds P. R. Kleindorfer et al. Cheltenham: Edward Elgar.

Serrano, I. R. 1994. *Civil Society in the Asia-Pacific Region.* Washington: CIVICUS.

Shiva, V. 1991. "The Greening of the Global Reach: Conflicts in Global Ecology." *Third World Resurgence* 14/15: 58–60.

Syman, A. 1997. "Asian Megacities: Bursting at the Seams." *Financial Times.* 19 September.

Thomas, C. 1992. *The Environment in International Relations.* London: Royal Institute of International Affairs.

UNDP (United Nations Development Programme). 1997. *Human Development Report 1997.* New York: Oxford University Press.

Wang, Y., Zhe, X., and Sun, B. 1993. *The Intermediate Strata in Society: Reforms and NGOs in China.* Beijing: China Development Press [in Chinese].

Willcocks, L. and Currie, W. 1998. *Information Systems at Work: People, Politics and Technology.* New York: McGraw Hill.

World Bank. 1996. *Rural Energy and Development: Improving Energy Supplies for Two Billion People.* Washington: World Bank.

World Bank. 1997a. *Environment Matters, Annual Review.* Washington: World Bank.

World Bank. 1997b. *World Development Report: The State in a Changing World.* New York: Oxford University Press.

WWF International. 1993. *The Southern Green Fund: Views from the South on the Global Environment Facility.* Gland: WWF International.

Young, O. R. 1994. *International Governance. Protecting the Environment in a Stateless Society.* Ithaca: Cornell University Press.

Young, O. R, ed. 1996. *The International Political Economy and International Institutions.* Cheltenham: Edward Elgar.

8

Environmental NGOs in an emerging global civil society

Helmut Breitmeier and Volker Rittberger

Environmental issues are among the most prominent when dealing with transnational non-governmental organizations. More than 1,400 environmental NGOs were officially accredited with the United Nations Conference on Environment and Development (UNCED) in Rio de Janeiro in 1992, and a total of about 7,000 NGOs took part, in one way or another, in the Global Forum organized as a special event for NGOs apart from the UN conference itself (Haas, Levy, and Parson 1995, 160; Jasanoff 1997, 579). The most significant development during the last two decades has been the dramatic increase of NGO activities outside formal international political processes. Outside international negotiations or the work of international organizations, NGOs operate as voices and agents of civil society *vis-à-vis* governments, state bureaucracies, and transnational corporations as they seek to come to grips with the threats to the human environment at the local, national, and global levels. For example, NGOs launched international campaigns against the degradation of environmental goods caused by practices like whale hunting, nuclear testing, or the clearing of tropical timber, and criticized states for their ineffective policies or transnational corporations for environmentally damaging production. It is the notion of environmental NGOs as a societal response to the erosion of democratic participation and accountability in internationalizing political processes that has prompted research to refocus attention on the transnational politics which had been an important but short-lived research topic in the 1970s.[1]

In addition to the participatory revolution brought about by NGOs outside formal political processes, international politics are also witnessing a change of roles that environmental NGOs play within formal international political processes. The post-Rio period has seen a continuous participation of NGOs within the political processes of the UN system, such as the work of the Commission on Sustainable Development (CSD) and other international organizations including notably the World Bank; and within Conferences of the Parties of a large number of international conventions for the protection of environmental goods. These international conventions increasingly provide for the participation of NGOs in treaty-based decision-making processes (Raustiala 1997, 723).

However, there are still complaints about NGOs' limited access to international bodies. One analyst has recently remarked on NGOs' access to UN bodies dealing with human rights issues that "even with respect to UN structures – that is, meetings with state representatives, officials or experts – which are open to NGOs, doors are never opened wide" (Dunér 1997, 308). Although such observations may also apply to many political processes in the field of the environment, one should note that access to, and participation in, such political processes differ widely. UNCED has certainly been one of the key events fostering participation of NGOs within the UN system, and especially the CSD has been praised for its "relative openness" towards NGOs (Conca 1996, 115).[2]

Current research on environmental NGOs focuses primarily on identifying the conditions for the growth of NGOs in the field of environmental politics, NGOs' behaviour *vis-à-vis* states and IGOs, and their role in international environmental negotiations.[3] This research seeks to answer the question of how and why NGOs have become seemingly successful players in environmental policy-making. However, it is still an open question how the research on NGOs can be linked with the broader theoretical debate in the discipline of international relations. Both realism and institutionalism analyse international politics only at the systemic level. Both theories consider states as the main actors in an anarchical international system.[4] Realists describe international politics as a model of billiard balls in which states are the only important actors (Waltz 1979). Therefore, the analysis of NGOs in international politics is irrelevant to realism. Institutionalism also rests on a state-centred analysis of international politics (Keohane 1989). The broadening of the system-level analysis of institutionalism by two-level games remained a metaphor and was not fully implemented by the institutionalist research community.[5] In contrast with realism and institutionalism, liberal theory deals with the impact of state-society relations in international politics. Although it is mainly a unit-level theory defined by the centrality "of individual rights, private property, and representative government" (Doyle

1997, 208), liberal theory transcends the analysis of the domestic level by incorporating transnational civil society.

Moravcsik (1997, 516–521) argues that a liberal theory of international politics comprises three core assumptions. First, individuals and private actors are the fundamental actors in international politics. Liberal theory analyses the political process with a bottom-up approach. The self-interested domestic and transnational actors are assumed to act as rational maximizers of material and immaterial welfare. Second, liberal theory conceives the state as a representative institution influenced by the activities of domestic actors rather than as an independent actor. These representative institutions act as transmission belts "by which the preferences and social power of individuals and groups are translated into state policy" (Moravcsik 1997, 518). Third, liberal theory presumes that state preferences determine state behaviour at the international level. States act as utility-maximizers since they seek to preserve the present welfare of their societies or try to enhance it in the future. Convergent state preferences will lead to coordination or even collaboration between states. By contrast, strong inter-state tension or even coercive interaction will be likely when the preferences of different states diverge or are totally incompatible. The (neo)liberal analysis focuses on mixed-motive situations with weak concerns about relative gains. In these mixed-motive situations states face a strong incentive for policy coordination, improving the welfare of every participating state as compared to unilateral policy adjustment. Realists concentrate on analysing mixed-motive situations with strong concerns about relative gains in which states face a weak incentive for policy coordination (Hasenclever, Mayer, and Rittberger 1997, 215).

Liberalism considers the interactions of actors at the unit and systemic levels. Compared with realism and institutionalism, it provides a theoretical framework for analysing the roles of NGOs in both domestic and international politics. This chapter will address questions about environmental NGOs and their roles in the evolving global civil society. When dealing with these research topics the chapter will also explore how the explanations offered by the current research on NGOs can be linked to liberal theory.

- Has growing self-organization of civil society changed the relationship between state and civil society or will it contribute to changing it in the future? Is the emergence of global civil society only (or also) a response of national civil societies to national governments' practices of shifting formerly domestic political decisions to the international level and thereby reducing the opportunities for political participation of their national civil societies (Scharpf 1991; Zürn 1996)?

- Can different types of NGOs be distinguished? Which of these different types of NGOs is most important for, or successful in, the field of environmental policy-making? What kinds of activities do they pursue in order to put pressure on states and international organizations to protect the environment?
- How competent are NGOs, and what kind of expertise can they contribute to international environmental policy-making? How does their dependency on funds from members and private and public (governmental and intergovernmental) donors influence their work?
- To what extent do environmental NGOs and economic interest groups influence each other? Are the relationships between both of them only competitive, or can they also cooperate?

This chapter will first discuss the relationship between state and civil society in international environmental politics. It will then distinguish different types of environmental NGOs and describe their activities that have an impact on environmental policy-making. Third, the chapter will address the competence of environmental NGOs and their dependency on financial resources. After having dealt with the relationship between environmental NGOs and economic actors, the analysis will be summarized.

Civil society and states in international environmental politics

Related to the worldwide salience of environmental problems, the emergence of a global civil society is a consequence of two different developments. First, the salience of environmental problems gives rise to societal actors demanding international collective management of these problems by national governments. Growing ecological interdependencies in the "global village" set the stage for international cooperation for the preservation of the environment, but does not make it certain. Certainly, collective action among states is often the only way to avoid the "tragedy of the commons" (Hardin 1968), or individual as well as collective suboptimal outcomes in a mixed-motive situation, but the incentives of free-riding should not be underestimated (Olson 1965).[6] For example, the riparian states of a regional sea can only protect the marine environment if they all agree to limiting the emission of pollutants into the regional sea. If one important riparian state refuses to go along with the limitation of marine pollution, other states will not tolerate being taken advantage of by a free-rider. In this case, states will hardly arrive at environmentally beneficial collective action. States will only succeed with environmental regime-building in the issue area if they can change the behaviour of a free-rider by offering positive, or threatening negative, incentives, such as financial and technical assistance, or political and economic sanctions. Civil society can support the activities of those states interested in establishing an environmental regime. Transnational environmental NGOs can collaborate with domestic environmental NGOs of the free-riding state and put the government under pressure to agree to the effective collective management of an international environmental problem.

Second, the growing need to establish international policy-making systems for the environment confronts national societies with the prospect of losing control over political processes, and of being deprived of governmental authorities which they can hold accountable for their (in)actions. Due to the transnational, or even global, character of many environmental problems, states deal with them more and more internationally rather than domestically. The last three decades have thus seen a significant increase of international conventions for environmental protection (UNEP 1993). Most of these multilateral treaties resulted from negotiations initiated by UN organizations, notably UNEP. Ratification of such international environmental treaties requires that states implement internationally agreed-upon policies and change administrative practices at the domestic level (Victor, Raustiala, and Skolnikoff 1998).

For example, legislation within the European Union dealing with issues such as exhaust fumes from automobiles or harmful substances in food has significantly increased, and the EU member states had to pass national legislation or take other steps to comply with EU law; moreover, this law-making has extended to other environmental issues for which the European Union had assumed the obligation to implement multilateral treaties, such as the Montreal Protocol on Substances that Deplete the Ozone Layer and its subsequent adjustments and amendments.

The outcomes of international environmental negotiations, or of programmes established by international organizations such as UNEP, affect domestic policies and constrain a national civil society's ability to influence the political process. Within multilevel negotiation systems governments retain the main authority for environmental foreign policies, whereas participation in, or control of, these political processes by societal actors, national parliaments, domestic courts, or subnational institutions runs the risk of being undermined. The practice of multilevel environmental negotiations can open up a democracy gap as national governments bring pressure to bear on national parliaments and courts to accede to, or to abide by, intergovernmental accords by pointing out that rejection could lead to both the failure of international collective action and a loss of international reputation, making it more difficult for the government to be accepted as an effective diplomatic player in the future.

Democracy consists of the possibility for democratic participation of the individual, and of the equality of these individuals guaranteed in constitutional law. Democracy can be defined as "the rule of the many according to the law" (Bienen, Rittberger, and Wagner 1998, 292). Within the nation-state the electorate of a democratic political system gives those parties a mandate for collective decision-making which are considered to represent the interests and values of the people. Although NGOs claim to represent national societies in international negotiations, they lack the legitimacy that domestic parties get from periodic general elections. NGOs can also pursue particular interests of their organizations or constituencies that may not always be identical with the public interest, nor do NGOs always provide procedures for democratic participation within their organizations (Schmidt and Take 1997, 18; Beisheim 1997, 23).

The internationalization of formerly domestic political processes undermines civil society's possibility of political participation. Although NGOs can contribute to bridging the democracy gap which derives from the shifting of political decisions from the national to the international level, they are not representatives of the "general will" of civil society. Therefore, the demand of civil society for political participation in global environmental governance can only be fulfilled if democracy at the global level will not only be open for participation of states and NGOs' delegates but also for citizens' elected representatives.

McGrew (1997, 241–254) distinguishes three different models of global democracy. First, the "liberal-democratic internationalist" model takes the report of the Commission on Global Governance (1995) as a starting point for proposals on the democratization of international politics. The Commission suggests a reform of existing institutions of international governance at the global and regional levels. It seeks to democratize the UN system and enhance the participation of civil society in the UN General Assembly by creating a People's Assembly and a Forum of Civil Society. The members of the proposed People's Assembly consist of delegates from national parliaments but not of representatives directly elected by the citizens of member states. While the measures suggested by the liberal-democratic internationalist model can contribute to bridging the gap between national parliaments, NGOs, and the United Nations, these measures fail to enhance the participation of the citizens of member states in global politics.

Second, the model of "cosmopolitan democracy" proposes a reconstruction of existing forms of global governance rather than only reforming them. It involves the demand of the liberal-democratic internationalist model for the democratization of international organizations, in which national civil societies have had at best a marginal influence so far (Held 1995, 111). The model of cosmopolitan democracy is consistent with the liberal-democratic internationalist model in so far as it suggests the creation of a second chamber of the UN General Assembly in the short term and the expansion of regional institutions of governance.[7] However, the measures suggested by the model of cosmopolitan democracy reach beyond those of the liberal-democratic internationalist model. Cosmopolitan democracy demands the creation of a true global parliament in the long term, of global referenda, and the incorporation of cosmopolitan democratic law into frameworks of governance at all levels. The nation-state will not be abolished by cosmopolitan democracy, but it will no longer operate as the only agency able to guarantee basic human and political rights and to allocate political values within its own borders. In contrast with the liberal-democratic internationalist model, the model of cosmopolitan democracy intends to facilitate the participation of the individual citizen in global politics. However, there is a danger that cosmopolitan democracy will lead to a devaluation of national parliaments, and will increase the geographical distance between the elected representatives and the electorate.

Third, the model of "radical communitarianism" denies the possibility of reforming existing institutions of global governance. The model posits that democracy cannot be achieved on a territorially delimited basis such as the nation-state, but on a functional basis. Functional authorities need to be created at the different local, national, regional, or global levels for dealing with matters related to a specific issue area (such as trade, environment, or health).[8] These functional authorities would be "directly accountable to the communities and citizens whose interests are directly affected by their actions" (McGrew 1997, 246). This model builds on a mode of politics where political decision-makers are exposed to strong pressure from the people affected by the decision-making. Scharpf (1992, 11–13) distinguishes between hierarchic-majoritarian and consensual modes of politics. Democratic legitimacy and the effectiveness of democratic decision-making can only be achieved in the hierarchic-majoritarian mode if there is a congruence between the people participating in, and affected by, the political decision-making. While the hierarchic-majoritarian mode of politics implies that the majority can outvote the minority, the consensual mode affords the balancing of diverging interests between the different actors. The functional authorities which the model of radical communitarianism provides for will prefer the consensual to the hierarchic-majoritarian mode of politics, since the model posits that the interests of the affected people should be reflected in the activities of these authorities. The model of radical communtarianism considers citizens' groups as important actors in politicizing social activities and mobilizing political participation by directly affected communities and individuals in the decision-making. The strong interaction between citizens' groups and the functional authorities can probably lead to a strengthening of the political participation of civil society. However, it remains an open question whether the functional authorities can effectively coordinate their activities beyond the realm of single issue areas. The inclusion of the affected communities in the decision-making can certainly lead to more democratic legitimacy, but it can also increase the number of actors in the political process and thus impair the effectiveness of democratic decision-making.

The emergence of a global civil society and the increasing practice of governments to deal with environmental problems through multilevel negotiations and other international institutions pose new critical questions for democratic theory (Dahl 1989; Sartori 1962) about the democratic representation of civil society by (environmental) NGOs, or, more generally, about the need for new mechanisms of political participation of civil society beyond the level of the nation-state. The three models of global democracy disagree on the influence conceded to civil society over the state. More democratic participation of civil society in global politics, such as environmental policy-making, implies a weakening of state control over society.

Towards a power shift from state to civil society?

What effects will growing ecological interdependencies and the creation of international environmental regimes have on global civil society in the future, especially with regard to its political influence on these processes? Are the activities of environmental NGOs an expression of a more fundamental shift in the relation between state and civil society? Since national governments are perceived to share power increasingly with business groups, international organizations, and even a multitude of citizens' groups, it has been asserted that the "steady concentration of power in the hands of states that began in 1648 with the Peace of Westphalia is over, at least for a while" (Matthews 1997, 50).

Although NGOs have been quite successful in challenging states in international political processes dealing with environmental issues since the first UN Conference on the Human Environment held in Stockholm in 1972, it is by no means certain that the frequency and strength of NGO activities have already led to a power shift in favour of civil society anywhere. On the contrary, states began negotiating environmental problems at the international level long before NGOs articulated their demands. Apart from the work of experts and technical or scientific NGOs which had been invited early on to take part in information-gathering about, and technical assessments and monitoring of, environmental hazards, states were first to seek collective action at the international level, and it was not until the mid-1980s that the number of non-governmental participants in international political processes increased commensurate with the frequency of intergovernmental negotiations on environmental issues. Governments have realized that they often gain from the activities of environmental NGOs within formal international political processes, since NGOs can provide information about policy options or reliable assessment of individual states' compliance, inform state delegations during negotiations about the actions of other delegations, publicize daily reports of the negotiations, help governments to convince domestic constituencies that they cannot be blamed for an unsatisfactory agreement or policy gridlock, and facilitate ratification of international environmental agreements (Raustiala 1997).

States can use the internationalization of environmental politics to preserve or strengthen their autonomy *vis-à-vis* domestic societies (Wolf 1998). The shifting of environmental policy-making from the domestic to the international level makes states more autonomous from their societies, since the negotiations and the process of political value allocation occur internationally, and domestic actors can influence the decision-making of governments in international negotiations much less than at the domestic level. In this respect, international negotiations provide an opportunity for states to agree on joint environmental policies which would normally not be accepted by their domestic societies. When granting NGOs increasing access to, and participation in, international environmental institutions, states decide on their own whether they want to reduce their autonomy from national societies, and they can always control the terms under which NGOs get involved. Governments were also increasingly aware that they can instrumentalize "green" NGOs for their purposes or form tacit coalitions with them in negotiations, as was the case of the United States and a number of NGOs like Friends of the Earth and Greenpeace when both were lobbying for stronger global regulation of ozone-depleting substances under the Montreal Protocol in the second half of the 1980s (Parson 1993; Rowlands 1995; Breitmeier 1996).

NGOs acting outside formal international political processes can constrain state autonomy. States are less autonomous *vis-à-vis* their societies when dealing with issues to which domestic societies assign great importance; in these instances it will be much easier for NGOs to mobilize societal support for their demands. Conversely, states have more leeway in their negotiations when the public pays less attention. A change in the importance attributed to environmental issues on the political agenda can also affect the work of NGOs. When issues have lost salience on the global or domestic political agendas, although states continue to negotiate environmental problems or implement internationally agreed-upon regulations domestically, NGOs will find it more difficult to inform and mobilize the public. As the number of international negotiations on environmental issues has increased, environmental NGOs certainly face difficulties in focusing public attention on issues that do not rank highly on the political agenda.

The technical character of many environmental problems constrains states' abilities to maintain their autonomy *vis-à-vis* their societies, because international management is impossible without the inclusion of domestic and transnational actors representing civil society. States need the scientific knowledge, technical expertise, the monitoring capacities, or the policy advice of NGOs for assessing the importance of the problem and the short- and long-term implications of policies designed for the preservation of the environment, developing policies for the management of environmental problems, or monitoring the compliance with international agreements. Most international research or monitoring programmes, like UNEP's Global Environment Monitoring System (GEMS) or the Cooperative Programme for Monitoring and Evaluation of the Long-range Transmission of Air Pollution in Europe (EMEP), rely on participation of experts and research institutes that can communicate their concerns about increasing environmental problems to decision-makers, to the public, or "green" NGOs. The work of assessment panels like the Intergovernmental Panel on Climate Change (IPCC) and scientific experts' contributions to the drafting of various chapters of Agenda 21 show that the growing number of environmental issues regarded as internationally important also afford participation of such actors within formal international political processes that can enhance the prospects for consensual knowledge about the cause-effect relationships in the issue area and the development of technical solutions (Haas 1992; Litfin 1994).

The power relationship between state and civil society has not yet undergone significant change. Put differently, the international activities of environmental NGOs have mainly resulted in preserving the balance of power between state and civil society rather than in changing this power relationship fundamentally in the latter's favour. Since NGOs have not yet weakened the predominance of the state system, the question arises of whether the assumption that civil society is already taking shape globally is tenable, indeed.

NGOs and the fragmentation of global civil society

The concept of "world civic politics" presumes the existence of a global society of citizens. It builds on Hegel's notion of a civil society and implies the existence of a sphere at the global level wherein "free association takes place between individuals. It is an arena of particular needs, private interests, and divisiveness but within which citizens can come together to realize joint gains" (Wapner 1996, 5). A definition of civil society emphasizes three relevant aspects (Rittberger, Schrade, and Schwarzer 1998). First, the aspect of uncoerciveness implies that the societal sphere is protected from governmental encroachment. Civil society possesses a degree of autonomy from the state. Second, the definition includes the notion of shared basic values and identity. Common norms and codes of behaviour are shaping the interaction of the members of civil society. Third, human association is another aspect of civil society. The formation of groups and the networking of different groups are important characteristics of civil society.

Civil society is, of course, not fully independent from the state. It interacts with the state and is permeated by laws and governmental or semi-governmental organizations. Global civil society conceived as a set of actors who are able to act spontaneously and organize themselves freely without states imposing their wills on them presupposes that the same states respect fundamental human rights, especially political and civil rights. For instance, the growth of activities of environmental NGOs in Asia is not only a consequence of increasing liberalization and world market integration, which have provided incentives for the development of the non-governmental sector, but is also driven by growing democratization of political systems in the region (Gan, this volume). Although democracy has been on the advance in the last decade,[9] "global civil society" is still far from denoting a political reality at the end of the twentieth century. At present, the concept should not blind the analyst to the large number of constraints that force us to conceive of global civil society as an at best incomplete or emergent, yet fragmented, society.

States differ with regard to their political systems. A fully developed global civil society would comprise national civil societies with basic democratic rights and the ability to act independently from state influence. World civic politics can only be achieved in a world of democracies. Between 1973 and 1990, the proportion of states in the world with democratic political systems has risen from 24.6 to 45.4 per cent (Huntington 1991, 26). Although many former socialist or authoritarian political systems have made the transition to democracy or are in the process of making this transition, democracy has not yet become the universally established practice of exercising public authority. Despite the impressive wave of democratization during the last three decades, reversions of fully developed democratic systems toward dictatorship or less developed forms of democracy cannot be excluded (Schmidt 1995, 185). As long as democracy cannot be established in many developing or newly industrialized countries, the OECD world remains the centre of global civil society.

In the field of the environment, the space of global civil society is currently filled primarily with actors from the societies of the Western liberal democracies; however, the recent influx of Southern NGOs should not be discounted. Western environmental NGOs have improved their collaboration on specific issues and reached agreement on many programmatic issues. For example, the climate policies of many industrialized countries in Europe and North America have been criticized by the Climate Network in Europe and the Climate Action Network in the United States, both representing a dozen organizations (Subak 1996, 60). Although Northern and Southern NGOs agree in principle on the preservation of environmental goods, programmatic consensus is much more difficult to achieve between them. The 1992 United Nations Conference on Environment and Development (UNCED) demonstrated that environmental NGOs do not always agree on the means for environmental protection (Johnson 1993). Northern and Southern NGOs, for example, had different views concerning the policies necessary for the preservation of the tropical forests. Also, Western environmental NGOs still have to learn that Southern interests in wildlife protection are different from, and more pragmatic than, those prevailing in Europe or North America. The 1997 Conference of the Parties to CITES revealed that Southern NGOs, although in favour of measures for the protection of elephants and rhinoceroses, had a preference for protection measures that take into account the needs of developing countries and the living conditions of their populations where, for example, newly increasing herds of elephants have already led to crop failures and the destruction of farmland.[10] Northern and Southern environmental NGOs also differ over cultural values and technical capabilities for communication. Since they operate in societies with different levels of economic development they have different views about the priority of economic development.

How can we link these findings to liberal theory? Research on environmental NGOs analyses, *inter alia*, how the activities of NGOs shape the preferences of the state. This corresponds with the liberal conceptualization of the state-society-relationship in which the state is an agency subject to the pressures of civil society. Liberal theory, however, is not confined to analysing the influence of civil society on the state. Skocpol (1985) rightly criticized pluralist conceptions of the state, for they limit their view to the societal input in governmental policy-making. Instead, Skocpol (1985, 9) conceives states as organizations whose goals "are not simply reflective of the demands or interests of social groups, classes, or society." States are also to some degree autonomous *vis-à-vis* their domestic societies. For instance, constitutional law often circumscribes the extent to which domestic society can control the foreign policy of the government. If the constitution stipulates that the parliament must approve of an international treaty before it can enter into force, governments will normally inform, and consult with, those parliamentary groups considered crucial for reaching a majority for ratification about the content of the negotiations at an early phase before the initiation of the process and during the various stages of negotiation. However, after the conclusion of international negotiation, parliaments usually cannot demand a reopening of negotiations and must give their assent or risk a diplomatic crisis. Furthermore, governments look after the interests of domestic economic actors in international negotiations often long before these actors realize the importance of the issues which are at stake. Even more strikingly, the process of European integration which led to the treaties of Maastricht 1991 and Amsterdam 1997 has revealed that governments agree on policies although some of them seem to lack the support of their domestic societies (Wolf 1997). In international environmental negotiations, governments often follow their own goals independent of the political pressure of civil society. For example, the British government prevented the European Community from consenting to an international protocol on the reduction of CFCs until 1987 because it gave more weight to the economic interests of the small CFC-producing industry than to those of environmental groups (Maxwell and Weiner 1993).

Types of NGOs: Advocacy and service organizations

Recent studies of NGOs have focused on identifying different types of NGOs based on their activities, ranging from making demands on states to offering their cooperation with them. This emphasis in NGO scholarship is based on the fact that there is still little systematic knowledge about what actions of which type of NGOs have the greatest impact on international political processes. The typology of NGOs previously suggested for the field of international peace and security may serve here as a starting point as well. Although environmental issues differ in many regards, a typology of NGOs consisting of advocacy organizations, service organizations, and transnational criminal organizations (TCOs) can contribute to making research on NGOs more comparable across a variety of issue areas (Rittberger, Schrade, and Schwarzer 1998).

Advocacy organizations can be understood as influencing, first of all, the process of political agenda-setting. NGOs educate the public, mobilize and organize citizens to show their concern about the issue(s) in question, and create pressure on, and lobby for their goals with, decision-makers. The main character of service organizations is to provide services to other organizations or groups and to contribute to implementing public policies. Unlike these two types of NGOs, transnational criminal organizations create and operate within a transnational extra-legal "governance" system. In addition to the enhancement of their interests in making illicit gains, a further goal of these NGOs consists in protecting themselves against state prosecution.

The analytic distinction between advocacy and service organizations loses much of its neatness when it is applied to the empirical world. Service organizations can, of course, contribute to placing an environmental issue on the political agenda; advocacy organizations, on the other hand, may also provide services to states and international organizations, but this is rather the exception. What distinguishes one type of NGO from the other is, therefore, not only the character of their main activities, but also the extent to which the activities of environmental NGOs tend to become politicized. NGOs with a strong advocacy orientation tend to challenge governments and their policies; therefore, they are likely to generate a more confrontational climate between themselves and states.

It is posited that two types of NGOs seem to be most important in the issue area of protecting the human environment: advocacy organizations and service organizations. Nonetheless, transnational criminal organizations cannot be ignored completely, since they are active in black markets for products whose production or use is strictly regulated or forbidden by international or national law. Recent cases involve the illicit trade in ivory from protected elephants or the smuggling of phased-out chlorofluorocarbons out of member states of the Montreal Protocol whose export controls for these substances are weak (Brack 1996; Werksman 1996). The practice of transboundary or transcontinental shipments of such products provides sufficient evidence to support the presumption that only organized groups are able to seize such products, to circumvent national customs clearance procedures, and to make deals with, and organize delivery to, buyers. Such organized groups must be distinguished from private companies which will normally not fall into the category of transnational criminal actors even when disposing of hazardous wastes illegally. Compared to the issue area of international security, such transnational criminal activities appear to be exceptional cases and to have a smaller negative impact on environmental protection.

Environmental advocacy organizations

Nearly any activity that can be subsumed under the category of advocacy may become manifest during the various phases of the policy-making process. Advocacy is often conceived of as aiming at influencing the process of agenda-setting, but it affects other phases of the policy-making process as well (Cobb and Elder 1972). NGOs seek to influence intergovernmental bargaining or to push states toward implementing internationally agreed-upon rules (Breitmeier et al. 1996a; 1996b). In the field of environmental policy-making, advocacy-type NGOs provide the public with information about the state of the environment gleaned from reports produced by research institutes, international organizations, or state agencies, thus generally operating as transmission belts for and interpreters of scientific knowledge. They often use sudden external shocks like accidents in nuclear power plants (Chernobyl) or chemical firms (Bhopal) as windows of opportunity for communicating their concern to the public and asking for decisive political action (Gordenker and Weiss 1996, 38–40).

While the activism of environmental NGOs certainly shapes political agendas, advocacy also aims at changing the ideational context of an issue and enhancing the sensitivity of national societies for a new problem-solving approach. NGOs are developing policy proposals and scenarios for long-term action in order to educate the public and decision-makers about the economic and financial consequences of their policy recommendations. Environmental legislation or negotiations will only gain momentum if legislators or negotiators and the public can be convinced that the policies suggested for dealing with the problem are economically and financially feasible. To gain acceptance for their policy recommendations and change the substance of public debates which, at least initially, are often dominated by arguments about costs and economic feasibility, NGOs have to change the ideational context of the issue area. Ideational and entrepreneurial leadership (Young 1994, 39–42) by NGOs can help to establish new world views about the value and use of environmental goods. For instance, the pressure that environmental NGOs have brought to bear on the World Bank with a view to modifying its lending policy for development projects in the Brazilian Amazon region which, until the early 1990s, were contributing to the destruction of tropical ecosystems has led the World Bank to reconsider its lending criteria and contributed to fashioning a new perspective on ecologically sustainable development (Reed 1997, 230–232).[11] Environmental NGOs can translate scientific findings into political demands and policy proposals, and they can act more independently and forcefully than international organizations.

Environmental NGOs have not shied away from confronting enterprises with demands for ecologically meliorative structural change of industrial production.[12] They can inform the public about environmentally sound products and encourage consumers to buy these rather than other products. Such a "bottom-up" approach can induce private firms to restructure their production if and when they realize that the markets for environmentally sound products will grow. In the early 1990s, for instance, Greenpeace made great efforts to persuade consumers to buy

CFC-free refrigerators manufactured by the East German firm Foron (*Der Speigel* 1993).[13] This campaign prompted other firms to change their line of production to CFC-free refrigerators and cooling systems. In addition, environmental NGOs can also talk private firms of a given industrial sector into establishing a voluntary code of conduct, making it easier for them to agree on producing less environmentally damaging products.[14]

The international context within which environmental NGOs have operated has changed significantly during the last decade. Ever since the release of the Brundtland Commission's report (WCED 1987), international environmental policy-making has moved into a higher gear. NGOs, *inter alia*, indirectly account for the increase of environmental negotiation processes and the establishment of new intergovernmental institutions dealing with environmental problems (such as the Global Environmental Facility and the Commission on Sustainable Development) as well as for the heightened salience of environmental policy within the European Union. At the same time, this changing international context has also posed a challenge to environmental NGOs, which had to adapt to the newly institutionalized policy-making processes at the international level; they had to learn how to educate the public about the new opportunities for environmental policy-making, and, at least to some extent, they had to cope with the newly posited link between environment and development. After UNCED, NGOs in many industrialized countries faced difficulties in keeping environmental issues on the political agenda due to economic recession, declining state revenues, and growing unemployment. Confronted with the rising salience of socio-economic issues, the prospects for environmental NGOs of keeping issues of environmental protection on the political agenda depend even more than usual on their access to the mass media and on external shocks.

Environmental NGOs have been among the first transnational actors adapting to changes in global telecommunications (Frederick 1993). They have used new communications media such as the Internet to create information networks and disseminate reports, press releases, etc. The new media provided them with opportunities for strengthening their impact on agenda-setting processes, for early warning on environmental problems, and for shortening the time span between problem identification and eliciting a policy response. While spectacular action often predominates the agenda-setting activities of some environmental NGOs such as Greenpeace, this kind of action will achieve its purpose only if the NGOs can persuade the mass media to report blockades of whalers, oil tankers, or ships loaded with hazardous wastes. Spectacular action of the same type cannot be repeated too often without losing its newsworthiness. Therefore, some environmental NGOs feel the pressure of being innovative in their public relations work in order to win the attention of the mass media and the loyalty of the public.[14] However, not every environmental NGO sees an advantage in spectacular action as a means of influencing agenda-setting processes, and even Greenpeace makes use of a wide range of agenda-setting activities, including softer forms of action. Dissemination of printed materials, issuing special reports, public hearings, and international conferences about an environmental issue are less spectacular but by no means less important methods of influencing agenda-setting processes.

Environmental service organizations

In addition to their advocacy role, NGOs have increasingly been reputed for their services. NGOs provide unpaid services to, or carry out commissioned work for, international organizations or national governments. It has been argued that more and more NGOs are "combining both strong market skills and orientation with a clear social commitment" (Gordenker and Weiss 1997, 444). Although NGOs are non-profit organizations, many of them carry out commissioned work for national governments, the United Nations, or other international organizations. International organizations, treaty secretariats, or other bodies established by the member states of an international environmental convention offer opportunities for environmental NGOs to perform management and service tasks. Probably the most striking example of how an environmental NGO can take on responsibility for the administration of an international legal convention is the 1971 Ramsar Convention on Wetlands of International Importance Especially as Waterfowl Habitat. This convention provides for the International Union for the Conservation of Nature (IUCN) to serve as the treaty secretariat. The convention specifies in Article 8 that IUCN "shall perform the continuing bureau duties under this Convention." International environmental regimes are not exclusively managed by state bureaucracies and the secretariats of international organizations; instead, NGOs have increasingly become involved in regime-related functions of monitoring and verification, technology transfer, or the enhancement of scientific knowledge (Victor et al. 1994, 17). Since the late 1970s, the number of independent and government-appointed scientists participating in the International Whaling Commission has more than doubled (Andresen 1998, 436).

NGOs occasionally perform important services by reassuring treaty members about compliance with the treaty injunctions irrespective of the legal status of these services (Breitmeier et al. 1996a, 114). They submit information directly to treaty bodies when members assess implementation, or they inform states about cases of non-compliance. They also inform the press and the public about the extent to which the ecological goals of a treaty have been achieved. Greenpeace often knows more about the practices of whale-hunting nations than certain member states of the 1946 International Convention for the Regulation of Whaling (Andresen 1998, 439–440). In general, NGO monitoring of state behaviour in the issue area of environmental protection provides an indispensable service to member states of an environmental treaty or regime when reviewing implementation and assessing compliance.

One of the most drastic changes in the role of environmental NGOs has occurred as a result of environmental concerns being explicitly taken into consideration by development aid agencies. Regional development banks like the ADB, international development aid programmes like the UNDP, and, in particular, church-based and other private development aid organizations have begun to assess *ex ante* the environmental consequences of the projects they fund in developing countries (Gan, this volume). The strategic intention underlying the concept of sustainable development takes on a concrete and visible form in the work of such private aid organizations, which, moreover, cooperate with local, national, and international environmental NGOs. For instance, the construction of irrigation systems in arid land zones must always consider that poor soils need balanced cultivation methods in order to protect them from overuse. Sustainable use of such irrigation systems financed by international development agencies or private aid organizations must also rely on expertise of local residents and of local, national, and international NGOs which can help to avoid negative environmental impacts in neighbouring areas produced by these irrigation systems.

Before concluding this section, it is necessary to explore again how liberal theory can contribute to analysing the roles of environmental advocacy and service organizations. Liberal theory considers the ideational context as a crucial factor influencing political processes at both domestic and international levels. It argues that ideas or moral visions can shape the preferences of decision-makers (Goldstein and Keohane 1993; Lumsdaine 1993). The analysis of the activities of advocacy and service NGOs suggests that both types can contribute to changing the ideational context. Therefore, research on the influence of ideas in world politics focuses, *inter alia*, on the activities of NGOs. Ideas can be defined as beliefs held by individuals (Goldstein and Keohane 1993, 7). Three types of beliefs can be distinguished. First, world views, such as the world religions, represent the most fundamental type of beliefs because these views affect people's identities and evoke deep emotions and loyalties. Environmental NGOs contributed to the establishment of a global environmental consciousness which has changed the relationship of people to the natural environment. Second, principled beliefs (for example, that racial discrimination is wrong) consist of normative ideas "that specify criteria for distinguishing right from wrong and just from unjust" (Goldstein and Keohane 1993, 9). The activities of environmental NGOs aim at establishing such principled beliefs (for example, that the hunting of elephants, rhinoceroses, or other endangered animals is wrong). The activities of Greenpeace created a principled belief that international whaling is immoral (Andresen 1998, 439). Finally, causal beliefs are beliefs about cause-effect relationships (for example, that an increasing atmospheric concentration of CFCs will cause the destruction of the stratospheric ozone layer with clearly recognizable consequences for the living beings on our planet). The activities of environmental advocacy and service organizations can help to generate such beliefs among the public or decision-makers. They contribute to, or publicize, the reports of international scientific panels assessing these cause-effect relationships. For example, the leading NGOs in the United States, such as the Natural Resources Defense Council and the Sierra Club, and other transnational environmental groups like Friends of the Earth and Greenpeace supported the hypothesis about the possible negative consequences of CFC emissions on the stratospheric atmosphere issued by Mario Molina and Sherwood Rowland (1974). These environmental NGOs publicized the results of the scientific panels established by UNEP and, with strong support from the scientific community, alerted civil society to the cause-effect relationship between CFCs and the destruction of the stratospheric ozone layer (Lobos 1987; Benedick 1991). Research on ideational leadership of environmental NGOs will have to consider the interactions of policy networks, including both transnational and purely domestic NGOs (Risse-Kappen 1995b, 188). The concept of the epistemic community (Haas 1989) provides a starting point for the analysis of policy networks in international environmental politics. For instance, several studies have shown that epistemic communities influenced the preferences of decision-makers during international environmental negotiations (Haas 1992).

Competence and levels of participation

One important part of a debate about the future relationship between civil society and the state is the question of whether NGOs are competent enough to take over responsibilities from states or international organizations. The competence of an environmental NGO does not only depend on skilled staff members, but also on the availability of financial resources. Furthermore, the size of an NGO's budget also determines its ability to participate at the local, regional, or international levels of environmental policy-making. The growing mobility of individuals moving back and forth between environmental NGOs and international or national governmental agencies indicates that many NGOs have gained a professional reputation for their expertise. Their acknowledged competence rests on their work on one or a few environmental issues and on meeting the challenge of demonstrating equal or even superior expertise than their counterparts in private firms or national governments (Knappe 1993; Greenpeace 1996). Environmental NGOs have realized that they will only be taken seriously as participants in policy-making if they can rely on professional staff input. Such insight has prompted many NGOs to add academic or other professional experts to their staff. Many activities subsumed under advocacy or service tasks could not be carried out without scientists, lawyers, or policy experts working as staff members of NGOs (Reiss 1990).

However, many environmental NGOs also suffer from structural constraints inherent in the trend toward policy-making at the international level which prevent their staff from making the utmost use of their competence. The small and financially weak environmental NGOs feel these constraints especially when international political processes overburden their travel budgets and thereby their ability to follow, monitor, and influence international negotiations. Although information on many multilateral political processes is now available on the Internet, close monitoring of, or even direct participation in, negotiations contributes to increasing the expertise of staff members because it offers opportunities for interaction with government representatives, officials of international organizations, other NGOs, and business groups. There is a clear divide between the big (and financially resourceful) NGOs like Greenpeace, Friends of the Earth, the Natural Resources Defense Council, or the German Bund für Umwelt und Naturschutz (BUND), on the one hand, and the small NGOs that operate with a small staff and a low budget, on the other. Scarce resources constrain the long-term study of single environmental problems, the observation of international policy-making, and the accumulation of institutional competence and memory. These resource constraints account for some of the failures of environmental NGOs to influence policy-making on less prominent issues, such as desertification (Corell 1996).

Environmental NGOs which are heavily dependent on fundraising for financing their activities and staff face another severe constraint. Financial support from individual donors can decrease if they cease to identify with the NGO's goals. Therefore, these organizations must focus on issues that at least some segment of civil society regards as urgently in need of being addressed. It is much easier to legitimize the work of NGOs vis-à-vis private donors if they can be convinced of the crucial role played by an NGO within well-known issue areas. Environmental NGOs need to create a "corporate identity" in order to impress both donors and many of their individual members with their policy relevance. One way of creating such an identity is to direct the NGO's activities toward issues which can be assumed to have high salience with the public. A case in point is the overwhelming attention that environmental NGOs in industrialized countries give to climate change, whereas other issues such as soil conservation or desertification tend to be neglected. Such trend-dependent behaviour limits an NGO's ability to deal with environmental issues over the long term. Sometimes it also reduces the ability of an NGO's staff to build up issue-specific expertise or preserve institutional memory.

The competence of an NGO also affects its ability to participate in multilevel environmental policy-making. At both the national and the international level, service organizations in particular have to demonstrate their ability and skills in order to be included in national or international projects, advisory groups, or assessment panels. Environmental education and project management at any level ranging from local to international require skilled experts with long-term professional experience. Competent staff members of environmental NGOs that are given the opportunity to participate in multilateral negotiations can often offer advice to national governmental delegations. Public or private research institutes regularly participate in international assessments of the state of an environmental problem, of the feasibility of alternative political solutions, and of the implementation of international programmes for the preservation of an environmental good (Greene 1998). These service organizations fulfil tasks that are concretely defined by states, treaty secretariats, or international organizations.

The work of a research-oriented environmental NGO runs the risk of being mainly determined by the interests of states and international organizations if it depends strongly on work paid for by national or international bureaucracies.[15] By contrast, advocacy NGOs are much more independent in deciding on the issues to which they would like to direct attention, and whether they want to work at the local, national, or international level. Some of them, like Greenpeace, establish bureaux in many developed and developing countries and focus their activities on all levels of policy-making. A strong infrastructure enables large NGOs to select experienced experts from their national bureaux for leadership positions in their international headquarters and vice versa.

Liberal theory provides a basis for further analysis of the role of individuals and groups in world politics. The competence of individual staff members can be crucial for the success or failure of NGOs in political agenda-setting, compliance monitoring, or the management of environmental projects commissioned by national governments or international organizations. Current research on NGOs primarily focuses on the relationships between states and non-state actors in world politics. Less attention has been paid to the structures of, and the decision-making processes in, international environmental NGOs. Studies of the composition and belief systems of NGOs' membership, staff, and leadership can shed further light on the representation of the different segments of civil society by NGOs.

NGOs versus economic actors

Both advocacy and service organizations do not only interact with national governments or international organizations, but communicate and collaborate with, or act against, economic actors as well. However, the relationships between environmental NGOs and private firms, associations of private companies, and trade unions have largely been ignored by NGO scholarship. What are the relationships between different types of environmental NGOs and economic actors? So far, research on environmental NGOs seems to proceed from the assumption that environmental NGOs and economic actors are adversaries with conflicting goals and different constituencies. Such a view ignores the fact that neither environmental NGOs nor associations of private firms or trade unions are homogeneous, let alone monolithic actors when pursuing their respective goals. In addition, the attitudes of both groups towards one another have undergone some change during the last decade, leaving both sides more open-minded to the views of the other. Villacorta (1997), for instance, explored the relationships of three development NGOs from Switzerland, the Netherlands, and the United States with the business sector. Her study suggests that there are "different options to pursue a relationship with business organizations, among them negotiation, collaboration, pressure, influence, exchange, and alliance building" (Villacorta 1997, 47). Furthermore, the interactions of NGOs with business organizations can lead to important shifts in the role of NGOs (such as increasing NGOs' participation in the market, emphasis on efficiency and professionalism, or education and lobbying). NGOs also face risks from enhancing their collaboration with economic actors. Such risks consist of becoming élitist or overemphasizing the logic of the market and "leaving aside other important dimensions like the advancement of social development, the strengthening of civil society, and the protection and preservation of the environment" (Villacorta 1997, 54).

Information exchange between NGOs and economic actors in particular has significantly increased, each side seeking at least to know more about the other side's view of an environmental problem and arguments for its preferred outcome from international environmental negotiations or national political processes. Private firms do not always share the same interests in particular environmental issues. Transnational economic interest groups like the World Business Council for Sustainable Development have shown that economic actors are moving towards seeking ways of reconciling ecological values with business interests (Schmidheiny 1992).

Environmental NGOs themselves occasionally disagree on political strategies. For instance, they can have different views on the best way of achieving the desired goal of environmental protection or on the extent to which a compromise agreed upon in intergovernmental negotiations should be welcomed or criticized. They can also disagree on their reactions to offers from "enlightened" economic actors for collaboration. "Pragmatic" environmental NGOs, whose pragmatism is built on the belief that environmental protection can be achieved within a market economy and that openness to discussing even divisive issues with political adversaries will promote the goals of environmental NGOs in the long term, even accept donations from private firms. "Fundamentalist" NGOs, which are much more opposed to a political approach accepting the rules of the market economy, argue that these contributions will make environmentalists dependent on their adversaries and will thwart environmental goals.

Economic actors can have different interests in an environmental issue and thus may have different attitudes toward environmental NGOs (see Table 8.1). First of all, they can be interested in preserving the status quo in an issue area in order to prevent changes of national policies. For instance, mining companies, owners of power plants, or trade unions of coal miners may form a coalition which insists on continuing with the use of fossil fuels for the production of electricity while opposing efforts to strengthen energy-saving measures, increase the production of nuclear energy, or raise the subsidies for the use of solar energy (Breitmeier 1996, 224). They can form international coalitions of industrial sectors and trade unions to prevent the enactment of strong measures for the reduction of greenhouse gases. Their relationship with environmental NGOs is therefore fraught with conflict and even hostility. Both camps – environmental as well as economic actors – mainly interact via the media and accuse each other of pursuing unrealistic goals. Obviously, constructive interaction between "traditional" economic interest groups and "fundamentalist" environmental NGOs is more difficult to achieve than between these economic interest groups and "pragmatic" NGOs.

Second, transnational firms can face strong uncertainty about their own interests when confronted with international environmental negotiations. These firms can earn money by fossil energy production as well as by using environmentally sound sources of energy. Their interest structure is a

Table 8.1 Relationship between different types of environmental NGOs and economic actors

		Environmental NGOs	
		Pragmatic NGOs	Fundamentalist NGOs
Economic actors	Status-quo-oriented interests	• Confrontation	• Hostility
	Mixed interests	• Occasional conflict • Exchange of information • Identification of common and divergent interests	• Occasional (severe) conflict • Exchange of information • Identification of common and divergent interests
	Environmentally like-minded interests	• Coalition-building since the interests of both converge • Private firms providing financial support for environmental NGOs	• Firms fear fundamentalist NGOs' potential to blame them for environmentally harmful activities

153

mixed one consisting of both traditional elements and elements of ecological compatibility. Therefore, transnational firms tend to be uncertain
about their own long-term business strategy and are undecided whether
they should support the traditional, ecologically incompatible interests of
coal miners, the oil industry, and owners of fossil fuel power plants, or
whether they should invest in new sources of energy with less harmful
effects to the atmosphere. Deregulation of the European energy market,
for instance, will increase the number of European or global players in
the energy market and therefore give rise to even more undecided players in the energy sector (Europäische Kommission 1996). Because information-gathering about possible future economic implications of any path
chosen by decision-makers in the issue area will be vital for such companies working under strong uncertainty about their future economic preferences, such undecided economic actors have a special interest in communicating with other important actors in the issue area. They will not
exclude communication with any actor from the environmentalist camp
and will exchange views with both pragmatic and fundamentalist environmental NGOs if they are ready for such an exchange.

Third, structural ecological change in Western industrialized countries
has spawned a growing industry with environmentally like-minded interests. Pollution abatement measures in many of these countries have
induced the ecological modernization of national industries focusing on
producing environmentally sound technologies and products. Transnational firms interested in selling new technologies with less harmful
effects on the global climate can create coalitions with environmental
NGOs, since the interests of both converge. Firms may hope that states
will agree on the international management of environmental pollution as
a means to create an even stronger demand for environmentally sound
products. Environmental NGOs and environmentally like-minded companies, however, still treat each other with scepticism. Transnational
firms still fear environmentalists, especially the fundamentalists, because
they credit them with the potential for blaming private firms for environmentally harmful practices, which often results in the loss of public
credibility with consumers.

Until the adoption of the Kyoto Protocol to the UN Framework Convention on Climate Change (UNFCCC) in December 1997, many industrialized countries had long opposed strict targets and timetables in the
climate change negotiations due to the dominance of powerful status-
quo-oriented domestic coalitions of firms and trade unions. The question
remains as to what extent the political work of environmental NGOs on
climate change accounted for the agreement of member states of the
UNFCCC on the reduction of greenhouse gases in developed countries

by 5 to 8 per cent below 1990 levels between 2008 and 2012.[16] Increasing communication and collaboration between environmental NGOs and economic actors have contributed to promoting environmentally like-minded interests and weakening coalitions of private firms such as the Global Climate Coalition in the United States, which launched a multi-million-dollar campaign to warn American consumers against the possible negative economic effects of internationally agreed-upon reduction measures a few months before the third Conference of the Parties to the UNFCCC convened in Kyoto.[17] Therefore, the political work of environmental NGOs will only pay off if they succeed in weakening the cohesion of the coalitions of status-quo-oriented economic actors in industrialized countries.

The liberal model of international politics pays strong attention to the interactions between transnational societal actors (Moravcsik 1997). Both types of actors, environmental NGOs and economic actors, are assumed to be rational and to be motivated by maximizing their own utility. Such a utilitarian approach rests on Bentham's notion of individuals as calculators "of pleasures and pains" (Doyle 1997, 226). It has been shown that both types of actors can be further distinguished. The pattern of interaction between the different types of environmental NGOs and economic actors is determined by the core interests of these actors. However, such a focus on the relationship between private actors in world politics cannot ignore the role of the state as a third strand in this network, for the state is capable of influencing the outcomes of the interactions between economic actors and environmental NGOs. It will depend on the ability of the state to defend its role against economic actors as a provider of public goods (such as social welfare, minimum wages, and preservation of the "commons" to civil society) whether the relative importance of private actors in world politics will grow further. At present, however, an analysis of international environmental politics that ignores the role of the state and of international organizations would lack reality.

Conclusion

Liberal theory provides a framework for analysing the interactions between state and civil society. National governments can, of course, lose autonomy towards their domestic societies when they see themselves confronted with the pressure of environmental NGOs in a particular issue area. However, states can also be conceived as actors seeking autonomy from their societies. The increasing number of internationalizing political processes opens up new opportunities for national governments to negotiate with other governments relatively uncontrolled by their societies. Since international and domestic politics are intertwined, states have been increasingly acting as coordinators between international and domestic bargaining (Scharpf 1991). The demands of transnational civil society actors for more democracy at the global level have opened up a discussion which forces democratic theory to extend its analysis beyond the state. While liberal theory has made important contributions to the lively academic debate about the "democratic peace" (Brown, Lynn-Jones, and Miller 1996), the democratization of international institutions and policy-making remains an open agenda for future research.

The analysis of the activities of environmental advocacy and service organizations suggests that states benefit from the resources provided by transnational civil society actors for environmental problem-solving. Service organizations can improve the effectiveness of state policies. Their competence is an important resource for states. Environmental NGOs have realized that their work requires professionalism to achieve their goals. As a result, they are increasingly credited with being competent actors by international organizations and national governments. The (non-)availability of financial resources also influences the competence of NGOs.

The agenda-setting activities of advocacy organizations are not always directed against states; instead they can perform the function of an early-warning system and alert the public and national governments about environmental problems. The demands of advocacy organizations for better participation in environmental policy-making and early information on international negotiations at the domestic level can, of course, create new challenges for domestic and international governance. Conveying environmental policies to the public has become essential to governments for securing the support of constituencies. Further research is needed to understand how the domestic public is influenced by transnational civil society actors.

The relationship between environmental NGOs and economic actors is one of the most promising fields for future research. Although the material interests of economic actors and the immaterial interests of environmental NGOs are often in opposition, both types of interests can also converge and encourage coalition-building among environmental NGOs and economic actors. Exploring the relationship between environmental NGOs and economic actors could generate knowledge about the ability of civil society for self-coordination. In this connection, civil society would comprise a sphere of private rules for environmental protection agreed upon between NGOs and economic actors without further state intervention. This kind of research will contribute to answering how much state regulation civil society needs for preserving the human environment.

Notes

1. Transnational relations became a buzzword with the publication of *Transnational Relations and World Politics* edited by Keohane and Nye in 1972 and their subsequent book *Power and Interdependence* published in 1977. Risse-Kappen (1995a, 7) argues that the former concept of transnational relations was "ill-defined" and makes an effort to refine it.
2. One example of NGOs' improved access to intergovernmental bodies is their participation in the UN General Assembly's Special Session to Review Agenda 21 held in New York in June 1997. On this occasion, Greenpeace and the Third World Network spoke as representatives of environmental NGOs and criticized state representatives for insufficient political achievements since Rio 1992. See United Nations (1997).
3. On the growing literature about environmental NGOs see Princen and Finger (1994); Morphet (1996); Raustiala (1997); Ringius (1997); Stairs and Taylor (1992); Weiss and Gordenker (1996).
4. For examples on realist and institutionalist explanations of international politics see Baldwin (1993); Hasenclever, Mayer, and Rittberger (1997); Keohane (1986).
5. On two-level games see Putnam (1988). An effort to apply this approach was made in the volume edited by Evans, Jacobson, and Putnam (1993).
6. On the distinction between collaboration and coordination games see Stein (1990). On the situation-structural approach to international regimes see Hasenclever, Mayer, and Rittberger (1997, 44–59) and Zürn (1992). See also List and Rittberger (1992; 1998) on different types of situation structures in the field of the environment and their differential conduciveness to cooperation.
7. For a critical discussion of the concept of cosmopolitan democracy and of other reform proposals regarding the United Nations see Bienen, Rittberger, and Wagner (1998).
8. On such functional approaches to democracy see Dryzek (1995) or Burnheim (1995).
9. Huntington (1991) describes the democratization of a large number of countries in the 1970s and 1980s, but points out that Asian and Islamic countries have been immune to more recent efforts of Western countries to support the democratization of political systems in Asia and in many African countries.
10. See *Frankfurter Allgemeine Zeitung*, 12 November 1997: 5.
11. A similar critique was directed by environmental NGOs against the construction of hydroelectric dam projects like the Narmada Dam in India and the Three Gorges Dam in China. See Gan's and Wapner's chapters in this volume.
12. In the 1980s, environmental NGOs in the United States were blaming the CFC-producing chemical firms for the damaging effects of CFCs on the stratospheric atmosphere and demanded a worldwide phasing out of CFC production (Breitmeier 1996, 141–143).
13. See *Der Spiegel* 1993.
14. See Wapner's chapter in this volume.
15. Turner (1998, 39) concludes that the "most important terrain for waging political struggle in the information age will be the field of public opinion. While representatives of social movements and NGOs may employ traditional strategies of political persuasion such as lobbying, their greatest power resides in their capacity to influence public values and norms on a global scale."

16. Gordenker and Weiss (1997, 448) argue that for international organizations the collaboration with service organizations has some advantages, since "NGO personnel are available without the customary long recruitment process or without long-term contracts. Their numbers can be expanded and contracted far more easily than is the case with permanent staff appointed to intergovermental secretariats or even those serving on limited UN contracts." However, subcontracting and outsourcing also create new problems for international organizations, since their influence on the execution and quality of commissioned work decreases.

17. The Kyoto Protocol is included in the report of the Third Conference of the Parties to the Framework Convention on Climate Change held in Kyoto from 1 to 11 December 1997. See United Nations FCCC/CP/1997/7/Add.1. In contrast with the obligation for the reduction of greenhouse gases, some developed countries are allowed by the protocol to stabilize their emissions (e.g., the Russian Federation) or to increase their emissions by 1 per cent (Norway), 8 per cent (Australia), or 10 per cent (Iceland).

18. See *International Herald Tribune*, 11 September 1997: 6.

REFERENCES

Andresen, S. 1998. "The Making and Implementation of Whaling Policies: Does Participation Make a Difference?" In *The Implementation and Effectiveness of International Environmental Commitments: Theory and Practice*, eds D. G. Victor, K. Raustiala, and E. B. Skolnikoff. Cambridge, MA: MIT Press.

Baldwin, D. A., ed. 1993. *Neorealism and Neoliberalism: The Contemporary Debate*. New York: Columbia University Press.

Beisheim, M. 1997. "Nichtregierungsorganisationen und ihre Legitimität." *Aus Politik und Zeitgeschichte* 43(97): 21–29.

Benedick, R. E. 1991. *Ozone Diplomacy: New Directions in Safeguarding the Planet*. Cambridge, MA: Harvard University Press.

Bienen, D., V. Rittberger, and W. Wagner. 1998. "Democracy in the United Nations System – Cosmopolitan and Communitarian Principles." In *Re-Imagining Political Community. Studies in Cosmopolitan Democracy*, eds D. Archibugi, D. Held, and M. Köhler. Oxford: Polity Press.

Brack, D. 1996. *International Trade and the Montreal Protocol*. London: Royal Institute of International Affairs.

Breitmeier, H. 1996. *Wie entstehen globale Umweltregime? Der Konfliktaustrag zum Schutz der Ozonschicht und des gobalen Klimas*. Opladen: Leske and Budrich.

Breitmeier, H., M. A. Levy, O. R. Young, and M. Zürn. 1996a. "International Regimes Database – Data Protocol." IIASA Working Paper WP-96-154. Laxenburg: IIASA.

Breitmeier, H., M. A. Levy, O. R. Young, and M. Zürn. 1996b. "The International Regimes Database as a Tool for the Study of International Cooperation." IIASA Working Paper WP-96-160. Laxenburg: IIASA.

Brown, M. E., S. M. Lynn-Jones, and S. E. Miller. 1996. *Debating the Democratic Peace: An International Security Reader*. Cambridge, MA: MIT Press.

Burnheim, J. 1995. "Power Trading and the Environment." *Environmental Politics* 4(4): 49–65.

Cobb, R. W. and C. D. Elder. 1972. *Participation in American Politics: The Dynamics of Agenda Building.* Baltimore: Johns Hopkins University Press.

Commission on Global Governance. 1995. *Our Global Neighborhood.* Report of the Commission on Global Governance. New York: Oxford University Press.

Conca, K. 1996. "Greening the UN: Environmental Organizations and the UN System." In *NGOs, the UN and Global Governance*, eds T. G. Weiss and L. Gordenker. Boulder: Lynne Rienner.

Corell, E. 1996. "The Failure of Scientific Expertise to Influence the Desertification Negotiations." IIASA Working Paper WP-96–165. Laxenburg: IIASA.

Dahl, R. A. 1989. *Democracy and its Critics.* New Haven: Yale University Press.

Der Spiegel. 1993. "Billige Tricks." *Der Spiegel* 47(25), 21 June, pp. 96–99.

Doyle, M. W. 1997. *Ways of War and Peace: Realism, Liberalism, and Socialism.* New York: W. W. Norton.

Dryzek, J. S. 1995. "Political and Ecological Communication." *Environmental Politics* 4(4): 13–30.

Dunér, B. 1997. "The Fight for Greater NGO Participation in the UN." *Security Dialogue* 28(3): 301–315.

Europäische Kommission. 1996. "Die Energie in Europa bis zum Jahre 2020." *Szenarien-Ansatz, Luxemburg: Amt für Amtliche Veröffentlichungen der Europäischen Gemeinschaften.*

Evans, P. B., H. K. Jacobson, and R. D. Putnam, eds. 1993. *Double-Edged Diplomacy: International Bargaining and Domestic Politics.* Berkeley: University of California Press.

Frederick, H. 1993. *Global Communication and International Relations.* Belmont: Wadsworth.

Goldstein, J. and R. O. Keohane. 1993. "Ideas and Foreign Policy: An Analytical Framework." In *Ideas and Foreign Policy. Beliefs, Institutions, and Political Change*, eds J. Goldstein and R. O. Keohane. Ithaca: Cornell University Press.

Gordenker, L. and T. G. Weiss. 1996. "Pluralizing Global Governance. Analytical Approaches and Dimensions." In *NGOs, the UN and Global Governance*, eds T. G. Weiss and L. Gordenker. Boulder: Lynne Rienner.

Gordenker, L. and T. G. Weiss. 1997. "Developing Responsibilities. A Framework for Analysing NGOs and Services." *Third World Quarterly* 18(3): 443–455.

Greene, O. 1998. "The System of Implementation Review in the Ozone Regime." In *The Implementation and Effectiveness of International Environmental Commitments: Theory and Practice*, eds D. G. Victor, K. Raustiala, and E. B. Skolnikoff. Cambridge, MA: MIT Press.

Greenpeace. 1996. *Das Greenpeace-Buch: Reflexionen und Aktionen.* Munich: C. H. Beck.

Haas, P. M. 1989. "Do Regimes Matter? Epistemic Communities and Mediterranean Pollution Control." *International Organization* 43(3): 377–403.

Haas, P. M. 1992. "Epistemic Communities and International Policy Coordination." *International Organization* 46(1): 1–35.

Haas, P. M., M. A. Levy, and E. Parson. 1995. "Appraising the Earth Summit. How Should We Judge UNCED's Success?" In *Green Planet Blues. Environmental Politics from Stockholm to Rio*, eds K. Conca, M. Alberty, and G. D. Dabelko. Boulder: Westview.

Hardin, G. 1968. "The Tragedy of the Commons." *Science* 162(3859): 1243–1248.

Hasenclever, A., P. Mayer, and V. Rittberger. 1997. *Theories of International Regimes.* Cambridge: Cambridge University Press.

Held, D. 1995. "Democracy and the New International Order." In *Cosmopolitan Democracy. An Agenda for a New World Order*, eds D. Archibugi and D. Held. Cambridge: Polity Press.

Huntington, S. P. 1991. *The Third Wave: Democratization in the Late Twentieth Century.* Norman: University of Oklahoma Press.

Jasanoff, S. 1997. "NGOs and the Environment: From Knowledge to Action." *Third World Quarterly* 18(3): 579–594.

Johnson, S. P. 1993. *The Earth Summit. The United Nations Conference on Environment and Development (UNCED).* London: Graham & Trotman.

Keohane, R. O, ed. 1986. *Neorealism and its Critics.* New York: Columbia University Press.

Keohane, R. O. 1989. "Neoliberal Institutionalism: A Perspective on World Politics." In *International Institutions and State Power: Essays in International Relations Theory*, ed. R. O. Keohane. Boulder: Westview.

Keohane, R. O. and J. S. Nye, eds. 1972. *Transnational Relations and World Politics.* Cambridge, MA: Harvard University Press.

Keohane, R. O. and J. S. Nye, eds. 1977. *Power and Interdependence: World Politics in Transition.* Boston: Little, Brown.

Knappe, B. 1993. *Das Geheimnis von Greenpeace.* Vienna: Orac.

List, M. and V. Rittberger. 1992. "Regime Theory and International Environmental Management." In *The International Politics of the Environment: Actors, Interests, and Institutions*, eds A. Hurrell and B. Kingsbury. Oxford: Clarendon Press.

List, M. and V. Rittberger. 1998. "The Role of Intergovernmental Organizations in the Formation and Evolution of International Environmental Regimes." In *The Politics of International Environmental Management*, ed. A. Underdal. London: Kluwer Academic Publishers.

Litfin, K. T. 1994. *Ozone Discourse: Science and Politics in Global Environmental Cooperation.* New York: Columbia University Press.

Lobos, M. S. 1987. "Thinning Air, Better Beware: Chlorofluorocarbons and the Ozone Layer." *Dickinson Journal of International Law* 6(1): 87–117.

Lumsdaine, D. H. 1993. *Moral Vision in International Politics: The Foreign Aid Regime 1949–1989.* Princeton: Princeton University Press.

Matthews, J. T. 1997. "Power Shift." *Foreign Affairs* 76(1): 50–66.

Maxwell, J. H. and S. L. Weiner. 1993. "Green Consciousness or Dollar Diplomacy? The British Response to the Threat of Ozone Depletion." *International Environmental Affairs* 5(1): 19–41.

McGrew, A. 1997. "Democracy Beyond Borders? Globalization and the Reconstruction of Democratic Theory and Politics." In *The Transformation of Democracy? Globalization and Territorial Democracy*, ed. A. McGrew. Cambridge: Polity Press.

Molina, M. J. and S. F. Rowland. 1974. "Stratospheric Sink for Chlorofluoromethans: Chlorine Atom Catalysed Destruction of Ozone." *Nature* 249: 810–812.

Moravcsik, A. 1997. "Taking Preferences Seriously: A Liberal Theory of International Politics." *International Organization* 51(4): 513–553.

Morphet, S. 1996. "NGOs and the Environment." In *The Conscience of the World: The Influence of Non-Governmental Organisations in the UN System*, ed. P. Willetts. London: Hurst.

Olson, M. 1965. *The Logic of Collective Action. Public Goods and the Theory of Groups*. Cambridge, MA: Harvard University Press.

Parson, E. 1993. "Protecting the Ozone Layer." In *Institutions for the Earth: Sources of Effective International Environmental Protection*, eds P. M. Haas, R. O. Keohane, and M. A. Levy. Cambridge, MA: MIT Press.

Princen, T. and M. Finger, eds. 1994. *Environmental NGOs in World Politics: Linking the Local and the Global*. New York: Routledge.

Putnam, R. D. 1988. "Diplomacy and Domestic Politics: The Logic of Two-Level Games." *International Organization* 42(3): 427–460.

Raustiala, K. 1997. "States, NGOs, and International Environmental Institutions." *International Studies Quarterly* 41(4): 719–740.

Reed, D. 1997. "The Environmental Legacy of Bretton Woods: The World Bank." In *Global Governance. Drawing Insights from the Environmental Experience,* ed. O. R. Young. Cambridge, MA: MIT Press.

Reiss, J. 1990. *Greenpeace: Der Umweltmulti – sein Apparat, seine Aktionen*. Munich: Heyne.

Ringius, L. 1997. "Environmental NGOs and Regime Change: The Case of Ocean Dumping of Radioactive Waste." *European Journal of International Relations* 3(1): 61–104.

Risse-Kappen, T. 1995a. "Bringing Transnational Relations Back In: Introduction." In *Bringing Transnational Relations Back In: Non-State Actors, Domestic Structures and International Institutions*, ed. T. Risse-Kappen. Cambridge: Cambridge University Press.

Risse-Kappen, T. 1995b. "Ideas Do Not Float Freely: Transnational Coalitions, Domestic Structures, and the End of the Cold War." In *International Relations Theory and the End of the Cold War*, eds R. N. Lebow and T. Risse-Kappen. New York: Columbia University Press.

Rittberger, V., C. Schrade, and D. Schwarzer. 1998. "Transnational Civil Society Actors and the Quest for Security: Introduction." In *International Security Management and the United Nations*, eds M. Alagappa and T. Inoguchi. Tokyo: UNU Press.

Rowlands, I. H. 1995. *The Politics of Global Atmospheric Change*. Manchester: Manchester University Press.

Sartori, G. 1962. *Democratic Theory*. Detroit: Wayne State University Press.

Scharpf, F. W. 1991. "Die Handlungsfähigkeit des Staates am Ende des zwanzigsten Jahrhunderts." *Politische Vierteljahresschrift* 32(4): 622–634.

Scharpf, F. W. 1992. "Einführung: Zur Theorie von Verhandlungssystemen." In *Horizontale Politikverflechtung. Zur Theorie von Verhandlungssystemen*, eds A. Benz, F. W. Scharpf, and R. Zintl. Frankfurt: M. Campus.

Schmidheiny, S. (with the World Business Council for Sustainable Development). 1992. *Changing Course: A Global Business Perspective on Development and the Environment*. Cambridge, MA: MIT Press.

Schmidt, H. and I. Take. 1997. "Demokratischer und besser? Der Beitrag von Nichtregierungsorganisationen zur Demokratisierung internationaler Politik und zur Lösung globaler Probleme." *Aus Politik und Zeitgeschichte* 43(97): 12–20.

Schmidt, M. G. 1995. "Der Januskopf der Transformationsperiode. Kontinuität und Wandel der Demokratietheorien." In *Politische Theorien in der Ära der Transformation*, eds K. von Beyme and C. Offe. Opladen: PVS.

Skocpol, T. 1985. "Bringing the State Back In: Analysis in Current Research." In *Bringing the State Back In*, eds P. B. Evans, D. Rueschemeyer, and T. Skocpol. Cambridge: Cambridge University Press.

Stairs, K. and P. Taylor. 1992. "Non-Governmental Organisations and the Legal Protection of the Oceans: A Case Study." In *The International Politics of the Environment. Actors, Interests, and Institutions*, eds A. Hurrell and B. Kingsbury. Oxford: Clarendon Press.

Stein, A. A. 1990. *Why Nations Cooperate: Circumstances and Choice in International Relations.* Ithaca: Cornell University Press.

Subak, S. 1996. "The Science and Politics of National Greenhouse Gas Inventories." In *Politics of Climate Change. A European Perspective*, eds T. O'Riordan and J. Jäger. London: Routledge.

Turner, S. 1998. "Global Civil Society, Anarchy and Governance: Assessing an Emerging Paradigm." *Journal of Peace Research* 35(1): 25–42.

UN (United Nations). 1997. Non-Governmental Liaison Service (NGLS). "Environment and Development File: Briefings on Agenda 21 Follow-Up III(15)." September.

UNEP (United Nations Environment Programme). 1993. *Register of International Treaties and Other Agreements in the Field of the Environment.* Nairobi: UNEP.

Victor, D. G., O. Greene, J. Lanchbery, J. Carlos di Primio, and A. Korula. 1994. "Review Mechanisms in the Effective Implementation of International Environmental Agreements." IIASA Working Paper WP-94-114. Laxenburg: IIASA.

Victor, D. G., K. Raustiala, and E. B. Skolnikoff, eds. 1998. *The Implementation and Effectiveness of International Environmental Commitments: Theory and Practice.* Cambridge, MA: MIT Press.

Villacorta, C. 1997. "Emergent Roles of NGOs: The Relationship with the Business for Profit Sector." Master's thesis, University of California.

Waltz, K. N. 1979. *Theory of International Politics.* Reading, MA: Addison-Wesley.

Wapner, P. 1996. *Environmental Activism and World Civic Politics.* Albany: State University of New York Press.

WCED (World Commission for Environment and Development). 1987. *Our Common Future.* Oxford: Oxford University Press.

Weiss, T. G. and L. Gordenker. 1996. "Pluralizing Global Governance: Analytical Approaches and Dimensions." In *NGOs, the UN and Global Governance*, eds T. G. Weiss and L. Gordenker. Boulder: Lynne Rienner.

Werksman, J. 1996. "Compliance and Transition: Russia's Non-Compliance Tests the Ozone Regime." *Zeitschrift für ausländisches öffentliches Recht und Völkerrecht* 56(4): 750–773.

Wolf, K. D. 1997. "Entdemokratisierung durch Selbstbindung in der Europäischen Union." In *Projekt Europa im Übergang? Probleme, Modelle und Strategien des Regierens in der Europäischen Union*, ed. K. D. Wolf. Baden-Baden: Nomos.

Wolf, K. D. 1998. "Die neue Staatsräson als Demokratieproblem in der Weltgesellschaft." In *Politische Theorie heute*, eds M. T. Greven and R. Schmalz-Bruns. Baden-Baden: Nomos.

Young, O. R. 1994. *International Governance. Protecting the Environment in a Stateless Society*. Ithaca: Cornell University Press.

Zürn, M. 1992. *Interessen und Institutionen in der internationalen Politik: Grundlegung und Anwendung des situationstrukturellen Ansatzes*. Opladen: Leske and Budrich.

Zürn, M. 1996. "Über den Staat und die Demokratie im europäischen Mehrebenenprozeß." *Politische Vierteljahresschrift* 37(1): 27–55.

FURTHER READING

Sand, P. A. 1997. "Das Washingtoner Artenschutzabkommen (CITES) von 1973." In *Internationale Umweltregime. Umweltschutz durch Verhandlungen und Verträge,* eds T. Gehring and S. Oberthür. Opladen: Leske and Budrich.

World Society Research Group. 1995. "In Search of World Society." Working Paper No. 1. Frankfurt: World Society Research Group (Technical University Darmstadt and Johann Wolfgang Goethe University).

Market forces and the environment

9

Market forces and environment: Introduction

Chung-in Moon

Human efforts to sustain higher living standards for ever-increasing numbers of people have been accompanied by two grave ecological consequences. One is ecological scarcity and the diminishing carrying capacity of the planet earth, and the other is pervasive environmental degradation stemming from the misuse and abuse of the ecosystem. While environmental degradation has seriously undermined the quality of life, ecological scarcity, especially involving such vital resources as food, water, and energy, has threatened the very foundation of organic survival of national populations and global populace. The latter is particularly critical not only because food, water, and energy are the basic requirements of life, but also because they serve as both inputs and outputs of economic development and improved quality of life (Paoletto 1997).[1]

The United Nations forecasts that the world population will increase to 12.5 billion by the year 2050 from the current level of 6 billion (Paoletto 1997). Despite advances in agricultural technology, feeding 12.5 billion people will not be easy because of natural limitations to food production, as well as a distorted pattern of distribution and consumption on the global scale. Unpredictable climatic changes, growing scarcity of water, and erratic demographic transition by region could complicate food security in the twenty-first century. Fresh water is also likely to pose a major environmental challenge for the next century. Water is not scarce, but it is unevenly distributed across the planet, making the dilemma more localized. A growing percentage of the world's population, especially in the third world, is deprived of access to clean drinking water and sanitation needs, which are the most fundamental to human survival. Moreover, in recent years disputes over the allocation of fresh water resources are escalating to violent intra-state and inter-state conflicts. The trend is likely to amplify in the coming century.

The global energy situation does not seem to be promising either. Although the recent oversupply of energy has defused the acuteness of the energy dilemma, a spectre of energy shortages could haunt human society in the medium and in the long run. Apart from the biophysical limitations embodied in the second law of thermodynamics,[2] energy consumption is on the rise, while the current energy glut has structurally impeded the development of alternative energy sources. Depressingly low energy prices, public concerns about safety, and technological barriers are hindering not only the promotion of soft energy paths (e.g., solar, wind), but also the development of nuclear power and fusion energy. At the same time, a vicious cycle of development, an increased demand for energy consumption, and extensive emissions of air pollutants are turning the energy issue into one of the major environmental problematiques in the twenty-first century.

Food, fresh water, and energy constitute the core of contemporary and future environmental concerns, all of which are intertwined through an intricate web of ecological interdependence. How can one cope with these environmental challenges? There are essentially two contending paradigms.[3] One is the technological-fix perspective, which is predicated on human ingenuity and adaptability (Kahn, Brown, and Martel 1976; Simon and Kahn 1984). Its proponents believe that the carrying capacity of the planet earth is not fixed but variable, and that human beings are capable of expanding the global ecological carrying capacity through knowledge and technology. Herman Kahn and Julian Simons, two leading futurists, point out that "because of increases in knowledge, the Earth's carrying capacity has been increasing through the decades and centuries and millennia to such a extent that the term carrying capacity has by now no useful meaning" (Simon and Kahn 1984, 45).

Human adaptation is manifested primarily through the logic of market forces, which plays a pivotal role in facilitating progress in knowledge and technology. In economic terms, scarcity simply denotes a situation in which certain goods are undersupplied while overdemanded. The disequilibrium can be easily corrected by market forces that respond through technological invention and innovation. Green Revolution, Blue Revolution, genetic engineering, and fusion technology are the hallmarks of technological responses to ecological scarcity through market mechanisms. Market forces are resilient enough to come up with alternative solutions to ecological scarcity and environmental degradation. What matters is incentive structure. If proper institutions are arranged in such a way as to assure profit incentives, markets can effectively overcome current and future ecological dilemmas by expanding the current carrying capacity through new frontiers of knowledge and technology.

The other approach is the sustainability perspective (Meadows and Meadows 1992; Harman 1979; Ophuls 1977; Pirages 1989; Postel 1994; Brown et al. 1996; Dobson 1995). Its proponents postulate that although technology and market forces can help manipulate ecological limits to accord with human preferences, the outright repeal of the limits is virtually impossible. Instead of removing or weakening limits through market forces and technology, they argue that the forces of growth should be weakened in harmony with the biophysical realities of a finite planet. Central to this approach is the concept of sustainability, which emphasizes the interlocking dynamics of resources utilization and destruction, regenerative capacity, and the collapse or preservation of ecosystems.[4] It involves three major dimensions. First is the ability to live within the boundaries of ecological limitations in the contemporary setting. The second involves inter-generational sustainability. Current needs should be met without depriving future generations of the resources necessary for their survival. Third is the concept of sustainability, which touches on the issue of intra-generational equity. A great portion of scarcity and human suffering arises more from the unequal distribution of resources than from scarcity *per se*. Thus, an equitable sharing of scarce resources emerges as a moral imperative.

According to this view, free markets are a powerful social invention for efficient allocation of scarce resources, but they cannot serve as a useful tool in ensuring sustainability. Decentralized, profit-maximizing agents of free markets seldom appreciate the meaning and value of sustainability. Neither future implications of current production and consumption nor intra-generational equity associated with the distribution of basic human needs is fully incorporated into the workings of market forces. Thus it becomes essential to restructure the operational logic of market forces in line with global sustainability; otherwise, it is impossible to escape from the sombre omens of the doomsday model.[5]

The chapters in this section converge with the sustainability perspective. They all share the view that scarcity problems involving food, fresh water, and energy are real and present and that market forces and technology alone cannot resolve the ecological dilemmas. Alternative ways of coping with the dilemmas should be actively sought.

Wilkening, Von Hippel, and Hayes argue that rapid industrialization and population growth have accompanied a substantial rise in energy demands, posing a major challenge for developing and developed nations in the twenty-first century. They present a rather pessimistic outlook by postulating that market forces cannot ensure long-term sustainability in energy use. The current operating logic of energy markets defies the issue of sustainability and is not ready to cope with future energy dilemmas. In order to secure energy sustainability, long-term objectives for energy supply and demand should be defined. International norms and values related to energy use should be altered, while energy-related institutions and infrastructure should be overhauled. Finally, there should be effective monitoring of progress towards sustainable energy.

In this process, experts and expert knowledge become a crucial factor in steering energy markets toward sustainability, since they can harness the power of the market by socializing ideas and practices of sustainability. Generating new knowledge on energy supply and demand, disseminating widely sustainable energy knowledge through the formation of epistemic communities, and applying such knowledge to market-related public and private sectors should constitute an integral part of new strategies for global energy sustainability. The authors conclude that the United Nations is uniquely positioned to act as a catalyst in creating, coordinating, and institutionalizing epistemic communities in service to the vision of sustainable energy.

In analysing the global fresh water dilemma, Peter Gleick notes that there is a sufficient amount of water to meet the needs and wants of every human being. But at regional, national, and local levels, imbalances between overall availability and growth in need and demand have emerged as a serious problem. Billions of people around the globe still suffer from a lack of basic sanitation services and clean drinking water, bearing serious implications for human health. Water is also posing a major threat to food security, due to diminishing water supplies as well as higher costs of water resulting from competition with industrial and other users. While excessive manipulation of the hydrological cycle has deepened the ecological crisis, the allocation of limited water supplies has increasingly been linked to inter- and intra-state conflicts.

Can market forces be conducive to resolving the global fresh water dilemmas? Gleick sees two conflicting faces of market forces in this regard. Market forces can serve as a valuable tool for conserving fresh water resources. Inadequate attention to the role of markets and subsequent failures in properly pricing water have led to excessive groundwater overdraft and wastes of fresh water. Thus, recognizing water as an economic good that is subject to the law of supply and demand can cure a great portion of fresh water dilemmas in many parts of the world. However, the application of market approaches in situations where non-economic values are high or where certain types of water needs or uses cannot be quantified is bound to fail, and may even create new problems. Local, national, and international intervention become essential in order to ensure the satisfaction of water as a basic human need. Gleick suggests several policy options: normative commitment to identify and meet basic human and ecosystem water needs; adoption of food policies within the boundary of water limitations; treatment of water as an economic resource; and participatory water management systems on the local, national, and even the international levels.

Drawing on the experiences of the Philippines and selected Asian countries, the chapter by Briones and Ramos explores the dimensions of food insecurity in developing countries. Despite a recent rise in food supply through progress in agricultural production technology, they argue that most developing countries still suffer acute and pervasive food insecurity, which has resulted from a lack of access to food rather than the actual production and supply of food. Limited and skewed access to food by a great majority of inhabitants in the third world is a product of both external and internal factors. While international pressures on liberalization of domestic agricultural markets through the settlement of the Uruguay Round of GATT have imposed unbearable constraints on the sustainable food production and distribution system, domestic, social, biophysical, and institutional factors have also contributed to aggravating food insecurity in developing countries. Briones and Ramos point out that rural poverty and illiteracy, environmental stress, and institutional and political distortions have not only undermined the foundation of domestic food production, but have also impeded people's access to adequate food. In their view, market forces are the primary causes of food insecurity rather than a solution to it.

New strategies should be devised for sustainable food production, distribution, and consumption. These include the systematic spread of technical advances to local farmers through education, public investment in the agricultural infrastructure, injection of profit motives in the minds of farmers, and the protection of small farmers by correcting unfair agricultural trade practices embodied in the GATT-Uruguay Round provisions, such as extensive farm subsidies in OECD countries. Briones and Ramos also draw attention to the importance of new partnerships and close cooperation between government and NGOs that would promote an empowering process for rural populations.

Common to the three chapters in this section is the belief that market forces alone cannot cope with the environmental dilemmas in the twenty-first century. Unruly market forces have severely undermined food security by distorting food production, distribution, and consumption in the developing world. Old inertia associated with the industrial paradigm has prevented energy markets from adopting the idea of sustainability, clouding the energy future in the twenty-first century. In the case of fresh water, market forces have a mixed outlook. Although market forces are deficient in satisfying basic water needs of the majority of inhabitants in developing countries, they can serve as an effective deterrent to overuse and misuse of scarce water resources.

In view of this, market forces and the environment are closely intertwined. In contrast to the technological-fix perspective, however, market forces are fundamentally flawed in coping with the environmental dilemma.

First, as long as the current pattern of population growth and conspicuous consumption continues, market forces and technology cannot ensure future sustainability. Technological progress might be able to abort major crises resulting from scarcity in the current generation, but cannot guarantee inter-generational sustainability since market forces rarely discount current consumption for the sake of future generations. Even if it is assumed that technology can fix the current and future scarcity dilemma, intended or unintended social and economic costs associated with it could wipe out its benefits. As the case of nuclear power development illustrates, the fallacy of the Faustian bargain could easily prevail (Ophuls 1977, 156–158).

Second, market forces often fail to take into account normative dimensions of resource scarcity. Food, water, and energy are the minimum requirements of basic human needs. Regardless of costs, human beings are entitled to them. As Beitz (1979, 136–142) aptly puts it, "those who are less advantaged for reasons beyond their control cannot be asked to suffer the pains of inequality when their sacrifices cannot be shown to advance their position with an initial position of equals." Market forces cannot effectively address this normative concern of distributive justice embedded in the allocation of food, water, and energy. It is all the more so because the production and consumption of these resources are heavily concentrated in the industrial North, and their equitable distribution is severely constrained by global capitalism.

Finally, food, water, and energy have the strong characteristics of public goods. Market mechanisms cannot resolve the undersupply or overexploitation of collective goods through free-riding behaviour. The tragedy of commons is likely to abound (Hardin 1968). In order to enhance the sustainability of food, water, and energy, there must be visible hands of national and global governance to correct market failures. Otherwise, market forces are likely to aggravate the scarcity problem in the future.

There are two viable ways of correcting market failures and enhancing ecological sustainability. One is to engineer the changes of the dominant social paradigm which defines social reality and shapes social expectation (Pirages 1989, 14). The environmental dilemma cannot be resolved by resorting to the old industrial paradigm which is heavily influenced by human ingenuity and cornucopian *Weltanschauung*, while defying sustainability. New norms, values, ideas, knowledge, and institutions should be developed and socialized so as to enhance global sustainability.

The other is the critical importance of global governance (Young 1994; 1997). Local and national governments alone cannot handle the dilemmas of market failures and distributive injustice. As with individual market agents, national governments are also obsessed with the maximization of short-term national interests rather than long-term global human interests. It is in this context that the role of the United Nations becomes all the more important. On the occasion of the Rio Earth Summit in 1992, which brought more than 150 nations and 1,400 NGOs to Rio, a new momentum was provided for the new sustainable pathway to our common future. However, enthusiasm generated through the Rio Summit has been withering away, while implementation of the Rio agenda has been stagnant. The United Nations should reverse the trend by taking a more active leadership role. Shaping a new global governance structure under the rubric of the United Nations will be the best way to resolve the current dilemmas and prevent the future calamities.

Notes

1. The terms "environment" and "ecology" are used interchangeably here. Environmental concerns such as air and water pollution, wastes, biodiversity, and climate change are being treated as a subset of the ecological system.
2. The second law of thermodynamics or entropy law refers to a natural process in which free energy degrades into bound energy. The law underscores the physical limitation to recycle non-renewable energy sources. See Georgescu-Roegen (1976, 4–7).
3. For a succinct discussion of the contending paradigms, see Dobson (1995), Pirages (1989), and Hughes (1985).
4. The best conceptual work on sustainability can be found in Daly (1992). Pirages (1977) and Goldin and Winters (1994) also offer useful overviews of sustainable society and sustainable development.
5. On the doomsday model, see Meadows and Meadows (1972; 1992).

REFERENCES

Beitz, C. R. 1979. *Political Theory and International Relations*. Princeton: Princeton University Press.

Brown, L. R., C. Flarin, H. Kane, L. Starke, and N. Lenssen. 1996. *Vital Signs: The Trends that are Shaping Our Future*. New York: W. W. Norton.

Daly, H., ed. 1992. *Steady-State Economics,* 2nd edn. London: Earthscan.

Dobson, A. 1995. *Green Political Thought*, 2nd edn. London and New York: Routledge.

Georgescu-Roegen, N. 1976. *The Entrophy Law and the Economic Process*. Cambridge, MA: Harvard University Press.

Goldin, I. and L. A. Winters, eds. 1994. *The Economics of Sustainable Development*. Cambridge: Cambridge University Press.

Hardin, G. 1968. "The Tragedy of the Commons." *Science* 162(3859): 1243–1248.

Harman, W. 1979. *An Incomplete Guide to the Future*. New York: Norton.

Hughes, B. B. 1985. *World Futures: A Critical Analysis of Alternatives*. Baltimore: Johns Hopkins University Press.

Kahn, H., W. Brown, and L. Martel. 1976. *The Next 200 Years*. New York: Williams Morrow.

Meadows, D. H. and D. Meadows, eds. 1972. *The Limits to Growth: A Report for the Club of Rome's Project on the Predicament of Mankind*. New York: Signet.

Meadows, D. H. and D. Meadows, eds. 1992. *Beyond the Limits: Global Collapse or a Sustainable Future*. London: Earthscan.

Ophuls, W. 1977. *Ecology and the Politics of Scarcity*. San Francisco: Freeman.

Paoletto, G. 1997. "Position Paper for the United Nations System in the 21st Century." Mimeo. Tokyo: UNU Press.

Pirages, D. 1977. *The Sustainable Society*. New York: Praeger.

Pirages, D. 1989. *Global Technopolitics*. Pacific Grove: Brooks-Cole.

Postel, S. L. 1994. "Carrying Capacity: Earth's Bottom Line." In *State of the World*, eds L. Brown et al. New York: W. W. Norton.

Simon, J. and H. Kahn, eds. 1984. *The Resourceful Earth*. Oxford: Basil Blackwell.

Young, O. R. 1994. *International Governance. Protecting the Environment in a Stateless Society*. Ithaca: Cornell University Press.

Young, O. R. 1997. *Global Governance*. Ithaca: Cornell University Press.

FURTHER READING

Daly, H. ed. 1973. *Toward a Steady-State Economy*. San Francisco: Freeman.

Hughes, B. B. 1993. *International Futures*. Boulder: Westview.

10

Sustainable energy in a developing world: The role of knowledgeable markets

Ken Wilkening, David Von Hippel, and Peter Hayes

Wise application of knowledge in service to a vision of sustainability can guide and invigorate a global economy and global energy network dominated by the free market system. Free markets are a powerful social invention for efficient allocation of scarce resources, but in and of themselves free markets cannot and will not produce sustainability. Free markets are not generators of collective vision. Creation of visions of sustainability is what might be called a "meta-market force," for it involves social, political, and cultural forces that fall outside the purview of market operation and conventional "non-market forces." Once created, visions of sustainability must be translated into practice. An essential, and often overlooked, aspect of the translation process is the role of knowledge. Knowledge mediates between vision and practice. "Sustainability knowledge" (knowledge produced in service to the goal of achieving a sustainable civilization) must be generated, synthesized, summarized, codified, disseminated, debated, reviewed, evaluated, brokered, applied, and entrenched for a sustainability vision to take root. A gargantuan task for the twenty-first century is to harness sustainability knowledge in all sectors of the global economy.

One sector is that of energy. The governing vision of sustainability in the energy sector is "sustainable energy," and knowledge related to sustainable energy must be harnessed in order to attain this vision. This chapter attempts to illuminate the role of knowledge in implementing the vision of sustainable energy in the marketplace.

175

There is no accepted definition of "sustainability."[1] Generally, use of the term acknowledges that things are out of balance in our current practices of living on earth, and that the imbalances, if not corrected, will diminish future generations' ability to live fulfilling lives. When applied to energy, the term sustainability acknowledges that current practices of energy extraction, transformation, and use are out of balance. Sustainability, therefore, is an overarching conceptual framework for steering the human race toward balanced practices of living and energy use. The framework is composed of at least four key dimensions: preservation of ecological integrity (the natural dimension); pursuit of human justice and equity (the social dimension); maintenance of peaceful community (the political dimension); and achievement of economic efficiency (the economic dimension). This chapter focuses primarily on the environmental and economic dimensions in relation to energy use, and considers their intersection in both developed and developing countries.

Worldwide growth in energy demand: Trends and projections

Economic and social development is invariably accompanied by an increase in the need for energy and "energy services." Energy services are services – provided through the use of fossils fuels, biomass, fissionable materials, or other energy sources – that help satisfy human needs and desires. Examples of energy services are almost unlimited. They include the boiling of drinking water in Nepal, grilling of tortillas in Mexico, firing of a tea cup in Japan, welding of a Tata automobile in India, and rocketing of an F-4 Phantom off an aircraft carrier in the Persian Gulf. The form of development that is most intimately associated with vast increases in the use of energy and energy services is "industrialization."

It is rapid industrialization, combined with large populations, in low-income countries, or in countries with economies in transition, that will probably drive the biggest future increases in energy use. Historically, in industrial economies, economic growth has been positively coupled with energy use. In the decades leading up to the 1970s there was essentially a linear relationship between economic growth and energy use. Though there seems to have been a "decoupling" from a linear relationship, there is still a "positive" relationship. In other words, an increase in GDP is still associated with an increase in energy use, although the ratio between the growth in the two quantities is often less than 1:1. In the developing world, in its almost unanimous drive to industrialize, there is also a "positive" relationship, although it is difficult to characterize because of the multiple forms and levels of development.[2]

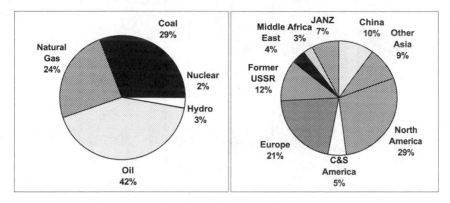

Source: British Petroleum statistics, spreadsheet file "fuelcons.wks." Here nuclear energy is counted as electricity output, not heat input; "C&S America" (Central and South America) includes Mexico; "JANZ" is Japan, Australia, and New Zealand; and "Other Asia" is all of Asia except China and Japan.

Figure 10.1. 1995 world energy use by fuel and region

As of 1995, the total amount of primary commercial fuels (including coal, petroleum, natural gas, hydroelectricity, and electricity from nuclear plants) stood at approximately 324 exajoules (EJ)[3], or about 7.74 billion tonnes of oil equivalent. Of this total, 53 per cent was used in OECD countries (sometimes referred to as the "industrialized" countries), 15 per cent in the countries of Central/Eastern Europe and the former Soviet Union, and 32 per cent in the rest of the world.[4] The "rest of the world" category includes virtually all of the lower-income countries of the world, including those in Africa, Central and South America, and much of Asia. Figure 10.1 shows the division of primary energy use in 1995 by fuel type and region or subregion, respectively. Oil accounted for the largest fraction of global energy use, followed by coal, natural gas, and primary electricity. North America was the region that consumed the greatest fraction of energy, followed by Europe, the former USSR, and China.

The global distribution of energy use has changed markedly, even over the last 10 years. Table 10.1 shows, for 1985, 1990, and 1995, the division of global primary energy use by fuel and country group. Although overall energy use in OECD countries and in the countries of Central/Eastern Europe and the former Soviet Union has grown only modestly – or even declined – over the last decade, growth in energy use in developing regions has been strong, particularly in China and other Asian countries. Note that the data in Table 10.1 do not include biomass fuels, which hold substantial shares of overall energy supply in many developing countries.

Table 10.1 World energy use trends, 1985–1995

Country group	Primary energy consumption, EJ						Fraction of primary energy consumption					
	Coal	Nat. gas	Oil	Nuclear	Hydro	Total	Coal %	Nat. gas %	Oil %	Nuclear %	Hydro %	Total %
1985												
OECD	37.9	32.2	69.5	4.3	4.3	148.2	26	22	47	3	3	100
Eastern Europe/ former USSR	21.9	23.3	21.1	0.7	0.9	68.0	32	34	31	1	1	100
Rest of world	28.1	6.9	26.7	0.2	2.1	64.0	44	11	42	0	3	100
Total world	87.9	62.4	117.3	5.3	7.3	280.2	31	22	42	2	3	100
1990												
OECD	39.6	36.1	76.8	5.8	4.3	162.5	24	22	47	4	3	100
Eastern Europe/ former USSR	19.9	27.7	21.2	1.0	0.8	70.8	28	39	30	1	1	100
Rest of world	34.5	10.2	33.3	0.4	2.6	81.0	43	13	41	0	3	100
Total world	94.0	74.0	131.4	7.1	7.9	314.4	30	24	42	2	3	100

Primary energy consumption, EJ   Fraction of primary energy consumption

Country group	Coal	Nat. gas	Oil	Nuclear	Hydro	Total	Coal %	Nat. gas %	Oil %	Nuclear %	Hydro %	Total %
	1995						1985					
OECD	37.9	42.4	80.4	6.9	4.6	172.3	22	25	47	4	3	100
Eastern Europe/ former USSR	13.5	22.2	12.0	0.8	1.1	49.6	27	45	24	2	2	100
Rest of world	41.1	14.4	42.7	0.5	3.4	102.1	40	14	42	1	3	100
Total world	92.6	78.9	135.1	8.2	9.1	323.9	29	24	42	3	3	100

Average annual growth rate, 1985–1995

Country group	Coal %	Nat. gas %	Oil %	Nuclear %	Hydro %	Total %
OECD	0.0	2.8	1.5	4.8	0.8	1.5
Eastern Europe/ former USSR	-4.7	-0.5	-5.5	1.5	1.6	-3.1
Rest of world	3.9	7.7	4.8	8.4	5.1	4.8
Total world	0.5	2.4	1.4	4.6	2.3	1.5

Projections and scenarios of future energy use suggest that the trend of the last decade of increasing use of fuels in "developing" regions relative to "industrialized" regions is likely to continue and possibly accelerate. Table 10.2 shows "Reference Case" projections published by the US Department of Energy's Energy Information Administration for global energy use by fuel and region in 2005 and 2015 (USDOE/EIA 1997).

Beginning in 1995, energy use in developing regions is projected to grow at an average rate of about 3.6 per cent per year through to 2015.[5] By 2015 energy use in developing regions increases to over 41 per cent of the global total from 32 per cent in 1995. Projections by other researchers show a similar pattern.[6]

This section establishes several critical facts: growth in energy use is coupled with growth in economic activity in an industrial economy, although the coupling may not necessarily be linear; economic activity in both developed and developing countries is projected to increase in the next two decades and hence energy use is also projected to increase; and developing countries' share of global energy use relative to that of industrialized countries is projected to increase. These facts combine to suggest that coping with the global impacts (ecological, social, economic, political, and technological) of energy use poses a major challenge for the twenty-first century, and will create energy dilemmas not only for developing nations but for developed nations as well.

Can market forces in the energy sector be harnessed to achieve long-term sustainability in energy use in both developed and developing countries, and thus to mitigate or prevent the potentially devastating impacts associated with rapid economic growth? Before attempting to answer this, it is necessary to examine more closely the character of the marketplace in the energy sector.

The global "Energy Market"

Global interdependence

One of the single most important economic changes in the world today is the phenomenal explosion in the use of free markets. There has been a dramatic shift away from "command-and-control" or "centrally planned" (socialist) economies to free market economies. Nothing better illustrates this point that the rush to free markets by the countries of Eastern Europe and the former Soviet Union, and China's experiment with free market practices. This monumental change means that the free market system, with all its goods and evils, is becoming both the world's dominant economic system and the system within which international energy relations are determined.

The explosion of free markets has intensified the phenomenon known as "global (economic) interdependence." Global economic interdependence in the energy sector is exemplified by the tremendous growth in internationally traded, financed, and produced forms of energy. It signals that in a very real sense one can talk about a global Energy Market (upper case) which ties together all energy-related market activities, whether local, national, international, or global in scale. The Energy Market stands in contrast to global energy markets (lower case) which tie together only internationally traded, financed, and produced energy. Global energy markets are a subset of the global Energy Market. The task of this chapter is to illuminate the role of knowledge in implementing the vision of sustainability in the global Energy Market. Before proceeding, however, it is necessary to examine the composition of the so-called Energy Market and its problems in dealing with sustainability issues.

Composition of the global Energy Market

The Energy Market consists of markets that encompass the buying and selling of fuels and the infrastructure within which the fuels are transformed and ultimately used to provide energy services. Energy markets range in scale from global (such as oil) to local (such as firewood). Some of the energy markets operating within the larger Energy Market are as follows.

Markets for fossil fuels

Markets for crude oil and petroleum products are global in scale, and are largely dominated by a relatively few major multinational companies and national crude oil suppliers. Coal markets are increasingly becoming global, although coal production in much of the world (including developing countries) has been traditionally state-owned. With the marked expansion of facilities for handling liquefied natural gas (LNG), the natural gas market has been shifting from primarily regional markets (using gas pipelines) to a nascent global market as well.

Markets for traditional renewable resources

Markets for biomass fuels have traditionally been local in nature, with individuals and small businesses doing the bulk of the trading. In some developing countries, markets for charcoal have become national in nature, sometimes even crossing international borders, and larger companies or cartels have sometimes become involved.

Table 10.2 USDOE/EIA projections of world energy use, 1995–2015

| Country group | Primary energy consumption, EJ | | | Fraction of total | | | Average annual growth, 1995–2015 |
| | | Projections | | 1995 % | Projections | | |
	1995	2005	2015		2005 %	2015 %	
Developing Asia							
Oil	24.5	39.0	55.1	35	35	35	4.1
Natural gas	5.1	15.1	22.9	7	13	14	7.8
Coal	38.6	55.3	76.8	55	49	48	3.5
Nuclear	0.4	0.7	1.1	1	1	1	5.0
Other	1.3	2.5	3.2	2	2	2	4.5
Total	69.9	112.6	159.1	100	100	100	4.2
Other developing nations							
Oil	22.3	29.9	38.0	54	58	58	2.7
Natural gas	10.3	13.0	17.9	25	25	27	2.8
Coal	6.5	6.5	7.5	16	13	11	0.7
Nuclear	0.1	0.1	0.1	0	0	0	3.5
Other	2.0	2.1	2.3	5	4	3	0.6
Total	41.2	51.6	65.8	100	100	100	2.4
Industrialized countries							
Oil	89.5	102.0	110.9	48	47	45	1.1
Natural gas	44.5	60.5	74.1	24	28	30	2.6
Coal	38.9	41.6	44.6	21	19	18	0.7
Nuclear	6.7	6.9	5.9	4	3	2	-0.7
Other	5.9	7.6	9.2	3	3	4	2.2
Total	185.6	218.5	244.6	100	100	100	1.4

| | Primary energy consumption, EJ | | | Fraction of total | | | Average annual growth, 1995–2015 |
| | | Projections | | | Projections | | |
Country group	1995	2005	2015	1995 %	2005 %	2015 %	
Eastern Europe/former USSR							
Oil	12.8	16.2	21.3	25	25	29	2.6
Natural gas	22.2	31.7	37.8	43	49	51	2.7
Coal	14.1	14.3	13.2	28	22	18	-0.3
Nuclear	0.9	0.9	0.8	2	1	1	-0.4
Other	1.1	1.1	1.4	2	2	2	1.4
Total	51.0	64.3	74.5	100	100	100	1.9
Total world							
Oil	149.0	187.2	225.2	43	42	41	2.1
Natural gas	82.1	120.2	152.7	24	27	28	3.2
Coal	98.2	117.7	142.1	28	26	26	1.9
Nuclear	8.1	8.6	7.9	2	2	1	-0.1
Other	10.3	13.3	16.1	3	3	3	2.2
Total	347.7	447.0	544.1	100	100	100	2.3

Source: USDOE/EIA, 1997. Figures for nuclear and "other" (mostly hydroelectric) fuel use were modified to reflect electricity output. Note that the USDOE/EIA energy consumption figures for 1995 are somewhat different from those published by British Petroleum – probably due to the use of different accounting practices.

Markets for conventional energy supply infrastructure

Large companies, including a number of multinational firms, dominate the provision of infrastructure for fuel extraction (coal, oil, and gas), for oil refining, for thermal, hydroelectric, and nuclear power generation, and for electricity transmission and distribution. Larger developing countries sometimes have their own industries for producing these types of equipment – particularly in smaller sizes – for both domestic use and export. Buyers of energy infrastructure have traditionally been state-owned companies or utilities, but there is a global trend toward the developers of energy facilities acting as facility owners and/or operators.

Markets for non-conventional/renewable energy supply infrastructure

The supply of infrastructure for renewable energy conversion – notably solar-photovoltaic and wind-power systems – has changed in recent years, with fewer and larger firms becoming dominant globally. Purchasers of renewable energy infrastructure vary in scale from individuals to nations.

Markets for end-use appliances and equipment

Most major electrical and gas appliances, motor vehicles, and other major energy-using devices tend to be manufactured by, or manufactured under licence to, large national or multinational corporations, while buyers are individuals/households, firms, and institutions.

Markets for energy-efficiency technologies

Sellers of energy-efficiency technologies are a combination of smaller and larger companies. Most of these devices are ultimately purchased by end-users (individuals, institutions, and businesses), although governments and utilities have sometimes played the role of "middle-man" in these markets.

Markets for capital

The availability of financial capital is an overarching consideration in the development and functioning of markets for fuels and especially infrastructure. In many cases, growth in demand for financing of energy infrastructure in developing countries is and will be well beyond the abilities of government and local financial institutions to provide. This means that external financing – multinational commercial and multilateral institutions – will have to fill the gap. Thus, the investment criteria of global financial institutions will play a large role in determining what type of energy systems evolve in developing countries, as well as how environmentally sustainable those systems are.

Actors in the global Energy Market

Energy sector actors in the above-described markets include the following.

Multilateral organizations and lenders

The United Nations, World Bank, Global Environment Facility, Asian, African and Inter-American Development Banks, Asia-Pacific Economic Cooperation (APEC) Forum, and other international and multinational organizations fulfil a number of roles in the energy sector of developing countries. These roles include funding research, development, and demonstration projects, providing or arranging financing for energy infrastructure, providing assistance with energy planning and energy-related economic development, tracking statistics from the energy sector, and transmitting information between various energy sector actors.

Multinational private corporations

Private corporations operating across national borders provide a substantial portion of the globally traded fuels, large energy installations, and energy demand equipment. Private corporations also play a major role in prospecting for and extracting fossil fuels, as well as in research, development, demonstration, and commercialization of new energy sector technologies. Also, industrial facilities in developing countries that are owned by multinational companies can be major demand centres for electricity and/or other fuels – thus, multinational companies can have substantial leverage in setting energy policy.

National corporations

State-owned corporations, including natural gas and electric utilities and oil and coal companies, have traditionally had a dominant role in the energy-supply sector in developing countries.

Larger private firms within nations

In some developing countries, large private firms serve as utilities and fuel suppliers, and also help shape both energy infrastructure and energy policy as suppliers of energy-using devices and as industrial/commercial consumers of fuels and energy sector equipment.

National research and development (R&D) institutions

Most industrialized nations and some developing countries have publicly and/or privately funded institutions devoted to aspects of energy technology development. Often these are organized by fuel type (such as the

Central Research Institute of the Electric Power Industry in Japan), or by other topic areas (such as the Beijing Energy Efficiency Centre in China).

National and subnational regulatory agencies

Domestic regulatory agencies are charged with setting energy and environmental standards, as well as with energy planning tasks. The regulation of energy pricing is a role often served by national agencies, although regulation in the energy sector is generally declining at present.

Non-governmental organizations

Interest groups outside of governments play various roles, including acting as advocates for consumer groups and indigenous peoples, as environmental "watchdogs," and as agents promoting (or opposing) particular energy technologies or paths.

Smaller private firms

Smaller private firms play multiple roles, including supplying technologies for energy conversion and energy demand equipment, supplying fuels such as biomass and charcoal, and consuming both fuels and energy-using devices.

"Local" communities

Local communities include state and provincial governments, cities, traditional villages, etc. These entities can act as buyers, sellers, and managers of energy. Traditional rural villages, for instance, administer traditional energy forms such as agricultural wastes, wood fuel, and charcoal produced locally, while at the same time administering industrial fuels such as electricity (in rural electrification schemes) and kerosene fuels sold in rural areas.

Individual consumers

Households and individuals are the final consumers of fuels and energy goods and services. As such, their preferences expressed via their "political votes," "monetary votes," and other economic/political actions help to determine which fuels and energy-consuming devices prevail in a particular country.

This description of energy markets and energy sector actors, while hardly complete, is sufficient to demonstrate that the operation of the marketplace in the energy sector is highly complex. The synergistic sum of all energy markets, forces that shape these markets, and actors within the markets, constitutes what is called the "Energy Market." It is this vast and loose-knit entity that must be made to function in a sustainable manner, and to which colossal amounts of sustainability knowledge must be applied in order to ensure its proper functioning.

Energy Market successes and failures

Making the Energy Market sustainable involves a two-pronged strategy – effectively deploying market forces where they do not currently exist (in other words, maximizing sustainability-directed market successes), and correcting failures in current markets (in other words, minimizing sustainability-inhibiting market failures). Knowledge has a central role in effecting both strategies. A few areas where market forces can be successfully deployed and where market deficiencies must be remedied are now discussed. The discussion proceeds from the global level to individual level.

Basic human needs

Eradication or major reduction of poverty is an essential requirement for the proper functioning of a globally sustainable economic system. Widespread poverty can undermine the global marketplace through such traumas as large-scale civil unrest, massive movements of people, or collapses of national governments. Because a market is ultimately based on considerations of economic efficiency, not human equity, even properly functioning markets have no incentive to eliminate poverty. It is up to regulators to subordinate the market to the imperative of meeting certain social sustainability criteria such as meeting basic human needs.[7] Energy markets can be created (as in the case of facilitating a switch from use of unhealthy or unsustainable traditional fuels, such as wood in deforested areas, to modern fuels, such as kerosene), and corrected (as in the case of taxing high-sulphur charcoal briquettes to encourage a shift to low-sulphur briquettes). Thus, knowledge needs to be developed and disseminated about the types and levels of energy-related needs and how best to meet them via market and non-market strategies.

Ecology and energy

Markets have failed so far to protect the earth's ecology.[8] Of all the symptoms of unsustainability in energy use, none may be more telling than the seemingly irreversible ecological impacts of energy use. It is impossible to eliminate all such impacts, but it is not impossible to keep impacts within the limits of ecological integrity. The global environmental impacts of modern energy use were first clearly recognized during the "environmental revolution" of the 1960s and 1970s. A complete rethinking of the relationship between energy use and ecological issues ensued, and led to such ideas as the "soft" energy path,[9] enhancing energy efficiency through approaches such as demand-side management,[10] and working toward a solar-based society. It is now widely accepted, if not realized in practice, that concerns about damage to ecological integrity must be considered in energy market decisions. Some of the threats to ecological integrity posed by fuel extraction, transformation, and use include global climate change, acid deposition, marine pollution, urban air pollution, water pollution, solid waste disposal, loss of biodiversity, displacement of animal/human populations, nuclear waste disposal, and nuclear weapons' proliferation. Generation and application of knowledge is a critical prerequisite for steering energy markets in the direction of ecological sustainability.

International regulation

International energy markets with no external regulation can be inefficient, environmentally destructive, and unsustainable. Regulation, if properly constructed, can provide a framework within which market forces are guided toward sustainability. The world is moving into an era of increased international regulation of energy-related sectors of the economy. For example, binding targets and timetables to reduce greenhouse gas emissions were agreed upon at the Third Conference of Parties (COP-3) of the Climate Change Convention in Kyoto, Japan, in December 1997. Also, increased global trade and the proliferation of environmental standards in different countries is forcing consideration of mechanisms like the ISO 14000 environmental certification process to ensure a level economic playing field in energy and other markets. And again, unsavoury corporate practices by some energy companies in remote areas, as well as the growing power of some multinational energy companies, are attracting regulatory attention. International regulation places a premium on accurate information and integrated knowledge.

National income accounts

Energy markets and market decisions are often significantly influenced by macroeconomic information such as is contained in national income accounts. However, the typical statistics on gross national product (GNP) and gross domestic product (GDP), as well as other macroeconomic parameters that are used to benchmark the health and wealth of an economy, do not usually measure changes in the human and environmental resource base upon which an economy is built. This deficiency can, for example, give the impression that a nation's economy is growing at a healthy rate, when in fact it is built largely upon depletion of human and environmental resources. Or it can give the impression that an economy is growing slowly when in fact it is successfully pursing socially and environmentally sustainable development. MacNeill, Winsemius, and Yakushiji (1991, 45) state the matter simply: "The introduction of indicators and appropriate revision of national accounting systems may be all that is required to correct public-sector economic decisions [which are lacking in a sustainability consciousness] in the long term, given the dominant focus of most governments on managing economic growth." The creation of "green" national income accounts can contribute to giving correct "sustainability signals" to energy markets. Green national income accounts require generation of substantial quantities of sustainability knowledge, such as sustainability indicators.

Full-cost pricing

The most important sustainability incentive in the energy sector is signalled through market prices. Full-cost pricing is the principle that producers must bear the full cost of all social and environmental damage incurred in producing and delivering a product above some minimum threshold. According to Tietenberg (1991, 214), "[i]mplementing the full cost principle would end the implicit subsidy that all polluting activities have received since the beginning of time." Full-cost pricing is similar to the "polluter pays" principle. The full-cost principle in the energy sector, as in other sectors, is knowledge intensive. It demands that the social and environmental costs of energy-related activities be made explicit, and that inappropriate subsidies are eliminated. The principle implies the imposition of "green" taxes.

"Sustainability" taxes

Even correcting unsustainable distortions in energy markets cannot take into account all external costs associated with energy production, transmission, and use. One way to correct prices is through "sustainability" taxes. Numerous taxes have been proposed and/or implemented. These include taxes on sulphur dioxide and carbon dioxide emissions, various other emission taxes, and taxes related to energy consumption levels. Emission taxes, for instance, force all polluters to face the same per-unit tax on emissions, and, if effectively employed, can result in a cost-effective (and possibly even efficient) allocation of pollution control responsibility. This outcome cannot be attained with the traditional command-and-control approach to regulation. A disadvantage of such taxes is that they put a financial burden on some firms, especially smaller firms, to the extent that they may go out of business. Similar to sustainability taxes are transferable permits or quotas schemes, such as those used in the sulphur dioxide emissions trading system enacted under the 1990 US Clean Air Act. All such tax and tax-related schemes demand high levels of information and knowledge input.

Energy planning and energy marketing

Energy planning is a tool to coordinate production and consumption of energy, and can be used either to encourage creation of new energy markets or to make current markets more sustainable. There must be a balance between free operation of markets and planning in the energy sector, and sustainability needs to become the byword in energy planning. One example of a sustainable energy-oriented planning tool is integrated resource planning (IRP). It goes without saying that knowledge plays a major role in such planning. Information on national and subnational patterns of energy supply and demand, energy resources and reserves, and technical and operating aspects of existing energy infrastructure, available in a transparent, consistent format, helps to identify opportunities for improvement of energy market operation. An example of a supplier of this type of information is ESource.[11]

Product life-cycle accounting

Energy markets are often deficient in the provision of sustainability information to large manufacturers. Sustainable energy markets require information that large manufacturers can use to make their production of goods sustainable. A promising approach for fusing economic efficiency with sustainability is product life-cycle accounting. Basically, this approach involves scrutinizing all production processes in an integrated fashion so as to identify opportunities to minimize wastes of energy and material, and in the process cut costs and pollutant emissions. Several national and multinational agencies have programmes to develop and encourage these sorts of economic/environmental "cradle-to-grave" accounting practices in industry. Needless to say, such accounting requires intense collection and organization of information and knowledge.

Sustainability information for the large consumer

Energy markets are often deficient in the provision of sustainability information to large consumers. Information on the technical (energy efficiency), environmental (pollutant emissions), and economic performance (capital and operating costs) of candidate energy technologies can help decision-makers in large organizations choose which energy supply options are suitable from a sustainability perspective. These types of data are available from equipment suppliers, regulatory agencies, and other non-governmental and institutional groups. Key issues in providing and using these data include data management, optimum usability for particular audiences, data "truthing" (making sure, for example, that manufacturers' claims are not exaggerated), and making sure that potential users are aware of information resources.

Sustainability information for the small consumer

Energy markets are often deficient in the provision of sustainability information to small consumers. Demand-side information to energy consumers (individuals, households, firms, and institutions) must be provided in order that they can make appropriate choices. Only if energy consumers have adequate information on the social and environmental ramifications of their choices of which fuels and energy-using devices to use can the promise of energy market efficiency and sustainability be fulfilled. Ways to provide environmental information to consumers include eco-labelling, "green pricing" of renewable electricity (a market-based technique for providing consumers with environmental information on their electricity bills), and information on the energy/environmental performance of a product, such as energy consumption rating systems for given types of appliances (refrigerators and air conditioners, for example).

Knowledge and sustainability in the Energy Market

Having surveyed some of the areas where energy markets succeed and fail in relation to the vision of sustainability, the chapter now turns to an examination of the role of knowledge in capitalizing on the successes and correcting the failures.

Knowledge and markets

The key question here is "How can knowledge related to sustainability be produced and incorporated into both public and private sector decision-making in ways that serve to configure, constrain, cajole, and coordinate market forces in the energy sector in the direction of a sustainable future?" Before plunging into this question, an understanding is needed of some of the elementary principles of the functioning (and "disfunctioning") of markets in relation to knowledge.

Hayek (1945, 520) succinctly stated the economic problem of society as:

not merely a problem of how to allocate "given" resources – if "given" is taken to mean given to a single mind which deliberately solves the problem set by these "data." It is rather a problem of how to secure the best use of resources known to any of the members of society for ends whose relative importance only these individuals know. Or, to put it briefly, it is the problem of the utilization of knowledge not given to anyone in its totality.

Thus, the economic problem of society is at root a problem of knowledge. There is no one "supermind" in society that can know the total resource base and how best to use it. Thus, how do resources get valued and distributed? The free market system solves this problem by capitalizing on the fact that the two end points in economic exchange – producers and consumers – know best the terms of exchange that suit their capabilities and preferences, although each possesses only scattered and fragmentary knowledge about the other. The ragged set of knowledge known to producer and consumer meets in a decentralized decision-making forum – the marketplace – and by equilibrating supply and demand via prices results in an orderly system for "efficient" allocation of scarce resources. The catch with current knowledge that informs the marketplace, though, is that it is deficient in one major respect – it is knowledge lacking in substantial sustainability content. This can be traced to the nature of the modern market system.

The modern market system is a product of the transition from feudalism to capitalism that occurred in Europe beginning around the thirteenth century, and is fundamentally based on the "commodification" of resources such as land and labour. Polanyi (1957) called the emergence of the modern market (or Market, as he designated it), the "Great Transformation." It transformed the ways in which goods were produced, in that it vastly expanded the range of commodities that could be traded in the marketplace. Under the system of commodification born of the Great Transformation, the information (or knowledge) content of a commodity came to be quintessentially expressed in its price. It also came to be expressed in the institutional structures that defined what constituted a commodity.

However, the prices and institutions of the modern market system do not reflect even the full range of existing knowledge, let alone generate the information needed to achieve sustainability. There are spheres in which markets do not function well. The most common way of terming the dysfunctional aspects of markets is as "market failures." Some market failures were discussed earlier. One of the most common market failures is "externalities." An externality implies that there is knowledge "external" to that which is contained in a commodity's price and which has been left out in figuring the price. For the purposes of this chapter, sustainability knowledge is the key knowledge left out. But what is sustainability knowledge? And how can it be injected into the marketplace?

Sustainability knowledge and the Energy Market

To implement the vision of sustainable energy using market forces requires three more-or-less distinct sets of knowledge – knowledge related to developing energy markets, making energy markets more efficient, and making energy markets sustainable. These constitute what might be called a "knowledge" ladder to sustainable energy.

The first step in the ladder is generating, disseminating, and applying knowledge to create energy markets which would best serve the goal of sustainability. "Market creation knowledge" can be employed in those countries, especially developing countries, which do not now have energy markets or which have only embryonic markets. For example, such knowledge may be deployed to set up a stock market in which stocks in energy service companies can be traded.

The second step in the ladder is generating, disseminating, and applying knowledge to make energy markets more efficient in those countries that already possess a well-functioning market system. "Market efficiency knowledge" can be employed, for instance, to deregulate energy markets. The state of California in the United States is engaged in an experiment to deregulate the electric utility industry to make it more efficient and possibly more sustainable.

The third step in the ladder is generating, disseminating, and applying knowledge to infuse energy markets with specific sustainability goals. For example, establishing national carbon dioxide emission ceilings may help stabilize the earth's climate.

One form of knowledge that cuts across all three knowledge sets is expert knowledge. Experts and expert knowledge have a key role to play in achieving a sustainable energy future. Experts include physical scientists, social scientists, policy analysts, planners, economists, medical doctors, lawyers, engineers, etc. One grouping of experts which is particularly important to achieving sustainability is known as epistemic communities.

Epistemic communities[12]

Epistemic (related to knowledge) communities are defined as groups of experts who generate policy-oriented expert knowledge relevant to a given issue area. These communities are bonded by common criteria as to what constitutes valid knowledge (for instance, the scientific method), and a common policy project (for instance, investigating global coral reef decline). Thus, they are collectives or networks of credentialled experts who engage in a policy mission. They are not merely engaged in "research," but research with a direct policy purpose. Epistemic communities are almost invariably multidisciplinary. Their level of operation may be local, national, international, or global. Their common policy project may be acid deposition in East Asia, clean coal technology in the United States, rural electrification in developing countries, or marine pollution in the Mediterranean. The essential function of epistemic communities is to generate policy-relevant knowledge on a select problem, which means they synthesize, summarize, interpret, and translate esoteric forms of technical knowledge into forms understood by policy-makers and lay people. The primary purpose of epistemic communities in the political world is to feed knowledge into the public sector to inform, among other things, decisions related to the marketplace. The relationship between epistemic communities, energy markets, and public sector governance institutions is illustrated in Figure 10.2.

Examples of energy-related epistemic communities include the Intergovernmental Panel on Climate Change (IPCC), the scientists associated with the Convention on Long-range Transboundary Air Pollution (LRTAP), and the economic and legal specialists who designed the sulphur dioxide emissions trading scheme in the 1990 US Clean Air Act. Epistemic communities exist for all three energy-market-related sets of knowledge in the knowledge ladder to energy sustainability. It is thus possible to generate a matrix of energy-sector-related epistemic communities classified in terms of knowledge type (market development, market efficiency, and market sustainability) and scale of operation (local, national, regional, global). This matrix is illustrated in Figure 10.3. One can imagine that each cell of Figure 10.3 contains the image portrayed in Figure 10.2, and that there are a vast range and number of epistemic communities parlaying knowledge between a wide variety of public and private sector institutions and actors.

To illustrate the power of epistemic communities to steer energy markets towards a sustainable path, three examples of them in action are now discussed.

The first example falls in the "regional scale/market sustainability knowledge" matrix cell, and relates to the development of the "critical-loads" approach to the acid deposition (acid rain) problem in Europe. Energy markets in Europe up until the mid-1980s did not account in any significant manner for the externalities associated with the emission of acidic substances due to fossil fuel combustion. The technique that a

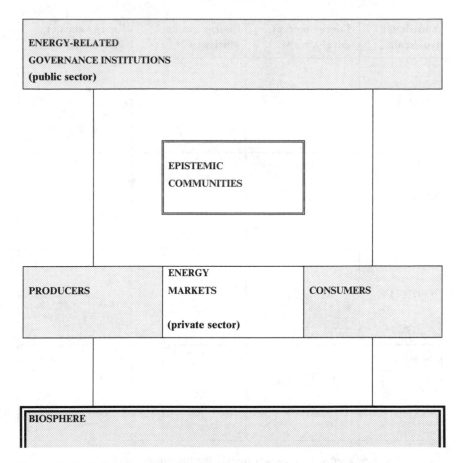

Figure 10.2. Epistemic communities, energy markets, and public sector governance institutions

European epistemic community of scientists devised to remedy this deficiency was a "sustainable energy indicator" called a critical load.[13]

Critical loads are but one example of a sustainable energy indicator. Such indicators have a major role to play in achieving energy sustainability. They are practical pointers, criteria, measures, standards, guidelines, or yardsticks that can be used to define and judge progress toward the sustainable energy vision. There are many types of indicators, including economic indicators such as local and national energy efficiencies per unit of economic output; social indicators such as levels of rural electrification; and environmental indicators such as carbon dioxide concentrations in the atmosphere. Because of the nature of the market system,

Knowledge type/scale	Energy market development	Energy market efficiency	Energy market substainability
GLOBAL			
REGIONAL			
NATIONAL			
LOCAL			

Figure 10.3. Knowledge and market matrix for the energy sector

it is imperative that a significant collection of quantitative sustainable energy indicators be developed. As has already been stated, the market is fundamentally based on the quantitative principle of commodification in which commodity transactions are mediated by "price" – a negotiated but nevertheless quantitative measure of consumer utility and producer profit. Thus, to mould itself to market dynamics, quantitative measures of energy sustainability must be generated. Much effort is already being expended in this direction. Organizations such as UNEP (in their Earth-watch programme), the World Resources Institute (in its annual *World Resources* publication), and the Worldwatch Institute (in its annual *State of the World and Vital Signs* series) are engaged in broad definition of sustainability criteria.

Science has assumed a role as arbiter of criteria of ecological sustainability, and epistemic communities have become formulators of such criteria. The formulation of the critical-loads approach by a European epistemic community associated with the acid deposition problem is evidence of this. A community of scientists related to the acid deposition problem in Europe first formed soon after the discovery of the problem in 1968. It expanded after the UN Conference on the Human Environment, or Stockholm Conference, in 1972, and was highly influential in the efforts leading to the signing of the Convention on Long-range Transboundary Air Pollution in 1979. For years the European acid deposition epistemic community cast about for an ecological sustainability criteria related to acid deposition that could be used by governments in making energy policy decisions. Although the idea of critical loads was first hit upon in Canada in the mid-1980s, it was the Europeans who seized upon it and crafted it into a policy tool. They laboured for almost a decade before it was finally accepted and formally used for the first time in the 1994 Oslo Sulphur Dioxide Protocol to the LRTAP. Since this time scientifically determined "critical loads" have become the normative base for international decision-making on the acid deposition issue in the region. Critical loads are not used to micromanage energy decisions in Europe. Instead, they provide an ecologically based tolerance of ecosystems to acidic pollutant inputs. It is left to the market to figure out how best to stay under the given tolerance level. Thus, critical loads have firmly situated themselves as an overarching framework within which regional and national energy policy decisions are made in Europe.

A second example of the power of epistemic communities to steer energy markets toward sustainability falls in the "national scale/market development knowledge" matrix cell of Figure 10.3, and relates to creation of markets for energy efficiency technologies in China. The Beijing Energy Efficiency Centre (BECon) was established in 1993 in a cooperative agreement between Chinese officials and the US Department of Energy, US Environmental Protection Agency, and the WWF. Among BECon's many activities is creating markets in China for "green lighting" technologies. An international epistemic community of green lighting experts, whose common policy objective is to generate policy-relevant knowledge for the Chinese government related to energy-efficient lighting, was instrumental in persuading the Chinese government to authorize in its Ninth Five-Year Plan a China Green Lighting Programme. The programme seeks, among other things, to create markets for energy-efficient lighting products. A key to creating such markets is technology transfer.

Technology transfer is a crucial element of the development of energy markets in developing countries. The transfer of technologies to increase energy (and economic) efficiency, reduce pollution and other environmental impacts, and generally support sustainable economic development has been touted as one way that industrialized and developing countries, working together, can address imperfections in global energy markets. Martin Bell, however, has pointed out that simply transferring technologies (hardware) is not enough (Hayes 1993). In addition to the knowledge of how to build and operate technologies, technology transfer should also provide the background knowledge, training, and organizational structure that will allow local personnel to learn about, work with, adapt, and upgrade technologies to fit local conditions better and to press worthwhile technologies into broader local use. Without this process of internalizing both technological "know-how" and "know-why," technology transfer is unlikely to reach its full potential. It is in the transfer of knowledge – know-how and know-why – that epistemic communities have a central role to play in the creation of markets. They help create the knowledge base that is essential for new markets to function.

The international "China green lighting" epistemic community consisting primarily of Chinese, US, and European experts has been a sparkplug for facilitating the transfer of knowledge (in addition to hardware) in the China Green Lighting Programme. Knowledge is transferred primarily through education and training of large-scale buyers, such as operators of buildings and public facilities, in the existence and use of green lighting. The community, in addition to engaging in education and training, has also been instrumental in holding an international symposium in China on green lighting technologies and applications, establishing a China Green Lights Centre in Beijing which displays products, organizes demonstration projects, and provides guidance on major investments made by the Chinese government in the lighting manufacturing sector. In sum, the epistemic community is helping establish markets in environmentally friendly and energy-efficient lighting products in China.

The third example of the power of epistemic communities to steer energy markets toward sustainability falls in the "local scale/market efficiency" matrix cell, and relates to deregulation of the electric utility industry in California in the United States. In the quest for removing utility monopolies in the United States, electric utilities are the latest deregulation experiment, following the removal of regulatory barriers in the telecommunications and natural gas industries. California embarked in January 1998 on a landmark experiment that will allow companies to compete to sell electricity to residential and business customers. Arguably, a freer (or less monopolistic) market for electricity will provide more choices (among them more "green" choices) and help cut prices. An epistemic community consisting primarily of economists, planners, and computer programmers drawn nationwide from academic institutions, government, and business has been at the centre of the deregulation experiment. The community is providing policy-relevant knowledge to state-level and federal-level policy-makers (for instance, state legislators, Congressional representatives, the California Public Utilities Commission, the Federal Energy Regulatory Commission, and the Department of Energy). It has been responsible for generating ideas such as the independent system operator (ISO), and the power exchange (PX). The ISO functions like an air traffic controller for energy and operates the state's transmission system. The PX acts as a spot market for electricity. The ISO and PX are independent of the utilities and thereby prevent a monopoly. The complex deregulation experiment in California is knowledge intensive, not hardware intensive, and the epistemic community has provided the key knowledge to bring it to fruition.

These three examples of energy-related epistemic communities demonstrate the critical role of experts and expert knowledge in guiding energy markets toward the vision of sustainable energy. Many other examples could be given. Markets to a degree solve a coordination problem; coordination of information on preferences and capabilities between the consumer and producer. Sustainable energy markets will have to solve another coordination problem; coordination of the welter of scattered epistemic communities whose expert knowledge is essential to sustainability. This expert knowledge coordination problem will be addressed in the concluding section.

Conclusion – The United Nations and epistemic communities

Energy, environment, and markets: the thread that can tie all these components together in the fabric of civilization in the twenty-first century is the vision of sustainability and its realization through knowledge used to guide and reconstitute energy markets. Sustainable energy knowledge is a fundamental tool for resolving multiple energy dilemmas in both developed and developing countries, and for addressing these energy dilemmas in the context of a highly complex, interdependent, and synergistically dynamic Energy Market.

A substantially greater effort is justified in the energy sector to design consciously interrelated, international, interorganizational, and interdisciplinary expert knowledge systems related to sustainability. A chief component of such knowledge systems is epistemic communities. Epistemic communities need to be created, coordinated, and institutionalized in both the public and private sectors. Knowledge is both a private and a public good. As a public good, the benefits of investing in knowledge generation and management cannot be fully captured by the private sector. Hence, private entities such as consumers or firms tend to under-invest in knowledge, particularly sustainability knowledge. Without public investment in sustainability knowledge and policy instruments to incorporate such knowledge into the formulation of market decisions, markets cannot be made sustainable.[14] Institutionalization of epistemic communities has been done in the case of the IPCC associated with the Global Climate Change Convention, and the working groups and task forces of the LRTAP, for instance.

The United Nations has a valuable role to play in catalysing the creation, coordination, and institutionalization of epistemic communities. The United Nations can, for example, connect and coordinate multiple and scattered epistemic communities that operate in each of the cells in Figure 10.3. One mechanism for coordination is to construct a loose global network of sustainable energy epistemic communities linked via the Internet by "information appliances" (PCs, network PCs, Web TVs, cellular phones, satellite technology, etc.). Modern information technology has the potential for effectively coordinating multiple epistemic communities.

Some suggested forms of UN support for epistemic community creation, coordination, and institutionalization are provided below. In many cases, the United Nations is uniquely qualified to provide the suggested support.

Ongoing support for research, analysis, and scholarship

The United Nations should provide continuing support for research and scholarship on energy market development, efficiency, and sustainability. In other words, the United Nations needs to continue funding the basic work of epistemic communities – research, analysis, and scholarship.

Support for building institutional capacity for epistemic community activities

UN support for knowledge capacity-building should be ongoing in each nation, but should stress development, within each country, of a stable core of sufficient expertise (located, for example, in universities or research institutes) to allow the perpetuation of human infrastructure. In general, high levels of education are necessary for all peoples to be able to participate in the sustainability and sustainable energy debates.

Support for regional coordination of epistemic communities

The United Nations should support programmes that bring together experts from nearby countries to work together to develop and support, for example, consistent responses to market forces, environmental monitoring networks, coordinated environmental policies, and coordinated medium- and long-range evaluation of national energy paths and scenarios,[15] as well as to share information on regional energy infrastructure, resources, and plans.

Support for global information resources

Global databases and knowledge bases need to be constructed. For instance, a number of databases of energy technologies, vendors, and other energy-related documents are available around the world, but a single source of comprehensive but usable, up-to-date, unbiased, and widely available information on the technical, economic, and environmental performance of a full range of energy sector measures and technologies is still lacking. The United Nations could help to support the compilation and dissemination of such knowledge bases and databases.

In conclusion, institutionalized and coordinated networks of epistemic communities, together with associated comprehensively designed knowledge systems, need to be more fully integrated into energy markets. The fusion of networks of epistemic communities with energy markets will lead to what the authors call "knowledgeable (energy) markets." The watchword of knowledgeable energy markets will be sustainability, not blind growth. The United Nations serves as a major catalyst for creating knowledgeable energy markets.

Notes

1. The World Commission on Environment and Development defined sustainability (or sustainable development) as: "development that meets the needs of the present without compromising the ability of future generations to meet their own needs" (WCED 1987, 43). The difficulty in reaching a consensus definition of sustainability, though, is demonstrated by the fact that one search of sustainable development definitions produced a list of 61 (Pezzey 1989).
2. The strong relationship between economic growth and energy use in both developed and developing countries is demonstrated by the almost linear relationship in the period from 1960 to 1990 between growth of worldwide electricity use and total global GDP; see Starr (1993).
3. One exajoule is equal to 10^{18} joules, or one billion gigajoules. An exajoule is equivalent to approximately 164 million barrels of oil, 24 million tonnes of oil, or 34 million tonnes of coal.
4. These data are from the British Petroleum (BP) website (www.bp.com), spreadsheet file "fuelcons.wks," visited on 13 August 1996. In this compilation the authors convert nuclear electricity generation to primary energy based on a direct conversion of electricity output to energy units, which is consistent with the treatment of hydroelectric energy but is different than the method used by BP.

5. Growth of energy use in developing regions is even more robust – 4.6 per cent per year from 1995 to 2015 – in the USDOE/EIA's "High Economic Growth" scenario.
6. See, for instance, IPCC (1992) and Fujime (1996).
7. Advocates of the basic-human-needs approach to development include Ghai et al. (1977) and Streeten (1981). In the area of energy and basic human needs one group of prominent advocates is Goldemberg et al. (1987).
8. Many excellent works discuss the major environmental impacts of energy use; see for example Ehrlich, Ehrlich, and Holdren (1977), Lazarus et al. (1995), and IPCC (1996a; 1996b; 1996c).
9. For example, see Lovins (1977).
10. For example, see Goldemberg et al. (1987).
11. ESource is a for-profit subsidiary of the Rocky Mountain Institute. It provides detailed, unbiased information to organizations on end-use technologies and applications. See http://www.esource.com.
12. See, for instance, Haas (1992; 1997).
13. The definition of a critical load adopted by the Executive Body of the LRTAP in 1988 is "a quantitative estimate of an exposure to one or more pollutants below which significantly harmful effects on specified sensitive elements of the environment do not occur according to present knowledge." An adjunct concept, "critical level," relates to ambient air concentrations of pollutants, not deposition values, and is defined as "concentrations of pollutants in the atmosphere above which direct adverse effects upon receptors, such as plants, ecosystems or materials, may occur according to present knowledge."
14. See Zarsky's chapter in this volume.
15. Some of the reasons for regional coordination in assembling and evaluating energy paths and scenarios include making more efficient use of regional resources, protecting regional environmental "commons," promoting trust and transparency in energy and environmental policy between countries, and learning from each other about different potential energy paths and options.

REFERENCES

Ehrlich, P. R., A. H. Ehrlich, and J. P. Holdren. 1977. *Ecoscience*. San Francisco: W. H. Freeman.

Fujime, K. 1996. "Long-Term Energy Supply/Demand Outlook for Asia APEC Nations." Bimonthly Report No. 137. Tokyo: Institute of Energy Economics.

Ghai, D. P., A. R. Khan, E. H. L. Lee, and T. Alfthan. 1977. *The Basic Needs Approach to Development*. Geneva: International Labour Organization.

Goldemberg, J., T. B. Johansson, A. K. N. Reddy, and R. H. Williams. 1987. *Energy for a Sustainable World*. Washington: World Resources Institute.

Haas, P. M. 1992. "Epistemic Communities and International Policy Coordination." *International Organization* 46(1): 1–35.

Haas, P. M, ed. 1997. *Knowledge, Power, and International Policy Coordination*. Columbia: University of South Carolina Press.

Hayek, F. A. 1945. "The Use of Knowledge in Society." *American Economic Review* 45(4): 519–530.

Hayes, P. 1993. "Constructing a Global Greenhouse Regime." In *The Global Greenhouse Regime: Who Pays?* eds P. Hayes and K. Smith. Tokyo: UNU Press.

IPCC (Intergovernmental Panel on Climate Change). 1992. *Emissions Scenarios for the IPCC, An Update*, Working Group 1 Report. Geneva: IPCC.

IPCC (Intergovernmental Panel on Climate Change). 1996a. *Climate Change 1995: The Science of Climate Change, Contribution of Working Group I to the Second Assessment Report of the Intergovernmental Panel on Climate Change.* New York: Cambridge University Press.

IPCC (Intergovernmental Panel on Climate Change). 1996b. *Climate Change 1995: Impacts, Adaptations, and Mitigation of Climate Change: Scientific-Technical Analyses, Contribution of Working Group II to the Second Assessment Report of the Intergovernmental Panel on Climate Change.* New York: Cambridge University Press.

IPCC (Intergovernmental Panel on Climate Change). 1996c. *Climate Change 1995: Economic and Social Dimensions of Climate Change, Contribution of Working Group III to the Second Assessment Report of the Intergovernmental Panel on Climate Change.* New York: Cambridge University Press.

Lazarus, M., D. Von Hippel, D. Hill, and R. Margolis. 1995. *A Guide to Environmental Analysis for Energy Planners.* Stockholm Environment Institute–Boston (SEI-B) Report. Boston: SEI-B.

Lovins, A. B. 1977. *Soft Energy Paths: Toward a Durable Peace.* Cambridge, MA: Ballinger Books.

MacNeill, J., P. Winsemius, and T. Yakushiji. 1991. *Beyond Interdependence: The Meshing of the World's Economy and the Earth's Ecology.* New York: Oxford University Press.

Pezzey, J. 1989. *Economic Analysis of Sustainable Growth and Sustainable Development*, Working Paper No. 15. Washington: World Bank Environmental Department.

Polanyi, K. 1957. *The Great Transformation: Political and Economic Origins of our Time.* Boston: Beacon Press.

Starr, C. 1993. "Global Energy and Electricity Futures." *Energy* 18(3): 225–237.

Streeten, P. 1981. *First Things First: Meeting Basic Needs in Developing Countries.* New York: Oxford University Press.

Tietenberg, T. H. 1991. "Managing the Transition: The Potential Role for Economic Policies." In *Preserving the Global Environment: The Challenge of Shared Leadership*, ed. J. T. Mathews. New York: W. W. Norton.

USDOE/EIA (US Department of Energy, Energy Information Administration). 1997. *International Energy Outlook, 1997*, Report No. DOE/EIA-0484(97). Washington: USDOE.

WCED (World Commission for Environment and Development). 1987. *Our Common Future.* Oxford: Oxford University Press.

11

Coping with the global fresh water dilemma: The state, market forces, and global governance

Peter H. Gleick

Over the past hundred years, growing populations and growing economic development have led to the need to regularize and tame the highly variable hydrologic cycle. The goals have been to reduce the impacts on humans of droughts and floods, to move water from water-rich areas to arid regions, to capture water in wet periods for use in dry periods, and to create the institutions necessary for addressing water-related problems. Enormous progress has been made in harnessing water resources to meet human needs. But this progress has come at a high economic and environmental price, and there still remain serious unmet needs.

Despite the billions of dollars spent on water supply systems worldwide, we are failing to keep up with the basic needs of much of the world's population. Others have documented the state of the world's fresh water resources and the problems caused by underuse, overuse, or misuse of water (Gleick 1993; 1998; Postel 1993; Clarke 1991; UNCNR 1996). The world faces many serious water problems. Among the greatest concerns are the inability to provide basic clean drinking water and sanitation services to billions of people, the risk that food production will fail to grow as fast as global population because of insufficient or inadequate water availability or quality, the possibility of inter-state or intrastate conflict over shared water resources, and the likelihood that global climatic changes will significantly affect water supply, demand, and quality in unpredictable ways.

The paradigm of development that has guided water resources planning and management during the twentieth century needs to be rethought in the light of these problems. Discussions about the need to develop new principles for addressing fresh water problems began 20 years ago at the ground-breaking conference on water at Mar del Plata, Argentina, and they have been further developed and refined at several important meetings since that time. Significant advances were made at the 1992 Dublin Conference in preparation for the Earth Summit in Rio de Janeiro. These principles were further discussed in the recent Comprehensive Assessment of the Freshwater Resources of the World (UNCFA 1997; Lundkvist and Gleick 1997).

One of those principles is that water must be considered an economic good. By giving water a price, and by better understanding the total (economic and non-monetary) costs of water supply and demand, decisions about investments and water policies can, theoretically, become more rational. In reality, however, including economic principles in water decision-making is necessary but not sufficient, and many water-related problems cannot be solved in this way. This chapter summarizes and elaborates on the major water issues facing the world and offers principles related to international and national governance and the role of market and non-market forces relevant for guiding water decisions into the next century.

Projections of future supply and demand

There is no such thing as a global water problem – all problems manifest themselves on smaller scales. For example, at the global average level, there is sufficient water to meet the needs and wants of every human being. At the continental level, per capita water availability still seems more than adequate, though large regional disparities appear. In Europe, each million cubic metres of water available per year is "shared" by over 150 people, on the average, while in South America only 25 people must share that much water (see Table 11.1).

At the national level, the differences are even more marked, with variations of several orders of magnitude. For example, one of the richest countries in Europe, measured by water availability, is Norway, with 10 persons per million cubic metres per year. At the other extreme is Turkey with nearly 1,000 persons per million cubic metres per year. Yet Turkey, compared to some of its Middle East neighbours, could be considered water rich (Gleick 1993; 1998; Engelman and LeRoy 1993; World Resources Institute 1996; Kelman 1996). And within countries, still larger variations in water availability, water distribution, water quality, and water use occur.

Table 11.1 Availability of fresh water by continent

Continent	Area (10^3 km^2)	Population (millions)	Runoff (km^3/year)	Availability (people/10^6 m^3/year)	Availability (m^3/person/day)
Europe	10,500	498	3,210	152	18
Asia	43,475	3,108	14,410	211	13
Africa	30,120	648	4,570	144	19
North and Central America	24,200	426	8,200	52	53
South America	17,800	297	11,760	25	108
Oceania	8,950	26	2,388	11	252
Total	135,045	5,003	44,540	114	24

Source: Shiklomanov 1993

Growing scarcity at the regional and local levels indicates imbalances between overall availability and growth in need and demand. These imbalances will have implications far outside the areas under stress. An important example is the issue of food production. If more and more countries do not have sufficient amounts of water to grow the food that they need, the deficit must be covered from somewhere else. And there must be arrangements, agreements, and institutions capable of creating a surplus big enough to cover the growing regional and local deficits, providing logistical capacity and procedures for the actual transfer of food and other essentials from surplus to deficit regions, and guaranteeing a political commitment to transfer food to deficit areas and the poor, even if people in these areas do not have the means to provide their own supply.

If these three preconditions are not at hand or met, the likely result in a growing number of areas is hunger and starvation, political and social instability, tension and conflict, serious ecological disruptions, and the mass exodus of people from depressed regions. In any case, the growing dependence on imports of food may soon begin to put upward pressure on market prices of many staples. Already now there are signs of a reverse in the trend of decreasing or stable food prices as compared to other commodities in international trade. Whether or not these trends continue depends in part on how regional and local water problems are addressed. Below, four critical water issues are discussed in more detail.

Unmet needs: Critical problems in water resources supply and demand

Water, basic needs, and human health

The ugly reality is that billions of people around the globe lack access to the most fundamental foundation of a decent civilized world: basic sanitation services and clean drinking water. As Akhtar Khan said, "Access to safe water and adequate sanitation is the foundation of development. For when you have a medieval level of sanitation, you have a medieval level of disease, and no country can advance without a healthy population" (Khan 1997, 5). For nearly 3 billion people, access to a sanitation system comparable to that of ancient Rome would be a significant improvement in their quality of life.

The failure to provide basic sanitation services and clean water to so many people is taking a serious toll on human health. In many developing countries, cholera, pneumonic and bubonic plague, dysentery, and other water-related diseases are on the upswing. Nearly 250 million cases are reported every year, with between 5 million and 10 million deaths. Diarrhoeal diseases leave millions of children underweight, mentally or physically handicapped, and vulnerable to other diseases. Yet the world is falling further and further behind in the efforts to provide these basic services. Between 1990 and 1997, an additional 300 million people were added to the rolls of those unserved by adequate sanitation services, a clear indication that the world community is failing to meet the most basic of needs.

In 1980, the United Nations launched the International Drinking Water Supply and Sanitation Decade, with the goal of providing clean drinking water and sanitation services to those without them. At that time, the UN estimated that 1.7 billion people did not have access to adequate sanitation services. Ten years later, at the end of the decade and after enormous effort, expense, and progress, 750 million of these underserved people had received new sanitation services, albeit at a pretty minimal level. During that same period, however, the population needing these services grew by almost exactly the same amount: 750 million people. In other words, population growth entirely wiped out the progress achieved in this area, and the official estimate in 1990 was that 1.75 billion people were still without access to adequate sanitation services. Unfortunately, the situation was even worse than that. Because of better data, more complete surveys, and population growth, current estimates are that more than 2.8 billion people are now without adequate sanitation services – half the world's population (Gleick 1998).

According to the United Nations there are also 1 billion people without access to clean drinking water, including nearly half of the population of Africa. Moreover, these global numbers hide some ugly regional problems. For example, the total populations in urban areas needing both clean water and sanitation grew over the decade, reflecting the massive and continuing migration to large urban centres in developing countries and the inability to provide necessary services there.

What are the implications of this inability to provide these services? Directly associated with poor sanitation services and unclean drinking water are the severe waterborne diseases: malaria, dysentery, cholera, and the many parasitic diseases found in Africa and Asia, such as schistosomiasis and guinea worm. Cholera is a good example. In all the years of the century up to 1990, there were rarely more than 100,000 cases of cholera reported annually, and usually between 30,000 and 70,000 cases a year. None of these was in Latin America, which had been free of cholera for over 100 years. In 1991, cholera exploded in the region: over 390,000 new cases were reported in 14 countries there, directly attributable to the failure to provide clean drinking water and adequate sanitation services. That same year there were over 590,000 cases worldwide, including over

100,000 cases in Africa alone, and tens of thousands caused by a new strain of epidemic cholera in Asia (Gleick 1998).

Food and water

The water "crisis," as described in the recent summary of the Committee on Natural Resources of the UN Economic and Social Council (UNCNR 1996), also includes serious concern over global and regional food security and sufficiency. Despite the massive development of irrigation infrastructure worldwide, nearly 1 billion people are still considered undernourished by the UN FAO, and there remain serious worries about the ability of the world community to meet future needs as well. In particular, finite water supplies and escalating demands, together with degradation of soil conditions and water quality, are contributing to concerns that society will fall further behind in the race to feed the earth's growing populations.

The 1992 Dublin Conference acknowledged the importance of food security concerns and suggested alternative approaches to ensure that future food goals are met:

Achieving food security is a high priority in many countries, and agriculture must not only provide food for rising populations, but also save water for other uses. The challenge is to develop and apply water-saving technology and management methods, and, through capacity building, enable communities to introduce institutions and incentives for the rural population to adopt new approaches, for both rainfed and irrigated agriculture (ICWE 1992).

In September 1997, a special session on food security at the Ninth World Water Congress in Montreal released a position statement that read in part:

The magnitude of the problem is enormous. Today some one billion people in the world do not have access to enough food. It now appears that half of the world's population by the year 2025 will live in water scarce regions, where food self sufficiency will be extremely difficult to achieve. A substantial food gap seems unavoidable in these regions ... Water tables are falling and rivers are running dry in many food-producing regions ... Despite uncertainties in both estimates of available fresh water due to deficiencies in global hydrological data, and in estimates of future water needs for food production, we know enough to be deeply concerned. Action is needed now (IWRA 1997).

The ultimate goal must be to grow sufficient food to meet the world's needs, somewhere, and to deliver that food where it is needed. Thus "global food security" is absolutely vital, while the goal of "national food self-sufficiency," where countries seek to produce all their food needs domestically, is increasingly unattainable and unnecessary. The view that every country must be largely responsible for its own food production hinders rational solutions to the problem of true food security.

Truly water-short regions cannot reliably depend on internal water resources to produce sufficient food to meet all domestic consumption. Water and agricultural experts in Israel, the western United States, and elsewhere have already acknowledged that increasing urban and industrial demands will continue to take water from the agricultural sector. Israel, for example, is beginning to assume that the only reliable long-term source of irrigation water may be water reclaimed from urban and industrial uses (Shuval 1996). The countries of the Persian Gulf that today depend on non-renewable fossil fuels to pump non-renewable fossil groundwater are already moving away from large-scale grain production and will be forced to shift more heavily to dependence on world grain markets.

Even countries formerly independent in food production, like China, are beginning to meet part of their food needs with purchases on the world market. As a result, a growing trade in water embodied in the purchase of foods and products produced elsewhere will continue to be seen. This embodied water – also called "virtual water" (Allen 1995) – represents the large-scale transfer of water from regions of water surplus to regions of water scarcity.

Several problems face developing countries wanting to meet significant food needs on the world market. First, availability of funds for use in purchasing food on the world market is often limited, because of the economic structure of developing countries, debt burdens, and lack of infrastructure. Second, growing pressure on global food markets has been predicted by some analysts, which may in turn raise market prices and increase competition for limited surpluses (see, for example, Brown and Kane 1994; Carruthers 1993; Kendall and Pimentel 1994; Postel 1993). These problems, in turn, force countries back toward national food self-reliance, at a high cost in both water and economic resources. Concerns about the risks of relying on foreign trading partners who may impose conditions on trade or food embargoes for political reasons must also be satisfactorily resolved. At the same time, others believe that there is substantial room to do better than we are doing today, and that continuing to provide all necessary food needs can be done with appropriate and achievable efforts (Mitchell and Ingco 1993; FAO 1993; Rosegrant and Agcaoili 1994).

Another fundamental shift in the global food situation is likely to be necessary from the point of view of water availability – a shift in diet away from water-intensive meat consumption in the more affluent nations. Diets that depend on meat for a significant proportion of protein and calories are far more water-intensive than diets higher in vegetable proteins. At present, nearly 40 per cent of all grain grown worldwide is used to feed animals. Eighty per cent of all corn production goes to animals. Reductions in livestock grain consumption in regions where irrigation is necessary would permit a shift in grain – and the water used to grow it – to direct human use. Current trends, however, are in the other direction, with more and more grain going to provide meat, at a high cost in water.

Water and ecosystems

A third component of the global water crisis is the ecological impact of human manipulation of the hydrological cycle. In part because of the lack of clearly defined legal water rights or firm guarantees for the environment, many aquatic ecosystems and individual species have become severely threatened or endangered. The recent disasters to the natural fisheries of Lake Victoria and the Aral Sea are but two examples. Overall, more than 700 species of fish have been recognized by international organizations as threatened or endangered. In just the last couple of years, many more have been added to the list, including several anadromous species, because of increasing pressures on water resources. Anadromous fisheries, in particular, are extremely vulnerable to changes in water supply and quality and to modifications in habitat (Covich 1993; Nash 1993).

While efforts are being made to identify basic ecosystem water requirements, there is little agreement about minimum water needs for the environment and few legal guarantees for environmental water have been set. Some limited efforts have been made to establish minimum requirements for certain threatened or high-priority ecosystems, but few criteria have been set, particularly in the developing world.

The ecosystems for which water is necessary include both natural ecosystems where there is minimal human interference and ecosystems that are already highly managed by humans. Societal decisions will have to be made regarding the degree to which these ecosystems should be maintained or restored and the indicators by which to measure their health. Examples of such decisions include identifying stretches of undisturbed rivers to protect, establishing minimum flow requirements in some river stretches, reallocating water from major water projects to the environment, and developing standards to protect wetlands and riparian habitats. Protecting natural aquatic ecosystems is not only vital for maintaining environmental health, but there are important feedbacks between these systems and both water quality and availability as well. The recent decision to place a cap on further development and diversions in the Murray-Darling river system in Australia (MDBMC 1996) and the complete revision of South African water law to include water for ecosystems as a fundamental priority (MWAF 1996) are two important examples of this new focus.

Traditional market mechanisms fail to address these problems and many of the proposed market solutions to water allocation problems will continue to fail in this area. Ultimately, allocations of water for the basic needs of ecosystems will have to be made on a governmental or regional level, with specific guarantees and protections accounting for climatic variability, seasonal fluctuations, basic human needs, and other factors. Management will have to follow an adaptive model where decisions are reviewed frequently based on the latest information and special efforts are made to avoid irreversible environmental consequences.

Water and security: Inter- and intrastate conflicts

As the twenty-first century approaches, water and water supply systems are increasingly likely to be both the objectives of military action and the instruments of war as human populations grow, as improving standards of living increase the demand for fresh water, and as global climatic changes make water supply and demand more problematic and uncertain (Gleick 1993; 1998). Where water is scarce, competition for limited supplies can lead nations to see access to water as a matter of national security. History is replete with examples of competition and disputes over shared fresh water resources: water resources have historically been both the objectives of inter-state conflict and the instruments of war.

Many rivers, lakes, and groundwater aquifers are shared by two or more nations. This geographical fact has led to the geopolitical reality of disputes over shared waters, including the Nile, Jordan, and Euphrates Rivers in the Middle East, the Indus, Ganges, and Brahmaputra in southern Asia, and the Colorado, Rio Grande, and Paraná in the Americas. Water and water supply systems have been the roots and instruments of war. Access to shared water supplies has been cut off for political and military reasons. Sources of water supply have been among the goals of military expansionism. And inequities in water use have been the source of regional and international frictions and tensions. These conflicts will continue – and in some places grow more intense – as growing populations demand more water for agricultural, industrial, and economic development (Gleick 1993).

Inter-state conflicts are caused by many factors, including religious animosities, ideological disputes, arguments over borders, and economic competition. Although resource and environmental factors are playing an increasing role in such disputes, it is difficult to disentangle the many intertwined causes of conflict. Identifying potential trouble areas does little good if there are no tools for mitigating the problem. International law for resolving water-related disputes must play an important role.

While various regional and international legal mechanisms, such as specific treaties and the new Convention on Non-Navigational Use of Shared International Watercourses (UN 1997), exist for reducing water-related tensions, these mechanisms have never received the international support or attention necessary to resolve many conflicts over water. Indeed, there is growing evidence that existing international water law may be unable to handle the strains of ongoing and future problems. In addition to improving international law in this area, efforts by the United Nations, international aid agencies, and local communities to ensure access to clean drinking water and adequate sanitation can reduce the competition for limited water supplies and the economic and social impacts of widespread waterborne diseases. In regions with shared water supplies, third-party participation in resolving water disputes, either through UN agencies or regional commissions, can also effectively end conflicts.

Not all water resources disputes will lead to violent conflict; indeed, most lead to negotiations, discussions, and non-violent resolutions. But in certain regions of the world water is a scarce resource that has become increasingly important for economic and agricultural development. In these regions, water is evolving into an issue of "high politics," and the probability of water-related conflict is increasing. Policy-makers and the military should be alert to the likelihood of conflicts over water resources, and to the possible changes in both international water law and regional water treaties that could minimize the risk of such conflicts.

Meeting basic needs for water

A distinction must be made between basic human and environmental "needs" for water and the much larger set of "wants" for water to provide additional goods and services. The overall demand for water includes a combination of basic "needs" and this larger set of "wants." "Need" for water exists independently of economic or political status and, in principle, it cannot be manipulated. More generally, "demand" typically refers to the economic and political demand that is expressed in terms of human desire, purchasing power, and degree of political empowerment and claims.

The goal of providing for basic human needs was officially recognized as early as the 1977 Mar del Plata Conference and continues to be an important unmet concern (UN 1978; 1992; ICWE 1992). The basic

Table 11.2 Water requirements for basic human needs

Purpose[1]	Basic water requirement (litres per person per day)
Drinking water[2]	5
Sanitation services	20
Bathing	15
Food preparation	10

Source: Gleick 1996
[1] Excluding water required to grow food.
[2] This is a true minimum to sustain life in moderate climatic conditions and average activity levels.

water requirement (BWR) described below and in Table 11.2 was designed to address the "need" part of this problem. Minimum needs have long been recognized by policy-makers in the form of the "lifeline tariff" being advocated in parts of the United States, some countries in Europe and Southern Africa, and elsewhere.

Recent efforts to integrate environmental issues and concerns with sustainable economic and social development have returned to the concept of meeting basic human needs first proposed nearly two decades ago. One of the most fundamental of those needs is access to clean water. Efforts to identify basic human needs for water have been made by UN agencies and international organizations in the past. More recently, a comprehensive definition of the BWR for domestic activities was put forth by the author (Gleick 1996). This definition recommends that 50 litres per person per day be provided to meet basic domestic water needs for drinking, sanitation, bathing, and food preparation. As part of this recommendation, international organizations, national and local governments, and water providers must play the leading role in meeting basic needs and should guarantee access to the BWR independently of an individual's economic, social, or political status.

Hundreds of millions of people, especially in developing countries, currently lack access to this BWR. Furthermore, rapid population growth and inadequate efforts to improve access to water ensure that this problem will grow worse before it grows better. A first step towards sustainable water use would be to guarantee all humans the water needed to satisfy their basic needs.

The broader level of demand for water – "wants" – can be changed and even reduced without necessarily diminishing the overall utility for the individual user of water. If users reduce their water demands, for instance through increased price or improved technology, well-being may nevertheless remain the same. The potential to increase efficiency – to reduce the volume of water used per unit of output – is quite significant in most productive uses of water, notably irrigated agriculture and industry. If the "freed" water can be used beneficially by others, this implies improved opportunities and increased utility for society at large.

Market and non-market solutions

The problems described above are very complicated, involving many different actors and driving forces. The solutions to those problems will, therefore, also be very complicated, and different approaches will apply to different actors and driving forces in myriad ways.

One of the principles to come out of each of the major water meetings, including the Mar del Plata and Dublin Conferences, is that effective water resource management requires treating water as an economic good. The Dublin statement, for example, says "water has an economic value in all its competing uses and should be recognized as an economic good."

Despite the call for water to be recognized as an economic good, there is little agreement about what this means or how the principle should be applied. At the most basic level, water should not be considered a free good – it should have a price, people should pay for it, and the price should reflect its true value, including environmental values. There are many examples worldwide where water has no price or is not paid for, and this leads to misuse of the resource. Ironically, there are also many examples where people in the developing world already pay far more for poor-quality water provided by vendors or private sellers than they would pay if they were supplied by more conventional municipal systems.

The largest single consumer of water is the agricultural sector, and water for agriculture is often heavily subsidized or even free. There are good reasons for this, including the desire of countries to maintain levels of rural employment and provide access to local markets for food, and for other social reasons. But too often, subsidies for agricultural water lead to inefficient and wasteful use of water, groundwater overdraft and contamination, and ecological destruction. Examples of the adverse impacts of cheap agricultural water can be seen in the devastation in the Aral Sea, the Colorado River delta in Mexico, the Nile Delta, and elsewhere. Groundwater overdraft is occurring in the Middle East, north China, India, and parts of the western United States – in large part because of market failures in properly pricing water.

The prevailing notion that provision of water should be free or subsidized and that water can be used without concern about the growing need and demand for water in other sectors is no longer acceptable. As long as precipitation, streamflow, or groundwater are plentiful in relation to overall demand, there is little reason to focus on complex allocation schemes or innovative market mechanisms for water management. Under such circumstances, the infrastructure needed to provide water might be comparatively simple and the necessary expenditure modest. When water is scarce, however, the social and environmental costs of greater and greater levels of water development rise. More and more of the world faces just such development constraints. When the ratio of use to overall availability increases, careful and rational water management, planning, and allocation become crucial.

Today, the construction of new water infrastructure requires increasingly expensive investment to produce an additional unit of water supply. This is partly due to the fact that the ratio of use to availability is high in most regions of the world and because most of the economically and environmentally appropriate sites for dams and storage facilities have already been developed (as have many uneconomic or environmentally inappropriate sites). Over time, therefore, distance from new water sources to users increases or the water requires increasingly expensive treatment.

More and more of the water used in the world, including water for food production, is provided through some kind of physical and institutional infrastructure that must be developed and reimbursed. Charges for that water need not be the same for every user – indeed, there is a long history of political support for various water-related subsidies, including cross-subsidies between various users and across different sectors – but the lesson of past developments is that some price must be paid and it is better if users pay the true costs.

There is thus a need to define better the different kinds of value (economic, health, social, etc.) that water use generates and to identify the various kinds of cost associated with water development, distribution, use, and treatment, including direct costs, opportunity costs, and hard-to-quantify environmental costs.

The failure of market forces in meeting water needs

As hinted above, markets for water are often limited and always incomplete. This raises the basic question: where is economics not enough? The application of economic principles alone fails in the areas of protecting ecosystems and environmental goods and services, in providing for basic human needs for water, and in resolving international disputes over shared water resources. Each of these problems also requires some form of government intervention, such as local or regional protections or policies.

But other questions also arise related to basic water needs and the role of markets. To what extent does a state have an obligation to provide its citizens with a basic water requirement? Is this obligation independent of ability to pay or other economic constraints? Should the international legal community consider the right to a certain level of fresh water to be a basic human right? How can the "environment" participate in water markets? What are appropriate subsidies, if any? For meeting basic human rights, international declarations made at Mar del Plata and the Earth Summit also suggest that states have the obligation to develop in such a way as to ensure that their use of fresh water is sustainable and adequate to meet the basic needs of its people, independent of ability to pay (Gleick 1996).

Water sufficient to meet basic needs should thus be an obligation of governments, water management institutions, or local communities. While in some regions governmental intervention may be necessary to provide for basic water needs, many areas will be able to use traditional water providers, municipal systems, or private purveyors within the context of market approaches. In some cases, however, governments or water providers may be unable to provide this amount of water using economic markets, because of rapid population growth or migration, the economic cost of water supply infrastructure in regions where capital is scarce, inadequate human resources and training, or even simple political incompetence. In such cases, the failure to provide this basic need must be considered a major human tragedy, and non-market intervention will be necessary. In particular, this means community or government direct action.

Institutional issues: Regional versus global governance

Water resources must now be recognized as a major determining factor for socio-economic development (UNCNR 1996). When human demands for water were low and when hydrological cycle behaviour and the climate were thought to be fairly predictable, water was one of the last things to be considered in the development decision-making process, if it was considered at all. Hydrologists and water managers tended to concentrate on gathering scientific knowledge about the hydrological cycle, paying little attention to socio-economic and environmental aspects or values, to the point that most development activities simply assumed that there would always be water available for growing needs.

Today, due to the increasing pressures on water resources and the recognized variability of the hydrological cycle and the climate, the position of water in the decision-making process has risen. Now, water must be considered in the context of development and security objectives, including the day-to-day management of water allocation for socio-economic activities and the preservation of natural ecosystems. It is now imperative that decision-makers in all sectors, and particularly those responsible for planning, make development decisions with explicit attention to water resources (Lundkvist and Gleick 1997).

Apart from increased concern within the policy domain, influential segments of society are showing a new interest in resource and environmental issues. Private and commercial sector interest in water affairs is growing. Environmental interests play an important role and community groups are increasingly seeking a say in water resource decisions (Gomez and Wong 1997). The new mix of partners concerned about water management and the new consensus about the myriad roles of water in development and for security represent an opportunity to address water problems in a more flexible and realistic manner.

Conclusions: Steps toward more sustainable water management and use

Identify and meet basic human and ecosystem water needs

Among the concepts raised nearly 20 years ago during the 1977 Mar del Plata Conference was that of meeting "basic needs." The 1992 Dublin Conference statement reiterated that principle, which was then strongly reaffirmed during the 1992 UNCED in Rio de Janeiro. International organizations, national and local governments, and water providers should adopt a BWR standard to meet basic needs, and guarantee access to it. Unless this basic resource need is met, large-scale human misery and suffering will continue and grow in the future, contributing to the risk of social and military conflict. Priority should be given to the unserved and underserved poor, who are at greatest risk. While these needs can be met in a market context, they must also be met where traditional markets fail.

National food policies must acknowledge water limitations

The view that all countries must be responsible for their own food production hinders rational solutions to the problem of true food security and leads to unsustainable use of water. By the late 1990s there were already many countries with insufficient water to grow all their own food and this situation will only get worse, not better. These countries go to world markets to meet their needs. The ultimate goal must be a world that grows sufficient food to meet the world's needs, somewhere, and the institutions and mechanisms to deliver that food where it is needed. Thus, countries without sufficient water resources realistically and dependably to produce sufficient food domestically must be able to meet needs through alternative reliable avenues. This requires a flexible combination of market and non-market institutions and a shift in the functioning of global trade, agricultural markets, and import-export policies. In particular, mechanisms to help shift poor water-short countries away from water-intensive agricultural production must be coupled with the development of robust trade or aid programmes. Some of the needed changes, like political guarantees against food embargoes and the development of adequate transportation and distribution systems, will not be produced through traditional market mechanisms. Over time, changes in diets and new forms for food production like "urban agriculture" can also play an important role in boosting global food security.

Water as an economic resource

Growing scarcity and water competition implies that water must be treated as an economic resource. Liberal provision of heavily subsidized water services is an invitation to waste and also means a significant drain on limited public funds and other resources. In order to meet basic human and environmental needs and stimulate long-term sustainable economic development, it is imperative that the notion of water as a free good be changed. The recognition of water as an economic resource, which was one of the cornerstones of the Dublin and Rio statements, implies that planners and users recognize the true value of water in all its competing uses and functions. Responsible and proper use requires, among other things, that charges and fees reflect the various costs for water with recognition of non-market values. Even modest steps in this direction have the potential to reduce and eliminate wasteful water use and allocations.

Water planning and decision-making

Water planning and decision-making should ensure representation of all affected parties and foster direct participation of affected interests. The principle that water planning and decision-making should involve the fullest participation by affected parties has been enunciated by international organizations and official water conference statements for nearly 20 years, going back to the 1977 Mar del Plata Conference. The goal was also one of the prime recommendations from the Dublin meeting.

Water development and management should be based on a participatory approach, involving users, planners and policy-makers at all levels. The participatory approach ... means that decisions are taken at the lowest appropriate level, with full public consultation and involvement of users in the planning and implementation of water projects (ICWE 1992).

Sustainable water planning and use should ensure comprehensive public representation, open and equitable access to information about the resources, and direct participation of affected interests in decisions about allocating those resources. The success of policies and programmes for water management, planning, and use now strongly depends on the extent to which the public becomes actively involved. Ways must also be found to incorporate and protect the interests of future generations – a fundamental criteria of sustainability as defined by the United Nations in Agenda 21.

Part of the idea of participatory decision-making must be the inclusion of mechanisms and institutions for dispute resolution. There has been progress on the international front in setting standards and principles for resolving conflicts over shared fresh water resources peacefully. In April 1997, the UN General Assembly approved the final Convention on the Law of the Non-Navigational Uses of International Watercourses – an international convention that had been negotiated over the past 30 years (UN 1997).

Article 7 of the Convention obliges states to take all appropriate measures to prevent harm to other states from their use of water. Article 8 obliges watercourse states to cooperate on the basis of equality, integrity, mutual benefit, and good faith in order to use and protect shared watercourses optimally. Article 33 offers provisions for guiding peaceful settlement of disputes by negotiation, mediation, arbitration, or appeal to the International Court of Justice. At the same time there are acknowledged limits to the ability of these standards to help settle disputes, and attention must continue to be focused here.

Management of the earth's water and other natural resources has increasingly been recognized by senior international policy-makers as inextricably linked with community prosperity and social and political stability. A wide range of both market and non-market solutions exist for many problems of misallocated or misused water, but insufficient attention has been paid to the proper application of these solutions. In the past, inadequate attention to the role of markets has caused significant misallocations and misuses of water. At the same time, application of market approaches in situations where non-economic values are high or where certain types of water needs or uses cannot be quantified also fails to resolve problems, and may often create more. These issues deserve more attention as the world moves into the twenty-first century.

REFERENCES

Allen, J. A. 1995. "Water in the Middle East and in Israel-Palestine: Some Local and Global Issues." In *Joint Management of Shared Aquifers*, eds M. Haddad and E. Feitelson. Jerusalem: Palestine Consultancy Group and the Truman Research Institute of Hebrew University: 31–44.

Brown, L. R. and H. Kane. 1994. *Full House: Reassessing the Earth's Population*

Carrying Capacity. Worldwatch Institute Environmental Alert Series. New York: W. W. Norton.

Carruthers, I. 1993. "Going, Going. Gone! Tropical Agriculture As We Know It." *Tropical Agriculture Association Newsletter* 13(3): 1–5, cited in A. F. McCalla. 1994. *Agriculture and Food Needs to 2025: Why We Should be Concerned.* Washington: Consultative Group on International Agricultural Research.

Clarke, R. 1991. *Water: The International Crisis.* London: Earthscan.

Covich, A. 1993. "Water and Ecosystems." In *Water in Crisis: A Guide to the World's Fresh Water Resources*, ed. P. H. Gleick. New York: Oxford University Press.

Engelman, R. and P. LeRoy. 1993. *Sustaining Water.* Washington: Population Action International.

FAO (Food and Agricultural Organization). 1993. "Agriculture: Towards 2010." Conference Paper C-93/24.

Gleick, P. H. 1993. *Water in Crisis: A Guide to the World's Fresh Water Resources.* New York: Oxford University Press.

Gleick, P. H. 1996. "Basic Water Requirement for Human Activities: Meeting Basic Needs." *Water International* 21(June): 83–92.

Gleick, P. H. 1998. *The World's Water 1998–99.* Washington: Island Press.

Gomez, S. V. and A. K. Wong. 1997. *Our Water, Our Future: The Need for New Voices in California Water Policy.* Oakland: Pacific Institute for Studies in Development, Environment, and Security.

ICWE (International Conference on Water and Environment). 1992. "The Dublin Statement on Water and Sustainable Development." International Conference on Water and Environment, Dublin, Ireland.

IWRA (International Water Resources Association) 1997. "Water Experts Express Grave Concerns about Future Global Food Security." Common position paper of the session Water Scarcity as a Key Factor in Food Security. Ninth World Water Congress of the IWRA, 1–6 September, Montreal, Canada.

Kelman, J. 1996. "Freshwater Availability in Large Cities of Brazil." Background memo, Chapter 4 Meeting in New York for the Comprehensive Global Freshwater Assessment.

Kendall, H. W. and D. Pimentel. 1994. "Constraints on the Expansion of the Global Food Supply." *Ambio* 23(3): 198–205.

Khan, A. H. 1997. "The Sanitation Gap: Development's Deadly Menace." In *The Progress of Nations 1997.* New York: United Nations (UNICEF).

Lundkvist, J. and P. H. Gleick. 1997. "Sustainable Water Strategies for the 21st Century." Policy paper for the Comprehensive Assessment of the Freshwater Resources of the World. Stockholm, Sweden: Stockholm Environment Institute.

MDBMC (Murray-Darling Basin Ministerial Council of Australia). 1996. "Setting the Cap: Report of the Independent Audit Group." Murray-Darling Basin Ministerial Council (November).

Mitchell, D. O. and M. D. Ingco. 1993. "The World Food Outlook." Draft paper, International Economics Department, World Bank, Washington.

MWAF (Ministry of Water Affairs and Forestry of South Africa). 1996. "Fundamental Principles and Objectives for a New Water Law in South Africa." Report to the Minister of Water Affairs and Forestry of the Water Law Review Panel (January).

Nash, L. 1993. "Environment and Drought in California 1987–1992: Impacts and Implications for Aquatic and Riparian Resources." Report, Pacific Institute for Studies in Development, Environment, and Security, Oakland, California.

Postel, S. L. 1993. *Last Oasis: Facing Water Scarcity*. New York: W. W. Norton.

Rosegrant, M. W. and M. Agcaoili. 1994. "Global and Regional Food Demand, Supply, and Trade Prospects to 2010." Paper presented at Population and Food in the Early Twenty-first Century: Meeting Future Food Needs of an Increasing World Population. International Food Policy Research Institute, 14–16 February, Washington, DC.

Shiklomanov, I. A. 1993. "World Fresh Water Resources." In *Water in Crisis: A Guide to the World's Fresh Water Resources*, ed. P. H. Gleick. New York: Oxford University Press.

Shuval, H. 1996. "Sustainable Water Resources Versus Concepts of Food Security, Water Security, and Water Stress for Arid Countries." Background paper, Workshop on Chapter 4 of the Comprehensive Global Freshwater Assessment of the United Nations.

UN (United Nations). 1978. *Water Development and Management. Proceedings of the United Nations Water Conference Mar del Plata, Argentina*, Vol. 1, Part 1. Oxford: Pergamon Press.

UN (United Nations). 1992. *Agenda 21: Programme of Action for Sustainable Development*. New York: United Nations.

UN (United Nations). 1997. "Convention on the Law of the Non-Navigational Uses of International Watercourses." Document A/51/869.

UNCFA (United Nations Comprehensive Freshwater Assessment). 1997. *Comprehensive Assessment of the Freshwater Resources of the World*. Stockholm: Stockholm Environment Institute.

UNCNR (United Nations Committee on Natural Resources). 1996. "Future Water Resources Management Issues and the Strategies and Policies that the International Community Should be Considering in Response." Document E/C.7/1996/6.

WRI (World Resources Institute). 1996. *World Resources 1996–97, The Urban Environment*. New York: Oxford University Press.

FURTHER READING

MNHW (Minister of National Health and Welfare). 1992. *Guidelines for Canadian Drinking Water Quality*. 5th edn. Ottawa: Canadian Government Publishing Center.

UNDP (United Nations Development Programme). 1994. *Human Development Report 1994*. Oxford: Oxford University Press.

UNICEF (United Nations Children's Fund). 1997. *The Progress of Nations 1997*. New York: United Nations.

Watson, R. T., M. C. Zinyowera, and R. H. Moss, eds. 1996. *Climate Change 1995: Impacts, Adaptations, and Mitigation of Climate Change: Scientific-Technical Analysis: Contribution of Working Group II to the Second Assessment Report of the Intergovernmental Panel on Climate Change*. Cambridge: Cambridge University Press.

12

Market forces and food security: The case of developing Asia

Angelina Briones and Charmaine Ramos

The world today has the capacity to produce more food than it can consume. However, millions of poor the world over are still unable to partake of this abundance of food supply, an irony most pronounced among low-income countries. The 1996 Rome Declaration states that food security exists only when all people, at all times, have physical and economic access to sufficient safe and nutritious food to meet their dietary needs and food preferences for an active and healthy life. This underscores the problem of food security today as primarily one of access and not only of availability.

Meanwhile, market forces are being unleashed throughout the world in sectors and ways that have a direct bearing on the food security problem as it poses itself today. These forces are manifested in two ways. First, trade barriers have gone down in agricultural commodities, including foodstuffs. The ratification of the General Agreement on Tariffs and Trade – Uruguay Round (GATT-UR) in 132 countries and the entry of the same into the World Trade Organization (WTO) signals an important epoch in global agricultural trade. In consonance with this development, several countries, especially in the Asian region, have moved away from policies aimed at achieving self-sufficiency in staple production; preferring instead to produce only part of their domestic needs while relying on imports for the balance. The 1996 World Food Summit also supports the view that food security can increasingly be met through imports and international trade in food. The FAO (1996b) has redefined food self-reliance to mean "reliance on trade to meet food needs" where it once meant supplementing domestically produced food with trade.

To be sure, world trade could indeed facilitate availability and access to food, with its potential to widen the food supply pool and drive food prices down. However, subjecting national food systems to the globalization process also poses new challenges and dilemmas to shaping food security policies at the national and international levels. One of these is the problems associated with the possible displacement of millions of smallholder food producers who comprise the bulk of the population in developing countries.

Second, the nature of state intervention in local food and agricultural markets is being reshaped from a regime of direct market participation through price controls and production procurement to one of crisis management and buffer stocking. In an effort to meet the conflicting goals of promoting cheap food and raw material prices and protecting national food systems, many developing countries used to employ market restrictions through quantitative quotas, price controls, the procurement operations of national marketing agencies, and export taxes and other levies. With the promulgation of structural adjustment policies in the 1980s, many of these measures were scrapped in favour of more market-friendly measures.

This chapter focuses on the first of these forces and delves into food and markets in developing Asia. Developing Asia has been at the centre of the global stage, first with its rise as an economic power in the 1980s and 1990s, and subsequently the current episode of financial crisis weakening many of its economies. This region offers an interesting showcase of how market forces have an impact on welfare objectives relevant to food security.

Against this backdrop, this chapter discusses the nature of the global food problem and how market forces influence it, and then zeroes in on developing Asia to assess considerations and constraints that these forces cannot address by themselves. The first section presents an overview of global food supply and distribution, and tackles the issue of food insecurity in developing countries. Section two examines market forces and international regimes as they affect food security in developing Asia. Section three deals with the domestic dimensions involving institutional and resource-related constraints that shape food security problems in developing Asia. In the concluding section, the chapter suggests a variety of policy options to cope with food insecurity in developing countries.

Understanding the food security problem: Global empirical dimensions

This chapter begins by looking at two sets of trends to ascertain the nature of global food scarcity. The first concerns food production and how it has kept pace with population growth. The second involves the movement of real food prices which indicates how global supply is keeping pace with demand. The chapter then verifies how these food availability indicators compare with some food consumption statistics.

World trends in food production and demand

Grain production outpaced population changes in the 1970s – a trend that heightened in the 1980s but appears to have reversed in the first five years of the 1990s (see Table 12.1). Throughout the 1970s, change in production was greater than change in population in practically all parts of the world except South America and Africa. The African situation improved in the 1980s – as with the rest of the world except South America. The dramatic increases in South American cereal-sector productivity only bore fruit in the 1990s, when it was the only region in the world where change in production outpaced change in population. According to the FAO (1996a), a considerable increase in plant production between 1970 and 1990 was due to increased productivity and improved yields and, to a lesser extent, an increase in cultivated area. The slowing of grain production in the 1990s, on the other hand, can be attributed to the exhaustion of land frontiers, such that further increases in production are bound to be technology-driven.

The role of productivity in boosting production between 1970 and 1990 is mirrored by the trends in average annual percentage change in productivity (see Table 12.2). Between 1971 and 1990, productivity growth was rising for all the economic groups and continental groups except Europe and Africa. The first half of the 1990s, in contrast, is characterized by slowing down in annual productivity increases, except in South America.

Despite this apparent slowing in cereal production, food production and food production per capita indices continue to be on a general upswing for most of the developing world (see Figure 12.1). The important exception is Africa, where, given the primacy of roots and tubers in the people's diet, production statistics pertaining to cereals may not be as important as the per capita food production index. Food production and per capita food production indices in North America and Europe in 1995 fell, compared to their position in 1985, to points approximating their

Table 12.1 Average annual percentage change in production and population; 1971–1995

	Average annual % change in production			Average annual % change in population		
	1971–1980	1981–1990	1991–1995	1971–1980	1981–1990	1991–1995
North America	4.43	4.52	−0.19	0.97	1.01	1.02
South America	1.95	1.23	6.15	2.31	1.99	1.63
Europe	3.66	1.26	−0.67	0.52	0.33	0.25
Africa	2.22	3.11	2.43	2.71	2.84	2.71
Oceania	6.39	9.02	10.27	1.62	1.54	1.39
Asia	2.81	3.34	1.36	2.10	1.89	1.98
World	2.76	2.44	−0.45	1.85	1.74	1.49
developed	2.89	2.03	−3.05	0.83	0.70	0.51
developing	2.74	3.12	1.76	2.25	2.08	1.79

Source: FAO 1997

Table 12.2 Average annual percentage change in productivity; 1971–1995

	1971–1980 %	1981–1990 %	1991–1995 %
North America	2.01	3.82	1.21
South America	1.12	1.70	5.60
Europe	3.74	1.85	0.33
Africa	2.46	0.61	−0.17
Oceania	2.06	8.43	4.83
Asia	2.39	3.12	1.70
World	2.10	2.52	0.01
developed	1.83	2.81	−1.47
developing	2.38	2.62	1.51

Source: FAO 1997

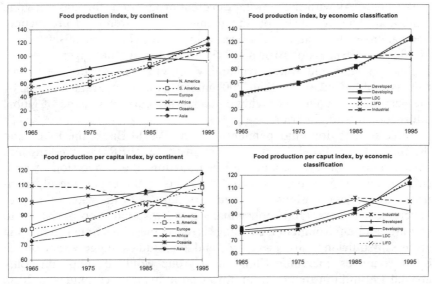

Source: FAO 1997

Figure 12.1. Food production and food production per capita indices, 1965–1995

1975 positions. The decline for developed countries, however, bears minimal impact to their populations in as much as their supplies still increasingly exceed their energy requirements. In North America, for instance, food supply exceeds energy requirements by almost 50 per cent (FAO 1996a). Per capita indices follow the direction of food production indices when countries are grouped according to their economic classification. However, continental grouping points to dramatic increases happening only in Asia and, to a lesser extent, South America.

Price movements

Trends and projections based on World Bank data suggest that the real price of food relative to industrial commodities has been on a downward trend throughout this century, declining by about 0.5 per cent every year. This implies that the global capacity to supply food has grown slightly more rapidly than global demand. The latest projections by the World Bank point to the continuation of this broadly balanced growth, with real prices in 2005 lower than those prevailing in the first half of the 1990s (Anderson et al. 1996).

However, there has been a spate of nominal increases in cereal prices in the 1990s. As with the slowing of cereal production, this has not gone unnoticed. The optimistic picture painted by the trends in production, population growth, and real prices prior to the 1990s is offset by the Malthusian warnings of Brown (1995), who projects that given expected declines in land and water availability for grain production in China, China would need more than 200 million tonnes of grain imports by the year 2030, a volume roughly equalling the current volume of global international trade in grain.

Three studies done independently by the World Bank, the FAO, and the International Food Policy Research Institute (IFPRI) – all taking into consideration concerns about land degradation, the conversion of agricultural land to industrial uses, and the limits to the expansion of irrigation – are far less pessimistic in their expectations of the capacity of producers, consumers, and policy-makers to respond appropriately to resource and environmental challenges (see Table 12.3). Small changes in grain self-sufficiency are projected, and the studies suggest that developing countries, including China, as a group would be importing only around 190 million tonnes from advanced industrial economies in 2010, doubling the volume of the early 1990s (Anderson et al. 1996).

The question of access

In view of these figures, the availability of food does not seem to pose any serious problem. As Table 12.4 illustrates, the proportion of the population who are food-deficient has been declining in all developing regions except inter-tropical Africa. However, has the availability of food ensured food security at the national and household levels?

Table 12.3 Grain self-sufficiency, various regions: Actual 1989–1991 and projected 2010

	Actual 1989–1991 %	Projected 2010, WB %	Projected 2010, IFPRI %	Projected 2010, FAO %
Advanced economies	128	136	124	128
Eastern Europe and former Soviet Union	88	105	102	102
All developing economies	91	86	88	89
East Asia	94	91	94	95
South Asia	100	90	97	97
Latin America	87	84	92	86
Sub-Saharan Africa	86	86	73	85
Middle East and North Africa	67	57	64	62

Source: World Bank from Mitchell and Ingco (1995), FAO from Alexandratos (1995), and IFPRI from Agcaoili and Rosegrant (1995) cited in Anderson et al. (1996).

Table 12.4 Estimates of food-energy deficiency in developing regions

Region	Period	% of food-energy-deficient persons in population	Number of food-energy-deficient persons (millions)
Inter-tropical Africa	1969–1971	38	103
	1979–1981	41	148
	1990–1992	43	215
Near East and North Africa	1969–1971	27	48
	1979–1981	12	27
	1990–1992	12	37
East Asia and South-East Asia	1969–1971	41	476
	1979–1981	27	379
	1990–1992	16	269
South Asia	1969–1971	33	238
	1979–1981	34	303
	1990–1992	22	255
Latin America and Caribbean	1969–1971	19	53
	1979–1981	14	48
	1990–1992	15	64

Source: FAO Sixth World Food Survey (1996) cited in FAO (1996a)

In reality, food availability has not been translated into food security. The absolute number of the hungry rose by as much as 17 per cent between 1980 and 1992. The trend is likely to continue. In 1992, 841 million people were deemed food-energy deficient – a figure comprising 20 per cent of the developing countries' population. The situation is most dire in the least developed countries where, despite an increase in global availability, per capita fat supply has risen only minimally, dietary energy supply has stagnated, and per capita protein supply has even declined.

What implications can be gleaned from these empirical trends? The first is that supply often has little to do with access. Food security continues to be a developmental problem and poverty remains the single most important obstacle to ensuring it at the national and household levels. The relative improvement in the performance of developing Asia compared to developing Africa in both production and, more importantly, consumption-side statistics points to the close relationship between economic development and the alleviation of hunger.

While supply cannot guarantee food security, the reverse is true enough. Food security cannot be attained without ample food supply. In view of continuing population growth, growing land scarcity, and mounting difficulties in achieving sustainable increases in food-crop yields, technological innovation remains a cornerstone in realizing long-run stability in food supply. For developing countries, the role of public investment in research and development can thus not be understated, as with the importance of institutions, infrastructure, and development of human resources in facilitating farmers' access to new technologies.

Finally, an increased involvement in international food trade is bound to be an important feature of the policy environment towards attaining food security goals. In a globalized food system, the fiscal capacity of nations to finance their food imports becomes a central issue. In developing countries where food producers are among the most food-insecure sectors, exposing their food markets to the vagaries of international trade poses new opportunities and challenges regarding their access to food.

Food and market forces – international regimes and national policies

The preceding section has demonstrated how the question of access is the central issue in food security. How, then, do market forces affect this problem? Food markets in developing countries have been traditionally protected. As the settlement of the GATT Uruguay Round (GATT-UR) has lifted the mercantilist overlay over the agricultural sector, however,

Table 12.5 Net trade balance in food (tonnes), 1965–1995

	1965	1975	1985	1995
Developed	(8,091,100)	15,294,000	40,766,000	106,323,800
Developing				
economies	13,142,870	(11,555,660)	(42,023,000)	(92,239,200)
Africa	3,272,740	(6,080,880)	(28,419,500)	(29,764,760)
Asia	(14,103,880)	(24,851,630)	(43,482,990)	(84,002,210)

Note: A negative trade balance points to net imports; positive points to net exports.
Source: FAO 1997

international market forces have begun to factor in the dynamics of food security in developing countries. This section is designed to elucidate the nature of agricultural liberalization followed by the GATT-UR agreement and trace impacts on objectives of food security in developing countries.

Trends in global food trade balances

Trends in global food trade balances point to the increased dependence of developing countries on food imports (see Table 12.5). Even though current levels of imports represent a minimal proportion of total consumption, the degree of dependence of developing countries on the international market, especially for grains, is expected to deepen. Rising income, especially in developing Asia, is expected to spur demand for both food and feed grains that may not necessarily be met by local production. The World Bank estimates that the developing countries' share in world food grains imports will reach 70 per cent by the year 2000.

Trends also suggest the dominant role of the developed world, despite falling rates of productivity and production, as a net food supplier – a role that is not likely to be relinquished in the near future. The World Bank envisages that the developing countries' share in world cereals exports will increase from 12.7 per cent in 1987 to only 14.4 per cent by 2000. Both the FAO and the World Bank posit that Argentina and Thailand are likely to remain the only significant third world suppliers of cereals. OECD countries, in contrast, are projected to increase their exports owing to their ecological, technological, and structural capacity (Brown and Goldin 1992).

The dependence of the developing world on developed countries for their food needs is not solely a result of natural comparative advantage shaped by factor endowment. Developed countries enjoy a structural advantage in food production through extensive agricultural price-support systems that not only encourage intensive farming methods, but also provide price support for virtually unlimited output, thus generating unprecedented surplus production. Prior to the ratification of GATT-UR, the United States and the European Union spent more than US$20 billion per annum on agricultural subsidies (Watkins and Windfuhr 1994). It is through these price-support systems that developed countries have been able to shape their dominance in food and feed grains trade to this day. The United States controls over three-quarters of the world market for corn. It also produces over 80 per cent of corn substitutes, such as soy and sorghum. Around one-third of US agricultural land is said to be used to produce for export markets. In an average year, exports account for 25 per cent of corn production, 40 per cent of wheat production, and 30 per cent of soy production. The European Union is the second major player in the basic food grains trade. The United States and the European Union together account for almost 50 per cent of world market shares for wheat.

The GATT-UR agreement and agricultural trade liberalization

The signing of the GATT-UR in 1994 represented an important epoch for many developing countries, which have long protected their food sector from the vagaries of international trade. The GATT-UR marks a watershed, in that agricultural trade has hitherto escaped previous GATT rounds. More importantly, the GATT-UR was launched in 1986 just as the world was reeling from the slump in agricultural prices caused by unprecedented levels of surplus production in the face of depressed world demand. The agricultural subsidy systems in developed countries were partly responsible for the surplus production. It was envisaged that market liberalization under GATT would remove market distortions caused by such price-support systems (see Table 12.6). The market-oriented approach to agricultural policy reform, which was embodied in the GATT-UR agreement, was expected not only to police international trade disputes, but also to bring international agricultural production back in line with demand.

The GATT-UR agreement is not likely to resolve market distortions, however. Moreover, food insecurity in developing countries is not likely to be alleviated either. The mandated 20 per cent reduction in the domestic support level would actually contribute to distorting global agricultural and food markets by legally permitting heavy subsidization in the developed world. Such a reduction has already been made up for by technological edge and concomitant productivity gains. And it would

Table 12.6 Key features of the GATT-UR

Domestic support reduction	• Reduction of trade-distorting subsidies equal to 20 per cent of aggregate measure of support (AMS), using 1986–1988 as the reference period • Remarks: provision does not apply where AMS does not exceed 5 per cent of the total value of agricultural production for developed countries and 10 per cent for developing countries
Export subsidies reduction	• For developed countries, reduction of export subsidies by 21 per cent for each product from its 1986–1990 average • For developed countries, reduction of budgetary expenditure on export subsidies by 36 per cent over six years • For developing countries, reduction by two-thirds of the above figures over 10 years • Remarks: food aid and unsubsidized exports exempted
Improved market access	• For developed countries, tariffication of all import restrictions and reduction by 36 per cent • For developing countries, reduction for each tariff line by at least 15 per cent over six years, increasing to 24 per cent over 10 years • For developing countries, introduction of minimum access requirements beginning at 3 per cent of domestic consumption and rising to 5 per cent by the end of the agreement • Remarks: under certain conditions, developing countries exempt from tariffication commitment where primary staples are concerned

Source: Watkins and Windfuhr (1994)

also allow too much flexibility in production baselines and the conversion of price support into GATT-exempt direct payments (Watkins and Windfuhr 1994). For instance, under the "Green Box" provisions of the agreement, direct income subsidies to farmers have been exempt from reductions on the ground that such payments are "decoupled" from production and thus not "trade-distorting." In reality, however, direct payments to European and US farmers are anything but decoupled from production because the profitability of the agricultural sector by and large hinges upon these transfers. Deficiency payments make up between one-fifth and one-third of US farm incomes (Bello 1997). The OECD estimates that each US farmer received an average transfer amounting to US$29,000 in 1995. The total subsidy given to EU farmers, US$97 billion, is equivalent to half the value of their production. The overall impact of subsidization by the United States and the European Union is that commodities are exported at prices which bear no relation to the real costs of production. Since the United States and the European Union are major grain producers and exporters, this has serious consequences for developing countries, now required by the GATT-UR to eliminate trade restrictions in agriculture and foodstuffs. Prices at which export activity takes place are the residual outcomes of Northern farm policies. International prices, as a consequence, are depressed relative to domestically produced grain in most developing countries, where farmers, in contrast, are subject to negative producer subsidies (Bello 1997).

Threats to food security arise from the potential livelihood losses of smallholder farm producers in developing countries, who must directly compete with subsidized food imports from developed countries. The mechanized and subsidized food systems of the North obviously bear little semblance to the predominantly smallholder production of the South. For the latter to be able to compete in the global arena, big strides will have to be made by developing countries in terms of technological breakthroughs in increasing and sustaining productivity, human resource development, and agricultural infrastructural support. The dislocation, meanwhile, has serious implications for the poverty-reduction efforts of low-income countries, where agricultural production accounts for some two-thirds of employment. This argument is usually assumed away in cases where the poor are net buyers of food. Increased national food supplies through relatively cheaper food imports could render net economic welfare gains. However, these gains are justifiable only if the welfare losses of smallholder producers are properly compensated. It is in this context that compensating mechanisms as a social safety-net emerge as an important policy concern.

Food security also becomes problematic because of an unsustainable dependence on food imports. As developing countries rely more on the international food market, their capacity to finance imports serves as a critical factor in ensuring food supply for their populations. Given that most developing countries suffer acute balance-of-payments deficits, increased food imports will considerably strain their foreign payment positions, eventually undermining macroeconomic standing. The trade-off between food security objectives and economic growth underscores the contemporary dilemma of developing countries. As a matter of fact, improved food security in developing Asia is related more to its ability to procure from the international market when compared with sub-Saharan Africa.

It should also be noted that the impact of subsidization in the US and EU farm sectors is measured in terms of not only the foreign exchange losses and fiscal burden of food imports but also erosion of traditional dietary patterns in importing nations. In sub-Saharan Africa, for example, imports of wheat and rice have been increasing by over 8 per cent per year, while production of local food staples such as cassava, sorghum, and millet has rapidly declined (Watkins and Windfuhr 1994). Gradual replacement of indigenous food groups by imported grain could severely undermine both nutritional balance and the cultural matrix embedded in traditional dietary patterns.

Beyond GATT and trade liberalization: The domestic front

It would nevertheless be wrong to overstate the role of Northern agricultural policies, and how the GATT-UR hinders food security in developing countries by institutionalizing such policies. Dilemmas of food insecurity in developing countries cannot be ascribed solely to exogenous variables such as GATT, agricultural liberalization, and subsidy in the North. Developing countries are equally to be blamed. Their urban-biased interventionist policies aimed at providing cheap food to underpin industrialization have marginalized the agriculture and food sectors. Policies associated with import-substituting industrialization (ISI) strategies, such as agricultural export taxation, the protection of manufactured goods, overvaluation of currencies, and skewed allocation of resources in favour of the urban, modern sector, are all seen to discriminate against the agricultural sector. Market reforms, such as those advocated by and enforced through the GATT-UR, could be conducive to correcting domestic distortions embodied in the ISI strategies and to enhancing food security objectives as long as they allow for the increased viability of the agricultural sector.

Freer flow of food imports could enhance national food security by assuring adequate supplies of food at cheaper prices. Freer trade could also help cope with food insecurity by facilitating faster agricultural growth and economic development. But food imports and freer trade, by and in themselves, cannot guarantee individual food security. Nor can food self-sufficiency be assured through freer market mechanism.

The Philippines' experience offers a classic example in this regard. The Philippines used to be self-sufficient in rice, but now as a result of agricultural liberalization has become a food-deficient developing country. Like some of its South-East Asian neighbours, the Philippines had to compromise food security by complying with the GATT-UR agreement as well as becoming a member of the World Trade Organization.

Food and markets in the Philippines

In 1994, the Philippine government concurred with the GATT-UR treaty and set the stage for liberalizing the importation of a wide range of agricultural commodities, including foodstuffs. The expected influx of food imports to follow its ratification triggered a national debate on the future of food security. Furthermore, ratification came at a time of very weak performance in the agricultural sector. In the 1960s and 1970s, the Philippines' agricultural sector registered the highest growth rate among the developing Asian countries. In the 1980s and early 1990s, however, it recorded the worst performance. Trends in growth rates of rice, corn, sugar-cane, and coconut, the four most important crops of the Philippines, are telling. While sugar-cane enjoyed a surge in the late 1980s due to conducive world prices, the rest went through a growth slump from the 1980s onwards. In the same period, the poultry and livestock and, to some extent, the fishery sectors became the major sources of growth in the beleaguered agricultural sector.

Other trends paint a dismal picture in terms of the sector's ability to supply the needs of a burgeoning population. Trends suggest that the agricultural frontier might already have reached the point of diminishing return as the expansion of arable land and permanent crop acreage stagnated in the 1980s. Much of the stagnation in the 1990s reflects uncertainty in property rights due to the unsuccessful implementation of agrarian reform and the resultant conversion of farm lands into nonagricultural uses (Lim 1996). Although productivity in major crops has generally been on the upswing since the 1970s, there have been worrisome movements since the 1980s. Rice yield growth was fastest in the 1970s as a result of the introduction of the Green Revolution. But it has been relatively stagnant since the mid-1980s, although the levels are currently still in pace with yield levels in most Asian countries except China and Indonesia. Corn yields, on the other hand, grew fastest in the 1980s with the introduction of high-yielding yellow feed-corn varieties, but were still among the lowest in Asia. Meanwhile, coconut yields have not recovered their levels of the late 1970s and have largely deteriorated since then.

These trends, along with declining agricultural relative prices, have led to the drop in agricultural output and its relative importance in national output. However, the sector continues to be the single most important source of livelihood for a large portion of the national population.

The liberalization of the agricultural sector through the GATT-UR has posed a paradoxical outlook to the farm sector in the Philippines. On the one hand, it could ease food insecurity by facilitating food imports in the face of declining production and the bleak prospects for the sector to catch up with population growth and demand. On the other, given the proportion of the population dependent on the agricultural sector, especially in corn and rice, the liberalization could easily deform the structural foundation of the domestic farm sector, and therefore undermine long-term prospects for food security (Lim 1996).

GATT and other liberalization measures

By how much will the GATT-UR measures open the Philippine agricultural sector? The tariff rates committed by the Philippine government are generally above the tariff levels prior to the ratification (see Table 12.6). Minimum access volumes in rice and corn represent a minimal amount of consumption and past levels of imports. Much of the threat, however, stems from how the implementation guidelines allow for increasing these volumes, without consultations with the producers, whenever there is a perceived shortage in corn and rice (in other words, when projected price is more than the border price by a rate equal to the average of the out-quota and in-quota tariff).[1]

However, the liberalization of the Philippine agricultural sector must be appreciated in the context of the economy-wide deregulatory framework, the regional trade agreements that the Philippines has entered into, and the agricultural modernization programme. In the 1980s, the government embarked on economy-wide and sector-specific reforms under the auspices of the World Bank's structural adjustment programmes, which were designed to improve economic efficiency and increase growth, while minimizing fluctuations in price levels. These reforms were also meant to correct the inherent bias of trade policies for industry and against agriculture. They included trade policy reforms to remove quantitative restrictions, lower average and limited dispersion of tariffs, eliminate implicit and explicit taxes on traditional exports, and abolish price controls on food and other essential consumer goods; liberalization of regulations on foreign investments; financial liberalization including the decontrol of interest rates and more liberal banking regulations; tax policy reforms to minimize inefficiencies and inequities in the tax structure, improve tax administration, and raise tax revenues; privatization to shift resources from the government to the private sectors; and currency devaluation to reduce the deficit in the balance of payments (Clarete 1992).

A tariff reform programme (TRP) was introduced in 1981, carrying out comprehensive tariff reductions in batches of five years. By the turn of the century, the programme aims to limit clusters to just 3, 10, and 20 per cent, with the exception of agricultural products whose quantitative restrictions have been subject to tariffs. The spread is expected to be further limited to only two categories: 3 and 10 per cent by 2003 and 3 and 5 per cent by 2004. These goals fall well within, if not well in advance of and beyond, the commitments called for not only by the GATT-UR but also the ASEAN Free Trade Area (AFTA) and the Asia-Pacific Economic Cooperation (APEC). For example, efforts are now under way to get rice and corn off the exclusion list of the Common Effective Preferential Tariff (CEPT).

It has been said that the GATT-UR binds the Philippine government's liberalization programme within an international framework. But it is also clear that the TRP is by far even more ambitious than the treaty.

Agricultural modernization

The Medium Term Agricultural Development Plan (MTADP) also provides impetus to the accelerated deregulation of the agricultural sector. Part of President Fidel Ramos's ballyhooed Philippines 2000 programme envisioned propelling the country towards Asian tiger growth rates. The MTADP aims at achieving two objectives: first, reducing by more than half the land currently used to cultivate corn and rice; and second, converting freed-up land for diversification to livestock and commercial crops, sectors being propped up for their potentials in the export market. To meet the country's food requirements, unprecedented growths in staple crop yields are being targeted. In corn, for instance, the programme is targeting tripling productivity rates before the end of the decade. The philosophy is to concentrate production where it is most efficient.

The failure of the government to address long-standing problems in the rural sector, such as agrarian reform and public investments in infrastructure and research and development, renders suspect the agricultural sector's ability to meet the productivity targets set by the programme. Nowhere is the failure more glaring than in the budgetary allocation the government sets aside for agriculture.

Public expenditure

Public expenditures in the agricultural sector went through a brief period of recovery in the late 1980s after bearing the brunt of contractionary policies in the 1970s. This quickly tapered off in the 1990s, with the share of expenditure on agriculture standing at a measly 4.5 per cent in 1995. A large chunk went to natural resources and environmental management, and rehabilitation of forest and fishery resources, as well as to rice price stabilization and the agrarian reform programme. Irrigation, to which close to 20 per cent of total infrastructure budget was allocated from 1974 to 1984, dropped sharply from the mid-1980s into the 1990s. Only about 30 to 40 per cent of public expenditure has been allocated for productivity-enhancing measures. Agricultural research is severely underfunded, with expenditure representing only 0.3 per cent of gross value added (GVA) compared to an average of 1 per cent among developing countries. Moreover, public expenditure continues to be disproportionately in favour of the rice sector, which accounts for less that 15 per cent of the agricultural GVA (David 1996).

Public expenditure allocations have not sufficiently focused on long-term productivity-enhancing investments which can reverse the declining competitive advantage of the sector. Without the government amply investing in productivity-enhancing measures, the shrivelling of agricultural land utilized for cereal production could only translate to the increased role of cereal imports. Therefore, even if it is argued that the GATT-UR does not substantially open the agricultural market, a tariff reform programme that goes beyond the tariffs inscribed by the treaty and an agricultural modernization programme that gives priority to cash crops and livestock production seem to augur for the increased role of food imports in the future.

Market forces

Much of the debate around market-driven agricultural policy is couched in terms of arguing whether market forces are good or bad for the sector. But such a track often leads to emotional diatribes about the sins and virtues of protectionism versus free markets. Rather than falling into this ideological trap, this chapter seeks to raise three major concerns that a developing country like the Philippines has to address in the face of agricultural trade liberalization.

First, what is the actual market situation, specifically in those sectors where local production stands to compete? There is the possibility that free market tenets do not actually hold in specific global markets, thus rationalizing the placement of national protective measures until international distortions are corrected. For instance, a comparison of total transfer per full-time farmer and per capita income in South Cotabato, Bukidnon, and Cagayan Valley, major yellow-corn-producing provinces in the Philippines, shows how subsidies in the North have posed unfair competition and have grossly distorted the image of a level playing field in the agricultural world market. Per capita incomes in Cagayan Valley (US$350), Bukidnon (US$224), and South Cotabato (US$293), major rice and corn producers in the Philippines, represent less than 1 per cent of total transfer per full-time farmer in the United States (US$19,000) and the European Union (US$29,000) in 1994 (OECD 1995 and UNDP 1995, cited in Watkins 1996).

Second, what are the institutional arrangements that underlie the Philippine agricultural sector's ill performance? This emphasizes that institutional arrangements may be as important, if not more, as free market forces in determining the ability of the sector to compete in the global arena. If non-market bottlenecks in the agricultural sector – like the agrarian reform problem and the inadequacy of investment into rural infrastructure such as farm-to-market roads and post-harvest facilities and into agricultural research and development that would increase rural productivity – are addressed properly, then the prospect of competing with food imports becomes less fearsome.

For example, the cost of marketing yellow corn in the Philippines is a major source of the said sector's cost disadvantage. While the marketing-to-total-cost ratio in Thailand stands at 27 to 32 per cent, the same falls within the range of 33 to 37 per cent in the Philippines (Setboonsarng and Rosegrant 1992). The sorry state of transportation infrastructure and storage facilities is the main culprit behind the high cost of marketing in the Philippines. The cost of bringing the produce from farm to user is very high, US$60 per tonne in the Philippines, compared to only US$12 in Thailand. Given that the yellow corn market is geographically segmented, the high cost of distribution makes it cheaper for the country to import yellow corn from Argentina, Thailand, and the United States than procure it locally.

Third, what safety nets are in place to alleviate problems and compensate the vulnerable sectors of food producers? This concern puts to the fore the idea that the distribution of benefits and losses is just as crucial as the projected efficiency gains from a policy of liberalization. The Philippines' GATT-related adjustment measures have been heavily criticized for lack of targeted safety-nets. Half of the 30 billion Philippines pesos (PhP) went to the infrastructure projects of the Department of Public Works and Highways. The Department of Agriculture and its affiliated agencies received less than 27 per cent of the total appropriation.

The more disturbing criticism is how some capital provisions of the GATT fund were appropriated for glaringly non-GATT adjustments-related projects. This goes to show that the fund earmarked for safety-nets was actually just a regular budget item in the General Appropriations Act with the budget title changed. No new appropriations were actually made expressly for adjustment measures. If the "questionable" projects (those projects that government would have implemented without the ratification of GATT) were stricken out, only PhP3 billion or 10 per cent of the figure allotted would be left for the fund (Montemayor 1995).

The Philippines case demonstrates that unruly market forces could easily disrupt the foundation of food security. But this is not to suggest the outright negation of market forces. Market liberalization ratified through the GATT-UR can significantly contribute to enhancing the agricultural sector in developing countries. Nevertheless, food producers in developing countries should also be properly and fairly equipped before they enter global competition. Correcting unfair subsidy provisions, realigning the institutional foundation, and ensuring social safety-nets for the displaced should be undertaken in tandem with the liberalization of the agricultural market. Otherwise, food security in developing countries can severely deteriorate.

Non-market constraints to food security in developing Asia

It has been argued that global food supply meets global food requirements, and international trade is an increasing source of food supply for the developing world. It has also been noted that food security hinges on access to food. This is a major concern in Asia, whose share of the world population is 58 per cent but whose share in food production is about 40 per cent. Developing countries in Asia have achieved consistently increasing trends in food production, but they have also been consistent net food importers since 1965, threatening food security.

Factors threatening food security in developing Asia are not limited to market forces such as agricultural market liberalization. Non-market factors, such as institutional and resources constraints, have severely impeded achieving food security. Against this backdrop, this section focuses on the domestic, non-market foundation of food security in Asian developing countries. Common to these countries is pervasive poverty among the rural populace, whose livelihood is dependent on agriculture and related fields. They are food producers but, ironically, are food-insecure. Why is this so? What would enable them to achieve household food security? Can the market be a major factor to draw them out of food insecurity? Answers are elucidated by examining the nature of poverty, institutional constraints to access, and resource-related constraints to food production in developing Asia.

Rural poverty and social constraints

The bulk of the world's population lives in Asia – as do the bulk of the world's poor (73 per cent). High population growth and widespread poverty and illiteracy characterize the social landscape of the lower-income countries of Asia. Only a good reading of the complexity and enormity of the situation can lead each government to policies and programmes that ensure food security, development, and growth that promotes people's welfare.

Asia is afflicted by both urban and rural poverty, but rural poverty accounts for three-quarters of the total. The rural poor have less or no access to basic services compared to their urban counterparts. Of the rural poor, the majority depend on agriculture for employment and income; hence, the poorest of the poor are the landless farm workers. This sector constitutes 45 per cent of the rural poor in India and 40 per cent in Bangladesh.

Illiteracy

Across Asia poverty has no greater contributory factor than illiteracy. It is most pronounced as a social burden in South Asia. As late as 1990, illiteracy in the region still exceeded 50 per cent, with women bearing the brunt. More than 70 per cent of women aged 25 or older are illiterate (Bardhan 1996). This is also the region that has 40 per cent of the world's poor and persistently high annual population growth (2 to 2.8 per cent). A notable exception is Sri Lanka, with a population growth of 1.5 per cent and illiteracy of only 12 per cent. East Asia and South-East Asia have better records of literacy, but are these a comfortable basis for complacency?

Simple literacy tests (reading and writing) have served well as a convention in the world's campaign to eradicate this social malignancy. With today's global concerns about the economy and environment (the Uruguay Round, the WTO, the Earth Summit, and Agenda 21), simple literacy should be replaced by functional literacy (read, write, compute, and comprehend). Functional literacy data are not readily available; hence, a focus on the Philippines scenario is given in Figure 12.2.

The environmental stress: The pressures of landlessness and poverty

Poverty and illiteracy drove masses of migrants to subsist on resources in upland areas and forestlands where there is minimal access to basic services. A large portion of these migrants consists of the landless and near-landless (tillers of less than 0.5 ha). To give a perspective view, two countries are taken as examples – the Philippines and India.

The Philippine rural scenario displays a complex mix of problems: landlessness, poverty, and rapid growth of a labour force that lacks skills

In 1994, the Philippines recorded a high simple literacy of 95 per cent of the total population between the ages of 10 and 64 years. Behind this impressive record, however, is the reality of a huge workforce confined to jobs of low productivity because of functional illiteracy. Of the 1994 population of 48 million (10 to 64 years old), average functional literacy was 83.8 per cent; average for women was 85.9 per cent and for men, 81.7 per cent (NSO 1994). The more relevant information with respect to food security and sustainability is rural functional literacy (RFL) from which rural functional illiteracy (RFI) is calculated as RFI in per cent = 100 − RFL in per cent. On the average RFI yielded a distressing figure of 42 per cent. Across 14 regions in the country, RFI gave a wide range of 31.8 to 60 per cent. Thus, even the lowest RFI means that one of every three persons in rural communities is functionally illiterate.

Figure 12.2. Functional literacy in the Philippines

for non-farm jobs. Social vent came in the form of migration. One portion went to urban centres and further swelled the urban poor, a second portion went to sugar and coconut farms where wages are below subsistence, and a third portion went to the upland areas with slopes greater than 18 per cent. The magnitude of upland migration is reflected by the hectarage of cropped upland, which increased more than sixfold from 0.58 million hectares in 1960 to 3.92 million hectares in 1987 (Cruz et al. 1992). In 1991, less than 3 per cent of the total number of farm owners accounted for more than 30 per cent of total farmland.

Indigenous peoples in upland and forested areas have their native way of ecologically working with nature, although at subsistence level. In contrast the migrants tilled the soil like they did in the flatlands, and caused extensive soil erosion. Meanwhile, scarcity of fuelwood drove the farmers to cut down trees and shrubs within reach. Magnify the scenario a million times and visualize the extent of eroded lands, loss of biodiversity, and accelerated deforestation. The scarred land snuffs the hope of the millions of upland children for a better life. The Department of Environment and Natural Resources has well-meaning programmes on reforestation, rehabilitation of watersheds, and innovative management of protected areas, but it is constrained by inefficiency and the pace of implementation. Some NGOs do productive work with the migrants, but they are like a few grains in a bucket of sand.

The Indian rural scenario is dominated by the same mix of problems: landlessness, poverty, and an unskilled labour force, but at higher intensity. Landless farm workers make up 45 per cent of the rural poor. Migration to the forestlands also became a natural vent for these people. At the beginning of the 1990s, about 300 million rural poor depended on forest resources for livelihood (Poffenberger 1990). Forest cover was estimated to be 63.9 million hectares (MEF 1991). The ecological impact of converting forestland into farm lots by millions of inhabitants is aggravated by their huge daily requirements of fuelwood for cooking and fodder for livestock. About 100 million livestock grazed on forestland with a carrying capacity of only 31 million (Collins, Sayer, and Whitmore 1991).

Forestland degradation is indeed an immense problem, but India has been fairly successful in pursuing innovative approaches to forest management. Implementation of partnerships between inhabitants and forestry departments facilitated by NGOs is a recognized feat achieved after many years of conflict.

Poverty alleviation

Poverty reduction causes an equivalent rise in food security at household level. Hence, governments across developing Asia gave priority attention to programmes on poverty alleviation. Based on their performance up to the early 1990s, Balisacan (1996) observed impressive annual rural poverty reduction (RPR) rates (1.38 to 2.19 per cent) for China, Indonesia, Malaysia, Thailand, Bangladesh, and India. Much lower annual RPR values (0.25 to 0.61 per cent) characterized Nepal, Pakistan, and the Philippines. Among countries in the first group, only China and Indonesia had annual RPR that slightly exceeded annual population growth (0.39 and 0.26, respectively). All the rest gave negative values, but the most negative were attributed to Nepal (−2.34 per cent), Pakistan (−2.19 per cent), and the Philippines (−2.05 per cent). Negative value indicates a net increase in the number of rural poor in spite of an often-cited achievement in poverty reduction.

In great contrast to the snail-paced RPR of these countries is the remarkable success of South Korea in handling its rural poverty. As early as 1970, South Korea had reduced rural poverty to 23.5 per cent, but strove further to reduce it to 6.5 per cent in 1988. Their determination to succeed was undaunted by the fact that 62 per cent of farms were less than one hectare in size.

The above consideration gave a priority role to the social and economic constraints of food security. Their role has always been masked by the dominant image of science and technology. Food producers who have been freed from social and economic shackles are better equipped to face biophysical and institutional constraints to food security.

Biophysical constraints

Food producers also have to contend with biophysical constraints to food production. Extension workers are useful agents but the farmers are the stakeholders. Biophysical constraints refer to the limiting effects of soil and water resources and agroclimatic conditions. Assessment and mapping of these constraints over agricultural lands in a geographic unit serve as a practical basis of policies, guidelines, and programmes for integrated management that may turn constraints into production assets. This is a perspective viewpoint on how relevant institutions perform their role in facilitating food production.

On a large scale, biophysical constraints are addressed by governments and corrective measures are implemented, otherwise food security is compromised. Typical examples of such programmes are infrastructure projects (large and small) to provide irrigation water to croplands over widespread drought areas and drain excess water in some waterlogged areas. In arid regions, desertification is one of the toughest problems that confronts government and public sectors. Practically speaking, it cannot be corrected by massive infrastructure investment but by the painstaking and slow process of establishing tree lines.

Table 12.7 Extent of major limitations for agriculture of soil resources in South-East Asia

Soil-related constraint	Percentage of land area	Area (million ha.)
No serious limitation	14	53.2
Mineral stress[a]	59	224.2
Excess water	19	72.2
Shallow depth	6	22.8
Drought	2	7.6

Source: Dent 1980
[a] Nutritional deficiencies or toxicities related to chemical composition or mode of origin.

In contrast to those biophysical constraints that are mitigated by government action, the soil constraints prevailing on farm lands are dealt with by farmers themselves. Resource-rich farmers are capable of overcoming constraints but poor families usually opt for subsistence farming by ignoring the situation. The latter option is a disastrous one on fragile lands.

For a cursory look at the extent of soil constraints in South-East Asia (Indonesia, Cambodia, Laos, Malaysia, the Philippines, Singapore, Thailand, and Viet Nam), the summary in Table 12.7 is useful. In over 380 million hectares, only 14 per cent of the land has no serious limitations. These are the prime agricultural lands. Serious limitations due to excess water (swamps, marshes, peat bogs, etc.), shallow depth (thin soil layers over bedrocks usually on steep slopes), and drought (sandy areas in arid climates) make land uneconomical to reclaim with current technologies.

The largest group of limitations (59 per cent) consists of various forms of mineral stress on plants, primarily due to soil nutrient deficiencies, nutrient imbalance, and toxicities of elements and substances. Some of these problems may be too severe to warrant reclamation but other problems can be corrected by technologies that have long been developed by agricultural researchers. The bottleneck is in their adoption and proper use by farmers. Again, poverty and functional illiteracy come into focus. They are the bottlenecks that can only be relieved substantially by an institutional framework designed to address social, economic, and technical needs/problems in their holistic occurrence and natural setting.

Institutional constraints

The issues of agriculture and food security are vital concerns to every agricultural country. A wide array of institutions have thus long been established, with wide-ranging functions such as agrarian reform, agricultural production and processing, credit, trade, education, research, extension, irrigation, and rural development. These institutions have long-standing bureaucracies but development priorities are often set by incumbent officials of the state. Beyond political dependence, however, the institutions have, over the years, fortified their framework in a way primarily geared to the preservation of their functioning (existence) rather than their functional objectives. Adjunct to their preservation, the institutions do not formulate and pursue policies not in consonance with the interest of ruling political and business élites.

Some institutions may have undergone reorientation in some functions or even changes in name, but still preservation of their existence is paramount. The new-found objectives are often used to endear the institutions to the people instead of striving harder to make people benefit from the institutions.

Economic prosperity has long been the aspiration of poor nations. For many past decades, however, the aspiring nations have not recognized the path-dependent nature of development and the culture dependence of this path. An outstanding example is education and research. In spite of burgeoning poverty and illiteracy among their people, governments of poor nations relentlessly invested huge resources in higher education up to postgraduate degrees following the narrowly specialized fields of the agricultural sciences. Meanwhile, the huge masses of poor and functionally illiterate farmers have been merely treated as passive recipients of technology. Contrary to this, NGOs have shown that there are alternative and innovative ways and means of harnessing the rural poor as active partners in development.

Conclusion: Coping with food insecurity

In view of the above discussion, the issue of food security goes beyond the question of supply and food balances. Ample domestic production and international trade can significantly alleviate food insecurity in developing countries. But the issue at stake is an equitable distribution of food within nations. There is no food security without access to food. Market forces alone cannot fully assure people's access to food. They should be harnessed and supplemented by more innovative domestic and international institutional arrangements. By way of conclusion, four major policy agendas are suggested below.

Education and the role of small farmers

In the past, developing countries and assisting international organizations focused primarily on science and technology and infrastructure needs of agriculture and food production. Since the 1970s, science and technology have demonstrated the high yield potentials of a continually increasing number of new breeds of plants and animals and new production technologies. Crop and livestock yields did increase, but there have been wide gaps between experimental plots and farmers' fields. Such yield gaps have been narrowed down by governments (like South Korea, Taiwan, and Japan) that gave equal attention to institutional, agrarian, and social reforms. Similar purposive reforms have not been pursued by most other countries in Asia. These are the countries whose yield gaps between experimental stations and farmers' fields remained wide. The few exceptions observed in recent years were achieved by governments that pumped in subsidies for production inputs.

In the light of empirical reality in developing countries, however, technology advances alone are not enough. One useful strategy would be to ensure that advances in science and technology are in the hands of farmers. Social and institutional reforms should now build up the knowledge and skills and productive capacity of food producers. The educational process requires innovative strategies and methodologies designed to cover tens or hundreds of millions of the rural populace. Non-farm skills should be apportioned to rural workers who are beyond the absorptive capacity of the agricultural labour force.

The educational process could be painstakingly slow due to low literacy, a dominating culture of passivity, and apparent hopelessness beyond subsistence. To follow traditional methods of non-formal education could defeat a noble purpose even at its initial stage. The educational process should explore creative, stimulating, and dynamic approaches; it should explore innovative strategies. The methodology should be participatory and evolutionary. Build-up of knowledge and skills should be relevant to prevailing resources and conditions in the locality; biophysical, social, cultural, and economic.

The education of small farmers is a key component of a broader strategy to ensure that agricultural and economic growth are linked to increases in household income. The baseline objective is to avoid growth-centric approaches that can result in negative boomerang effects. For instance, while the technology package spread by the Green Revolution did bring about unprecedented production increases in Asia, evidence also points to the fact that greater access to credit and fertilizer subsidies among larger farms shifted benefits to larger growers, victimizing small farmers. This illustrates fundamental limits to market solutions to food insecurity in developing countries. A visible hand of the state should be able to correct market failures (Gershman 1998).

Public investment and market participation

The sincerity of the state in embarking on a massive educational programme could be ascertained by carrying out simultaneous infrastructure projects such as farm-to-market roads, irrigation or water-impounding facilities, and drainage systems. These are part and parcel of the state's overall development programme for the sustainability of agriculture and food production.

Granted that infrastructure projects and educational programmes are already in place, there is still one overriding and motivating force that could accelerate the people's quest for knowledge and skills. This is a visible access to a market system that provides fair prices and decent incomes to farm households. The motivating force of market opportunities on farmers' education has been a long-standing observation in Taiwan and Japan during the formative years of their agricultural development. Government-sponsored training courses were deemed inadequate by farmers who had been motivated by good market prices. They preferred to pay and enrol in certain specialized training courses that gave them additional skills and sharpened their edge of competitiveness.

In the same vein, it has long been a practice among farmers in rich countries to donate private funds for research and development on commodities of their choice. Such varying levels of quest for new knowledge and technical skills are practically motivated by profit. At the present time, however, the profit motive shares its prominence with sustainability concerns for the resource base that produces the food.

Forming new partnerships

The question of food security and sustainability cannot be solely dealt with by market forces and the state. There must be a new form of partnership among the state, farmers, and NGOs. NGOs in the field of agriculture have shown quite a successful track record in grassroots education, research and development, and other forms of extension services to the farm sector. For instance, a Philippine NGO, Farmer-Scientist Partnership for Development, which was established in 1986 to respond to farmers' needs for new rice cultivars, came out with a research-cum-training project where farmers developed more than 50 new rice cultivars. Aside from saving on time, money, and resources, the farmers could obtain unique knowledge and skill (rice breeding) on varied aspects of sustainable and diversified farm systems. Likewise, NGOs can play an effective role in enhancing food security and sustainability in developing countries.

Linking domestic and international arenas

While free market rhetoric is being used to fashion international free trade agreements, this chapter has shown that some elements go against the spirit of genuine free market reforms. Developing countries in Asia should play a more active role in calling for steeper cuts in both explicit and implicit subsidies to agricultural exports from the OECD countries, principally the European Union and the United States. They must also be aggressive in invoking provisions of the GATT-UR to defend smallholder production. Japan and South Korea have been able to utilize sanitary and photosanitary considerations convincingly against the influx of chemically treated imported fruits and vegetables, and in the process assist their own fruit and vegetable growers (Bello 1997). The scheduled WTO review on the agricultural accord in 1999 offers an excellent opportunity for developing Asia to ventilate its agenda. The Cairns Group, a group that emerged during the Uruguay Round negotiations composed of the Philippines, Australia, New Zealand, Argentina, and other medium-sized agricultural exporting countries, is also a potential avenue for the articulation of the same. In addition, developing countries in Asia and the world should more actively seek coordinated efforts through the United Nations, the best venue through which structural reforms of the agricultural sector in developing countries can be assisted.

It has been observed that in poor countries which have achieved food security, the strategies "seem to be based upon creating the political, social and economic conditions under which ambitious programmes of public support are undertaken with determination and effectiveness" (Dreze and Sen 1989, cited in Gershman 1998). This chapter has outlined some of those conditions which are by no means complete. In the final analysis, food insecurity is as much a political concern as an economic one, which market-related reforms in trade and fiscal policies alone cannot comprehensively address.

Notes

1. The implementing guidelines of the minimum access volume (MAV) stand among the most criticized aspects of the agreement. Even as it is touted to be a "freer market" mechanism, its logic is not governed at all by free market principles. David (1996) cites how the guidelines tend to counter the spirit of tariffication in as much as (a) access to imports under MAV is not bid out but is based on historical market shares in the initial year, thus quota rents will accrue to those granted access; (b) whenever there is a perceived shortage as described in the introduction to this chapter, MAV will be increased but the increase will have to be approved by Congress; (c) the National Food Authority (NFA) is both an MAV consolidator and a member of the MAV management team, thus it can provide indirect pressure for importation to be coursed through it; and (d) all revenues derived from MAV in-quota tariff duties are earmarked by Congress for rural infrastructure, research, and development programme proposals coming from the private sector, including agricultural and agri-business groups representing the producers of commodities where quantitative restrictions have been lifted.

REFERENCES

Agcaoili, M. and M. Rosegrant. 1995. "Global and Regional Food Supply: Demand and Trade Prospects to 2010." In *Population and Food in the Early Twenty-first Century*, ed. N. Islam. Washington: IFPRI.

Alexandratos, N. 1995. "The Outlook for World Food and Agriculture to Year 2010." In *Population and Food in the Early Twenty-first Century*, ed. N. Islam. Washington: IFPRI.

Anderson, K., B. Dimaranan, T. Hertel, and W. Martin. 1996. "Asia Pacific Food Markets and Trade in 2005: A Global, Economy-wide Perspective." Paper presented at the Conference on Food and Agricultural Policy Challenges for the Asia Pacific, 1–3 October, Manila, Philippines.

Balisacan, A. 1996. "Agricultural Growth and Rural Poverty in Developing Countries of Asia and the Pacific." In *Rural Poverty Alleviation and Sustainable Development in Asia and the Pacific*. Bangkok: ESCAP Rural and Urban Development Division.

Bardhan, P. 1996. "Efficiency, Equity and Poverty Alleviation: Policy Issues in Less Developed Countries." *The Economic Journal* 106: 1344–1356.

Bello, W. 1997. "Strategic Policy for Food Security." *Public Policy* 1(1).

Brown, L. R. 1995. *Who Will Feed China: Wake-up Call for a Small Planet.* Worldwatch Environmental Alert Series. London: Earthscan.

Brown, M. and I. Goldin. 1992. *The Future of Agriculture: Developing Country Implications.* Paris: OECD Development Centre Studies.

Clarete, R. 1992. "Structural Adjustment and Agriculture: Developing a Research Analytical Framework." Working Paper No. 92–91. Makati, Philippines: Philippine Institute for Development Studies.

Collins, M., J. Sayer, and T. Whitmore, eds. 1991. *The Conservation Atlas of Tropical Forests: Asia and the Pacific.* London: Macmillan.

Cruz, M. C., C. Meyer, R. Repetto, and R. Woodward. 1992. *Population Growth, Poverty and Environmental Stress: Frontier Migration in the Philippines and Costa Rica.* Washington: World Resources Institute.

David, C. 1996. "Agricultural Policy and the WTO Agreement: The Philippine Case." Paper presented at the Conference on Food and Agricultural Policy Challenges for the Asia Pacific, 1–3 October, Manila, Philippines.

Dent, F. J. 1980. "Major Production Systems and Soil-Related Constraints in Southeast Asia." In *Soil-Related Constraints to Production in the Tropics*. Los Banos, Philippines: International Rice Research Institute.

Dreze, J. and A. Sen. 1989. *Hunger and Public Action.* New York: Oxford University Press.

FAO (Food and Agricultural Organization). 1996a. "Food Security and Nutrition." Provisional version of Technical Paper No. 10, World Food Summit. Rome: FAO.

FAO (Food and Agricultural Organization). 1996b. "Rome Declaration on World Food Security." World Food Summit. Rome: FAO.

FAO (Food and Agricultural Organization). 1997. FAO Statistical Database. Internet ⟨http://www.fao.org⟩.

Gershman, J. 1998. "Beyond Markets and Protectionism: Politically Incorrect Reflections on Entitlements, Empowerment and Food Security." Paper presented at the Freedom from Debt Coalition Conference on Food Security, 30–31 March, Silang, Cavite, Philippines.

Lim, J. 1996. "Issues Concerning the Three Major Agricultural Crops and GATT." In *The General Agreement on Tariffs and Trade: Philippine Issues and Perspectives*, ed. J. Reyes. Manila: Philippine Peasant Institute.

MEF (Ministry of Environment and Forests). 1991. *The State of Forest Report*. India: Dahra Dun.

Mitchell, D. O. and M. D. Ingco. 1995. "Global and Regional World Food and Agricultural Prospects." In *Population and Food in the Early Twenty-first Century*, ed. N. Islam. Washington: IFPRI.

Montemayor, R. 1995. "The GATT Masterplan Budget: A Litany of Broken Promises." Speech delivered before the Tenth Congress of the Philippine House of Representatives, Metro Manila, Philippines.

NSO (National Statistics Office), in coordination with Department of Education, Culture and Sports (DECS), Philippines. 1994. *Functional Literacy, Education and Mass Media Survey (FLEMMS)*. Metro Manila: NSO and DECS.

OECD (Organization for Economic Cooperation and Development). 1995. *Agricultural Policies, Markets and Trade in OECD Countries*. Paris: OECD.

Poffenberger, M., ed. 1990. *Forest Management Partnerships: Regenerating India's Forest*. Executive summary of Workshop on Sustainable Forestry, 10–12 September, New Delhi. New Delhi: The Ford Foundation and Indian Environmental Society.

Setboonsarng, S. and M. Rosegrant. 1992. "Comparative Analysis of Production and Marketing of Corn in the Philippines and Thailand." In *The Philippine Corn/Livestock Sector: Performance and Policy Implications*, eds M. Rosegrant and L. Gonzales. Washington: IFPRI.

UNDP (United Nations Development Programme). 1996. *Human Development Report 1996*. New York: UNDP.

Watkins, K. 1996. "The European Union's Common Agricultural Policy (CAP) and Impact of the Northern Food System on the South." Paper presented to the South-East Asian NGO Conference on Food Security and Fair Trade, 13–16 February, University of the Philippines, Quezon City, Philippines.

Watkins, K. and M. Windfuhr. 1994. "Agriculture in the Uruguay Round: Implications for Sustainable Development in Developing Countries." WWF International Discussion Paper. Gland: Worldwide Fund for Nature.

FURTHER READING

ADB (Asian Development Bank). 1995. *Key Indicators of Developing Asian and Pacific Countries*. Oxford: Oxford University Press.

ADB (Asian Development Bank). 1996. *Key Indicators of Developing Asian and Pacific Countries*. Oxford: Oxford University Press.

Ahmed, S. 1995. "Fertilizer Use in Asia: How High Can It Rise?" In *Proceedings of APO-FFTC Seminar on Appropriate Use of Fertilizer in Asia and the Pacific*. Tokyo: Asian Productivity Organization.

Ange, A. L. 1993. "Rice Yields and Fertilizer Use in Asia." Paper presented at the Seventeenth Consultation on the FAO Fertilizer Programme, 9–13 May, Islamabad, Pakistan.

Balisacan, A. 1995. *Agriculture in Transition: Arresting Poverty in the Rural Sector*. Tokyo: Institute of Development Economics.

Bulatao, R., E. Bos, M. T. Vu, and E. Massiah. 1990. *1989–1990 World Population Projection*. Washington: World Bank.

FAO (Food and Agricultural Organization). 1994. *Production Yearbook*. Rome: FAO.

FAO (Food and Agricultural Organization). 1996. "Food Requirements and Population Growth." Provisional version of Technical Paper No. 10, World Food Summit. Rome: FAO.

Putzel, J. 1996. "A Comparative Assessment of Governance and Food Security." Paper presented at the South-East Asian NGO Conference on Food Security and Fair Trade, 13–16 February, Quezon City, Philippines.

UNDP (United Nations Development Programme). 1995. *Human Development Report 1995*. New York: UNDP.

World Bank. 1986. *Poverty and Hunger*. Washington: World Bank.

World Bank. 1996. *World Development Report*. Washington: World Bank.

Regional arrangements

13

Environmental governance – the potential of regional institutions: Introduction

Muthiah Alagappa

The traditional role of regional institutions has been in the areas of peace, security, and economic development. The significance and role of regional arrangements in maintaining international peace and security, for example, are recognized in the UN Charter. Chapter 8 of the Charter details the role of regional arrangements in the context of the UN system for maintaining international peace and security. In practice, peace and security are among the key concerns of regional organizations in all parts of the world. Similarly, regional arrangements to promote economic development have been common since 1945. Regional environmental cooperation, however, is relatively new and can be traced to the 1970s. Since then regional arrangements and agencies pertaining to the environment have proliferated in nearly all parts of the world. Increasing awareness of environmental problems and their growing magnitude, and recognition of the transnational character of many of these problems and the close interconnection between environment and socio-economic development, account for the growth in environment-related regional arrangements. Regional institutions are becoming an important component of the global architecture for environmental governance.

The role and effectiveness, and hence the significance, of regional institutions, however, vary widely. They depend on the nature of the problem (global issues, specific regional or subregional concerns, bilateral problems, or issues of concern within state boundaries), the level at which it is addressed, and the nature of the specific regional institution and its capacity to address such problems. All these factors vary widely. In practice, therefore, the role of regional institutions in managing the environment is not uniform across regions and subregions. Some, like those in Western Europe, are more effective and have a much higher role capacity than those in other regions and subregions.

Recognizing the existence of such variations, this overview and the three chapters that follow describe and analyse the role and place of regional institutions in environmental governance in general terms, on the understanding that the role of specific institutions will have to be determined on the basis of their respective strengths and weaknesses, and the nature of the problem to be dealt with. The overview and chapters address three key questions.

• What roles can and do regional institutions play in managing environmental concerns?
• What explains their effectiveness or non-effectiveness?
• How do regional agencies relate to other actors like the state, global institutions, the private sector, and NGOs who are also involved in managing the environment?

One must begin by defining regional arrangements and agencies. Regional arrangements or regionalism (these two terms are used interchangeably in this chapter) may be defined as "cooperation among governments or non-governmental organizations in three or more geographically proximate and interdependent countries for the pursuit of mutual gain in one or more issue areas" (Alagappa 1997, 423). Regional agencies refer to formal and informal regional organizations (with physical and organizational infrastructure, staff, budgets, etc.) with responsibility for implementing regional arrangements. Such agencies may be regionwide, sometimes spanning a continent like the Organization of American States (OAS) and the Organization of African Unity (OAU), or may be subregional like the Association of South-East Asian Nations (ASEAN), the Southern Common Market (MERCOSUR) in Latin America, the Southern African Development Community (SADC), and the Commonwealth of Independent States (CIS) that comprises the republics of the former Soviet Union. Regional agencies are usually coterminous with regional arrangements, but not necessarily so. The term "institutions" is used in this chapter to cover both regional arrangements and agencies.

Regional environmental arrangements may be sector-specific, like the 1979 Geneva Convention on Long-range Transboundary Air Pollution and the 1992 Helsinki Convention on the Protection and Use of Transboundary Watercourses and International Lakes. Or they may be case-specific like the Nile Basin Action Plan, the Treaty for Amazon Cooperation, and the Convention for the Protection of the Mediterranean Sea

Against Pollution. Sectoral and case-specific arrangements are often interrelated, with the former providing an umbrella framework for the latter. Sectoral and case-specific arrangements may lead to the creation of separate specialized agencies or they may be nested in existing multi-purpose regional institutions like the European Union, the OAS, the OAU, MERCOSUR, and ASEAN.

What role for regional institutions?

In generic terms, regional institutions can play a number of roles, including:
- provision of high-level forums to map the regional environmental agenda, articulate regional goals, and build relevant regional norms;
- facilitation of regional input into the formulation of global conventions and the implementation of such conventions through their translation into regional conventions and national action plans;
- development and management of regional initiatives and action plans to address transboundary environmental problems in the region;
- mediation of disputes between member states; and
- harmonization of national efforts on issues that fall under the domestic jurisdiction of member states.

Provision of high-level forums

Nearly every region and subregion has one or more ministerial-level forums on the environment. A Permanent Commission has been established by the OAS to promote and coordinate environmental cooperation in the Americas. Latin America has its own high-level forum in the annual Meeting of the Ministers of the Environment that is organized in cooperation with UNEP's Latin America regional office. The high-level policy forums in Africa include the African Ministerial Conferences on the Environment (AMCEN) established in 1985 under the auspices of UNEP, the African Economic Community (AEC) established within the framework of the OAU and the 1992 Abuja Treaty, and the Council of Arab Ministers Responsible for the Environment (CAMRE). In Asia, the forum for Asia-Pacific Economic Cooperation (APEC) has periodic meetings of environment ministers. Beginning with the Dobris Conference in 1991, pan-Europe ministerial-level conferences have been held regularly. Subregional organizations have their own ministerial-level forums.

These forums play an important role in identifying critical regional concerns, mapping the regional environmental agenda, articulating and building consensus for regional goals and norms, identifying opportunities for regional cooperation, and facilitating such cooperation. The first pan-European Conference of Environmental Ministers that took place in 1991 in Dobris (in the then Czechoslovakia), for example, initiated the preparation of the first pan-European assessment and development of an environmental plan for all of Europe. Subsequent conferences in this process were held in 1993, 1995, and 1998. The 1995 Sofia Declaration endorsed the Environmental Programme for Europe (EPE), based on the Dobris Assessment that was prepared in response to the request of the 1991 conference. The EPE is linked to Agenda 21, adopted at the Rio Summit in 1992. Another concrete outcome of this process is the endorsement in Lucerne in 1993 of the Environment Action Plan for Central and Eastern Europe (EAP/CEE). This programme was developed by an international task force composed of the European Commission, the World Bank, and the OECD, and the European Union provides a methodology for integrating environmental concerns into the economic transitions of the CEE countries. The three key components of the programme are setting priorities, strengthening institutional capacity, and developing cost-effective financing for environmental action.

In the Americas, the OAS adopted the Inter-American Programme of Action for Environmental Protection in 1991 (Munoz 1992, 33–41). In addition to stating the objectives, principles, and tasks of the OAS in environmental protection, the programme identified the measures that should be taken by individual member states as well as through regional cooperation. The purposes of high-level forums are nicely summed up by the stated objectives of the annual Meeting of the Ministers of Environment. These include mapping and guiding the implementation of the environmental agenda in Latin America, identifying opportunities for regional cooperation in environmental matters, achieving greater effectiveness and coherence in regional planning and implementation of the global environmental agenda, and adoption of common positions on topics of importance to the region (UNEP 1995).

Input into and implementation of global conventions

A key role of high-level forums is the forging of common regional positions on global issues like the depletion of the ozone layer, climate change, and biodiversity loss. They can identify the regional dimensions of the problems, formulate priorities, and present regional perspectives at global forums. The OAU, for example, submitted a comprehensive report entitled "African Common Position on Environment and Development" to the Earth Summit in 1992 as its contribution to Agenda 21. In the course of negotiating a global convention, regional agencies can advance the collective interests of member states by seeking to influence the terms of the related conventions. The European Community, for example, played a key role in the formulation of the 1985 Vienna Convention for Protection of the Ozone Layer, the 1987 Montreal Protocol on Substances that Deplete the Ozone Layer, and the 1992 UN Framework Convention on Climate Change (UNFCCC). The role of the European Community and later the European Union in this regard, however, may be rather unique. Unlike other regional arrangements, a key goal of the European Union is economic as well as some form of political and legal integration. Its member states are legally bound by various treaties, beginning with the 1957 Treaty of Rome, to agree on common positions. The European Union can be granted a political mandate by its member states to negotiate on their behalf, and they are bound to comply with the negotiated instrument. The European Union also has the necessary institutional and financial resources, and the technical expertise, to pursue specific goals in global forums. Other regional agencies are not so advantaged and they have not been active players at the global level. Often member states of such regional organizations have acted jointly under the label of developing countries, while states like the United States and Japan have acted in their individual capacities. This was the case, for example, in the third UNFCCC Conference of the Parties meeting in Kyoto in December 1997, where negotiations were essentially among four parties: the European Union, the United States, Japan, and the developing countries. The unity of the latter group rested on their common goal to secure the commitment of developed countries to cut their emissions of greenhouse gases while seeking to maintain the exemption granted to developing countries under the Berlin Mandate.

Although the role of regional agencies in the developing world may be limited in the formulation phase of global conventions, they can play a larger role in integrating global programmes into existing regional policy frameworks, and, where necessary and feasible, developing additional initiatives or measures in light of local knowledge and conditions. They can also coordinate and assist in the translation of global conventions into national action plans through information-sharing, education and training schemes, and capacity-building in member states. Finally, regional agencies can monitor implementation of global conventions, assess their effectiveness, and prepare regional reports.

This has been the case in Asia, for example, in relation to the global Convention on Biological Diversity. The ASEAN Agreement on the Conservation of Nature and Natural Resources establishes a regional framework on biological diversity conservation and sustainable use. The framework seeks to enhance the protection and conservation of heritage areas and endangered species, and strengthen research and development capacities in member states. In South Asia the South Asian Cooperative Environment Programme's (SACEP) strategy and action programme (1992–1996) includes biodiversity as a priority area. It has plans in the areas of conservation of wildlife, corals, mangroves, deltas, and coastal areas. The ADB initiated efforts to translate the recommendations of the global convention on biodiversity through financial assistance to member countries. Indonesia, for example, was a recipient of an ADB loan and technical assistance in 1992 to conserve biodiversity in an area covering about 500,000 hectares.

The African Common Perspective and Position on Biological Diversity adopted by AMCEN in 1994 stipulates the strategy on biological diversity for Africa. It seeks to develop expertise, establish regional research institutes, and strengthen institutional capacity in this issue area. In combating land degradation, another critical concern in Africa, several regional programmes have been instituted to implement the UN Convention to Combat Desertification. Subregional organizations like the SADC, the Inter-State Committee for Drought Control (CILSS), the Economic Community of West African States (ECOWAS), the Intergovernmental Authority on Development (IGAD), and the African Development Bank have also taken initiatives to strengthen regional cooperation in combating land degradation. AMCEN has an important role in combating desertification though its Committee on Deserts and Arid Lands.

Initiatives on region-specific concerns

Apart from their role in formulating and implementing global conventions, regional agencies may also develop and manage programmes on issues which are of concern to the region but not covered by global conventions. This was the case, for example, with respect to the issue of transboundary air pollution in Europe. The efforts of the Scandinavian states, though initially resisted by some EC countries including Britain and Germany, led eventually to the adoption of the 1979 (European) Convention on Long-range Transboundary Air Pollution. A number of protocols have been adopted under this framework. Under the 1985 Helsinki Protocol, member states undertook to reduce their sulphur emissions by the end of 1993 to at least 30 per cent below 1980 levels. Under the 1988 Sofia Protocol, they undertook to stabilize nitrogen oxide emissions at 1987 levels by the end of 1994. The 1991 Geneva Protocol concerned control of emissions of volatile organic compounds or their transboundary fluxes and the 1994 Oslo Protocol sought to reduce sulphur emissions further. In 1998 two new protocols were adopted on heavy metals and persistent organic pollutants.

Regional arrangements have been instituted in Latin America to manage large ecosystems such as Amazonia, the Andes, the Central American tropical forests, the Southern Pacific, and the Caribbean small island states. The Treaty of Amazon Cooperation, for example, established a Special Commission for the Amazonian Environment that operates eight environmental programmes in the affected states. Similarly, action has been taken in Africa at the subregional level in the management and use of international waters and their basins. The SADC has a Protocol on Shared Watercourse Systems. Action plans exist for the management of the Zambezi River basin, Lake Chad basin, and the Okavango. Action plans exist in Europe for the management of many seas including the Aral, Baltic, Black, and Mediterranean Seas as well as some major river basins including the Danube and the Rhine. In South-East Asia, with the assistance of the UNDP, the riparian states negotiated the Agreement on Cooperation for the Sustainable Development of the Mekong River Basin in 1995 and established the Mekong River Commission. The agreement stipulates the principles for sustainable development, utilization, management, and conservation of the water and related resources, and the institutional, financial, and management issues relating to the Mekong River Commission.

Mediation of bilateral disputes

At the bilateral level, regional institutions can play a mediator role in disputes among member states. The European Union, for example, was instrumental in the resolution of the dispute between Hungary and Slovakia over the construction of two dams in the Danube River basin. In the wake of the 1989 political revolution, both Czechoslovakia and Hungary, faced with domestic protests from environmental groups, decided to abandon their respective dam projects to generate electricity. The dam project in Czechoslovakia (now in Slovakia) was very near completion. Subsequently, however, Czechoslovakia decided to go ahead and finish the project. Citing ecological concerns, Hungary objected vehemently and vowed to stop completion of the project. Following the failure of bilateral negotiations, the European Union was asked in April 1992 to mediate the conflict. For several reasons, including the inability of the scientific community to agree on the nature and extent of the environmental damage, the European Union could not mediate the dispute by itself. It was, however, successful in defusing political tensions (which became more acute with the spilt of Czechoslovakia in 1993 and Slovakia's publicly declared intention to finish the project and fill the reservoir) and in persuading both countries to submit the matter to the jurisdiction of the International Court of Justice. The European Union's success was in part due to the leverage it had over Hungary and Slovakia, both of which desire EU membership. Acceptance of the principles and norms that inform the behaviour of EU states was a way of demonstrating their readiness for such membership.

Provision of technical assistance and harmonization of national legislation

Regional institutions can also play a role in some matters, like the management of toxic waste disposal, that are essentially within the domestic jurisdiction of member states. Regional conventions in such areas may set standards and provide technical assistance in the enactment of national legislation, and in monitoring the implementation of such legislation. They may also regulate the international dimensions of such problems. The ASEAN Strategic Plan of Action on the Environment, for example, emphasizes the promotion of environmentally sound management of toxic chemicals and hazardous waste in member states and the control of transboundary movement of hazardous waste. Strategy 7 of the strategic plan seeks to establish regional guidelines for assessing highly polluting industries and for the safe handling of potentially harmful chemicals entering the ASEAN region. In Central America, the Central American Commission for Environment and Development (CCAD) joined forces with the Central American Inter-Parliamentary Commission on the Environment (CICAD) to help set up regional networks of NGOs and government bodies to monitor the dumping of wastes. An agreement was signed in 1992 by seven countries to ban the importation or the international transportation of hazardous material. In Africa, the 1991 Bamako Convention on the Ban of the Import into Africa and the Control of Transboundary Movement and Management of Hazardous Wastes within Africa outlaws the importation of any hazardous waste into Africa.

Supporting functions and services

In addition to the above roles, regional institutions can provide a number of support functions and services that are critical to the success of global and regional initiatives as well as national action plans. These include:
- capacity-building through the development of regional databases and information-sharing systems, as well as regional training schemes;
- providing access to environmentally clean technologies and production processes;
- arranging funding support; and
- fostering interface among and the development of regional networks of governments, knowledge communities, NGOs, grassroots organizations, and other actors.

The development of reliable and mutually accepted data is crucial to the identification of common problems and forging consensus on policy measures necessary to address such problems. For a number of reasons, including human, institutional, and financial resource constraints, the national production of data is difficult. Moreover, the accuracy of such data is often contested by other parties. In North-East Asia, for example, studies by Japanese scholars suggest that China is a major source of wet sulphate deposition in Japan. Studies by Chinese scholars, on the other hand, suggest that China only accounts for 3.5 per cent of Japan's total sulphur deposition. Clearly, joint research activities by scientists from affected countries as well as from other states and agencies would help in producing a mutually acceptable database and facilitate the development of joint policies (Streets et al. 1999). Such collaborative studies, initially by the European Air Chemistry Network created in 1956 by the International Meteorological Institute, and later by the OECD and the European Community, were critical in the development of joint policy measures to address the acid rain problem in Europe. Europe now has a clear policy of promoting access to and sharing information on the environment. The 1995 Sofia Ministerial Conference endorsed the UN-ECE Guidelines on Access to Environmental Information and Public Participation in Environmental Decision-Making, and has recommended that it be developed into a convention. Agencies created to implement the UN-ECE guidelines include the European Information and Observation Network of the European Environmental Agency (EEA), and UNEP's Environment and Natural Resources Information Networking (ENRIN) programme. There have been efforts in other regions as well to develop regional databases and regional information-sharing schemes. ASEAN, for example, has established an information-sharing network on the transboundary movement of toxic chemicals and hazardous waste.

Closely related to this function is that of regional education and training to develop expertise and strengthen regional and national institutional capacities. The Central American Commission for Environment and Development, for example, initiated a project in 1994 to train the staff of government environmental agencies in participatory methods for policy formulation. In South-East Asia, ASEAN, with financial and technical assistance from the ADB, has instituted several training and information-sharing schemes in areas like the standardization of national environmental legislation, water quality management and industrial pollution, and appropriate technology transfer within the region.

Environmentally clean technologies and processes are critical to the success of regional and national action plans. For reasons alluded to earlier, individual states are often not in a position to fund and develop such technologies on their own. Acting collectively they have better prospects for both local development and the acquisition and transfer of such technologies from more developed states and regional institutions. One of the objectives of the Inter-American Programme of Action for Environmental Protection is to "sponsor and support projects for design and use of technologies that further environmental protection."

Arranging financial support is another critical function that can be undertaken by regional institutions. Most regions have development banks that now include an environmental portfolio. Regional banks like the European Bank for Reconstruction and Development (EBRD) and the ADB have funded studies and supported specific projects, some of which have been noted in earlier discussion. In addition, regional institutions can also facilitate funding support for regional and national action plans from other regional agencies and states.

Finally, regional agencies, by serving nesting and cross-fertilization functions, have played a catalytic role in fostering cooperation among governments, NGOs, scientific communities, and other actors. The Central American Commission for Environment and Development, for example, brings together representatives of governments, NGOs, grassroots groups, and international agencies to discuss, analyse, and develop policy proposals and action plans in the areas of forestry and toxic waste disposal. Similarly, in Europe regional participatory networks, involving national governments, regional and international organizations, and NGOs are gaining strength. An advanced example of this is the BALLERINA network of the Baltic Sea.

How effective are regional institutions?

The preceding discussion identified the roles that can be undertaken by regional institutions. But, as noted earlier, regional institutions vary widely in terms of their goals and capabilities. In practice, relatively few regional institutions have been effective in fulfilling all their stated roles. The most effective regional environmental institutions are located in Western Europe. Environmental considerations have become a central concern of the European Union, and the European Commission now has enforcement powers. In 1997, for the first time in its history, the European Commission brought proceedings against member states for failing to implement judgements of the European Court of Justice in five cases concerning failure to comply with Community environmental law. Most member states in question have since rectified the relevant national legislation. Western European institutions enjoy certain advantages: peace and stability in the region; a long history of regional cooperation that is grounded in strong political and legal commitments from member states; well-developed regional and national institutions and governing structures; adequate financial resources and technical expertise; comprehensive and up-to-date environmental data and information; and an impressive range of environmental policy options, both tested and implemented.

Regional institutions in many other parts of the world are not so blessed, and have been much less effective, especially in implementation. Because of the many constraints confronting regional institutions in developing countries, many programmes have been only partially implemented or remain unimplemented. Though somewhat extreme, the case of the Inter-Governmental Authority on Development (IGAD) in East Africa, established in 1986 and whose primary focus is drought and desertification control, is instructive. With the exception of its food security project that was implemented with funds from Italy, all other IGAD programmes were stillborn. To revitalize IGAD, a special summit meeting of the heads of state and government was convened in 1996, and several subregional environmental projects have been submitted to the international community for consideration. The constraints on IGAD included lack of peace and security in the subregion, lukewarm support from member states, lack of democratization and grassroots participation, lack of funds, and lack of expertise and capacity at national and regional levels. Such constraints are characteristic of most regional and subregional institutions in Africa, and their implementation record for regional conventions is rather poor.

Even where the expertise and resource constraints are much less severe, as in the case in South-East Asia, regional environmental institutions have been only partially effective. Political considerations have hampered effectiveness. The ASEAN states, for example, instituted a framework for cooperation to address the severe haze problem in the region caused by forest fires in Indonesia. The 1994 ASEAN Cooperation Plan on Transboundary Pollution outlines the efforts to be undertaken at the national and regional levels. Each member state undertook to enhance national capabilities to deal with forest fires. The ASEAN states agreed to share knowledge and technology in the prevention and mitigation of forest fires and to establish a cooperative mechanism to combat such fires. The ASEAN plan, however, was and still is not legally binding. For it to work all parties must act in good faith, but this has not been the practice. The polluter state, Indonesia, did not take the required action and political inhibitions prevented the other states from confronting Indonesia over this matter. Many aspects of the ASEAN plan therefore remained underdeveloped and unimplemented. When the haze recurred in 1997, although it was more severe and occasioned a regional emergency with health and safety implications, the ASEAN states were unable to address the problem. Likewise, the North-East Asian states (China, Japan, and the two Koreas) have yet to develop a cooperative framework to address the acid rain problem that confronts this subregion. Apart from the lack of a history of regional cooperation in the subregion, cooperation to address this issue is hindered by political tensions, a lack of political will, especially on the part of China, and the lack of a common data point. A further constraint arises from the fact that regional organizations and schemes are largely bureaucratically driven, lacking the participation of scientific communities and civil society organizations.

However, not all regional institutions in developing regions have been ineffective. The CCAD, for example, has been quite successful in discharging its mission to promote policy coordination, harness funding, build new institutions, foster information-sharing, and encourage citizens' participation in addressing environmental programmes in the subregion. Generally, regional agencies appear to be quite successful in providing high-level forums and in formulating regional goals and conventions, but their implementation record is mixed if not poor. This should not be interpreted to mean that regional institutions cannot play a significant role in environmental governance; only that they may be more effective in some roles than others, and that effectiveness varies widely across regions and subregions. Moreover, while the limitations must be recognized, necessary action must also be taken to build up the capacities of regional institutions in the developing world. With the necessary support these institutions can play a key role in complementing the roles of the other actors in managing environmental problems.

How do regional institutions relate to the other actors?

Regional institutions, like other intergovernmental organizations, are creations of states. They can only be as strong as is desired by member states. Except for the European Union, regional organizations do not have independent political, legal, or resource bases. They cannot command support or compliance on their own accord. It is therefore imperative that regional institutions act in conjunction with other actors including member states, international organizations like the United Nations and its specialized agencies such as UNEP and the UNDP, international and regional financial institutions like the World Bank, the ADB, and the EBRD, and NGOs and other grassroots organizations. In other words, to be successful regional institutions must be an integral part of a multilayered arrangement that spans several levels. They must also bring together a multitude of international, governmental, private sector, NGO, and grassroots actors at the regional and subregional levels. The nesting, interface, and cross-fertilization functions of regional institutions are critical. The successful examples cited in the previous two sections illustrate this contention. Further, each regional institution must find its own specific niche by fulfilling a critical need or function that cannot be effectively provided by the other actors.

Environmental problems are the product of several factors, like population growth, economic development, and political conflict, and they have several dimensions, including environmental, economic, social, cultural, and political. In light of the multifaceted causes and dimensions, an integrated approach is critical. Environment management must form an integral part of broader arrangements that are concerned with managing political, economic, and security affairs in the region. Effort must be made to incorporate environmental concerns into the agenda of these bodies and develop the necessary policies and institutions in the context of the existing regional policy and institutional frameworks. Lyuba Zarsky, in her chapter, for example, argues the case for lodging the environmental goals in relation to energy use in the Asia-Pacific in the context of regional economic organizations. Similarly, Egbert Tellegen in his chapter makes the case for linking energy conservation and waste minimization to trade and financial aid from Western Europe. In addition to facilitating an integrated approach, this route will ensure that environmental problems receive the attention of high-level political leaders, thus fostering political and institutional support for regional environment initiatives and action plans.

This, however, does not and should not preclude specialized regional agencies, although their task should be limited to implementing global and regional initiatives and plans, and, as noted earlier, they should be integrated into the existing regional framework. The integrated approach and institutional structure will also prevent duplication and turf conflict, as well as conserve and pool limited resources. An integrated approach is most advanced in Europe, where environmental considerations have been effectively integrated into other community policies, in particular the energy policy and common agricultural policy. In 1996–1997 the European Union took initiatives on subjects such as the auto-oil programme, CO_2 and vehicle emissions, and the internalizing of external costs, in particular through the directive on the reduction of the sulphur content of fossil fuels. Other integrated EU strategies include those against acidification and biodiversity. An integrated approach is also the practice in several other regions and subregions. The need now is to elevate this approach to the level of a norm and encourage all regional and subregional agencies to become environmentally conscious and incorporate environmental concerns as an integral part of their agendas and policies.

Conclusion

The foregoing discussions suggests two conclusions. One, regional and subregional cooperation can augment the roles and effectiveness of other actors (global institutions, the nation-state, NGOs, and the private sector) in implementing international conventions on global issues like climate change and ozone depletion, as well as take a lead role in addressing regional or subregional-specific concerns like land degradation, food security, international rivers management, and acid rain. They may mediate bilateral disputes among member states and provide technical assistance in the development of national legislation. They can also perform a number of supporting functions and services, like the development of databases, information-sharing networks, and regional education and training schemes, sponsoring clean technology projects, arranging funding support, and fostering regional networks among NGOs and experts. Regional environmental cooperation, however, is still relatively new and, except in Western Europe, still at an early stage. Regional institutions, especially those in the developing world, face numerous difficulties and their track record is, at best, mixed. For them to function effectively, they require the support of their member states as well as the support and assistance of global institutions and the rich nations.

Notwithstanding their limitations, regional institutions can be and have been a critical force in raising national and regional awareness of environmental problems and in urging the need for and benefits of cooperation in addressing such problems. Regional arrangements and agencies are becoming more significant and they have the potential to become an important component of the global environment architecture. The United Nations should foster the development of regional agencies in the management of environmental concerns, and should seek to integrate them into its institutional framework for the formulation and implementation of global conventions as well as the management of region-specific problems.

The second conclusion is that environmental concerns and policies must be embedded in the larger regional picture, and institutional and policy frameworks. Environmental problems have multiple causes and implications, and successful implementation of environmental policies hinges upon a variety of factors that span the political, economic, and security arenas. They cannot therefore be addressed in isolation. An integrated approach that connects environmental concerns to the more urgent concerns like development and security is critical to the effective implementation of environmental initiatives. It is imperative to encourage the inclusion of environmental concerns into the agenda of existing multipurpose regional institutions that are concerned with the manage-

ment of political, security, and economic affairs, and to develop environmental policies in the context of the broader regional institutional and
policy frameworks. The multifaceted nature of environmental problems
and their resolution also requires regional institutions to act in concert
with other actors, especially the parliamentarians, the private sector, the
scientific community, NGOs, and grassroots organizations. They must not
only serve as a vertical link between the state and global institutions but
also as a horizontal link fostering cross-fertilization among these and
other actors at the national and subnational levels.

As noted earlier, in light of the wide variations across regional institutions in terms of authority, goals and priorities, institutional capacity,
financial resources, and expertise, the specific roles and tasks of regional
institutions can only be ascertained in specific contexts. In line with this
understanding, the ensuing three chapters investigate the possibilities and
limitations of regional cooperation in three regions: the Asia-Pacific,
Central and Eastern Europe, and sub-Saharan Africa. Lyuba Zarsky's
chapter argues that the next 10 to 15 years present a crucial window of
opportunity to lay the foundations for more environmentally sustainable
energy use in Asia. She advocates the case for the high-energy-consuming
Asia-Pacific states to develop a long-term market-oriented regional energy plan that integrates environmental considerations. The development
of such a plan must include input from the scientific community, the
business community, and environmental advocacy groups. Egbert Tellegen's chapter investigates the role of regional cooperation in energy
conservation and waste minimization in Central and Eastern Europe. He
argues that preventive environmental policy has not figured as prominently as it should in Western European assistance to Central and Eastern Europe. To stimulate preventive environmental measures he makes
the case to link aid-giving and trade to energy conservation and waste
minimization. Gregory Myers's chapter reviews the role of African regional organizations in addressing land and natural resource degradation. Because of weaknesses at the national level, regional organizations
may on the surface appear to have an important role to play in resource
management and conservation in Africa. Myers, however, cautions
against unrealistic expectations. African regional organizations suffer
many weaknesses. Further, regional organizations cannot force policy
changes on states. The drive for change, in his view, must come from
below: from local communities and civil society. The task of regional
organizations, according to Myers, is to create "enabling environments"
to facilitate the interaction of government and civil society. To promote
bottom-up change, he asserts that regional organizations should facilitate
discussion about land policy and property rights among all related actors
and act as conduits of information and ideas.

REFERENCES

Alagappa, M. 1997. "Regional Institutions, the UN and International Security: A Framework for Analysis." *Third World Quarterly* 18(3): 421–442.

Munoz, H., ed. 1992. *Environment and Diplomacy in the Americas.* Boulder: Lynne Rienner.

Streets, D. G., G. R. Carmichael, M. Amann, and R. L. Arndt. 1999. "Energy Consumption and Acid Deposition in Northeast Asia." *Ambio* 28(2): 135–143.

UNEP (United Nations Environment Programme). 1995. *Final Report of the Ninth Meeting of Ministers of the Environment of LAC.* 21–26 September, Havana, Cuba.

FURTHER READING

Tay, S. 1997. "Haze and ASEAN Cooperation," *The Straits Times Weekly Edition.* 4 October.

14

Energy and the environment in Asia-Pacific: Regional cooperation and market governance

Lyuba Zarsky

Energy use in Asia will grow dramatically over the next decade and for the foreseeable future. As a whole, the Asian region (South and East Asia) is expected to use 133 per cent more commercial energy in 2010 than it did in 1995 (Fesharaki, Clark, and Intaraprovich 1995, 2). In East Asia, commercial energy demand will double. Electricity generating capacity in China alone is expected to nearly quadruple (IEA 1996, 13).

If the future looks like the past, rising Asian energy use based on coal and oil will create severe, possibly irreversible, environmental and health problems, as well as heighten concerns about energy supply security. As in other parts of the world, sustainable energy development in Asia requires that dependence on fossil fuels be reduced. However, some of the leading alternatives, especially nuclear and hydro, pose their own environmental and security problems.

The explosive hunger for energy is prompting a move away from centralized state planning and towards greater reliance on markets to meet demand for energy supplies and capital for energy infrastructure. The transition towards markets will present governments with new roles, policy imperatives, and options. Given the increasing level of market interdependence, the most powerful policy instruments – those which shape market incentives – will be those undertaken collectively.

This chapter examines the role of regional cooperation in nudging markets toward an energy path which enhances both environmental and supply security. The first section profiles the trend towards markets and describes the energy-security-environment nexus and the policy dilemmas it creates. The second section analyses energy-environmental market failures and develops a broad policy framework for regional energy cooperation . The third section describes and evaluates initiatives towards energy cooperation in Asia, both within regional institutions and on a project basis.

One hundred years of smoke and smog? The energy picture in Asia

Energy demand in Asia is driven primarily by rapid economic growth, which generates increases in energy use by industry, transport, and household sectors, including newly electrified rural areas. Demographic factors are also important: over 4 billion people will be living in Asia by 2010, an increasing number of them in cities. By 2025, over half of the Asian populace will be urban, up from only 35 per cent in 1995 (WRI 1996, 150).

Energy demand projections are derived from projected GDP growth rates. Extrapolating from a decade-long economic boom, the International Energy Agency projected in 1996 that GDP in China would grow annually by 9 per cent between 1995 and 2005 and by 7 per cent between 2005 and 2010. For the rest of (developing) East Asia, the corresponding projections were 6.6 per cent and 5.9 per cent (Grollman 1996).

These projections were made before Asia's financial crisis, which, at least in the short term, will dampen economic growth, energy demand, and power sector investment. Nonetheless, the economic "fundamentals" point towards sustained industrialization, urbanization, growth in personal transport, and rural electrification – all of which add up to increased energy use. According to one "post-crisis" estimate, primary energy demand in Asia will increase at an annual rate of 4–5 per cent through to 2010 – double the global rate (Yergin, Eklof, and Edward 1998, 38). Moreover, environmental problems are already pressing even at current levels of demand. The slowdown in growth may even exacerbate environmental problems, as governments cut environmental budgets (Nautilus Institute 1997).

Moving towards markets

Throughout Asia, the trend at the macroeconomic level is towards liberalization and market opening. In the Asian countries hardest hit by the financial crisis – South Korea, Thailand, and Indonesia – this trend will accelerate as a result of the conditions for bail-out by the International

Monetary Fund. Financial markets in particular will get an overhaul. In the energy sector, the two crucial markets are those for energy supplies and power sector financing.

Besides stimulating economic growth and the overall demand for energy, macro-level liberalization will affect the energy sector in two broad ways. First, it will enhance the efficiency of energy use. Through more open markets, Asians will generally have access to more efficient producer and consumer goods. Secondly, a greater reliance on markets will encourage policies and forms of governance more appropriate to markets, including the energy sector. Better governance is important in both stimulating investment and integrating environmental objectives.

The investment demands of increased energy use are staggering. By one estimate, annual investments required to meet Asia's power demand over the next decade are projected to be some US$600 billion – over 62 per cent of the world's projected power sector investments (Bakthavatsalam 1995). By another estimate, in North-East Asia alone (China, Japan, Taiwan, and North and South Korea) the investment requirements of the power sector are projected to average US$72 billion per year for the next 15 years – a total of US$1.8 trillion (Razavi 1997, 1). By any estimate, the capital requirement is huge and has raised concerns about where the capital will come from.

In nearly all the developing countries of Asia, the power sector has historically been dominated by and financially dependent upon the central government. Domestic capital markets remain largely undeveloped, unable to tap domestic sources for large-scale investment. In the past, Asian governments looked to multilateral financing agencies such as the World Bank and the ADB as primary sources of power sector financing. However, given the scale of the required capital and the current "cut government spending" political climate, multilateral banks will at best play a brokering role.

The recognition of these constraints by Asian governments has triggered substantial changes in methods of financing to allow the private sector – both domestic and foreign – to invest in power generation. The increasing role of independent power producers (IPPs) means that the power sector, while still in large part a government monopoly, is moving towards being market-based (Razavi 1997). In China, for example, foreign investment accounted for 18 per cent of power sector investment in 1995, up from only 6.4 per cent in 1985 (Razavi 1997, 5). India, the Philippines, Japan, Thailand, and South Korea have all begun to open up their electric power industries.

The trend towards markets is also evident in energy supply strategies. While there are large reserves of coal in China, India, South-East Asia, and Australia, growing energy demand has created a new and growing dependence on oil imports. Virtually all Asian countries either are already or will soon be net importers of oil. China, for example, traditionally a major oil exporter, has become since 1993 a net importer at the rate of 600,000 barrels per day and is projected to increase its oil imports fivefold by 2010 (Calder 1997, 24). Indonesia, long the largest oil exporter in South-East Asia, will probably become a net oil importer between 2000 and 2005 (Calder 1997, 24). The shortfall between India's domestic crude oil production and oil consumption is nearly 900,000 barrels per day (US EIA 1997). Overall, imports accounted for 59 per cent of Asia-Pacific oil supplies in 1995. By 2010, oil import dependence, primarily on the Middle East, will increase to 77 per cent (Fesharaki, Banaszak, and Kang 1997, 8).

Apart from oil, energy supplies in East Asia are met largely via intra-regional markets, including Australia (see Figure 14.1). There is a substantial intra-regional trade in coal and liquefied natural gas (LNG), as well as in oil. The primary exporters are Indonesia and Australia and the primary importers are Japan, South Korea, and Taiwan. The demand for natural gas, which accounted for 9 per cent of energy use in 1995, is met almost entirely within the region. Excluding China, about two-thirds of coal demand is met by imports and three-quarters of imports are supplied within the region (Grollman 1996, 14).

The trend towards greater reliance on markets to fulfil energy needs in Asia is evident not only at the lofty heights of the power sector but also at the level of the rural and urban poor. Processes of modernization and urbanization are increasingly replacing non-commodified, traditional energy sources such as biomass, animal, and human power with commodified, often fossil-fuel-based, forms of energy. The move up the "energy ladder" has implications for both environment and equity (UNDP 1997, 8–10).

The energy-security-environment nexus

The expected surge in energy demand in Asia – and the ways in which the demand is met – will have enormous implications not only within but beyond the region. On the one hand, increasing energy use will bring welfare benefits to millions of Asians, as well as to economies throughout the world, which will gain export markets. Job creation and rising standards of living are important aspects of sustainable development.

On the other hand, the region's growing hunger for energy resources will create new forms of insecurity and could potentially inflame relations between major powers within and beyond the region. Moreover, given Asia-Pacific's current dependence on fossil fuels, its highly inefficient and technologically backward power sector, and its weak environmental

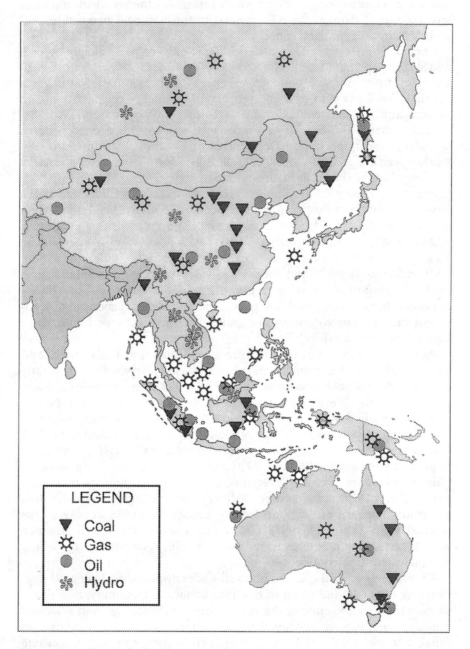

Figure 14.1. East Asia-Pacific region: Strategic energy resources

management capacities, a future which resembles the past will rain massive ecological damage on Asia, primarily through acid deposition, and globally through climate change.

Current energy demand in Asia-Pacific is met overwhelmingly by coal and oil. In 1995, coal and oil accounted for 46 and 38 per cent respectively of total primary commercial energy consumption. Natural gas accounts for 9 per cent of primary commercial energy consumption, and nuclear and hydro account for 5 and 2 per cent respectively. In India, domestic coal, which has a high ash content, accounts for over 55 per cent of energy consumption (US Department of Energy 1997). In China, the world's leading coal producer, coal accounts for 77 per cent of energy consumption, as shown in Figure 14.2 (Streets 1997, 10).

Emissions from coal-fired power plants, especially in China and India, have resulted in widespread acid deposition both within and beyond national borders. Acid deposition occurs when emissions of pollutants, including sulphur and nitrogen, interact with water and oxygen in the atmosphere to produce sulphur dioxide, which reacts in the atmosphere with hydroxyl radicals and then with water to become sulphuric acid (SO_3). Transported by air currents, the pollutants mix and are finally deposited back on the earth's surface. The chemical reactions and depositions may be fairly close to the source of emissions – or hundreds of kilometres downwind.

Acid deposition is an especially pressing problem in India and North-East Asia. In India, sulphur dioxide levels in nearly all cities greatly exceed international standards (US EIA 1997). In North-East Asia, according to the World Bank/ADB RAINS-Asia model, sulphur dioxide emissions totalled 14.7 million tonnes in 1990. Under a "business-as-usual" scenario, sulphur dioxide (SO_2) emissions will more than double by 2010 and nearly triple by 2020; emissions of nitrogen oxide (NO_x) will more than triple between 1990 and 2020 (Streets 1997, 12). Even under a "higher efficiency forecast" scenario, in which governments make targeted efforts to increase energy efficiency and institute reasonable fuel substitution measures, sulphur dioxide emissions would double in the next 30 years (US EIA 1997). Given that Europe and North America have taken strong measures to reduce acid rain, Asia will emerge as the dominant emitting continent.

The impacts of acid rain are not well understood, since ecological degradation is usually the result of multiple variables. Generally, acid deposition is believed to modify the rate of nutrient leaching from soils and biomass; diminish or destroy fish populations; affect soil bacteria and fungi; increase uptake of heavy metals such as cadmium; and exacerbate pre-existing stresses such as pesticide contamination. The increase in emissions of nitrogen oxide may be especially problematic. Initial studies

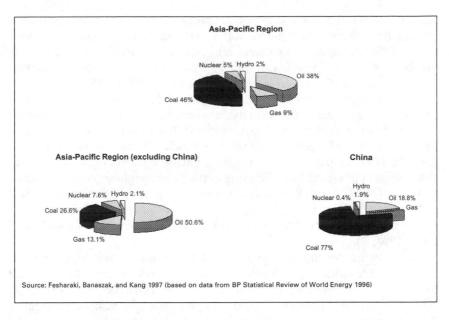

Figure 14.2. Primary commercial energy consumption by source, 1995

have suggested that the increase in NO_x emissions and fertilizer use in North-East Asia may lead to ozone levels sufficiently high to threaten rice, wheat, and corn production (Carmichael and Arndt 1997, 22).

The sensitivity of a particular ecosystem to the effects of acid deposition varies. North-East Asia is especially vulnerable due to the combination of high deposition and sensitive soils and vegetation (Bhatti and Streets 1992). Coal-related emissions also jeopardize human health by causing respiratory problems. By the end of the 1980s, the annual environmental and health cost of direct acid rain damage in the worst-affected areas of China was estimated to be 16 billion yuan (US$2 billion) (Sinton 1997, 2).

Acid rain is a problem not only within but also between countries in Asia. In North-East Asia, sulphur emissions emanating from China deposit acid in Japan, North Korea, South Korea, and the Sea of Japan. According to RAINS-Asia, China accounted for some 37 per cent of Japan's sulphur deposition and 34 per cent of North Korea's in 1990 (Carmichael and Arndt 1995, 33).

In addition to acid rain, Asia's future heavy reliance on coal and oil to fuel energy will produce a large volume of greenhouse gas emissions, especially carbon. In 1992, China was second only to the United States in total carbon dioxide emissions; India was the world's sixth largest emitter.[1] Cumulatively, the United States and the European Union are responsible for the lion's share of the stock of carbon dioxide emissions in the atmosphere. The United States, for example, has generated four times more emissions than China and nearly 14 times more than India (WRI 1996, 319). In terms of the annual flow of emissions, however, China is the world's second largest emitter (WRI 1996, 318).

While a large increase in the use of fossil fuels, especially coal, will undermine environmental security, an increased thirst for oil presents another kind of security problem: vulnerability to supply disruption and price volatility. The primary source for crude oil imports is the Middle East. In 1997, 76 per cent of total Asia-Pacific crude imports came from that region. Given the large refining capacity throughout Asia, including in Japan, China, South Korea, India, and Singapore, oil requirements will continue to be met through imports of crude oil. By 2005, the Middle East's share is projected to rise to 90 per cent (Fesharaki, Banaszak, and Kang 1997, 9).

The growing dependence on Middle East oil may make Asian importers vulnerable to supply disruption and monopolistic pricing, as happened in the heyday of the OPEC cartel in the 1970s (Greene 1997, 18). Most Asian nations do not have well-developed strategic reserve stockpiles. Even if, as some analysts argue, market interdependence reduces vulnerability to supply disruption (Yergin, Eklof, and Edward 1998, 44), Asia's growing dependence on Middle East oil may have broad geopolitical repercussions, since it will generate a level of interdependence much higher than that prevailing between the Middle East and the West (Calder 1997, 25).

Concerns about environmental impacts and supply/price security have prompted interest in other cleaner fuels, especially natural gas, nuclear power, and hydro. While growing in absolute terms, the share of oil in electricity generation in Asia-Pacific will slip from about 15 per cent in 1993 to only about 5 per cent in 2010. The share of nuclear, on the other hand, is projected to increase from 12 to nearly 14 per cent, hydro from 15.5 to nearly 17 per cent, and natural gas from about 12 to about 14 per cent (Fesharaki, Clark, and Intaraprovich 1995, 1).

While they would help to reduce air pollution, both nuclear power and hydro generate their own security and environmental problems. For nuclear power, the overriding problems are safety and the potential proliferation of nuclear weapons, especially given the region's undeveloped capacities for spent-fuel management and the lack of a regional spent-fuel management regime (Von Hippel and Hayes 1997). In the absence of such a regime, the widespread adoption of nuclear power could accelerate a nuclear arms race.

Japan, China, Taiwan, India, Pakistan, South Korea, and North Korea all have nuclear power programmes; Indonesia and Thailand may join the group soon. Moreover, proposals in Japan to move towards a "plutonium economy" based on closed-cycle plutonium reactors have generated widespread environmental and security concerns in Asia.

Large-scale hydro power, on the other hand, often entails substantial social and ecological costs. Social costs include displacement of communities, sometimes affecting millions of people, as well as loss of agricultural, fishing, tourism, and other resources. Ecological impacts can broadly be categorized as impoundment effects – deforestation, loss of vegetation, and other consequences of flooding large areas of land required for storage reservoirs – and barrier effects, especially loss of migratory fish species. There is also a health risk, since reservoirs often provide habitats suited to disease vectors. Moreover, large-scale hydro dams pose a risk of large-scale flooding should the dam crack or break (Hirsch 1997).

Given the nexus of source-related environment and security issues, the most attractive energy sources to fuel Asia's energy growth are natural gas – of which there are substantial reserves in the region – renewables (mini-hydro, wind, solar, photovoltaics, tidal, biomass, and geothermal), and energy efficiency. The widespread use of natural gas, however, will require a huge investment in infrastructure to transport and distribute – via either pipeline or transmission lines – gas (or gas-fired electricity) from fields in the northern regions of China, Central Asia, the Russian Far East, and South-East Asia (see Figure 14.1).

The role of renewables is still very small. However, four Asia-Pacific nations – India, Japan, China, and Australia – are pursuing renewable resources for electricity generation on a large scale (Fesharaki, Clark, and Intaraprovich 1995, 5). Moreover, small-scale renewable energy technologies can offer proven and environmentally benign alternatives to grid-based power. In India, fewer than 40 per cent of households are connected to the grid (Bakthavatsalam 1995).

Nonetheless, like a shift to natural gas, a major shift towards renewable energy sources is some way off into the future. In the short to medium term, that is the next 10–20 years, coal will continue to dominate the Asian region and short-term policy imperatives will revolve around ways to make the use of coal cleaner and more efficient, as well as to substitute cleaner fuels for coal and oil as much as possible.

There is also substantial room to improve energy efficiency. India uses 60 per cent more energy per dollar of GDP than the world average (US Department of Energy 1997). China uses 20 times as much primary energy to produce a dollar of economic product as does Japan. Only part of the difference stems from the different industrial structures of the two economies. The rest stems from inefficient equipment and outmoded practices (Sinton 1997, 8). The widespread embrace of the best available technology – even if for only new plants – would provide a significant environmental benefit.

Regional environmental governance of energy markets

The anticipated explosion in energy demand in Asia poses dilemmas for policy-makers. It will be difficult simply to meet the demand at all – to mobilize the required finance and channel it into well-managed and efficient power projects. The deeper challenge is to meet the demand in ways which at once promote human health and environmental security, enhance supply security, and encourage (or at least do not undermine) prospects for inter-state peace and stability. In other words, if it is not to create new sets of intractable problems, energy planning must be based on integrating security and environmental, as well as economic, objectives. Given the past large investment in (dirty) coal and imported oil (and nuclear power, especially in Japan), and the long lead times required to develop and disseminate alternatives, this challenge can fully be met only over the long term – perhaps 20 to 50 years.

The central policy imperative is to develop the capacity for scenario-based strategic planning – in other words, to define overarching, integrated objectives for the development path of the energy sector. From environmental, security, and geopolitical points of view the heart of such a scenario should be to reduce dependence on fossil fuels.

Guided by a long-term "fossil-free future" scenario, an ensemble of policy initiatives can be designed which fulfil short- and medium-term energy sector objectives while at the same time promoting a transition to renewables.[2] Without a long-term strategy, policies and resultant energy choices will be skewed towards the status quo or towards crisis management. Crucial strategic investments in transition fuels like natural gas may be foregone.

In the short term, environmental security objectives should be to embrace demand-side management and enhance the efficiency of energy use throughout the economy; to make the use of coal as clean and efficient as possible; to invest in the development of natural gas and renewables; to substitute cleaner fuels for coal and oil wherever feasible; to reduce dependence on Middle East oil; and to phase out nuclear power and, in the interim, make its use as safe as possible.

Achieving these short- and long-term objectives will require new roles for the state in enabling and governing markets to achieve desired energy sector objectives. Governments will need to design market-oriented policy instruments, as well as mechanisms to gather and apply scientific information and interface with business, communities, and other stake-holders. The key question for this chapter is what should or could be the scope of regional, as against national or global, approaches to integrated strategic energy planning.

Transborder resources and externalities

The most compelling rationale for regional energy cooperation arises when energy resources, markets, and/or energy-related environmental impacts are transboundary. In both South-East and North-East Asia, including Siberia and the Russian Far East, there are significant reserves of natural gas and oil. The primary markets, however, are in North-East Asia. Developing and distributing the gas is a cross-border undertaking (Paik 1995). In addition to primary resource development and management of regional commons, nations may also find economic advantage in integrating electricity grids on a regional basis.

Energy-related environmental pollution, including acid deposition, crosses national boundaries in Asia and requires regional cooperation to monitor emissions. In addition, pooling scientific efforts regionally can reduce the costs of mitigating the effects of acid rain and building management capacities where they are weakest. Most important, significant differences in the costs of reducing emissions in different countries provide scope and incentive for adopting regional as against purely national strategies.

Globalization and market failures

Geography-based incentives for regional cooperation exist regardless of the particular character of the economy. A new rationale emerges when economies are market-based and increasingly integrated. The growing openness of Asia's economies to trade and foreign investment – especially in the power sector itself – suggests that energy sector choices will be increasingly guided by domestic and global market forces. Without proper governance, however, markets have three major failings, all highly relevant to energy sustainability and security.

The first failing, now commonly understood, lies in the fact that market prices do not – and perhaps cannot fully – incorporate social costs. For fossil fuels, externalities include local air pollution, atmospheric pollution and the costs of climate change, marine pollution, and the costs of war in maintaining supply. The inclusion of these externalities in market prices, however partially and imperfectly, would change millions of energy production and consumption decisions every day.

The second problem with markets is that, to be efficient, market decisions must be based on perfect information. When it comes to ecological and health impacts of production and consumption, the state of the art is that requisite information is imperfect or even inherently unknowable. Moreover, information often takes the character of a public good. Because the benefits of investing in information cannot be fully captured privately, private entities such as consumers or firms tend to underinvest in gathering it. Without public investment in information and policy instruments to incorporate it in market decisions, markets are flying blind when it comes to gauging the environmental and health costs and benefits of energy choices.

The third failing of markets is that they do not incorporate the future, and tend to guide production and consumption decisions according to a short-term rationality. However, many important and desirable economic outcomes, including technology development, are path-dependent: decisions taken today shape the options for tomorrow. Markets value the future only in terms of foregone consumption (net present value), but not in terms of foregone benefits due to today's consumption. From a long-term point of view, the optimal use of fossil fuels would be as a bridge towards non-fossil-fuel sources. Without policy intervention, markets will not chart such a course and may even foreclose options.

These three failings – in pricing, information, and strategic planning – generate a fundamental weakness of markets, which is that they are riddled with prisoner's-dilemma-type situations: what makes sense at the micro level of the individual does not add up to social rationality at the macro level. It is up to good governance, incorporating both formal and informal rules and norms, to create an institutional framework which can channel the enormous power of markets towards social goals, including a more ecologically sustainable future. In Asia, a framework for energy governance is probably the single most important component of a path towards sustainable development.

Developing such a framework is primarily the role of government. The unilateral policy-making capacities of national governments in governing energy supply and financial markets, however, are conditioned and constrained by global market forces. On the one hand, market openness means that local prices for goods, services, and financial assets are determined, or at least influenced, by international prices. On the other hand, pressures to be competitive in export markets and to attract foreign investment dampen policy initiatives which would impose significant costs on producers or investors. Purely domestic policy initiatives – such as a national carbon tax to improve energy pricing – become "stuck in the mud" of competitiveness concerns. Rules of market behaviour, including energy regulatory requirements and standards, are increasingly pushed by markets towards international convergence.[3]

Global markets, in short, like global ecosystems, require global governance. Global governance, however, is extremely complex. There are some 190 nations in the world, split along many divides. Negotiations are costly and difficult. Regional approaches to energy governance, as one analyst argues, "encourage the break-up of the 'global cooperation' problem into smaller and more manageable pieces" (Grollman 1997). Moreover, when markets – for primary energy supplies, electricity, or power sector financing – are themselves primarily regional, there is a strong rationale for regional approaches to governance.

Regional policy framework

A framework for regional environmental governance of energy in Asia would focus first on developing a broad regional consensus for energy policy; and secondly on generating the institutional and policy framework to implement it. In Europe, this two-part approach underlay the development of the European Energy Charter.

A regional institutional framework would incorporate at least five key policy targets: rational pricing; environmental guidelines for financial markets and innovative financing instruments for cleaner fuels and technologies; the convergence of energy regulations and standards, including energy efficiency standards; investment in scientific information, including mapping renewable resources; and the creation of a strong interface between government, the scientific community, environmental advocates, and the public.

Pricing

Rational pricing strategies entail policy instruments to internalize environmental externalities in energy prices. Currently, however, domestic Asian and global energy prices not only exclude externalities but include subsidies to fossil fuels. In China and India, for example, subsidies to electricity make consumer prices about 40 per cent below the world price; for fossil fuels, prices are about 25 per cent below world prices (World Bank 1995). Ending subsidies to the coal sector and promoting freer trade in coal would help to substitute low-sulphur coal imports, including from Australia, for high-sulphur domestic coal (Anderson 1993).

While embracing world fossil fuel prices would promote more rational energy choices, the deeper problem is that world prices are themselves skewed by direct and indirect financial and environmental subsidies. Both OECD countries and developing countries subsidize energy, including fossil fuels. According to one estimate, energy sector subsidies in the OECD are nearly US$150 billion per year (De Moor and Calamai 1997).

While there are broad domestic social and economic benefits to ending fossil fuel subsidies, adjustment costs make subsidy reform politically difficult. Collective action at the regional level to reduce subsidies would "level the playing field" and help governments overcome domestic political opposition. As a recent OECD study concluded, "Overcoming opposition to subsidy reform will be substantially easier if countries can be convinced to react *together*, rather than *separately*, in reducing subsidies/ tax concessions to particular industries or sectors" (Runge and Jones 1996).

The economic logic for the removal of subsidies to fossil fuels is unimpeachable. Subsidies for renewables, on the other hand, might be justified on the basis of social benefits (positive externalities). In India, a "medium" level of governmental support would increase the share of renewables in total power generation capacity to about 8 per cent by 2015, while a "high" level of support would increase the renewables share to about 12 per cent (Bakthavatsalam 1995, 1).

Financial markets

Perhaps more than any other single factor, the character of power sector investment will affect the environmental future of Asia. If capital markets can be structured so as to be environmentally sensitive, they will be a powerful channel for improving ecological and public health. If they remain environmentally blind, financial markets will be channels for ecological degradation.

According to the RAINS-Asia "best available technology" scenario, for example, sulphur emissions in North-East Asia could be cut by nearly 70 per cent between 1990 and 2020.[4] The key is in mobilizing capital markets to deliver the best available coal-burning technologies and cleaner fuels. One approach might be for governments collectively to set guidelines which require social and environmental impact assessments and mitigation strategies for power sector projects. They could also require public hearings or other avenues of public input into the design and construction of resource development projects and power plants.

Broad rules to govern investment are emerging at the global level. The OECD attempted to negotiate a Multilateral Agreement on Investment (MAI), which aimed to eliminate domestic barriers to foreign investors. However, environmental (and social) parameters were excluded from MAI obligations, sparking widespread criticism among environmental groups and leading ultimately to the collapse of the MAI effort. Governments in Asia could move the process forward by promoting their own environmental guidelines for investment.[5]

Creating innovative financial instruments is another way governments can channel capital markets towards environmental goals. The primary goal of such instruments is to find ways to capture "public goods" benefits of investment in cleaner technologies when markets, governments, or multilateral development banks (MDBs) are reluctant to finance them. One innovative proposal currently being explored by the Nautilus Institute is a financial guarantee mechanism for technology risk in China (Razavi 1997).

Regulations and standards

Reflecting different histories and socio-economic conditions, energy regulations and standards vary widely in the Asian region. Market integration, however, creates pressures for standards to converge. The crucial policy issues are, first, how to nudge convergence upwards toward a higher (rather than a lower) level of environmental performance; and secondly, how to manage an upward-convergence process in a way which recognizes the region's diverse needs and capacities.

Information

Deepening and broadening the energy-environment information base in Asia is a crucial and immediate task for regional cooperation. One of the most pressing needs is to map the region's energy resources, especially renewable sources. There is also a need for more information about the sources, quantities, and effects of emissions, and for effective monitoring networks to be put in place.

A wise investment must extend beyond acquiring knowledge to learning to use it, especially for planning purposes. The embrace of common planning tools at a regional level would enhance medium- and long-term planning capabilities and could provide great benefits in terms of energy resource and product development, as well as policy design.

Scientific and stakeholder input

The integration of environmental with economic and security objectives in energy planning requires a much broader level of expertise than an economic- (or security-) driven approach alone. In particular, it is crucial to bring the judgement and knowledge of the scientific community into the policy debate. While scientists were the primary force in stimulating Asian awareness of acid rain, energy planning and policy decisions in Asia continue to be dominated by energy policy experts with little training or knowledge of ecological sciences.[6]

Other key contributors to the debate include environmental advocates, as well as consumer, community, and other citizen groups. Environmental groups are often a source of innovative policy ideas, as well as a transmission vehicle for information and communication flows between governments and communities (APEC SOM 1997). Moreover, a vibrant regional network outside the official lines of government can explore politically sensitive issues and help to build popular support for a regional energy strategy. Without popular support, political will for a regional institutional energy framework – including public investment in information and energy price adjustments – may not materialize.

Regional energy initiatives

The Asia-Pacific region spans a large swathe of the world and the world's population. It is not a geographically determined entity. The parameters of "Asia-Pacific" tend to be drawn – and drawn differently – by researchers, depending on what they are trying to illuminate; or by regional organizations, depending on their political or economic goals and constraints. For the United Nations, the "region" is bounded by ESCAP (the Economic and Social Commission for Asia and the Pacific), which spans some 56 countries from East Asia and the South and West Pacific to South Asia and Turkey.[7] The extensive geographic span of ESCAP is reflected in its broad tasks, which focus primarily on information exchange and capacity-building, and its comprehensive issues areas, which sweep from poverty alleviation to human rights.

From the UN point of view, there are several "subregions" in Asia, which, largely through nurturing by ESCAP and the UNDP, have developed programmes for environmental, including energy, cooperation. These include the North-East Asian Regional Environment Programme and the South Asian Cooperative Environmental Programme of the South Asia Association for Regional Cooperation (SAARC).

Many of the environmental goals of energy market governance, however, may best be achieved by lodging them in the institutional context of regional economic organizations, especially those focused on trade and investment. Such institutions are already self-consciously developing rules of market behaviour. Although they are focused primarily on macroeconomic policy, energy-environment policies can parallel and gain momentum from the regional policy-creation effort. "An ecologically sustainable regional energy strategy," concludes one analyst, "would require an institutional framework comparable in scale and scope to agreements on commerce and trade" (Grollman 1996, 5).

The leading economic organization in the region is the Asia-Pacific Economic Cooperation forum (APEC), which links 21 countries around the Pacific Rim spanning from East Asia and Australia to North and South America.[8] Within the trans-Pacific APEC region, some 70 per cent of trade and 65 per cent of investment is intra-regional. Led by the United States and its Western allies, APEC economies have embraced a vision of "free and open trade and investment" by 2010 for developed and 2020 for developing countries (Yamazawa 1994, 201–211).

In the aftermath of the financial crisis of 1997, APEC lost momentum and its future agenda and effectiveness are not clear. While trade and investment liberalization continue to be its primary focus, APEC also operated on a second "track" devoted to economic and technical co-operation. Dubbed the "eco-tech" track, this tranche of APEC work included in the early 1990s a strong focus on the environment, as well as on human resource development, small and medium-sized business development, and other issues of social concern. Moreover, in 1994 APEC embraced – at least rhetorically – the principle of integration of economy and environment and charged all 10 of APEC's working groups, including the Energy Working Group, to incorporate environmental concerns into their work agendas (Zarsky and Hunter 1997). Of all the groups, the Energy Working Group is the most active and broad-ranging on both liberalization and environmental issues.

Other regional organizations which are on a path to market integration include the 10-member ASEAN, which is pursuing the creation of an ASEAN Free Trade Area (AFTA); and SAARC, which agreed in 1993 to form a South Asia Preferential Trading Arrangement (Kalpage 1996).

Cooperation among two or more states in the region is also occurring outside the umbrella of regional institutions, and is aimed especially at the transborder development of energy resources. Consortia of companies and states are emerging to develop the huge natural gas reserves in South and Central Asia, as well as to explore offshore oil reserve in the Russian Far East, South China Sea, and elsewhere.

This section describes cooperative initiatives both within the region's institutional umbrellas and on a project basis.

APEC

Based on a consensus model of decision-making, APEC is a forum for building norms and encouraging common regional goals. It is not an arena in which formal agreements are negotiated but acts as a "talk shop" to promote broad policy shifts and stimulate Asian regionalism. However, as the only Asian regional organization to include North and South American countries, its agenda is strongly influenced by the United States and its process by an "East-meets-West" dynamic.

In APEC, the United States and its Western allies press hard for liberalization, while many East Asian countries, including Japan, emphasize eco-tech cooperation to promote economic development. Even when the Western economies embrace and/or lead an eco-tech initiative, such as developing a regional programme of action on environmentally sustainable development, they do so in the context of opening markets.

Environmental and energy cooperation at APEC are encased within the discourse of "public-private partnership," "commercial technology transfer," and the removal of "market distortions" which stand in the way of efficiency. Japan's attempts to promote "development cooperation" based on non-market development assistance principles have largely faltered. Energy cooperation at APEC is thus primarily a product of the market-opening thrust of Western APEC countries generally, especially by suppliers of energy resources and energy technologies, in competition with Japanese suppliers for East Asian markets.[9] Secondly, it is a vehicle to promote learning, information exchange, and capacity-building, including on environmental management aspects of energy development.

Institutionally, APEC addresses energy issues via two vehicles: a regional Energy Cooperation Working Group (EWG), chaired by Australia and Japan; and ad hoc meetings of energy ministers. The EWG is assisted by five expert groups which concentrate on particular aspects of the EWG's agenda and which relate to its five strategic themes: energy data and outlook; clean fossil energy; energy efficiency and conservation; new and renewable energy technologies; and minerals and energy exploration and development. The expert groups and the EWG as a whole sponsor seminars, workshops, and other meetings to exchange information and promote common views. Between January and June 1998, for example, the EWG's calendar of events included 14 separate meetings, four of them relating to environmental dimensions of energy development (APEC Energy Working Group 1997).

The primary goal of the EWG is to promote freer trade in energy and greater access by foreign investors to the power sector. At the Energy Ministerial in August 1997, the Australian Chair of the EWG listed APEC's key challenges as improving market transparency and removing barriers to trade in energy products and services; mobilizing sufficient capital for power infrastructure demand; adjusting energy policies to reflect market dynamics and reduce business costs and investment risks; and "mitigat[ing] any adverse environmental impacts" (Higgins 1996, 1). Environmental cooperation, he suggested, was a "prime example where regional cooperation can be beneficial," and he proposed initiatives such as adopting environmental impact mitigation criteria as a standard component for planning and energy project evaluation, and multilateral joint ventures for reducing greenhouse gas emissions. In conclusion, he suggested an "accelerated programme of work" on energy-environmental issues.

Acceleration is very much what the programme needs. Despite the adoption of 14 Energy Principles in 1996 (see Figure 14.3), environmental

1. Emphasize the need to ensure energy issues are addressed in a manner which gives full consideration to harmonization of economic development, security, and environmental factors.

2. Pursue policies for enhancing the efficient production, distribution, and consumption of energy.

3. Pursue open energy markets for achieving rational energy consumption, energy security, and environmental objectives, recommending action in the appropriate forum of APEC to remove impediments to the achievement of these ends.

4. Recognize that measures to facilitate the rational consumption of energy might involve a mix of market-based and regulatory policies, with the relative components of the mix being a matter for the judgement of individual economies.

5. Consider reducing energy subsidies progressively and promote implementation of pricing practices which reflect the economic cost of supplying and using energy across the full energy cycle, having regard to environmental costs.

6. Promote regular exchange of experience on the various policies being used by member economies to achieve a more rational energy consumption.

7. Ensure that a least-cost approach to the provision of energy services is considered.

8. Promote the adoption of policies to facilitate the transfer of efficient and environmentally sound energy technologies on a commercial and non-discriminatory basis.

9. Encourage the establishment of arrangements for the development of human resource skills relevant to the application and operation of improved technology.

10. Enhance energy information and management programmes to assist more rational energy decision-making.

11. Encourage energy research, development, and demonstration to pave the way for cost-effective application of new, more efficient, and environmentally sound energy technologies.

12. Promote capital flows through the progressive removal of impediments to the funding of the transfer and adoption of more energy-efficient and environmentally sound technologies and infrastructure.

13. Promote cost-effective measures which improve the efficiency with which energy is used but reduce greenhouse gases as part of a suggested regional response to greenhouse gas emissions.

14. Cooperate, to the extent consistent with each economy's development needs, in the joint implementation of projects to reduce greenhouse gas emissions consistent with the Climate Change convention.

Figure 14.3. APEC (non-binding) Energy Principles

issues have taken a back seat in the working group behind the active promotion of coal – albeit cleaner coal – and generally a supply-driven, fossil-fuel-based approach to energy (Grollman 1997). Although a host of workshops, seminars, and expert groups have pondered the relationship of environmental and economic costs and benefits, the working group has been slow to recognize the need for a long-term, integrated regional energy strategy.

One problem is that, like the rest of APEC, the Energy Working Group and the Energy Ministerials are dominated by diplomats and civil servants. There has been some success in expanding the involvement of the business community in the EWG and an Ad Hoc Business Forum has been established. One of the strengths of the EWG is the informal networking between and among business people and government, as this promotes business. However, scientists, environmental groups, and other stakeholders have no regular interface with either the EWG or the Ministerials. As a result, efforts in the early 1990s to propel a sustainable development agenda at APEC dissipated (Zarsky 1998).

Besides building a more robust regionalism, the involvement of NGOs provides a source of innovative ideas. In July 1997, for example, the International Institute for Energy Conservation, an NGO with a regional office in Bangkok, sponsored a forum on Asia Regional Cooperation on Energy Efficiency Standards and Labelling (IIEC 1997). The forum drew participants from 13 countries to explore the contentious and difficult issues involved in creating national, regional, and international energy efficiency standards regimes. The forum recommended regional cooperation in the development of an energy efficiency testing infrastructure, as well as on the alignment of energy efficiency testing methods between Asian and international procedures.

A new initiative spawned by (but independent of) the Energy Working Group is the Asia-Pacific Energy Research Centre. Based in Tokyo, the Centre will produce an annual "regional energy outlook" as well as specific research projects. The research will focus on medium- to long-term issues associated with energy supply security and the environmental consequences of energy use (APEC Energy Working Group 1997). If the Centre emerges as a dynamic and independent builder of information resources – and a vibrant vehicle for a broader public policy debate – it could make a significant contribution towards a regional energy strategy. However, if it is captured by supplier interests or bureaucrats, it will do little to build regional momentum.[10]

SAARC

The South Asian Association for Regional Cooperation encompasses seven countries south of the Himalayas: India, Pakistan, Bangladesh,

Bhutan, Nepal, Sri Lanka, and the Maldives. Established in 1985 at a summit held in Dhaka, Bangladesh, SAARC's main goal is "to accelerate economic and social development" through regional cooperation (SAARC 1997a).

A focus on the environment has threaded SAARC's history. Environment and Meteorology is one of 11 areas of cooperation in SAARC's Integrated Programme of Action, each of which has a technical committee. In 1991, the sixth SAARC summit approved a study on "Causes and consequences of natural disasters and the protection and preservation of the environment." In 1992, designated as SAARC's Year of the Environment, a host of programmes were identified, including ones on energy and environment. In 1993, the Technical Committee on Environment included within its purview a focus on the "Greenhouse effect and its impact on the region" (SAARC 1997b).

Regional cooperation could go far towards meeting South Asian energy needs and enhancing environmental issues, as well as energy supply and security. The water resources of the Himalayas are enormous. The hydro power potential of Himalayan rivers flowing through Nepal alone has been estimated at 83,000 MW. The hydro power potential in India, Bangladesh, and Pakistan has been estimated to be 70,000 MW, 1,772 MW, and 21,000 MW respectively (Dash 1996, 9). The development of hydro power, especially in an environmentally and socially sensitive manner, will require states to cooperate in managing the water resource, amassing the requisite investment capital, and designing electricity distribution systems. In Bhutan, the Chukha hydro project was recently completed with assistance from India.

Another significant regional energy source is natural gas. Recent discoveries in Bangladesh suggest that current proven reserves are in the range of 283–340 billion cubic metres and could well be above 1,700 billion cubic metres (Mohan 1997). The gas would find a ready export market in India, which is eager to diversify its energy supply resources away from its dependence on Middle East oil. There could also be an integrated regional market encompassing the eastern and north-eastern states of India, Bangladesh, Bhutan, and Nepal.

Despite the lure of economic and environmental benefits, SAARC has not been effective in garnering regional cooperation for energy resource development – nor, indeed, on any component of its Integrated Action Programme. Stuck in the quagmire of Indo-Pakistani conflict, SAARC has avoided controversial issues, including the contentious "upstream-downstream" issues of water development. Lacking political will, as well as financial resources for implementation, programmes of action have remained stuck at the level of seminars and rhetoric. "Since 1985," concludes Kishore Dash of the East-West Center, "SAARC has evolved slowly but continuously both in terms of institutions and programmes.

However, it is true that most of the programmes and achievements of SAARC exist on paper" (Dash 1996, 2).

Mahbub-al Haq, head of the Human Development Centre in Islam-abad and author of the first "Human Development Report in South Asia, 1997," is even more unceremonious: "So far, SAARC has been a bureaucratic organisation with ceremonial summits that are expensive photo opportunity sessions for national leaders." However, he concludes, "it can be the future" (Pradhan 1997). Hope for SAARC is based on optimism for a new era of reduced conflict between India and Pakistan.

Moreover, the shift in macroeconomic policies towards market liberal-ization, especially in the context of growing energy requirements, will change incentives: the potential for commercial gains will raise the cost of conflict and increase the benefits of cooperation. The new discoveries of natural gas in Bangladesh, for example, along with economic liberaliza-tion and deregulation of the petroleum sector, generated a 10 fold in-crease in US investment in Bangladesh in 1997. After 25 years, cumula-tive US investment amounted to US$20 million. In 1997 alone, it jumped to US$200 million, primarily for oil and gas development (Mohan 1997).

Cooperation between India and Bangladesh to develop and utilize natural gas could create a new subregional "eastern" tilt to South Asian politics, which have previously been dominated by the "western" Indo-Pakistani axis. Energy cooperation could also breathe life into the South Asia Preferential Trading Agreement (SAPTA): intra-regional trade and investment has been modest and stagnant to date. The embrace of greater energy cooperation, in short, could be, in the near future, a driving force for wider South Asian subregional and even regional cooperation.

ASEAN

The Association of South-East Asian Nations is made up of 10 countries: Brunei, Cambodia, Indonesia, Laos, Malaysia, Myanmar, the Philippines, Singapore, Thailand, and Viet Nam. Formed in the 1960s primarily to foster security cooperation, ASEAN emerged in the 1990s as an engine for regional economic cooperation. The proposed ASEAN Free Trade Area (AFTA) aims to create an integrated zone for foreign investment by minimizing internal barriers to trade and creating common external tariff and investment policies. Moreover, with its "ASEAN-plus" formula of regular consultations with its primary economic and security partners, including the United States, India, China, and the European Union, ASEAN plays an important political role in regional affairs. In recent years, the ASEAN Regional Forum has emerged as the region's over-arching forum for discussion of security affairs in South-East and North-East Asia.

Regional energy cooperation is nothing new to ASEAN's agenda. In July 1997, ASEAN energy ministers, at their fifteenth meeting, approved a Medium-Term Programme of Action on Energy Cooperation, which extends from 1995 to 1999. The action plan has six objectives: to implement existing energy cooperation programmes; to develop indigenous, non-oil energy resources: to strengthen regional institutions through training and research; to establish an ASEAN policy framework; to synchronize ASEAN activities related to energy; and to promote sustainable self-supporting ASEAN cooperation on issues of common concern (ASEAN 1997).

The action plan identified seven sectors for enhanced energy cooperation, including electricity, coal, oil and gas, new and renewable sources of energy, energy conservation, energy and environment, and energy policy and planning. The energy ministers also declared 1998 as ASEAN Energy Efficiency and Conservation Year (ASEAN 1997).

For the countries of ASEAN, like the rest of Asia, key energy issues involve reducing supply dependence on the Middle East, developing new sources of energy, especially gas, and improving the access of poor and rural communities to energy resources. Indicating the high priority of energy issues, there is a focal point on energy within the ASEAN secretariat. In addition to cooperating in the exploration and development of new energy sources, the primary work of ASEAN to date has been on information exchange and capacity-building. Funded by the European Community, ASEAN has established the ASEAN-EC Energy Management Training and Research Centre. In a concerted effort to encourage business sector interest and investment, Malaysia hosted the first ASEAN Energy Business Forum in 1997, which drew some 230 public and private sector participants.

Like other regional organizations, ASEAN has had difficulty in moving workplans from design and agreement to implementation. The ambitious sweep of the workplans may be especially hard to implement in the current fiscally constrained post-financial-crisis era. Among the regional projects under way are the Trans-ASEAN Gas Pipeline and the ASEAN Power Grid Interconnection projects, both under the auspices of the heads of the ASEAN power utilities/authorities.

Outside of the ASEAN rubric, regional energy cooperation in South-East Asia has focused on cross-border development of energy resources, especially the Natuna gas project in the South China Sea. The Natuna gas fields, which lie within the disputed Spratley Island group, are estimated to contain reserves of 178 billion cubic metres of natural gas. The project is being developed by Indonesia's state-owned Pertamina oil and gas company, with Exxon, Mobil Oil, and several Japanese companies (*Straits Times* 1997).

Development of the Natuna gas fields, however, will probably be stymied by South-East Asia's financial crisis. In late 1997, for example, Thailand announced that it did not need the energy resources and withdrew from its purchasing agreement. Territorial disputes within the South China Sea could also put a drag on development. A part of the lucrative Natuna project lies in a disputed "grey area" claimed by both Indonesia and China. Despite Chinese assurances, Indonesia deploys reconnaissance aircraft and naval patrols to protect the project from military action by China.

North-East Asia

North-East Asia is the least institutionally developed region in Asia. Geographically, the region might be considered to encompass the north-eastern provinces of China, the far eastern provinces of Russia, Japan, North and South Korea, Mongolia, and Alaska. However, given that cooperation between states lies within the realm of the national, not provincial, governments, the region is usually considered to encompass simply China (and sometimes Taiwan as well), and, depending on the purpose of the description, Russia. Moreover, in UN terms, the United States is in North America. The fledgling North-East Asian Regional Environment Programme nurtured by the UNDP and ESCAP thus includes Japan, the two Koreas, Mongolia, China, and Russia.

Energy-related issues, most prominently the mitigation of acid deposition and the development of cross-border oil and natural gas reserves, top the list of regional priorities for environmental cooperation. The reduction of acid deposition would also reduce North-East Asia's greenhouse-related emissions.

The scale and cross-border nature of the acid deposition problem suggests that there are strong incentives for regional energy cooperation in North-East Asia. However, the political divides are deep. Until 1991, the region was split by the Cold War and economic opportunities languished. Moreover, North and South Korea remain technically in a state of war and historical animosities arising from Japan's occupation of Korea and China have not fully abated.

Most important in terms of solving collective action problems, regional institutions in North-East Asia are undeveloped. When Europe and North America encountered acid deposition problems, they were much richer institutionally than North-East Asia is today. In Europe, the European Union provided a forum, while the United States and Canada have a rich set of communication channels. Even research forums or networks are still lacking or in their infancy in North-East Asia.[11]

Nonetheless, the region is rapidly becoming more economically integrated and the pace of economic integration is likely to accelerate. With increasing market openness, it is predicted that trade and investment flows within the region will boom. According to one estimate, the value of trade within North-East Asia will more than double between 1995 and 2000 and triple by 2010 (Kap-Young, Kubayashi, and Takahasi 1995). Economic integration has prompted greater interest in regional cooperation, and a kind of "soft regionalism" is emerging.

A number of energy-related regional initiatives have emerged since 1991. The North-East Asian Regional Environment Programme selected energy-related air pollution as the first of three priority areas, and has developed pilot demonstration clean coal projects. There are also a host of bilateral initiatives, primarily between Japan and China, involving the monitoring of acid deposition and, through Japanese official development assistance, financing of clean coal technology.

In Europe, acid rain was tackled in part via a regional convention to reduce emissions. China, however, is not open to a regional agreement at this time, although it is interested in other forms of regional cooperation (Sinton 1997). With the support of the Japanese government, a regional acid deposition monitoring network has been created. Another proposal is to establish a joint fund to cover the incremental cost of abatement technology in those facilities where the greatest benefit would be achieved (Streets 1997, 8).

Another approach is for the United States and Japan, as the dominant suppliers of energy technology and finance, to collaborate in establishing innovative regional financing mechanisms for clean coal and fuel substitution. Aimed primarily at China, such mechanisms could also be utilized to promote energy efficiency and reduce incentives for nuclear power in North Korea (ESENA 1997).

In addition to reducing acid rain, there are strong incentives for regional cooperation in developing the large reserves of natural gas and oil in China, Siberia, and the Russian Far East (see Figure 14.1). Located in remote regions of Russia and China, extracting these resources and getting them to the heavily populated coastal areas in China, Japan, and Korea will be highly capital-intensive. Regional cooperation is needed to manage not only the crossing of borders but also the garnering of large investment funds and the allocation of the resources.

The construction of a large-scale gas field and 4,100 km pipeline from Irkutsk in Siberia to Ulaanbaatar, Beijing, and Seoul, for example, will require an estimated investment of US$11 billion. Recently, South Korea, China, Russia, and Japan agreed to exchange letters of intent to develop the Siberian gas field. When completed, the gas field would provide 30 billion cubic metres of natural gas to China, Russia, and Korea annually for 30 years at a much lower price than liquefied petroleum gas. However, there is a long lead time: under the best scenario, the pipeline would not be ready until 2006 (*Korea Herald* 1997). Moreover, given the high level of requisite inter-state cooperation and the enormous financial requirement, some analysts consider the pipeline scheme to be a pipe dream and recommend transmission lines instead.

In addition to reserves in the interior, there are significant oil and gas resources offshore, especially near Sakhalin Island in the Sea of Okhotsk in the Russian Far East. To date, exploration has yielded discovery of 273 million tonnes of oil and 878 billion cubic metres of gas. Unexplored offshore reserves are estimated to contain an additional 450 million tonnes of oil and 700 billion cubic metres of gas.

Lacking the requisite capital and technology, the Russian Federation offered international tenders for the development of Sakhalin hydrocarbon resources. Sakhalin I is a US$15 billion consortium led by Exxon and including a group of Japanese firms led by the Japan National Oil Corporation, as well as two Russian partners. Sakhalin II, a US$10 billion consortium, is led by the US company Marathon and includes McDermott, Royal Dutch Shell, Mitsui, and Mitsubishi (Rosenthal and Mischenko 1998).

Regional cooperation will be needed not only to extract the resources but to ensure that their development does not generate an ecological catastrophe. To date, extraction has been constrained by severe climatic conditions, including an icing period of up to nine months a year and ice thickness reaching 1.5–2 metres. The depth of the sea in drilling areas can reach 30–50 metres. Moreover, the area is one of high seismic activity, and tsunamis and severe wind sheer are common in the summer months. Most important, fiscal resources for environmental protection are scarce in Russia and institutions for environmental governance rudimentary.

Conclusion

Regional cooperation could be an important vehicle to promote more sustainable and secure production and use of energy in Asia. The growing reliance on markets – for energy resources, electricity, and power sector financing – suggest that market governance is a crucial component of a regional energy strategy. The first step, however, is to develop a regional consensus about the goals and objectives of energy policy – in the long as well as the short term. Such a consensus should be built on the integration of environmental and security concerns with economic objectives in an energy strategy.

The development of a regional – or even subregional – consensus will not be easy. The region is wracked by political animosities, perhaps most strongly in South Asia, and a lack of common language. Significant gaps in economic development and political power, along with historical memories of (Japanese) occupation and fears of (Chinese) expansionism create undercurrents of mistrust. In many countries in Asia, there is still little opportunity for critics and innovators – either inside or outside government – to have their say.

Nonetheless, perceptions of common good, as well as economic and financial incentives to cooperate, are becoming stronger. A new kind of social group is emerging: people born after the Second World War who have travelled in Asia, been educated in the West, speak English, and have a highly developed sense of social and environmental concerns. These people are beginning to wield influence in professional and governmental circles and may form the core for a new style of leadership and regionalism in Asia on environmental issues and beyond. Developing regional institutional mechanisms which enhance their voices in regional dialogue, both official and unofficial, is the most pressing need.

Notes

1. WRI (1996, 326–327). On a per capita basis, carbon dioxide emissions from the United States were more than seven times those from China.
2. For an excellent exposition of this argument, see Grollman (1997).
3. For a fuller exposition of the argument, see Zarsky (1997a).
4. The scenario assumes that all major point sources of emissions (existing and new, industrial and power) install state-of-the-art desulphurization systems and that all other users of fossil fuels switch to lower-sulphur fuels. Even under a somewhat less ambitious "advanced control technology" scenario, in which desulphurization technology is applied only to new power plants and there is a modest level of fuel switching, sulphur emissions could be cut or stabilized. See Streets (1997, 12–14).
5. A non-binding investment code adopted by APEC included a provision which eschewed the practice of lowering environmental standards in order to attract investment. See APEC (1995, Annex 3).
6. For an interesting look at the role of Asian scientists in creating an "epistemic community' on the issue of acid deposition, see Wilkening (1997).
7. A complete list of ESCAP's regional and associate members can be found on http://unescap.org/stat/statdata/apinfig.htm.
8. APEC's members are Australia, Brunei, Canada, Chile, China, Hong Kong, Indonesia, Japan, Malaysia. Mexico, New Zealand, Papua New Guinea, Peru, the Philippines, Russia, Singapore, South Korea, Taiwan, Thailand, Viet Nam, and the United States.
9. At the APEC Leaders' Summit and ministerial meetings in Vancouver in November. 1997, energy was one of nine sectors identified for "fast track liberalisation." *APEC Currents*, The Australian APEC Study Centre, http:/www.arts.monash.edu.au/ausapec/newsletter/Curr7.htm.
10. For an analysis of the problem of bureaucratic stagnation in the environmental cooperation side of APEC, see Zarsky (1997b).
11. One attempt is the Energy, Security, Environment in North-East Asia project (ESENA), which links scholars and policy-makers in Japan and the United States in an effort to develop joint regional policy initiatives. The project is directed by the Nautilus

Institute for Security and Sustainable Development and the Center for Global Communications in Tokyo. See http://www.nautilus.org/ESENA.

REFERENCES

Anderson, K. 1993. "Economic Growth, Environmental Issues, and Trade." In *Pacific Dynamism and the International Economic System*, eds C. F. Bergsten and M. Noland. Washington: Institute for International Economics.

APEC. 1995. *Implementing the APEC Vision*. Third Report of the Eminent Persons Group (August).

APEC Energy Working Group. 1997. "APEC Energy Working Group." Internet: ⟨http://www.dpie.gov.au/resources.energy/energy/apec/index.html⟩.

APEC SOM (Senior Officials Meeting). 1997. "Engagement with Civil Society Organizations by Multilateral Organizations." 18 August.

ASEAN. 1997. *Programme of Action on Energy Cooperation*. Internet: ⟨http://www.asean.or.id/economic/paenergy.htm⟩.

Bakthavatsalam V. 1995. "Financing India's Renewable Energy Boom." Paper presented at Conference on the Changing Politics of International Energy Investment, Royal Institute of International Affairs, 4–5 December, London. Internet: ⟨http://www.crest.org/renewables/ireda/bakthavatsalamtalk.html⟩.

Bhatti N. and D. Streets. 1992. "Acid Rain in Asia." *Environmental Management* 16(4).

Calder, K. E. 1997. "Fueling the Rising Sun, Asia's Energy Needs and Global Security." *Harvard International Review* 19(3): 24–31.

Carmichael, G. R. and R. Arndt. 1995. "Long Range Transport and Deposition of Sulfur in Asia." In *RAINS-Asia: An Assessment Model for Acid Rain in Asia*. Washington: World Bank.

Carmichael, G. R. and R. Arndt. 1997. "Deposition of Acidifying Species in Northwest Asia." Energy, Security, and Environment in North-East Asia Project (ESENA), Nautilus Institute for Security and Sustainable Development.

Dash, K. C. 1996. "The Political Economy of Regional Cooperation in South Asia." *Pacific Affairs* 69(3): 1–13.

De Moor, A. and P. Calamai. 1997. *Subsidizing Unsustainable Development, Undermining the Earth with Public Funds*, San Jose, Costa Rica: Earth Council.

ESENA (Energy, Security, and Environment in North-East Asia). 1997. Internet ⟨http://www.nautilus.org/esena/⟩.

Fesharaki, F., A. C. Clark, and D. Intaraprovich. 1995. "Energy Outlook to 2010: Asia-Pacific Demand, Supply, and Climate Change Implications." *Asia Pacific Issues* 19 (April).

Fesharaki, F., S. Banaszak, and W. Kang. 1997. "Energy Supply and Demand in Northeast Asia." Paper presented to the Seventh Meeting of the Northeast Asia Economic Forum, 17–21 August, Ulaanbaatar, Mongolia.

Greene, D. L. 1997. "Economic Scarcity, Forget Geology, Beware Monopoly." *Harvard International Review* 19(3): 16–19.

Grollman, N. 1996. "Energy Dynamics and Sustainable Development in the East Asia-Pacific Region." Issues Paper No. 7. Melbourne: Australian APEC Study Centre.

Grollman, N. 1997. "The Energy Subregion as a Basis for Greenhouse Policy." *Energy Policy* 25(4): 459–467.

Higgins, R. 1996. "Energy Challenges for the Asia Pacific Region." Address to PECC Meeting, 26–27 August, Sydney, Australia.

Hirsch, P. 1997. "The Nam Theun Dam in Laos: Conflicts Over Development Plans for the Mekong River Region." Mimeo, Department of Geography, University of Sydney, New South Wales.

IEA (International Energy Agency). 1996. *World Energy Outlook*. Paris: OECD. Quoted in N. Grollman. 1996. "Energy Dynamics and Sustainable Development in the East Asia-Pacific Region." Issues Paper No. 7. Melbourne: Australian APEC Study Centre.

IIEC. 1997. "Communique." Forum on Asia Regional Cooperation on Energy Efficiency Standards and Labelling, Bangkok, 14–16 July, ⟨http://www.iiec. org/pubs/89.html⟩.

Kalpage, S. 1996. "SAARC Moves Slowly Forward." *The Sunday Times* (New Delhi), 29 December, ⟨http://www.lacnet.org/suntimes/961229/gnes.html⟩.

Kap-Young, J., S. Kubayashi, and H. Takahasi. 1995. "International Trade in Northeast Asia: Past, Present and Future." Working Paper No. 1, Project on Economic Cooperation in Northeast Asia. Tokyo: Sasakawa Peace Foundation.

Korea Herald. 1997. "Korea to Develop Siberian Gas Field, Pipeline with Three Countries." 22 October.

Mohan, C. R. 1997. "The 'Emerging East.'" *The Hindu*, 11 December.

Nautilus Institute. 1997. "Environmental Conservation Budget Cut in Half." *Connectivity Monitor* 13, 24 October.

Paik, K. W. 1995. *Gas and Oil in Northeast Asia, Policies Projects and Prospects*. London: Royal Institute of International Affairs.

Pradhan, S. 1997. "South Asia: Last Chance for World's Poorest Region." Inter Press Service, 30 April.

Razavi, H. 1997. "Innovative Approaches to Financing Environmentally Sustainable Energy Development in Northeast Asia." In *Energy, Security and Environment in North-East Asia (ESENA)*. Nautilus Institute for Security and Sustainable Development (January).

Rosenthal, E. and V. Mischenko. 1998. "Environmental and Cultural Conflicts over Offshore International Oil Leases off Sakhalin Island, Russian Far East." In *Design Options for an International Environmental Ombudsman*. Costa Rica: Earth Council.

Runge, F. C. and T. Jones. 1996. "Subsidies, Tax Disincentives and the Environment: An Overview and Synthesis." In *Subsidies and Environment, Exploring the Linkages*. Paris: OECD.

SAARC. 1997a. "South Asian Association for Regional Cooperation." Internet: ⟨http://www.saarc.com/index.html⟩.

SAARC. 1997b. "Integrated Program of Action." Internet: ⟨http://www.south-asia.com/saarc/c2.htm⟩.

Sinton, J. E. 1997. "China's View of Acid Rain in Northeast Asia and Regional Cooperation Strategies for Mitigation." Energy, Security, and Environment in North-East Asia Project (ESENA), Nautilus Institute for Security and Sustainable Development.

Straits Times. 1997. "India to Deploy Jets to Protect Gas Field." 12 August.

Streets, D. G. 1997. "Energy and Acid Rain Projections for Northeast Asia." Energy, Security and Environment in North-East Asia Project (ESENA), Nautilus Institute for Security and Sustainable Development, ⟨http://www.nautilus. org/papers/energy/streets/ESENA/1.html⟩.

UNDP (United Nations Development Programme). 1997. *Energy After Rio, Prospects and Challenges*. New York: United Nations Publications.

US Department of Energy. 1997. "India: Economics, Demographics, and Environment." Internet: ⟨http://www.eia.doe.gov/emeu/cabs/indiaindiach1. htm#ENGECON⟩.

US EIA (US Energy Information Administration). 1997. "Country Analysis Briefs – India." Internet: ⟨http://www.eia.doc.gov/emeu/cabs/india/eglance.gis⟩.

Von Hippel, D. and P. Hayes. 1997. "Two Scenarios of Nuclear Power and Nuclear Waste Production in Northeast Asia." Nautilus Institute for Security and Sustainable Development. Internet: ⟨http://ww.nautilus.org/ESENA⟩.

Wilkening, K. E. 1997. *The Role of Scientists and Scientific Knowledge in Policymaking on the Acid Deposition Issue in Europe, North America and East Asia*. PhD dissertation, University of Wisconsin-Madison.

World Bank. 1995. *Monitoring Environmental Progress, A Report on Work in Progress*, Washington: World Bank Environmentally Sustainable Development Unit.

WRI (World Resources Institute). 1996. *World Resources 1996–97, The Urban Environment*, New York: Oxford University Press.

Yamazawa, I. 1994. "On Pacific Economic Integration." In *Asia Pacific Regionalism: Readings in International Economic Relations*, eds R. Garnaut and P. Drysdale. Canberra: Japan Research Centre, Australian National University.

Yergin, D., D. Eklof, and J. Edward. 1998. "Fuelling Asia's Recovery." *Foreign Affairs*, March/April.

Zarsky, L. 1997a. "Stuck in the Mud? Nation-States, Globalisation and the Environment." In *Globalisation and the Environment Preliminary Perspectives*. Paris: OECD.

Zarsky, L. 1997b. "Heading for the Doldrums? APEC and the Environment." *Connectivity Monitor* 1(10). Internet: ⟨http://www.nautilus.org/trade/monitor/ apec/index.html⟩.

Zarsky, L. 1998. "APEC, Globalization, and the 'Sustainable Development' Agenda." *Asian Perspectives* 22(2).

Zarsky, L. and J. Hunter. 1997. "Environmental Cooperation at APEC: The First Five Years." *Journal of Environment and Development* 6(3): 222–251.

FURTHER READING

Blake, D. W. 1996. *Regional Cooperation for Power Infrastructure*. Report to the APEC Energy Working Group. Canberra: APEC.

Michaelis, L. 1996. "The Environmental Implications of Energy and Transport Subsidies." In *Subsidies and the Environment, Exploring the Linkages*. Paris: OECD.

Zarsky, L. 1995. "Environmental Cooperation and Sustainable Development in Northeast Asia." In *Economic and Regional Cooperation in Northeast Asia*. Chicago: University of Chicago Press.

15

Regional environmental cooperation and preventive environmental policy in Central and Eastern Europe

Egbert Tellegen[1]

One of the heritages of the former communist regimes in Central and Eastern Europe is environmental decay. The old political system has disappeared but many hot-spots of dangerous forms of environmental pollution have remained. The process of economic transformation has led to a drastic reduction of production and consumption and, as a consequence, to the decline of some forms of pollution. In spite of that, it has also resulted in a deterioration of existing forms of environmental control. On top of this the introduction of a Western-style market economy implies new forms of environmental stress, varying from disposables replacing returnable packing to growing quantities of cars, roads, and traffic pollutants.

All sorts of environmental problems in Central and Eastern Europe have been frequently described and analysed in recent years. The primary interest of this chapter is the role of regional cooperation in environmental problem-solving. The chapter begins with a short discussion of relatively old forms of international cooperation in the fields of measurement and abatement of air and water pollution, followed by a discussion on European environmental cooperation since 1989 and the role of environmental issues in the extension of the European Union. The latter part of the chapter is devoted to recent developments in regional cooperation to reduce energy use and waste production. Environmental problems in Central and Eastern Europe have often been defined as problems of inefficient and wasteful use of natural resources. A main, if not the most important, challenge for environmental policy in this part of the world is to reduce the excessive use of natural resources such as minerals and fossil fuels. For this reason, the discussion of regional environmental cooperation will focus on developments in the fields of energy conservation and waste minimization.

The territory

The term "Central and Eastern Europe" is used to refer to those European countries that were governed by communist regimes until the revolutionary changes of 1989 and the disintegration of the Soviet Union and Yugoslavia. It is not intended to offer equal or, in size or number of inhabitants, proportional attention to the different parts of Central and Eastern Europe.

Early forms of regional cooperation

Cooperation within Western and Eastern Europe

Forms of regional environmental cooperation developed within Western and Eastern Europe long before the fall of the Berlin Wall in 1989. In Western Europe both the Council of Europe and the European Community were active in the fields of environmental and nature protection. The Council of Europe, founded in 1949, has been mentioned as "the first broadly based international body to have the environment on its work programme" (Haigh 1987, 373). It developed activities in the fields of nature conservation and environmental pollution control. The European Economic Community, founded in 1957, gradually extended its competence to environmental issues, if only in order to avoid economic advantages for countries with low environmental standards. In Eastern Europe, Bulgaria, Czechoslovakia, Hungary, Poland, Romania, and the Soviet Union worked together in the Council for Mutual Economic Assistance (COMECON), which was founded in 1949. Within COMECON both bilateral and multilateral forms of cooperation developed (Lisitzin 1987). In 1988 a common declaration between the European Community and COMECON was signed, followed by a special environmental conference in Sofia in 1989 (Baker 1996, 157). East-West cooperation on single environmental issues started much earlier, and will be discussed below.

Transboundary air pollution

The reduction of air pollution has long been recognized as a common interest of Eastern and Western European countries, even though some countries suffer more from transboundary air pollution than others. Both natural conditions (in particular prevailing wind directions and sensitivity of ecosystems) and economic activities in neighbouring countries (such as energy production and other industrial activities) may contribute to these differences. Among the European countries, Russia is a net importer of air pollution, most of which originates from other members of the former Eastern bloc (Kljoev 1997, 6).

In 1975 the Helsinki Conference on Security and Cooperation in Europe (CSCE) took place. After that meeting, the Soviet Union wanted to continue the process of détente in fields other than human rights and arms control, and proposed to discuss environment, energy, and transport issues (Levy 1993, 81). In 1979, negotiations within the framework of the Economic Commission for Europe (ECE) of the United Nations led to the adoption of the Convention on Long-Range Transboundary Air Pollution (LRTAP). This convention was ratified by 32 countries in Eastern and Western Europe and North America (the United States and Canada). Even before 1979, the ECE had already initiated the development of a European Monitoring and Evaluation Programme (EMEP) for transboundary air pollution. Under the umbrella of EMEP, Meteo Synthesising Centres were founded in Moscow (known as MSC-East) and Oslo (known as MSC-West) (Van der Weij 1993, 37). Research was concentrated at the International Institute for Applied Systems Analysis (IIASA) in Laxenburg, Austria.

Within the framework of the LRTAP convention, various protocols were adopted to cover different air pollutants. In 1985, 18 countries signed the Helsinki Protocol and thereby committed themselves to reducing SO_2 emissions by 30 per cent by 1993, as compared with the level of emissions in 1980. Under the 1988 Sofia Protocol, the signatories were committed to stabilizing NO_x emissions to 1987 levels by the year 1994. A third protocol, signed in Geneva in 1991, aims to limit emissions of volatile organic compounds (VOCs) in 1999 to a level 30 per cent below that applying in 1988 (Hordijk 1991). All the Western countries and most of the Eastern European countries had reached the 30 per cent SO_2 reduction target in 1993. Many Western countries achieved a much larger reduction of SO_2 emissions.

In 1994, the member states of the LRTAP agreed upon a new SO_2 reduction plan. The new plan was not emission-oriented but effect-oriented. In other words, the aim was no longer to achieve equal reductions in emissions in all member states, but to reduce local depositions as far as is necessary not to surpass critical loads. The concept of a critical load has been defined as "a quantitative estimate of an exposure to one or more pollutants below which significant harmful effects on specified elements of the environment do not occur according to present knowledge" (Amann et al. 1992, 1186). This new policy is based on maps of critical loads for different parts of Europe (Hettelingh, Downing, and de Smet 1991). There are great differences in the critical loads applying to different areas, based, for example, on the different types of soils in these areas.

It is clear that this new policy makes international cooperation much more complicated. Local depositions are often highly dependent on emissions in other countries, and the necessary level of reduction may therefore differ among member states because of the different effects in other member states. A logical consequence of the effect-oriented approach would be the creation of a common European fund from which investments in pollution reduction would be paid in order to reduce the most extreme deviations from the critical loads, wherever these are in Europe.

As early as 1985, the Austrian Minister of Environmental Protection, Kurt Steyer, suggested creating a common fund for SO_2 emission abatement in the framework of the LRTAP treaty. At the time, opponents of this idea argued that Eastern European countries should not be granted subsidies for taking environmental measures as long as a large part of their state budget was still devoted to military spending. Nevertheless, even though the Cold War has now come to an end, such a common fund has not yet been created. Western financial institutions do offer financial aid to individual countries to reduce local and transboundary air pollution, but cooperation within the LRTAP convention remains limited to joint studies of the scale and effects of air pollution and the definition and evaluation of policy targets. Even so, the modest scope of LRTAP cooperation should not be interpreted as a complete lack of effectiveness. In the context of the LRTAP, "weak rules permitted strong consensus building powers, whereas strong rules would have generated hostility on the part of governments" (Levy 1993, 76). The same author characterized LRTAP cooperation as "tote-board diplomacy": "The protocols were tote-boards showing who was responsible and who was not" (Levy 1993, 77). LRTAP protocols put external and internal pressure on countries who remain off the tote-board or who fail to comply with accepted reduction targets.

Transboundary water pollution: The Baltic Sea

Between Eastern and Western Europe, the Baltic Sea is the most "transboundary" sea. Abatement of transboundary pollution of the Baltic Sea has been recognized as a common interest of Western and Eastern European countries for a long time.

The Baltic Sea is surrounded by Germany, Denmark, Sweden, Finland, Russia, the three Baltic republics, and Poland. Main pollutants of the Baltic Sea are discharges of municipal and industrial waste water.

In 1974 the countries surrounding the Baltic Sea signed the Helsinki Convention on the Protection of the Baltic Sea. This agreement is usually abbreviated as HELCOM (referring to the executive commission of the convention). In 1992, a revised Helsinki agreement was signed by 12 states.

Before the fall of communist regimes, common efforts to protect the Baltic Sea were limited mainly to the prevention of pollution by ships. The protection of national sovereignty and secrecy hindered inclusion of land-based activities and inland waters as sources of pollution, and was in particular resisted by the Soviet Union. In the revised 1992 version of HELCOM these sources are included. "This new approach was revolutionary in the sense that the national, separate approach, which left a lot of room for national negligence, was given up. The national sovereignty was no longer seen as an argument against joint action" (Van der Weij 1993, 101). Another new development starting around 1990 was the participation of NGOs in HELCOM. Greenpeace received observer status at the end of the 1980s, followed by the WWF and the Coalition Green Baltic, consisting of 15 Baltic NGOs, in 1991. A third new element was the involvement of international banks: the EBRD, the European Investment Bank, the Nordic Investment Bank, and the World Bank. The former principle that every country should pay for the reduction of its own contribution to pollution of the Baltic Sea was given up (Van der Weij 1993, 101–102). In 1992, together with the new convention, a common action programme was formulated (EAP 1993). Since the start of the programme in 1992 15 hot spots have been deleted following proactive measures (Helsinki Commission 1997).

Compared to East-West cooperation in the frame of the LRTAP to reduce air pollution, the scope of cooperation in the frame of HELCOM is much larger. NGOs are involved, priorities of emission reductions are indicated, and banks are engaged to provide the necessary financial means to transform priorities into practical measures.

The "Environment for Europe" process

The fall of the Berlin Wall and the end of the Soviet Union in 1991 gave a strong impetus to East-West European environmental cooperation. Environmental issues played a crucial role in the revolt against communist regimes in Central Europe and in the struggle for independence in the European republics of the Soviet Union. In Western Europe environmental concern was growing and environmental issues reached a prominent place on political agendas in the early 1990s. Under these favourable circumstances, a new form of pan-European environmental cooperation, the so-called "Environment for Europe" process, was initiated by Eastern and Western European states. A guiding role in this process was played by pan-European conferences of ministers of the environment, which were held in Dobris (former Czechoslovakia) in 1991, in Lucerne (Switzerland) in 1993, and in Sofia (Bulgaria) in 1995 (Klarer and Francis 1997, 28–36). The most recent conference took place in Aarhus (Denmark) in June 1998. Among the outcomes of the first conference in Dobris was a pan-European Environmental Action Plan, which was adopted at the Lucerne Conference in 1993 (EAP 1993) and the so-called Dobris Assessment, an all-European investigation of environmental conditions, pressures, and problems, which was published in 1995 (Stanners and Bourdeau 1995). During the Sofia Conference six areas of further cooperation were chosen. Unlike the earlier Environmental Action Plan, which was primarily a Western initiative, the Sofia initiatives were proposed by Eastern European countries and they play a leading role in their further development. An example of concrete measures to improve environmental quality is offered by the Sofia initiative on local air pollution. It is chaired by the Bulgarian Minister of Environment and has its secretariat at the Regional Environment Centre in Szentendre near Budapest. It promotes cooperation at national and municipal levels. Part of this Sofia initiative is a total phase-out of leaded petrol in all European countries. A special Task Force Group under the auspices of the UN Economic Commission for Europe and chaired by the Danish Ministry of Environment and Energy prepared a declaration for the total phase-out of leaded petrol in Europe, which was adopted at the Aarhus Conference.

Like environmental cooperation around the Baltic Sea, widely different institutions are involved in this pan-European environmental cooperation: states, international and supranational organizations, international financial institutions, and non-governmental environmental and business organizations. "The Environment for Europe process presents a formidable platform for contact and cooperation between East and West with the representation of all mentioned countries and organizations. The Environment for Europe process is unique, no similarly comprehensive effort exists in other policy areas" (Klarer and Francis 1997, 28). There can be no doubt about the fact that this pan-European cooperation has stimulated information-gathering on hot-spots of environmental pollution and other environmental problems, and the development of knowledge of and experience with environmental legislation, strategies, and policy instruments. Nevertheless, it cannot be denied that there is growing criticism in Central and Eastern European countries of the ways in which financial aid from the West, such as the EU programmes PHARE (Poland Hungary Assistance for Reconstruction of Economy) and TACIS (Technical Assistance Commonwealth of Independent States), has been spent. Too much has been spent on investigations by Western consultancy firms and too little on investments in local public facilities and industry. Even in Poland, the country which received by far the largest amount of financial environmental support from the PHARE programme, the share of financial support from the West accounted for less than 5 per cent of total environmental expenditure in the 1990–1994 period (Kolk and Van der Weij 1998).

The accession of new member states to the European Union

The European Union has played a crucial role in environmental cooperation with Central and Eastern European countries. It did and does so for widely different reasons, summarized by Baker (1996, 152). Among them are economic considerations: the fear of competition within the European Union by Eastern European enterprises with low pollution costs; the risk of transfer of Western European enterprises to Eastern European areas with low environmental standards; the opening up of business opportunities for transfer of ecological technology and enterprises in Eastern Europe; and the relatively low costs of emission reduction in Eastern Europe in cases of transboundary air and surface water pollution. Nevertheless, all these considerations are not enough to give environmental protection top priority in cooperation between the European Union and Central and Eastern European states. At the end of the 1990s the environmental euphoria of the early 1990s is over in both Eastern and Western Europe. Central and Eastern European countries no longer need environmental issues to oppose the communist government in their national capital or in Moscow. In Western Europe the environmental issue has lost its prominent place on policy agendas in favour of issues like unemployment, crime, and entrance into European monetary union.

Under these less favourable circumstances the European Union initiated a process of eastward extension. This process started with bilateral European agreements with many individual countries, offering a prospect of full membership. However, not all the countries that have signed a European agreement with the European Union can hope for EU membership in the near future. In 1997 the European Commission published its Agenda 2000, according to which only five countries should be selected for a first round of eastward extension of the European Union: the Czech Republic, Estonia, Hungary, Poland, and Slovenia.

There is a contradiction in the attitude of the European Union towards Eastern European future member states regarding environmental matters. On the one hand, new countries are expected to integrate the whole so-called *acquis communautaire*. On the other hand, it is completely clear that it will take decades before even the five selected countries can fulfil the requirement of full adoption of European environmental legislation and environmental standards (Eisma 1997). One may even wonder whether it is useful that countries in another part of Europe and in another period simply take over the environmental "infrastructure" which has been developed at other places and under different circumstances (Baker 1996, 158). The European Union was founded as an economic union, and to date economic interests prevail over environmental considerations. There is a real possibility that some countries will obtain full membership although they are far from integrating the environmental *acquis communautaire*. This would be a signal to other countries with the ambition to obtain full membership of the European Union not to put much effort into improvement of environmental legislation and policy (Eisma 1997, 5).

Official EU statements stress the necessity to integrate "ecology" and "economy" by means of preventive environmental policies. In reality, EU support to Central and Eastern Europe is far more economically than ecologically directed, and more oriented to monitoring and legislation than to integrative and preventive environmental policy measures.

The need for preventive environmental policies

Effective environmental policy requires more than just exchange of environmental information and implementation of environmental legislation and policy. This is particularly the case in the former communist states, where scientific knowledge was available and environmental quality standards were high but where technology and management were in a poor state. This backwardness resulted in wasting materials and energy. For good reasons, the authorities of the communist countries defined environmental problems primarily as problems of irrational use of natural resources. Time and again the excessive use of materials and energy in production processes was criticized (Tellegen 1989). "We spent, in fact we are still spending far more on raw materials, energy, and other resources per unit of output than other developed nations. Our country's wealth in terms of natural and manpower resources has spoiled, one may even say corrupted us" (Gorbachev 1987, 85). This failure became a major driving force behind the process of *perestroika*. This is reason enough to focus on regional cooperation in the fields of energy conservation and waste minimization as a means to stimulate both economic efficiency and environmental improvement in Central and Eastern Europe.

Energy conservation

Energy: A crucial issue

Use of energy plays an important role in widely different forms of environmental stress, nature destruction, and related social tensions. In Central and Eastern Europe the excessive air pollution in the Black Triangle (Germany, Poland, and the Czech Republic), the destruction of nature in northern Siberia, the conflicts between Hungary and Slovakia regarding the canalization of the River Danube, and last but not least the Chernobyl catastrophe are examples of the environmental and social impact of the use of energy.

Final energy consumption per capita in general is not very different from the West, but compared to the low level of consumption in those countries energy consumption can be called excessive.[2] The disintegration of Central and Eastern European planned economies was followed by a drastic decline of economic activities and energy use, but it is reasonable to expect a growing energy consumption when the period of economic decline is followed by an era of economic growth. In Hungary, the decrease of energy consumption came to an end in 1992 (Lehoczki and Balogh 1997, 138).

For many years solutions for problems of shortages and damages caused by the use of particular sources of energy have been found by switching from one energy source to another. Nowadays it has become clear that all forms of energy use which are based on fossil or fissile fuels lead to environmental degradation and environmental risks. The reduction in use of these sources of energy is achieved in three different ways:

• supply efficiency improvement
• use of renewable energy sources
• reduction of end-user demand.

They are usually brought together under the banner of "energy conservation," although strictly speaking this term is incorrect in the case of implementation of renewable energy.

Large improvements are possible in these three areas of energy conservation in Central and Eastern Europe. Some examples are mentioned below.

Supply efficiency improvement

A sector in which energy efficiency can be considerably improved is the supply of heat in buildings. The existing highly centralized systems can be changed or replaced by more efficient decentralized supply systems (Martinot 1995; OECD/IEA 1995; Batov 1996; Matrosov 1997). The

Russian cities Rostov-on-Don and Vladimir are among the places where this decentralization of heat supply has already been put into practice (Matrosov and Goldstein 1996, 4).

Use of renewable energy sources

There are great possibilities for use of renewable energy sources in Central and Eastern Europe. Recently it was estimated that renewable energy sources (wind and hydro power, solar energy, and energy from biomass) could have provided 30 per cent of the total energy consumption of Romania in 1995 (Dinica 1997). Russia has a long tradition of using wind power for electricity generating (Gol'man 1991; Larin 1991). Energy supply in remote areas and local autonomy have been recently mentioned as arguments for further introduction of wind energy in both Russia and the Ukraine (Sjpil'rain 1997, 10; Martinot 1995, 68). The Ukrainian government has supported the development of wind energy as part of its conversion policy (Martinot 1995, 79; Golubenko and Tsyganov 1997).

Reduction of end-user demand

In Central and Eastern European countries, with their long tradition of highly centralized energy supply, low energy prices, absence of metering of energy consumption, and limited possibilities to influence individual energy consumption, there are huge possibilities to reduce end-user demand for energy. Measures to reduce end-user demand are often combined with measures to improve energy efficiency. In Russia, the district of Chelyabinsk introduced the notion of an "energy contract" by means of which energy conservation services can be paid for through energy savings (Livinsky 1997, 51).

Forms of East-West energy cooperation

There is a worldwide interest in the development of energy supply in the countries of the former Soviet Union and other Central and Eastern European states. As a consequence of the nuclear catastrophe at Chernobyl in 1986 and the presence of other unsafe nuclear power plants, Western countries have become strongly interested in the development of nuclear energy in Eastern Europe. Governmental and non-governmental organizations from abroad strived for the complete closure of the power plant at Chernobyl (of which two blocks remained in operation after the catastrophe and one block is still in operation today) and other dangerous nuclear power plants. To stimulate the closure or safer operation of 22 unsafe nuclear power plants in Armenia, Bulgaria, Lithuania, the Ukraine, Russia, and Slovakia, the G-7 group of industrial nations created the Nuclear Safety Account in 1993. This fund is financially supported by 15 countries. In 1996 it offered a grant of 118 million ECU to the Chernobyl nuclear power plant to get the plant closed by the year 2000.

On the other hand, Western enterprises that were not able to sell nuclear power plants in the West developed strong interests in the continuity and extension of nuclear power in Central and Eastern Europe. Development of nuclear power in Central and Eastern Europe thus became a topic in which many interest groups with often widely conflicting interests became involved.

The necessity to import fossil fuels on the one hand, and the need to remain independent of foreign powers (in particular, the Middle East) on the other, stimulated East-West inter-state cooperation. In December 1994, 49 countries signed the Energy Charter Treaty in Lisbon. Its main purpose is the guaranteed delivery of fossil fuels (in particular oil and gas) from the East to the West by means of investment protection, liberal trade connections, transit facilities, and dispute settlement. Added to the charter is a special protocol on energy efficiency and related environmental aspects. The latter element is more a statement of intentions than a guiding principle, let alone a legally binding and enforceable rule. The treaty entered into force in 1998, after it received the thirtieth instrument of ratification.

In the meantime, Western European countries were and are involved in several energy conservation projects in Central and Eastern Europe.

Energy conservation projects

In the past 10 years a variety of energy conservation projects have been initiated in Central and Eastern Europe, with support from Western Europe.

Energy efficiency demonstration zones

National states, international financial institutions, the European Union and its programmes for financial support, and different branches of the United Nations work together in the Energy Efficiency 2000 project. One of the activities of this programme has been the development of energy efficiency demonstration zones. The demonstration zones have been created in several Eastern European countries. In Russia, environmental zones were financially supported by Germany, the United Kingdom, the United States, Norway, and the World Bank.

Energy centres

The Thermie Programme of the European Union started in 1992. Its aim is to promote market penetration of EU energy-efficient technologies throughout Europe. For that purpose it has founded 14 energy centres in Central and Eastern European countries.

The European Commission Baltic Renewable Energy Centre was established in Poland in 1994. Its main tasks consist of gathering and dissemination of information.

Urban energy efficiency projects

In 1994, the Netherlands Agency for Energy and the Environment, called NOVEM, and the Italian company CESEN started the PHARE Regional Energy Programme, "Improvement of urban energy efficiency through multilateral cooperation and development of networks." The report on the first part of the study contains the results of 18 projects. To illustrate how successful projects to reduce final energy consumption can be, the results of two of the projects are given below.

- Energy management for school buildings in Tallinn, Estonia. This was a project in which the cities of Tallinn, Kiel (Germany), and Aarhus (Denmark) participated. The purpose of the project was to reduce energy consumption in a school by 15 to 20 per cent. It included both technical improvements such as the tightening of windows and the renovation of ventilation, heating, and electrical systems, and social activities like energy management training and raising public awareness. In the school in which the pilot project took place, energy consumption was reduced by 39.7 per cent within one year (NOVEM/ CESEN 1997, 29–32).
- Improving the energy performance of residential dwellings in Stary Smokovec, Slovakia. In this project the cities of Glasgow and Dublin participated. The purpose of this project was formulated as follows:

> To incorporate energy efficient design improvements into the reconstruction of a residential dwelling block in Slovakia, in order to achieve an energy reduction of 40 per cent; to combine training in insulation techniques with the actual refurbishment of residential dwellings; to increase householder energy awareness through developing and delivering of local energy advice activities and services (NOVEM/CESEM 1997, 39).

Within this project energy savings of 47.88 per cent were reached within one year (NOVEM/CESEM 1997, 39–42).

Constraints on energy conservation

Although it is perfectly clear that there are great possibilities for energy conservation in Central and Eastern Europe, investments in energy conservation are meagre compared to investments in energy production. For what reasons?

The dominance of supply-side options

Discrepancies between supply of and demand for energy can be reduced by changing supply or changing demand. Both from an economic and an environmental viewpoint, so-called "demand-side management" often has to be preferred over "supply-side management." In other words, in cases of shortage of energy, reduction of energy use is often a better option than increasing the supply of energy. Experiences in Western countries have indicated that there are strong vested interests which hinder the shift from supply- to demand-side management. The same can be said of Central and Eastern European countries and the financial aid from the West to these countries.

Foreign direct investment projects in the field of energy are mainly concentrated in oil and gas exploration and extraction in Russia, Kazakhstan, and Azerbaijan, with some in oil drilling in Albania, Hungary, Latvia, and Romania, and hardly any in energy conservation (including renewable energy sources) (Brendow 1996, 543).

The importance of countervailing power

In order to stimulate energy conservation, strong countervailing power counteracting the supply-side options of organizations with vested interests in the growth of energy use should be developed. This can be done in particular by two types of institutions: environmental and energy conservation NGOs and national and international governmental organizations.

Environmental and energy conservation NGOs can inform their Central and Eastern European counterparts about different forms of energy conservation and the ways in which they can be successfully implemented. In fact, they are already doing so. By means of the Internet and other forms of information technology, knowledge about any successful experience with energy conservation can be made available to local environmental groups and individual interested citizens in Central and Eastern Europe.

"Joint implementation" in cooperation with Central and Eastern European countries is a policy instrument by means of which Western European countries and the European Union as a whole can fulfil obligations to contribute to worldwide reduction of CO_2 emissions. It is cheaper to reduce CO_2 emissions in Eastern and Central Europe than in Western Europe.

Waste minimization

Waste problems during and after the Soviet period

The dumping of large amounts of waste was considered to be an urgent environmental problem in the centrally planned economies. In the former

Soviet Union waste problems were vividly described in newspapers like *Izvestija* and *Pravda*, and in the weekly magazine *Literaturnaja Gazeta*. Waste reduction and even wasteless production policies were propagated. One of the most important advocates of a wasteless production process, and a member of the Academy of Sciences, described this ideal "as perhaps one of the most attractive economic – and at the same time ecological – concepts of the closing years of this century." He expected that in the twenty-first century, environmental pollution in whatever form will be "considered an unusual event" (Laskorin 1984, quoted in Tellegen 1986, 232).

In reality, the fall of the Iron Curtain aggravated some waste problems in Central and Eastern Europe. It stimulated the import of hazardous waste from Western countries. In general there are no vested interests in receiving polluted air or water from neighbouring countries. However, the same cannot be said of receiving waste from abroad, because money is paid for it. Waste may be imported legally or illegally, with or without the consent of the public authorities of the receiving countries. In both cases this may be opposed by NGOs and less organized local groups of individual citizens.

As early as 1989, the Basel Convention on the Control of Transboundary Movements of Hazardous Wastes and their Disposal was adopted. It entered into force on 5 May 1992.

The main provisions of the convention call for the following action by states:
1. Information exchange with other parties on waste exports and imports, through designated national authorities.
2. The prohibition of waste exports to countries that are not party to the convention or to countries which are party to the convention but which have not expressly authorized waste imports.
3. The licensing and supervision of persons transporting or disposing of waste.
4. The packaging, labelling and transport of waste in accordance with international rules and standards.
5. Cooperation on the environmentally sound management of waste.
6. Mutual information in the event of accidents during the transboundary movement of waste (EAP 1993, V1–21).

Nevertheless, as a consequence of the revolutions which took place in 1989, the same year as that in which the convention was adopted, Central European countries have become a favourite destination for hazardous waste from Western countries. In fact, transport of hazardous waste to this area started earlier. The former German Democratic Republic, Poland (Bernstorff and Puckett 1992), and Romania (Bernstorff and Totten 1992) are among the countries to which hazardous waste was transported. Local groups, often supported by international organizations like Greenpeace, have been successful in preventing or interrupting imports of waste from the West. Sometimes the waste was sent back to the country from where it came. Nowadays rules regarding export from EU countries to other countries are stricter than in the past and will probably reduce legal and illegal export of waste from the West to the East in the future.

Cleaner industrial production and products

From both a technological and a sociological perspective the development of environmental measures by industrial enterprises in advanced (post-) industrial societies can be characterized as a process of internalization. The "internalization" of environmental technology can be illustrated by the development of technological measures to reduce air pollution. In the past, high chimney stacks were built to dilute and spread industrial air pollution. The next step was the introduction of so-called end-of-pipe technology. Filters were installed in stacks and air pollution was transformed into solid waste. The third phase in this development was the introduction of clean(er) production processes, combined with the use of clean(er) materials within production processes. Corrective technology at the end of the production process was replaced by preventive technology within the production process. Cleaner production has been defined as "the continuous application of an integrated preventative environmental strategy to processes and products to reduce risks to humans and the environment" (Verspeek 1996, 78). As a social process the development of cleaner production in recent years can be defined as the transfer from a defensive or compliance approach to an offensive or innovative approach. As long as a compliance approach prevails, the necessity to reduce emissions in order to obey fixed standards of governmental environmental policy will be the starting point for environmental measures within enterprises. Ways will be looked for to conform, with the least cost and effort, to the standards formulated by others. When an innovative approach is followed the starting point is the design of production processes which best fit both economic and ecological criteria. In the past decades great successes with such an innovative approach have been reached in many countries (Groenewegen 1996; Van Berkel 1996). In many cases it was possible to take preventive measures that created economic-ecological win-win situations. "Pollution prevention pays" was the principle on which many environmental innovations in industry were based. In general, the more complicated process of environmental improvement of products is preceded by the environmental improvement of production processes (Reijnders 1996, 28)

Cleaner production and sustainable product development are supported by the United Nations. The UNEP cleaner production programme started in 1990 (Aloisi de Larderel 1995), and the UNEP working group on sustainable product development was founded in 1994 (Van Weenen 1997).

Cleaner production programmes in Central and Eastern Europe

In recent years programmes for clean(er) production have been put into practice in Central and Eastern Europe with the support of Western European countries.
- The Norwegian Society of Chartered Engineers initiated cleaner production programmes in Poland, the Czech Republic, and Slovakia (Nedenes 1994; Dobes 1997).
- The World Environmental Centre (WEC) initiated projects in Poland, the Czech Republic, Slovakia, Hungary, Romania, Bulgaria, Estonia, Latvia, and Lithuania (Lindhqvist and Rodhe 1994, 4–5).
- The Danish government supported industrial waste minimization projects in Poland, Hungary, and the Baltic states (Lindhqvist and Rodhe 1994, 5).

Barriers to cleaner production in Central and Eastern Europe

The introduction of cleaner production in Central and Eastern Europe is hindered by different barriers (Csalagovits 1997). It may sound strange, but their simplicity and cheapness sometimes seem to be a handicap for cleaner production measures. In Lithuania so-called "good housekeeping measures" suffer from "a fixation on technical solutions by production managers, low status associated with such measures, difficulties in motivating the staff, an embarrassment that these rather simple measures had not been thought of earlier, and a general failure to recognize their importance" (Staniskis 1996, 46). Another barrier is the lack of a tradition of efficiency improvement measures in former planned economies (Lindhqvist and Rohde 1994, 10). Interestingly enough, not only the remnants of centralized decision-making in the past but also the contemporary absence of state power in the field of environmental protection have a negative influence on the development of cleaner production (CP). "The effectiveness of CP programmes is often constrained by the absence of an appropriate national framework containing long term environmental policies and strategies, by uncoordinated use of economic incentives and penalties, and lack of appropriate regulations and enforcement strategies" (Wangen 1996, 19).

Efficiency improvement is not enough

Much has been written about the disastrous state of the environment in Central and Eastern Europe in recent years. Before and after the fall of communism, lack of efficiency in the use of materials and energy has been considered as the main cause of environmental decay. The presence of large undisturbed natural areas with a great biodiversity in Central and Eastern Europe, and the fact that the use of natural resources per capita in general is not higher than in Western Europe, have been mentioned less often. There is almost no difference of opinion about the necessity of greater efficiency of resource use in order to improve environmental quality in Central and Eastern Europe. But the net effect of these improvements may be more than counteracted by the introduction of elements of a Western lifestyle in fields like household consumption, transport, and recreation. The production of cars, the construction of highways, and, as a consequence, the deterioration of public transport systems offer just one example of the environmentally damaging effects of East-West cooperation in Europe. However, it is beyond the scope of this chapter to discuss how Central and Eastern Europe could be protected against the devastating environmental effects of a Western lifestyle.

Recommendations: Aid and trade

This chapter has presented the development of different types of environmental cooperation in Europe. This cooperation started with exchange of information and formulation of policy targets by states. In a later stage, widely different organizations became involved and money was made available for pilot studies and treatment of hot-spots of environmental pollution in Central and Eastern Europe.

Preventive environmental policy which is propagated so often in official documents does not strongly profit from Western support to Central and Eastern Europe. Initiatives in that direction have been taken and successes have been achieved, but they play a minor role in the actual development of energy consumption and waste production in that part of Europe. What can be done to stimulate preventive environmental measures in these fields? Only a brief answer will be given to this question.

Aid

Financial support to Central and Eastern European countries should be related more directly to preventive environmental measures like energy conservation and waste minimization. The creation of so-called "revolving funds" could be a useful way in cases in which preventive measures can be paid back by reduction of costs. Energy conservation measures can be paid back by savings on the energy bill. Waste minimization measures may also lead to a reduction of payments for pollution or for materials that are no longer wasted. In cases of extreme environmental stress, subsidies for preventive measures can be justified even if the costs cannot be paid back in a reasonable period of time. In such cases at least part of the subsidy should only be paid after the proposed measures have proven to be effective.

Trade

The most important driving force behind environmental policy measures within the European Union has always been the avoidance of market distortions by differences in the environmental policy measures of the different member states. Energy conservation and waste minimization could also play a role in trade measures. Trade can be influenced not only by national states and supranational organizations such as the European Union, but also by NGOs. They can try to convince consumers not to buy the products of factories which are wasting materials and energy. It is clear that this is an extremely complicated matter in which different quite respectable though contradictory policy goals can come into conflict with each other. Nevertheless, when the so often stated ambitions of preventive environmental policies really are put in practice, these types of measures probably cannot be avoided.

Notes

1. The author is greatly indebted to Gert van der Meer, Ckees van Oijen, Linda Pietersen, and Stephan Slingerland for critical comments on an earlier draft of this text and to Gemmeke Caron, Ante Matser, Jord Neuteboom, Jeroen Splinter, and Frans Verspeek who provided much of the literature which has been used in preparing this chapter.
2. For data on Russia, see OECD/IEA 1995, 43.

REFERENCES

Aloisi de Larderel, J. 1995. "Making it Happen." *Our Planet* 7(6): 19–21.
Amann, M., L. Hordijk, G. Klaassen, W. Schipp, and L. Sorensen. 1992 "Economic Restructuring in Eastern Europe and Acid Rain Abatement Strategies." *Energy Policy* 20(12): 1186–1197.

Baker, S. 1996. "The Scope for East-West Cooperation." In *Prospects for Environmental Change*, eds A. Blowers and P. Glasbergen. London: Arnold.

Batov, S. 1996. *Individual Heat Metering Systems Implementation in District Heated Dwellings in Bulgaria. Experiences from Pilot Projects. 1992–1996.* Sofia: Technical University.

Bernstorff, A. and J. Puckett. 1992. *Poland: The Waste Invasion.* Amsterdam: Greenpeace International Waste Trade Campaign.

Bernstorff, A. and K. Totten. 1992. "Romania: The Toxic Assault." *Waste Imports 1986–92.* Hamburg: Greenpeace Germany.

Brendow, K. 1996. "Foreign Direct Investments (FDI) in Energy and Electricity Projects in the Economies in Transition." *EDF/UNIPEDE.*

Csalagovits, A. O. 1997. "Municipal Cleaner Production Policy in the Czech Republic." EPCEM Project Report 1997/1. Interfaculty Department of Environmental Science, University of Amsterdam.

Dinica, V. 1997. "The Estimation of Romania's Potential for Renewable Energy Resources." Masters thesis, Central European University, Budapest.

Dobes, V. 1997. "Promoting Cleaner Production – Experiences from the Czech Republic." *The Bulletin* (quarterly newsletter of the Regional Environmental Centre for Central and Eastern Europe) 7(1): 10.

EAP (Environmental Action Programme). 1993. "Environmental Action Programme for Central and Eastern Europe (1993)." Document submitted to the Ministerial Conference, 28–30 April, Lucerne, Switzerland.

Eisma, D. 1997. "Draft Opinion (Rule 147) for the Committee on Foreign Affairs, Security and Defence Policy on Agenda 2000." European Parliament. 22 September.

Gol'man, I. 1991. "Vetrodoei vsje strany, ob'edinjajtes'!" *Energija, Ekonomika, Technika, Ekologija* 8: 17–23.

Golubenko, N. and V. Tsyganov. 1997. "The Working, Creation and Work of Wind Electric Plants of Middle Power in SDO 'Yuzhnoye'." Paper presented at the NATO Advanced Research Workshop on Conversion and Ecology, 24–27 April, Dnepropetrovsk, Ukraine.

Gorbachev, M. 1987. *Perestroika: New Thinking for Our Country and the World.* London: Collins.

Groenewegen, P., ed. 1996. *The Greening of Industry. Resource Guide and Bibliography.* Washington: Island Press.

Haigh, N. 1987. "Collaborative Arrangements for Environmental Protection in Western Europe." In *Environmental Policies in East and West*, eds G. Enyedi, A. J. Gijswijt, and B. Rhode. London: Taylor Graham.

Helsinki Commission. 1997. "Protecting the Baltic Sea." *The Bulletin* (quarterly newsletter of the Regional Environmental Centre for Central and Eastern Europe) 7(1): 5.

Hettelingh, J. P., R. J. Downing, and P. A. M. de Smet. 1991. "Mapping Critical Loads for Europe." CCE Technical Report No 1. RIVM Report No 259101001. Bilthoven, Netherlands.

Hordijk, L. 1991. "Use of the RAINS Model in Acid Rain Negotiations in Europe." *Environmental Science and Technology* 25(4): 596–602.

Klarer, J. and P. Francis. 1997. "Regional Overview." In *The Environmental Challenge for Central European Economies in Transition*, eds J. Klarer and B. Moldan. Chichester: John Wiley & Sons.

Kljoev, N. 1997. "Vnesjnie i vnutrennie ugrozy ekologii rossii." *Pridoda i ljudi* 4(41): 2–8.

Kolk, A. and E. Van der Weij. 1998. "Financing Environmental Policy in Central and Eastern Europe." *Environmental Politics* 7(1): 53–68.

Larin, V. 1991. "Tsjto den' grjadoesjtsjij nam gotovit?" *Eneregija, Ekonomika, Technika, Ekologija* 10: 50–51.

Laskorin, B. 1984. "Bez otkhodov" (Wastage-free). Interview in *Izvestia*, 3 and 7 June.

Lehoczki, Z. and Z. Balogh. 1997. "Hungary." In *The Environmental Challenge for Central European Economies in Transition*, eds J. Klarer and B. Moldan. Chichester: John Wiley & Sons.

Levy, M. A. 1993. "European Acid Rain: The Power of Tote-Board Diplomacy." In *Institutions for the Earth. Sources of Effective International Environmental Protection*, eds P. M. Haas, R. O. Keohane, and M. A. Levy. Cambridge, MA: MIT Press.

Lindhqvist, T. and H. Rodhe, 1994. "Evaluation of Waste Minimisation Initiatives in Central and Eastern Europe." In *Introducing Cleaner Production in Eastern Europe,* eds T. Lindhqvist and H. Rodhe. Proceedings of an invitational expert seminar, 8–9 September, Kaunas University of Technology, Lithuania, sponsored by UNEP, Kaunas University of Technology, and the Department of Industrial Environmental Economics, Lund University (Sweden).

Lisitzin, E. N. 1987. "Collaborative Arrangements for Environmental Protection in European Socialist Countries." In *Environmental Policies in East and West*, eds G. Enyedi, A. J. Gijswijt, and B. Rhode. London: Taylor Graham.

Livinsky, A. 1997. "Regional Legal Framework for Energy Efficiency." In *Russia's Energy Efficient Future: A Regional Approach*. OECD/IAE Conference proceedings, 25–26 September, Chelyabinsk, Russian Federation. Paris: OECD.

Martinot, E. 1995. "Energy Efficiency and Renewable Energy in Russia: Perspectives and Problems of International Technological Transfer and Investment." PhD dissertation, University of California, Berkeley.

Matrosov, Y. 1997. "In the South Urals and in the Lower Don Basin, Houses Will Consume Less Heat." *Energy Efficiency* (quarterly bulletin of the Center for Energy Efficiency, Moscow) January–March: 8–10.

Matrosov, Y. and D. Goldstein. 1996. "New Approaches to Energy Conservation in Russia's Regions." *Energy Efficiency* (quarterly bulletin of the Center for Energy Efficiency, Moscow) July–September: 4–5.

Nedenes, O. S. 1994. "The Norwegian Industrial Transfer of Know-how Programmes on Waste Minimization/Cleaner Production to Central and Eastern European Countries." In *Introducing Cleaner Production in Eastern Europe*, eds T. Lindhqvist and H. Rodhe. Proceedings of an invitational expert seminar, 8–9 September, Kaunas University of Technology, Lithuania, sponsored by UNEP, Kaunas University of Technology, and the Department of Industrial Environmental Economics, Lund University (Sweden).

NOVEM/CESEN. 1997. "The Urban and Regional Energy Efficiency Programme." Final Report, Round 1.

OECD/IEA. 1995. *Energy Policies of the Russian Federation.* Paris: OECD.

Reijnders, L. 1996. *Environmentally Improved Production Processes and Products: An Introduction.* Dordrecht: Kluwer.

Sjpil'rain, E. E. 1997. "Netraditsionnye vosobnovljaemye istotsjniki energii." *Energia, Ekonomika, Texnika, Ekologija* 5: 6–14.

Staniskis, J. 1996. "CP Programs and Projects in Lithuania." *Opracowanie Autorskie*: 39–46

Stanners, D. and P. Bourdeau, eds. 1995. *Europe's Environment.* The Dobris Assessment. Copenhagen: European Environment Agency.

Tellegen, E. 1986. "The Soviet Press on Wastage, Conservation and Recycling." *Zeitschrift für Umweltpolitik & Umweltrecht* 3(86): 231–246

Tellegen, E. 1989. "Perestroika and the Rational Use of Materials and Energy." *The Environmental Professional* 11(2): 142–151.

Van Berkel, C. W. M. 1996. "Cleaner Production in Practice." PhD dissertation, University of Amsterdam.

Van der Weij, E. 1993. *Soviet International Environmental Politics.* Amsterdam: University of Amsterdam Department of International Relations and Institute of Central and Eastern European Studies.

Van Weenen, H. 1997. "Sustainable Product Development: Opportunities for Developing Countries." *UNEP Industry and Environment* January–June: 14–20.

Verspeek, F. 1996. "Capacity Building for Transfer of Cleaner Production Practices and Technologies." *Opracowie Autorskie*: 75–88.

Wangen, G. 1996. "Capacity Building in Cleaner Production in the Baltic Region." *Tema Nord 1996.* Copenhagen: Nordic Council of Ministers.

FURTHER READING

Blatt Bendtsen, U. and M. Chodak. 1997. "Good-bye to Leaded Petrol." *Environment for Europe Newsletter* 1.

Enyedi, G., A. J. Gijswijt, and B. Rhode, eds. 1987. *Environmental Policies in East and West.* London: Taylor Graham.

Klarer, J. and B. Moldan. 1997. *The Environmental Challenge for Central European Economies in Transition.* Chichester: John Wiley & Sons.

Tellegen, E. 1996. "Environmental Conflicts in Transforming Economies: Central and Eastern Europe." In *Environmental Problems as Conflicts of Interests*, eds P. B. Sloep and A. Blowers. London: Arnold.

16

African regional organizations and environmental security

Gregory W. Myers

The purpose of this chapter is to review the role that African regional organizations have played in addressing environmental issues, particularly land and natural resource degradation. The chapter will draw lessons from three organizations: the Inter-State Committee for Drought Control (CILSS), the Intergovernmental Authority on Development (IGAD), and the Southern African Development Community (SADC). Each organization represents countries in three different regions of the continent with unique environmental concerns, objectives, and strategies for addressing them.

Following this introduction, the chapter examines the role of property rights in land degradation, and particularly how land tenure policy can be used to address environmental concerns as well as other social problems. As such, the focus on land tenure reform is used as a criterion to determine the efficacy of regional organizations in dealing with transboundary environmental concerns. The next section reviews efforts of the CILSS, IGAD, and the SADC in addressing environmental regional concerns, particularly noting the ways, if any, in which they consider property rights and resource tenure security as variables in achieving their objectives. The chapter will conclude with a brief discussion of lessons learned.

In all three regions land degradation, desertification, and deforestation are critical issues. There are more than 2 billion hectares of arid land in Africa. More than two-thirds of the continent's land is desert or dry zones, and becoming increasingly degraded and unusable. Aside from climatic variations, much of the continent's land degradation is due to deforestation and other types of resource misuse as a result of social problems or policies.

Deforestation in Africa is caused by a number of factors, including land clearing for agriculture and cutting trees for fuelwood and other uses. The FAO estimates that approximately 13,000 square kilometres of African forests disappear each year (FAO 1985; 1995). Since 1960 it is estimated that 18 per cent of African forests have disappeared (WRI 1997), and in many locations the process is accelerating. This is of course exacerbated by official population growth rates for the continent that average at least 3 per cent per year.

In addition to deforestation, other social forces contribute to degradation. Numerous pre- and post-Cold War conflicts in Africa have had either a direct or indirect impact on the environment. Wars contribute to environmental damage as much as, if not more so than, natural disasters. Over the last few decades conflicts have occurred or are taking place in a majority of countries, involving a majority of the continent's populations. These conflicts have been in the Horn of Africa (Somalia, the Sudan, Ethiopia, and Eritrea), southern Africa (Mozambique, Angola, parts of South Africa, and the Democratic Republic of Congo, formerly known as Zaire), West Africa (Liberia and Sierra Leone) and East Africa (Rwanda and Burundi), to name only a few. This list does not include major civil disturbances in Algeria, Kenya, Nigeria, Uganda, and most recently Guinea-Bissau.

Wars destroy fragile ecosystems, wildlife populations, forests, and farmland. Wars also destroy economies and infrastructures, and displace populations. The United Nations High Commissioner for Refugees (UNHCR) estimates that there are currently at least 8 million displaced people in Africa (UNHCR 1997). Unofficial estimates of displaced populations in Africa are remarkably higher. For example, in Mozambique during the civil war in that country, estimates of internally and externally displaced populations reached as high as 4 million people, or better than 25 per cent of the population (Drumtra 1993; Myers 1994). In several countries, displacement continues beyond a single generation so that displacement becomes a way of life.

Displaced populations have an impact on resource use and conservation. First, humanitarian efforts following or during conflicts frequently take precedence. Prevention of starvation and genocide is paramount over resource conservation. Populations are often settled or self-settle in areas that are perceived to be secure. These areas are frequently already overpopulated. The increased burden on the environment usually results in resource mining of trees, land, and wildlife. Typically, once the conflict ends displaced populations are reluctant to return home, and when they finally do, permanent residents left behind are faced with an over-exploited environment. It is not uncommon in recent African conflicts for there to be post-war waves of displaced populations as people and communities seek to capture new economic opportunities or abandon areas that are no longer sustainable.

In many African countries, as a result of wars, poor economic and social policy, overpopulation, and many other factors, standards of living have decreased significantly, while hunger, misery, and population displacement are conditions that have become the norm. These stresses often force rural communities to abandon "traditional" or "customary" resource conservation practices and overexploit resources for survival.

Beyond these causes, market globalization may also have mixed consequences for political stability and environmental sustainability. Globalization is creating opportunities for many states to capitalize on new economic opportunities, and focus on broader political and social issues. For example, processes of globalization have given some former economic "basket cases" in Africa, like Uganda, access to new markets and technology. Along with market and political reforms this has helped to promote dramatic economic growth and market efficiencies in this country over the last few years.

At the same time, market globalization may also created economic and political pressures in many emerging economies, as well as some established or developed ones, which could negatively affect resource use and conservation, leading to resource mining. There is greater pressure than ever for the emerging markets in Africa to open their doors to trade regionally and internationally. This will increase with the US government spearheading programmes like "Trade not Aid." While this may have many benefits, many African countries only have natural resources to trade in exchange for the commodities that they purchase. This often leads to resource mining in timber and forest products, wildlife and fish, and minerals.

In southern Africa there are already concerns that South African businesses, in some cases in partnership with Mozambican operations, are over-hunting wildlife reserves and fishing grounds in Mozambique. South Africa's need to compete in a broader international economic arena, let alone within the region, may lead to both economic and environmental shocks in many of its trading partners. This imbalance between South Africa's commercial power and the strength of the comparatively poorer nations in the region may facilitate resource mining by South African businesses in the region. There is already evidence that South African businesses are exploiting weak regulatory structures in neighbouring countries to acquire and exploit massive tracts of land and other resources.

As a result of these numerous pressures – social and climatic – resource degradation is increasingly problematic for many communities in Africa. Global and regional organizations have focused on environmental concerns in Africa for nearly three decades, with varying degrees of success. Before turning to a discussion about the ways in which the CILSS, IGAD, and the SADC have focused on resource degradation, brief criteria for analysis must be established.

Property rights and natural resource management

A premise of this chapter is that land and natural resource tenure security is an integral part of sound land-use management and natural resource conservation. Land tenure or property rights that are inappropriate for a given economy or social structure will lead to overexploitation of resources and contribute to resource degradation, among other outcomes (Thiesenhusen 1991; Southgate, Sanders, and Ehui 1990; Black 1994). This is particularly so if the tenure rights are viewed as weak, discouraging long-term investment and local-level management decisions. Conversely, where policies for use of land and natural resources are relevant to economic and political structures and conditions, and are participatory in nature, investors and other resource users tend to make long-term and efficient investments that promote sounder resource use and higher levels of production. In addition, clear tenure rules that are understood by all tend to reduce the chances of mismanagement of resources, corruption, and resource conflict.

In many developing countries, the balance between the objectives of the state and those of private interests or civil society are not always even or congruent. The state and élite bureaucrats are often predatory, restricting popular decision-making about resource use and downstream benefits accrued from the exploitation of resources. Further, the state's capacity and will to enforce national regulatory laws in the face of private predators are not always evident. States have vested interests in maintaining control over valuable natural resources. These "national interests" often lead them to construct or enforce tenure systems that are not always in the best interests of the economy or the environment.

Most countries in Africa nationalized control over land and other natural resources following independence. This was done in the name of nationalism or progressivism, or in reaction to colonialism. Laws were also often enacted as a reaction to national political struggles between old and newer power structures: urban educated élite versus rural chiefs, to name one example. In some countries, such as Mozambique, post-independence land reforms were a rejection of all the old ways, colonial and pre-colonial. Despite these nationalization campaigns, or as a result of them, resources were misused and mismanaged, and economies suffered. Environmental degradation continued at an alarming rate throughout the continent. At the same time, these policies contributed to political instability.

In the last few years policy-makers have increasingly become aware of the problems and limitations of the nationalized economies and property systems – recognizing connections between property rights, economic growth, and conservation. As a result a number of African countries have begun to discuss or experiment with different property rights systems that permit greater transparency, market interaction, and popular participation in decisions about resource use and management. Consequently, property rights reforms, particularly for land, water, and forestry, have become part of national and regional-level discussions about conservation programmes in Africa. The CILSS, IGAD, and the SADC have, to a lesser or greater extent, included tenure reform issues as part of their objectives. The analysis that follows looks at the way the CILSS, IGAD, and the SADC have focused on land and natural resource tenure issues as part of their efforts to address resource degradation within their respective regions

Land tenure reform (including secure access to, and decentralized control of, resources) is also seen increasingly as relevant to political stability in many countries. There is a growing discussion focusing on the causal linkages between environmental degradation and civil conflict. Evidence from numerous countries suggests linkages on the one hand between subnational and international conflict and, on the other hand, resource scarcity and insecurity of resource tenure. Numerous cases from Africa demonstrate this relationship, including Rwanda, Somalia, the Sudan, and Ethiopia (Homer-Dixon 1991; 1994; Myers 1997b; African Rights 1993; Besteman and Cassanelli 1996).

A second premise of this chapter is that there are significant connections between property rights, sound resource management, and stable political structures. The more regional organizations link environment, resource access and security, and governance issues, the more they will enjoy more stable and robust economies and political institutions. This chapter will also look at the way the CILSS, IGAD, and the SADC have, if at all, focused on resource tenure security as a variable in conflict or conflict prevention, and by extension environmental degradation.

Regional organizations and the environment

Beginning in 1972, the UN Conference on the Human Environment focused world attention on global environmental concerns. Africa was particularly singled out as a potential "hot-spot." The 1972 conference was followed by numerous other environmental forums and treaties. It also led to the development of UNEP, which has itself created numerous other global and regional programmes, conferences, and forums. Many of these also focused on environmental issues, and many others that were created for other purposes have, over the years, modified their foci to include environmental concerns.

One organization created by the United Nations, the World Commission on Environment and Development (WCED), argued in 1987 that a concept of "sustainable development" was needed. This position was quickly adopted by regional organizations, particularly those in the developing world, and later followed by discussions about greater popular participation by target populations in regional organization management.

In 1987, the WCED recommended a second UN-sponsored global conference on the environment, which would more broadly address environmental issues and include wider participation. This recommendation eventually led to the 1992 UN Conference on Environment and Development (UNCED, also know as the Earth Summit) in Rio de Janeiro.

Despite these numerous forums, international and regional bodies have had limited success in addressing national and transboundary environmental problems. Indeed, in many instances the overall global environmental picture is significantly worse than it was in 1972 (Halpern 1992). For example, despite massive bilateral and multilateral assistance, environmental destruction has not been halted in many African countries. In the Sahel, desertification continues, and has become worse as a result of natural and manmade disasters over the last two decades (Bohrer and Hobbs 1996).

This apparent gap between global conservation objectives and continued environmental degradation suggests that past strategies have not been successful. It may not be that more financial and "expert" human resources are required to mitigate these trends, but rather a rethinking about the role that global and regional organizations should play in addressing this concern. Experiences from three African regional organizations are revealing.

The CILSS

The Inter-State Committee for Drought Control was formed in 1974 and is composed of nine countries (Burkina Faso, Cape Verde, Chad, Guinea-Bissau, Mali, Mauritania, Niger, Senegal, and the Gambia). The Committee's functions are many and have changed over time, but focus largely on natural resource management and conservation. The CILSS is an interesting example of a regional organization that has continued to evolve over the years since its establishment.

The CILSS has three characteristics that set it apart from other regional organizations. First, it was formed specifically in response to an environmental crisis, the 1968–1974 Sahelian drought and famine. Second, the CILSS began operations by concentrating on rural and "least-developed" sectors of the economies in the region, as opposed to most other regional organizations that are established to promote trade and commercial development. And third, the CILSS has a unique relationship with the donor community via a sister organization, the Club du Sahel.

The Club du Sahel, which is part of the OECD, was approved by member states in 1976. In addition to Sahelian representatives, the Club is composed of bilateral and multilateral donors including the World Bank and the UNDP. The Club's main functions are to coordinate policy dialogue and assistance between donors and recipients (mainly the CILSS), and to prevent overlapping and competing programmes and objectives.

Despite years of substantial financial assistance from the Club (and other bilateral and multilateral assistance), and work within the organization and between it and member states, the region is nowhere near its initial goals of achieving self-sustaining economic development, food self-sufficiency, and desertification control. But this does not mean that the organization has not seen success, nor that it does not have the potential to achieve success in the long term. Indeed, thus far some of its greatest accomplishments have been to refocus the way it looks at environmental issues, particularly linking resource security and conservation, and how it strives to make discussion more participatory and decentralized. This success has been predicated on a series of moves within the organization that began following its inception.

This CILSS process, particularly with regard to resource management and control, has evolved over many years. As stated above, beginning with its inception in 1974 it focused on rural issues, and particularly environmental degradation as a result of drought. For 10 years following inception the organization had some success (increased donor assistance and more focused attention, better knowledge about environmental issues affecting the region, and regional institution-building). But the organization also realized that, despite these efforts, conditions were worsening. Hence, member states began to focus attention on developing greater understanding of linkages between factors in complex environmental problems.

In 1984, with the Nouakchott Conference in Mauritania, the CILSS recognized the need for greater community participation by emphasizing increased involvement of local populations in development projects. In

1989 the CILSS moved a step forward with the Segou Round Table on Local-Level Natural Resource Management in the Sahel, held in Segou, Mali.

This meeting focused greater attention on land tenure security as part of the overall environmental problem faced by the region, and for the first time really began to expand participation in the discussion process. Segou brought together representatives from government, rural communities, donors, and NGOs. The main premise of this meeting was to begin a discussion about the need for a shift in the locus of power among Sahelian states to achieve sustainable development (Freudenberger 1994). The Segou Declaration recognized the necessity of decentralization, but stopped short of recommending specific mechanisms for achieving this.

The next steps came in 1994 with the Praia Regional Conference on Tenure and Decentralization, held in Praia, Cape Verde. Conference delegates noted that between the conferences in Segou and Praia, environmental conditions had continued to deteriorate and desertification was worse in the Sahel. Delegates in Praia noted that past declarations had not gone far enough to achieve national-level reforms. Not surprisingly then, conference organizers subtitled the conference, "to achieve democratic, participative and decentralized management of natural resources in the Sahel" (cited in Freudenberger 1994). As with Segou, rural resources users were not only considered as the main target beneficiaries of policy reform, but also as participants in discussion about the nature of reforms and how they should be implemented.

The successes of these conferences (Nouakchott, Segou, and Praia) were supported by nine different national-level activities from 1991 to 1994. These ranged from technical assistance and research focusing on desertification and other environmental issues to conferences and seminars in the nine CILSS countries.

Praia, like preceding conferences, created opportunities for cross-sectoral and cross-boundary discussions, as well as for donor, NGO, and government coordination. It did not attempt to set national-level objectives. It ended without a clear mandate, or even a strategy for addressing the multifaceted problems faced by the members regarding natural resource management and decentralization. A follow-up meeting was scheduled for later the same year to take place in Kenya. This meeting, attended by a few "key" people from the CILSS and the Club du Sahel, developed a three-year action plan for the CILSS.

Clearly, the push to slow and eventually reverse environmental degradation must come from a number of directions. It might be facile to suggest that the regional organization should push harder to encourage reform that will lead to faster changes, ensuring environmental security and reducing desertification. Indeed, one might ask why Praia ended without a clear mandate? Or better still, why after all these years the CILSS is no closer to achieving its target objectives than it was when it first began operation.

The answer is that environmental transformation and reform of natural resource management in the CILSS must not only come from within each member country, but also from rural dwellers who themselves use the resources. This would then suggest greater participation in the discussion process, and eventual decentralized and democratized control over resource management and the benefits that accrue from exploitation and conservation. In this regard, the CILSS has best helped by coordinating actions, creating opportunities for discussion among members, and giving rural groups and individuals opportunities to confront national political structures; but it has not dictated or enforced "decisions" made at the regional level. To do so would probably have undermined goals and marginalized rural voices. Further, members have used the CILSS to initiate discussion of problems and solutions that are often not politically acceptable (at least initially) in their own countries. A prime example is the discussion about the relationship between environmental conservation and land tenure reform.

Members have also used the forum to judge, and in some cases follow, the experiences of other member states. For example, Senegal's decentralization (and democratization) efforts to transfer control over resources to local and more democratic institutions have been a long process, marked by political tensions and setbacks within Senegal that continue to this day. Nevertheless, Senegal has achieved a remarkable degree of success, beginning in 1964 with its programmes to develop locally elected councils which have responsibility for, among other duties, managing resources.

It is clear that other countries in the region have watched and learned from Senegal's experiments. Guinea and Niger have enacted (or are in the processes of enacting) forest legislation that grants increased rights to local populations living in the area of forests. Chad, Burkina Faso, and Mali have also engaged in constructive environmental policy reform programmes based upon examples derived from other members. Most notably, the development of forest codes has included the opinions of local populations, as well as facilitating the participation of local populations in the management of forest resources and the benefits from the exploitation of those resources. In conjunction with the CILSS, almost all member states have begun national-level dialogues about property rights reform and more localized participation in resource management.

In addition, the organization has been more successful than others in creating options for member consideration, rather than strict-rule guidelines at the regional level that cannot be followed. For example, the 1990 CILSS Food Aid Charter promotes food security among member states. However, as the past Executive Director of the CILSS, Brah Mahamane, states, "the Charter does not seek to force member countries to follow a strict 'modus operandi'. Each country operates within its own political, institutional and economic constraints" (CILSS and OECD 1993, 4).

The first premise articulated in the introduction of this chapter is that environmental degradation is related to, in part, the nature of property rights systems and the degree to which these systems secure tenure rights and democratize control over resources and the benefits from resource exploitation and conservation. In this case, the CILSS has made important forward progress in generating discussion among member states about these linkages, thus the organization may yet achieve its initial and refined objectives to reduce desertification and achieve economic self-sufficiency in the future.

Where the CILSS has been most criticized is in the workings of its national-level coordinating committees (CONACIL). The Club du Sahel has been critical of the way member states control the committees, particularly their attempts to silence national committees' public discussions. On the other hand, member states have argued that the CONACIL are disruptive and interfere with national-level objectives and politics. These criticisms explain potential tensions between regional "goals" and regional "needs," and further illustrate that regional solutions will not necessarily come from regional organizations, but from the people who live within these regions themselves.

IGAD

The Inter-Government Authority on Drought and Development (IGADD) was formed in 1986. Comprised initially of six countries in the Horn and eastern Africa (Djibouti, Ethiopia, Kenya, Somalia, the Sudan, and Uganda), its initial focus was on food security, drought, desertification, and other transboundary environmental issues. In 1993 Eritrea joined the group and in 1995 the body was "revitalized" and renamed the Inter-Governmental Authority on Development (IGAD).

Like West Africa, this region has experienced severe climatic conditions that have led to famine, death, and population displacement of several hundreds of thousands of people in the last two decades. Perhaps more importantly, the region has been home to some of the worst and longest-running civil violence on the continent. These wars have also contributed to population displacement, death, and environmental destruction.

IGAD differs from the CILSS in several ways. First, it is substantially younger. Second, IGAD has more provisions that focus on economic and commercial linkages throughout the region, mirroring other African regional organizations. Third, it has far fewer financial resources than the CILSS. Fourth, the member states are not as homogeneous as are those in the CILSS. Finally, it faces a number of ongoing civil battles within and between member states that undermine its work.

Between 1986 when IGAD (IGADD) was formed and 1995 when the body was revitalized, IGAD accomplished few of its central tasks. The high number of armed conflicts in the region and the massive number of displaced people forced the organization to become more involved in conflict resolution and humanitarian efforts as prerequisites to achieving any of its other environmental or economic growth objectives.

The second premise presented in the introduction to this chapter is that there is a relationship between property rights, resource management, and political stability, or in the case of the IGAD countries, violence. Conservation and sustainability cannot be achieved without proper resource rights, and as long as wars continue in the region, populations are killed and displaced and financial resources are focused on humanitarian efforts. IGAD has apparently begun to move in this direction, as it has increasingly sought help from bilateral and multilateral donors to mediate ongoing conflicts in the region.

The new 1995 charter authorized the body to promote economic integration in the subregion, in accordance with the Common Market for Eastern and Southern Africa and the African Economic Community. More importantly, the revitalized group recognized the relationships between environmental issues, particularly environmental security and sustainability, economic development, and peace. The new charter included two key provisions on capacity-building for conflict prevention, resolution, and management; and the alleviation and mitigation of refugee problems.

Just as it was reviewing its agenda, in 1994 IGAD adopted the Declaration of Principles for the Settlement of Conflict in the Sudan. The government of the Sudan rejected IGAD's initial offers to mediate the conflict and pursued a separate track of "peace within." In 1997 the Sudan finally agreed to participate in an IGAD discussion on peace, but has failed to implement human rights guarantees in the southern part of the country – a minimum requirement in the peace process. Nevertheless, IGAD has continued to provide a forum for discussion between combatants and between donors and member states. IGAD has also been involved in attempts to mediate the conflict in Somalia, which have also been supported by major bilateral and multilateral institutions. IGAD has recently become involved in the latest round of violence between Ethiopia and Eritrea.

While none of these efforts thus far has resulted in complete success, they have moved the conflicts to the forefront of the agenda of an organization that was created to address regional environmental and food security concerns. They have also helped to focus global attention on resolution of the conflicts as part of any other work in the region.

Again, in defence of IGAD, regional organizations historically have had little success in preventing or stopping inter-state conflicts once they begin, particularly in Africa where institutions are relatively poor and weak. Perhaps more importantly, there is a strong bias against inter-state interference by other African countries. This is institutionalized in the terms of the OAU. Nevertheless, until the violence issues are resolved in the Sudan, Somalia, and now between Ethiopia and Eritrea (let alone smaller conflicts that are brewing elsewhere in the region), IGAD's effectiveness to address regional environmental concerns, particularly transboundary issues such as desertification and deforestation, will remain limited.

Despite its limited successes thus far, IGAD, like the CILSS, has worked diligently in the last few years to decentralize its approach and the programmes that it recommends. The Sahara and Sahel Observatory has provided linkages between the CILSS and IGAD, hosting conferences and seminars for members and specialists from both organizations. The Observatory has been particularly keen on helping IGAD to study the land tenure lessons learned by the CILSS over the past few years. Studying the "successes" of the CILSS and other organizations, IGAD has attempted to develop a better understanding of the region's environmental problems through research and dialogue, and it has worked to be more inclusive in seminars and conferences.

In addition, IGAD has decentralized other environmental programmes as they evolve. For example, following the 1994 IGAD Eleventh Session of the Council of Ministers, the organization has sponsored two regional programmes in response to the 1994 UN Convention to Combat Desertification. These programmes supported environmental education and enhanced public awareness across the region. Not only did they recommend a new school curriculum focusing on environmental education, but more importantly articulated the need for greater local community participation in the management of resources and conservation efforts.

As in the discussion on the CILSS, it is problematic to assume that IGAD will or should resolve regional environmental problems. It may be more effective to consider the ways that IGAD can provide forums for members to come together and discuss ways that these issues should be addressed at a more localized level and in a more participatory and democratized way.

At the end of the day, environmental concerns such as land degradation, desertification, and deforestation in the region will continue so long as the fighting continues and rural dwellers themselves do not have the chance to assume ownership responsibility for the changes that must take place. But more importantly, IGAD has an opportunity to help members and member populations to see that when discussion about natural resources and participation is truly localized and democratized, the fighting may well stop. In effect, IGAD must help members to see the connections between the two premises articulated in the introduction to this chapter.

The SADC

The SADCC, the Southern Africa Development Coordination Conference, was established in 1980. Initially it was a "front-line" organization for states bordering on South Africa during apartheid and that country's destabilization campaign. Its objectives were primarily to reduce economic dependence on South Africa by its members.

The Southern African Development Community (SADC) was formed in 1992 and comprises 14 states: Angola, Botswana, Lesotho, Malawi, Mauritius, Mozambique, Namibia, South Africa, Swaziland, Tanzania, Zambia, and Zimbabwe. The reformation came as the civil war in Mozambique was coming to a close, and both Mozambique and South Africa were headed toward reconciliation and democratic elections. In 1997 the Seychelles and the Democratic Republic of Congo joined the organization. The SADC is now, theoretically, an economic alliance, fostering regional economic development and integration.

The SADC is significantly different than the other two regional organizations discussed, and these differences colour the way in which it operates and its likely success as a regional organization, particularly its success in addressing regional environmental concerns. First, as noted above, the SADC (as the SADCC) was initially created as a buffer organization against South African commercial (and political) domination. Second, when it was formed the region was experiencing severe violence, much of it perpetrated or instigated by South Africa. Third, the region is composed of countries with great economic and commercial potential, and significant differences among members. The South African economy alone is larger than many of the combined economies of the region, and is viewed by many policy-makers as the engine of regional growth. Fourth, the private sector plays a much larger role in many SADC economies, and participates in or influences SADC discussion and objectives. Fifth, where the SADC was formed to focus on commercial concerns, both the CILSS and IGAD were formed largely to address environmental issues. In many ways, the SADC appears to operate as a collection of disparate countries with unequal objectives that are located in the same region, whereas members of the CILSS and IGAD are relatively homogeneous and have come together to address significant environmental and political threats.

The SADC region has one of the fastest-growing urban populations in the world. The region suffers from intense land pressures, particularly on rangeland. Deforestation, soil loss, increased use of marginal lands, and land degradation are a few of the more severe environmental problems facing the region. In addition, many countries (including Angola, Mozambique, South Africa, and recently the Democratic Republic of Congo) have experienced widespread violence over the last two decades that has resulted in massive displacement of local populations and concomitant environmental abuse.

The organization does aspire to address regional environmental issues, including pollution, soil erosion, desertification and drought, water conservation, and wildlife management and protection, but it does so more with an eye to the commercial impacts of good resource management and conservation. Many, if not all, of its environmental programmes contain objectives which promote commercial growth of resource use.

The SADC created an Environment and Land Management Sector which integrates environment, land management, conservation, and production. This programme focuses on resource management, soil conservation, training, education, and extension. In addition it focuses on marketing services, incentives, and financing. As water is a scarce commodity in the region, and unevenly distributed, the SADC also created a Water Sector. The SADC has an Early Warning System and a Food Security Unit to monitor weather and food production respectively. The SADC developed a Wildlife Sector programme, based on the premise that sustainable exploitation of wildlife and wildlife products will contribute significantly to regional economic growth. In addition to being an important supplement to human nutrition, wildlife exploitation can (and already does in some member countries) provide considerable income generation through eco-tourism, safari hunting, and game ranching. Finally, the SADC developed a Forestry Sector to promote regional self-sufficiency in forest products; protect, manage, and control forest resources; and enhance productivity and the commercial value of trees.

As in the CILSS, the SADC has attempted to provide a forum for studying and discussing the individual and collective environmental problems and programmes of member countries that, theoretically, impact on the region. Successful programmes in individual countries have become models for other members. South Africa has recently launched several new local-level initiatives to bring rural farmers and herders into the management structure of the country's natural resources. This programme may have been in part influenced by the success of the Land Board system in Botswana. Many countries, including Mozambique, Malawi, Zambia, and South Africa, are talking about the Campfire programme in Zimbabwe, a programme for community-based wildlife management.

The SADC has proved to be a relatively open and democratic institution, focusing resources on discussion about critical regional problems, including environmental and ecological concerns. It has incorporated the views of member states and has worked to include the views of some subnational groups. In addition, the SADC has included the private sector as an important focal point, demonstrating linkages that the private sector should/could play in regional economic growth and transboundary environmental issues.

For all these positive accomplishments, there are some serious real and potential problems in the way this organization addresses environmental and other social problems which set it apart from the CILSS and IGAD. First, there are obviously vast differences in wealth and economic potential between member states (as well as within some). The economic power and potential of South Africa outweighs the economic and commercial capacity of many members combined. The difference between South Africa and Malawi or Mauritius, for example, is enormous. Even with good intentions, South Africa has the potential to drive development (including natural resource management) in a way that may be more beneficial to South Africa and its citizens than to other countries in the region. Moreover, as South Africa is the economic driving force in the region, its own domestic economic objectives will greatly influence the SADC's objectives. South Africa's economic objectives focus on job growth and business expansion. Environmental affairs are not a national priority. One could conclude that the SADC is not truly a regional organization, but simply a front for advancing South African commercial interests (Holland 1995). This degree of economic difference and power between members does not exist in CILSS or IGAD.

Second, while South Africa has worked hard in the post-apartheid period to develop regional-friendly policies, South African businesses and entrepreneurs have the potential to undermine fragile economic and social programmes elsewhere in the region via aggressive attempts to capture markets and access to resources, and this can have severe negative environmental repercussions. For example, in the last few years South African entrepreneurs have moved north into Mozambique,

Angola, Tanzania, and Namibia seeking access to markets and to land and other natural resources at vastly discounted prices. Many of these forays have already resulted in distorted markets and in displaced or marginalized populations (see Myers and Meneses 1995; Myers, Eliseu, and Nhachungue 1998 for discussions of South African investments in Mozambique).

Land markets, both legal and illegal, are springing up all over the region. This is taking place in countries that do not have a history of market liberalization, particularly the marketing of land or other natural resources, or strong regulatory institutions. Resource abuse in these cases is not uncommon.

It remains to be seen how the members of the SADC will capitalize on opportunities created by the new wealth unleashed in the post-apartheid period, while preventing the goals of the organization from being hijacked by one member's needs or objectives, or being overrun by South African capital. At the same time, policies or programmes that work in South Africa, as the dominant member, may not necessarily be appropriate to the needs of other member countries with far weaker economic and political structures. The commercial sector should play an important role in any programmes addressing environmental and other social concerns, but government should ensure that the real cost of resources is accurately reflected in their prices, and be wary of ways in which unregulated businesses may undermine weak political institutions and lead to overexploitation of resources, among other abuses.

And finally, it is clear that the SADC has not encouraged or insisted that regional discussions should include rural or community participants from member countries in the same way that the CILSS has or that IGAD is trying to do. To be more than just a regional business association, the SADC will need to focus more attention on inclusion and participation, as the CILSS has done.

Lessons learned

Environmental issues are often low priorities in many countries in Africa. Ministries or other government agencies dealing with environmental issues (including land and water) are often the weakest politically, with little or no clout to influence national policy. Staff training and human resources are either non-existent or extremely weak. Frequently, African governments have little knowledge of their country's resource base and limited experience in managing it.

Moreover, weak states are often unable, or unwilling, to implement decisions made at international, regional, or national levels, particularly if they affect an already fragile political structure. In other instances, national governments benefit from internal weaknesses or confusions, manipulating their own economic systems to satisfy short-term objectives. At the same time, urban-based élites can often gain access to resources cheaply through exploitation of weak or accommodating political structures.

Throughout Africa the phenomenon of land concessions or grants by the state to élites has exploded, resulting in massive, or potentially massive, population displacement and landlessness. Displacement often leads to overcrowding in other areas and overexploitation of scarce resources. For example, in Mozambique, recent research has revealed that the state in the post-war period following 1992 has granted concessions, or is in the processes of granting concessions, that total at least 25 per cent of the country's land space. In some areas of the country marked by rich and fragile resource bases, concessions cover more than 50 per cent of the total land space, and in a few extreme cases, more than 100 per cent of the total land area (Myers 1997a). This type of cronyism takes place to the disadvantage of long-term growth, political stability, and environmental sustainability.

While national governments may adopt or agree to global or regional objectives and treaties, they do not always abide by these decisions once they return home. For example, in 1995, two years after the Earth Summit, 12 ministers of environment and other senior government officials from 17 eastern and southern Africa states called upon member governments to ratify environment-related conventions and agreements. They identified eight global, regional, and subregional treaties that had not been effectively implemented or had been ignored altogether. One group convened by the African Ministerial Conference on the Environment (AMCEN) and UNEP focused on the Convention on Biological Diversity. In this group, as a subset of the Earth Summit group, numerous biological diversity zones were recognized and participants agreed to protect certain fragile ecological areas. Nevertheless, member states routinely violated the provisions and spirit of this and other environmental treaties after the conference.

A blatant example took place in southern Mozambique, in Matatuine District along the border between Mozambique and South Africa, in 1995. Parts of an area stretching along the coast from south of Durban in South Africa up north through southern Mozambique were declared a biological diversity zone. This area includes Matatuine District in southern Mozambique, and is home to thousands of hectares of pristine forest and bush land, a natural elephant corridor, fragile wetlands and riverine areas, and other scarce flora and fauna (Myers and Meneses 1995). Despite the fact that both countries were signatories to the Convention on

Biological Diversity, Mozambique facilitated land "distributions" to dubious South African and other foreign investors that have challenged the ecological integrity of the zone on the Mozambican side of the border.

Despite these weaknesses at the national level, or as a result of them, regional organizations do have an important role to play in the area of resource management and conservation. However, observers must be clear on what they can be expected to accomplish successfully and, moreover, what they should be expected to do.

If national governments are unable or unwilling to resolve serious environmental problems, protecting their own heritage and the environmental integrity of their region, why not rely on regional institutions to encourage or "force" changes in policy and practice among member states? For example, why not rely on regional organizations to use market restrictions or benefits as a tool to enforce member compliance?

The experiences of the CILSS, IGAD, and the SADC demonstrate not only that policy changes cannot be forced on member states from above, but more importantly that the drive for change must come from local communities and civil society. Consequently, the more regional organizations are able to create "enabling environments" where governments and civil society come together on relatively neutral grounds to discuss politically sensitive issues, the more they will be able to address issues that broadly affect the region. At the same time, the more regional organizations are able to act as conduits for information and ideas, particularly involving rural resource users, the more there will be a "democratizing effect" which will eventually force change from the ground up.

If a central criterion for addressing land degradation in Africa is the nature of property rights systems – that is if communities and individuals have clear, defensible, and transactable rights, which are appropriate to their specific economic and political structures – then a test for the success of a regional organization in addressing environmental concerns would be the degree to which it supports or promotes discussion about land policy and property rights within the region.

Clearly, the CILSS meets this criterion by promoting both land tenure discussions among members and decentralized participation in that discussion process. IGAD has also moved in this direction, but has also been forced to focus more on the role of subnational and inter-state violence as an inhibitor to sound regional environmental management. It remains to be seen if IGAD will be able to link environmental sustainability successfully with regional peace through a more elaborated discussion of land policy issues. And finally the SADC, which appears to least meet the criteria established in the introduction to this chapter, has focused more on the role of the private sector in addressing environmental concerns.

While the market may well be the best determinant in how resources are managed and exploited, it remains to be seen if all partners within the SADC may equally benefit from this perspective.

In summary, while regional organizations cannot be expected to cure regional problems, they can be expected to do the following.

- Create opportunities for dialogue among member states about environmental issues that are often politically, economically, and culturally sensitive within member states.
- Create opportunities for more localized (and democratized) participation by groups that are normally disregarded or marginalized in public discussions about the environment and other issues held within member states. These groups include NGOs, women's groups, and minority political and social groups.
- Create opportunities for similar or like-minded transborder groups with similar objectives to define common interests and strategies.
- Foster environmental policy and practice transformation within and across member states through long-term educational, research, and dialogue processes that create demand for change from the ground up.

In conclusion, policy affecting transboundary environmental issues, particularly land use and degradation, will only come from a long-term process of dialogue, negotiation, and education in which civil society and government participate. The role of regional organizations should be to provide information, policy options, and a forum for participatory discussion. Multilateral and bilateral institutions can facilitate the success of regional organizations by developing programmes that are more regional in nature, cutting across boundaries, and by creating a level arena in which political discourse can take place.

REFERENCES

African Rights. 1993. *Land Tenure, the Creation of Famine, and Prospects for Peace in Somalia*. Discussion Paper No. 1. London: African Rights.

Besteman, C. and L. V. Cassanelli, eds. 1996. *The Struggle for Land in Southern Somalia: The War Behind the War*. Boulder: Westview Press.

Black, R. 1994. "Forced Migration and Environment Change: The Impact of Refugees on Host Environments." *Journal of Environmental Management* 42(3): 261–277.

Bohrer, K. and M. Hobbs. 1996. *Post-Praia Progress Towards Tenure Security and Decentralization: Review of CILSS Member Country Legislative Reforms*. Madison: Land Tenure Center, University of Wisconsin-Madison.

CILSS and OECD. 1993. "The Food Aid Charter for the Countries of the Sahel." CILSS and OECD.

Drumtra, J. 1993. "No Place Like Home: Mozambican Refugees Begin Africa's Largest Repatriation." USCR Issue Paper, December. Washington: US Committee for Refugees.

FAO (Food and Agricultural Organization). 1985. *Tropical Forestry Action Plan.* Rome: FAO.

FAO (Food and Agricultural Organization). 1995. "Forest Resources Assessment – 1990: Global Synthesis." FAO Forestry Paper 124. Rome: FAO.

Freudenberger, M. S. 1994. *Tenure and Decentralization Policy Dialogue and the GTZ in East Africa: Lessons Learned from the CILSS/Club.* Madison: Land Tenure Center, University of Wisconsin-Madison.

Halpern, S. 1992. "United Nations Conference on Environment and Development: Process and Documentation." Providence: Academic Council for the United Nations.

Holland, M. 1995. "South Africa, SADC, and the European Union: Matching Bilateral with Regional Policies." *Journal of Modern African Studies* 33(2): 263–283.

Homer-Dixon, T. F. 1991. "On the Threshold: Environmental Changes as Causes of Acute Conflict." *International Security* 16(2): 76–116.

Homer-Dixon, T. F. 1994. "Environmental Scarcities and Violent Conflict: Evidence from Cases." *International Security* 19(1): 5–40.

Myers, G. 1994. "Competitive Rights, Competitive Claims: Land Access in Post-War Mozambique." *Journal of Southern African Studies* 34(1).

Myers, G. 1997a. *Land Tenure Security in Zambezia Province: A Report to the Zambezia Agricultural Development Project (ZADP) – World Vision International Mozambique.* Maputo: World Vision.

Myers, G. 1997b. "Resource Security, Democratization, and Conflict Resolution." LTC Paper. Land Tenure Center, University of Wisconsin-Madison.

Myers, G., J. Eliseu, and E. Nhachungue. 1998. *Five Years of Peace – Five Years of Insecurity: Land Tenure in Manica and Tete Provinces.* Maputo: Amoterra and Danida.

Myers, G. and C. Meneses. 1995. *Elephants in the Trees: Land and Resource Administration in Southern Maputo Province.* Maputo: Land Tenure Center Project.

Southgate, D., J. Sanders, and S. Ehui. 1990. "Resource Degradation in Africa and Latin America: Population Pressure, Policies, and Property Arrangements." *American Journal of Agricultural Economics* 72(5): 1259–1263.

Thiesenhusen, W. 1991. "Implications of the Rural Land Tenure System for the Environmental Debate: Three Scenarios." *Journal of Development Studies* 26(1): 1–24.

UNHCR. 1997. "State of the World's Refugees." Internet: ⟨http://www.unhcr.ch/refworld/publ/state/97/toc.htm⟩.

WRI (World Resources Institute). 1997. *Combating Desertification: Agenda 21.* Washington: World Resources Institute.

FURTHER READING

Courthra, G. 1997. "Subregional Security: The Southern African Development Community." *Security Dialogue* 28(2): 207–218.

Doos, B. R. 1994. "Environmental Degradation, Global Food Production, and Risk for Large-scale Migrations." *Ambio* 23(2): 124–130.

Elbow, K. 1994. "Report on the CILSS/Club du Sahel Regional Conference on Land Tenure and Decentralized Management of Natural Resources in the Sahel." Madison: Land Tenure Center, University of Wisconsin-Madison.

Hesselinger, G. 1994. *Land Tenure and Natural Resource Management in the Sahel: Experiences, Constraints and Prospects.* Paris: CILSS/OECD Club du Sahel.

Land Tenure Center. 1998. *Country Profiles of Land Tenure: Africa 1996.* Madison: Land Tenure Center, University of Wisconsin-Madison.

Mwangi, W. 1996. "A Revitalized IGAD, But What is in Store?" *EcoNews Africa* 5(24).

Permanent Interstate Committee for Drought Control in the Sahel. 1990. "The Food Aid Charter for the Countries of the Sahel." Paris: OECD/Club du Sahel.

Westing, A. H. 1991. "Environmental Security and its Relation to Ethiopia and Sudan." *Ambio* 20(5): 168–171.

International organizations and the environment

17

Intergovernmental organizations and the environment: Introduction

Michael W. Doyle and Rachel I. Massey

Many environmental problems have increased in severity during the second half of the twentieth century. Pesticide use has increased, species have become extinct, soils have become depleted. While environmental problems have proliferated, so too have intergovernmental organizations intended to address them. In 1972, the UN Conference on the Human Environment explicitly put the environment on the international agenda and laid the groundwork for the establishment of an intergovernmental organization: UNEP. Fifteen years later, the Brundtland Commission's 1987 report, *Our Common Future*, highlighted an increased appreciation for the intersectoral nature of environmental problems and emphasized the close relationship between economic development and environmental concerns (WCED 1987). In 1989, the General Assembly established the UN Conference on the Environment and Development (UNCED). After two years of preparatory committee meetings in Nairobi, Geneva, and New York, this conference convened at the heads-of-state level at the Earth Summit in Rio in June 1992. One important result of UNCED was the establishment of a high-level coordinating and agenda-setting Commission on Sustainable Development (CSD). The CSD was mandated to pursue the integrated agenda of development and environment identified by the Brundtland Commission, further defined at the Rio Summit, and set out in Agenda 21.

The chapters in this section examine the history, mandate, and activities of three intergovernmental organizations that have been active participants in the formation of the global environmental agenda. UNEP is the oldest and core UN agency with a specifically environmental mandate. The CSD is a relatively new international environmental organization, founded in response to the new sustainable development agenda set by UNCED. Finally, the World Bank is an influential international organization whose core mandate is not concerned with environmental protection, but whose activities have a major effect on prospects for the international coordination of environmental protection. The chapters examine how the mandate, the configuration, and the resources of each organization have influenced its ability – as well as the collective ability of intergovernmental organizations in aggregate – to address global environmental problems. While each chapter evaluates one organization individually, the larger purpose of this collective undertaking is to evaluate whether existing organizations together meet the need for a coordinated approach to protecting the global environment.

Theoretical context: Evaluating international organizations

The field of political science has produced a variety of theoretical insights that are applicable to the cases discussed here. This section provides a very brief overview of some definitions and concepts that are central to the discussion that follows.

Basic definitions

Political scientists make distinctions among harmony, deadlock, coordination, and cooperation (Oye 1985). As Oye argued, harmony exists when parties carry out activities unilaterally that are in their individual interests and that result in mutual benefit. Deadlock persists when parties choose policies in their individual interests that result in conflict regardless of what others are prepared to choose. Both outcomes can explain many instances of what is taken to be "cooperation" success and failure that is incorrectly attributed to coordination and cooperation. Real coordination implies that although parties share a common interest in an outcome, they would not achieve that outcome without some conscious act of mutual agreement (as when traffic rules specify which side of the street cars drive on). Finally, real cooperation denotes that parties have worked together to accomplish something and that divergent interests have been taken into account and collective action problems overcome. As the tasks undertaken by the organizations discussed in this volume are considered, it will be useful to take note of the extent to which they reflect simple harmony or simple discord, or, in more complicated ways, codify or formalize coordination or create the conditions for the more difficult task of cooperation.

Another distinction of significance for this discussion is that between institutions and organizations. Oran Young makes a strong argument for keeping this distinction clear at all times. Institutions, as defined by Young, are "social practices consisting of easily recognized roles coupled with clusters of rules or conventions governing relations among the occupants of those roles" (Young 1989, 32). This definition is very broad. Examples of institutions, according to this definition, include both treaties and less formalized understandings among individuals or nations that guide behaviour. He defines organizations, on the other hand, as "material entities possessing physical locations (or seats), offices, personnel, equipment, and budgets." Young notes that an organization is often created in tandem with the creation of an institution – of which it may constitute a subset or which it may be responsible for administering – but that both institutions and organizations may also be free-standing. Furthermore, he points out, it is important not to assume automatically that all international cooperative arrangements must be embodied in or accompanied by an organization. Indeed, some purposes are best achieved by means of a decentralized regime that is not administered by a single organization – or, indeed, by any organization at all. As the organizations discussed here are considered, one should be aware of how they are interrelated with institutions. The relationship is clearest in the case of the CSD: the organization is specifically intended to promote adherence to the more general institution of Agenda 21 and the other commitments signed at Rio. UNEP has been an active agent in forming institutions itself; however, it cannot really be said to be the creature, instrument, or implementing body of any single overarching institution. Finally, the World Bank as an organization is clearly not part of any specific environmental regime. It is a creature of the international economic regime, broadly conceived, that was established at Bretton Woods. Despite the collapse of the Bretton Woods system, its goal of trade liberalization and the promotion of economic growth worldwide continues in part through organizations, such as the World Bank, to which it gave rise.

As the functions these three organizations serve are considered, as well as the areas they fail to cover, it will be helpful to keep this distinction in mind. In particular, it may be the case that some of these functions clearly require an actual organization to carry them out, whereas other goals might best be achieved by a decentralized institution.

Institution-building with and without hegemony

One perspective on international cooperation is the realist perspective. Many realists would argue that the term "international organization" is an oxymoron. International politics among equal sovereigns is, according to some views, essentially anarchic. Given the sovereign independence of the component states, what must be studied is how states are either dominated and thereby organized or not dominated and thereby disorganized.

Realists describe a world defined by anarchy and characterized by a constant struggle for relative gain among states (Grieco 1990). In this world, cooperation can emerge only when there is a hegemon, one state with sufficient power to create and enforce it. If a cooperative international system serves the interests of the hegemon, then the hegemon will bear whatever costs are necessary, including the costs of coercion, to perpetuate cooperation. Thus, hegemony produces a situation in which one state is powerful enough to maintain the essential rules governing inter-state relations, and willing to do so.

States do, however, share some interests. The analysis of a complicated world in which states share some interests and are not dominated by concerns for relative power belongs to two principal schools of thought inspired by a more liberal outlook on world politics. The first, functionalism, studies the ways in which states organize themselves to promote cooperation, establishing regimes and institutions which serve the limited common purposes that states are willing to acknowledge. In the functionalist paradigm, international organizations are seen as agents, forums, or instrumentalities of states' interests. The second approach, neofunctionalism, notes the equally obvious fact that international organizations are actual organizations with budgets, headquarters, staffs, and, most notably, their own set of interests. Moreover, the gap between states and international and transnational organizations (IOs and TNOs) is not as vast as international law would make it appear. How many heads of state would not trade their influence, budget, and degree of autonomy with those of the World Bank, the International Monetary Fund, or even General Motors? International organizations are themselves actors with interests and agendas. Like a state, an international organization can grow or decline; like a state, it can dominate, facilitate, or collapse. Robert Keohane's book, *After Hegemony*, argues in this vein that states can achieve cooperation without a hegemon. When states are enjoying peace and relative compatibility of interests, they may establish institutions that help them to maintain good communication and the tools for successful cooperation even at a later point when interests diverge and new challenges arise (Keohane 1984).

Functionalist and neofunctionalist perspectives on cooperation

Functionalism considers states to be the primary actors of significance, and organizations to be forums or instrumentalities of states' interests. Functional theories of cooperation assert that actors have both common and competitive interests and organizations are the instruments through which states pursue their interests in coordination and cooperation. Within this framework, it is possible to identify the conditions under which these organizations are most likely to be successful. Organizations will succeed if they have clear, fixed purposes; if there are high returns on expertise; if clear property rights can be delineated; if there are coherent constituencies with clear interests; and if problems are simple and divisible and yet connected. The functionalist perspective on international organizations is well illustrated in some of the insights of game theory and economics.[1]

The classic works of functionalism, including David Mitrany's *A Working Peace System* (Mitrany 1966), were discursive treatments of how positive and negative interdependence ("spillover") could create a need for increasing the scope and capacity of international cooperation. But formal analogies sharpen the logic underlying the functionalist thesis. The most famous story illustrating the problem of functional organization is George Akerlof's "Market for Lemons." The market for used cars is a market for "lemons" – the American slang for a malfunctioning automobile. Buyers tend to assume that used cars are lemons (patched-up and painted wrecks) and consequently are willing to pay very little for them. Sellers who own good cars are consequently unwilling to sell because they do not receive the fair and true value of the car. Thus only lemons are put on the market; and sellers who would like to sell and buyers who would have liked to buy a valuable used car are left disappointed by market failure. If only there existed a reliable rating agency that distinguished the good used cars from the lemons, argues Akerlof, all would be better off (Akerlof 1984).

In situations of coordination, therefore, where states have symmetrical interests in pursuing a common good or avoiding a bad, reliable information alone can be sufficient to ensure coordination. Organizations that provide reliable information are valued and necessary, and so such organizations are created. For example, knowing the true value of the used car would enhance the prospect of more and better sales; and developing countries that can purchase non-polluting technology for the same price as a polluting technology will presumably do so as long as they can be assured that the costs are truly the same and the environmental benefits are positive. Providing this information is one part of UNEP's technical advisory mandate.

Where states have common interests but also incentives to defect from common strategies, or where the interests shared by a number of states may have distributional consequences that differ, then states may have a long-run interest in establishing organizations that sanction short-run defections (by reputational or material losses such as aid conditionality).

Sometimes assigning property rights is sufficient to achieve efficient coordination. If all countries have the same right to pollute, licences to pollute can be sold internationally to those industries that find clean-up most costly and the funds can be used for sustainable development in countries whose clean-up is less costly or which are below their national quotas. An organization that monitors and enforces this pollution market would be effective and valued, just as the used car buyer would have benefited from a reliable rating agency with the power to penalize cheating.

Finally, many common purposes require infrastructure – research, monitoring, training, conferences – and sharing the expenses on a regular basis would allow this to be created, especially when no country benefited enough individually to make the cost worthwhile, thus overcoming the "free-rider" problem in creating infrastructure. Organizations in the functionalist view improve coordination and cooperation and themselves grow in competence, authority, and budget through "spillover." As Mitrany (1966) argued, successful cooperation that furthers common interests in turn creates incentives for more coordinated and cooperative activity.

Neofunctionalism, which evolved from functionalism, highlights international organizations as actors in their own right, possessing their own interests and agendas. From this perspective, initially developed by Ernst Haas, the budgets, headquarters, staffs, and – most notably – the interests of organizations themselves affect the ways in which international interactions play out (Haas 1968). In the neofunctionalist view, an international organization is a hierarchical structure with purposes, direction, and the capacity to change. It may have a constituency and it exists within a constraining environment, but neither of these factors completely defines its purposes or its capacities. Some functional interests are not automatically fulfilled; "spillovers" become stalled or even "drain" away. From this perspective, an organization's success in fulfilling its mandate may be attributed not only to its instrumental value but also to its ability to build on existing capacity (staff and capital), on the quality of leadership of the organization, on taking entrepreneurial advantage of an opaque and uncertain but pluralist political environment that allows the organization to grow, and on the advantages flowing from experience and time to learn. The influence of the United Nations in the 1960s, for example, would be seen from this perspective as being due not to its utility to the great powers but rather to the inspirational leadership of Secretary-General Dag Hammarskjöld. Similarly, UNEP's survival far off the beaten international track in Nairobi can be attributed not only to its third world constituency but also to the effective coalition-building of Mostafa Tolba, who led the organization for 16 years.

Almost all international organizations should be evaluated first by their instrumental value: they would not exist but for their instrumental value to states. But many would not survive but for a capacity to innovate and grow. And they would not meet global needs were it not for an ability to innovate beyond the lowest common denominator of currently perceived state interests. Thus both the functionalist and the neofunctionalist perspectives can provide helpful insights into the activities of and challenges facing international environmental organizations.

Insights from cooperation theory: Start small; start with the easy; interact face to face

A variety of insights into the functioning of international environmental organizations may be derived from game theory studies of cooperation and bargaining. One area into which some interesting recent studies provide insight is that of the optimal size for an organization or an agreement in its early stages of development. George Downs (1998) employs a simple model to demonstrate that the number of actors party to an agreement at its outset is likely to affect how deep that agreement will be in the long term. In particular, he shows that if the number of parties is small at the start, they can achieve an agreement that is deeper than it would be if there were more parties to the agreement, and that the deepness of the agreement will then persist as more parties join. The lesson of this model is that it may be best to "start small"; it may be best to focus on achieving a relatively deep agreement among a small number of states than to worry initially about including a large number of states in the agreement.

A related insight from cooperation theory is that it may be important to start with the tasks that are easiest. Solving a simple problem may allow countries to lay the foundations for later, more difficult work; coordination may serve as an avenue into cooperation.

Empirical studies on cooperation suggest that the simple fact of face-to-face interaction also increases people's ability to agree with one another. In an experiment where individuals are allowed to talk with one another before beginning to bargain on an assigned problem, their probability of agreement rises even if they are not allowed to discuss the actual subject of the bargaining exercise. What this may imply for international environmental organizations is that just creating forums for conversation on international environmental problems may make it easier for countries to reach agreement on measures requiring international coordination. So to whatever extent an international environmental organization fosters or encourages or catalyses conversation among representatives of countries that need to cooperate in order to achieve environmental goals, it is worth having those organizations. This mitigates the force of the complaint that a lot of organizations never accomplish anything, people in them just talk a lot. It may be that this very talking is central to whatever environmental protection successes have been seen.

Lessons from enforcement: Do not over-police

Game theory analyses of cooperation also provide some interesting insights into the problem of enforcement. In *Optimal Imperfection*, for example, George Downs and David Rocke (1995) discuss the ways in which enforcement mechanisms affect those countries that do adhere to an agreement but then have to discipline a defector from the agreement. They point out that enforcement is costly for those having to discipline the defector. Thus they may be likely to avoid engaging in agreements from which they expect there will be defection. Downs and Rocke consider the hypothetical case of three countries that are polluting a body of water. Two of the countries want to agree on a pollution abatement treaty, and they expect to have the capacity to adhere to the agreement. They have to decide whether they should include the third country in the agreement. Downs and Rocke show that if there is significant uncertainty about the third state's future capacity to adhere to the agreement, it may be better for the two states that are confident in their own capacity to go ahead with a bilateral agreement and let the third country simply be a free-riding bystander. The reason is that if the third country defects, the other two will have to punish it. In this hypothetical scenario, the only means of enforcement available to them is to stop adhering to the agreement themselves – that is, to become polluters of the body of water themselves. What this means is that by including the third country in their treaty, they might end up collectively producing more pollution than they would if the treaty were bilateral. Obviously it will not always be the case that increasing pollution of one's own will be the primary possible means of punishment; but the example can be extended in various ways to other sorts of punishment – the point being that states must undertake costly measures in order to adhere to enforcement provisions, and that they must take this into account when they decide whether they might want to join an agreement. This has an effect on the utility of including enforcement measures in international environmental agreements.

According to the "managerial" perspective, enforcement provisions are seen as being largely irrelevant: as long as violations are due to a lack of state capacity to adhere to an agreement, which appears to be the case in the majority of examples, the threat of punishment will not significantly affect the likelihood of defection. The "transformationalist" perspective takes this view to an extreme. Going beyond the view that the enforcement provisions may be irrelevant, theorists in this tradition suggest that enforcement provisions may actually be counterproductive because they may make states reluctant to join agreements. Thus it is premature to claim that organizations and individuals responsible for forging environmental agreements should actually avoid including enforcement provisions.[2]

Questions

The following overarching questions run through the chapters in this section and are addressed further in the Conclusion to the section. Do intergovernmental organizations adequately cover the range of global environmental challenges? In what way can and should the role of these organizations be enhanced? How do the organizations discussed here interact with one another to cover the map of global environmental problems? Are there inefficient overlaps – areas where organizations duplicate one another's efforts? Are there synergies, where multiple organizations are tackling the same problems in different and complementary ways? Finally, are there gaps that all these organizations fail to cover?

Most basically, do the organizations discussed here, in combination with those mentioned briefly in this chapter, have the potential to solve the major environmental challenges that face the international community? Are there clear ways in which these organizations can and should be strengthened? Or is there a need for a different sort of international organization – a global environmental organization that would perform a role analogous to the WTO's role in regulating trade?

Notes

1. See Keohane (1984), especially chapter 6, "A Functional Theory of Regimes."
2. George Downs (1998) concludes that enforcement provisions may not be necessary in order for an agreement to be worthwhile; but that, on the other hand, there is not good evidence that the inclusion of enforcement mechanisms is actually counterproductive.

REFERENCES

Akerlof, G. 1984. *An Economic Theorist's Book of Tales: Essays that Entertain the Consequences of New Assumptions in Economic Theory.* New York: Cambridge University Press.

Downs, G. W. 1998. "Enforcement and the Evolution of Cooperation." *Michigan Journal of International Law* 19(2): 319–344.

Downs, G. W. and D. M. Rocke. 1995. *Optimal Imperfection? Domestic Uncertainty and Institutions in International Relations.* Princeton: Princeton University Press.

Grieco, J. 1990. *Cooperation Among Nations.* Ithaca: Cornell University Press.

Haas, E. B. 1968. *Beyond the Nation-State: Functionalism and International Organization.* Stanford: Stanford University Press.

Keohane, R. O. 1984. *After Hegemony: Cooperation and Discord in World Political Economy.* Princeton: Princeton University Press.

Mitrany, D. 1966. *A Working Peace System.* Chicago: Quadrangle Books.

Oye, K. 1985. "Explaining Cooperation under Anarchy: Hypotheses and Strategies." *World Politics* 38(1): 1–24.

WCED (World Commission for Environment and Development). 1987. *Our Common Future.* Oxford: Oxford University Press.

Young, O. R. 1989. *International Cooperation: Building Regimes for Natural Resources and the Environment.* Ithaca: Cornell University Press.

18

The UN Environment Programme at a turning point: Options for change

David L. Downie and Marc A. Levy

The UN Environment Programme was created as direct consequence of the 1972 UN Conference on the Human Environment. The first international organization dedicated to environmental protection, UNEP's mandate was to act as a focal point for environmental action and coordination within the UN system. It would promote international cooperation in the field of the environment and recommend appropriate policies. It would also provide general policy guidance for the direction and coordination of environmental programmes within the UN system.

Today, 27 years later, UNEP faces a series of challenges that could threaten its very existence. There is no doubt that UNEP has had its share of successes, but there have been dramatic changes in international environmental policy-making in recent years and UNEP has not demonstrated the ability to keep pace. Chronic financial problems, the absence of a clear focus and mission for the institution, problems of location, and management difficulties have all contributed to the erosion of UNEP's participation in the international environmental policy-making process.

This chapter examines options for UNEP in assisting the management of global environmental problems. It does not go so far as to recommend a particular package of reforms. Instead, the more modest aims are to provide an overview of the problems, to clarify potential choices for improvement, and to formulate an initial framework within which to judge future action.

To this end, the chapter's first section outlines the significant challenges facing the organization; challenges which threaten its continued relevance to international environmental management. The second section reviews functions that UNEP has performed well in the past, thereby demonstrating the value of saving the organization. The third section outlines several potential roles for UNEP within the UN system that might improve its contribution to the management of global environmental problems. The final section then outlines some changes that would be necessary, within both UNEP and the international community as a whole, to allow the organization to play these roles.

It should be emphasized that many of these points are currently under active discussion within UNEP, within the UN system, and within the global environmental community as whole.[1] Consequently, to avoid early obsolescence, this chapter does not delineate or place its analysis within the context of specific, ongoing reviews of UNEP. Such a discussion would easily be overtaken by events. The intent of the chapter, rather, is to provide an outline of the challenges facing UNEP as it enters the twenty-first century as well as a framework for evaluating and participating in the ongoing debate regarding its future.

UNEP

When it was created in 1972, UNEP's programme had seven priority areas: human settlements and habitats (later spun off into the UN Centre for Human Settlements (Habitat) – UNCHS); health of people and their environment; terrestrial ecosystems and their management and control; environment and development; oceans; energy; and natural disasters.[2] UNEP was intended to serve as a catalyst in developing and coordinating an environmental focus in other organizations, rather than initiating its own large programmes in these areas. UNEP's role was to remind others of, and help them to take into account, all the environmental interactions and ramifications interconnected with their work. Many thought that the lack of such a cross-sectoral, interdisciplinary view had led to many environmental problems in the first place.

Despite its broad mandate, UNEP has a smaller staff and budget than most UN organizations. Its size is traceable both to its original purpose, which is to be catalytic rather than programmatic, as well as to its status as a "programme" rather than a "specialized agency." As such, UNEP lacks the independent status of such organizations, and member states fund UNEP's budget on a voluntary basis rather than under the mandatory assessment process that supports the specialized agencies. This situation has produced significant financial uncertainty for UNEP, including increasing budgetary shortfalls in recent years.

UNEP is headquartered in Nairobi, Kenya, and has smaller regional offices around the world. It reports to the UN General Assembly through the Economic and Social Council. UNEP's internal organizational structure centres on its Governing Council and Secretariat.

The Governing Council consists of 58 states who serve for three-year terms on the basis of equitable geographic distribution.[3] It meets biennially and is charged with promoting environmental cooperation; providing policy guidance and coordination of environmental programmes in the UN system; reviewing the world environment situation; and promoting the contributions of relevant scientific and other professional communities to producing and using environmental knowledge.

UNEP's Secretariat is headed by an Executive Director (ED). The ED is elected by the General Assembly, upon the nomination of the UN Secretary-General. UNEP has had only four Executive Directors: Maurice Strong, who had been Secretary-General of the 1972 Stockholm Conference, served as ED from 1973 to 1975; Mostafa Tolba led the organization for most of its history, from 1976 to 1992; Elizabeth Dowdeswell was ED from 1993 to 1997; and Klaus Töpfer, the current ED, took office on 1 February 1998.

The ED provides support to the Governing Council, coordinates programmes under the guidance of the Council, offers advice to other UN organs, secures cooperation from the scientific community, and assists the promotion of international environmental cooperation. The ED also suggests medium-range and long-range planning issues to the Governing Council regarding UN work in the environment, and brings the Governing Council's attention to any matter he believes requires its consideration.

Dimensions of the current crisis

UNEP has achieved remarkable success in its 25 years, but faces a number of challenges that, in sum, are so severe that they constitute a crisis for the organization. This section outlines the most significant of these challenges: changes in the agenda and organizational structure of international environmental politics; the absence of a clear focus and mission for the institution; chronic financial shortfalls; problems of location; and management difficulties.

Changed international environmental agenda

Some of UNEP's challenges are signs of progress in international environmental policy. Indeed, some are the direct result of the organization's successes. The dramatic increase in the breadth and density of the international environmental agenda counts among these.

At the time of its creation in 1972, UNEP's agenda contained few issues that were global in scope and only a few dozen environmental treaties had been negotiated. Since then about 100 additional environmental treaties have entered into force, and by one count more than 40 of these were negotiated directly under UNEP's auspices (Haas 1995, 654). Increasingly these are global treaties, which adds obvious layers of complexity to their negotiation and implementation. They include agreements to protect the ozone layer, prevent climate change, protect biodiversity, and combat desertification.

Thus, whereas in the 1970s UNEP was seeking to shape an international agenda that had relatively large openings and which few other actors were trying to influence, today the agenda is densely packed and a wide diversity of actors have become expert at gaining influence within it. The result is that the international environmental agenda has acquired a breadth and depth that makes it impossible for UNEP to shape, manage, and coordinate all of its aspects. There are simply too many issues and too many complexities within environmental politics for an organization with UNEP's limited size, budget, and expertise to address them all well. At the same time, however, the failure to do so produces dissatisfaction with the organization.

The obvious irony is that the same forces which make the international agenda more difficult to influence have also increased the demand for UNEP to help coordinate it. The 1987 report of the World Commission on Environment and Development (Brundtland Report) had explicitly called for strengthening UNEP in response to the growing needs (WCED 1987). And Agenda 21, approved in 1992 at the UN Conference on Environment and Development (UNCED), confirmed UNEP's role in "promoting environmental activities and considerations throughout the United Nations system," and gave it lead responsibility for developing international environmental law (Imber 1994, 110). However, Agenda 21 proved less effective at strengthening UNEP than at broadening the international agenda and spawning the creation of a potential competitor, the Commission on Sustainable Development.

Changed organizational structure in international environmental affairs

UNEP faces challenges from a diverse array of other international organizations involved in environmental management. These organizations began working on environmental affairs as the international environmental agenda expanded, as more issues required management, and as more activities required implementation. As a result, UNEP faces competition from organizations that did not exist when it was created or did not work on environmental issues until recently.

Among the organizations now working on environmental affairs are several discussed in this volume. Recently created institutions include the Global Environment Facility (GEF), the Commission on Sustainable Development (CSD), and issue-specific treaty secretariats such as the Biodiversity, Climate, and Ozone Secretariats. Long-standing organizations that have significantly expanded activities related to monitoring or protecting the environment include the FAO, the UNDP, the UN Industrial Development Organization (UNIDO), the World Bank, the World Meteorological Organization (WMO), and, to a lesser degree, the global trade regime centred around the WTO. Each of these organizations competes, explicitly or in more *de facto* ways, with UNEP and each other for environmental monitoring, project implementation, regime management, and issue coordination activities and the donor dollars that support them. As these organizations in most cases already enjoy better funding, more central locations, clearer and stronger mandates, and greater support from the international community than does UNEP, they offer significant challenges to UNEP's ability to play a lead role or even a unique role in environmental affairs.

Absence of a clear focus, mission, and role for UNEP

The lack of a clear mission represents the third major challenge facing UNEP. Given the crowded field, perhaps it is not surprising that UNEP's specific role in environmental politics – and even within the UN system – is increasingly unclear. However, it is striking the extent to which UNEP's ultimate purpose and its place in international environmental management remain unresolved. This problem stems from failures by UNEP to delineate specific activities as its foci, and by the United Nations as an institution and the global community as a whole to organize international environmental management more coherently.

Many criticisms of UNEP argue that much of the organization's current crisis stems from its tendency to take on too many tasks that dilute its overall impact. A 1997 internal oversight assessment report stressed this point, but it has also been a consistent criticism throughout its history.[4] Certainly a review of UNEP's vision of itself and its recent activities does indicate an incredibly wide range of activities for such a financially constrained organization.[5] The most recent statement by UNEP's Governing Council regarding UNEP's mandate delineates a very broad and diverse set of missions for the organization (UN 1997a, section I). The organization's report to the June 1997 Rio+5 special session of the General

Assembly, for example, reported on significant activities relevant to every single chapter of Agenda 21 (UN 1997a, section II B; UNEP 1996b). Moreover, in a candid note to the Governing Council, former Executive Director Dowdeswell acknowledged that UNEP's activities do not reflect either a sense of clear priorities or an understanding of UNEP's comparative advantage:

A rigorous review of current activities reveals a number that are no longer on the leading edge or represent sufficient added value given the scarce resources of UNEP. Others are self-perpetuating, continuing long after "catalysis" should have been completed. Furthermore, activities once undertaken by UNEP, such as certain types of coordination, may now be better accomplished by others (UNEP 1996b, section 31).

UNEP's lack of a clear mission also results from a lack of commitment to the organization and the failure by the international community to organize clearly the management of environmental issues. For example, other organizations have been allowed to expand their activities into areas perhaps more appropriate for UNEP. More telling, however, is that a new body, the CSD, has been given responsibility for some of UNEP's formal agenda.[6] Thus, UNEP's lack of a clear role, as well as the increased competition it faces, reflect a broader uncertainty by the international community regarding how it wishes to organize multilateral environmental institutions.

Financial shortfalls

UNEP has always been on a tenuous financial footing. As a programme, it depends on voluntary contributions, as opposed to mandatory assessments, for the bulk of its budget. This uncertainty has constrained UNEP's budget to small rates of growth compared to the growth in its agenda. UNEP's budget is also much smaller than those of other UN organizations involved in environmental affairs.

Moreover, in recent years UNEP experienced funding shortfalls and has been unable to fund even its limited budget, necessitating cutbacks. For example, although UNEP was able to spend US$160 million from its Environment Fund in the 1994–1995 biennium, it lowered its 1996–1997 budget to US$137 million. It then reduced that figure even further to US$102 million after contributions failed to materialize (UNEP 1996a, 9). A striking example of the impact of such budget shortfalls was a letter that the UNEP Chemicals Office sent to governments, industry, NGOs, and academic institutions in 1998 asking for financial donations so that it could continue to organize negotiations on a global treaty regulating persistent organic pollutants (UNEP Chemicals 1998). One external assessment observes that the financial uncertainties and shortfalls have produced a vicious circle:

Managers and their staff are engaged in paring down their programmes and because of the time and energy it takes, they have had less time left to do environmental work. This has led to a reduction of discernible results, leading to reduced donor confidence and lower contributions and in turn to further paring down of programmes (UN 1997b, 8).

Location

UNEP's home office is located on a beautiful campus in Kenya just north of Nairobi. As the first and one of only two UN agencies headquartered in a developing country, UNEP's location is an important political statement.[7] At the same time, however, Nairobi has proven to be a liability in UNEP's attempts to play a central and coordinating role in environmental affairs.[8]

Travel to UNEP headquarters is complicated and time-consuming for most of the world's environmental diplomats. The Internal Oversight Services concluded that senior UNEP staff spend too much time travelling (UN 1997b), something that may be inevitable for any organization given a strong coordinating role at the global level but based in Nairobi.

Electronic, voice, and mail communications with officials outside Kenya have, until recently, been surprising inadequate, unreliable, and expensive.[9] Although new satellite systems should relieve some of these problems, communications can still be difficult and decades of inadequate service have already exacted a political toll. The time difference to New York and Washington, and thus the headquarters of the United Nations, the UNDP, the CSD, the GEF, and the World Bank, further complicates efficient communication and coordination. Security concerns in Nairobi have also increased and proven an obstacle to attracting and retaining top personnel. Local political support by the government of Kenya is sometimes uneven. Even the difficulties of local transportation can complicate holding large international conferences at UNEP headquarters despite the relatively high quality of its conference facilities.

Management difficulties

Observers, drawing on first-hand accounts by UNEP staff, claim that in the past few years the internal management environment in UNEP has suffered. The most intensive review of UNEP's management is a sharply critical assessment prepared by the Office of Internal Oversight Services

(UN 1997b). It reports a range of management problems, including confusing organizational structures, inadequate attention to performance indicators, poor relations between senior management and staff, inefficient hiring practices, and lack of transparency in decision-making processes. While the report notes other factors hindering UNEP's effectiveness (including several of those outlined in this section), it is striking in the degree to which it singles out uneven management practices as accentuating current problems. While the tone of that particular report appears overly strident, it is widely accepted that UNEP faces management problems.[10]

While it is not possible to judge the cause of UNEP's current management difficulties, it is worth noting that at least some of the blame lies in the history of the organization, especially its initial and long-standing reliance on charismatic leaders. Tolba, by far the longest-serving ED, established an environment in which UNEP's greatest results, and even its day-to-day operation, were highly dependent on his energy, charisma, and intellect rather than on a set of management practices or an organizational culture that could endure beyond his inevitable departure.[11] Dowdeswell attempted to introduce regularized and transparent management practices but ultimately could not resolve all the outstanding difficulties, many of which continued to worsen. Her rejection of the Tolba model of personally dominating the organization met with initial success, but the management structure she put in place did not, in the opinion of some observers, resolve all the problems of confusing organizational structures, inadequate attention to performance indicators, inefficient hiring practices, or the organization's lack of a clear mission and focus.

Yet in some ways, many of these difficulties can be traced to management problems endemic throughout the UN system or to UNEP's location, its precarious financial situation, and the lack of a clear mission and commitment assigned to it by the international community. It will be major challenge for the current ED, Töpfer, to address these structural and interrelated problems. Moreover, it is unclear if he can solve the management issues without the full support of the international community in addressing the budget issue and articulating and supporting a clear role for UNEP.

Why UNEP is worth saving

These challenges impede UNEP's ability to contribute to the development and implementation of international environmental policy, and could even threaten its continued existence.[12] Although it is rare for international organizations, especially UN bodies, to disappear, this remains a possibility for UNEP. Its status as a "programme" gives it an unusually weak claim on financial resources. As noted, the CSD now has responsibility for some of UNEP's agenda, and many other bodies, such as the UNDP and the World Bank, have radically strengthened their environmental activities so that UNEP's claim to fulfilling a unique functional role has diminished. All these features make it easier to imagine governments letting UNEP disappear today, whereas it would have been an implausible alternative only five years ago.

For that reason it is worth exploring where UNEP has played an especially important role in helping manage environmental problems. This would allow a case to be made for keeping the organization alive. By now a conventional wisdom has emerged regarding UNEP's contribution. Two functions in particular dominate this consensus – collecting, analysing, and disseminating environmental data, and serving as a catalyst for environmental cooperation.[13]

Collecting and disseminating environmental information

From the beginning, UNEP was designed to play an important role in collecting data on environmental change, monitoring long-term trends, and assessing the state of critical natural resources. Some of UNEP's most influential activities in this area include establishing the Global Environment Monitoring System (GEMS), which collects environmental data; creating the International Referral System (INFOTERRA) to help disseminate environmental information; and operating the International Register of Potentially Toxic Chemicals (IRPTC) to promote effective regulation of hazardous chemicals.

UNEP routinely receives high marks for carrying out these information-related functions.[14] The IRPTC was instrumental in helping to improve the way hazardous chemicals are managed in developing countries, and in facilitating the adoption of a prior informed consent (PIC) regime governing the export of such chemicals. GEMS (now known as "State of the Environment Reporting") has not fully lived up to its potential, but the shortcomings are attributable almost entirely to low levels of funding. The need for such information remains high and no other organization has stepped in to collect it.

UNEP also participates in and publishes its own periodic overviews of environment indicators (UNEP 1997). On a smaller scale, UNEP has emerged from time to time to assist in the collection of more specific environmental data when other organizations were unwilling to do so. It provided funding for the European Monitoring and Evaluation Programme (EMEP), originally created by the OECD and which collects data on acid rain in Europe, after the OECD decided to cease its participation. This was vital in keeping EMEP alive long enough for other actors to realize their interest in it. Indeed, EMEP is recognized as playing a vital role in European efforts to manage acid rain.[15]

Serving as a catalyst for international environmental cooperation

Since Stockholm, UNEP has played an important role in several complicated issue areas by helping the international community create and expand international treaties that, by all accounts, have produced better collective management than if they had not existed. UNEP had a direct role in promoting the creation of a series of efforts to protect regional seas, one of the most influential being the Mediterranean Action Plan. A total of 10 regional seas programmes were created under UNEP's auspices, and the initiative is widely considered a success.[16]

UNEP also played a key leadership role in catalysing and coordinating international efforts to create and expand the Montreal Protocol and other international agreements to protect stratospheric ozone, widely considered one of the most effective international responses to an environmental problem.[17] UNEP helped to initiate international action as early as 1977 by calling for and coordinating a series of scientific and political meetings that set the international agenda, functioned to build consensus on the existence and seriousness of the problem, and became the procedural foundation for creating the regime.[18] UNEP then sustained international activity when interest in ozone depletion waned significantly during the early 1980s.

In the late 1980s and 1990s, UNEP acted as a facilitator, making it easier for states to conclude individual agreements by creating and maintaining a particular structure to the negotiations and providing organizational assistance that reduced transaction costs. UNEP also functioned as a negotiation manager, actively pushing negotiators toward a robust regime by offering strong control proposals, undercutting the arguments of regime opponents, building consensus, and applying political pressure. Finally, UNEP has become an important contributor to regime administration, performing valuable organizational tasks, helping to implement regime rules, and managing the review process.

Other conventions in which UNEP played a prominent role include the 1973 Convention on Trade in Endangered Species of Wild Fauna and Flora (CITES), the 1989 Basel Convention on the Control of Transboundary Movements of Hazardous Waste and their Disposal, and the 1992 Convention on Biodiversity. Currently, UNEP is attempting to manage negotiations aimed a creating a global treaty regulating persistent organic pollutants (POPs).[19]

This catalytic role results from efforts by UNEP's Governing Council, which meets every other year, and by the Secretariat, especially the ED. The Governing Council's main role in this regard is to identify critical issues for international attention and mandate negotiations or discussions that can lead to treaties. While environmental treaties do not require such intervention from the Governing Council to come into existence (the UN Framework Convention on Climate Change was the result of a UN General Assembly resolution, for example), having the Governing Council meet regularly to identify gaps and set priorities meets a clear need of the international system. No other body engages in this kind of agenda-setting. Although the CSD does have some overlap, it has not played the same kind of role.[20]

The ED's role is more idiosyncratic. Stories are legion of Tolba's leadership skills and their instrumental effects at key junctures in various environmental negotiations. When the Montreal Protocol negotiations seemed stalled in early 1987, for example, Tolba convened a meeting in Warzberg, Germany, in which key scientists were asked for the first time to apply a common dataset to competing models of ozone depletion. When the results converged much more closely than had prior model runs, Tolba used the information to undermine opposition to cutting CFC production and to move the negotiations forward.[21]

Clarifying UNEP's role: Options for change

If UNEP's past actions prove it can make a positive contribution but the challenges it faces make UNEP's current configuration untenable, then what options appear most promising for moving forward? At the broadest level, two distinct strategies can be identified. One option is to refocus UNEP more narrowly, emphasizing those functions for which it has a proven comparative advantage and shedding others. In this option, much of UNEP's structure remains unchanged but its role is more clearly articulated and its operations focused around a much smaller set of functions. The other broad strategy would be to alter UNEP's structure fundamentally and increase its financial resources and decision-making power by significant amounts.

Creating a more focused UNEP with clearly defined functions within international environmental affairs

There are three main candidates for inclusion in a streamlined UNEP: environmental information, negotiation management, and international coordination and catalysis.

Environmental information

UNEP is not the only organization collecting, disseminating, and assessing environmental information. However, it is the only one with the responsibility for approaching these tasks with regard to the entire range of environmental issues as faced by all nations of the world. Other bodies participating in these tasks adopt a narrower focus, whether sectorally or geographically. For issues where national governments or international organizations are sufficiently mobilized, environmental information tends to be collected without UNEP's help. However, there remains a need for an international organization that takes the big picture into account, collecting baseline information before widespread concern develops, and with coverage that is global, not concentrated in spots of already-high capacity.

One prominent example is water. Several assessments have pointed to safe drinking water as one of the most pressing environmental issues facing the world.[22] Yet there are very poor data on access to water and water quality. The best water quality data are UNEP's, yet these are severely limited in coverage and comparability. Even for such a high-profile issue as deforestation, the availability of comparable, comprehensive data is quite spotty.

Given adequate resources, a reorientation of its staff, and improved technical capabilities, UNEP could fulfil its environmental information mandate far more effectively. Doing so would meet all the relevant criteria for what a streamlined UNEP ought to focus on – UNEP is good at it, the world needs it, and no one else is doing it.

Negotiation manager

As discussed above, UNEP has proven effective in initiating and managing the creation and expansion of international environmental agreements. If such roles were formalized, UNEP would become the acknowledged UN unit with responsibility for initiating and sustaining international negotiations, for facilitating agreements by lowering transaction costs, for managing negotiations toward stronger agreements, and for overseeing administration of the agreements by the individual secretariats. By focusing on treaty development and eliminating many other activities, UNEP could build upon past strengths and provide clarity within the international community regarding which organization would be responsible for these tasks.[23]

Global environment coordinator and catalyst

The international system clearly needs a greater degree of coordination with regard to the international environmental agenda than is currently being provided. The benefits from improved coordination would include the following.

- Systematic assessments of how well the international agenda meets global needs. The status quo favours attention to a few high-profile conventions (especially the UNFCCC) without regard to the merits of contending issues.
- More efficient division of labour among international agencies. The status quo encourages redundancy as agencies compete with each other for a share of limited resources.
- Exploration of potential zones of agreement that cut across issues. The status quo has the potential for individual issues to reach dead ends.
- Consideration of potentially useful linkages across sectors in the international system (for example, linking trade, aid, and environment). The status quo makes such linkage hard because environmental issues cannot compete on equal footing with economic issues.

UNEP possesses the potential to play a greater role in providing such coordination than it has in the past. The Internal Oversight Services assessment concluded that helping to coordinate the activities of the various convention secretariats should be a major focus for UNEP. More ambitiously, the Brundtland Commission in 1987 explicitly concluded that "UNEP's catalytic and coordinating role in the UN system can and should be reinforced and extended" (WCED 1987, 321). The recent revision of UNEP's governance structure, which created a "High-level Committee of Ministers and Officials in Charge of the Environment," is a step in the right direction.[24] This new body, which will meet once a year to provide guidance to the Governing Council and the ED, will give member states a more direct role in UNEP's steering function and permit UNEP to play a more direct role in coordinating the international environmental agenda. Finally, the 1998 Report of the Secretary-General's Task Force on Environment and Human Settlements called for the establishment of a UN system-wide Environmental Management Group to be chaired by the ED of UNEP, a system that could enhance UNEP's coordinating influence (UN 1998a).

However, there are other pressures mitigating greater levels of coordination, and UNEP should therefore enter such waters cautiously. Coordination appeals to actors who focus on overall public goods and who consider the sorts of benefits enumerated above to be paramount. However, actors with narrower interests at stake often dominate the environmental agenda. For many national governments and international agencies, public interests compete with private interests, most of which centre around competitive pressures for influence and shares of resources. For that reason, governments and agencies often undermine efforts at effective coordination because it would threaten their ability to reap private benefits.[25] Indeed, there are signs that some governments and agencies may not want significantly greater coordination. They place the secretariats of new international conventions far apart. They lodge few complaints regarding the failure of the CSD to develop a workable agenda. And they blithely accept the creation of new international bodies (such as the GEF and the CSD) when concern for coordination would dictate more caution about avoiding redundancy and overlap.

It could be a mistake, therefore, for a streamlined UNEP to devote the bulk of its resources to serving a coordinating and catalytic role without a clear, strong, and well-financed consensus within the UN system and the international community as a whole that it should do so. There are things UNEP can and should do in this area without such a commitment but it is probably close to the limit of its potential, especially as compared to the information and negotiation-management functions.

Creating a "super-UNEP" or "World Environment Organization"

The rationale for radically reshaping UNEP into a body with much greater financial resources, with the ability to make broad policy decisions more easily and effectively, and with more clout among national governments and other UN agencies has gained adherents over the past few years. Sometimes this proposal appears explicitly as a recommendation for converting UNEP into such an organization (UNEP 1996c). Other times the proposal envisions a new organization to which UNEP would be subordinate.[26] In terms of evaluating the merits of such an organization, the two variants can be considered together. While there are non-trivial strategic considerations involved in choosing between a "super-UNEP" or a new "World Environmental Organization," these considerations have more to do with the political calculus of how best to arrive at a powerful environmental organization. Both variants of this proposal envision a similar organization fulfilling similar functions.

Proponents of this vision believe that there are significant benefits in greater coordination. They also find UNEP incapable of providing those benefits as currently structured because it is too weak to contend successfully with more powerful pressures resisting coordination. Therefore, the logical route to effective coordination lies in the creation of a much stronger environmental body. This argument is not without merit.

At the same time, however, there are good reasons to believe that a super-UNEP or World Environmental Organization would fail to live up to the expectations of its proponents. These reasons can be understood by some explicit reflection about the Bretton Woods institutions that are in many ways a model for such proposals. Two key factors help explain the effectiveness of the Bretton Woods institutions. First, there was and continues to be a rough consensus on both the goals of these institutions (Western-style economic development) and the means to achieve them (following precepts of neoclassical economics). To be sure, there is disagreement and debate over these issues, but when looking at the big picture it is striking how much agreement exists. Second, political power is not divided equally in these institutions, but instead concentrated in the wealthiest nations (mainly by linking decision-making power to the size of financial contributions).

Any World Environmental Organization would lack these facilitating conditions. There would probably be no operating consensus on either goals or means. Instead, as is clear to many observers of efforts to implement Agenda 21, there would be continued disagreement over an enormous range of issues, masked only superficially by a bland common commitment to "sustainable development." And it is virtually unthinkable that any new global environmental agency that desired broad membership would be able to adopt a decision-making procedure that did not spread political power more evenly across nations. Taken together, these two conditions would hamstring a World Environmental Organization with a tendency to get bogged down in self-serving disputes over ends and means, and with an inability to make use of effective leadership to overcome stalemates. While creative leaders might make occasional good use of a World Environmental Organization, as Tolba did at times with UNEP, it is clear nonetheless that such an organization would not operate as effectively as the Bretton Woods institutions that inspired its form.

Preliminary judgements: Three requirements for success

As mentioned in the introduction, this chapter does not offer a judgement about which option for change is best, but seeks instead to frame the choices clearly. Each option emphasizes a particular function or package of functions on which UNEP should concentrate while jettisoning others. For the first it is providing policy-relevant information and interpretations of information. For the second it is initiating and managing new agreements. For the third it is steering the international agenda and brokering agreements among weakly coordinated actors. The fourth option encompasses the functions of the first three and adds the additional functions of providing the capacity to produce authoritative collective decisions and provide compliance procedures broadly conceived.

The merits of these and other proposals are likely to be debated for some time. Trial balloons and trial programmes will be developed, but the final resolution of UNEP's status, UNEP's role, and the proper organization of institutions involved in international environmental management – a system that already includes the CSD, the FAO, the GEF, the UNDP, UNEP, the World Bank, treaty secretariats, and others – will take some time. This debate should be judged by evaluating four specific questions: how serious is the need within the international community for the functions UNEP is asked to perform; how well has UNEP performed those specific functions in the past; how effectively might other organizations be able to provide these functions if UNEP does not; and will UNEP have the full support, clear mandate, and necessary resources to carry out these functions successfully?

Again, although this chapter does not advocate specific policy changes, preliminary evidence suggests that UNEP should narrow its operations to focus almost exclusively on information gathering, dissemination, and analysis; negotiation management; and a quite limited amount of system-level coordination. Focusing on these roles would help clarify UNEP's place within the UN system and could prove the most productive in contributing to the management of global environmental problems. It would also build upon UNEP's existing strengths, its past successes, and its 27 years of institutional momentum, advantages lacking in the CSD, one of UNEP's chief competitors. However, for UNEP to survive and function effectively in any of these roles several changes must occur.

Putting UNEP on a more secure financial footing

Whatever rationale there may have been for restricting UNEP to largely voluntary contributions made on a biennial basis (and that rationale was always weak on merits), this arrangement is clearly counterproductive for any constructive scenario of UNEP's future. Turning UNEP into a specialized agency could have the desired effect of requiring mandatory contributions. However, there will be strong pressures against such a move, as there have been throughout UNEP's history. The other agencies always resisted proposals to put UNEP on a more equal footing, and over the past five years have improved their track records in environmental issues enough to give them strong ammunition to counter any review of the question.

However, it is possible to give UNEP far more financial security without turning it into a specialized agency. The simplest strategy would be to negotiate a legal agreement making members' contributions to UNEP's Environment Fund legally binding. This is a commonly used device. For example, the European Monitoring and Evaluation Programme, a subsidiary body of the Convention on Long-range Transboundary Air Pollution, is financed through a 1984 protocol to LRTAP. While such protocols improve on strictly voluntary contributions by making payments legally binding, the common practice of countries falling into arrears on required contributions makes it an imperfect strategy. There is talk of creating new, more automatic mechanisms for financing international environmental measures. However, most observers consider their adoption unlikely in the short term, and the specialized agencies will surely fight to obtain their own access to such resources.[27]

Relocating UNEP headquarters physically or virtually

UNEP was located in Nairobi as part of the political bargain that made its creation possible.[28] There was never a strong expectation that such a setting would be a boost to the organization's effectiveness. In fact, some argue that it makes more sense to believe that UNEP's founders, overall, hoped that the Nairobi location would keep the organization marginalized and weak (Von Moltke 1996, 57). There are by now good reasons for revisiting the consequences of that decision. For UNEP to play a more effective role as an information provider, negotiation manager, and coordinating broker among multiple organizations and stakeholders, it must have better communications links (both electronic and transport) and perhaps be physically closer to secretariats and other bodies.

Moving UNEP may be impossible politically and there are significant political benefits in maintaining its headquarters in a developing country. However, any hope of improving UNEP must include a massive improvement in its electronic communications. UNEP should be provided with state-of-the-art satellite communications systems so that it can have easy, reliable, and inexpensive-to-operate data, voice, and visual communications with the rest of the world. The troubles associated with UNEP's current location may or may not be sufficient arguments to move its headquarters, but they are clearly sufficient arguments to upgrade UNEP's facilities.

Developing a clear and accepted mandate

Whatever plan is agreed upon regarding UNEP's future, it will not succeed unless the UN system and the international community as a whole agree on UNEP's new mandate. The new structure must be clear, broadly supported, and fully implementable. This means that UNEP and only UNEP will be primarily responsible for the tasks to which it is assigned. Other institutions will have to accept that UNEP will be given some of their former responsibilities in exchange for assuming some of UNEP's. The Secretary-General and the major donors will have to agree to implement fully and maintain the new organizational structure for a sufficient amount of time to allow evaluation of its impact. Without such full support, any changes to UNEP's operational focus will fail to overcome the challenges facing the organization and UNEP will continue to wither and eventually expire.

Conclusion: UNEP at a turning point

UNEP faces a series of challenges that threaten its continued relevance to international environmental management. These include a tremendous expansion in the agenda and organizational structure of environmental politics; competition from larger, better financed, and more effectively located institutions; the absence of a clear focus and mission; chronic financial shortfalls; problems of location; and management difficulties.

Despite these threats, UNEP's past successes as an information provider and negotiation catalyst and coordinator argue for the value of saving the organization. This chapter does not go so far as to recommend a particular package of reforms. However, the authors believe that preliminary evidence suggests the most productive measures would centre on narrowing UNEP's operations to focus almost exclusively on information gathering, dissemination, and analysis; negotiation management; and a quite limited amount of system-level coordination. Other activities would be jettisoned and new resources and expertise obtained to concentrate on the smaller set of tasks. For this transformation to occur successfully, however, UNEP's facilities would have to be significantly upgraded, its chronic financial difficulties would have to be resolved, and, perhaps most importantly, it would have to receive a clear and broadly accepted mandate from the UN system and the international community.

Notes

1. See, for example, the Report of the UN Task Force on Environment and Human Settlements (UN 1998a; Töpfer 1998); the report of the Secretary-General on implementing conventions related to environment and sustainable development (UN 1998d); the special session of the UNEP Governing Council on the subject in May 1998 (UNEP 1998b, and related information at the UNEP website ⟨http://www.unep.org⟩); and the relevant discussion during the Fifty-third UN General Assembly (UN 1998b; 1998c) and during the Twentieth Session of the UNEP Governing Council in February 1999.
2. General discussions of UNEP and its history include Haas 1995; McDonald 1990; UNEP 1998a; and the information contain on UNEP's homepage ⟨http://www.unep.org⟩. Broader discussions of the management of environmental issues within the UN system as a whole, including UNEP's history and role, include Thacher 1992; Birnie and Boyle 1992, 32–64, especially 39–53; Birnie 1993; French 1995b; Von Moltke 1996.

3. Sixteen countries are from the African Group (the informal name given to UN member states from Africa for the purpose of distributing appointments an a geographic basis), 13 from the Asia and Pacific Group, six from the Eastern European Group, 10 from the Latin America and Caribbean Group, and 13 from the Western Europe and Others Group (which includes Australia, Canada, New Zealand, the United States, and Western European countries).

4. Representative references include McCormick 1989, 110.

5. See, for example, ⟨http://www.unep.org/unep/about.htm⟩ viewed on 18 November 1998.

6. See Pamela Chasek's chapter in this volume.

7. Habitat is also located in Nairobi on the same campus with UNEP.

8. This summary reflects years of private conversations with UNEP officials and other individuals involved in international environmental policy-making and implementation.

9. In addition to Downie's extensive personal experiences in this regard, travel and communications difficulties are a common complaint of UNEP officials and many who interact with the organization. Indeed, officials in different UNEP offices complain about the difficulty and expense of even exchanging faxes with colleagues in North America, South America, Europe, and Asia.

10. In addition to the information obtained in personal communications, examples include the public clashes between UNEP headquarters and the secretariat of the Convention on Biological Diversity, and the regular difficulties approving budgets.

11. This is a common observation about Tolba. See, for example, Imber 1994, 77.

12. Although such comments were once very rare, observers now discuss this as a possibility. See, for one example, Pearce 1997, 11.

13. While claims that UNEP played vital roles in performing these functions are so commonplace as to be practically banal, the authors are not aware of any effort to assess their validity systematically. Certainly enough evidence exists from particular cases, such as the Mediterranean Action Plan, the Montreal Protocol, and efforts to control hazardous chemicals, to make the claims plausible. But it has not yet been demonstrated how different the world would have been if UNEP had not been present to play these roles.

14. See, for example, the assessments summarized in McCormick 1989, 123.

15. For a broader discussion of the European acid rain regime, including UNEP's contribution, see Levy 1993.

16. For a broader discussion of UNEP's regional seas programme see Haas 1991. For a detailed discussion of the Mediterranean Action Plan see Haas 1990.

17. For discussions of the creation, expansion, impact, and reputation of the Montreal Protocol, including details of UNEP's contributions, see Downie 1990; Benedick 1991; Haas 1992; Parson 1993; Downie 1996. A specific discussion of UNEP's role as outlined in this section can be found in Downie 1995.

18. These early efforts helped to produce the "World Plan of Action on the Ozone Layer," the "Coordinating Committee on the Ozone Layer," and, in 1982, the start of formal global negotiations.

19. For information on the POPs negotiations see Downie 1999, and the UNEP Chemicals homepage ⟨http://irptc.unep.ch/pops/⟩.

20. See the discussion by Pamela Chasek in this volume.

21. For more discussion see Downie 1996, 286–287 and 348–350; Downie 1995, 178–179; Litfin 1994, 112–113.

22. See, for example, World Bank 1992 or the Comprehensive Freshwater Assessment at ⟨gopher://gopher.un.org:70/00/esc/cn17/1997/off/97 – 9.EN⟩.

23. Such a role would not be without challenges. Many of the previous successes in this area can in some ways be traced to Tolba's influence and it could be difficult, although not

impossible, to institutionalize successful negotiation management. Also, relationships between UNEP and the individual treaty secretariats have been testy at times. However, such troubles do not eliminate the very real benefits to be gained from a single organization having the responsibility to help coordinate their activities.

24. This change was approved at the nineteenth session of UNEP's Governing Council, which ended on 9 April 1997.

25. A clear example of this pattern is seen in Connolly, Gutner, and Bedarff 1996.

26. For example, see the proposal by Brazil, Germany, Singapore, and South Africa, discussed in Deen 1997. For an extended argument for such a body, see Esty 1994, 73–98.

27. Some mechanisms for automatic financing, for example taxes on international financial transactions, are reviewed in French 1995a and French 1995b.

28. The Stockholm Conference did not determine where the UNEP Secretariat should be located, instead putting the decision into the hands of the General Assembly. However, third world delegations made it clear that they wanted the secretariat located in a developing country, arguing that no UN agency had yet been headquartered in a developing country. By the time the General Assembly session started in September, five front-runners had emerged (from the 13 countries that had requested to host UNEP): Austria, India, Kenya, Switzerland, and the United States. Developing countries feared that a split between their final candidates would result in the organization being placed in Europe or the United States. As part of the political manoeuvering, the Kenyan government informed India that if India did not withdraw its proposal, Kenya would expel all Indians from Kenya. Since Uganda, under Idi Amin, had taken similar action only a few years before, the threat was taken seriously. India withdrew, and when the issue went to a vote in the General Assembly, the united bloc of developing countries handily overcame the numerically inferior and still split voting bloc of developed countries (McDonald 1990).

REFERENCES

Benedick, R. E. 1991. *Ozone Diplomacy: New Directions in Safeguarding the Planet.* Cambridge, MA: Harvard University Press.

Birnie, P. W. 1993. "The UN and the Environment." In *United Nations, Divided World*, eds A. Roberts and B. Kingsbury. New York: Oxford University Press.

Birnie, P. W. and A. E. Boyle. 1992. *International Law and the Environment.* Oxford: Oxford University Press.

Connolly, B., T. Gutner, and H. Bedarff. 1996. "Organizational Inertia and Environmental Assistance to Eastern Europe." In *Institutions for Environmental Aid*, eds R. O. Keohane and M. A. Levy. Cambridge, MA: MIT Press.

Deen, T. 1997. "Environment-UN: New Global Green Body Proposed." Inter Press Service, 25 June.

Downie, D. L. 1990. "Descendants of the Montreal Protocol: Clues to the Causes of International Cooperation and Regime Change." Presented at the annual meeting of the Southern Political Science Association, November, Atlanta, Georgia.

Downie, D. L. 1995. "UNEP and the Montreal Protocol: New Roles for International Organizations in Regime Creation and Change." In *International*

Organizations and Environmental Policy, eds R. V. Bartlett, P. Kurian, and M. Malik. Westport: Greenwood Press.

Downie, D. L. 1996. *Understanding International Environmental Cooperation: Lessons from the Ozone Regime*. Doctoral dissertation, University of North Carolina, Chapel Hill.

Downie, D. L. 1999. "POPs Puzzles: Conflicts of Interest and Theory in Creating a New Regime." Presented at the annual meeting of the International Studies Association, 16–20 February, Washington.

Esty, D. C. 1994. *Greening the GATT: Trade, Environment, and the Future*. Washington: Institute for International Economics.

French, H. F. 1995a. "Forging a New Global Partnership." In *State of the World, 1995* ed. L. R. Brown. Washington: Worldwatch Institute.

French, H. F. 1995b. *Partnership for the Planet: An Environmental Agenda for the United Nations*. Worldwatch Paper 126. Washington: Worldwatch Institute.

Haas, P. M. 1990. *Saving the Mediterranean: The Politics of International Environmental Cooperation*. New York: Columbia University Press.

Haas, P. M. 1991. "Save the Seas: UNEP's Regional Seas Programme and the Coordination of Regional Pollution Control Efforts." In *Ocean Yearbook Vol. 9*, eds E. M. Borgese, N. Ginsburg, and J. R. Morgan. Chicago: University of Chicago Press.

Haas, P. M. 1992. "Banning Chlorofluorocarbons: Epistemic Community Efforts to Protect Stratospheric Ozone." *International Organization* 46: 187–224.

Haas, P. M. 1995. "United Nations Environment Programme." In *Conservation and Environmentalism: An Encyclopedia*, ed. Robert Paehlke. New York: Garland Publishing.

Imber, M. F. 1994. *Environment, Security and UN Reform*. New York: St. Martin's Press.

Levy, M. A. 1993. "European Acid Rain: The Power of Tote-Board Diplomacy." In *Institutions for the Earth: Sources of Effective International Environmental Protection*, eds P. M. Haas, R. O. Keohane, and M. A. Levy. Cambridge, MA: MIT Press.

Litfin, K. T. 1994. *Ozone Discourse: Science and Politics in Global Environmental Cooperation*. New York: Columbia University Press.

McCormick, J. 1989. *Reclaiming Paradise: The Global Environmental Movement*. Bloomington: Belhaven.

McDonald, J. W. 1990. "Global Environmental Negotiations: The 1972 Stockholm Conference and Lessons for the Future." American Academy of Diplomacy Occasional Paper OP-S (January).

Parson, E. 1993. "Protecting the Ozone Layer." In *Institutions for the Earth: Sources of Effective International Environmental Protection*, eds P. M. Haas, R. O. Keohane, and M. A. Levy. Cambridge, MA: MIT Press.

Pearce, F. 1997. "Environment Body goes to Pieces." *New Scientist*, 15 February.

Thacher, P. S. 1992. "The Role of the United Nations." In *The International Politics of the Environment*, eds A. Hurrell and B. Kingsbury. Oxford: Oxford University Press.

Töpfer, K. 1998. *United Nations Task Force on Environment and Human Settlements*. Nairobi: UNEP.

UN (United Nations). 1997a. "Review and Appraisal of the Implementation of Agenda 21: Contribution of the United Nations Environment Programme to the Special Session." United Nations document A/S-19/5. Internet ⟨gopher://gopher.un.org/00/ga/docs/S-19/plenary/As19–5.EN⟩ (visited 11 November 1998).

UN (United Nations). 1997b. "Note by the Secretary-General" prepared for Fifty-first session of the General Assembly, Agenda Items 112 and 141, "Review of the Efficiency of the Administrative and Financial Functioning of the United Nations," and "Report of the Office of Internal Oversight Services on the Review of the United Nations Environment Programme and the Administrative Practices of its Secretariat, including the United Nations Office at Nairobi." Document A/51/810.

UN (United Nations). 1998a. "Environment and Human Settlements: Report of the Secretary-General." Document A/53/463.

UN (United Nations). 1998b. "Environment and Sustainable Development: Report of the Second Committee." Document A/53/609/Add.6.

UN (United Nations). 1998c. "General Assembly Fifty-third Session, Agenda Item 30: UN Reform: Proposal and Measures. Report of the Secretary-General on Environment and Human Settlements. Detailed Debate." Unpublished mimeo.

UN (United Nations). 1998d. "Ways and Means of Undertaking the Review of Progress made in Implementing Conventions Related to Sustainable Development: Report of the Secretary-General." Document A/53/477.

UNEP (United Nations Environment Programme). 1996a. "Revised Proposals for 1996–1997 and Proposals for 1998–1999" (prepared for Nineteenth Session, Nairobi, 17 January–7 February 1997, Item 7 of provisional agenda, "The Environment Fund and Administrative and Other Budgetary Matters"). Document UNEP/GC.19/22.

UNEP (United Nations Environment Programme). 1996b. "Implementation by UNEP of Agenda 21: Note by the Executive Director" (prepared for Nineteenth Session, Nairobi, 17 January–7 February 1997, Item 5 of provisional agenda, "Preparations for the 1997 Review and Appraisal of Agenda 21"). Document UNEP/GC.19/INF.17.

UNEP (United Nations Environment Programme). 1996c. "Contribution of the Governing Council of the United Nations Environment Programme to the Special Session of the General Assembly in 1997" (prepared for Nineteenth Session, Nairobi, 17 January–7 February 1997, Item 5 of provisional agenda, "Preparations for the 1997 Review and Appraisal of Agenda 21"). Document UNEP/GC.19/30.

UNEP (United Nations Environment Programme). 1997. *Global Environmental Outlook*. New York: Oxford University Press.

UNEP (United Nations Environment Programme). 1998a. *From Action to Vision: UNEP since UNCED*. Nairobi: UNEP.

UNEP (United Nations Environment Programme). 1998b. "Report of the Governing Council on the Work of its Fifth Special Session, 20–22 May 1998." General Assembly, Official Records, Fifty-Third Session, Supplement No. 25. Document A/53/25.

UNEP Chemicals. 1998. "E-mail/Telefax Letter" from J. Willis, Director, UNEP Chemicals, 5 October 1998. Unpublished, author's files.

Von Moltke, K. 1996. "Why UNEP Matters." In *Green Globe Yearbook of International Cooperation on Environment and Development*. Oxford: Oxford University Press.

WCED (World Commission for Environment and Development). 1987. *Our Common Future*. Oxford: Oxford University Press.

World Bank. 1992. *World Development Report 1992: Development and the Environment*. New York: Oxford University Press.

19

The UN Commission on Sustainable Development: The first five years

Pamela S. Chasek

In 1992 the UN Conference on Environment and Development changed the international environmental agenda. For the first time, the UN system examined both environmental protection and economic development on an equal footing at the same conference. The results of the Earth Summit, as UNCED was popularly called, embodied in the global programme of action, Agenda 21, the Rio Declaration on Environment and Development, and the Non-legally Binding Authoritative Statement of Principles for a Global Consensus on the Management, Conservation, and Sustainable Development of All Types of Forests (the "Forest Principles"), tried to promote and operationalize this concept of sustainable development and change the way the international system looks at the relationship between the environment and economic development.

At the international level, the main responsibility for monitoring the implementation of the Rio accords and sustainable development fell to the Commission on Sustainable Development. This Commission, which was called for in Agenda 21 and established by UN Resolution 47/191 in December 1992, was given three broad responsibilities:

- to review progress at the international, regional, and national levels in the implementation of recommendations and commitments contained in the final documents of UNCED, namely Agenda 21, the Rio Declaration on Environment and Development, and the Forest Principles;
- to elaborate policy guidance and options for future activities to follow up UNCED and achieve sustainable development; and

- to promote dialogue and build partnerships for sustainable development with governments, the international community, and the major groups identified in Agenda 21 as key actors outside central government who have a major role to play in the transition towards sustainable development, including women, youth, indigenous peoples, NGOs, local authorities, workers' and trade unions, business and industry, the scientific community, and farmers, to ensure effective follow-up of UNCED (UN 1993a).

How well the Commission has succeeded in fulfilling its mandate and further advancing the sustainable development agenda is the subject of debate. While there are numerous ways to evaluate the success or failure of any organization, there are two major challenges in evaluating the work of the CSD. First, it is still a relatively young intergovernmental body without a significant track record. Second is the fact that the Commission is a different beast to everyone who is involved in or observes its work. Just like the three blind men who come across an elephant, each person who examines the work of the CSD has a different opinion as to what exactly we are talking about when we discuss the UN Commission on Sustainable Development.

With this in mind, the purpose of this chapter is to evaluate the work of the CSD during its first five years. The first part of the chapter will examine the history of the Commission and its work. The evaluation itself will examine the Commission's effectiveness in fulfilling its mandate, and its role in setting and coordinating the international sustainable development agenda. The chapter concludes with an examination of the overall strengths and weaknesses of the Commission, and policy recommendations aimed at strengthening the work of the CSD, including the need to streamline its agenda, encourage accountability and peer review, break out of the North-South schism, and mobilize greater political will at all levels.

History of the CSD

The CSD is one of the major institutional outcomes of UNCED, which was held in Rio de Janeiro, Brazil, in June 1992. Agenda 21 provided for the creation of the CSD in Chapter 38:

In order to ensure the effective follow-up of the conference, as well as to enhance international cooperation and rationalize the intergovernmental decision-making capacity for the integration of environment and development issues and to examine the progress in the implementation of Agenda 21 at the national, regional and international levels, a high-level Commission on Sustainable Development should be established in accordance with Article 68 of the Charter of the United Nations (UN 1992, 275).

Agreement in Rio about the creation of the CSD was achieved in spite of considerable opposition from many Northern governments, including the United Kingdom and the United States, who opposed on principle the creation of any new body in the UN system. This position was eventually overridden, in large part as a result of the persistence of a number of Southern and other Northern governments and a number of NGOs (Bigg and Dodds 1997). In the autumn of 1992, the Forty-seventh UN General Assembly debated the role and modalities of the CSD and, after much haggling, adopted Resolution 47/191, "Institutional arrangements to follow up the United Nations Conference on Environment and Development," which established the CSD as a functional commission of the Economic and Social Council (ECOSOC).

The Commission consists of 53 member states elected by ECOSOC for a three-year term with seats allocated on a regional basis: 13 for African states; 11 for Asian states; 10 for Latin American and Caribbean states; six for Eastern European states; and 13 for Western European and other states. One-third of the members are elected annually and outgoing members are eligible for re-election. Other states, organizations of the UN system, and accredited intergovernmental organizations and NGOs can attend as observers.

The Commission held its first substantive session in New York from 14 to 25 June 1993. Malaysian Ambassador Ismail Razali was elected chairman and presided over an exchange of information on the implementation of Agenda 21 at the national level. The CSD also adopted a Multi-Year Thematic Programme of Work for the period 1993–1997. This work programme integrated the 40 chapters of Agenda 21 into nine thematic clusters: (a) critical elements of sustainability (including trade and environment, sustainable consumption, combating poverty, demographic dynamics, and sustainability); (b) financial resources and mechanisms; (c) education, science, transfer of environmentally sound technologies, cooperation, and capacity-building; (d) decision-making structures; (e) roles of major groups; (f) health, human settlements, and fresh water; (g) land, desertification, forests, and biodiversity; (h) atmosphere, oceans, and all kinds of seas; and (i) toxic chemicals and hazardous wastes.

Clusters (a) to (e), which are broadly cross-sectoral in nature, were to be considered by the Commission annually, while clusters (f) to (i), which are sectoral in nature, were to be considered on a multi-year basis: (f) and (i) in 1994, (g) in 1995, and (h) in 1996. According to the work programme, in 1997 the Commission would conduct an overall review of the progress achieved in the implementation of Agenda 21 to prepare for the Nineteenth UN General Assembly Special Session (UNGASS) to assess progress in implementing Agenda 21.

At its first session, the Commission also recognized the need for intersessional work to address some of the more contentious issues that the CSD would discuss in 1994, namely finance and technology transfer. Delegates agreed to establish an "*ad hoc* open-ended intersessional working group" to be composed of government experts to assess and suggest specific measures to enhance the implementation of Agenda 21 in these two areas. The 1993 session of the CSD also set up reporting processes to channel information on efforts to implement Agenda 21 into the CSD for review; allowed a number of governments to offer to host meetings that addressed various parts of the CSD agenda; agreed on other matters involving financial assistance and technology transfer; and addressed progress made by various parts of the UN system towards incorporating Agenda 21 into their operations (Bigg and Dodds 1997; CSD 1993b).

The second session of the CSD was held from 16 to 27 May 1994, under the chairmanship of former German Environment Minister Dr Klaus Töpfer. Delegates widely acknowledged the need for effective intersessional work to prepare for the next session of the Commission and the CSD took the decision to extend the mandate of the intersessional working groups, so that one group would prepare for the 1995 discussion on land resource issues and the second group would focus on finance and technology transfer. There was much support for intersessional meetings hosted by governments and other organizations to address issues on the CSD's agenda. The 1994 session also adopted decisions on chemical safety; greater cooperation with governing bodies of international organizations, the Bretton Woods institutions, and the WTO; the need for better financing and technology transfer to support Agenda 21 implementation; and the need to change contemporary patterns of consumption and production that are detrimental to sustainable development.

With regard to the CSD's working methodology, delegates emphasized the importance of continuous exchange of information on practical experience gained by countries, organizations, and major groups; ongoing work on the elaboration of realistic and understandable sustainable development indicators that can supplement national reporting;[1] and the need for a dialogue-oriented approach, including the use of panel discussions and other means by which information could be shared and the expertise of a wide range of actors could be sought (Bigg and Dodds 1997; CSD 1994).

At its 1995 session, which met from 11 to 28 April 1995 under the chairmanship of former Brazilian Environment Minister Henrique Calvalcanti, the Commission held more dialogue sessions and panel discussions. Fifty-three countries produced national reports and more than 50 ministers and high-level officials attended the session. One of the most notable accomplishments was the establishment of the Intergovernmental

Panel on Forests to formulate options for action to support the management, conservation, and sustainable development of all types of forests and report back to the CSD in 1997. The Commission also established a work programme on consumption and production patterns; called for a review of the mechanisms for transferring environmentally sound technologies; agreed on a timetable for the formulation of sustainable development indicators; promoted an integrated approach to the planning and management of land resources; recognized the need to analyse the potential effects of environmentally related trade issues; recognized that poverty eradication is an indispensable requirement of sustainable development; and encouraged initiatives at the national and international levels, including action to phase out the use of leaded gasoline (Bigg and Dodds 1997; CSD 1995).

The fourth session of the CSD, chaired by Bulgarian Deputy Prime Minister and Minister for Economic Development Rumen Gechev, met from 18 April to 3 May 1996, completed its multi-year review of Agenda 21, and began to assess its own current and future role. As in 1995, there was a day dedicated to the work of major groups and more panel discussions. The CSD endorsed the Global Plan of Action on protecting the marine environment from land-based activities, which was adopted in November 1995. The Commission also urged governments to pilot the 126 indicators developed by the CSD Secretariat in conjunction with governments, UN agencies, and major groups. The CSD also addressed the relationship between the WTO provisions and trade measures for environmental purposes, including those relevant to multilateral environmental agreements (Bigg and Dodds 1997; CSD 1996).

The fifth session of the CSD, which met from 7 to 25 April 1997 under the leadership of Mostafa Tolba (Egypt), prepared a comprehensive document to be adopted by UNGASS in June 1997. Governments agreed that although some progress had been made in terms of institutional development, international consensus-building, public participation, and private sector actions, the global environment continues to deteriorate and the commitments in the UNCED agreements have not been fully implemented.

Five years after the Earth Summit in Rio, delegates reconvened in New York from 23 to 27 June 1997 for UNGASS to review the implementation of Agenda 21. This meeting served as a review and assessment of the work of the Commission, and how the UN system, governments, local authorities, NGOs, and international organizations were implementing key components of Agenda 21 and moving toward sustainable development. UNGASS delegates adopted a "Programme for the Further Implementation of Agenda 21" and called on the CSD to:

- make concerted efforts to attract greater involvement in its work by ministers and high-level national policy-makers responsible for specific economic and social sectors;
- continue to provide a forum for the exchange of national experiences and best practices in the area of sustainable development;
- provide a forum for the exchange of experiences on regional and subregional initiatives, and regional collaboration for sustainable development;
- establish closer interaction with international financial, development, and trade institutions.
- strengthen its interaction with representatives of major groups; and
- organize the implementation of its next multi-year programme of work in the most effective and productive way (Carpenter et al. 1997b, 10).

Delegates also agreed on a new five-year work plan, culminating with the next comprehensive review of progress achieved in the implementation of Agenda 21 in the year 2002.

Has the CSD accomplished its mission?

Unlike many functional commissions of ECOSOC, the CSD was given a very broad mandate and programme of work. Therefore, there is quite a lot of room for interpretation and evaluation of what the CSD has accomplished after its first five years. This section examines the Commission's effectiveness in accomplishing the three major goals of its mission, as set out by General Assembly Resolution 47/191.[2]

Review progress in the implementation of Agenda 21

On a purely technical level, the CSD's first multi-year programme of work reviewed the implementation of each chapter of Agenda 21, the Forest Principles, and, to a lesser extent, the Rio Declaration. Within this context, the CSD attempted to monitor implementation at the national, regional, and international levels. At the national level, the CSD assessed progress through the submission of national reports and the exchange of national experiences. From the beginning, governments had a number of concerns about national reporting. Many developing-country delegations stressed that this information should be voluntary, and that the Secretariat should not set guidelines or a standardized format for the reports. Members of the Group of 77 did not want anyone to examine the individual reports or make comparisons between them (Chasek, Goree, and Jordan 1993a). This was largely because developing countries did not want to create a situation where development aid would be linked to national reporting. Others, such as Australia and the Nordic countries, believed that the reports should be limited to the topics being discussed during a particular year and should be as concise as possible (Chasek, Goree, and Jordan 1993b).

While the final resolution adopted by the CSD (CSD 1993a) listed guidelines that the Secretariat should follow on preparing the information to be included in the analysis of national information, it is left to individual governments to decide on the degree of detail and regularity of their reporting to the CSD, thus maintaining the voluntary nature of national reporting (Bergesen and Botnen 1996). However, the reporting requirements proved to be too vague to facilitate a comprehensive reporting process. The Secretariat continued to work closely with governments to evaluate and improve the reporting process (Verheij and Pace 1997). However, although more countries have submitted reports each year, their contents are still difficult to compare and even harder to verify. Furthermore, the questions in the reports do not always address the issues that are most important, and it is not always clear what exactly the Secretariat wants to measure. The national reports submitted have been few in number, of uneven quality, and not always linked to the political debates among ministers within the Commission. The summaries produced by the Secretariat are based on insufficient coverage and presented in such general terms that it is impossible to draw meaningful conclusions from them. As a result, they appear to play a marginal role when the Commission meets (Bergesen and Botnen 1996).

On the positive side, the CSD has actually been able to move towards a crude form of peer group review by instituting the practice of having governments give presentations and allowing other governments and major groups to comment. Furthermore, the CSD has managed to gain greater acceptance for the use of indicators to monitor progress towards sustainable development. As part of the implementation of the Work Programme on Indicators of Sustainable Development adopted by the CSD at its third session in April 1995, a working list of 134 indicators and related methodology sheets has been developed and is now ready for voluntary testing at the national level. The aim of the CSD is to have an agreed set of indicators available for all countries to use by the year 2000.

With regard to reporting on progress in the implementation of Agenda 21 at the international level, the majority of UN agencies, organs, and programmes have incorporated relevant recommendations from Agenda 21 into their work programmes. Information on these activities has been provided to the CSD both in the form of special reports prepared by a specific agency and through the reports prepared by the task-manager system instituted by the Inter-Agency Committee on Sustainable Development (IACSD). A different UN agency or department is responsible for preparing, in collaboration with concerned organizations, coordinated inputs for the consolidated analytical reports of the Secretary-General, which will focus on common UN system strategies for the implementation of Agenda 21 and identify areas for further action for consideration by the CSD (UN 1993b).

Elaborate policy guidance and options for future activities

The CSD's record in elaborating policy guidance and options for future activities to follow up UNCED and achieve sustainable development is a mixed one. On the one hand, when one looks at the cumbersome and politicized mechanics of accomplishing anything within the UN system, it is hard to imagine how a body such as the CSD can come up with any real policy guidance at all. The CSD's hands are particularly tied on issues such as finance and technology transfer, where the North-South divide is as wide as ever.

Yet there are some areas where the CSD has been successful in providing policy guidance. The first is forests. The establishment of the Intergovernmental Panel on Forests (IPF) in 1995 is seen by many as a watershed event that has helped to focus the international dialogue on forests. Eleven intergovernmental processes supported the work of the IPF and over 200 comprehensive technical reports were prepared in conjunction with its work. The IPF's deliberations built international consensus and formulated approaches for action on the majority of issues under consideration.[3]

Another success story is the Comprehensive Freshwater Assessment. At its second session in 1994, the CSD requested preparation of a Comprehensive Assessment of the Freshwater Resources of the World, to be submitted at its fifth session in 1997. This assessment provides an overview of major water quantity and quality problems, with the aim of helping people understand the urgent need to deal with these issues before they become even more serious. In spite of its limitations, the available information provides the basis for a broad understanding of the problems facing various regions of the world, and of the nature and magnitude of the global implications of not dealing with these problems.[4] Furthermore, the assessment led the Commission to make fresh water one of its priority issues in the second five-year work programme.

While governments have identified new things that they want to do, the bigger question remains: "Is anyone listening?" Is the CSD having an impact outside of the UN basement? A number of NGOs believe that the CSD needs a more strategic process, including greater involvement of experts, national-level officials from the capitals, and stakeholders at the local level. While the CSD has succeeded in attracting far more NGOs, ministers, and representatives from national capitals than any other ECOSOC commission, the vast majority of delegates – especially those from developing countries – are diplomats. The job of the diplomat is to negotiate, not always to understand the technical issues under negotiation. The diplomats often do not consult their capitals or the people who actually understand various environmental and development problems. Thus, the CSD debates are often characterized by North-South rhetoric. According to members of the NGO community, if the CSD is to be truly effective in the area of providing policy guidance, there should be additional funding to support the attendance of people from capitals so as to move towards substance and away from rhetoric.

Promote dialogue and build partnerships for sustainable development

Of all three areas, the CSD seems to have best accomplished its goal of promoting dialogue and building partnerships for sustainable development between governments, the international community, and major groups.[5] One of the major accomplishments of the Rio process was the breakthrough in the participation of NGOs and other major groups. Their participation gives a real vitality to the work of the CSD, particularly through the convening of side events and dialogue sessions. Some have gone so far as to say that the CSD is the most successful commission in the UN system because of the fact that it promotes dialogue between governments, intergovernmental organizations, and major groups.

During CSD-5, for the first time, there were formal dialogue sessions between governments and each of the major groups. While not everyone was satisfied with these sessions, specifically with the fact that few government delegates participated and the way in which the results of the sessions were used by the Commission, they represented a significant step in institutionalizing major groups into the work of the Commission. The general purpose of these dialogue sessions is to bring a sense of reality into the CSD. Governments are not the only ones implementing Agenda 21 and working to achieve sustainable development. Each of the major groups is also a stakeholder, and has success stories to report and problems to bring to the table.

This partnership-building within the CSD has also had an effect on the domestic agenda in some states. The CSD is one of the few UN bodies capable of generating an NGO reaction or a backlash in national capitals. While not every country has NGO representatives present during the work of the CSD, those that do must watch their backs. If the NGOs do not like what their government representatives are saying, they will report on this to their constituencies at home, who will in turn put pressure on the government to explain or even change its position. In many UN bodies, governments have no one watching them and can say whatever they want, but not in the CSD. In the Commission there must be a delicate equilibrium between national interests, international role-play, and the domestic agenda. The NGOs have made sure of this.

Yet there are still some problems. First, not every major group is equally represented in the work of the Commission. While the dialogue with NGOs, women, and youth has improved – and with it an improvement in these groups' understanding of the process – the dialogue with some of the other groups has never really taken off. In the cases of other major groups, particularly business, indigenous peoples, farmers, and trade unions, the CSD is attracting members of umbrella organizations but not members of the actual groups. In other words, the "diplomats" for the sector are attending, rather than the rank-and-file membership. Finally, very few major groups from developing countries are represented at the CSD. Many of them cannot afford to attend or are unaware of the importance of the CSD. As a result, a certain amount of outreach to major groups is still necessary.

Second, in spite of the increased attendance of major groups at the CSD and the convening of dialogue sessions and other events, there is still concern that governments are not listening. While some major group representatives, especially members of the Women's Caucus, have become very effective at lobbying government delegates and ensuring that their views are represented in the decisions, many other major groups feel that although they contribute to sustainable development, they have little impact on the work of the CSD.

Finally, there are some government delegates who are concerned that major groups are no longer able to distinguish between their role as lobbyists and their lack of a role as decision-makers. No matter how much access is given to major groups at the CSD, they are still observers. The decisions rest with governments, who hopefully have the basis for making those decisions. Many major groups come to the CSD with inflated expectations. Instead of observing what is going on, reporting to their own constituencies, and trying to influence policy-makers at home, some major group representatives behave like UN diplomats and spend their time trying to influence the text under negotiation. Some government delegates argue that they must remember that a lot of advocacy work needs to be done at home. NGOs and major group representatives respond that advocacy work also has to be done at the CSD and, to have the greatest impact, they must participate in the drafting of text to the greatest extent possible. These issues regarding the appropriate role for major groups are now resonating throughout the entire UN system.

Critical assessment of the CSD

While the major focus of the CSD during its first five years was to monitor the implementation of the Rio agreements, its purpose is not only to look back to what has been accomplished since 1992. The CSD also has a role to play in setting the international sustainable development agenda and acting as a coordinating body within the UN system on environment and development issues. The Commission has had varying levels of success in these areas, but since the CSD is an intergovernmental body, the onus of responsibility ultimately rests in the hands of the member governments. In fact, unless its member governments are ready to act on a particular issue, the CSD will accomplish little. During its first five years the CSD did find that the time was ripe for governments to act in several areas and, as a result, the Commission can report some success. Yet, in far more cases, the CSD has not yet proven to be a major force outside the UN system.

Agenda-setting

Given its position as a highly visible and well-attended UN commission, the CSD has an opportunity to play a pivotal role in setting the international sustainable development agenda. But how does one measure the CSD's effect on agenda-setting? Has the CSD generated greater concern for an issue already on the international agenda? Has the CSD put any new issues on the international agenda? Has the CSD directed attention to the links between issues that were formerly considered separately? Has the CSD promoted more sophisticated priority-setting among the many issues on the international agenda?

   To a certain extent, some CSD delegates and observers believe that the Commission has been successful in generating greater concern for issues on the international sustainable development agenda. By creating the Intergovernmental Panel on Forests, the CSD was able to focus the forest issue and create more understanding that forests are owned by someone and give a livelihood to many people. Fresh water resources and energy are two issues that did not receive much attention in Rio and are now at the top of the international agenda (at least the CSD's agenda for the period 1998–2001), largely due to the work of the Commission. Similarly, the CSD's discussions on sustainable production and consumption patterns and the need for technology transfer, education, and capacity-building in developing countries have raised the profiles of these issues. However, when it comes to putting new issues on the international agenda, the CSD has not been as successful. Some argue that the CSD has put the issues of transport and tourism on the agenda, and has advanced the discussions on finance so that new issues such as private direct investment, airline fuel taxes, and a tax on foreign financial transactions have been added to the international sustainable development agenda. Others argue that UNEP has contributed and will continue to contribute much more to agenda-setting due to its scientific and technical capabilities. But given the wide range of sustainable-development-related issues that could be placed on the agenda, these issues are only the tip of the iceberg.

Perhaps the area where the CSD, which is a political rather than a technical body, can have the greatest impact in agenda-setting is in directing attention to links between issues and promoting more sophisticated priority-setting. In fact, many had hoped that this would be the primary role of the CSD. Yet the Commission has had only a modicum of success in these two areas. The CSD's first multi-year thematic programme of work was designed to try to draw out the links between related sectoral issues and address cross-sectoral issues in terms of the sectors under review. For example, during its 1995 session the CSD examined all the sectoral issues related to land resources (agriculture, forests, desertification, biodiversity, and mountains), and it was hoped that the cross-sectoral discussions on issues such as finance, technology transfer, consumption and production patterns, education, and capacity-building would be discussed in terms of land resources as well. While the Commission's intentions were admirable, its execution was not so successful. Governments continued to differentiate their statements and their negotiating strategies on both the cross-sectoral and sectoral issues. The debate on finance was rarely able to get beyond the call for new and additional financial resources and the achievement of the UN target of 0.7 per cent of GNP for official development assistance, much less focus on finance for a particular sector. This was due, in part, to the composition of government delegations and the lack of issue linkage at the national level.

The one area where there was some success in issue linkage was in some of the government-sponsored intersessional meetings. In many of these meetings, which provide expert input into the work of the CSD, participants have drawn out these linkages in finance, fresh water resources, forests, sustainable production and consumption, and other issues. However, while the results of these meetings are submitted to the CSD and become part of the official record, the level and quality of debate in the Commission rarely does justice to the work of these expert meetings. So, although linkages are being advanced outside the CSD, the intergovernmental political process has not yet been able to surmount the rhetoric to make the necessary progress in this aspect of agenda-setting.

During its first five years, the CSD can be described as having a marked lack of priorities, not to mention a lack of effectiveness in priority-setting. This was in large part due to the nature of the multi-year programme of work that stressed the overall review of the implementation of Agenda 21 over priority-setting. However, the Special Session of the General Assembly adopted a new multi-year programme of work for the CSD for the period 1998–2002 that does reflect both prioritization and a streamlining of its ambitious agenda. Each year the overriding issues will be poverty and consumption and production patterns. In 1998 the sectoral theme was "Strategic Approaches to Freshwater Management" and the cross-sectoral theme was to be transfer of technology, capacity-building, education, science, and awareness-raising. In 1999 the sectoral theme is oceans and seas and the cross-sectoral theme is consumption and production patterns. In 2000 the sectoral theme will be integrated planning and management of land resources and the cross-sectoral theme will be financial resources, trade, and investment and economic growth. The sectoral theme in 2001 will be atmosphere, energy, and transport and the cross-sectoral theme will be information for decision-making and participation and international cooperation for an enabling environment. The 2002 session is to complete a comprehensive review (UN 1997). For each sectoral and cross-sectoral theme different chapters of Agenda 21 have been identified as the main issues for an integrated discussion under the theme. The main question that remains is whether governments will be able to address these issues in a cross-sectoral, cross-ministry nature and focus on the stated priority issues. It is important to reiterate that the CSD is an intergovernmental body, and unless the individual governments have the political will to move the dialogue forward, the CSD will not be in any position to prioritize issues or set the international sustainable development agenda.

Overall, the CSD does not have a particularly strong record in agenda-setting. Examples of the areas where the Commission has played an agenda-setting role include the global fresh water assessment and the Intergovernmental Panel on Forests. The CSD has also identified areas where major gaps existed in the international discussion of sustainable development, including such sectors as energy, transport, and tourism. Nevertheless, the CSD's record in agenda-setting must also be viewed within the context of the Commission's overall purpose. Not everyone thinks that the CSD's role is to set the international agenda, and many agree that this is more of a job for UNEP. Perhaps the CSD is better placed to play more of an advocacy role – to put political pressure on national governments and the international system to respond to the challenges of sustainable development – rather than to set the agenda.

Role of the CSD as a coordinating body within the UN system

It was envisaged that implementation of Agenda 21 would require the active involvement of all relevant international institutions, both within and outside the UN system, that deal with specific economic, social, or environmental dimensions of sustainable development. However, the CSD was never seen as *the* body that would coordinate the work of the UN system. Instead, paragraph 38.13(a) of Agenda 21 gave the CSD a monitoring role, stating that the CSD should:

monitor progress in the implementation of Agenda 21 and activities related to the integration of environmental and developmental goals throughout the United Nations system through analysis and evaluation of reports from all relevant organs, organizations, programmes and institutions of the United Nations system dealing with various issues of environment and development, including those related to finance (UN 1992).

Similarly, paragraph 21 of UN General Assembly Resolution 47/191, which established the CSD:

requests all specialized agencies and related organizations of the United Nations system to strengthen and adjust their activities, programmes and medium-term plans, as appropriate, in line with Agenda 21, in particular regarding projects for promoting sustainable development, in accordance with paragraph 38.28 of Agenda 21, and make their reports on steps they have taken to give effect to this recommendation available to the Commission and the Economic and Social Council in 1993 or, at the latest, in 1994 (UN 1992).

This language leaves the onus of responsibility for implementing Agenda 21 with the relevant agencies themselves, although it does give the CSD the opportunity to review such actions. However, the real work at the inter-secretariat level has been led and coordinated through the Inter-Agency Committee on Sustainable Development (IACSD).

The IACSD was established in October 1993 by the Administrative Committee on Coordination (ACC) – the highest inter-agency body of the United Nations, chaired by the Secretary-General, and consisting of the heads of organizations in the UN system. The IACSD meets twice a year and reports to the ACC.[6] The role of the IACSD is to identify major policy issues relating to UNCED follow-up by the UN system, and to advise the ACC on ways and means of addressing them so as to ensure effective system-wide cooperation and coordination in the implementation of Agenda 21 and other UNCED outcomes, including the CSD, and their follow-up. To accomplish this, task managers have been appointed from the organizations of the UN system. They are responsible for inter-agency coordination, catalysing joint initiatives, identifying common strategies, preparing reports for the CSD, and exchanging information under the CSD's work programme (UN 1993c).

The UN Division for Sustainable Development provides secretariat services for both the CSD and the IACSD. As a result, the work of these two bodies – one intergovernmental and political and one inter-agency and functional – has been closely coordinated. Thus, the CSD is linked "both vertically and horizontally" to other parts of the UN system (Bigg and Dodds 1997, 21). Vertically, the Division for Sustainable Development reports to the Under-Secretary-General for Economic and Social Affairs,[7] who in turn assists the Secretary-General. Horizontally, it relates to UN agencies, programmes, and bodies, and takes part in the work of the IACSD.

While the primary responsibility for UN system coordination has rested with the IACSD, the CSD has had an impact on that inter-agency body and on the roles of the agencies in implementing Agenda 21. When it adopted its first multi-year thematic programme of work, the CSD created nine thematic clusters. The CSD originally introduced these thematic clusters to facilitate its own review of Agenda 21 implementation. However, these same clusters have been used to assess the capacity of UN agencies to contribute to Agenda 21 programming, and have been used by coordinating authorities to evaluate agency programming. Furthermore, the reports of the task managers have been presented and reviewed on the basis of these clusters in the CSD's multi-year thematic review process. Thus it could be said that the CSD has had an effect on coordination, since its multi-year thematic review procedure has permeated every aspect of the UN inter-agency coordination process (Henry 1996).

Strengths and weaknesses

Like any organization, the CSD has its own strengths and weaknesses that will have an impact on its future. The CSD has a number of strengths that have contributed to making it the unique body it is. To some degree, one can say that the strengths of the CSD are the same as the strengths of the United Nations as a whole: it is a forum that brings together all the countries of the world on an equal standing. However, the CSD's main strengths are in the ways it stands out from the rest of the UN system. Unlike the UN General Assembly and other bodies, there are fewer rigid formats and there is a truly open attitude about the participation of NGOs and major groups.

The CSD has also proven to be a real catalyst for policy action in numerous areas. Among other things, the CSD has motivated numerous government-sponsored meetings and workshops related to the implementation of Agenda 21; fostered coordination on sustainable development within the UN system; helped to defuse much of the resistance to national reporting that was evident in Rio; and galvanized NGO and major group activities and action aimed at sustainable development at the international, national, and local levels (Bernstein et al. 1995). Unlike many UN bodies, the CSD has attracted a mixture of ministers and fairly high-level NGOs on an annual basis. In addition, through its innovative working methods the CSD has managed to add vitality to the international sustainable development debate and keep the "spirit of Rio" and Agenda 21 alive. Many also credit the strong and committed Secretariat, which has been primarily responsibly for the preparation of comprehensive documentation, the development of sustainable development indicators, compilation of national reporting information, and integration of the work and contributions of major groups into the CSD process, with the success of the Commission. The commitment of the member governments, the Secretariat, the major groups, and the rest of the UN system has enabled the CSD to create a political forum with political leadership, as well as a space for new ideas, new thinking, and new forms of interaction between stakeholders and governments and between the local and global levels.

Nevertheless, like any organization, the CSD also has its weaknesses. A number of observers have commented that many of the decisions or resolutions adopted by the CSD are vague and not particularly action-oriented. Unfortunately, this is something that plagues much of the UN system. To build consensus in any multilateral negotiation process where there are so many disparate concerns to be met, sacrifices have to be made in order to reach an agreement. Perhaps the biggest obstacle to strengthening the CSD's decisions is the North-South schism over environment and development issues. Like many UN commissions or programmes that deal with economic development issues, the polarized positions of the 130 developing countries who negotiate as a bloc within the "Group of 77" and the developed countries have had a major impact on the work of the CSD. The Group of 77 continues to hold the entire sustainable development agenda hostage to fulfilment of developed country commitments to increase official development assistance and to provide, in general, "new and additional financial resources." As a result, much of the work of the CSD results in these "lowest common denominator" agreements.

The fact that the CSD is a subsidiary body of ECOSOC has given it an inherent weakness. The CSD's decisions have to be endorsed by ECO-

SOC and then forwarded on to the General Assembly. This serves to weaken the impact that the CSD can have on the international community and national governments. Furthermore, as a functional commission of ECOSOC the CSD does not have its own implementing process, nor any mechanisms to hold governments accountable.

While the CSD attracts many ministers each year, most are ministers of the environment. To be truly effective in setting the sustainable development agenda, the CSD must also attract and involve ministers of foreign affairs, finance, trade, agriculture, development or development assistance, forests, and so on. Similarly, the CSD does not garner the attention of the Bretton Woods institutions or the WTO to the level at which they should be involved. Finally, the CSD has given insufficient attention to the key linkages between environment and development issues. This is due in part to the fact that governments themselves are divided along sectoral lines, and that it is very difficult for the CSD to address an integrated agenda truly when the member governments are unable to do so.

Finally, there is the issue of the CSD's relationship to UNEP. Since its creation, there has been concern about the overlapping and duplicative functions of the CSD and UNEP. The fact that the two organizations have different mandates and different structures must not be forgotten. UNEP plays a more catalytic and scientific role than the CSD by identifying critical issues for international attention and mandating negotiations or discussions that can lead to treaties.[8] The CSD plays more of a coordinating role that is enhanced by the location of the Secretariat and the meetings at UN headquarters in New York, and the close cooperation with the IACSD and major groups. In fact, some have gone so far as to say that the CSD could eventually eclipse ECOSOC as the main coordinating and political body on economic, social, environmental, and development affairs. UNEP and the CSD should be able to co-exist if they focus on their inherent comparative advantages and strengths rather than compete with one another.

Final thoughts and recommendations for the future

So where does the CSD go from here? If any informal consensus exists on the future of the CSD, it is that the CSD definitely has a future. There is no question that the CSD has established itself as an essential part of the process for reviewing implementation of Agenda 21 and advancing the sustainable development agenda. Yet there are a number of ways in which the CSD can increase its effectiveness.

Streamline the agenda

Now that the first multi-year programme of work has come to a close, the CSD has taken the opportunity to streamline its agenda for the next five years. Rather than embarking on another comprehensive review of Agenda 21, the CSD will instead focus on a selected number of issues. In essence the CSD will try to fill in the gaps in the UN system where no single agency currently has responsibility, such as fresh water resources, oceans, energy, transportation, tourism, and sustainable production and consumption. Furthermore, the CSD will try to avoid duplicating any work that is currently under way in other forums, specifically the conferences of the parties to the major environmental conventions. Hopefully, this increased focus will in turn foster greater dialogue and more action-oriented proposals than the CSD has been able to generate thus far.

Encourage greater accountability and peer review

To increase the effectiveness of the CSD in both monitoring the implementation of Agenda 21 and advancing the international sustainable development agenda, governments must feel more accountable for their actions and this can be accomplished through a certain level of peer review. National reporting must be enhanced and countries should play a role in reviewing these reports. Developing countries should examine developing countries so as to avoid any North-South finger-pointing. Similarly, the CSD must continue to foster increased dialogue within countries (between ministries and between governments and major groups), between countries, between governments and the UN system, and among UN agencies and programmes.

Break out of the North-South schism

Ambassador Ismail Razali, President of the Fifty-first General Assembly, told UNEP's High-Level Segment in February 1997, "Agenda 21 and the CSD will only bring about sustainable, equitable, and ecologically sound development if we can break out of the North-South schism ... the real political challenge is to reshape North-South relations" (Razali 1997). The negotiations on finance during the CSD suggest that states are not only failing to break out of the North-South schism, but that the schism is increasingly polluting the UN's response to sustainable development with suspicion. For developing countries, the decline in overseas development assistance since 1992, and attempts during CSD-5 to switch the burden of international funding for sustainable development to private sector investment, which developed countries argue is a case of acknowledging actuality, have helped to discredit the very concept of "sustainable development" (Carpenter et al. 1997a). If both developed and developing countries can move beyond these issues, the CSD will become more effective at promoting policy dialogue. Until this happens, the North-South agenda will continue to dominate the sustainable development agenda.

Mobilize political will

If the CSD is to be truly successful, it must – in the words of former UN Secretary-General Boutros Boutros-Ghali – mobilize the "political will, intellectual leadership, and partnerships" necessary to transform sustainable development into policies and practices on the ground (Boutros-Ghali 1993). In other words, the CSD needs to oblige governments to take the necessary action at the international level, but perhaps more importantly at the national and local levels. Thus far, the CSD has made some progress in mobilizing the international community, governments, and major groups to advance the sustainable development agenda, but much more needs to be done. While dialogue is and should be the focus at the international level, action – and the political will needed to promote and support it – must take place at the national and local levels.

During its first five years, the CSD has managed to generate over 400 pages of negotiated text. But these are only words, and words they will remain until the CSD manages to translate them into action. Now, in the aftermath of the Special Session of the General Assembly that received its own mixed reviews, and at the beginning of a new five-year work programme, the CSD will need to increase its effectiveness and continue to develop new and innovative working methods to maintain its position at the centre of the sustainable development debate. As the *Earth Negotiations Bulletin* commented in its summary of CSD-5, the CSD must "deliver a renewed political mandate to translate popular concern into urgent and concrete instructions to politicians, translate the information-rich assessments into unequivocal action plans, and translate illusions of top-down sovereign authority and competence into partnerships that span a globalizing world" (Carpenter 1997a: 13).

Notes

1. This was considered to be a major accomplishment, since two years earlier in Rio many developing countries were not willing even to discuss the creation of sustainable development indicators for fear that their use would compromise national sovereignty over natural resources and the environment.

2. This evaluation of the first five years of the CSD is based on a review of the existing literature on the Commission as well as a series of interviews with UN, governmental, and non-governmental representatives who have participated in the work of the Commission since its establishment in 1992. The majority of the people interviewed asked that their comments be treated as "off the record." As a result, no one will be cited directly, but the author would like to thank the following people and institutions for their contributions: Oscar Avalle, GEF Secretariat, Gunilla Bjorkland, Stockholm Environment Institute, Felix Dodds, UNED-UK, Alison Drayton, Government of Guyana, Paul Hofseth, Government of Norway, Ambassador Bo Kjellén, Government of Sweden, Peter Padbury (Canada), Andrey Vasilyev, UN Division for Sustainable Development, and Marilyn Yakowitz, OECD.
3. For more information on the work of the IPF, see United Nations. "The Report of the Intergovernmental Panel on Forests on its Fourth Session" (E/CN.17/1997/12), 20 March 1997 ⟨gopher://gopher.un.org:70/00/esc/cn17/ipf/session4/97---12.EN⟩ (visited 15 January 1998).
4. The Comprehensive Freshwater Assessment (document E/CN.17/1997/9) can be found on the Internet at ⟨gopher://gopher.un.org:70/00/esc/cn17/1997/off/97--9.EN⟩ (visited 15 January 1998).
5. Major groups, as defined by Agenda 21, include women, youth, indigenous peoples, NGOs, local authorities, workers' and trade unions, business and industry, the scientific community, and farmers.
6. Participants in the work of the IACSD include the UN Department for Economic and Social Affairs, the UN Department for Development Support and Management Services, the UN Department for Economic and Social Information and Policy Analysis, the UN Office of Legal Affairs, the UN Department of Humanitarian Affairs, the UN Centre for Human Settlements, the Regional Economic Commissions, UNCTAD, UNEP, UNICEF, the UNDP, the UNFPA, the UN International Drug Control Programme, the UNHCR, the ILO, the FAO, UNESCO, the WHO, the World Bank, the IMF, the WMO, WIPO, UNIDO, the IAEA, and secretariats of the major environmental conventions.
7. Until mid-1997, the Division for Sustainable Development was a part of the Department for Policy Coordination and Sustainable Development. With the first phase of UN reform activities during the summer of 1997, the department's name was changed to the Department for Economic and Social Affairs.
8. See Downie and Levy's chapter on UNEP in this volume.

REFERENCES

Bergesen, H. O. and T. K. Botnen. 1996. "Sustainable Principles or Sustainable Institutions? The Long Way from UNCED to the Commission on Sustainable Development." *Forum for Development Studies* 1: 35–61.

Bernstein, J., P. Chasek, P. Doran, and V. Hulme. 1995. "Summary of the Third Session of the UN Commission on Sustainable Development: 11–28 April 1995." *Earth Negotiations Bulletin* 5(42).

Bigg, T. and F. Dodds. 1997. "The UN Commission on Sustainable Development." In *The Way Forward: Beyond Agenda 21*, ed. F. Dodds. London: Earthscan.

Boutros-Ghali, B. 1993. Speech before the UN General Assembly, New York (2 November). Quoted in J. Blumenfeld, "The United Nations Commission on Sustainable Development." *Environment* 36(10): 5.

Carpenter, C., P. Doran, K. Schmidt, and L. Wagner. 1997a. "Summary of the Fifth Session of the UN Commission on Sustainable Development: 8–25 April 1997." *Earth Negotiations Bulletin* 5(82).

Carpenter, C., P. Doran, K. Schmidt, and L. Wagner. 1997b. "Summary of the Nineteenth United Nations General Assembly Special Session to Review Implementation of Agenda 21: 23–27 June 1997." *Earth Negotiations Bulletin* 5(88).

Chasek, P., L. J. Goree VI, and R. Jordan. 1993a. "CSD Highlights: Tuesday, 15 June 1993." *Earth Negotiations Bulletin* 5(4).

Chasek, P., L. J. Goree VI, and R. Jordan. 1993b. "Summary of the First Session of the Commission on Sustainable Development: 14–25 June 1993." *Earth Negotiations Bulletin* 5(12).

CSD (Commission on Sustainable Development). 1993a. "Exchange of Information Regarding the Implementation of Agenda 21 at the National Level." (E/CN.17/1993/L.3/Rev.1) 22 June.

CSD (Commission on Sustainable Development). 1993b. "Report of the Commission on Sustainable Development on its First Session." (E/CN.17/1993/3/Add.1).

CSD (Commission on Sustainable Development). 1994. "Report of the Commission on Sustainable Development on its Second Session." (E/CN.17/1994/20).

CSD (Commission on Sustainable Development). 1995. "Report of the Commission on Sustainable Development on its Third Session." (E/CN.17/1995/36).

CSD (Commission on Sustainable Development). 1996. "Report of the Commission on Sustainable Development on its Fourth Session." (E/CN.17/1996/38).

Henry, R. 1996. "Adapting United Nations Agencies for Agenda 21: Programme Coordination and Organisational Reform." *Environmental Politics* 5(1): 1–24.

Razali, I. 1997. Speech to UNEP Governing Council, Nairobi, February.

UN (United Nations). 1992. "Institutional arrangements to follow up the United Nations Conference on Environment and Development." General Assembly Resolution 47/191. Internet ⟨gopher://gopher.un.org/00/ga/recs/47/191%09%09%2B⟩ (visited 25 August 1997).

UN (United Nations). 1993a. United Nations Department for Policy Coordination and Sustainable Development. "Terms of Reference: Commission on Sustainable Development." Internet ⟨http://www.un.org/dpcsd/dsd/csdback.htm⟩ (visited 25 August 1997).

UN (United Nations). 1993b. "Report on the Second Meeting of the Inter-Agency Committee on Sustainable Development" (ACC/1993/24). Internet ⟨gopher://gopher.un.org: 70/00/inter/iacsd/93-24.en⟩ (visited 15 January 1998).

UN (United Nations). 1993c. United Nations Department for Policy Coordination and Sustainable Development. "Terms of Reference: Inter-Agency Committee for Sustainable Development." Internet ⟨http://www.un.org/dpcsd/dsd/iacsdref.htm⟩ (visited 28 September 1997).

UN (United Nations). 1997. "Overall Review and Appraisal of the Implementation of Agenda 21: Report of the Ad Hoc Committee of the Whole of the Nineteenth Special Session." Document A/S-19/29.

Verheij, M. S. and W. R. Pace. 1997. "Reviewing the Spirit of Rio: The CSD, Agenda 21, and Earth Summit +5." Report published by the International NGO Task Group on Legal and Institutional Matters (INTGLIM).

20

The World Bank's environmental agenda

Mikiyasu Nakayama

At the 1997 UN General Assembly Special Session on the Environment, James D. Wolfensohn, the President of the World Bank, emphasized the following set of global environmental problems: climate change, biodiversity and sustainable forestry, desertification and land degradation, water, and ozone depletion (World Bank 1997a). He stated:

These [responses to global environmental issues] are not fringe activities. They are central to meeting human needs and reducing poverty. I wholeheartedly commit the Bank to do all it can to forge a global partnership to promote equitable approaches to global environmental issues, and to do so quickly. Time is not on our side. This agenda cannot afford to wait.

The World Bank consists of the International Bank for Reconstruction and Development (IBRD) and the International Development Association (IDA). The aim of the organization is to help its borrowers reduce poverty. The IBRD and the IDA make loans to borrower governments for projects and programmes that promote economic and social progress so that people may live better lives. The IBRD, established in 1945, lends only to credit-worthy borrowers and only for projects that promise high real rates of economic returns to the country. The IBRD borrows most of the money its lends in capital market across the globe. The IDA was established in 1960 to provide assistance to poorer developing countries that cannot meet the IBRD's near-commercial terms. The IDA provides credits to the poorest countries – those with an annual per capita GNP of US$785 or less. IDA credits carry no interest. Unlike the IBRD, most of the IDA's funds are contributed by developed countries (World Bank 1997c).

Environmentally sustainable development is one of the World Bank's fundamental objectives. The World Bank invests in projects with primarily environmental objectives, in addition to its regular investment portfolio. The World Bank is also an implementing agency of the Global Environment Facility (GEF) and the Multilateral Fund for the Montreal Protocol (MFMP), which are two important global financing mechanisms established to assist developing countries in addressing global environmental concerns (World Bank 1996).

Some of the projects funded by the World Bank in the past were criticized by environmentalists, even in the late 1960s, in terms of the World Bank's negligence over the environmental impacts of the projects it supported (Mikesell and Williams 1992). A review of 25 years of the World Bank's history (Mason and Asher 1973) suggested that environmental aspects external to the projects (such as increased incidence of waterborne disease resulting from projects that change the pattern of water distribution and usage) had not been seriously considered by the World Bank at the project preparation stage.

There is little doubt that the World Bank is much better prepared to work on environmental issues than it was a decade ago. The number of environmental staff members, both for development of environment-oriented projects and for review of ordinary lending projects from the environmental point of view, has increased from five in the mid-1980s to around 300 today. A vice-presidency for environmentally sustainable development was established in 1993. The World Bank is now the world's largest lender to the developing world for the environment. The World Bank's lending for environmental projects amounted to US$11.6 billion in the 1997 fiscal year, while it was just US$30 million in 1986 (World Bank 1997c).

Moreover, the World Bank has shown its willingness to "mainstream" global environmental concerns into its regular lending and non-lending service, and take a major intellectual and policy leadership role (World Bank 1997a).

An essential question that must be addressed is whether the existing mechanisms within the World Bank are adequate to deal with environmental issues, and what sort of room remains for the institution to further enhance its capacity. This chapter does not intend to touch upon all the environmental issues associated with the World Bank's activities. It rather aims at pointing out a few somewhat "generic" or institutional issues within the system of the World Bank in dealing with environmental matters. Three such issues will be discussed in the following sections.[1]

Upward harmonization or pollution displacement

There is no reason not to believe that a Bank-financed project is in general "cleaner" than other projects of the same sort in the developing world. For example, a World Bank document (World Bank 1995) mentions that the Bank-financed coal-fired thermal power plants implemented over the last ten years are significantly less carbon-intensive than the same sort of projects not financed by the World Bank. That is, the Bank-financed thermal power plants consume less carbon per unit of energy produced.

This difference is due largely to the environmental conditions attached to the Bank-financed projects. A loan agreement between the World Bank and a borrower is usually accompanied by conditions which the borrower is obliged to observe. Often, some of these conditions relate to environmental standards; an example would be emissions standards for a thermal power station. The standards specified tend to be more stringent than those that would hold domestically under other circumstances. As long as a borrower sticks to the conditions, Bank-financed projects are destined to be "cleaner" than others.

One of the major aims of applying tighter standards to a Bank-financed project is "upward harmonization" of environmental standards within a country, in that a Bank-financed project is supposed to serve as a vehicle to improve environmental standards in a developing nation. The idea is that if the World Bank were to compromise the level of standards in accordance with the borrower's perceived capacity, it may increase a risk of downward harmonization of standards, which leads to a deterioration of the environment in the developing world.

Is environmental conditionality really instrumental in improving environmental standards in developing countries? In other words, does the World Bank's model of "upward harmonization" work in practice?

The idea seems too optimistic, at least under some circumstances. Take a coal-fired thermal power plant as an example. In a large country which produces both "clean" and "dirty" coals, the government may selectively provide the Bank-financed power plant with "clean" coal, so that the power station can maintain the emission standards (such as SO_x and NO_x concentration) requested by the World Bank. In this case, "dirty" coal is fed into other power plants which are not subject to the tighter environmental standards. This "displacement of pollution" arrangement is, from the viewpoint of the government, the most cost-effective way of sticking to the conditions specified by the World Bank.

It is questionable, under such circumstances, whether the Bank-financed power station could function as a locomotive towards environmental "upward harmonization" in the country. A rather pessimistic scenario is that the government abandons the effort to provide the Bank-financed power plant selectively with "clean" coal as soon as the last World Bank evaluation mission has left the country. This viewpoint stems from the fact that the conditions attached to a particular project may provide little incentive for the borrower to apply the same "high standards" for the entire nation.

This problem is partly due to the fact that an ordinary environmental assessment (EA) does not examine "indirect" impacts of a particular project on the borrower as a whole: in this case, investigating whether a Bank-financed "clean project" could improve the "upward harmonization" within the same sector by providing the government with some incentives. The importance of "sectoral" EA has been stressed by the World Bank (World Bank 1995), so that environmental issues of a particular sector could be analysed in relation to policies, institutions, and development plans. However, even existing sectoral EA methodologies do not seem adequate to evaluate the impact of a Bank-financed project (with environmental conditions attached) on activities "downstream" of the sector in question.

Another important question to ask about environmental conditionality is whether the environmental requirements specified in a particular project are realistic for the borrower or not. In other words, have the conditions been developed in accordance with the institutional capacity of countries in the developing world and the availability of properly trained staff? Needless to say, the conditions attached to a project are unlikely to be adhered to if the borrower lacks sufficient human resources as well as institutional and legal frameworks.

Does the World Bank have enough working knowledge about the capacity of borrowers, to the extent that a rational judgement could be made about the feasibility of environmental conditions attached to a particular project (provided borrowers are sincerely willing to implement the conditions)? Only a limited number of sectoral EAs have been conducted within the framework of the World Bank's lending operation for a particular project (World Bank 1995), and it sounds too optimistic to believe that the World Bank has working knowledge about the institutional capacity of the borrower.

Attaching many conditions to a project does not necessarily lead to better environmental protection in the borrowing country than would a smaller number of conditions. Environmental conditions to be attached to a project should thus be based on sound grounds to believe that the borrower is willing to observe the conditions, hopefully even after completion of the project, and also equipped with sufficient human resources to implement them successfully.

For this purpose, the World Bank should conduct more sectoral EAs in a borrowing country to assess the capacity of the country in various sectors, and carefully examine whether the environmental conditions attached to a project are rational and implementable for the particular borrower.

Lack of mechanisms to deal with transboundary issues

There is reason to believe that the World Bank is now better equipped with mechanisms to deal with global environmental issues than it was, say, a decade ago. The GEF is the major instrument for this purpose.[2] It is a financial mechanism that provides grant and concessionary funding to recipient countries for projects and activities that address climate change, biological diversity, international waters, and depletion of the ozone layer. The GEF covers the difference (or increment) between the costs of a project undertaken with global environmental objectives in mind, and the costs of an alternative project that a country would have implemented in the absence of global environmental concerns. The World Bank management approved 70 projects in more than 50 countries, totalling GEF grant commitments of US$670 million, between the GEF's inception in 1991 and February 1997 (World Bank 1997b).

Are the GEF and other similar mechanisms sufficient to allow the World Bank to deal with various aspects of the global environment? Is the World Bank sufficiently prepared to tackle environmental issues, which are transboundary in nature, not necessarily "global," and could be solved only through the collaboration of related countries?

The latest list of the World Bank's environmental projects (World Bank 1997a) includes 85 projects under the category of the "Global Environment Facility Investment Work Programme." Of these, only seven projects are designated as "regional," two projects are under the "global" category, and all the rest are activities within a single country. To be more precise, the two "global" projects are the pilot phase and replenishment of the "Small and medium scale enterprise programme." Of seven "regional" projects, three are "Oil pollution management projects in seas," two are "Ship-generated waste management," and the remaining two projects concern "Community-based natural resource and wildlife management" and "Lake Victoria environmental management."

This list of "global" and "regional" projects suggests that issues which can only be solved with a regional and collaborative initiative have not yet been adequately addressed by the World Bank, even with the aid of the GEF.

This may stem from the fact that the World Bank system has been tailored, in principle, for planning and implementation of its lending operation. The lending operation is essentially a matter to be negotiated and agreed upon between one particular borrower and the World Bank. Mechanisms to deal with a "regional" issue, in which more than one country ought to be involved, are thus generally lacking within the system. It is also the case with environmental issues. The lack of such a mechanism is fatal in dealing with regional problems, which can only be solved through collaboration among countries in the region.

Take the transboundary water resources issue as an example. The water resources and related environment of the world are under enormous stress (GEF 1995). Though efficient use and effective conservation of water resources are required in various water systems, attaining such goals is difficult in international water bodies, because it requires cooperation among riparian countries. Riparian conflicts hamper the ability of many countries to utilize shared water resources optimally (Kirmani and Le Moigne 1997).

Some 60 per cent of the world's population live in the watershed of an international water system. The global community is thus in need of modalities to deal with international water bodies in a much better way, in terms of both water quantity and quality. As in armed conflicts among nations, international organizations are expected to serve as a mechanism to mitigate conflicts among riparian countries, with a view to more rational management of the shared water system. However, international organizations as a whole, let alone the World Bank, have so far had very limited success in serving such a function. In only a few exceptional cases, such as UNEP's initiative in formulation of the Zambezi Action Plan (adopted by riparian countries of the Zambezi River basin in 1987) and the UNDP's role as mediator among basin countries of the Mekong River in the early 1990s (towards a new framework of cooperation adopted in 1995 by riparians), were international organizations instrumental in the formulation of an agreement among basin countries (Nakayama 1997).

The Indus Water Treaty adopted in 1960 by India and Pakistan is still regarded as the only "success story" of the World Bank in transboundary fresh water bodies, in that the World Bank successfully acted as mediator between two riparian countries and that it let the riparian countries agree upon the ways and means of sharing the water resources of the Indus River. The World Bank has, however, made few direct interventions in international water affairs in the 37 years thereafter (Kirmani and Rangeley 1994).

The case of the Aral Sea basin may be a good example in this context. The World Bank (in practice) took over from UNEP in 1992 the leading role in dealing with the environmental disaster of the Aral Sea region. The activity was initiated by UNEP in 1989 in response to a request by the former Soviet Union. It was then expected that the World Bank could serve as a coordinator, both among basin countries and within the donor community, so that an integrated regional scheme would be developed and implemented to cope with the environmental disaster. The Aral Sea Basin Unit was established in the World Bank to administer certain donor funds and ensure international coordination. The progress thereafter has been, to say the least, not as fast as it was hoped to be. Though the lending operation of the World Bank was initiated in all the basin countries (former republics of the Soviet Union in Central Asia), the development of a regional environmental programme and its implementation to deal with the Aral Sea problem has experienced a substantial delay. In particular, the idea of the World Bank coordinating donors has encountered difficulties, and a planned meeting of donors was postponed by a few years. The meeting was at last organized in October 1997, though not as a "donors' meeting" but just as a "meeting of participating bodies."

The Aral Sea Basin Unit was abolished, even before the "meeting of participating bodies," without establishing a fully fledged action programme, with support from donors, to combat the environmental disaster. This partly stemmed from the lack of support for the activity of the Aral Sea Basin Unit from other operational units, presumably because developing lending operations could be conducted independently of the Aral Sea Basin Unit's efforts. In other words, there were only limited incentives within the World Bank to promote the initiatives of the Aral Sea Basin Unit as a flagship of the World Bank as a whole.

What is apparently lacking within the World Bank is a functioning mechanism to deal with environmental issues of a transboundary nature, with due support from other operational units. In this context, could an ad hoc mechanism such as the now-defunct Aral Sea Basin Unit really be functional and instrumental? The institutional framework of the World Bank has been optimized for country-by-country lending operations. It thus generally lacks built-in incentives within the system to work on regional issues, as shown by the project portfolio of the past GEF projects.

A rational answer to this issue is establishing a new (and not ad hoc) built-in institutional framework to deal with transboundary issues. However, the feasibility and/or desirability of establishing such a mechanism should be judged from various viewpoints. For example, promoting regional collaboration (for the sake of a transboundary environmental problem) may let the World Bank use ordinary lending projects either as "carrot" or "stick," as was in practice the case with the World Bank's "success story" in the Indus River basin (Nakayama 1997). Conducting such an operation for the purpose of solving transboundary environmental issues may provoke a burning controversy both within and outside of the World Bank, for it would constitute a major departure from the present World Bank mode of operation.

The role of the World Bank as an international organization should therefore be re-examined in this regard; namely whether the World Bank is really the best actor (among various international institutions) to deal with transboundary environmental issues.

Environmental assessment for programme lending

The staff of the World Bank have been required, since 1989, to classify all proposed investment projects in accordance with their potential impacts on the environment. The classification depends on the type, location, sensitivity, scale, nature, and magnitude of potential impacts. Category A projects are supposed to have significant, irreversible impacts on environments that are sensitive and diverse (World Bank 1997a). The projects under this category are subject to a full EA. Category B projects may have less significant impacts than those under Category A, and few if any of the impacts are irreversible. An EA is not mandatory for Category C projects, which are supposed not to have adverse environmental effects.

Of 598 projects screened by the World Bank between 1993 and 1995 for their potential environmental impacts, 67 projects (11 per cent) were classified as Category A, 242 (40 per cent) projects were classified as Category B, and the remaining 289 projects (48 per cent) were classified as Category C (World Bank 1995). Category A projects were concentrated in the agriculture, energy and power, transport, urban, and water and sanitation sectors.

It is remarkable that all the 19 Category A projects approved by the World Bank (IBRD/IDA in this case) are "project" type of lending, and no "programme" lending falls under this category. The programme lending in this context represents loans for structural reform and sector reform, commonly known as structural adjustment loans (SALs).

Most of the World Bank's loans are for specific projects. However, under the assumption, which is based on past experiences, that projects have a high rate of failure in an unstable or distorted economic environment, the World Bank initiated the SAL for borrowers in the early 1980s. The SAL is designed to support basic changes in economic, financial, and other policies; these may include a greater reliance on market forces; reduced government price interventions and subsidies; limits on public sector involvement in industrial and agricultural production; a better business environment and greater reliance on the private sector; a more open trading system to provide a better yardstick for efficiency; and stimulus for competition and export growth.

The adjustment lending in 1995 amounted to 24 per cent of the World Bank's commitments, which is some 10 times larger than the controversial lending for construction of large dams (which forms a 2 or 3 per cent share of the World Bank's overall portfolio).

It has been a matter of dispute between NGOs and the World Bank whether SALs have had adverse environmental effects or not, in particular for low-income groups in a country. A WWF International report (Reed 1992) examined the consequences of SALs in three countries (Côte d'Ivoire, Mexico, and Thailand) and concluded that the development paths these three countries pursued had created high levels of environmental degradation and generated unnecessary waste and loss of national wealth. On the other hands, a report by the World Bank (Munasinghe and Cruz 1995) reviewed several cases, with a view to identifying the broad relationship between economy-wide policies and the environment, and offered recognition of the generally positive environmental consequences of economy-wide policy reforms.

At this stage there is no clear-cut answer to the question of whether SALs improve or degrade the environment; a lot more effort and time is required to establish a solid view.

An important question to ask, however, is why no such programme lending (i.e. SAL) has been found in Category A projects, despite the fact that the magnitude of structural reform and sector reform programmes are, in terms of the amount of funds, much larger than a single project for one hydroelectric power station? This has been a matter of dispute among NGOs and lending institutions such as the World Bank.

Has the World Bank developed EA methodologies that are applicable for programme lending operations? Such loans could have much larger impacts, in accordance with the amount of funds involved, than loans for a single project. The cause-and-effect relationship of SALs ought to be quite complicated, for SALs may affect various sectors in various forms within a country. The analytical frameworks employed for both of the previously mentioned reports (WWF International and the World Bank) seem rather empirical and experimental. Without a solid methodology, it may be hard for a project officer or an environmental specialist to put a SAL project into Category A.

It is safe to say that existing knowledge about estimating possible impacts of SALs may be insufficient to develop a functional EA methodology for such a programme lending operation. However, now that a quarter of World Bank loans fall under this category, it seems imperative to put more resources to work on this issue. It is even surprising to the author that although SALs have been condemned by NGOs as great threats to the environment in various countries, very few quantitative (or numerical) analyses have ever been conducted by those involved (i.e. NGOs and lending institutions), and that there is therefore still no working knowledge to develop an EA methodology to deal with SALs.

The solution to this issue may be rather simple, and probably the easiest to implement (among the three issues discussed in this chapter), for it is just a matter of resources (both human and financial) available to elaborate an EA methodology to deal with SALs, and such measures would not require a philosophical debate on the way of thinking (as in the case with upward harmonization or pollution displacement) nor a fundamental review of the mandate of the World Bank as an international organization (as with the lack of a mechanism to deal with transboundary issues).

Conclusion and considerations

Three issues related to the environment, which need further institutional enhancement and methodological advancement within the World Bank, have been examined from the viewpoint of identifying possible solutions.

The issue raised under "Upward harmonization or pollution displacement" seems rather generic in the system, for it relates to the philosophy of environmental conditions. It may require some fundamental changes within the system, in the context of the way of thinking about the possible "trickle-down effect" of Bank-financed projects in the developing world. Improvements could be achieved by putting more human and financial resources (such as more sectoral EAs in the borrowing countries) into the existing institutional framework of the World Bank.

The issue of "Lack of mechanisms to deal with transboundary issues" must require some drastic and rather fundamental (in terms of the mandate of the organization) changes to the present institutional and operational framework of the World Bank. Achieving a solution is simply more difficult and may require more efforts and resources than the first issue. The feasibility of possible solutions within the World Bank to this issue should be examined from various viewpoints, as mentioned above, including the mandate of the World Bank.

The rather limited success of UNEP in implementation (after having the agreement adopted by riparian countries) of the Zambezi Action Plan (Nakayama 1997) may suggest that the present catalytic role of UNEP is not sufficiently functional for transboundary environmental issues, while the "super-UNEP" or "World Environmental Organization" may not be a solution in this regard as suggested by Downie and Levy in their chapter in this volume. The World Bank could still be found the best-situated international organization to work on transboundary environmental issues, as implicitly hinted by Downie and Levy, but it is still an open question subject to various debates in the future.

The issue mentioned in "Environmental assessment for programme lending" apparently requires more research efforts in developing solid EA methodologies to encompass the rather complex cause-and-effect relation of the impacts of SALs, because they involve a nationwide reform policy. The solution thus may simply depend on the availability of resources (both human and financial) for the research efforts needed.

Solutions for these problems may not necessarily be mutually compatible: for example, changing the institutional framework of the World Bank for the sake of working on transboundary issues (shifting more human resources from country operation into regional operation, for example) might be feasible only at the cost of enhancing its capacity to deal with the SAL-related matter, which is particularly an issue for a single country.

Institution-wide review is apparently needed to give priority to these issues, which are currently not adequately addressed in the system, so that the World Bank could make best use of its finite financial and human resources to cope with national, regional (transboundary in the context of this chapter), and global environmental issues. Sharing of environmental responsibilities with other international (bilateral and multilateral) organizations should also be examined to find an optimized solution, in the framework of international organizations as well as the donor community as a whole. Such discussions are particularly required about the ways and means of dealing with transboundary environmental issues, for it is not clear at this stage if the World Bank should make rather drastic (even regarding its institutional mandate) and costly (in terms of resources available within the system) changes for the sake of working on the issue.

Notes

1. This chapter is based on interviews conducted with several staff members of the World Bank, both in environmental and non-environmental sections, in addition to a literature survey of relevant documents. The author wishes to express his thanks to those interviewees, who will remain anonymous, for their assistance.
2. GEF projects and programmes are managed through three implementing agencies: the UN Development Programme (UNDP), the UN Environment Programme (UNEP), and the World Bank.

REFERENCES

GEF (Global Environment Facility). 1995. *Scope and Preliminary Operational Strategy for International Waters.* Washington: Global Environment Facility.

Kirmani, S. and G. Le Moigne. 1997. "Fostering Riparian Cooperation in International River Basins." World Bank Technical Paper No. 335. Washington: World Bank.

Kirmani, S. and R. Rangeley. 1994. *International Inland Waters.* World Bank Technical Paper No. 239. Washington: World Bank.

Mason, E. S. and R. E. Asher. 1973. *The World Bank since Bretton Woods.* Washington: Brookings Institution.

Mikesell, R. F. and L. Williams. 1992. *International Banks and the Environment.* San Francisco: Sierra Club Books.

Munasinghe, M. and W. Cruz. 1995. *Economywide Policies and the Environment: Lessons from Experience.* World Bank Environment Paper No. 10. Washington: World Bank.

Nakayama, M. 1997. "Successes and Failures of International Organizations in Dealing with International Waters." *International Journal of Water Resources Development* 13(3): 367–382.

Reed, D. 1992. *Structural Adjustment and the Environment.* Boulder: Westview.

World Bank. 1995. *Mainstreaming the Environment.* Washington: World Bank.

World Bank. 1996. *Environment Matters, World Bank Environmental Projects: July 1986–June 1996*, Washington: World Bank.

World Bank. 1997a. *Environment Matters*, Annual Review. Washington: World Bank.

World Bank. 1997b. *Advancing Sustainable Development: The World Bank and Agenda 21.* Washington: World Bank.

World Bank. 1997c. *Annual Report 1997.* Washington: World Bank.

21

Intergovernmental organizations and the environment: Looking towards the future

Michael W. Doyle and Rachel I. Massey

This conclusion revisits the questions posed in the introduction to this section, drawing on the insights provided by the previous three chapters. What have these studies taught us about how existing intergovernmental environmental organizations should be evaluated? Do they suggest that environmental protection is best furthered through the strengthening of existing institutions, by the expansion or revamping of environmental organizations, or by the creation of one or more additional organizations? When the possibility of creating a new organization or expanding an existing one is considered, it is tempting to think in terms of an active combination of a catalytic, agenda-setting role with actual programme development and management. The impression that emerges from the material presented in this volume, however, suggests that neither agenda-setting nor programme development is lacking in existing organizations. On the other hand, there are important areas that do not appear to be covered by any existing organization. In particular, the challenges posed by increasing economic integration may create the need for a new intergovernmental environmental organization.

The organizational environment

This section briefly discusses the activities of other intergovernmental organizations that work to coordinate environmental protection on a

411

global scale. By noting the work of organizations whose mandates bring them into the same realm as those discussed by the preceding three authors, understanding may be enhanced of which areas of environmental protection are well covered by existing organizational structures and which are in danger of being neglected.

The long-standing mandate of the FAO,[1] founded in 1945, includes the promotion of environmental protection. Currently, the organization places particular emphasis on sustainability in both agriculture and the exploitation of forest and marine resources. The FAO has facilitated the adoption of several important conventions relating to environmental protection, including the FAO International Code of Conduct on the Distribution and Use of Pesticides (1985), the Code of Conduct for Responsible Fisheries (1995), and the Global Plan of Action on Plant Genetic Resources (1996).

Another organization with a significant role in coordinating international efforts at environmental protection is the United Nations Children's Fund (UNICEF), founded in 1946. Although UNICEF's mandate does not explicitly include environmental issues, various items in its mandate necessitate by extension that it takes the environment into account. The basic goal of the organization is to ensure the protection of children's rights and the promotion of their welfare. In the period leading up to the year 2000, the organization is focusing largely upon infant and child mortality rates, access to drinking water, sanitation, primary education, and women's literacy.[2] UNICEF works for environmental protection both at the international and at the local level and was an active participant in UNCED, where it lobbied to include measures protecting children in Agenda 21. Since 1992, UNICEF has participated in a number of other international conferences, where it has emphasized the need to address environmental problems that affect children's health and safety. At the local level, programmes specifically focused on the preservation of the natural environment have become increasingly prominent among UNICEF's projects. UNICEF promotes, among other things, the adoption of clean-energy technologies such as solar stoves at the household level; the development of sustainable agriculture initiatives that improve household food security; and the protection of forest resources at the village level. These programmes serve multiple purposes, at once increasing food and income security for rural families, improving children's nutrition, and promoting the protection of the resources upon which children's welfare ultimately depends. UNICEF's urban projects have also focused increasingly during this decade upon the ways in which pollution affects children's health.

The UNDP is another organization whose original mandate does not specifically mention environmental protection but which has had to adopt the cause of environmental protection in order properly to fulfil its mandate. Just as the promotion of children's welfare requires attention to the health of the ecosystems upon which children depend, similarly an organization concerned with development must give its attention to developing nations' abilities to husband scarce environmental resources. In addition to incorporating environmental projects into its individual country programmes, the UNDP is a major participant in a number of international environmental protection projects. In the aftermath of UNCED, the UNDP established the "Capacity 21" programme to help individual countries develop the capacity to implement Agenda 21 domestically. Along with UNEP and the World Bank, the UNDP is responsible for managing the GEF, which provides funding for sustainable development and environmental impact abatement initiatives in developing countries. The UNDP is also responsible for implementing funds through the Multilateral Fund of the Montreal Protocol to help developing countries phase out and develop alternatives to ozone-depleting substances. In addition, the UNDP operates a "Sustainable Development Networking Programme," which facilitates the exchange of information on individual countries' approaches to sustainable development. Finally, the UNDP has developed a system of "environmental management guidelines" and a "companion training programme," which help to standardize approaches to environmental protection within a wide variety of individual programmes.

The World Health Organization (WHO) operates two major environmental programmes: Promotion of Environmental Health (PEH) and Promotion of Chemical Safety (PCS). The PEH programme includes subprogrammes on urban environmental health, rural environmental health, and global and integrated environmental health. The PCS programme has four components: chemical risk assessment, chemical risk communication, chemical risk reduction, and strengthening of national capabilities in and capacities for management of chemicals. The PCS programme also collaborates with the International Labour Organization (ILO) and UNEP in executing the International Programme on Chemical Safety (IPCS).

Many other intergovernmental organizations address global environmental problems as well. While it is not possible to discuss the activities of each in detail here, brief note can be taken of some of them. The World Food Programme, created to coordinate the provision of food aid and help solve food-related crises, takes an interest in environmental protection issues to the extent that they affect individual countries' and communities' food security. Other organizations whose mandates lead them frequently to take an interest in global environmental problems include the UN Educational, Scientific, and Cultural Organization

(UNESCO), the International Fund for Agricultural Development (IFAD), the ILO, and the International Maritime Organization (IMO). The work of certain other organizations is entirely concerned with a specialized aspect of global environmental protection. The World Meteorological Organization (WMO), for example, coordinates research and information-sharing relating to the global climate, and the International Atomic Energy Agency (IAEA) works to control the proliferation of substances associated with atomic energy production. In a different arena, the GEF, founded in 1991, exists to distribute resources from the developed to the developing world for the advancement and dispersal of environmentally sound technologies. Established by the UNDP, UNEP, and the World Bank, the GEF currently provides funding under four windows: global climate change, ozone depletion, biological diversity, and international waters. It also supports the Framework Convention on Climate Change, the Convention on Biological Diversity, and the Montreal Protocol on Substances that Deplete the Ozone Layer. Finally, a number of other intergovernmental bodies have an influence on global environmental protection efforts although their mandates do not lead them directly to participate in environmental agenda-setting. Thus, for example, both the IMF and the WTO are responsible for making decisions that may have significant environmental repercussions. Moreover, the European Union and the OECD both devote substantial attention to the development of environmental protection plans.

It is clear from this short review that many intergovernmental organizations in addition to UNEP, the CSD, and the World Bank take an interest in global environmental protection. Although a certain amount of duplication could increase efficiency and foster best practices, some areas are covered so thoroughly that additional attention from an organization such as UNEP or the CSD is likely to be redundant and might even be counterproductive. For example, the FAO has served an important role as the facilitator of international environmental agreements. As the organizations discussed here continue to develop their own roles in international environmental protection, they should take account of this ability in the FAO to catalyse environmental action, and should attempt to enhance and encourage the further development of that ability. Similarly, functions such as those that the UNDP has served – especially the promotion of information-sharing and the standardization of methodologies for solving environmental problems – are essential. As long as the UNDP is able to carry out these functions adequately, it may be unnecessary for an organization such as UNEP to attempt to duplicate that role. Rather, UNEP, the CSD, and the World Bank should attempt to fulfil whatever role the UNDP fails to fulfil in this regard. For example, it is possible that the services provided by the UNDP for developing countries are not duplicated by any organization concerned with the role of developed countries. It may also be that no existing international organization is ideally suited to the dissemination of best environmental technology or the encouragement of technological leapfrogging. These, then, are gaps to which UNEP, the CSD, and the World Bank should attend, whether by taking charge of relevant activities themselves or by creating new forums where these activities can occur.

Gaps in the coverage of global environmental problems

How do the World Bank, UNEP, and the CSD interact with other organizations to cover the map of global environmental problems? Are there inefficient overlaps – areas where organizations duplicate one another's efforts? Are there synergies, in which multiple organizations are tackling the same problems in different and complementary ways? Finally, are there gaps that all these organizations fail to cover? Some progress towards answering these questions can be made by reviewing their mandates and activities.

The CSD

As was seen in Chasek's chapter, the mandate of the CSD is to review progress in the implementation of agreements that resulted from the Rio Conference; to elaborate policy guidance; and to promote dialogue among a long list of relevant actors, ranging from governments to farmers. On reviewing the list of areas the CSD plans to cover in its current five-year plan, one might conclude that no gaps remain. The CSD plans to cover four major physical categories of environmental problems (fresh water, oceans, land, and atmosphere) in four years, and has also apportioned among those years all the major conceptual themes that may be relevant to the solution of these problems. Technology, capacity, education, science, awareness, consumption, production, economics, decision-making, participation, and cooperation are all to be considered. To search for omissions in this list would be counterproductive. However, the very fact that so many topics are slated to be "covered" in four years clearly indicates that none of the topics is likely to be addressed in concrete terms. The CSD is unlikely to be found coordinating international watershed protection forums in 1999, because it will already have moved on from fresh water management to oceans and seas; nor is it likely to have catalysed a new treaty on ocean dumping by 2000, because it will be hurrying on to its consideration of land resources.

Two conditions must hold in order for a mandate as broad as that of the CSD to produce valuable results. First, the CSD's dialogue sessions must be planned in such a way that they serve a clear purpose. There must be a clear understanding about whether their goal is to lay the groundwork for more concrete negotiations to be undertaken in the future; to "brainstorm," producing ideas upon which other organizations will act; or simply to ensure face-to-face contact among environmental policy-makers from around the world. While all these purposes are valid, each implies a different approach and should be expected to pose different challenges. Assuming that this condition is met, the CSD seems well positioned to fulfil the role of providing for a global "discussion" of the major areas of environmental protection challenges. However, the second condition for effectiveness is that some other organization or set of organizations should be committed to pursuing and putting into practice the ideas generated in the CSD's sessions. It is not clear that the international institutional capacity exists for this condition to be fulfilled.

UNEP

UNEP, as Downie and Levy explain, appears to have a number of institutional advantages over the CSD, increasing the likelihood of its accomplishing substantial tasks. It has existed since 1972, and thus has had the opportunity to develop some institutional momentum. It has also had an active long-term leadership; during his 16 years as leader of the organization, Mostafa Tolba took what Robert Haas has referred to as a classic, neofunctionalist, "entrepreneurial" role in a variety of international negotiations (Haas 1995, 654). UNEP's mandate is also somewhat more limited than that of the CSD. While the CSD is charged with promoting communication among all actors concerned with environment and development, UNEP is expected to coordinate and catalyse environmental protection activities among UN agencies. While it has not done everything conceivable, UNEP has accomplished some significant tasks over the course of its existence.

The World Bank

Comparing mandates one may find, for example, that the CSD has taken care of forests and UNEP has taken care of desertification while no organization has adequately covered ocean pollution. But, as Nakayama's chapter points out, one must also watch for gaps – not in particular, concrete areas of environmental protection, but rather in methods of analysing environmental protection. Nakayama suggests that the World Bank as first and foremost a national economic development organization focuses its methodologies of environmental assessment too much on individual projects and not enough on the larger environmental profile of a country or region. Here there may be room for better coordination with UNEP or the CSD.

Unlike the CSD and UNEP, the World Bank was not established with the specific purpose of promoting environmental protection and environmentally sound development. Rather, in the World Bank's case environmental concerns are an addendum to, or a check on, a central agenda that was originally elaborated without explicit regard for environmental concerns. The World Bank has adopted the practice of attaching environmental conditions to its loans, and requiring projects in developing countries to meet environmental standards that would apply in developed countries. This policy is intended to promote "upward harmonization" of environmental standards internationally. Nakayama points out, however, that a developing country may meet World Bank standards simply by diverting its polluting practices to other projects – for example, using "clean" coal in a Bank-funded power plant but simply shunting its "dirty" coal to other plants rather than ceasing to use it.

While the CSD and UNEP focus on broad themes of environmental protection, the World Bank focuses on specific projects that are of economic significance. When it analyses the potential environmental effects of a project and seeks ways to mitigate them, it focuses on the details of that project. Gaps can emerge between sweeping evaluations of international environmental performance, on the one hand, and detailed analysis of individual projects, on the other. Could coordination between the World Bank and UNEP, for example, produce more coherent evaluations of the macro-level environmental effects of World Bank projects in a given region?

Mandates and capacities

One useful approach to evaluating international environmental organizations may be to consider whether each organization's mandate is appropriate to the structure and constituency of the organization, and vice versa. Chasek comments, for example, that CSD meetings are mainly attended by environment ministers, and suggests that attendance should be made broader. Another possible recommendation might be that the CSD's mandate be reformulated in terms of its actual constituency. Presumably a single organization cannot build partnerships among all groups simultaneously. But if an organization such as the CSD could turn its dialogue function into improved coordination among environmental ministers or their envoys, it might enjoy some genuine successes.

One overarching lesson is that the mandate should fit the organization, and vice versa. An organization such as the CSD, with ample global attention and an able, but not expert, staff, is basically designed to run annual conferences. It is best suited to the articulation, mobilization, and high-level coordination of effort – not for carrying out complex programmes of action. Others, such as UNEP, have more staff and a more autonomous organization for determining expert consensus, training, and sectoral decision-making. The World Bank, with masses of financial expertise and financial resources for implementation, has the rare potential actually to put into effect the courses of action that have been agreed upon.

"Institutional overload"

In their edited collection of studies on international environmental institutions, *Institutions for the Earth*, Haas, Keohane, and Levy (1993) suggest a second standard for evaluating organizational effectiveness. They note that international environmental protection efforts suffer from "institutional overload." So many organizations and treaties exist relating to environmental protection that government officials are spread thin attempting to participate in, understand, evaluate, and find ways to comply with all of them. International environmental arrangements would benefit from what Haas, Keohane, and Levy refer to as an equivalent to a "most-favoured nation" status: a set agreement that two or more states can agree to adopt to govern their relations and that does not have to be worked out anew each time. They note, however, that there is no clear way to standardize the process of agreeing upon environmental protection measures in the way there is to standardize trade agreements.

The future of international environmental organizations

Do the institutions which have been considered have the potential to solve whatever environmental problems should theoretically be soluble? Should the focus be on strengthening these institutions? Or is there a need for a different sort of international organization – a "super-UNEP" of the sort Downie and Levy allude to, a global environmental regime with a role analogous to the WTO's role in regulating trade?

Intergovernmental environmental organizations: Managing globalization

The term "globalization," frequently employed though seldom carefully defined, refers to increasing economic and social integration among countries. It implies increasing trade openness and capital mobility, as well as the ever-increasing interconnectedness of distant parts of the world through communication technologies and travel. Globalization leads to interaction and interdependence among locations and polities once so remote that the domestic policies of one had little or no relevance for another.

The advance of economic and social integration has spawned a considerable literature on the possible implications of globalization for individual countries' autonomy in domestic policy decisions. Topics range from the choice of macroeconomic and social welfare policies to the establishment of environmental and labour standards (see, for example, Rodrik 1997 concerning possible constraints on social welfare policy). Environmental standards are one area of domestic policy that may be increasingly affected by international dynamics as globalization progresses. The liberalization of both trade and investment regimes, for example, can potentially create downward pressure on individual countries' environmental standards. As trade openness increases, firms are increasingly vulnerable to competition from outside their home country's borders. Firms that cut costs by imposing negative environmental externalities on the communities in which they are located may enjoy a competitive advantage over those that do not; and those whose home countries insist on high environmental standards may find themselves at a disadvantage. Furthermore, even if firms are not under severe competitive pressure, capital mobility as well as ease of transport and communication may increase their ability to extract concessions from the state. The easier it is for a firm to relocate from one country to another, the greater is its bargaining power in relation to the state. Thus one effect of globalization may be downward pressure on environmental standards exerted by firms that enjoy the option of relocating.

The competition that may arise among states as each seeks to attract mobile industry is sometimes referred to as creating a risk of a "race to the bottom." According to the view represented by this term, each state has a strong incentive to lower its environmental standards in order that industry will be willing to locate within it, bringing employment and economic growth. Most students of these dynamics agree that the term "race to the bottom" is a misnomer; states are unlikely actively to lower standards by repealing existing environmental protection laws. Daniel Esty has suggested that international competition may, however, produce a "regulatory chill" or "political drag" – a stagnating or dampening effect, in which states fail to enforce their environmental protection laws or avoid adding new regulations to their books (see, for example, Esty 1994a). Thus, in Esty's view, even if states do not actively lower standards, international competitive pressures may be a significant constraint on the abilities of states to protect their environments.

Empirical studies have suggested that in fact industry competitiveness is not significantly affected by environmental standards.[3] On the other hand, these studies have focused primarily on a limited industry category: highly polluting industries based in the United States (see Pearson 1996). Little empirical work has been done, for example, to test whether these patterns hold true for natural-resource-based industries in developing countries. Furthermore, although thorough empirical studies have not shown evidence of competitiveness effects, some researchers have found evidence that governments nonetheless act as though such effects existed (Leonard 1988). Esty cites anecdotal evidence that competitiveness concerns were an obstacle to environmental regulation by individual states; among other examples, he cites the difficulty that legislators encountered in both the United States and the European Union when they attempted to increase taxes on fossil fuel use (Esty 1994a; Esty and Geradin 1998).

Despite the proliferation of organizations concerned in one way or another with coordinating international environmental protection efforts, no organization exists that is clearly capable of addressing the particular problems that may arise with globalization. Decisions that once had only domestic significance now affect and are affected by corresponding domestic policy decisions in other countries; yet countries lack a forum within which to bring these policies into balance with one another. This lack suggests that although many intergovernmental organizations already work on environmental protection, it may nonetheless be reasonable to create one more.

Visions of a Global Environmental Organization

The idea of creating a Global Environmental Organization (GEO), with a broad mandate for adjudication analogous to that of the WTO, has arisen at many junctures but has never been successfully pursued (Ayling 1997). Recent work by Daniel Esty provides an overview of the benefits that might be achieved through the creation of such an organization (Esty 1994a; 1994b). Esty lists three principal rationales for establishing a GEO: to deal with transboundary environmental externalities; to achieve economies of scale in research and promote common goals through information-sharing; and, finally, to reduce the "political drag" through which international competitiveness concerns can inhibit the development of environmental protection policies within individual countries. In Esty's view, the current array of intergovernmental organizations is ill-equipped to solve global environmental problems. UNEP, he argues, is far from adequately prepared to coordinate international cooperation over a wide range of environmental issues. The CSD is handicapped by the optimistic breadth of its mandate:

Since Agenda 21 covers every imaginable environmental issue without differentiating priorities and often reflects contrary points of view, [the CSD's] mission is a bit like being told to follow up on the Bible (Esty 1994b, 292).

Multiple other organizations also make attempts to solve environmental problems, but often with competing or incompatible methodologies. Thus while many organizations exist, in aggregate they fail to meet the challenges of global environmental protection.

Esty argues that in order to achieve effective environmental protection, it may be helpful for states to have a way to "tie their hands." According to this view, an important function of an international environmental organization is to let governments make commitments that will help them adhere to welfare-enhancing domestic policies even when powerful members of their constituencies oppose them. When governments wish to promote trade liberalization, they may be impeded by domestic protectionist interests; but by "tying their hands" through international commitments, they may give themselves the wherewithal to withstand protectionist demands. Similarly, governments wishing to legislate for environmental protection may encounter vocal opposition from industry or interests that stand to lose from tighter controls on pollution or natural resource depletion. In these circumstances, if governments can make a credible show domestically of having international commitments they cannot contravene, their ability to legislate for environmental protection may be enhanced.

Esty proposes that a GEO should emulate selected characteristics of a variety of currently existing organizations. The WHO is a good model for effective international coordination of transboundary problems; its successful efforts to eradicate certain infectious diseases relied in part on well-targeted assistance to developing countries. A GEO should, further, be endowed with a staff of individuals highly skilled in technical areas; in this respect it could be modelled on the OECD, the FAO, or the World Bank. A GEO would also require a secure source of significant funding.

Esty's portrait of a hypothetical future GEO is optimistic; in particular, if currently existing intergovernmental environmental organizations are underfunded, it is difficult to imagine where the funding for an ambitious new intergovernmental project might be found. The authors would suggest, in fact, that any new intergovernmental organization should be designed in such a way as to be able to carry out a limited but clear set of goals with relatively little funding. While an organization may grow into its mandate over time, there is a significant advantage to beginning with a realistic mandate and, therefore, the prospect of measurable successes. Furthermore, an organization that successfully accomplishes some limited tasks with minimal funding may always grow as new sources of support become available; but an organization designed to rely on large amounts of capital may not easily adapt itself to reduced support.

One means by which the problems of limited resources and "institutional overload" may be addressed simultaneously would be to pursue another idea that Esty puts forward. He suggests that if a GEO is to be created, it should be accompanied by the consolidation or elimination of several currently existing organizations concerned with environmental protection. Again, of course, this undertaking is much easier to propose than to carry out. Aside from the well-known propensity of organizations to focus on perpetuating their own existence when it is threatened, a potential source of problems is the fact that each currently existing organization has a distinct organizational history and "personality." While it is difficult to dismantle an organization, it may be even more difficult to achieve the seamless union of organizations that were previously distinct. The hierarchies and habits of individual organizations do not disappear automatically; and the staff of organizations forced to merge may have difficulty working together effectively. Thus even the relatively simple prospect of merging organizations with overlapping mandates is likely to be complicated in practice and poses the small but serious risk that vital institutional abilities may be lost in the process.

Summing up

Will environmental protection best be furthered through the strengthening of existing institutions, or by the creation of one or more additional organizations? The mere proliferation of organizations is not in itself useful: there are plenty of organizations already. The point noted above by Haas, Keohane, and Levy (1993) about "institutional overload" alerts us to a risk: the more different organizations there are that are trying to develop approaches to environmental problems, the more different kinds of regimes they may establish that states must navigate. If predictable rules and easily recognized roles and norms are among the central aspects of successful international institutions, this multiplicity of international organizations concerned with environmental problems may be counterproductive. The fashion of recent years, as the neofunctionalists would have predicted, has been for organizations to add "environment" to their list of concerns wherever and whenever possible. If this serves in part to confuse issues, so states do not know where to look for guidance and norms relating to environmental protection, then this fashion of concern may not produce results much better than those which international apathy would yield.

However, areas do remain to which no organization is explicitly dedicated. As has been seen, one such area is the ambiguous relationship between trade and environmental agreements. In recent years, a number of trade measures taken in the name of environmental protection have been rejected by the WTO as inappropriate barriers to trade. When the functionalist principles of trade liberalization and environmental protection collide and conflict, which should take precedence, or what body should adjudicate between them? Although many different organizations make efforts to promote environmental protection, their efforts may be superseded by decisions arrived at by the WTO, an organization whose mandate was developed without reference to environmental protection. Jeffrey Dunoff has argued that the WTO's current practice of adjudicating on environmental issues that may fall outside its mandate will eventually undermine the organization's legitimacy (Dunoff 1997; 1998). Thus while some environmental organizations suffer from mandates larger than their capabilities, the WTO, like the World Bank, takes responsibility for issues that go beyond its mandate. This may suggest that the world does need a new intergovernmental organization: one endowed with the means to adjudicate environmental questions in a way member states consider legitimate.

A second insight suggested by the material reviewed here, however, runs in the opposite direction. It has been seen that existing intergovernmental organizations, even those not officially intended to solve environmental problems, have developed considerable capacities to solve environmental problems within clearly defined conceptual boundaries. Other intergovernmental organizations have developed the complementary ability to catalyse and coordinate the creation of important environmental agreements. The lesson here is that these abilities, in some cases developed over the course of decades, are a significant resource. A new organization intended to collect many functions under one roof might not equal the capabilities of these existing organizations. It is essential that existing capabilities should not be ignored or undermined in the name of centralization and standardization. Thus, while certain issues point in the direction of either creating a new environmental organization or radically changing and expanding an existing organization, they do not mean that a new organization should take over roles fulfilled by organizations that already exist. Abilities developed over decades should not be superseded in the interests of centralization.

If a new intergovernmental organization is to be created, it is essential that its founders recognize the importance of the relationship between mandate and capabilities. The easy trap into which optimists may fall is that of mandating a new organization to accomplish tasks of which it is simply not capable. To create a new organization with an unrealistically ambitious mandate could actually undermine the cause of international environmental protection, by expanding still further the disarticulated array of environmental regimes that states confront. Even if its ultimate purpose is to match the WTO in influence and visibility, a new intergovernmental environmental organization should be endowed with a relatively limited, and realistic, mandate to, in effect, "start easy." This will make it possible to evaluate the new organization's successes and failures clearly; and to push the organization towards maximum effectiveness in promoting international cooperation for environmental protection.

Finally, although the strength of intergovernmental organizations may always be somewhat mitigated by the difficulty of enforcement, it is possible that as economic integration increases, intergovernmental organizations will be an increasingly important means through which states may be able to develop policy. To the extent that globalization may reduce states' autonomy – whether by constraining their fiscal and monetary policy options or by making it harder to impose stringent environmental regulations on industry – intergovernmental organizations may be the means through which states can regain or maintain their policy-making abilities. Thus while a GEO might be seen as infringing on national sovereignty in problematic ways, it might in the end actually enhance states' sovereignty. It might allow them collectively to pursue environmental protection policies that none would be able to maintain alone.

Notes

1. Information on intergovernmental organizations other than UNEP, the CSD, and the World Bank is drawn from Bergesen and Parmann (1997) and from the texts of presentations by organization representatives at the Rio Plus 5 Conference in New York in 1997.
2. Most of these areas of concern are closely linked to environmental issues; while the link through water quality and sanitation is obvious, women's literacy is also central to many aspects of local environmental protection.
3. For overviews of relevant studies, see Jaffe et al. (1995), Dean (1992), and Pearson (1985; 1996).

REFERENCES

Ayling, J. 1997. "Serving Many Voices: Progressing Calls for an International Environmental Organization." *Journal of Environmental Law* 9(2): 243–269.

Bergesen, H. O. and G. Parmann, eds. 1997. *Green Globe Yearbook of International Cooperation on Environment and Development: 1997.* New York: Oxford University Press.

Dean, J. 1992. "Trade and the Environment: A Survey of the Literature." In *International Trade and the Environment*, ed. Patrick Low. Washington: World Bank.

Dunoff, J. L. 1997. "Trade and Recent Developments in Trade Policy and Scholarship – and their Surprising Political Implications." *Journal of International Law and Business* 17: 759–774.

Dunoff, J. L. 1998. "Rethinking International Trade." *University of Pennsylvania Journal of International Economic Law* 19(2): 347–389.

Esty, D. C. 1994a. *Greening the GATT: Trade, Environment, and the Future.* Washington: Institute for International Economics.

Esty, D. C. 1994b. "The Case for a Global Environmental Organization." In *Managing the World Economy: Fifty Years After Bretton Woods*, ed. P. B. Kenen. Washington: Institute for International Economics.

Esty, D. C., and D. Geradin. 1998. "Environmental Protection and International Competitiveness: A Conceptual Framework." *Journal of World Trade* 32(3): 5–46.

Haas, P. M. 1995. "United Nations Environment Programme." In *Conservation and Environmentalism: An Encyclopedia*, ed. Robert Paehlke. New York: Garland Publishing.

Haas, P. M., R. O. Keohane, and M. A. Levy, eds. 1993. *Institutions for the Earth: Sources of Effective International Environmental Protection.* Cambridge, MA: MIT Press.

Jaffe, A. B., S. R. Petersen, P. R. Portney, and R. N. Stavins. 1995. "Environmental Regulation and the Competitiveness of US Manufacturing: What Does the Evidence Tell Us?" *Journal of Economic Literature* 33(1): 132–163.

Leonard, J. H. 1988. *Pollution and the Struggle for the World Product: Multinational Corporations, Environment, and International Comparative Advantage.* New York: Cambridge University Press.

Pearson, C. S. 1985. *Down to Business: Multinational Corporations, the Environment, and Development.* New York: World Resources Institute.

Pearson, C. S. 1996. "Theory, Empirical Studies, and their Limitations." In *Asian Dragons and Green Trade: Environment, Economics, and International Law*, eds S. S. C. Tay and D. C. Esty. Singapore: Asia-Pacific Centre for Environmental Law.

Rodrik, D. 1997. *Has Globalization Gone Too Far?* Washington: Institute for International Economics.

FURTHER READING

Brown Weiss, E. 1993. "International Environmental Law: Contemporary Issues and the Emergence of a New World Order." *Georgetown Law Journal* 81(3): 675.

Esty, D. C. 1996. "Revitalizing Environmental Federalism." *Michigan Law Review* 95(3): 570–653.

Esty, D. C. and A. Dua. 1997. *Sustaining the Asia Pacific Miracle: Environmental Protection and Economic Integration.* Washington: Institute for International Economics.

Esty, D. C. and D. Geradin. 1997. "Market Access, Competitiveness, and Harmonization: Environmental Protection in Regional Trade Agreements." *The Harvard Environmental Law Review* 21(2): 265–336.

Haas, P. M. and D. McCabe. Forthcoming. "Amplifiers or Dampeners: International Institutions and Social Learning in the Management of Global Environmental Risks." In *Learning to Manage Global Environmental Risks: A Comparative History of Social Responses to Climate Change, Ozone Depletion and Acid Rain*. Social Learning Group. Cambridge, MA: MIT Press.

Keohane, R. O. 1997. "Problematic Lucidity: Stephen Krasner's 'State Power and the Structure of International Trade.'" *World Politics* 50 (October): 150–170.

Kindleberger, C. 1973. *The World in Depression: 1929–1939*. Berkeley: University of California Press.

Kuhlow, M. L. 1998. "Environmental Side Agreements to Trade Treaties: A New Model of Environmental Policy-Making?" *Journal of Public and International Affairs* 9 (Spring): 128–144.

Low, P., ed. 1992. *International Trade and the Environment*. Washington: World Bank.

McNamara, K. R. 1998. *The Currency of Ideas: Monetary Politics in the European Union*. Ithaca: Cornell University Press.

Mundell, R. 1960. "The Monetary Dynamics of International Adjustment under Fixed and Flexible Exchange Rates." *Quarterly Journal of Economics* 74: 227–257.

Remmer, K. L. 1997. "Theoretical Decay and Theoretical Development: The Resurgence of Institutional Analysis." *World Politics* 50 (October): 34–61.

Ruggie, J. G. 1983. "International Regimes, Transactions, and Change: Embedded Liberalism in the Postwar Economic Order." In *International Regimes*, ed. S. Krasner. Ithaca: Cornell University Press.

Young, O. R. and G. Osherenko. 1993. *Polar Politics: Creating International Environmental Regimes*. Ithaca: Cornell University Press.

Conclusion

The global environment in the twenty-first century: Prospects for international cooperation

Pamela S. Chasek

The earth's environment faces critical threats as we enter the twenty-first century. Economic development and population growth, coupled with high levels of consumption by affluent members of society, on the one hand, and abject poverty on the other, have stretched to the limit our planet's ability to absorb environmental abuses. If current trends continue, anthropogenic environmental problems, including climate change, desertification, deforestation, ozone depletion, biodiversity loss, shortages of fresh water, depleted fisheries, persistent organic pollutants, hazardous and solid wastes, and air pollution, could bring us to the brink of ecological disaster. Yet, in spite of the potential political, social, and economic consequences of environmental degradation, the environment remains a politically contested issue at the global, national, and local levels.

States are the final determinants of the outcomes of global environmental issues. States are responsible for adopting national and international policies that directly and indirectly affect the environment. States also decide which issues are considered by the international community and negotiate the international legal instruments that create global environmental regimes. However, non-state actors also exert major and increasing influence on global environmental politics. International and regional organizations help to set the global environmental agenda, initiate and mediate the process of regime formation, and cooperate with developing countries on projects and programmes that directly affect the environment. NGOs work to influence agenda-setting, international environmental negotiations, national environmental policies, and trade and economic policies that have an impact on the environment (Porter and Brown 1996). Market forces affect the overall framework in which environmental issues are addressed, and influence the means by which states attempt to resolve transnational environmental problems.

This book has examined the roles of these different actors *vis-à-vis* the environment during the last quarter of the twentieth century. But the question still remains, can the existing locus of actors find the proper solutions to current and future environmental problems? Related questions, first put forth in the Introduction, include the following. What will be the nature of the issues that will have to be addressed in the next century? What should be the role of the United Nations? Is there a better model for international cooperation to address environmental issues? This Conclusion will attempt to answer these questions, although, as is the case in any predictive exercise, these questions give rise to new ones – questions that may not yet have any answers.

Issues to be addressed in the twenty-first century

A number of issues have been raised in this volume about the future role of the United Nations and other actors with regard to the environment. While this is by no means a comprehensive list of environment-related issues to be addressed by the international community, it does reflect some issues of concern emerging from the preceding chapters.

Environmental problems compete with other problems for public attention

One of the biggest problems in resolving and preventing environmental crises is that environmental problems compete with other significant problems for public attention – and often lose the battle. As Kohli, Sørensen, and Sowers noted in their introduction to the section on states, "There is no uncontested consensus that environment problems are very serious and need to be addressed immediately. This lack of consensus is as true to individual states in both the developing and the developed world as it is to the international actors, including the United Nations." Environmental problems struggle for political recognition with other issues internationally, within governments, and also within populations. People need a healthy environment, but they also need food, shelter, and a number of other things. While fundamentally linked, in the short and medium run these different objectives may appear to conflict.

At the state level, as Evans points out, conventional approaches to the political economy of the state suggest little in the way of positive strategies. Realist analysis of the ways in which states use their power as sovereigns to maximize the "national interest" suggests pessimistic conclusions when it comes to environmental problems. It is not only global environmental issues, like the ozone layer, that will be neglected if the traditional logic of competing sovereign states prevails. States primarily concerned with enhancing their sovereign power are also unlikely to address domestic environmental issues successfully. Again, it is only in the long run that economic and military prowess depend on sound environmental policy.

Evans argues further that if traditional state-centred politics have little to offer in the environmental arena, calls for curtailing the role of the state offer even less. The "natural" logic of markets leaves environmental improvements as undersupplied collective goods and degradation as a negative externality for which both producers and consumers will try to avoid responsibility. Shifting incentives in a way that forces private economic actors to pay real attention to environmental issues implies more state involvement, not less. A central question is thus to determine how states and the public can constructively focus on environmental problems.

Finding a role for civil society in global environmental governance

The second section of this book, on civil society, raises the issue of the role of civil society in global environmental governance. What should the relationship be between civil society and the UN system? In his chapter, Wapner points out that NGOs greatly influence the way the international system addresses environmental issues. There are literally thousands of NGOs throughout the world working for environmental protection, and they devote significant resources to their campaigns. NGOs expend tremendous effort lobbying states and influencing international regime formation and implementation. But their efforts do not stop there, nor are such strategies undertaken separate from a host of other forms of political practice. NGOs aim to reorient human practices at all levels of collective life. To do so, they enlist the governing power not simply of states but also of economic and sociocultural forces that significantly influence human activity.

From his experience with Asian NGOs, Gan makes his own observations on the role of NGOs. First, NGOs will continue to create new social linkages, or webs of contacts, and help establish and improve relationships between the general public and governments, international agencies, the private sector, and the scientific community. Second, the diversification of NGOs will continue to increase in both scope and speed. Their influence will reach increasing numbers of people, and their power will be further strengthened by wider participation of the general public.

While NGOs are gaining power and recognition in the international arena, the United Nations remains an organization of states, with only a limited role for civil society. In some cases it can be argued that some states actually fear expanding the role of civil society in international organizations, as it may undermine their own sovereignty. Nevertheless, civil society, particularly in the form of community-based organizations and NGOs, is playing an increasingly important part in protecting the earth's environment. Their voices must be heard and supported at the state, regional, and international level. The challenge, therefore, lies in devising an acceptable arrangement that will allow the formal participation of civil society in international arenas such as the United Nations without threatening state sovereignty.

Conflicts between energy production or use and environmental sustainability

The conflict between energy production or use and environmental sustainability is likely to be one of the main environmental issues of the twenty-first century. A number of the chapters in this book, including the chapters by Gan, Goldemberg, Sims, Wilkening, Von Hippel, and Hayes, and Zarsky, address various issues related to energy.

The global energy situation does not seem to be promising. The earth's capacity to absorb energy-related pollution will be exceeded before energy shortages become a problem. Energy consumption is on the rise, while the current energy glut has structurally impeded the development of alternative energy sources. At the same time, a vicious cycle of development, an increased demand for energy consumption, and extensive emissions of air pollutants are turning the energy issue into one of the major environmental problematiques in the twenty-first century.

As Sims points out, if the pursuit of environmental responsiveness is inherently a collective enterprise, so too is the monitoring of emerging energy systems. Private interests have strong incentives to monitor profitability, which is one aspect of efficiency. States have incentives to measure the overall efficiency of energy use and effectiveness of its distribution. Environmental responsiveness is a shared concern of states, market-led forces, and the citizens who use energy in their daily lives. Because of its extensive experience with environmental technology and informal education about its use and effects, the United Nations can and probably will be a catalyst in crystallizing both goals and standards for environmental responsiveness in the twenty-first century.

Market forces are fundamentally flawed in coping with the environment

The third section of this book stresses the belief that market forces alone cannot cope with environmental dilemmas in the twenty-first century. Briones and Ramos argue that unruly market forces have severely undermined food security by distorting food production, distribution, and consumption in the developing world. Wilkening, Von Hippel, and Hayes state that old inertia associated with the industrial paradigm has prevented energy markets from adopting the idea of sustainability, clouding the energy future in the twenty-first century. In the case of fresh water, according to Gleick, market forces have a mixed outlook. Although they are deficient in satisfying the basic water needs of the majority of inhabitants in developing countries, market forces can serve as an effective deterrent to overuse and misuse of scarce water resources.

First, as long as the current pattern of population growth and conspicuous consumption continues, market forces and technology cannot ensure future sustainability. Second, market forces often fail to take into account normative dimensions of resource scarcity. Third, market mechanisms cannot resolve the undersupply or overexploitation of collective goods through free-riding behaviour. The tragedy of commons is likely to abound, unless market failures are corrected and ecological sustainability is enhanced.

Improving global environmental governance

It is clear from the chapters in the fifth section of this book that existing international organizations have not been totally effective in improving environmental protection on a global scale. UNEP has been hindered by its limited mandate, lack of resources, and physical location. The CSD has too broad a mandate and no enforcement powers. Environmentally sustainable development is now considered to be one of the World Bank's fundamental objectives, but the World Bank was never intended to be the focal point of international environmental governance. There is an ongoing debate about whether to expand UNEP's powers into what Downie and Levy call a "super-UNEP," to create a new Global Environmental Organization, as argued by Esty (1994a; 1994b) and outlined by Doyle and Massey in this volume, or to maintain the status quo.

At the same time, there is a school of thought that regional environmental cooperation may be a better solution to certain types of transboundary environmental issues. The fourth section of this book looks at a sample of regional organizations in Central and Eastern Europe, Asia, and sub-Saharan Africa. As Alagappa explains, since the 1970s regional arrangements and agencies pertaining to the environment have proliferated in nearly all parts of the world, and are becoming an important component of the global architecture for environmental governance. The role and effectiveness, and hence the significance, of regional institutions, however, vary widely. They depend on the nature of the problem (global issues, regional or subregional-specific concerns, bilateral problems, or issues of concern within state boundaries), the level at which it is addressed, the nature of the specific regional institution, and its capacity to address such problems. All these factors vary widely. In practice, therefore, the role of regional institutions in managing the environment is not uniform across regions and subregions.

Representatives of regional organizations and arrangements are increasingly participating in global environmental regimes, institutions, and forums. This participation often serves in turn to strengthen regional organizations. One global agreement, the UN Agreement on Straddling Fish Stocks and Highly Migratory Fish Stocks, actually recognizes, supports, and incorporates the work of various regional fisheries agreements. Yet this agreement is the exception rather than the rule. In other areas, such as forests, there is vehement disagreement among states, NGOs, and regional and global organizations about the need for a global, legally binding agreement on the sustainable management of all types of forests. Some argue that regional agreements are more appropriate given the different types of forests and ecosystems around the world. Others believe that a global instrument is needed to harmonize the various regional and national arrangements and codify what exactly comprises "sustainable forest management." There is no consensus on the relationship between most global organizations or institutions and regional arrangements, which types of arrangements are appropriate for different situations, and how they should relate to the concept of global environmental governance.

Recommendations: What is the role of the United Nations?

There is no shortage of books and articles that contain recommendations about what the United Nations can do to address the world's environmental problems effectively. Some experts call for convening more conferences and negotiating more treaties. Some support strengthening existing institutions, while others prefer the establishment of new institutions. There are calls to expand the UN's work in new areas, such as energy, fresh water resources, and sustainable tourism. So what does this volume add to the debate? The following list of recommendations put forth by the authors identifies possible actions that the United Nations and the other major actors in the international system can take, and proposes a set of realistic goals for the twenty-first century.

Inform and educate international policy-makers

There is a variety of ways in which the UN system can continue and enhance its contributions in the field of environmental accountability. The UN system has already played a proactive role in bringing environmental issues to international attention, particularly through member agencies such as the UNDP, UNEP, the UNU, and UNIDO. Through publications, research, workshops, and training sessions, these agencies have sought to build and disseminate conceptual models and practical measures that integrate environmental and development concerns. These activities also provide an important networking function, bringing scientists and professionals from developing countries together to share ideas and difficulties, as well as providing additional training and funding. The UN system should continue to promote such activities, because a well-informed and well-educated international system of policy-makers and experts is the first step towards formulating effective solutions to global environmental problems.

Influence member governments to play more environmentally responsible roles

An international organization is only as strong as its member states. Therefore, to improve the effectiveness of international organizations at tackling environmental issues it is necessary to encourage governments of member countries to play more environmentally responsible roles. How can the UN system promote this? One way is through provision of information about environment-friendly technologies and modes of production. This must remain a key focus of UN endeavours, especially those that might deliver the simultaneous provision of competing public goods. As stressed by Evans, "small injections of new knowledge can play an important role in arriving at positive resolutions." The United Nations has already assisted in the spread of alternative energy technologies, particularly wind and solar community development projects, notes Sims. This role could be expanded from technical assistance *per se* to other forms of incentive-building. For instance, one of Goldemberg's most innovative suggestions is that developing countries aggregate their demand for environmentally friendly technologies such as photovoltaics; since most technologies exhibit exponentially declining cost curves when mass marketed, such demand might spur multinational and domestic energy companies to cheaper production and more research and development. Such a process could be facilitated by cooperation between UN agencies such as the UNDP or UNEP on the one hand, and selective member states on the other.

Build capacity and the use of appropriate technology in member states

UN member states, particularly developing ones, often lack the capacity to address their environmental problems adequately. Sims points out that specific areas where expertise is needed include planning and the reconciliation of local, regional, and national priorities and capabilities, and also in demonstrating, monitoring, maintenance, and evaluation of energy technologies. Such tasks will draw upon the extensive experience of international agencies and, particularly, the United Nations, which has actively assisted the spread of energy technologies that are widely viewed as environmentally responsive, rather than the massive but environmentally controversial projects of the past. As a result, the United Nations offers vast experience with wind and solar energy technology and their use in rural areas of low-income countries. Its staff and advisers with general expertise in community development can assist both official and agency technical specialists and local community representatives.

The possibilities for "leapfrogging" that Goldemberg describes for technological adaptation can also apply to governmental tasks. Institutional development concerning environmental supervision and the diffusion of knowledge about experiences with environment-friendly policies at all political levels is of paramount importance. Some initiatives have already emerged, such as UN sponsorship of guidelines to handle hazardous waste in developing countries; such tasks should be expanded.

Address the potentially environmentally hazardous effects of globalization

Increasingly, the challenge for UN agencies is to address the potentially environmentally hazardous effects of globalization. This could be done by UN-sponsored proposals for reforms in international trade regimes, especially devising mechanisms to address issues of environmental accountability. Eventually, however, cooperation of states will be important, because integral to such a project is the promotion of national systems of environmental accounting and auditing for investments, including the innovative use of tax incentives for environmental entrepreneurs.

Assist in the diffusion of innovations across national boundaries

In his chapter, Evans argues that "a state-society synergy image suggests a fluid political arena in which solutions to environmental problems emerge out of creative conflicts between local communities and state agencies." Indigenous innovation is the most likely source of such solutions, but if each locality has to "reinvent the wheel" then problems may evolve more rapidly than local innovations are replicated. Public institutions or community/NGO networks at the national level may help diffuse innovations across localities, but the degree to which cities in different countries and regions share similar problems is striking, and diffusing innovations across national boundaries is likely to depend on supranational organizations.

Since collective solutions to environmental problems involve, almost by definition, ideas from which the returns are not amenable to private appropriation through markets, corporations are not the best choice as vehicles. Ideas that could be put into practice by communities on their own may be most effectively spread by international NGOs. But if implementation depends on the joint action of communities and government agencies, UN agencies, which appear at the local level as a peculiar hybrid of global NGOs and supranational state agencies, may well have a special aptitude for complementing the local dynamics of state-society synergy.

Enable NGOs to act as agents to empower the people

According to Gan, the increasing involvement of NGOs in environmental activities provides good opportunities for both the United Nations and the international development assistance community. Through increasing participation of NGOs in the design, consultation, operation, and evaluation of development projects, these institutions will be able to act as agents to empower people at the lower levels of society. With more incentives to support the NGO sector, greater social equilibrium could be achieved. It can be expected that NGOs will assume many of the conventional mandates that are usually performed by governments and specialized UN agencies. What represents the so-called global civil society is the inclusion of people's voices and needs.

Wilkening, Von Hippel, and Hayes take this argument one step further and state that the United Nations has a valuable role to play in catalysing the creation, coordination, and institutionalization of epistemic communities. The United Nations can, for example, connect and coordinate multiple and scattered epistemic communities. Some suggested forms of UN support for epistemic community creation, coordination, and institutionalization include ongoing support for research, analysis, and scholarship; support for building institutional capacity for epistemic community activities; support for regional coordination of epistemic communities; and support for global information resources. In many cases, the United Nations is uniquely qualified to provide the suggested support.

Allow greater NGO access within the political processes of the UN system

The post-Rio period has seen a continuous participation of NGOs within some political processes of the UN system, such as the work of the CSD and of other international organizations including the conferences of the parties to a large number of international environmental conventions. These international conventions increasingly provide for the participation of NGOs in treaty-based decision-making processes. However, there are still complaints about NGOs' limited access to international bodies.

In their chapter, Breitmeier and Rittberger cite the work of the Commission on Global Governance, which suggests a reform of existing institutions of international governance at the global and regional levels. It seeks to democratize the UN system and enhance the participation of civil society in the UN General Assembly by creating a People's Assembly and a Forum of Civil Society. The members of the proposed People's Assembly consist of delegates from national parliaments but not of representatives directly elected by the citizens of member states. Whether or not such a People's Assembly is created, it is essential to provide NGOs with a voice in the international arena since they are instrumental in implementing any environmental programmes, action plans, or agreements.

Correct market failures and enhance ecological sustainability

Moon argues that there are two viable ways of correcting market failures and enhancing ecological sustainability. One is to engineer changes in the dominant social paradigm which defines social reality and shapes social expectation. New norms, values, ideas, knowledge, and institutions should be developed and socialized so as to enhance global sustainability. The other is the critical importance of global governance. Local and national governments alone cannot handle the dilemmas of market failures and distributive injustice. National governments are obsessed with the maximization of short-term national interests rather than long-term global human interests. It is in this context that the role of the United Nations becomes important. The United Nations must take on a more active leadership role. Shaping new global governance structures under the rubric of the United Nations will be the best way to resolve the current dilemmas and prevent future calamities.

Augment the roles and effectiveness of other actors through regional cooperation

According to Alagappa, regional and subregional cooperation can augment the roles and effectiveness of other actors (global institutions, states, NGOs, and the private sector) in implementing international conventions on global issues like climate change and ozone depletion, as well as take a lead role in addressing regional or subregional-specific concerns like land degradation, food security, international rivers' management, and acid rain. Regional organizations may mediate bilateral disputes among member states and provide technical assistance in the development of national legislation. They can also provide a number of supporting functions and services, like the development of databases and information-sharing networks, regional education and training schemes, sponsorship of clean technology projects, arrangement of funding support, and fostering of regional networks among NGOs and experts. Regional environmental cooperation, however, is still relatively new and, except in Western Europe, still in an early stage. Regional institutions, especially those in the developing world, face numerous difficulties and their track record is, at best, mixed. In order to function effectively, they require the support of their member states as well as the support and assistance of global institutions and the rich nations.

Notwithstanding their limitations, regional institutions can be and have been a critical force in raising national and regional awareness of environmental problems and in urging the need for and benefits of cooperation in addressing such problems. Regional arrangements and agencies are becoming more significant, and have the potential to become an important component of the global environment architecture. The United Nations should foster the development of regional agencies in the management of environmental concerns, and seek to integrate them into its institutional framework for the formulation and implementation of global conventions as well as the management of region-specific problems.

Address environmental concerns and policies within the larger regional picture

Environmental concerns and policies must be embedded in the larger regional picture, and institutional and policy frameworks. Environmental problems have multiple causes and implications, and successful implementation of environmental policies hinges upon a variety of factors that span the political, economic, and security arenas. They cannot be addressed in isolation. An integrated approach that connects environmental concerns to the more urgent concerns like development and security is critical to the effective implementation of environmental initiatives. It is imperative to encourage the inclusion of environmental concerns into the agenda of existing multipurpose regional institutions that are concerned with the management of political, security, and economic affairs, and to develop environmental policies in the context of the broader regional institutional and policy frameworks. The multifaceted nature of environmental problems and their resolution also requires regional institutions to act in concert with other actors, especially parliamentarians, the private sector, the scientific community, NGOs, and grassroots organizations. They must not only serve as a vertical link between the state and global institutions, but also as a horizontal link fostering cross-fertilization among these and other actors at the national and subnational levels.

However, as Zarsky points out, the development of a regional – or even subregional – consensus is not easy. Different regions of the world are wracked by political animosities and lack of a common language. Significant gaps in economic development and political power create undercurrents of mistrust. In many countries there is still little opportunity for critics and innovators – either inside or outside government – to have their say. The United Nations may have a role to play in assisting in the establishment of regional institutions, especially in areas and on issues where regional cooperation may actually accomplish more than global cooperation.

Encourage greater cooperation between existing international organizations

While UNEP was envisioned as the central focus of UN environmental activities, the reality is that many UN specialized agencies, programmes, and funds are active on environmental issues. UNEP was supposed to coordinate these activities, but never quite succeeded in this area during its first 25 years. The CSD was also given a mandate to coordinate system-wide activities and has made some progress in this area. Nevertheless, a certain amount of system-wide review is still needed to determine priorities and ensure that they are adequately addressed by the international system.

International cooperation

While this list of issues and possible solutions focuses primarily on the UN system, the crux of the matter is that managing the environment demands high levels of cooperation and policy coordination. This includes cooperation at all levels, from the village or community level to the state, regional, and global levels. Cooperation must involve all types of actors – individuals, NGOs and community-based organizations, states, regional arrangements, and international organizations. The problem is that the necessary vertical and horizontal cooperation is often lacking.

Vertical cooperation involves communication between those who manage natural resources at the local level, NGOs, states, appropriate regional arrangements, and international organizations. There needs to be a balance between the "top-down" approach of mandating environmental sustainability and the "bottom-up" approach of listening to the voices of the people. At times it appears as though the UN system is operating in its own "ivory tower." During the negotiation and adoption of resolutions and treaties, delegates often forget the impact (or lack thereof) that their deliberations will have "on the ground." The debate over the wording – and even the placement of commas – is far more political than practical. It is important for international bodies to understand and recognize what is happening in the trenches, and do what is necessary to promote sustainability that works. Not only do there need to be improved mechanisms to get local-level input into international deliberations, but there must be improved efforts by the United Nations and other international bodies to disseminate information, technology, and financial assistance at the state and local levels to ensure greater and more effective implementation of environmental programmes.

Global environmental protection must begin at the community and bioregional level. Local watersheds, ecosystems, and microclimatic conditions are among the primary objects of bioregional protection, and their alteration by human activities is much easier to understand from the vantage point of local communities than from the macro perspective of global ecology. Moreover, if it is true that global threats to the environment require supranational policy responses, the empowerment of local communities may provide needed checks and counterbalances to reassure citizens interested in democracy that environmental stewardship does not necessarily imply authoritarian forms of global government (Hempel 1996, 6).

Horizontal cooperation involves communication between states, between international organizations, or between regional arrangements. For example, a number of different environmental treaty bodies, including the UN Framework Convention on Climate Change, the Convention on Biological Diversity, the Convention to Combat Desertification, the Ramsar Convention, and others are attempting to improve coordination and cooperation. States that share common ecosystems, such as countries in the Amazon Basin, or the members of the Inter-State Committee for Drought Control (CILSS), the Intergovernmental Authority on Development (IGAD), and the Southern African Development Community

(SADC) in Africa, which are described in Myers's chapter, are forming organizations or regional environmental cooperation agreements.

One area where greater horizontal cooperation is needed is between environmental organizations and development-oriented organizations. Environmental issues have appeared increasingly on the agendas of development-oriented institutions including the UNDP, the World Bank, the regional multilateral development banks, and such specialized agencies as the WHO, the WMO, the FAO, UNESCO, UNIDO, and the UN Regional Economic Commissions. The "greening" of these bodies has been a welcome step, but the integration of environmental considerations in their programmes clearly needs to go further. The Inter-Agency Committee on Sustainable Development has brought together the UN bodies concerned with these issues and helped to coordinate their work. But more needs to be done.

The United Nations, as the only organization in the world with universal membership, is well placed to promote both vertical and horizontal cooperation. According to the UN Task Force on Environment and Human Settlements' June 1998 report, the main roles of the United Nations in the field of environment are to:

- facilitate intergovernmental consensus and international cooperation on environmental components of policies and actions for sustainable development, including legally binding commitments;
- promote support, especially from developed to developing countries, so as to facilitate the implementation of agreed environmental action plans, especially Agenda 21;
- involve, encourage, and support relevant "stakeholders" so that they make their appropriate contribution at global, regional, national, and local levels;
- monitor and assess existing and emerging environmental problems, alert policy-makers and the public to them, and advocate and coordinate measures and action to tackle these problems and their causes, thereby reducing future risks;
- provide support and resources to enable the effective implementation of global and national commitments relating to the environment, and to build capacity for environmental action in developing countries (UN 1998).

If the UN system were to operate along these lines in both theory and practice, it could make great strides in increasing vertical and horizontal cooperation, as well as in achieving the ultimate goal – effective management of the planet's natural resources and environment.

But is there a better model for international cooperation? Some argue that shaping a new global governance structure will be the best way to resolve current environmental dilemmas and prevent future calamities.

But it is important to remember that global governance does not necessarily mean a centralized world government. Although the successful design of global environmental governance will depend a great deal on the efforts of national leaders, the design itself is likely to relegate nation-states to a position of declining influence in world affairs. Both the global and the local ends of the political spectrum must be strengthened in order to achieve effective environmental governance. This means that some of the environmental authority currently reserved by sovereign states may have to be redistributed to supranational entities and local communities, simultaneously (Hempel 1996, 6). Whether or not this becomes the scenario in the future remains to be seen.

There is no doubt that international action will continue to be essential in meeting the environmental challenges of the twenty-first century. The UN system is well placed to play a central part in this action, but it will not be successful unless it actively cooperates with other components of society and remembers the need to act both locally and globally.

REFERENCES

Esty, D. C. 1994a. *Greening the GATT: Trade, Environment, and the Future.* Washington: Institute for International Economics.

Esty, D. C. 1994b. "The Case for a Global Environmental Organization." In *Managing the World Economy: Fifty Years After Bretton Woods*, ed. P. B. Kenen. Washington: Institute for International Economics.

Hempel, L. C. 1996. *Environmental Governance: The Global Challenge.* Washington: Island Press.

Porter, G. and J. W. Brown. 1996. *Global Environmental Politics*, 2nd edn. Boulder: Westview.

UN (United Nations). 1998. "Environment and Human Settlements: Report of the Secretary-General." Document A/53/463.

Acronyms

ACC	Administrative Committee on Coordination
ADB	Asian Development Bank
AEC	African Economic Community
AEI	Asian Energy Institute
AFTA	ASEAN Free Trade Area
AMCEN	African Ministerial Conferences on the Environment
AMS	aggregate measure of support
APEC	Asia-Pacific Economic Cooperation
ASEAN	Association of South-East Asian Nations
BIG/GT	biomass integrated gasifier/gas turbine
BWR	basic water requirement
CAMRE	Council of Arab Ministers Responsible for the Environment
CDM	Clean Development Mechanism (UNFCCC)
CEDAE	Companhia Estadual de Águas e Esgotos
CEPT	Common Effective Preferential Tariff
CERES	Coalition for Environmentally Responsible Economies
CEST	condensing-extraction steam turbine
CCAD	Central American Commission for Environment and Development
CFCs	chlorofluorocarbons
CICAD	Central American Inter-Parliamentary Commission on the Environment

442

CILSS	Inter-State Committee for Drought Control
CIS	Commonwealth of Independent States
CITES	Convention on International Trade in Endangered Species
COMECON	Council for Mutual Economic Assistance
CONACILs	CILSS coordinating committees
COP	Conference of the Parties (UNFCCC)
CNS	National Council of Rubber Tappers (Brazil)
CSCE	Conference on Security and Cooperation in Europe
CSD	United Nations Commission on Sustainable Development
CSE	Centre for Science and Environment (India)
DOE	Department of Energy (United States)
EA	environmental assessment
EAP/CEE	Environment Action Plan for Central and Eastern Europe
EBRD	European Bank for Reconstruction and Development
EC	European Community
ED	Executive Director (UNEP)
ECE	United Nations Economic Commission for Europe
ECOSOC	United Nations Economic and Social Council
ECOWAS	Economic Community of West African States
EEA	European Environmental Agency
EMEP	Cooperative Programme for Monitoring and Evaluation of the Long-range Transmission of Air Pollution in Europe
ENRIN	Environment and Natural Resources Information Networking
EPA	Environmental Protection Agency (US)
EPE	Environmental Programme for Europe
ESCAP	Economic and Social Commission for Asia and the Pacific
EU	European Union
EWG	Energy Cooperation Working Group (APEC)
FAO	Food and Agriculture Organization
FECAM	Fundo de Controle Ambiental
FEEMA	Fundação Estadual de Engenharia do Meio Ambiente
FIRJAN	Federação das Indústrias do Estado do Rio de Janeiro
GATT	General Agreement on Tariffs and Trade
GDP	gross domestic product
GEF	Global Environment Facility
GEMS	Global Environment Monitoring System
GEO	Global Environmental Organization

GNP	gross national product
GVA	gross value added
HELCOM	Helsinki Convention on the Protection of the Baltic Sea
IACSD	Inter-Agency Committee on Sustainable Development
IAEA	International Atomic Energy Agency
IBRD	International Bank for Reconstruction and Development
IDA	International Development Association
IFAD	International Fund for Agricultural Development
IFPRI	International Food Policy Research Institute
IGAD	Intergovernmental Authority on Development
IGO	intergovernmental organization
IIASA	International Institute for Applied Systems Analysis
ILO	International Labour Organization
IMF	International Monetary Fund
IMO	International Maritime Organization
INFOTERRA	International Referral System
INGO	international non-governmental organization
IO	international organization
IPCC	Intergovernmental Panel on Climate Change
IPCS	International Programme on Chemical Safety
IPF	Intergovernmental Panel on Forests
IPPs	independent power producers
IPPUC	Instituto de Pesquisa e Planejamento Urbano de Curitiba
IRP	integrated resource planning
IRPTC	International Register of Potentially Toxic Chemicals
ISI	import-substituting industrialization
ISO	independent system operator
IUCN	International Union for the Conservation of Nature
LNG	liquefied natural gas
LRTAP	Convention on Long-range Transboundary Air Pollution
MAI	Multilateral Agreement on Investment
MAV	minimum access volume
MDB	multilateral development bank
MERCOSUR	Southern Common Market
MFMP	Multilateral Fund for the Montreal Protocol
MITI	Ministry of International Trade and Industry (Japan)
MSC	Meteo Synthesising Centres
MTADP	Medium Term Agricultural Development Plan
NFA	National Food Authority
NFFO	Non-Fossil Fuel Obligation
NGO	non-governmental organization
NOVEM	Netherlands Agency for Energy and the Environment

OAS	Organization of American States
OAU	Organization of African Unity
OECD	Organization for Economic Cooperation and Development
OECF	Overseas Economic Cooperation Fund (Japan)
OSPARCOM	Oslo and Paris Commission
PACE	Professional Association for China's Environment
PCS	Promotion of Chemical Safety
PEH	Promotion of Environmental Health
PHARE	Poland-Hungary Assistance for Reconstruction of Economy
PIC	prior informed consent
POPs	persistent organic pollutants
PR	progress ratio
PV	photovoltaics
PX	power exchange
RFI	rural functional illiteracy
RFL	rural functional literacy
RPR	rural poverty reduction
SAARC	South Asia Association for Regional Cooperation
SACEP	South Asian Cooperative Environment Programme
SAL	Structural Adjustment Loan
SAPTA	South Asia Preferential Trading Agreement
SADC	Southern African Development Community
SEB	state electricity board
SDPC	State Development Planning Commission (China)
TACIS	Technical Assistance, Commonwealth of Independent States
TERI	Tata Energy Research Institute
TNO	transnational organization
TOE	tonnes of oil equivalent
TRP	tariff reform programme
UNCED	United Nations Conference on Environment and Development
UNCHS	United Nations Centre for Human Settlements (Habitat)
UNCNR	United Nations Committee on Natural Resources
UNDP	United Nations Development Programme
UNEP	United Nations Environment Programme
UNESCO	United Nations Educational, Scientific, and Cultural Organization
UNFCCC	United Nations Framework Convention on Climate Change

UNGASS	United Nations General Assembly Special Session
UNHCR	United Nations High Commissioner for Refugees
UNICEF	United Nations Children's Fund
UNIDO	United Nations Industrial Development Organization
UR	Uruguay Round of the GATT negotiations
URBS	Urbanização de Curitiba
VOCs	volatile organic compounds
WCED	World Commission on Environment and Development
WEC	World Environment Centre
WFS	World Food Summit
WHO	World Health Organization
WMO	World Meteorological Organization
WRI	World Resources Institute
WTO	World Trade Organization
WWF	Worldwide Fund for Nature

Contributors

Muthiah Alagappa is the Director of Studies at the East-West Center in Honolulu. He has a PhD from the Fletcher School of Law and Diplomacy, Tufts University. His research interests include international relations theory, international politics of the Asia-Pacific region, government and politics in South-East Asia, and the interaction of the United Nations with regional institutions.

Helmut Breitmeier is a senior research scholar at the Institute for Political Science, Darmstadt University of Technology (Germany). He received his PhD from the University of Tübingen in 1994. He is the author of *Wie entstehen globale Umweltregime? Der Konfliktaustrag zum Schutz der Ozonschicht und des globale Klimas* (1996). His scientific work encompasses research on international regimes and inter-

national environmental politics. His current work focuses on the creation of an international regimes database and the consequences of participation of international NGOs for national democracies.

Angelina M. Briones has a PhD in soil science from the College of Tropical Agriculture, University of Hawaii. She is a member of the faculty of the College of Agriculture at the University of the Philippines Los Banos. She is a founding member of the Farmers-Scientists Partnership for Development (FSPD) and has actively worked since 1986 as a member of the multidisciplinary team of researchers/scientists in a project popularly called MASIPAG, which enables rice farmers to develop new rice cultivars.

Pamela S. Chasek has a PhD in international studies from the Paul H. Nitze School of Advanced Inter-

447

national Studies, Johns Hopkins University. She is the founder and editor of the *Earth Negotiations Bulletin,* a reporting service on UN environment and development negotiations. She is also an adjunct professor at Columbia University's School of International and Public Affairs and Manhattan College. Her research focuses on the process of multinational environmental negotiations.

David L. Downie is Assistant Professor of Political Science and International Affairs at Columbia University. Since 1994 he has also served as Director of Environmental Policy Studies at Columbia University's School of International and Public Affairs. His research focuses on international environmental regimes, including their develop-ment, content, and comparative efficacy, and international organi-zations. His issue-area specialities include ozone depletion policy and persistent organic pollutants.

Michael W. Doyle is Director of the Center of International Studies and Professor of Politics and Interna-tional Affairs at Princeton Univer-sity. He is the author of *Empires* (Cornell), *Ways of War and Peace* (W. W. Norton) and other books, and is a member of the Research Advisory Committee of the UNHCR and the Advisory Committee of the Lessons Learned Unit of the UN Department of Peace-keeping Operations.

Peter Evans is Chancellor's Professor and Chair of the Sociology Depart-ment at the University of California, Berkeley. His recent books include *State-Society Synergy: Government*

Action and Social Capital in Development (edited) (U. C. Berkeley, 1997) and *Embedded Autonomy: States and Industrial Transformation* (Princeton University Press, 1995). He is currently working on an edited collection entitled *Livable Cities: The Politics of Urban Livelihood and Sustainability.*

Lin Gan is a senior research fellow at the Center for International Climate and Environmental Research – Oslo (CICERO), University of Oslo, Norway. He has been a project leader in research to analyse the development and dissemination of renewable energy technologies in China and India, and a project to study sustainable development of transportation systems and greening of the automobile industry in China. He is currently taking a leave of absence to work at the Worldwide Fund for Nature (WWF), China Programme. He is the leader of the Climate and Energy Programme, being responsible for projects related to climate change, energy conservation, and the development and dissemination of renewable energy technologies in China. Dr. Gan received his PhD in Public Administration from Roskilde University, Denmark, in 1995, and did his post-doc at the International Institute for Applied Systems Analysis (IIASA) in Austria in 1996–1997.

Peter H. Gleick is co-founder and President of the Pacific Institute for Studies in Development, Environ-ment, and Security. He is a leading expert on global fresh water resources. Dr Gleick received a

MacArthur Foundation Research and Writing Fellowship in 1988 to explore the implications of global environmental changes for water and international security. He serves on a wide range of national and international scientific and advisory panels and is widely published. His latest book is *The World's Water 1998–1999* (Island Press, 1998).

José Goldemberg earned his PhD in Physical Science from Universidade de São Paulo, of which he is a former Rector and Full Professor. He served as the President of the Brazilian Association for the Advancement of Science and as the Secretary of State for Science and Technology, Secretary of the Environment, and Minister of State of Education of the Federal Government of Brazil until August 1992. He has authored many technical papers and books on nuclear physics, environment, and energy.

Peter Hayes is a senior researcher at the Nautilus Institute, a non-profit research and education institute. He has a doctorate from the Energy and Resources Group at the University of California, Berkeley. Professionally active as an environment and energy consultant in developing countries (working for UNEP, the ADB, the World Bank, the Canadian International Development Research Council, the US Agency for International Development, and the UNDP), he also writes widely about security affairs in the Asia-Pacific region.

Atul Kohli is a Professor at the Woodrow Wilson School of Politics, Princeton University. He holds a PhD from the University of Califor-

nia, Berkeley. His publications include *Democracy and Discontent: India's Growing Crisis of Governability*, and *The State and Poverty in India: The Politics and Reform*. He is currently working on a comparative project on the role of governments in facilitating economic development.

Marc A. Levy is Lead Project Scientist, Socioeconomic Data and Applications Center, at CIESIN in the Columbia University Earth Institute. He is also CIESIN's Acting Director for Science Applications. Levy has taught political science and international environmental policy at Williams College and Princeton University. He has published on the effectiveness of international environmental institutions, on policies to reduce European acid rain, and on environment-security connections. He is a member of the US Task Force on State Failure, which has assembled and analysed data on environmental, political, and economic change and their role as potential precursors of political instability. Levy is co-editor (with Robert O. Keohane and Peter M. Haas) of *Institutions for the Earth* (MIT Press, 1993) and co-editor (with Keohane) of *Institutions for Environmental Aid* (MIT Press, 1996).

Rachel Massey is a graduate student in the Woodrow Wilson School of Public and International Affairs at Princeton University.

Chung-in Moon is Professor of Political Science and Director of the Center for International Studies, Yonsei University, Seoul. He has published 11 books and over 120 articles in edited volumes and such scholarly journals as *World Politics, World Development*, and *International Studies Quarterly*. His most recent publication is *Democracy and the Korean Economy* (Hoover Press, 1999, with Jongryn Mo).

Gregory W. Myers is an expert on natural resource policy, land tenure, land access, and population resettlement. He has a PhD in Development Studies from the Land Tenure Center, School of Agriculture and Life Sciences, University of Wisconsin-Madison. From 1986 to 1998 he worked concurrently as an independent consultant, and as an employee of the Land Tenure Center. From 1998 to the present he has worked as an independent consultant. He has developed and conducted research programmes and fact-finding missions for US and foreign governments and international agencies on social and political policy, natural resource access and management, population resettlement, privatization, democratization, and complex emergencies. He has also negotiated foreign national legal codes and policy reform for natural resource access in numerous countries. Dr Myers is widely published on natural resource and public policy issues.

Mikiyasu Nakayama is a Professor of the United Graduate School of Agricultural Science, Tokyo University of Agriculture and Technology, Japan. He is interested in environmental monitoring and management of river and lake basins. He received his BA (1980), MSc (1982), and PhD (1986) from the University of Tokyo. He served

as a programme officer in UNEP between 1986 and 1989, and has also served as an adviser and expert for several UN organizations (UNEP, UNCHS, UNCRD, and UNU), as well as for NGOs such as IUCN and ILEC. From 1989 to 1998 he taught water resources management and its international and environmental aspects at Utsunomiya University. From 1994 to 1996 he was "on loan" to the North African Department of the World Bank to deal with water resources management projects in Morocco, Tunisia, and Iran.

Charmaine G. Ramos is a research fellow of the Management and Organizational Development for Empowerment (MODE), a non-governmental research institution based in the Philippines. She is a lecturer in development theories and international economics at the Miriam College. She acquired her MA in Economics at the University of the Philippines-Diliman.

Volker Rittberger is Professor of Political Science and International Relations and Director of the Center for International Relations/ Peace and Conflict Studies, University of Tuebingen, Germany. He received his PhD from Stanford University in 1972. He has numerous publications in the field of international relations theory, international institutions, and foreign policy analysis.

Holly Sims is an Associate Professor at the State University of New York in Albany, and North American Co-Editor for Public Administration and Development. She holds a

PhD in Political Science from the University of California, Berkeley. Her current research focuses on China's environmental stewardship, renewable energy use in China and India, and economic crisis and environmental change in Cuba.

Georg Sørensen is Professor of Political Science at the University of Aarhus, Denmark. Recent books include *Democracy and Democratization* (Westview, 1998) and *An Introduction to International Relations* (with Robert Jackson) (Oxford University Press, 1999).

Jeannie Sowers is a PhD candidate in the Department of Politics at Princeton University. She is writing a dissertation on environmental politics in Egypt.

Egbert Tellegen is Professor of Environmental Science at the Department of Eastern European Studies, University of Amsterdam. He received his PhD in Sociology from the State University of Utrecht in 1962. From 1976 until the end of 1998 he headed the Interfaculty Department of Environmental Science of the University of Amsterdam. Recent publications include "Environmental conflicts in transforming economics: Central and Eastern Europe" in P. Sloep and A. Blowers, *Environmental Problems as Conflicts of Interest* (Arnold, 1996), and *Society and its Environment: An Introduction* (with Maarten Wolsink) (Gordon and Breach Science Publishers, 1998).

David Von Hippel is a Nautilus Institute associate based in Eugene, Oregon. David holds a PhD in Energy and Resources from the University of California, Berkeley. His work with the Nautilus Institute has centred around energy and environmental issues in Asia, and particularly in North-East Asia. In addition to his work with Nautilus, he has worked with a number of private and public agencies, including the World Bank, the United Nations, a domestic (US) gas utility, and the Tellus Institute (Boston).

Paul Wapner is an Associate Professor in the School of International Service at the American University, Washington, DC. He is the author of *Environmental Activism and World Civic Politics* (SUNY Press, 1996) and co-editor of *Principled World Politics: The Challenge of Normative International Relations at the Millennium* (Rowman and Littlefield, 2000 forthcoming).

Kenneth E. Wilkening is energy/environment/security programme officer at the Nautilus Institute. His work focuses on the intersection of energy, environment, and security issue areas in North-East Asia. He received his PhD from the Institute for Environmental Studies at the University of Wisconsin-Madison, where he specialized in Asian international environmental policy. His interests include the role of science and culture in international policy-making, the transboundary air pollution issues in Europe, North America, and East Asia, and sustainability-based concepts of energy and environmental security.

Lyuba Zarsky directs the Globalization and Governance Program of the Nautilus Institute and has written widely on trade, investment, and the environment in Asia.

Index

acid rain
  see also transboundary pollution
  Asia 265–266, 276–277
  China 277
  Europe 263, 295
  impacts of 276–277
  India 276
  North-East Asia 295
Administrative Committee on Coordination
  391
Africa
  African Ministerial Conferences on the
    Environment (AMCEN) 257, 338
    biodiversity 260
    combating desertification 260
  Campfire programme, Zimbabwe 336
  conflicts 323, 331–332, 335
  deforestation 323
  desertification 260, 322–323
  effects of globalization 324
  Inter-Governmental Authority on
    Development (IGAD) 331–334
  Inter-State Committee for Drought
    Control (CILSS) 327–331
  Intergovernmental Authority on
    Development (IGAD) 265
  land reforms 326, 338, 339
  political weakness 337–338
  property rights 325–326

  Protocol on Shared Watercourse Systems
    261
  refugees 323–324
  regional organizations 322–340
  role of regional institutions 339
  South Africa, economic power 324, 334,
    336–337
  Southern Africa Development
    Community (SADC) 334–337
  Southern Africa environmental problems
    335
  Zambezi Action Plan 404, 408
Agenda 21 139, 220, 258, 345, 347
  child protection measures 412
  creation of CSD 358, 378, 379
  CSD's monitoring role 391, 395
  implementation of 381, 382–385, 390,
    392, 393
  negotiation of 4
  participation of NGOs 386
  review of 382
  thematic clusters 380
  UNEP's mandate 358
Agreement on Straddling Fish Stocks and
    Highly Migratory Fish Stocks 432
agriculture
  biophysical constraints 244–245
  farmers in developing countries 234
  farm subsidies 233–234, 239

Japan 248, 249
small farmers 246–247
soil constraints 244–245
Taiwan 248
trade liberalization 232–235
air pollution
see also acid rain, transboundary
pollution
cleaner industrial production 315
Central and Eastern Europe 302–304
Amazonia
rubber tappers 92
Treaty of Amazon Cooperation 261
Anacostia Watershed Society 91
Antarctic and Southern Oceans Coalition
93
Aral Sea Basin Unit 405
Asia
acid rain 265–266, 276–277
Agreement on Cooperation for
Sustainable Development of Mekong
River Basin 261
Asia Regional Cooperation on Energy
Efficiency Standards and Labelling
290
dependence on fossil fuels 273–276
Economic and Social Commission for
Asia and the Pacific (ESCAP) 286
economic growth 111
energy pricing 283–284
energy resources 275, 291–296
energy sector development 111–113
energy-security-environment nexus
274–280
food security 223–249
greenhouse gas emissions 277–278
haze problems 265
hydro power potential 291
illiteracy 242
market forces 281–283
market liberalization 272–274
Mekong River Commission 261
Mekong River project 404
natural gas resources 291, 292, 293–294,
295–296
non-governmental organizations (NGOs)
109–126
oil insecurity 276
oil resources 296
population 272
power sector funding 273, 284–285
primary generating sources 278

projected GDP 272
projected growth in energy use 271, 272
regional energy initiatives 286–296
regional energy policy framework
283–286
rural migration 242–243
rural poverty 241–244
soil constraints 245
traditional medicine 102–103
transborder resources 281
transboundary pollution 281
Asia-Pacific Economic Cooperation
(APEC) 286–290
Energy Principles 289
Energy Working Group 287, 288, 290
Asia-Pacific Energy Research Centre 290
Asian Development Bank (ADB)
biodiversity efforts 260
funding Asian power sector 273
links with NGOs 123–124
Meralco Distribution Project 124
Three Gorges Dam 116
Asian Energy Institute 117
Association of South-East Asian Nations
(ASEAN) 292–294
biological diversity 259–260
Cooperation Plan on Transboundary
Pollution 265
databases 263
Energy Business Forum 293
Free Trade Area 287, 292
legislation standardization 263
Medium-Term Programme of Action on
Energy Cooperation 293
toxic waste management 262

Baltic Sea
Coalition Green Baltic 305
Helsinki Convention on Protection of the
Baltic Sea (HELCOM) 305
pollution 304–305
Bangladesh
natural gas resources 291, 292
rural poverty 241
Basel Convention 96, 314, 364
Beijing Energy Efficiency Centre 114, 186,
197–198
biomass
biomass integrated gasifier/gas turbine 73
markets for 181
use as energy source 72–73
use in Asia 111–112

Boutros-Ghali, Boutros 396
Brazil
    Amazonian rubber tappers 92
    biomass integrated gasifier/gas turbine 73
    carbon emissions 72
    Curitiba transport system 48–51
    ecological capital 51–54
    energy policy 26, 30, 44–45
    pollution control in Rio 45–48
    São Paulo sewerage system 55–57
    use of ethanol 72
    World Bank lending policy 144
Brent Spar campaign 98–100
Bund für Umwelt und Naturschutz
        (Germany) 149

Cairns Group 249
Calvalcanti, Henrique 381
carbon emissions 67–68, 93–94
cellular telephones 71
Central American Commission for
        Environment and Development 262,
        263, 264, 266
Central American Inter-Parliamentary
        Commission on the Environment
        262
Central and Eastern Europe
    see also Europe
    aid to 317–318
    air pollution 302–304
    Baltic Sea pollution 304–305
    cleaner industrial production 315–316
    Council for Mutual Economic Assistance
        (COMECON) 302
    energy conservation 311–313
    energy use 309–310
    Environment for Europe process
        305–307
    Environmental Action Plan 306
    environmental problems 301–302,
        308–309
    European Union membership 307–308
    nuclear power 310–311
    Poland Hungary Assistance for
        Reconstruction of Economy
        (PHARE) programme 306–307, 312
    renewable energy sources 310
    toxic waste 314–315
    trade with 318
    waste minimization 313–316
Centre for Science and Environment,
        carbon production estimates 93–94

CEREC Principles 100–101
China
    acid rain 277
    Beijing Energy Efficiency Centre 114,
        186, 197–198
    clean coal technologies 295
    electricity generating capacity 271
    energy efficiency 279
    energy policy 22–39
    energy pricing 283
    food security 210, 228
    Green Lighting Programme 197–198
    greenhouse gas emissions 277–278
    oil imports 274
    power sector funding 273
    Professional Association for China's
        Environment 117
    State Development Planning Commission
        114
    Three Gorges Dam 26, 34–35, 115–116
    use of coal 23, 276
    Xiaolangdi Dam 116
CILSS see Inter-State Committee for
        Drought Control
civil society
    see also international politics
    Forum of Civil Society 135
    fragmentation of 139–142
    Hegelian concept 139–140
    international environmental politics
        133–142
    power shift away from states 137–139
    role in environmental management
        20–21, 58–60, 428–429
    role in global governance 83–84
    role of NGOs 130–157
    UN People's Assembly 135
Climate Action Network (US) 141
Climate Network 141
climate change
    carbon production estimates 93–94
    CFC campaign 148
    Intergovernmental Panel on Climate
        Change (IPCC) 139, 194
    Montreal Protocol 77, 96–97, 134, 138,
        143, 259, 400, 413, 414
        UNEP's role 364, 365
    role of regional institutions 260
    UN Framework Convention on Climate
        Change (UNFCCC) 77–78, 154–155,
        188, 414
        Kyoto negotiations 259

Club du Sahel 328–331
coal
  clean technologies 24–25
  pollution displacement 401–402
  use in China 23, 276
  use in India 23, 33, 276
Coalition Green Baltic 305
Commission on Global Governance 135
Commission on Sustainable Development
    (CSD)
  Agenda 21 policing role 347
  agenda-setting 388–390
  competition with UNEP 359, 365, 370,
    394
  Comprehensive Freshwater
    Assessment 385, 390
  coordinating role 391–392
  coordination with World Bank 417
  creation of 345, 358, 378, 379–380
  critical assessment 388–392
  delegates 385–386
  effectiveness of 383–387
  fifth session 382, 385
  first session 380–381
  fourth session 382
  future recommendations 394–396
  history of 379–383
  implementation of Agenda 21 382–385
  integration in UN system 391–392
  Intergovernmental Panel on Forests
    381–382, 385, 388, 390
  lack of agenda 368
  links with NGOs 131
  mandate 415–416, 417, 420–421, 438
  membership 380
  methodology 382
  mobilizing political will 396
  national reporting 383–384, 393
  North-South schism 393, 395–396
  participation of NGOs 386–387
  partnership building 386–387
  policy guidance 385–386
  programme of work 380
  responsibilities 378–379
  responsibility for UNEP agenda 360, 363
  role of NGOs 145
  second session 381, 385
  Strategic Approach to Freshwater
    Management 390
  strengths 392–393
  third session 381–382, 384
  weaknesses 393–394, 420–421

Convention on Biological Diversity
    259–260, 364
Convention on International Trade in
    Endangered Species (CITES) 96,
    102, 141
  UNEP's role 364
Convention on Long-range Transboundary
    Air Pollution (LRTAP) 194, 197,
    303–304, 370
  role of regional institutions 260
Convention on Non-navigational Use of
    Shared International Watercourses
    213, 220
cooperation theory 351–352
Council for Mutual Economic Assistance
    (COMECON) 302
Council of Europe 302
Curitiba
  ecological capital 51–54
  transport system 48–51
Czechoslovakia, Danube River dispute 261,
    309

desertification
  Africa 322–323
  AMCEN Committee on Deserts and
    Arid Lands 260
  Club du Sahel 328–331
  Inter-Governmental Authority on
    Development (IGAD) 265, 331–334
  Inter-State Committee for Drought
    Control (CILSS) 327–331
  Sahara and Sahel Observatory 333
  Sahel 327
  tree planting 244
  UN Convention to Combat
    Desertification 260, 333
developing countries
  food security 171, 228–230
  GDP per capita 66–67
  Group of 77 383, 393
  national reporting 383–384
  role at Kyoto 259
  role of UNDP 414–415
  technological leapfrogging 19, 20, 71, 74,
    415
    obstacles to 78
Dobris Assessment 306
Dowdeswell, Elizabeth 357, 360
  management style 362
Dublin Conference 205, 209, 215, 218,
    219

Earth Summit *see* UN Conference on
    Environment and Development
    (UNCED)
Eastern Europe *see* Central and Eastern
    Europe
Economic and Social Commission for Asia
    and the Pacific (ESCAP) 286
Economic and Social Council (ECOSOC)
    380, 393–394
economic forces
    see also market forces
    role in environmental management
        97–101
Energy Charter Treaty 311
energy intensity 29
energy policy
    Brazil 26, 30, 44–45
    China 22–39
    efficient development 36–38
    environmental responsiveness 34–36
    India 22–39
    market-led systems 30–34
    performance criteria 24–25
    state-led systems 25–30
    United States 30, 31, 36
energy use
    1995 figures 177
    Asia 111–113
    basic human needs 187
    biomass 72–73
    capital funding 184–185
    Central and Eastern Europe 309–310
    conflict with environmental sustainability
        430
    consumption levels 78
    creating environmental problems 64–65
    critical loads 195, 197, 303–304
    demand for energy 176–180
    demand-side management 313
    deregulation of European market 154
    development in Asia 111–113
    Energy Market 180–199
    energy conservation 311–313
    energy glut 168
    energy planning 190
    energy supply infrastructure 184
    energy-efficient technologies 184
    environmental problematique 168
    fossil fuels in Asia 273–276
    fuel type 177
    full cost pricing 189
    intensity 66–71
    international regulation 188

knowledge/market matrix 196
    market forces 187–199, 281–283
    national income accounts 188–189
    photovoltaics 73–74
    pricing 189, 283–284
    product life-cycle accounting 190
    projections 180, 182–183, 271, 272
    rapid industrialization 176
    regional 177
    regional governance 280–286
    regulations and standards 285
    regulatory authorities 186
    relationship with ecology 187–188
    role of epistemic communities 193–201
    role of NGOs 109–126
    supply-side management 313
    sustainability information 190–191
    sustainability taxes 189–190
    sustainable 175–176, 191–199
    trends in 177–179
Environment for Europe process 305–307
Environment Protection Agency (US) 197
Environmental Programme for Europe
    258
environmental management
    bottom-up approach 439
    competition for public attention 428–429
    economic forces 97–101
    energy production 430
    future prospects 427–441
    gaps in global coverage 415–418
    global governance 431
    globalization 418–420
    institutional overload 418, 422
    intergovernmental organizations 411–424
    international cooperation 427–441
    lack of coherence 359
    market forces 43, 168–173, 431
    pollution displacement 401–403
    problems encountered 64–65
    regional institutions 431–432
    role of civil society 20–21, 58–60,
        429–430
    role of NGOs 83–89, 104–105, 124–126,
        155–157, 429–430
    role of states 15–21, 25–39, 42–45,
        57–60, 76–78
    role of United Nations 6–7, 19–21, 38,
        39, 59–60, 170, 173, 428, 432–438
    role of World Bank 408–409
    sustainability perspective 169
    techological-fix perspective 168–169
    upward harmonization 401–403, 417

environmental NGOs *see* non-governmental
  organizations (NGOs)
epistemic communities 193–201
Estonia, energy efficiency projects 312
ethanol (ethyl alcohol) 72–73
Europe
  see also Central and Eastern Europe,
    European Union
  acid rain 263, 295
  Conference of Environmental Ministers
    257–258, 263
  Council of Europe 302
  effectiveness of regional institutions
    264–265
  Environment for Europe process
    305–307
  Environmental Action Plan 306
  Environmental Programme for Europe
    258
  European Economic Community 302
  solving acid rain problem 263
  water supply 205
European Air Chemistry Network 263
European Economic Community 302
European Monitoring and Evaluation
    Programme (EMEP) 139, 303,
    363–364, 370
European Union
  see also Europe
  acquis communautaire 307–308
  Danube River dispute 261–262, 309
  environmental initiatives 267
  environmental protection legislation 134
  farm subsidies 233–234, 239
  global conventions 259
  new member states 307–308
  role at Kyoto 259
  Thermie Programme 311–312
  trade with Central and Eastern Europe
    318
  world grain market 232

Farmer-Scientist Partnership for
    Development (Philippines) 248
FEEMA (Fundação Estadual de
    Engenharia do Meio Ambiente)
    45–48
Food and Agriculture Organization (FAO)
  competition with UNEP 359
  deforestation in Africa 323
  environmental activities 414
  food price movements 228
  food production/demand trends 225–228

food trade balances 231
  mandate 412
  model for World Environment
    Organization 421
food security
  agricultural trade liberalization 232–235
  Asia 223–249
  biophysical constraints 244–245
  Cairns Group 249
  China 210, 228
  developing countries 228–230
  domestic/international links 248–249
  farmers in developing countries 234
  food availability 228–230
  food price movements 228
  food production/demand trends
    225–228
  food trade balances 231–232
  food-energy deficiency 229
  GATT Uruguay Round 223, 230,
    232–237, 240, 249
  grain self-sufficiency 229
  institutional constraints 245–246
  Inter-Governmental Authority on
    Development (IGAD) 265
  international trade 223–224
  market forces 230–235, 239–241
  market participation 247–248
  measures to promote 246–249
  non-market constraints 241–246
  partnerships 248
  Philippines 235–241
  public investment 247–248
  role of small farmers 246–247
  Rome Declaration 223
  rural migration 242–243
  rural poverty 241–244
    reduction 244
  water supply 209–211, 218–219
  World Food Programme 413
  World Food Summit 223–224
  World Trade Organization 223, 235
forests
  deforestation in Africa 323
  Forest Principles 4, 378, 383
  Intergovernmental Panel on Forests
    381–382, 385, 388, 390
  need for global agreement 431
fossil fuels
  see also coal
  environmental problems 64–66, 75
  markets for 181
  use in Asia 273–276

fresh water *see* water supply
Friends of the Earth 92, 94, 149
  CFC campaign 148
  Montreal Protocol 97, 138
  Three Gorges Dam 116
  whaling campaign 103

Gechev, Rumen 382
General Agreement on Tariffs and Trade
  (GATT), Uruguay Round 171, 223,
  230, 232–237, 240, 249
  key features 233
Global Climate Coalition (US) 93, 155
Global Environmant Facility (GEF) 359,
  400, 403, 413
  activities 414
  biomass integrated gasifier/gas turbine
  73
  campaign against 119
  role of NGOs 145
  Small Grants Programme 123
Global Environment Monitoring System
  (GEMS) 139, 363
Global Environmental Organization *see*
  World Environment Organization
Green Belt movement, Kenya 91–92
greenhouse gases 154–155, 277–278
  emission levels 77–78
  role of regional institutions 260
  sustainability taxes 189–190
Greenpeace 149, 150
  1994 budget 92
  Brent Spar campaign 98–100
  CFC campaign 144–145, 148
  credibility 94
  HELCOM 305
  links with Asian NGOs 119
  Montreal Protocol 138
  public relations activities 145–146
  seal hunting campaign 103–104
  toxic waste campaign 95–96, 314–315
  whaling campaign 103, 147, 148

Hammarskjöld, Dag 350
Helsinki Convention on Protection of the
  Baltic Sea (HELCOM) 305
Helsinki Protocol 303
Hungary, Danube River dispute 261–262,
  309
hydro power
  Danube River dispute 261, 309
  ecological impacts 279

environmental responsiveness 34–35
Narmada Dam 85, 115
potential of Himalayas 291
social costs 279
Three Gorges Dam 26, 34–35, 115–116
use in Asia 278
World Bank funding 406
Xiaolangdi Dam 116

India
  acid rain 276
  energy efficiency 279
  energy policy 22–39
  energy pricing 283, 284
  Narmada Dam 85, 115
  oil imports 274
  rural migration 243
  rural poverty 241
  Tata Energy Research Institute (TERI)
  114, 117
  use of coal 276
Indonesia
  oil imports 274
  Prokasih programme 122
Indus Water Treaty 404, 405
Inter-Agency Committee on Sustainable
  Development 384–385, 391–392, 394
Inter-American Programme of Action for
  Environmental Protection 258, 264
Inter-Governmental Authority on
  Development (IGAD) 265, 331–334
  links with CILSS 333
Inter-State Committee for Drought Control
  (CILSS) 327–331
  links with IGAD 333
Intergovernmental Panel on Climate
  Change (IPCC) 139, 194
Intergovernmental Panel on Forests
  381–382, 385, 388, 390
International Atomic Energy Agency
  (IAEA) 414
International Bank for Reconstruction and
  Development (IBRD) 399–400
  see also World Bank
International Development Association
  (IDA) 399–400
  see also World Bank
International Fund for Agricultural
  Development (IFAD) 414
International Fund for Animal Welfare 103
International Institute for Energy
  Conservation 290

International Labour Organization (ILO) 413, 414
International Maritime Organization (IMO) 414
International Monetary Fund 414
International Programme on Chemical Safety 413
International Referral System (INFOTERRA) 363
International Register of Potentially Toxic Chemicals (IRPTC) 363
International Union for the Conservation of Nature (IUCN) 146
International Whaling Commission 146
international cooperation 2–7
ISO 14000 188
international non-governmental organizations (INGOs) see non-governmental organizations (NGOs)
international organizations
  see also international politics
  evaluation 346–353
international politics
  see also states
  cooperation theory 351–352
  cosmopolitan democracy 135–136
  definitions 346–347
  enforcement 352–353
  free-riding states 133–134
  functionalist perspective 348–350
  hegemony 347–353
  international organizations 346–353
  liberal theory 132, 141, 147–148, 150–151, 155–157
  liberal-democratic internationalist model 135
  neofunctionalist perspective 350–351
  radical communitarianism 136–137
  realist perspective 347–348
  regional institutions 255–269
  role of NGOs 131–142
  water supply 217–218

Japan
  acid deposition monitoring 295
  agricultural development 248, 249
  nuclear power 279
  role at Kyoto 259

Kenya
  Green Belt movement 91–92
  UNEP headquarters 361

Kyoto Protocol 77–78, 154, 188

LRTAP see Convention on Long-range Transboundary Air Pollution

Mar del Plata Conference 205, 213, 215, 217, 218, 219
market forces
  energy use 187–199, 281–283
  environmental management 431
  food security 230–235, 239–241
  globalization 281–283, 419–420
  market failures 281–283, 436–437
  role in environmental management 43, 168–173
  water supply 215–217
Mendes, Chico 92
Meralco Distribution Project, Philippines 124
Montreal Protocol 77, 96–97, 134, 138, 143, 259, 400, 413, 414
  UNEP's role 364, 365
Mozambique
  biodiversity infringements 338–339
  land reforms 325–326, 338
  overexploitation of natural resources 324, 336–337

Narmada Dam 85, 115
nation-states see states
Natuna gas fields 293–294
Natural Resources Defense Council (US) 92, 148, 149
networks
  Asian NGOs 285–286
  BALLERINA 264
  Central American Commission for Environment and Development 264, 266
  Environment and Natural Resources Networking programme 263
  epistemic communities 200–201
  fostered by regional institutions 268
  non-governmental organizations (NGOs) 92–93, 116–117, 118–120, 145
  Sustainable Development Networking Programme 413
non-governmental organizations (NGOs)
  accountability 94
  advocacy organizations 142–146
  agents of civil society 130, 435–436

non-governmental organizations (NGOs)
(cont.)
Asian energy sector development
109–126
Asian power sector 285–286
campaigning in Asia 85
characteristics of 121
competence 148–151
definition of 89–92
energy use watchdogs 186
engaging economic forces 97–101
engaging social mores 101–104
financial power 92
fragmentation of civil society 139–142
fundamentalist 152–154
fundraising 149–150
greater empowerment 435–436
implementation of Agenda 21 386
influence on states 94–97, 138
levels of participation 148–151
limitations of 117–118
links with aid agencies 123–124, 131
links with governments 120–122
links with private sector 122
links with scientific community 122–123
lobbying 114–116
mediating 116–117
Montreal Protocol 96–97, 138
networking 92–93, 116–117, 118–120,
145
participation in CSD activities 386–387
participation in UN system 436
participation in UNCED 130, 131
political spectrum 90
pragmatic 152–154
promoting food security 246, 248
relations with economic actors 151–155
relations with regional institutions 266,
268
research-oriented 113–114
role in environmental management
83–89, 104–105, 124–126, 155–157,
429–430
role in international politics 131–142
schism between Northern and
Southern 93–94, 141
service organizations 142–143, 146–148
types of 142–145
use of new communications
technology 145
World Bank structural adjustment
loans 407
North Korea, nuclear power 295

North-East Asia Regional Environment
Programme 294, 295
Norway
Brent Spar campaign 99–100
water supply 205
nuclear power
Central and Eastern Europe 310–311
International Atomic Energy Agency
(IAEA) 414
Japan 279
North Korea 295
use in Asia 278–279

Organization of American States (OAS),
Inter-American Programme of
Action for Environmental Protection
258
Oslo and Paris Commission (OSPARCOM)
99
ozone depletion see climate change,
greenhouse gases

Philippines
agricultural modernization 238
Farmer-Scientist Partnership for
Development 248
food security 171, 235–241
grain production 236
illiteracy 242
market forces 239–241
Meralco Distribution Project 124
public expenditure 238–239
rural infrastructure 239–240
rural migration 242–243
World Bank structural adjustment
programme 237
photovoltaics 73–74
Poland Hungary Assistance for
Reconstruction of Economy
(PHARE) programme 306–307,
312
pollution
see also acid rain, air pollution, climate
change, water pollution
critical loads 195, 197, 303–304
global 76
local 74–75
regional 75–76
Rio de Janeiro 45–48
population
Asia 272
forecasts 167
refugees in Africa 323

poverty
  see also food security
  Asia 241–244
  Bangladesh 241
  India 241
  rural 241–244
  rural poverty reduction 244
  South Korea 243
power supply
  faulty distribution 28–29
  inefficiency 29–30
Professional Association for China's
      Environment 117
progress ratio 74–75
Prokasih programme, Indonesia 122
Promotion of Chemical Safety programme
      413
Promotion of Environmental Health
      programme 413

Ramsar Convention on Wetlands 146
Razali, Ismail 380, 395
regional institutions 255–269
  Africa 322–340
  Asian energy initiatives 286–296
  Baltic Sea pollution 304–305
  conflict mediation 332–333
  cooperation in Central and Eastern
      Europe 301–318
  databases 263
  definition of 256
  dispute mediation 261–262
  effectiveness 255–256, 264–266
  Environment for Europe process
      305–307
  environmental governance of energy
      markets 280–286
  European air pollution 302–304
  expectations of 340
  fostering networking 268
  global conventions 258–260
  high-level forums 257–258
  regional agencies 256
  regional arrangements 256–257
  regional initiatives 260–261
  relations with other actors 266–267
  role in environmental management
      257–264, 431–432
  role of United Nations 437–438
  support services 262–264
  sustainable development concept 327
  technical assistance 262
  UN Charter 255

Rio Conference *see* UN Conference on
      Environment and Development
      (UNCED)
Rio de Janeiro, pollution control 45–48
Rio Declaration 4, 378, 383
Russia
  air pollution 303
  decentralization of heat supply 310
  energy savings 310
  Sakhalin oil and gas fields 296
  waste minimization 313–314
  wind power 310

Sahara and Sahel Observatory 333
Sahel
  Club du Sahel 328–331
  desertification 327
  Praia Conference 329, 330
  Segou Round Table 329
Sakhalin oil and gas fields 296
sanitation *see* water supply
São Paulo, sewerage system 55–57
scientific community
  links with NGOs 122–123
  role in Asia 285
Sea Shepherds Conservation Society
      103
Senegal
  decentralization process 330
  land fertility 91
sewerage *see* water supply
Sierra Club 148
Slovakia
  Danube River dispute 261–262, 309
  energy efficiency projects 312
Sofia Protocol 303
Somalia, peace negotiations 332
South Africa, economic power 324, 334,
      336–337
South America
  Treaty of Amazon Cooperation 261
  water supply 205
South Asia Association for Regional
      Cooperation (SAARC) 290–292
South Asia Preferential Trading Agreement
      287, 292
South Asian Cooperative Environment
      Programme 260
South Korea
  agricultural development 249
  rural poverty 243
Southern Africa Development Community
      (SADC) 334–337

State Development Planning Commission
(China) 114
state-society synergy 18–19, 44–45, 58–60
states
see also international politics
autonomy of 141–142
common interests 348
free-riding 133–134
globalization 418–420
growth in democracy 140
influenced by NGOs 94–97, 138
international environmental politics
133–142
power shift to civil society 137–139
role in environmental management
15–21, 25–39, 42–45, 57–60, 76–78
steel industry 71–72
Steyer, Kurt 304
Stockholm Conference 3, 92, 137, 197,
326–327, 345
formation of UNEP 355
Strong, Maurice 357
Sudan, peace negotiations 332
sustainability knowledge 175, 191–199
Sustainable Development Networking
Programme 413

Taiwan, agricultural development 248
Tata Energy Research Institute (TERI)
114, 117
technological leapfrogging 19, 20, 71, 74,
415
obstacles to 78
technology transfer 197–198, 263–264,
311–312, 435
third world cities
Curitiba 48–54
sustainability 42–45, 57–58
Three Gorges Dam 26, 34–35, 115–116
Tolba, Mostafa 350, 357
Commission on Sustainable Development
382
leadership 362, 365, 369, 416
Töpfer, Klaus 357, 362, 382
Torrey Canyon disaster 3
toxic waste
African initiatives 262
ASEAN initiatives 262
Basel Convention 96, 314, 364
Central American initiatives 262
Central and Eastern Europe 314–315
prevention of international trade 95–96

transboundary pollution 2, 94
acid rain in Asia 276–277
acid rain in Europe 263
air pollution in Europe 302–304
ASEAN Cooperation Plan on
Transboundary Pollution 265
Asia 281
Baltic Sea 304–305
Convention on Long-range
Transboundary Air Pollution
(LRTAP) 194, 197, 303–304, 370
European Monitoring and Evaluation
Programme (EMEP) 139
haze in South-East Asia 265
role of regional institutions 260
water resources 404
World Bank mechanisms 403–406
transnational criminal organizations
142–143
transport systems, Curitiba 48–51
Turkey, water supply 205

UN Conference on Environment and
Development (UNCED) 84, 93, 122,
145, 173, 327, 345
"African Common Position" report 258
agreements not implemented 382
creation of CSD 378, 379
dissent among NGOs 141
follow-up by UN system 391
national reporting 383–384, 393
participation of NGOs 130, 131
participation of UNICEF 412
role of CSD 378–379
scope of 4–5
UNEP's mandate 358
water supply 217, 218
UN Educational, Scientific, and Cultural
Organization (UNESCO) 413–414
UN Environment Programme (UNEP)
355–372
1994 budget 92
absence of clear mission 359–360
accomplishments 416
African biological diversity 338
agenda-setting 390
Aral Sea pollution 404
Brundtland Commission report 367
CFC campaign 148
challenges facing 355–356, 357–362
cleaner industrial production 315
communications facilities 371

competing organizations 358–359
competition with CSD 359, 370, 394
coordination with World Bank 417
disseminating environmental
    information 363–364, 366
Earthwatch programme 196
Environment and Natural Resources
    Networking programme 263
Environmental Management Group 367
Executive Director 357
expansion of powers 431
financial status 356, 360–361, 370–371
formation of 3, 355
Global Environment Facility (GEF) 413,
    414
Global Environment Monitoring System
    (GEMS) 139, 363
Governing Council 357
inadequacies 420
initiating multilateral treaties 134
International Referral System
    (INFOTERRA) 363
International Register of Potentially
    Toxic Chemicals (IRPTC) 363
international catalyst 364–365, 366–368
international environmental agenda
    357–358
location 357, 361, 371
management difficulties 361–362
mandate 356, 358, 371–372, 418, 438
Montreal Protocol 364, 365
negotiations manager 366
options for change 365–372
organizational crisis 357–362
persistent organic pollutants 364
role of 362–369
size 356
Tolba's leadership 350, 357, 362, 365,
    369, 416
water supply data 366
World Environment Organization
    368–369
Zambezi Action Plan 404, 408
UN Environmental Management
    Group 367
UN Framework Convention on Climate
    Change (UNFCCC) 77–78, 154–155,
    188, 414
Kyoto negotiations 259
UN Industrial Development Organization
    (UNIDO) 359
UN Office of Internal Oversight Services

361–362, 367
UN Development Programme (UNDP)
    environmental activities 412–413,
        414–415
    Global Environment Facility (GEF) 413,
        414
    Mekong River project 404
    Montreal Protocol 413
    Sustainable Development Networking
        Programme 413
United Kingdom
    Brent Spar campaign 99–100
    delay in reducing CFCs 142
    Non-Fossil Fuel Obligation 76–77
    opposition to CSD 380
United Nations Children's Fund (UNICEF)
    412
United Nations
    Administrative Committee on
        Coordination 391
    capacity-building 434
    democratization of system 135–136
    diffusion of innovations 435
    Division for Sustainable
        Development 392
    educating policy-makers 433
    empowering NGOs 435–436
    enhancing ecological sustainability
        436–437
    globalization 434
    influencing governments 433–434
    international cooperation 438–441
    lack of coherence in environmental
        management 359
    links with NGOs 125–126
    market failures 436–437
    official development assistance target 389
    People's Assembly 135
    regional cooperation 437–438
    relations with regional institutions 268
    role in environmental management 6–7,
        19–21, 38, 39, 59–60, 170, 173,
        432–438
    role of epistemic communities 199–201
    Task Force on Environment and Human
        Settlements 440
    water supply problems 208
United States
    deregulation of electric utilities 193,
        198–199
    energy policy 30, 31, 36
    farm subsidies 233–234, 239

United States (cont.)
  greenhouse gas emissions 277–278
  Natural Resources Defense Council 92
  opposition to CSD 380
  role at Kyoto 259
  "Trade not Aid" 324
  "wise use" movement 93
  world grain market 232

water *see* hydro power, water pollution,
      water supply
water pollution
  Aral Sea 404–405
  Baltic Sea 304–305
  Convention on Non-navigational Use of
      Shared International Watercourses
      213, 220
  Indus Water Treaty 404, 405
  Mekong River project 404
  transboundary issues 404–405
  Zambezi Action Plan 404, 408
water supply
  access to fresh water 167–168, 170–171,
      208
  basic water requirement (BWR)
      213–214, 218
  Comprehensive Freshwater Assessment
      385, 390
  conflicts over 212
  CSD sectoral theme 390
  distribution by continent 206
  Dublin Conference 205, 209, 215, 218,
      219
  ecosystems 211–212
  Europe 205
  fisheries 211
  food security 209–211, 218–219
  health implications 207–209
  hydrological cycle 211
  infrastructure development 216
  international politics 217–218
  Mar del Plata Conference 205, 213, 215,
      217, 218, 219
  market forces 215–217
  planning 219–220
  problems of 204–205
  projections 205–207
  sanitation services 207–208
  São Paulo sewerage system 55–57
  UNEP data 366
wildlife
  Asian traditional medicine 102–103

bear gall bladders 102
  Campfire programme, Zimbabwe 336
  Convention on International Trade in
      Endangered Species (CITES) 96,
      102, 364
  overexploited in Mozambique 324
  protection for elephants 141
  seal hunting campaign 103–104
  Southern Africa 335
  whaling campaign 103
Wolfensohn, James D. 399
Women's Caucus 387
World Bank
  Aral Sea pollution 404–405
  Baltic Sea pollution 305
  Bretton Woods creation 347
  campaign to reform 93
  Club du Sahel 328
  competition with UNEP 359
  coordination with CSD 417
  coordination with UNEP 417
  Environmental Programme for Europe
      258
  environmental agenda 363, 399–409
  environmental assessments 402, 406–408
  environmental effectiveness 416–417, 418
  environmental mandate 430
  food price movements 228
  food trade balances 231
  funding Asian power sector 273
  funding criteria 78, 110, 144, 401–402
  funding dam construction 406
  funding environmental projects 400
  future role 408–409
  Global Environmant Facility (GEF) 400,
      403, 413, 414
  global projects 403
  Indus Water Treaty 404, 405
  institutional review 409
  links with NGOs 123, 131
  model for World Environment
      Organization 421
  Montreal Protocol 400
  Narmada Dam project 115
  Philippines structural adjustment
      programme 237
  pollution displacement 401–403
  reforms in India 32
  regional projects 403
  relations with regional institutions 266
  structural adjustment loans 406–408
  Three Gorges Dam 116

transboundary issues 403–406
upward harmonization 401–403, 417
water resources 404–405
World Business Council for Sustainable
    Development 152
World Commission on Environment and
    Development (WCED) 327, 358
World Environment Organization 368–369,
    408, 418, 420–422, 424, 431
World Food Programme 413
World Food Summit 223–224
World Health Organization (WHO) 413,
    421
World Meteorological Organization
    (WMO) 359, 414
World Resources Institute 196
    carbon production estimates 93
World Trade Organization (WTO) 359,
    414, 418, 423, 424
    review of agricultural accord 249

food security 223, 235
World Water Congress 209
Worldwatch Institute 196
Worldwide Fund for Nature (WWF) 94
    1994 budget 92
    Asian traditional medicine 102–103
    Beijing Energy Efficiency Centre 197
    Convention on International Trade in
        Endangered Species (CITES) 96
    HELCOM 305
    links with Asian NGOs 119–120
    Three Gorges Dam 116
    whaling campaign 103
    World Bank structural adjustment
        loans 407

Xiaolangdi Dam 116

Zambezi Action Plan 404, 408
Zimbabwe, Campfire programme 336